AN INTRODUCTION TO SOCIOLINGUISTICS

RONALD WARDHAUGH
AND JANET M. FULLER

SEVENTH EDITION

WILEY Blackwell

This seventh edition first published 2015
© 2015 John Wiley & Sons, Inc.

Edition History: Basil Blackwell Ltd (1e 1986); Blackwell Publishers Ltd (2e 1992, 3e 1998, and 4e 2002); Blackwell Publishing Ltd (5e 2006, 6e 2010)

Registered Office
John Wiley & Sons Ltd, The Atrium, Southern Gate, Chichester, West Sussex, PO19 8SQ, UK

Editorial Offices
350 Main Street, Malden, MA 02148-5020, USA
9600 Garsington Road, Oxford, OX4 2DQ, UK
The Atrium, Southern Gate, Chichester, West Sussex, PO19 8SQ, UK

For details of our global editorial offices, for customer services, and for information about how to apply for permission to reuse the copyright material in this book please see our website at www.wiley.com/wiley-blackwell.

The right of Ronald Wardhaugh and Janet M. Fuller to be identified as the authors of this work has been asserted in accordance with the UK Copyright, Designs and Patents Act 1988.

Library of Congress Cataloging-in-Publication Data
Wardhaugh, Ronald.
  An introduction to sociolinguistics / Ronald Wardhaugh and Janet M. Fuller. – Seventh edition.
    pages cm.
  Includes bibliographical references and index.
  ISBN 978-1-118-73229-8 (pbk.)
1. Sociolinguistics.   I. Fuller, Janet M., 1962-   II. Title.
  P40.W27 2015
  306.44–dc23

                              2014030512

A catalogue record for this book is available from the British Library.

Cover image: Willie Rodger, *The Kiss*, 1995, oil on canvas. © Willie Rodger, RSA RGI DUniv., 1995, reproduced by kind permission. Private Collection / Bridgeman Images

Set in 10.5/13 pt MinionPro-Regular by Toppan Best-set Premedia Limited
Printed in Singapore by C.O.S. Printers Pte Ltd

1   2015

AN INTRODUCTION TO
SOCIOLINGUISTICS

Blackwell Textbooks in Linguistics

The books included in this series provide comprehensive accounts of some of the most central and most rapidly developing areas of research in linguistics. Intended primarily for introductory and post-introductory students, they include exercises, discussion points and suggestions for further reading.

Contents

Companion Website

This text has a comprehensive companion website which features a number of useful resources for instructors and students alike.

Instructors

- Chapter-by-chapter discussion points
- Solutions and sample answers to the explorations and exercises in the text.

Students

- Chapter-by-chapter study guide
- List of key terms
- Annotated key links.

Visit **www.wiley.com/go/wardhaugh/sociolinguistics** to access these materials.

List of Figures

List of Tables

Preface

When I was asked to work on the seventh edition of *An Introduction to Sociolinguistics* I jumped at the chance, having often used the textbook myself and knowing it was something I would be proud to have my name on. As I worked on the project, my respect for Ronald Wardhaugh only grew; the depth and breadth of his knowledge provides the basis for these chapters. While I am responsible for the content of this textbook, this project was only possible because I had as a starting point such excellent material.

The changes I have made are both thematic and organizational. Throughout the text, I have sought to incorporate research which reflects contemporary social theories, in particular social constructionist and critical approaches, as applied to the study of language in society. Further, I have sought to position sociolinguists as potential actors and activists, not objective observers who necessarily remain outside of the worlds they study; this perspective culminates in the final section, which has been titled 'Sociolinguistics and Social Justice.'

In terms of chapter layout, some re-arrangement of the materials will be apparent to those who have used the textbook in the past. The first section contains chapters on the same topics, although with some different titles to the sixth edition. The second section has been updated, but retains its focus on variationist sociolinguistics. The section now titled 'Language and Interaction' contains chapters on ethnography, pragmatics, and discourse analysis. The final section on social justice continues to include chapters on language and gender (and sexuality) and language policy and planning, but also a chapter focusing on language and education in sociolinguistic research.

Finally, the seventh edition of *An Introduction to Sociolinguistics* also has an accompanying website, where students can find a review guide, vocabulary lists, and links to related websites for each chapter. There are also materials for instructors, including discussion topics and guides to the explorations and exercises that are provided in the textbook.

May your introduction to sociolinguistics be the beginning of new interests and insights!

Janet M. Fuller

Acknowledgments

I would like to thank several friends and colleagues for taking the time to consult with me on topics in their expertise during the writing of this book – Matthew Gordon, on variationist sociolinguistics; Michael Aceto, on pidgin and creole linguistics; and Heike Wiese, on *Kiezdeutsch* 'neighborhood German.' Their support was much appreciated.

I am further indebted to Southern University of Illinois, and especially the Department of Anthropology, for granting me the sabbatical during which I did most of the work on this book, and to the John F. Kennedy Institute at the Freie Universität Berlin, and especially Director Irwin Collier, for support while on my sabbatical in 2013–2014.

This project could not have been carried out without the valuable feedback on this revision from Ronald Wardhaugh, and the help with content, formatting, and other logistics from the staff at Wiley-Blackwell. Their support and assistance was much appreciated.

Finally, as always I am grateful to my children for inspiration: Arlette, who has always helped me question everything I thought I knew, and Nicholas, who provided me with encouragement, explanations of pop culture, and tech support throughout this project.

1

Introduction

> ## Key Concepts
>
> How to define and delineate the study of sociolinguistics
>
> What it means to 'know' a language
>
> How language varies across speakers and within the speech of one person
>
> The social construction of identities
>
> The relationship between language and culture
>
> Research design and methodologies for sociolinguistics research

Sociolinguistics is the study of our everyday lives – how language works in our casual conversations and the media we are exposed to, and the presence of societal norms, policies, and laws which address language. Since you are reading this book, you may already have some idea what the study of sociolinguistics entails; you may already have an interest in, and knowledge about, regional dialects, multilingualism, language policy, or non-sexist language. And we will cover all of these topics, along with many others – what social class and ethnicity might have to do with language use, why we do not always 'say what we mean,' the role of language in education.

But we would like to encourage readers to approach the study of sociolinguistics not as a collection of facts, but as a way of viewing the world around you. In sociolinguistics, we seek to analyze data so that we can make generalizations about

An Introduction to Sociolinguistics, Seventh Edition. Ronald Wardhaugh and Janet M. Fuller.
© 2015 John Wiley & Sons, Inc. Published 2015 by John Wiley & Sons, Inc.

language in society, but also to question both our findings and the very process of doing research. Take, for instance, the topic of nicknames. There is a stereotype that men use nicknames and women do not, exemplified in the following joke:

> If Diana, Natalie, Naomi, and Maria meet for lunch, they will call each other Diana, Natalie, Naomi, and Maria. But if Matt, Peter, Kirk, and Scott go out for a brewsky, they will call each other Dutch, Dude, Doofus, and Pencil.

We could investigate this sociolinguistic phenomenon by surveying people about their nicknames and also observing or recording interactions in which they are addressed by close friends and family members. We might find, indeed, that the men in our study are often called nicknames, while the women rarely are. But we would like to go deeper than this generalization; why do we ask this question in the first place? Why do we assume that the categories of 'men' and 'women' are socially relevant? What is it about nicknames that makes using them, or not using them, significant social behavior? And even if most men are called by a nickname and most women are not, how do we explain the existence of individual men who do not have nicknames, and the individual women who do?

Thus, while in sociolinguistics we do analyze speech with the goal of making generalizations, we also question these generalizations and examine how they, in turn, influence how we use language. In short, sociolinguistics is not a study of facts (e.g., men call each other nicknames) but the study of ideas about how societal norms are intertwined with our language use (e.g., what it means to be a male or female member of a particular society may influence the terms we use to address each other).

We will come back to these points repeatedly: language, society, and sociolinguistic research findings must all be viewed in their social contexts, interpreted, and redefined. To begin, however, we will offer a starting point for discussing language in society. By **society**, we mean a group of people who are drawn together for a certain purpose or purposes; this is a rather vague and broad term, and throughout this book we will be engaged in discussing how to draw meaningful boundaries around a group of speakers for the purposes of studying their language. We use the term **language** to mean a system of linguistic communication particular to a group; this includes spoken, written, and signed modes of communication.

These terms are, as you will undoubtedly have noted, inextricably intertwined. A society must have a language or languages in which to carry out its purposes, and we label ways of speaking with reference to their speakers. This connection is inevitable and complex; our purpose here is to study the relationship between language and society in more specific ways which help us more clearly define and understand both the social groups and the ways they speak.

In this introductory chapter, we will present some of the basic concepts in the field of sociolinguistics: what it means to 'know' a language, the nature of differences across and within languages, the importance of social group membership in language use, and different ideas about the relationship between the worldviews of these groups and the languages they speak. Further, we will outline the field of study in terms of approaches and methodologies.

Knowledge of Language

When two or more people communicate with each other, we can call the system they use a **code**. We should also note that speakers who are multilingual, that is, who have access to two or more codes, and who for one reason or another shift back and forth between these languages in some form of multilingual discourse (see chapter 4) are also using a linguistic system, but one which draws on more than one language. The system itself (or the **grammar**, to use a well-known technical term) is something that each speaker 'knows,' but two very important issues for linguists are (1) just what that knowledge comprises and (2) how we may best characterize it.

In practice, linguists do not find it at all easy to write grammars because the knowledge that people have of the languages they speak is extremely hard to describe. Anyone who knows a language knows much more about that language than is contained in any grammar book that attempts to describe the language. One of the issues here is that grammar books tend to be written as **prescriptive** works; that is, they seek to outline the standard language and how it 'should' be spoken. What sociolinguistics and linguistic anthropologists do is provide **descriptive** grammars of languages, which describe, analyze, and explain how people actually speak their languages.

One example of this difference can be found in the *less/fewer* distinction. Prescriptively, *less* should be used with non-count nouns, such as water, rice, or money; *fewer* is used with count nouns (or noun phrases) such as drops of water, grains of rice, or pesos. So something may be worth *less money*, but it costs *fewer pesos*. Descriptively, however, this distinction does not hold; *less* is often used with count nouns. Most notable is the common sign at US grocery stores indicating that certain cashier lines are for patrons with 'ten items or less.' Chances are you will also hear people saying things like *there were less students present today than yesterday*, although of course there may be some dialects of English where this distinction is still commonly employed.

While linguists are aware of prescriptive rules of language as dictated in reference grammars, the focus of linguistics is not prescriptive rules but the rules inside the heads of speakers which constitute their knowledge of how to speak the language. This knowledge that people have about the language(s) they speak is both something which every individual who speaks the language possesses and also some kind of shared knowledge. It is this shared knowledge that becomes the abstraction of a language, which is often seen as something which exists independent of speakers of a particular variety.

Today, most linguists agree that the knowledge speakers have of the languages they speak is knowledge of something quite abstract. It is a knowledge of underlying rules and principles which allow us to produce new utterances. It is knowing what is part of the language and what is not, knowing both what it is possible to say and what it is not possible to say. Communication among people who speak the same language is possible because they share such knowledge, although how it is shared and how it is acquired are not well understood. Individuals have access to it and constantly show that they do so by using it properly. As we will see, a wide range of skills and activities is subsumed under this concept of 'proper use.'

Competence and performance

Confronted with the task of trying to describe the grammar of a language like English, many linguists follow the approach associated with Chomsky, undoubtedly the most influential figure in linguistics for the last half century. Chomsky distinguishes between what he has called **competence** and **performance**. He claims that it is the linguist's task to characterize what speakers know about their language, that is, their competence, not what they do with their language, that is, their performance. The best-known characterization of this distinction comes from Chomsky himself (1965, 3–4) in words which have been extensively quoted:

> Linguistic theory is concerned primarily with an ideal speaker–listener, in a completely homogeneous speech-community, who knows its language perfectly and is unaffected by such grammatically irrelevant conditions as memory limitations, distractions, shifts of attention and interest, and errors (random or characteristic) in applying his knowledge of the language in actual performance. This seems to me to have been the position of the founders of modern general linguistics, and no cogent reason for modifying it has been offered. To study actual linguistic performance, we must consider the interaction of a variety of factors, of which the underlying competence of the speaker–hearer is only one. In this respect, study of language is no different from empirical investigation of other complex phenomena.

Pinker (2007, 74) points out the consequences of such a view: 'Though linguists often theorize about a language as if it were the fixed protocol of a homogeneous community of idealized speakers, like the physicist's frictionless plane and ideal gas, they also know that a real language is constantly being pushed and pulled at the margins by different speakers in different ways.' It is just such 'pushing and pulling' that interests Labov, arguably the most influential figure in sociolinguistics in the last fifty or so years. He maintains (2006, 380) that 'the linguistic behavior of individuals cannot be understood without knowledge of the communities that they belong to.' This is the focus of sociolinguistics, and what makes it different from Chomskyan linguistics. We are primarily concerned with real language in use (what Chomsky calls performance) not the language of some ideal speaker (i.e., an idealized competence). This distinction is reflected in methodological differences; syntacticians such as Chomsky will often use **grammatical judgments** to get at competence, while sociolinguists tend to use recordings of language use (see section below on methodologies, and chapter 11 on Discourse Analysis).

The knowledge that we will seek to explain involves more than knowledge of the grammar of the language, for it will become apparent that speakers know, or are in agreement about, more than that. Moreover, in their performance they behave systematically: their actions are not random; there is order. Knowing a language also means knowing how to use that language, since speakers know not only how to form sentences but also how to use them appropriately. There is therefore another kind of competence, sometimes called **communicative competence**, and the social aspects of that competence will be our concern here.

Exploration 1.1: Grammatical Judgments

Here are a number of statements that can be 'tagged' to make them into questions. Add a tag question to each with the tag you would be most likely to use and also add any other tags you might also use or think others might use. See (1) for an example of a potential answer. Indicate for each example which tag you believe to be the prescriptively 'correct' tag, or if you might associate certain tags only with certain types of speakers. Compare your results with those of others who do this task. If there are differences in your answers, how can you explain them? Do such differences challenge the idea of a shared communicative competence?

1.   He's ready, *isn't he?*
     Other possible tags: 'innit,' 'ain't he.'
     Prescriptively 'correct' tag: 'isn't he.'
2.   I may see you next week, …?
3.   No one goes there any more, …?
4.   Either John or Mary did it, …?
5.   Few people know that, …?
6.   You don't want to come with us, …?
7.   I have a penny in my purse…?
8.   I'm going right now, …?
9.   The baby cried, …?
10. The girl saw no one, …?

Variation

The competence–performance distinction just mentioned is one that holds intriguing possibilities for work in linguistics, but it is one that has also proved to be quite troublesome, because the performance of different speakers, and the same speaker in different contexts, can vary quite a lot. For instance, speakers in some areas of the Midwestern United States might utter sentences such as 'The car needs washed' while others would say 'The cars needs to be washed' or 'The car needs washing.' Further, an individual speaker might use all three of these constructions at different times. (These different structures for expressing the same meaning are called **vari-ants**; this term will be discussed in more detail in chapter 6.) For sociolinguists, this **linguistic variation** is a central topic. The language we use in everyday living is remarkably varied. There is **variation** across speakers, that is, reflections of different ways that people speak in different regions or social groups, but also variation within the speech of a single speaker. No one speaks the same way all the time, and people constantly exploit variation within the languages they speak for a wide variety of purposes. The consequence is a kind of paradox: while many linguists would like to view any language as a homogeneous entity, so that they can make the strongest possible theoretical generalizations, in actual fact that language will exhibit consid-erable internal variation. One claim we will be making throughout this book is that variation is an inherent characteristic of all languages at all times, and the patterns exhibited in this variation carry social meanings. (See the link to a website which provides an overview of the field, the sociolinguistics page for the PBS series *Do You Speak American*, in the materials associated with chapter 1 in the web guide to this textbook.)

The recognition of variation implies that we must recognize that a language is not just some kind of abstract object of study. It is also something that people use. Although some linguists, following Chomsky's example, are focused on what lan-guage (as an abstraction) is, sociolinguists have argued that an *asocial* linguistics is scarcely worthwhile and that meaningful insights into language can be gained only if performance is included as part of the data which must be explained in a com-prehensive theory of language. This is the view we will adopt here.

We will see that while there is considerable variation in the speech of any one individual, there are also definite bounds to that variation: no individual is free to do just exactly what he or she pleases so far as language is concerned. You cannot pronounce words any way you please, inflect or not inflect words such as nouns and verbs arbitrarily, or make drastic alterations in word order in sentences as the mood suits you. If you do any or all of these things, the results will be unacceptable, even gibberish. The variation you are permitted has limits, and these limits can be described with considerable accuracy. For instance, we can say, 'It is the fence that the cow jumped over,' which is comprehensible if somewhat stilted, but most speak-ers would agree that 'the fence jumped the cow over' does not follow English word order rules and is largely incomprehensible. Individuals know the various limits (or norms), and that knowledge is both very precise and at the same time almost entirely unconscious. At the same time, it is also difficult to explain how individual speakers acquire knowledge of these norms of linguistic behavior, because they appear to be much more subtle than the norms that apply to such matters as social behavior, dress, and table manners.

Our task will be one of trying to specify the norms of linguistic behavior that exist in particular groups and then trying to account for individual behavior in terms of these norms. This task is particularly interesting because most people have no conscious awareness of how their linguistic behavior is conditioned by social norms. We will also see how the variation we find in language allows changes to occur over time and often points to the direction of change. A living language not only varies, it changes.

Exploration 1.2:   Variation in Greetings

How do you greet your friends, your family, your colleagues, your professors and your acquaintances? Are there different verbal exchanges as well as different embodied practices (e.g., air kisses, shaking hands, fist bump)? Does the situation matter – that is, do you greet your family differently if you have not seen them for a long time, or friends in different ways depending on whether you run into each other by accident on campus or if you are meeting for dinner? Are there ways of greeting, either that you use or that you do not use, that index membership in particular groups? Are there ways of greeting that you find inappropriate – in general, or for particular addressees or in particular situations? Compare your own repertoires and practices with those of the other students in your class.

Speakers and Their Groups

In order to talk about how speakers use language, we must talk about both individuals and groups, together with the relationships between people within and across groups. One of the current ways of thinking about this focuses on speaker identities. The term **identity** has been used in a variety of ways in both the social sciences and lay speech. In the current social theory, identities are not fixed attributes of people or groups but are dynamically constructed aspects which emerge through discourse and social behavior. Although we do look at identities of individuals, what we are primarily concerned with is *social* identity: 'Identity is defined as the linguistic construction of membership in one or more social groups or categories' (Kroskrity 2000, 111). Our special focus is on how language constructs speaker identity.

In such a view, identities are not preconceived categorical affiliations such as 'male' or 'female' but nuanced ways of being that we construct; while we may indeed reference such categories, our identities are not simply a matter of listing demographic identifiers (e.g., 'single white female, 45, architect, nature lover'). So while a speaker may introduce a comment by saying *As a mother* …, thus explicitly referencing this aspect of her identity, what will emerge is a more nuanced picture of what type of mother she is – for example, protective, feminist, one who encourages independence, one who is concerned with the upward mobility of her children. Named social categories are not our identities but concepts we use to construct our identities.

Further, our identities are fluid and we do not have a single identity but multiple levels of identity, and shifting and sometimes even conflicting identities which emerge in different contexts. To continue the example above, the speaker may reference her identity as a mother but then also focus on how she identifies strongly with her profession and struggles to balance this with the demands of parenthood; this may be intertwined with her gender identity and her social class identity. In another conversation, this same speaker might focus on her political affiliations to construct a different aspect of her identity.

Likewise, group identity categories are constantly being negotiated. What it means to be the member of a particular social category (e.g., 'gay', 'educated', 'Latino') may vary over time, space, and situation, and how particular speakers identify with or are assigned to these categories may also vary. We will revisit this concept of multiple identities throughout this text because it is highly relevant to our study of language in society.

So far, we have said that the term 'society' refers to a group of people unified through some purpose; other concepts such as 'speech community', 'social network', and 'community of practice' will be found in the pages that follow (see especially sections devoted to these concepts in chapter 3). We will see how these are useful if we wish to refer to groups of various kinds, since it is among groups that individuals form relationships or reject such a possibility. The groups can be long-lasting or temporary, large or small, close-knit or casual, and formally or informally organized. This is, therefore, another level of complexity we must acknowledge in the pages that follow as we refer to 'middle class', 'women', 'speakers of Haitian Creole', 'teenagers', and so on. We must remember that these categorizations also have a process side to them: all must be enacted, performed, or reproduced in order to exist. Socioeconomic class, gender, language background, and age are only important aspects of our identities and groups if we choose to organize our lives in that way; in some contexts they may not be salient social categories and we may instead see ourselves as members of groups based on racial identification, sexual orientation, national belonging, or membership of a particular formal social group (e.g., a Choir, a professional association, or a fox hunting club).

In all of the above we must recognize that **power** has a significant role to play; it undoubtedly has a key role to play in how we choose to identify ourselves and how we form groups with others. Power is 'the ability to control events in order to achieve one's aims' (Tollefson 2006, 46) and is also 'the control someone has over the outcomes of others' (Myers-Scotton 2006, 199). It is pervasive in society and never completely absent, although it is exercised on a continuum from extremely brutal to most subtle. It may be exercised and resisted through words as well as deeds.

Bourdieu (1991) conceives of languages as symbolic marketplaces in which some people have more control of the goods than others because certain languages or varieties have been endowed with more symbolic power than others and have therefore been given a greater value. For example, speaking – and especially writing – what is considered the standard language in a given community (see discussion of this in chapter 2) is often necessary to gain employment, may open doors in terms of finding housing, and may lend the speaker more authority even in casual conversations. We cannot escape such issues of power in considering language, social relationships, and the **construction of social identities**. In chapter 2, we will address the issue of standard languages and issues of societal power; in chapter 11 we will discuss the interaction of language and power within social relationships; in chapter 12 we will address gendered aspects of power; and in chapters 13 and 14 we will discuss institutionalized power relationships between the speakers of particular languages (or particular varieties of languages).

Solidarity refers to the motivations which cause individuals to act together and to feel a common bond which influences their social actions. Thus the concept of solidarity is intertwined with both identity formation and group formation. We know that people can unite for all kinds of reasons, some of which they may not even be able to articulate, and the consequences may be great or small. We will also look at some of the consequences for language behavior. For instance, in the next chapter, we will discuss how a sense of belonging contributes to the classification of a particular code as a language or a dialect. In chapter 3, we will look more at how people use language to construct their identities as members of particular groups. Much variationist work (discussed in chapters 6–8) rests on the idea that the use of particular linguistic features corresponds with desired membership in particular social groups; in chapters 9 and 11, we look at how this can be examined with qualitative methods.

Exploration 1.3: Idiolects

An idiolect is an individual's way of speaking, including sounds, words, grammar, and style. The first author of this book, Wardhaugh, speaks in such a way that he is regarded as North American almost everywhere he goes but in certain aspects shows his origins in the north of England. He pronounces *grass* and *bath* with the vowel of *cat*, does not pronounce the *r*'s in *car* and *cart*, and distinguishes the vowels in *cot* and *caught* (and pronounces the latter word exactly like *court*). He also distinguishes the vowels in *Mary*, *merry*, and *marry*. He sometimes pronounces *book* to rhyme with *Luke*, and finds he has to watch his pronunciation of *work* because he has a 'relic' Geordie pronunciation homophonous to *walk*.). He now says words like *tune*, *duke*, and *news* like *toon*, *dook*, and *nooz* (but when, as a young man, he served in the Duke of Wellington's Regiment, he used to say *Jook*). In vocabulary he knows Geordie dialect words like *bumler* 'bumble bee,' *canny* 'nice,' *gob* 'mouth,' *hinny* 'honey,' *lug* 'ear,' *plodge* 'wade,' and *tettie* 'potato' but no longer uses them. His grammar, both written and spoken, is that of Standard English.

Try to characterize your own speech in a similar way, identifying the aspects of your background and exposure to different ways of speaking which you believe influence your speech. How does your description compare to others in the class, and with what others say about you?

Language and Culture

There is a tradition of study in linguistic anthropology which addresses the relationship between language and **culture**. By 'culture' in this context we do not mean 'high culture,' that is, the appreciation of music, literature, the arts, and so on. Rather, we adopt Goodenough's well-known definition (1957, 167): 'a society's culture consists of whatever it is one has to know or believe in order to operate in a manner acceptable to its members, and to do so in any role that they accept for any one of themselves.' Such knowledge is socially acquired: the necessary behaviors are learned and do not come from any kind of genetic endowment. Culture, therefore, is the 'know-how' that a person must possess to get through the task of daily living; for language use, this is similar to the concept of communicative competence we introduced above. The key issue addressed here is the nature of the relationship between a specific language and the culture in which it is used.

Directions of influence

There are several possible relationships between language and culture. One is that social structure may either influence or determine linguistic structure and/or behavior. Certain evidence may be adduced to support this view. For instance, given the evidence of the **age-grading** phenomenon (i.e., young children speak differently from older children, and, in turn, children speak differently from mature adults), we could argue that the social organization of age groups influences the language used in these groups. Another possible piece of evidence for this direction of influence is studies which show that the varieties of language that speakers use reflect such matters as their regional, social, or ethnic origin and possibly even their gender.

In both cases it might be that social structures account for – possibly even determine – linguistic differences.

A second possibility is directly opposed to the first: linguistic structure and/or behavior may either influence or determine social structure or **worldview**. This is the view that is behind the **Whorfian hypothesis**, which we will discuss in more detail in the next section. Such a view is behind certain proposed language reforms: if we change the language we can change social behavior, for example, a deliberate reduction in sexist language will lead to a reduction in sexist attitudes.

A third possible relationship is that the influence is bi-directional: language and society may influence each other. Certain language reforms can also be seen as relying on this perspective; the reforms are made because of changes in societal norms, for example, awareness that generic 'he' is not inclusive may increase the power of female speakers, enabling them to claim inclusion. Consequently, language change and a greater awareness of gender equality co-occur, hand in glove as it were.

A fourth possibility is to assume that there is no relationship at all between linguistic structure and social structure and that each is independent of the other. A variant of this possibility would be to say that, although there might be some such relationship, present attempts to characterize it are essentially premature, given what we know about both language and society.

The Whorfian hypothesis

The claim that the structure of a language influences how its speakers view the world is today most usually associated with the linguist Sapir and his student Whorf, a chemical engineer by training, a fire prevention engineer by vocation, and a linguist by avocation. However, it can be traced back to others, particularly to Humboldt in the nineteenth century. Today, the claim is usually referred to as 'Linguistic Determinism,' the 'Linguistic Relativity Hypothesis,' the 'Sapir–Whorf Hypothesis,' or the 'Whorfian Hypothesis.' We will use the last term since the claim seems to owe much more to Whorf than to anyone else.

Sapir acknowledged the close relationship between language and culture, maintaining that they were inextricably related so that you could not understand or appreciate the one without a knowledge of the other. Whorf took up Sapir's ideas but went much further than saying that there was merely a 'predisposition'; in Whorf's view the relationship between language and culture was a deterministic one; the social categories we create and how we perceive events and actions are constrained by the language we speak. Different speakers will therefore experience the world differently insofar as the languages they speak differ structurally.

One claim is that if speakers of one language have certain words to describe things and speakers of another language lack similar words, then speakers of the first language will find it easier to talk about those things. We can see how this might be the case if we consider the technical vocabulary, that is, **register** (see discussion of this in chapter 2) of any trade, calling, or profession; for example, physicians talk more easily about medical phenomena than those without medical training because they have the vocabulary to do so. A stronger claim is that, if one language makes distinctions that another does not make, then those who use the first language will more readily perceive the relevant differences in their environment. If you must classify camels, boats, and automobiles in certain ways, you will perceive camels, boats, and automobiles differently from someone who is not required to make these differentiations. If your language classifies certain material objects as long and thin and others as roundish, you will perceive material objects that way; they will fall quite 'naturally' into those classes for you.

This extension into the area of grammar could be argued to be a further strengthening of Whorf's claim, since classification systems pertaining to shape, substance, gender, number, time, and so on are both more subtle and more pervasive. Their effect is much stronger on language users than vocabulary differences alone. The strongest claim of all is that the grammatical categories available in a particular language not only help the users of that language to perceive the world in a certain way but also at the same time limit such perception. They act as blinkers: you perceive only what your language allows you, or predisposes you, to perceive. Your language controls your worldview. Speakers of different languages will, therefore, have different worldviews.

Whorf's work on Native American languages led him to make his strongest claims. He contrasted the linguistic structure of Hopi with the kinds of linguistic structure he associated with languages such as English, French, German, and so on, that is, familiar European languages. He saw these languages as sharing so many structural features that he named this whole group of languages Standard Average European (SAE). According to Whorf, Hopi and SAE differ widely in their structural characteristics. For example, Hopi grammatical categories provide a 'process' orientation toward the world, whereas the categories in SAE give SAE speakers a fixed orientation toward time and space so that they not only 'objectify' reality in certain ways but even distinguish between things that must be counted, for example, trees, hills, waves, and sparks, and those that need not be counted, for example, water, fire, and courage. In SAE, events occur, have occurred, or will occur, in a definite time, that is, present, past, or future; to speakers of Hopi, what is important is whether an event can be warranted to have occurred, or to be occurring, or to be expected to occur. Whorf believed that these differences lead speakers of Hopi and SAE to view the world differently. The Hopi see the world as essentially an ongoing set of processes; objects and events are not discrete and countable; and time is not apportioned into fixed segments so that certain things recur, for example, minutes, mornings, and days. In contrast, speakers of SAE regard nearly everything in their world as discrete, measurable, countable, and recurrent; time and space do not flow into each other; sparks, flames, and waves are things like pens and pencils; mornings recur in twenty-four-hour cycles; and past, present, and future are every bit as real as gender differences. The different languages have different obligatory grammatical categories so that every time a speaker of Hopi or SAE says something, he or she must make certain observations about how the world is structured because of the structure of the language each speaks. (We should note that Malotki (1983) has pointed out that some of Whorf's claims about the grammatical structure of Hopi are either dubious or incorrect, for example, Hopi, like SAE, does have verbs that are inflected for tense.)

Pinker (1994, 59–67) has no patience at all for any of Whorf's ideas. He says that Whorf's claims were 'outlandish,' his arguments were circular, any evidence he gave for them was either anecdotal or suspect in some other way, and all the experiments conducted to test the ideas have proved nothing. More recently, he says (2007, 143) that a convincing experiment 'would have to show three things: that the speakers of a language find it impossible, or at least extremely difficult, to think in the way that the speakers of another language can; that the difference affects actual reasoning to a conclusion rather than a subjective inclination in hazy circumstances; and that the difference in thought is caused by the difference in language, rather than merely being correlated with it for some other reason such as the physical or cultural milieu.'

More recently, Deutscher (2010a, 2010b) has revisited the Whorf hypothesis, noting some of the obvious problems with this hypothesis: 'If the inventory of ready-made words in your language determined which concepts you were able to understand, how would you ever learn anything new?' However, he further discusses some recent research which provides evidence for the connection between language and worldview. One example is that speakers of a remote Australian aboriginal tongue, Guugu Yimithirr, from north Queensland, do not make use of any egocentric coordinates (i.e., deictic words such as 'left,' 'right,' 'behind,' 'in front of') but instead rely solely on the cardinal directions of east, west, north, and south. Research on this language prompted recognition of the same phenomenon in languages of other far-flung places such as Bali, Namibia, and Mexico. Deutscher uses this research not to make strong claims about linguistic relativity, but to urge readers to recognize how deeply encoded some sociolinguistic differences may be, advising us that 'as a first step toward understanding one another, we can do better than pretending we all think the same.'

We will let Franz Boas (1911) and Edward Sapir (1921) have some final cautionary words on this topic. Boas pointed out that there was no necessary connection between language and culture or between language and race. People with very different cultures speak languages with many of the same structural characteristics, for example, Hungarians, Finns, and the Samoyeds of northern Siberia; and people who speak languages with very different structures often share much the same culture, for example, Germans and Hungarians, or many people in southern India, or the widespread Islamic culture. We can also dismiss any claim that certain types of languages can be associated with 'advanced' cultures and that others are indicative of cultures that are less advanced. As Sapir observed on this last point (1921, 219), 'When it comes to linguistic form, Plato walks with the Macedonian swineherd, Confucius with the head-hunting savage of Assam.'

Exploration 1.4:   Translatability

If you speak more than one language or dialect, are there certain words or phrases which you feel you cannot translate into Standard English? What are these words or phrases – are they simply words for things which are not part of the cultures of the English-speaking world, or concepts or idioms not found in English? What does the view of particular words as 'untranslatable' indicate about the connection between language and worldview?

Correlations

It is possible to claim a relationship between language and social structure without making claims about causality, and such correlational studies have long formed a significant part of sociolinguistic work. Gumperz (1971, 223) has observed that sociolinguistics is an attempt to find correlations between social structure and linguistic structure and to observe any changes that occur. Chambers (2002, 3) is even more direct: 'Sociolinguistics is the study of the social uses of language, and the most productive studies in the four decades of sociolinguistic research have emanated from determining the social evaluation of linguistic variants. These are also the areas most susceptible to scientific methods such as hypothesis-formation, logical inference, and statistical testing.' The approach to sociolinguistics which focuses on such correlations and the quantitative analysis of them is often called **variationist sociolinguistics** and will be discussed in chapters 6–8.

It is important to note that correlation only shows a relationship between two variables; it does not show ultimate causation. To find that X and Y are related is not necessarily to discover that X causes Y (or Y causes X). For example, to find that female speakers use more standard features than male speakers in a given community does not prove that being female causes a speaker to speak in a more standard manner (see chapter 7 for a discussion of how such findings have been interpreted, and chapter 12 for a broader discussion of language and gender). We must always exercise caution when we attempt to draw conclusions from such relationships.

When we observe how varied language use is we must search for the causes. Chambers (2003, 226) notes, 'Upon observing variability, we seek its social correlates. What is the purpose of the variation? How is it evaluated in the community? What do its variants symbolize?' Ultimately, the goal of sociolinguistics is to address the social meanings of language use, and correlation with social variables is one way to address this question.

The Boundaries of Sociolinguistics

Some investigators have found it appropriate to try to introduce a distinction between sociolinguistics (or **micro-sociolinguistics**) and the **sociology of language** (or **macro-sociolinguistics**). In this distinction, (micro-) sociolinguistics is concerned with investigating the relationships between language and society with the goal being a better understanding of the structure of language and of how languages function in communication; the equivalent goal in the sociology of language is trying to discover how social structure can be better understood through the study of language, for example, how certain linguistic features serve to characterize particular social arrangements. Hudson (1996, 4) has described the difference as follows: sociolinguistics is 'the study of language in relation to society,' whereas the sociology of language is 'the study of society in relation to language.' In other words, in sociolinguistics we study language and society in order to find out as much as we can about what kind of thing language is, and in the sociology of language we reverse the direction of our interest. Using the alternative terms given above, Coulmas (1997, 2) says that 'micro-sociolinguistics investigates how social structure influences the way people talk and how language varieties and patterns of use correlate with social attributes such as class, sex, and age. Macro-sociolinguistics, on the other hand, studies what societies do with their languages, that is, attitudes and attachments that account for the functional distribution of speech forms in society, language shift, maintenance, and replacement, the delimitation and interaction of speech communities.'

The view we will take here is that both sociolinguistics and the sociology of language require a systematic study of language *and* society if they are to be successful. Moreover, a sociolinguistics that deliberately refrains from drawing conclusions about society seems to be unnecessarily restrictive, just as restrictive indeed as a sociology of language that deliberately ignores discoveries about language made in the course of sociological research. So while it is possible to do either kind of work to the exclusion of the other, we will look at both kinds. Consequently, we will not attempt to limit the scope of this book only to studies which are considered sociolinguistics in a narrow sense. Rather, we wish to include a broad spectrum of approaches and ideas which have been used in the study of language in society.

A further distinction which is sometimes made is that between sociolinguistics and **linguistic anthropology** (Fuller, the second author of this text, has a background in and affiliation with anthropology as well as linguistics, and thus brings this perspective to the study of sociolinguistics). Recent work (Duranti 2003, Gumperz and Cook-Gumperz 2008, Bucholtz and Hall 2008) has noted the fuzziness of the distinction between these two fields, arguing that there is considerable overlap in theory, themes, methodologies, and history. Ethnography of communication has long been an area of overlap between these two fields (and others); current approaches to the study of identities and language ideologies also blur the distinction between sociolinguistics and linguistic anthropology. In chapter 9, we will discuss several ethnographic approaches which focus on language in society, including ethnography of communication. This is qualitative research and thus methodologically very different from quantitative variationist work; it also tends to address the question of the social meaning of language use less in terms of correlation with the social categories associated with the speaker, and more in terms of how speakers use language to carry out their social lives (including but not limited to positioning themselves as members of particular social categories). Further, other approaches to discourse analysis which have similar aims will be introduced in chapter 11.

There is also a growing amount of work called **critical sociolinguistics** (Singh 1996, Kress 2001) that takes what we will call an 'interventionist' approach to matters that interest us; we will discuss its findings in more detail in the final section of this book. This approach derives from critical theory, which is concerned with 'the processes by which systems of social inequality are created and sustained. Of particular interest is inequality that is largely invisible, due to ideological processes that make inequality seem to be the natural condition of human social systems' (Tollefson 2006, 43). Two of its principal exponents are Fairclough (1995, 2006) and van Dijk (2003), who champion an approach called 'critical discourse analysis', the topic of a section in chapter 11. This work focuses on how language is used to exercise and preserve power and privilege in society, how it buttresses social institutions, and how even those who suffer as a consequence fail to realize that many of the things that appear to be 'natural' and 'normal' are culturally constructed and not inevitable; it is power relations in society that determine what is defined as 'normal.' The claim is that politics, medicine, religion, education, law, race, gender, academia, and so on can be understood for what they really are only within the framework of critical discourse analysis because such systems maintain unequal distributions of wealth, income, status, group membership, education, and so on. Fairclough (2001, 6) expresses what he sees as the failure of sociolinguistics to deal with such matters as follows: 'Sociolinguistics is strong on "what?" questions (what are the facts of variation?) but weak on "why?" and "how?" questions (why are the facts as they are?; how – in terms of the development of social relationships of power – was the existing sociolinguistic order brought into being?; how is it sustained?; and how might it be changed to the advantage of those who are dominated by it?).' He insists that: 'The tradition of critical research in the social sciences focuses upon what are widely seen as the big issues and problems which people face in their lives in order to arrive at an understanding of the present which can illuminate possibilities for a better future and inform struggles to achieve it' (2006, 162).

This is very much an ideological view. Its proponents maintain that all language use is ideological as are all investigations, that is, that there is no hope of an 'objective' or 'neutral' sociolinguistics. Consequently, critical discourse analysis claims the high ground on issues; it is 'a resource for people who are struggling against domination and oppression in its linguistic forms' (Fairclough, 1995, 1) and 'it is not enough to uncover the social dimensions of language use. These dimensions are the object of moral and political evaluation, and analysing them should have effects in society: empowering the powerless, giving voices to the voiceless, exposing power abuse, and mobilising people to remedy social wrongs' (Blommaert 2005, 25).

As this overview has made clear, there are many different perspectives, approaches, topics, and methodologies within the broad field of sociolinguistics. In the next section, we will introduce some issues involved in this last area, methodologies, which are relevant for all study of language in society.

Methodological Concerns

Sociolinguistics should encompass everything from considering 'who speaks (or writes) what language (or what language variety) to whom and when and to what end' (Fishman 1972, 46). It must be oriented toward both data and theory: that is, any conclusions we come to must be solidly based on evidence, but should also make theoretical contributions. Above all, a research project should begin with a research question, but that question must be one that can be answered with socio-linguistic data. We must collect data for a purpose and that purpose should be to find an answer, or answers, to an interesting question. Questions phrased in ways that do not allow for some kind of empirical testing have no more than a speculative interest.

Thus, those who seek to investigate the possible relationships between language and society must have a twofold concern: they must ask good questions, and they must find the right kinds of data that bear on those questions. Here are some types of sociolinguistics studies we will discuss in this book:

- **correlational studies**, i.e., those that attempt to relate two or more variables (e.g., certain linguistic forms and social-class differences, see chapters 6–8);
- **microlinguistic studies**, i.e., those that typically focus on very specific linguistic items or individual differences and uses in order to search for possibly wide-ranging linguistic and/or social implications (e.g., the distribution of *singing* and *singin'*; see chapters 2 and 7);
- **discourse analysis**, i.e., studies of conversational structure and how speakers use language for their social purposes (e.g., how we begin and end conversations and how this is dependent on the relationship between interlocutors; see chapter 11);
- **macrolinguistic studies**, i.e., studies that examine large amounts of language data to draw broad conclusions about group relationships (e.g., choices made in language planning; see chapter 14);
- **critical analyses**, i.e., studies that seek to assess how language is used to create and perpetuate power structures; such studies may focus on discourse or larger patterns of language use and thus overlap with discourse analysis or macrolin-guistic studies (e.g., how people talk about multilingualism could be analyzed in discourse, or language planning and policies related to multilingualism; see chapters 11 and 12–14).

Data

Since sociolinguistics is an empirical science, it requires a solid database. As we will see, that database is drawn from a wide variety of sources. These include censuses, documents, surveys, interviews, and recordings of interactions in both public and private spheres. Some data require the investigator to observe or record 'naturally occurring' linguistic events, for example, conversations, or gain access to written texts and interactions (as discussed in chapter 11); others require the use of various elicitation techniques to gain access to the data we require or different varieties of experimental manipulation, for example, the matched-guise experiments referred to in chapter 4. Some kinds of data require various statistical procedures, particularly when we wish to make statements about the typical behavior of a group, for example, a social class; other kinds seem best treated through such devices as graphing, scaling, and categorizing in non-statistical ways, as in dialect geography (see chapter 6); still others rely on interpretive analyses which draw on evidence from ethnographic research and/or transcripts of interactions (see chapters 9 and 11).

Labov has written of what he calls the **observer's paradox**. He points out (1972b, 209–10) that the aim of sociolinguistic research is to find out how people talk when they are not being systematically observed, but the data are available only through systematic observation. In chapter 7 we will discuss this paradox and certain research methodologies which seek to overcome this quandary. However, we note that while many sociolinguists are focused on vernacular speech, this is only one area of interest in the field of sociolinguistics as a whole. Many other types of language use, from speech in public domains to interviews and written documents, can be the object of study in sociolinguistics.

Research design

Because of the varied methods and research questions in sociolinguistics, the concerns in research design are quite varied. In some cases, when arguments are based on a **quantitative** analysis, it is necessary to pay attention to **sampling** techniques, error estimation, and the confidence level, that is, the **level of significance** with which certain statements can be made. As we will see (chapters 6–7), sociolinguists try to meet these statistical demands when they are required. In these cases, the findings often show trends in correlations between social and linguistic variables. An issue in such research is generalizability, that is, to what extent the findings of a particular study can be applied to a broader population.

However, **qualitative** research also forms part of sociolinguistic research, particularly in critical and interactional sociolinguistics, where the goal is to analyze language as cultural behavior. In this case, the generalizations are not about how particular groups of people speak, but how language is used to perform social functions.

A recurring concern, then, must be with the theoretical framework that is the basis for research, and how the research questions, methodology, analysis, and findings all fit into this framework. In this respect sociolinguistics is like all other sciences.

Finally, researchers must try to assess how they themselves might influence the language use around them, and how they may bring their own biases and assumptions to their analyses and claims. We must also consider these possibilities when we assess the work of others and be critical consumers of everything we see, hear, and read. A healthy skepticism is essential.

Overview of the Book

Sociolinguistics is inherently interdisciplinary; people working on sociolinguistic research as we define it may come from a diverse range of disciplines, including linguistics, sociology, anthropology, psychology, and education. We will observe that there are many interconnections between sociolinguistics and other disciplines and also between concerns which are sometimes labeled **theoretical** and others which are said to be **applied**. At the very least, sociolinguistics is a socially relevant variety of linguistics, but it is probably much more. You will be able to form your own views on these issues as we proceed through the various topics treated in the chapters that follow.

These chapters are organized within four general topics. However, there will be considerable moving back and forth with cross-referencing within topics and among topics. Inter-relationships are everywhere, and our themes will recur across the discussions of dialects, multilingualism, discourse, and social justice.

Part I, Languages and Communities, deals with some traditional language issues: trying to separate languages from dialects and looking at types of regional and social variation within languages (chapter 2); trying to figure out what kinds of 'groups' are relevant when we study language use (chapter 3); examining multilingual language use (chapter 4); and reviewing the codes that may develop in such contact situations (chapter 5).

Part II, Inherent Variety, addresses the concerns which are factors in language variation (chapters 6–7) and what these might show us about how languages change (chapter 8).

Part III, Language and Interaction, is concerned with research on language as cultural behavior. In it we will outline some of the traditions of this study based on ethnography (chapter 9), topics in the field of pragmatics which overlap into sociolinguistics (chapter 10), and research of a discourse analytical nature (chapter 11).

Part IV, Sociolinguistics and Social Justice, looks into three areas of life in which sociolinguistics offers us some hope of understanding pressing problems (and which some sociolinguists argue require our deliberate intervention). Language, gender, and sexuality, one of the great 'growth areas' in language study, is the first of these (chapter 12). Sociolinguistics and education is the second (chapter 13). Language planning and policy issues, including the spread of English world-wide and the 'death' of many languages, is the third (chapter 14).

Chapter Summary

This chapter provides an introduction to the field of sociolinguistics as well as to some of the major themes that will recur throughout this textbook. We propose broad definitions for the terms 'language' and 'society,' introduce the concepts of 'identities,' 'power,' and 'solidarity,' and explore the possible relationships between language and culture, most notably the Whorfian hypothesis. Because of the inter-disciplinary nature of the field of sociolinguistics, we also address how it fits into various disciplines and how it overlaps with linguistic anthropology and sociology of language. We note that the field includes work on topics such as critical socio-linguistics, pragmatics, and discourse analysis. Finally, we turn to concerns in meth-odology, stressing that there is no one best method, but that research must be designed to answer specific research questions.

Exercises

1. Look at the list of grammar rules below. Write an essay defending the use of one of these 'incorrect' grammatical constructions. Why do you think using these constructions is justifiable? Explain how the difference between these rules and natural speech demonstrates the difference between descriptive and prescriptive grammars.

    Prescriptive rules and examples:
    *   Never end a sentence with a preposition; use 'whom' instead of 'who' in object position. Example of a violation:
        Who did you give it to? ('Correct' speech: 'To whom did you give it?')
    *   Adverbs (words which modify a verb or adjective) should end in -ly (unless they are irregular, e.g., *fast-fast* or *good-well*). Examples of violations:
        Come quick! The house is on fire! ('Correct' speech: 'come quickly')
        That's a real nice dress you're wearing. ('Correct' speech: 'really nice')
        You read so slow! I'm already done with the chapter! ('Correct' speech: 'you read so slowly')
    *   The correct expression is 'It is I,' not 'It's me.'
    *   The verb 'lie' (past tense 'lay') means that something is in a prone posi-tion; the verb 'lay' (past tense 'laid') means that something is being put into a prone position. Examples of violations:
        It's laying on the table.
        Just lie it down there.

2. Politically correct (PC) language. Below are some examples of so-called PC language. Think about why these terms have been suggested, which ones have been widely adopted, and what attitudes exist toward some of these linguistic terms. What beliefs about the relationship between language and culture are reflected in the suggestion and adoption of or resistance to PC language?

Firefighter (formerly 'fireman')

Server (formerly 'waiter/waitress')

Banned (formerly 'blacklisted')

Differently-abled (formerly 'disabled')

Homemaker (formerly 'housewife')

Native Americans (formerly '[American] Indian' or 'Red Indians')

Happy Holidays (instead of 'Merry Christmas')

3. Communicative competence. Look at the following joke about British sayings and what they really mean. Discuss how this depiction of cross-cultural miscommunication illustrates the concept of communicative competence.

WHAT THE BRITISH SAY	WHAT THE BRITISH MEAN	WHAT FOREIGNERS UNDERSTAND
I hear what you say	I disagree and do not want to discuss it further	He accepts my point of view
With the greatest respect	You are an idiot	He is listening to me
That's not bad	That's good	That's poor
That is a very brave proposal	You are insane	He thinks I have courage
Quite good	A bit disappointing	Quite good
I would suggest	Do it or be prepared to justify yourself	Think about the idea, but do what you like
Oh, incidentally / by the way	The primary purpose of our discussion is	That is not very important
I was a bit disappointed that	I am annoyed that	It doesn't really matter
Very interesting	That is clearly nonsense	They are impressed
I'll bear it in mind	I've forgotten it already	They will probably do it
I'm sure it's my fault	It's your fault	Why do they think it was their fault?
You must come for dinner	It's not an invitation, I'm just being polite	I will get an invitation soon
I almost agree	I don't agree at all	He's not far from agreement
I only have a few minor comments	Please rewrite completely	He has found a few typos
Could we consider some other options	I don't like your idea	They have not yet decided

(source: http://www.telegraph.co.uk/news/newstopics/howaboutthat/10280244/Translation-table-explaining-the-truth-behind-British-politeness-becomes-internet-hit.html)

Further Reading

Crystal, David (2008). *A Dictionary of Linguistics and Phonetics*. Oxford: Wiley-Blackwell.
  This is a very readable reference work on linguistics and phonetics; it is useful for a
  quick definition of basic terms and concepts.
Duranti, Alessandro (ed.) (2009). *Linguistic Anthropology: A Reader*. 2nd edn. Oxford:
  Wiley-Blackwell.
  This volume presents readings on major topics in linguistic anthropology; an excellent
  reference and the place to begin gaining background on a particular topic.
Fasold, Ralph. W. (1984). *The Sociolinguistics of Society*. Oxford: Blackwell.
Fasold, Ralph. W. (1990). *The Sociolinguistics of Language*. Oxford: Blackwell.
  This two-volume treatment of issues in language and society is a classic text and a
  comprehensive treatment of the topics in the field in the 1970s and 1980s.
Meyerhoff, Miriam (2006). *Introducing Sociolinguistics*. London: Routledge.
  An introduction to sociolinguistics textbook covering a wide range of topics and
  approaches to the field but with a more variationist focus.
Mesthrie, Rajend, Joan Swann, Ana Deumert, and William L. Leap (2009). *Introducing Socio-
  linguistics*. Edinburgh: Edinburgh University Press.
  An introduction to sociolinguistics textbook by multiple authors, including examples
  from a wide range of languages and cultures and different approaches to the study of
  language in society from variationist to critical sociolinguistics.
Sherzer, Joel (1987). Discourse-Centered Approach to Language and Culture. *American
  Anthropologist* 89(2): 295–309.
  This is a foundational article about the relationship between language and culture from
  a linguistic anthropological perspective.

For further resources for this chapter visit the companion website at

 www.wiley.com/go/wardhaugh/sociolinguistics

References

Blommaert, J. (2005). *Discourse*. Cambridge: Cambridge University Press.
Boas, F. (1911). Introduction. *Handbook of American Indian Languages*. Washington, DC:
  Smithsonian Institution. In D. H. Hymes (ed.) (1964), *Language in Culture and Society:
  A Reader in Linguistics and Anthropology*. New York: Harper & Row.
Bourdieu, P. (1991). *Language and Symbolic Power*. Cambridge, MA: Harvard University
  Press.
Bucholtz, M. and K. Hall (2008) All of the Above: New Coalitions in Sociocultural Linguis-
  tics. *Journal of Sociolinguistics* 12(4): 401–31.
Chambers, J. K. (2002). Studying Language Variation: An Informal Epistemology. In J. K.
  Chambers et al. (eds.), *The Handbook of Language Variation*. Oxford: Blackwell.
Chambers, J. K. (2003). *Sociolinguistic Theory: Linguistic Variation and its Social Significance*.
  2nd edn. Oxford: Blackwell.
Chomsky, N. (1965). *Aspects of the Theory of Syntax*. Cambridge, MA: MIT Press.

Coulmas, F. (ed.) (1997). *The Handbook of Sociolinguistics*. Oxford: Blackwell.

Deutscher, Guy (2010a). *Through the Language Glass: Why the World Looks Different in Other Languages*. New York: Metropolitan Books.

Deutscher, Guy (2010b) Does your language shape how you think? *New York Times* August 29.

Duranti, Allessandro (2003). Language as Culture in U.S. Anthropology: Three Paradigms. *Current Anthropology* 44(3): 323–47.

Fairclough, N. (1995). *Critical Discourse Analysis*. London: Longman.

Fairclough, N. (2001). *Language and Power*. 2nd edn. London: Longman.

Fairclough, N. (2006). *Language and Globalization*. New York: Routledge.

Fishman, J. A. (1972). The Sociology of Language. In P. P. Giglioli (ed.), *Language and Social Context: Selected Readings*. Harmondsworth, England: Penguin Books.

Goodenough, W. H. (1957). Cultural Anthropology and Linguistics. In P. L. Garvin (ed.), *Report of the Seventh Round Table Meeting on Linguistics and Language Study*. Washington, DC: Georgetown University Press.

Gumperz, J. J. (1971). *Language in Social Groups*. Stanford, CA: Stanford University Press.

Gumperz, J. J. and J. Cook-Gumperz (2008). Studying language, culture, and society: Sociolinguistics or linguistic anthropology? *Journal of Sociolinguistics* 12(4): 532–45.

Hudson, R. A. (1996). *Sociolinguistics*. 2nd edn. Cambridge: Cambridge University Press.

Kress, Gunther (2001). From Saussure to Critical Sociolinguistics: The Turn towards a Social View of Language. In Margaret Wetherell, Stephanie Taylor, and Simeon J Yates (eds.), *Discourse Theory and Practice: A Reader*. London: SAGE, 29–38.

Kroskrity, Paul (2000). Identity. *Journal of Linguistic Anthropology* 9(1–2): 111.

Labov, W. (1972). *Sociolinguistic Patterns*. Philadelphia: University of Pennsylvania Press.

Labov, W. (2006). *The Social Stratification of English in New York City*. 2nd edn. Cambridge: Cambridge University Press.

Malotki, E. (1983). *Hopi Time: A Linguistic Analysis of the Temporal Concepts in the Hopi Language*. Berlin: Mouton.

Myers-Scotton, C. (2006). *Multiple Voices*. Oxford: Blackwell.

Pinker, S. (1994). *The Language Instinct: How the Mind Creates Language*. New York: William Morrow.

Pinker, S. (2007). *The Stuff of Thought*. New York: Viking.

Sapir, E. (1921). *Language: An Introduction to the Study of Speech*. New York: Harcourt, Brace.

Singh, R. (ed.) (1996). *Towards a Critical Sociolinguistics*, vol. 125. Amsterdam: John Benjamins.

Tollefson, J. W. (2006). Critical Theory in Language Policy. In T. Ricento (ed.), *An Introduction to Language Policy*. Oxford: Blackwell.

van Dijk, T. A. (2003) Critical Discourse Analysis. In D. Schiffrin, D. Tannen, and H. E. Hamilton (eds.). *The Handbook of Discourse Analysis*. Oxford: Blackwell.

Part I
Languages and Communities

Strange the difference of men's talk.

Samuel Pepys

Choice words, and measured phrase, above the reach
Of ordinary men, a stately speech.

William Wordsworth

Correct English is the slang of prigs who write history and essays.

George Eliot

Language is by its very nature a communal thing; that is, it expresses never
the exact thing but a compromise – that which is common to you, me and
everybody.

T. E. Hulme

It is impossible for an Englishman to open his mouth without making some
other Englishman despise him.

George Bernard Shaw

Speech is civilization itself.

Thomas Mann

2

Languages, Dialects, and Varieties

Key Concepts

The difference between a language and a dialect

Defining a standard language

Defining dialects by region: drawing geographical boundaries

Development of ethnic dialects

Varieties defined according to their forms and functions: styles, registers, and genres

We stated in the introductory chapter that all languages exhibit internal variation, that is, each language exists in a number of varieties and is in one sense the sum of those varieties. We use the term **variety** as a general term for a way of speaking; this may be something as broad as Standard English, a variety defined in terms of location and social class, such as lower-class New York City speech, or something defined by its function or where it is used, such as legalese or cocktail party talk. In the following sections, we will explore these different ways of specifying language varieties and how we define the terms 'language,' 'dialect' (regional and social), 'style,' 'register,' and 'genre.'

An Introduction to Sociolinguistics, Seventh Edition. Ronald Wardhaugh and Janet M. Fuller.
© 2015 John Wiley & Sons, Inc. Published 2015 by John Wiley & Sons, Inc.

Language or Dialect?

For many people there can be no confusion at all about what language they speak. For example, they are Chinese, Japanese, or Korean and they speak Chinese, Japanese, and Korean, respectively. In these cases, many people see language and ethnicity or nationality as virtually synonymous (Coulmas 1999). However, for many people, there is no one-to-one correlation between these categories; some people are both Chinese and American, or may identify as simply Canadian, not Korean-Canadian, regardless of what languages they speak.

Most speakers can give a name to whatever it is they speak. On occasion, some of these names may appear to be strange to those who take a scientific interest in languages, but we should remember that human naming practices often have a large 'unscientific' component to them. Census-takers in India find themselves confronted with a wide array of language names when they ask people what language or languages they speak. Names are not only ascribed by region, which is what we might expect, but sometimes also by caste, religion, village, and so on. Moreover, they can change from census to census as the political and social climate of the country changes.

Linguists use the term **vernacular** to refer to the language a person grows up with and uses in everyday life in ordinary, commonplace, social interactions. We should note that so-called vernaculars may meet with social disapproval from others who favor another variety, especially if they favor a variety heavily influenced by the written form of the language. Therefore, this term often has pejorative associations when used in public discourse.

Haugen (1966) has pointed out that **language** and **dialect** are ambiguous terms. Although ordinary people use these terms quite freely in speech, for them a dialect is almost certainly no more than a local non-prestigious (therefore powerless) variety of a 'real' language. In contrast, scholars may experience considerable difficulty in deciding whether one term should be used rather than the other in certain situations. How, then, do sociolinguists define the difference between a dialect and a language?

First, we need to look at the history of these terms. As Haugen says, the terms 'represent a simple dichotomy in a situation that is almost infinitely complex.' The word 'language' is used to refer either to a single linguistic norm or to a group of related norms, and 'dialect' is used to refer to one of the norms.

A related set of terms which brings in additional criteria for distinction is the relationship between what the French call *un dialecte* and *un patois*. The former is a regional variety of a language that has an associated literary tradition, whereas the latter is a regional variety that lacks such a literary tradition. Therefore, *patois* tends to be used pejoratively; it is regarded as something less than a dialect because it lacks an associated literature. Even a language like Breton, a Celtic language still spoken in parts of Brittany, is called a *patois* because it lacks a strong literary tradition and it is not some country's language. However, *dialecte* in French, like *Dialekt* in German, cannot be used in connection with the standard language, that is, no speaker of French considers Standard French to be a dialect of French, and in German to tell someone they speak a *Dialekt* means that they do not speak Standard German (called *Hochdeutsch* 'High German'). In contrast, it is not uncommon to find references to Standard English as being a dialect – admittedly a very important one – of English.

Haugen points out that, while speakers of English have never seriously adopted *patois* as a term to be used in the description of language, they have tried to employ both 'language' and 'dialect' in a number of conflicting senses. 'Dialect' is used both for local varieties of English, for example, Yorkshire dialect, and for various types of informal, lower-class, or rural speech. The term 'dialect' often implies nonstandard or even substandard, when such terms are applied to language, and can connote various degrees of inferiority, with that connotation of inferiority carried over to those who speak a dialect. This is part of what we call the **standard language ideology**, and we will have more to say about it below.

In the everyday use of the term, 'language' is usually used to mean both the superordinate category and the standard variety; dialects are nonstandard and subordinate to languages. Sociolinguists view this issue somewhat differently; every variety is a dialect, including the standard variety, and there is an increasing trend toward discussing discrete languages as ideologically constructed rather than linguistically real entities (Blommaert 2010, Garcia 2009; also, see chapter 4 for further discussion).

Mutual intelligibility

The commonly cited criterion used to determine if two varieties are dialects of the same language or distinct languages is that of **mutual intelligibility**: if speakers can understand each other, they are speaking dialects of the same language; if they cannot, they are speaking different languages. However, there are several problems with this criterion. First, mutual intelligibility is not an objectively determined fact (Salzman et al. 2012, 170). For example, some speakers of (standard) German can understand (standard) Dutch, while others may find it incomprehensible. Your ability to understand someone who speaks differently from you may vary according to your experience with different ways of speaking.

Second, because there are different varieties of German and Dutch, and they exist in what is called a **dialect continuum** (see discussion of this below), speakers of some varieties of German can understand varieties of Dutch better than they can understand other varieties of German! Historically, there was a continuum of dialects which included what we now call the different languages of German and Dutch. The varieties which became standardized as the languages of the Netherlands and Germany, Standard Dutch and Standard German, are no longer mutually intelligible for many speakers. However, in the border area, speakers of the local varieties of Dutch and German still exist within a dialect continuum and remain largely intelligible to one another. People on one side of the border say they speak a variety of Dutch and those on the other side say they speak a variety of German, but linguistically these varieties are very similar. There are important sociopolitical distinctions, however. The residents of the Netherlands look to Standard Dutch for their model; they read and write Dutch, are educated in Dutch, and watch television in Dutch. Consequently, they say they use a local variety, or dialect, of Dutch in their daily lives. On the other side of the border, German replaces Dutch in all equivalent situations, and the speakers identify their language as a dialect of German. The interesting linguistic fact is that there are more similarities between the local varieties spoken on each side of the border than between the one dialect and Standard Dutch and the other dialect and Standard German, and more certainly than between that German dialect and the south German and Swiss and Austrian dialects of German. Thus, situations in which there is a dialect continuum make it apparent that the lines drawn between languages are not based on linguistic criteria.

The third problem with using mutual intelligibility as the criterion for status as a dialect or a language is that even without a dialect continuum, there are many examples of named, distinct languages that are mutually intelligible. Hindi and Urdu are considered by linguists to be the same language in its spoken form, but one in which certain differences are becoming more and more magnified for political and religious reasons in the quest to establish different national identities. Hindi is written left to right in the Devanagari script, whereas Urdu is written right to left in the Arabic–Persian script. Hindi draws on Sanskrit for its borrowings, but Urdu draws on Arabic and Persian sources. Large religious and political differences make much of small linguistic differences. The written forms of the two varieties, particularly those favored by the elites, also emphasize these differences. They have become highly symbolic of the growing differences between India and Pakistan (see King 2001 for more details on this historical development). As far as everyday use is concerned, it appears that the boundary between the spoken varieties of Hindi and Urdu is somewhat flexible and one that changes with circumstances. This is exactly what we would expect: there is considerable variety in everyday use but somewhere in the background there is an ideal that can be appealed to, proper Hindi or proper Urdu. This ideal is based on a sociopolitical ideology of the language, and on different social identifications of the speakers, not on any clear and objective linguistic difference.

Another example showing the sociopolitical division of language is the story of Serbian and Croatian. In what was once Yugoslavia, now divided by the instruments of ethnicity, language, and religion, the language was called Serbo-Croatian. During the time of President Tito it was a country that claimed to have seven neighbors, six constituent republics, five nationalities, four languages, three religions, two scripts, and one Tito. However, the two largest groups, the Serbs and the Croats, failed to agree on most things. After Tito's death, the country, slowly at first and increasingly more rapidly later, fell into fatal divisiveness. Linguistically, Serbo-Croatian is a single South Slav language used by two groups of people, the Serbs and Croats, with somewhat different historical, cultural, and religious backgrounds. There is a third group in Bosnia, a Muslim group, who also speak Serbo-Croatian, and religious differences thus also contributed to the divisions which led to the eventual bloodshed. Finally, there is a very small Montenegrin group who also speak a variety which was incorporated into Serbo-Croatian. The Serbian and Croatian varieties of Serbo-Croatian are known as *srpski* and *srpskohrvatski*, respectively. The actual differences between them involve different preferences in vocabulary rather than differences in pronunciation or grammar. That is, Serbs and Croats often use different words for the same concepts, for example, Serbian *varos* and Croatian *grad* for 'train.' The varieties are written in different scripts (Roman for Croatian and Cyrillic for Serbian), which also reflect the different religious loyalties of Croats and Serbs (Catholic and Orthodox). As conflict grew, differences became more and more important and the country and the language split apart. Now, in Serbia, people speak Serbian just as they speak Croatian in Croatia. Serbo-Croatian no longer exists as a language of the Balkans (Pranjković 2001). Now that there is a separate Bosnia the Bosnians call their variety *bosanski* and Montenegrins call their variety *crnogorski* (Carmichael 2002, 236, Greenberg 2004). The situation became even more complicated when Kosovo declared its independence from Serbia in 2008. But the complications here are clearly sociopolitical, not linguistic.

There are other, less dramatically politically charged examples of how mutually intelligible varieties are considered different languages. We have already mentioned German and Dutch; we can also add the situation in Scandinavia as further evidence. Danish, Norwegian (actually two varieties), and Swedish are recognized as different languages, yet it is common for speakers of these languages to each speak their own language to each other and still be able to communicate (Doetjes 2007, Gooskens 2006, Schüppert and Gooskens 2010). Linguistic overlap between these three languages is clearly enough to make communication feasible for most speakers – in other words, they are more similar to each other than some dialects of German are to each other – but the social and political boundaries foster the continued distinction of these varieties as separate languages.

The fourth reason that mutual intelligibility cannot be used as the sole means of distinguishing dialect versus language status is that there are sometimes unintelligible dialects which are identified by their speakers as being the same language. You may be aware of varieties of English you cannot understand, for instance. A particularly interesting instance of unintelligibility of dialects occurs with what we call Chinese, which is generally accepted to include two main sub-categories of varieties, Cantonese and Mandarin. Although they share a writing system, Mandarin and Cantonese are not mutually intelligible in spoken discourse; written characters are pronounced differently in these varieties although they maintain the same meaning. Yet speakers of Mandarin and Cantonese consider themselves speakers of different dialects of the same language, for to the Chinese a shared writing system and a strong tradition of political, social, and cultural unity form essential parts of their definition of language (Kurpaska 2010).

Likewise, speakers of different regional varieties of Arabic often cannot understand one another's dialects, but are all oriented toward common standard forms (Modern Standard Arabic, with its basis in Classical Arabic). Although some native speakers of some varieties of Arabic might not understand a radio broadcast in Modern Standard Arabic (Kaye 2001), no one questions the categorization of these disparate dialects as one language, because of the religious, social, historical, and political ties between the cultures in which they are spoken.

The role of social identity

Sociolinguists claim that the defining factor in determining whether two varieties are considered distinct languages or dialects of the same language is sociopolitical identity, not linguistic similarity or difference. Orientation toward a particular standard language and, often, an associated national identity, is what makes speakers identify as speakers of language X or Y.

In direct contrast to the above situation, we can observe that the loyalty of a group of people need not necessarily be determined by the language they speak. Although Alsatian, the dialect of German spoken in the Alsace (France), is now in decline, for many generations the majority of the people in Alsace spoke their German tongue in the home and local community. However, their loyalty was and is unquestionably toward France; speaking a Germanic dialect did not mean they identified with Germany. They look to France not Germany for national leadership and they use French, not German, as the language of mobility and higher education. However, everyday use of Alsatian has been a strong marker of local identity, and for a long time was an important part of being Alsatian in France (Vassberg 1993).

The various relationships among languages and dialects discussed above can be used to show how the concepts of **power** and **solidarity** help us understand what is happening. Power requires some kind of asymmetrical relationship between entities: one has more of something that is important, for example, status, money, influence, and so on, than the other or others. A language has more power than any of its dialects. The standard is the most powerful dialect but it has become so because of non-linguistic factors. 'A language is a dialect with an army and a navy' is a well-known observation. Standard English and Parisian French are good examples. Solidarity, on the other hand, is a feeling of equality that people have with one another. They have a common interest around which they will bond. A feeling of solidarity can lead people to preserve a local dialect or an endangered language in order to resist power, or to insist on independence. It accounts for the persistence of local dialects, the modernization of Hebrew, and the separation of Serbo-Croatian into Serbian and Croatian.

Part of having power is having the ability to impose your way of speaking on others as a, or the, prestigious dialect, that is, a standard language. The process through which a standard language arises is primarily a sociopolitical process rather than a linguistic one; this is the topic of the next section of this chapter.

Exploration 2.1:   Naming Varieties

How do you usually describe the different languages/dialects that you speak? Did reading the section on language versus dialect make you think about the varieties you master any differently? Provide an outline of your linguistic repertoire, including information about the commonly used names for the language(s) you speak, any information about the specific variety(ies) of the language(s) you are more comfortable in, if you consider yourself a 'native speaker' of the language(s), how you learned your language(s), and what assumptions you think others might make about you based on the way you speak. Compare impressions with others in the class.

Standardization

One of the defining characteristics mentioned above about the distinction between 'dialect' and 'language' has to do with standardization. If you see yourself as a speaker of German, you orient to Standard German, not Standard Dutch, even if Standard Dutch might be linguistically more similar to your native dialect. Thus the process of standardization and the ideology involved in the recognition of a standard are key aspects of how we tend to think of language and languages in general. People tend to think of a language as a legitimate and fixed system which can be objectively described and regard dialects as deviations from this norm. This is the standard language ideology but, as we will see, it is only one way that we can think about a language and its varieties.

Standardization refers to the process by which a language has been codified in some way. That process usually involves the development of such things as grammars, spelling books, and dictionaries, and possibly a literature (see chapter 14 for further discussion of language planning processes). We can often associate specific items or events with standardization, for example, Wycliffe's and Luther's translations of the Bible into English and German, respectively, Caxton's establishment of printing in England, and Dr Johnson's dictionary of English published in 1755. Standardization requires that a measure of agreement be achieved about what is in the language and what is not.

The standard as an abstraction

It is a mistake to think of a standard language as a clearly demarcated variety which can be objectively determined. Lippi-Green (2012) writes about 'the standard language myth,' citing Crowley's (2003) work on the standard as an 'idealized language.' One of the points Lippi-Green makes is that most people (i.e., non-linguists) feel strongly that they know what the standard language is 'much in the same way that most people could draw a unicorn, or describe a being from *Star Trek's* planet Vulcan, or tell us who King Arthur was and why he needed a Round Table' (Lippi-Green 2012: 57).

Lippi-Green also states that we see the standard as a uniform way of speaking; although some regional variation might be allowed (see below for further discussion), social variation is not considered acceptable within anything labeled as the standard. Furthermore, once we have such a codification of the language we tend to see standardization as almost inevitable, the result of some process come to fruition, one that has also reached a fixed end point. Change, therefore, should be resisted since it can only undo what has been done so laboriously. The standard variety is also often regarded as the natural, proper, and fitting language of those who use – or should use – it. It is part of their heritage and identity, something to be protected, possibly even revered. Milroy (2001, 537) characterizes the resulting ideology as follows: 'The canonical form of the language is a precious inheritance that has been built up over the generations, not by the millions of native speakers, but by a select few who have lavished loving care upon it, polishing, refining, and enriching it until it has become a fine instrument of expression (often these are thought to be literary figures, such as Shakespeare). This is a view held by people in many walks of life, including plumbers, politicians and professors of literature. It is believed that if the canonical variety is not universally supported and protected, the language will inevitably decline and decay.'

This association with the standard as simultaneously the goal of all speakers and something which is created by (and accessible to) only the educated elite is also noted by Lippi-Green. She further points out that what is meant by 'educated' is never specified; indeed, it is quite circular since the standard is spoken by educated people, and we consider them educated because they speak the standard.

The connection to education goes in both directions, because once a language is standardized it is the variety that is taught to both native and non-native speakers of the language. It takes on ideological dimensions – social, cultural, and sometimes political – beyond the purely linguistic ones. In Fairclough's words (2001, 47) it becomes 'part of a much wider process of economic, political and cultural unification … of great … importance in the establishment of nationhood, and the nation-state is the favoured form of capitalism.' According to the criteria of association with a nation and its economic, political, and cultural capital, both English and French are quite obviously standardized, Italian somewhat less so, and varieties associated with sub-groups within a society, such as the variety known as African American English, not at all.

Exploration 2.2:   Standard Pronunciation?

How do you pronounce the following words? (They are presented in groups to bring out particular contrasts that are present in some dialects but not others; try to pronounce these words naturally, but do note if you are aware of pronunciations different from your own.) Do you consider some pronunciations nonstandard? Compare your assessments with others in the class; does what is considered 'standard' vary from one region to the next?

but, butter, rudder	*calm, farm*
bad, bed, bid	*which, witch*
pen, pin	*Mary, merry, marry*
cot, caught, court	*do, dew, due*
happy, house, hotel, hospital	*news, noose*
tune, lute, loot	*picture, pitcher*
suet, soot	*morning, mourning*

The standardization process

In order for a standard form to develop, a norm must be accepted; as discussed above, that norm is an idealized norm, one that users of the language are asked to aspire to rather than one that actually accords with their observed behavior. However, it is perceived as a clearly defined variety.

Selection of the norm may prove difficult because choosing one vernacular as a norm means favoring those who speak that variety. As noted by Heller (2010), language can be viewed not as simply a reflection of social order but as something which helps establish social hierarchies. Thus it is not just that a variety is chosen as the model for the standard because it is associated with a prestigious social identity, but that it also enhances the powerful position of those who speak it, while diminishing all other varieties, their speakers, and any possible competing norms.

Because the standard is an abstraction, attitudes toward and associations with the normative forms are all-important. A group that feels intense solidarity may be willing to overcome great linguistic differences in establishing a norm, whereas one that does not have this feeling may be unable to overcome relatively small differences and be unable to agree on a single variety and norm. Serbs and Croats were never able to agree on a norm, particularly as other differences reinforced linguistic ones. In contrast, we can see how Hindi and Urdu have gone their separate ways in terms of codification due to religious and political differences.

The standardization process itself performs a variety of functions (Mathiot and Garvin 1975). It unifies individuals and groups within a larger community while at the same time separating the community that results from other communities. Therefore, it can be employed to reflect and symbolize some kind of identity: regional, social, ethnic, or religious. A standardized variety can also be used to give prestige to speakers, marking off those who employ it from those who do not, that is, those who continue to speak a nonstandard variety. It can therefore serve as a kind of goal for those who have somewhat different norms; Standard English and Standard French are such goals for many whose norms are dialects of these languages. However, as we will see (particularly in chapters 6–8), these goals are not always pursued and may even be resisted.

The standard and language change

Standardization is also an ongoing matter, for only 'dead' languages like Latin and Classical Greek do not continue to change and develop. The standardization process is necessarily an ongoing one for living languages. The standardization process is also obviously one that attempts either to reduce or to eliminate diversity and variety. However, it would appear that such diversity and variety are 'natural' to all languages, assuring them of their vitality and enabling them to change (see chapter 8). To that extent, standardization imposes a strain on languages or, if not on the languages themselves, on those who take on the task of standardization. That may be one of the reasons why various national academies have had so many difficulties in their work: they are essentially in a no-win situation, always trying to 'fix' the consequences of changes that they cannot prevent, and continually being compelled to issue new pronouncements on linguistic matters. Unfortunately, those who think you can standardize and 'fix' a language for all time are often quite influential in terms of popular attitudes about language. One issue today is the influence of texting and computer-mediated communication on the language, and there are always those who are resistant to new developments. Take, for instance, an article in the online version of the *Daily Mail* titled 'I h8 txt msgs: How texting is wrecking our language,' in which the author writes about '… the relentless onward march of the texters, the SMS (Short Message Service) vandals who are doing to our language what Genghis Khan did to his neighbours eight hundred years ago. They are destroying it: pillaging our punctuation; savaging our sentences; raping our vocabulary. And they must be stopped.' Such attitudes about languages are not in keeping with how sociolinguists view language; as we have discussed above, internal variation is inherent to all languages, and all languages keep changing.

Standard English?

It is not at all easy for us to define Standard English because of a failure to agree about the norm or norms that should apply. For example, Trudgill (1995, 5–6) defines Standard English as the variety:

- Usually used in print
- Normally taught in schools
- Learned by non-native speakers
- Spoken by educated people
- Used in news broadcasts

Note that this definition revolves around how it is used, not the particular features of the language, as Standard English is constantly changing and developing. Trudgill also points out that the standard is not the same as formal language, as the standard can also be used colloquially (see below for a discussion of formal and informal styles).

Historically, the standard variety of English is based on the dialect of English that developed after the Norman Conquest resulted in the permanent removal of the Court from Winchester to London. This dialect became the one preferred by the educated, and it was developed and promoted as a model, or norm, for wider and wider segments of society. It was also the norm (although not the only variety) that was carried overseas, but not one unaffected by such export. Today, written Standard English is codified to the extent that the grammar and vocabulary of written varieties of English are much the same everywhere in the world: variation among local standards is really quite minor, so that the Singapore, South African, and Irish standard varieties are really very little different from one another so far as grammar and vocabulary are concerned. Indeed, Standard English is so powerful that it exerts a tremendous pressure on all such local varieties; we will return to this topic in chapter 14 in our discussion of language planning and policy. However, differences in the spoken varieties exist and are found everywhere in the world that English is used and, while these differences may have been reduced somewhat in the British Isles, they may actually have increased almost everywhere else, for example, within new English-speaking countries in Africa and Asia.

The standard–dialect hierarchy

As we have just seen, trying to decide whether something is or is not a language or in what ways languages are alike and different can be quite troublesome. However, we usually experience fewer problems of the same kind with regard to dialects. There is usually little controversy over the fact that they are either regional or social varieties of something that is widely acknowledged to be a language. That is, dialects are usually easily related to the standard variety because of the latter's sociopolitical salience.

Some people are also aware that the standard variety of any language is actually only the preferred dialect of that language: Parisian French, Florentine Italian, or the Zanzibar variety of Swahili in Tanzania. It is the variety that has been chosen for some reason, perhaps political, social, religious, or economic, or some combination of reasons, to serve as either the model or the norm for other varieties. It is the empowered variety. As a result, the standard is often not called a dialect at all, but is regarded as the language itself. It takes on an ideological dimension and becomes the 'right' and 'proper' language of the group of people, the very expression of their being. One consequence is that all other varieties become related to that standard and are regarded as dialects of that standard but with none of its power. Of course, this process usually involves a complete restructuring of the historical facts.

We see a good instance of this process in Modern English. The new standard is based on the dialect of the area surrounding London, which was just one of several dialects of Old English, and not the most important since both the western and northern dialects were once at least equally as important. However, in the modern period, having provided the base for Standard English, this dialect exerts a strong influence over all the other dialects of England so that it is not just first among equals but rather represents the modern language itself to the extent that the varieties spoken in the west and north are generally regarded as its local variants. Historically, these varieties arise from different sources, but now they are viewed only in relation to the standardized variety.

A final comment seems called for with regard to the terms language and dialect. A dialect is a subordinate variety of a language, so that we can say that Texas English and Swiss German are, respectively, dialects of English and German. The language name (i.e., English or German) is the superordinate term. We can also say of some languages that they contain more than one dialect; for example, English, French, and Italian are spoken in various dialects. If a language is spoken by so few people, or so uniformly, that it has only one variety, we might be tempted to say that language and dialect become synonymous in such a case. However, another view is that it is inappropriate to use dialect in such a situation because the requirement of subordination is not met. Consequently, calling something a dialect of a particular language implies that that language has at least two dialects, but calling something a language does not necessarily entail that it has subordinate dialects.

Regional Dialects

Regional variation in the way a language is spoken is likely to provide one of the easiest ways of observing variety in language. As you travel throughout a wide geographical area in which a language is spoken, and particularly if that language has been spoken in that area for many hundreds of years, you are almost certain to notice differences in pronunciation, in the choices and forms of words, and in syntax. There may even be very distinctive local colorings in the language which you notice as you move from one location to another. Such distinctive varieties are usually called **regional dialects** of the language.

Dialect continua

This use of the term dialect to differentiate among regional varieties can be confounded by what is called a **dialect continuum**, in which there is gradual change of the language. Over large distances the dialects at each end of the continuum may well be mutually unintelligible, although speakers can easily understand people in neighboring areas. In these cases, it was (and still is) possible to travel long distances and, by making only small changes in speech from location to location, continue to communicate with the inhabitants. (You might have to travel somewhat slowly, however, because of the necessary learning that would be involved!) It has been said that at one time a person could travel from the south of what is now Italy to the north of what is now France in this manner. It is quite clear that such a person began the journey speaking one language and ended it speaking something entirely different; however, there was no one point at which the changeover occurred, nor is there actually any way of determining how many intermediate dialect areas that person passed through. For an intriguing empirical test of this idea, one using recent phonetic data from a continuum of Saxon and Franconian dialects in the Netherlands, see Heeringa and Nerbonne (2001). They conclude that the traveler 'perceives phonological distance indirectly' (2001, 398) and that there are 'unsharp borders between dialect areas' (2001, 399).

In such a distribution, which dialects can be classified together under one language, and how many such languages are there? As we have suggested above, this distinction is based more on social identity and political boundaries than on linguistic criteria. The hardening of political boundaries in the modern world as a result of the growth of states, particularly nation-states rather than multinational or multiethnic states, has led to the hardening of language boundaries. Although residents of territories on both sides of the Dutch–German border (within the West Germanic continuum) or the French–Italian border (within the West Romance continuum) have many similarities in speech even today, they will almost certainly tell you that they speak dialects of Dutch or German in the one case and French or Italian in the other. Various pressures – political, social, cultural, and educational – may serve to harden state boundaries and to make the linguistic differences among states more, not less, pronounced.

Dialect geography

When a language is recognized as being spoken in different varieties, the issue becomes one of deciding how many varieties and how to classify each variety. **Dialect geography** is the term used to describe attempts made to map the distributions of various linguistic features so as to show their geographical provenance. For example, in seeking to determine features of the dialects of English and to show their distributions, dialect geographers try to find answers to questions such as the following. Is this an *r*-pronouncing area of English, as in words like *car* and *cart*, or is it not? What past tense form of *drink* do speakers prefer? What names do people give to particular objects in the environment, for example, *elevator* or *lift*, *carousel* or *roundabout*? We calls such features **variables**, as there are variable (i.e., varied and changing) ways of realizing them. For example, the past tense of *drink* might be *drank* or *drunk*, or the words for the fuel you put in an automobile could be *petrol* or *gas*.

Sometimes maps are drawn to show actual boundaries around such variables, boundaries called **isoglosses**, so as to distinguish an area in which a certain feature is found from areas in which it is absent. When several such isoglosses coincide, the result is sometimes called a **dialect boundary**. Then we may be tempted to say that speakers on one side of that boundary speak one dialect and speakers on the other side speak a different dialect. We will return to this topic in chapter 6.

Everyone has an accent

Finally, the term dialect, particularly when it is used in reference to regional variation, should not be confused with the term **accent**. Standard English, for example, is spoken in a variety of accents, often with clear regional and social associations: there are accents associated with North America, Singapore, India, Liverpool (Scouse), Tyneside (Geordie), Boston, New York, and so on. However, many people who live in such places show a remarkable uniformity to one another in their grammar and vocabulary because they speak Standard English and the differences are merely those of accent, that is, how they pronounce what they say.

One English accent has achieved a certain eminence, the accent known as **Received Pronunciation** (RP), the accent of perhaps as few as 3 percent of those who live in England. (The 'received' in Received Pronunciation is a little bit of old-fashioned snobbery: it meant the accent allowed one to be received into the 'better' parts of society!) This accent is of fairly recent origin (see Mugglestone 1995), becoming established as prestigious only in the late nineteenth century and not even given its current label until the 1920s. In the United Kingdom at least, it is 'usually associated with a higher social or educational background, with the BBC and the professions, and [is] most commonly taught to students learning English as a foreign language' (Wakelin 1977, 5). Those who use this accent are often regarded as speaking 'unaccented' English because it lacks a regional association within England. As Hughes et al. (2005, 3) say: 'Because of its use on radio and television, within Britain RP has become probably the most widely understood of all accents. This in turn means that the learner who succeeds in speaking it, other things being equal, has the best chance of being understood wherever he or she goes in the British Isles.' Other names for this accent are the Queen's English, Oxford English, and BBC English. However, there is no unanimous agreement that the Queen does in fact use RP. Harrington et al. (2000) point out that an acoustic analysis of her Christmas broadcasts since 1952 showed a drift in her accent 'toward one that is characteristic of speakers who are younger and/or lower in the social hierarchy.' She 'no longer speaks the Queen's English of the 1950s.' Today, too, a wide variety of accents can be found at Oxford University, and regional accents also feature prominently in the various BBC services.

Trudgill (1995, 7) has pointed out what he considers to be the most interesting characteristics of RP: the speakers who use it do not identify as coming from a particular region, nor is the variety associated with a particular region, except that it is largely confined to England. Further, it is possible to speak Standard English but not speak RP; hence our characterization of it as an accent and not a dialect. As Bauer (1994, 115–21) also shows, RP continues to change. One of its most recent manifestations has been labeled 'Estuary English' (Rosewarne 1994) – sometimes also called 'Cockneyfied RP' – a development of RP along the lower reaches of the Thames reflecting a power shift in London toward the worlds of finance, entertainment, sport, and commerce and away from that of inherited position, the Church, law, and traditional bureaucracies.

It is also interesting to observe that the 1997 *English Pronouncing Dictionary* published by Cambridge University Press abandoned the label RP in favor of BBC English even though this latter term is not unproblematic, as the BBC itself has enlarged the accent pool from which it draws its newsreaders. One consequence of this policy is that some people see old standards as being eroded, that is, their own power base being threatened. A letter writer to the *Daily Telegraph* in October 1995 informed readers that 'Sir Harold Nicolson looked forward, in 1955, to an age when all classes would "speak English as beautifully and uniformly as they do upon the BBC." Forty years on, though, the Corporation has abandoned its old manner of speech in favour of the all-too-aptly named "classless" accent, which, though certainly uniform, is far from beautiful.'

The development of Estuary English is one part of a general leveling of accents within the British Isles. The changes are well documented; see, for example, Foulkes and Docherty (1999), who review a variety of factors involved in the changes that are occurring in cities. One feature of Estuary English, the use of a **glottal stop** for a 't' sound (Fabricus 2002), is also not unique to that variety but is spreading widely, for example, to Newcastle, Cardiff, and Glasgow, and even as far north as rural Aberdeenshire in northeast Scotland (Marshall 2003). Watt (2000, 2002) used the vowels in *face* and *goat* to show that Geordie, the Newcastle accent, levels toward a regional accent norm rather than toward a national one, almost certainly revealing a preference for establishing a regional identity rather than either a very limited local identity or a wider national one. Recent research (see Coupland 2007, 97–9) also shows that while British people in general still have a high regard for RP they also like Scottish- and Irish-accented English. However, they do not like the accents of cities such as Glasgow, Birmingham, and Liverpool, nor do they like Asian- or German-accented English. Most people like their own accents whatever they are and seem content with them. Coupland says of accent variation: the 'social meanings … are clearly multidimensional, inherently variable, and potentially unstable' (2007, 99).

The most generalized accent in North America is sometimes referred to as **News-caster English**, the accent associated with announcers on the major television networks, or **General American**, a term which emphasizes its widespread accept-ance and lack of regional association (see the website for this chapter to find a link to the discussion of Standard American English in the *Do You Speak American?* PBS production). Lippi-Green (2012, 62) endorses the use of the term SAE (**Standard American English**), while recognizing that it is a 'mythical' beast and idealizes a homogeneous variety. There is no official definition of what forms are included in SAE in terms of accent or grammar; as noted by Pinker (2012), 'The rules of stand-ard English are not legislated by a tribunal but emerge as an implicit consensus within a virtual community of writers, readers, and editors. That consensus can change over time in a process as unplanned and uncontrollable as the vagaries of fashion.' It is also often recognized that there are regional standards in US English; for example, while **r-lessness** may be considered standard in Boston or Atlanta, it is not in Chicago; /ai/ **monophthongization** (e.g., the pronunciation of the vowel in the pronoun 'I' to sound more like 'Ah') is heard by newscasters in southeastern parts of the United States but not farther north or west.

As a final observation we must reiterate that it is impossible to speak English (or any other language) without an accent. There is no such thing as 'unaccented English.' RP is an accent, a social one rather than a regional one. However, we must note that there are different evaluations of the different accents, evaluations arising from social factors not linguistic ones. Matsuda (1991, 1361) says it is really an issue of power: 'When … parties are in a relationship of domination and subordination we tend to say that the dominant is normal, and the subordinate is different from normal. And so it is with accent. … People in power are perceived as speaking normal, unaccented English. Any speech that is different from that constructed norm is called an accent.' In the pages that follow we will return constantly to lin-guistic issues having to do with power.

Social Dialects

The term dialect can also be used to describe differences in speech associated with various social groups or classes. An immediate problem is that of defining **social group** (see chapter 3) or **social class** (see chapter 6), giving proper weight to the various factors that can be used to determine social position, for example, occupation, place of residence, education, income, 'new' versus 'old' money, racial or ethnic category, cultural background, caste, religion, and so on. Such factors as these do appear to be related fairly directly to how people speak. There is a British 'public-school' dialect, and there is an 'African American' dialect found in many places in the United States; we will elaborate on **ethnic dialects** in the next section.

Whereas regional dialects are geographically based, social dialects originate among social groups and are related to a variety of factors, the principal ones apparently being social class, religion, and race/ethnicity. In India, for example, caste, one of the clearest of all social differentiators, quite often determines which variety of a language a speaker uses. In a city like Baghdad in a more peaceful era than at present the Christian, Jewish, and Muslim inhabitants spoke different varieties of Arabic. In this case the first two groups used their variety solely within the group but the Muslim variety served as a lingua franca, or common language, among the groups. Consequently, Christians and Jews who dealt with Muslims used two varieties: their own at home and the Muslim variety for trade and in all inter-group relationships.

Studies in **social dialectology**, the term used to refer to this branch of linguistic study, examine how ways of speaking are linked to social differences within a particular region. Socio-economic class is a main factor which will be addressed at length in chapters 6–8. Another factor in social dialectology which has received a great deal of attention is race/ethnicity; we will focus on African American Vernacular English, about which a wealth of sociolinguistic research has been carried out, and also present information about Latino Englishes in the Unites States, which are emerging as an important focus in the study of ethnic dialects. First, however, we will introduce a German social dialect which is controversial both in German society and among sociolinguists, a case which brings to the forefront the concerns inherent to social dialectology.

Kiezdeutsch 'neighborhood German'

The term *Dialekt*, 'dialect' in German, as mentioned above, has historically been used solely to refer to regional varieties. While sometimes stigmatized, these dialects are at the same time integral to regional identities and seen as deeply, essentially German. While a body of literature on *Gastarbeiterdeutsch* ('guest worker German') emerged beginning in the 1970s, this variety was identified as a second language or a 'pidginized' variety of German, and very clearly spoken by immigrants (e.g., Keim 1978, Pfaff 1980), and thus, not a German *Dialekt*. Subsequently, a body of research about multilingual language practices of multiethnic groups of urban youths in Germany showed that multilingual practices were common among urban youths of many backgrounds (e.g., Auer and Dirim 2003, Kallmeyer and Keim 2003); while this research did show that such practices were not unique to children of immigrant background, it also did not suggest that multilingual discourse was something quintessentially German. However, when *Kiezdeutsch*, a way of speaking associated with multiethnic neighborhoods, was described as a German dialect (Wiese 2010, 2012), resistance to the idea of recognizing this way of speaking as a variety of the German language became apparent. The controversies surround this work, both in academic circles and in public discourses, exemplify the issues in social dialects in general. These issues include the label applied to the variety, identifying the features of the variety, correlations with demographic factors, and the process of the development.

In the case of *Kiezdeutsch*, this term was chosen by researchers because other terms used to refer to the variety in everyday speech were inaccurate (e.g., *Türkendeutsch*, 'Turks' German') and potentially offensive (e.g., *Kanak Sprak*, derived from a derogatory term for foreigners [*Kanak* or *Kanaker*], and nonstandard spelling/pronunciation of German *Sprache* 'language'). However, as this case illustrates, no term is perfect. The term *Kiez* varies regionally in how it is used; in Berlin it is commonly used in a positive manner to refer to one's neighborhood, indicating it is where one feels at home, but in Hamburg the term is used to refer to one particular neighborhood, the so-called red light district. As we will see in our discussion of African American Vernacular English and Latino Englishes below, labels for varieties are often problematic and sites of controversy; this issue will also be discussed further in the next chapter as we attempt to define social groups.

While certain features of *Kiezdeutsch* do not seem to be disputed, the development and status of these features are. Wiese argues that although *Kiezdeutsch* does include some lexical items from languages other than German (often, Turkish), it is not a mixed language; instead, the grammatical features have their roots in the German language. She refers to *Kiezdeutsch* as a German dialect. Auer (2013, 36) disputes this, saying it is simply a youth style of speaking which is not used consistently enough to be considered a dialect, and suggests that there are features indicating 'unsichere Beherrschung der deutschen Morphologie' ('uncertain mastery of German morphology'). Similarly, Jannedy (2010) calls *Kiezdeutsch* a 'multi-ethnolectal youth language,' and not a social dialect.

Popular opinion about nonstandard social dialects is often that these ways of speaking are lazy, sloppy, and degenerate. Wiese (2012) aims at convincing a general audience that the features of *Kiezdeutsch* are part of normal language development and variation, not a bastardization through foreign influence, but this position has caused great consternation for many readers, who do not want to accept that a new dialect is possible (see Wiese 2014 for an analysis of this public discourse).

Who speaks *Kiezdeutsch* is also represented in the literature in different ways. There is agreement that its speakers generally live in multiethnic neighborhoods, and it is referred to as a youth language, but whether it is indeed limited to young speakers has not been conclusively demonstrated. Auer (2013) discusses the speakers of *Kiezdeutsch* as socially marginalized youths of immigrant background, while among Wiese's research participants are speakers with German backgrounds who are monolingual German speakers (as well as speakers of other ethnic or national backgrounds who are monolingual German speakers).

Finally, the process of the development of this variety is controversial. It is often assumed to be the result of language contact, meaning that the features are borrowed from other languages, especially Turkish (e.g., Auer 2013). Wiese (2010, 2012) argues for a somewhat difference scenario: that this situation of language contact has created a fertile environment for internally motivated language change (see chapters 5 and 8 for discussions of contact variety development and language change more broadly).

What is clear is that *Kiezdeutsch* is a variety which has developed as an ingroup language; the development and use of *Kiezdeutsch* is intertwined with the identities of the speakers. As will be discussed for ethnic dialects, the identification with a group is a key element in the development of a social dialect.

Ethnic dialects

So-called ethnic dialects do not arise because members of particular ethnic groups are somehow destined to speak in certain ways; like all other social dialects, ethnic dialects are learned by exposure and anyone, regardless of their ethnic identification or racial categorization, might speak in ways identified as 'African American Vernacular English' or 'Chicano English.' The connection between race/ethnicity/nationality and linguistic variety is one that is entirely socially constructed, it is in no way linked to any inherent attributes of a particular group.

The processes that create ethnic dialects are poorly understood, and much research remains to be done into how and why they develop (we will also address this topic in chapters 6 and 7). However, we do know that ethnic dialects are not simply foreign accents of the majority language, as many of their speakers may well be monolingual speakers of the majority language. Chicano English, for example, is not English with a Spanish accent and grammatical transfer, as many of its speakers are not Spanish speakers but English monolinguals. Ethnic dialects are ingroup ways of speaking the majority language.

One study which gives us insights into the motivations for the development of an ethnic dialect was done by Kopp (1999) on Pennsylvania German English, that is, the English spoken among speakers of what is commonly called 'Pennsylvania Dutch,' which is a German dialect which developed in certain regions of Pennsylvania. Kopp analyzes a variety of features associated with speakers of Pennsylvania German in both sectarian (i.e., Amish and Mennonite) and nonsectarian communities. He discovers what at first seems to be a paradoxical pattern: although the sectarians are more isolated from mainstream society, and they continue to speak Pennsylvania German, their English has *fewer* phonological features that identify them as Pennsylvania German speakers than the nonsectarians, who are integrated into the English mainstream and less likely to be speakers of Pennsylvania German. So the nonsectarians, who are in many cases English monolinguals, exhibit more phonological features reminiscent of a Pennsylvania German accent in their spoken English than the sectarians! As Kopp explains, this makes perfect sense when we think of language as providing a way to construct identity. The sectarians speak Pennsylvania German, and thus can use that language to create group boundaries; the nonsectarians, who increasingly do not speak Pennsylvania German, have only their variety of English to use to construct themselves as members of a particular ethnic group.

Although Pennsylvania German English developed largely in rural areas, many ethnic dialects are urban phenomena. Cities are much more difficult to characterize linguistically than are rural hamlets; variation in language and patterns of change are much more obvious in cities, for example, in family structures, employment, and opportunities for social advancement or decline. Migration, both in and out of cities, is also usually a potent linguistic factor.

In research which examines the complexities of urban speech, Jaspers (2008) also addresses some of the ideological issues at stake in the study of ethnic dialects. He addresses the practice of naming particular ways of speaking as **ethnolects**, pointing out that it is indicative of the ideological positions of the sociolinguists doing the research themselves. Labeling and describing a particular way of speaking as an ethnic dialect implies a certain homogeneity about the variety and its speakers, and it inevitably also places the dialect and the group who speaks it outside the mainstream. Jaspers writes (2008, 100):

> The point is not that code-establishment and naming as such should be frowned upon, but that they limit our understanding of inner-city social and linguistic practices, and that they have ideological consequences sociolinguists should take into account. As an alternative, I have advocated that ethnolect be regarded as a useful term for speakers' perceptions of particular ways of speaking (and of course, some scholars of ethnolects are already attending to perceptions of this kind), with the understanding that speakers' perceptions, and the names they develop for them, do not necessarily correspond to systematic linguistic differences (and vice versa).

The following discussion of African American Vernacular English and Latino Englishes attempts to incorporate these disparate perspectives. In doing so, we seek to describe a fascinating linguistic phenomenon, the development and spread of a linguistic variety that is linked to a particular racial group without contributing to **essentialist** ideas about social groups or making simplistic descriptions of languages.

African American Vernacular English

Interest in African American Vernacular English (AAVE) grew in part out of the observation that the speech of many Black residents of the northern United States, in New York City, Philadelphia, Washington, DC, Baltimore, Detroit, and Chicago, resembles the speech of Blacks in southern states in many respects, yet differs from the speech of Whites in their respective regions. To some extent, this similarity is the result of the relatively recent migrations of Blacks out of the south; in another, it is just one reflection of long-standing patterns of racial segregation only now slowly changing, patterns that have tended to separate the population of the United States along color lines. Linguists have referred to this variety of speech as *Black English*, *Black Vernacular English*, and *African* or *Afro-American English*. Today, probably the most-used term is *African American Vernacular English*, and we will use this term (abbreviated as AAVE), although in our discussions of research by particular authors we will use whatever term they used. (The term *Ebonics* – a blend of *Ebony* and *phonics* – has also recently achieved a certain currency in popular speech, but it is not a term we will use in discussion of sociolinguistic research.) It should be also noted that variation in AAVE according to region (e.g., Hinton and Pollock 2000,Wolfram and Thomas 2008), age (e.g., Rickford 1999, Wolfram and Thomas 2002), and social class (e.g., Linnes 1998, Weldon 2004, Wolfram 2007) have also been studied and that these form an essential aspect of ongoing research.

Exploration 2.3:   Naming Varieties, Again

Why do you think the variety we are referring to as 'AAVE' has been referred to with so many different terms? Why have researchers chosen to use 'Black,' 'Afro-American,' or 'African American' to describe this variety at different times? Why is the term 'Vernacular' introduced to describe this way of speaking? In what ways can you link these naming practices to our discussion of the relationship between language and worldview from chapter 1?

Features of AAVE

The features of AAVE which have been researched include phonological, morphological, and syntactic characteristics (see also chapters 6 and 7 on variationist studies for discussions of research on this topic). We will focus here primarily on features which have been found to be specific to AAVE and which have been researched extensively over several decades. This is not, we stress, an exhaustive list of features nor an indepth coverage of the research on their variation (please see the reference in the Further Reading section to find more research on this topic). The aim of this section is to make our readers aware of some of the characteristics of this dialect.

On the phonological level, consonant cluster reduction has often been noted (e.g., from Labov 1972 to Wolfram and Thomas 2008); words such as *test*, *desk*, and *end* may be pronounced without their final consonants. (See chapter 7 for a discussion of earlier work on consonant cluster deletion in AAVE.) Other phonological features commonly found in varieties of AAVE include **r-lessness**, and **/ai/ monophthongization**, and realization of 'th' sounds as /t/, /d/, /f/, /v/ or /s/ (Thomas 2007), although these features are found in other varieties of English in North America and around the world.

Some of the most salient and frequently researched features of AAVE have to do with **verbal -s marking**. This involves the presence or absence of the suffix -*s* on finite verbs. In Standard English dialects, -*s* marking is only on third-person singular verbs (e.g., *She likes cheese*). In AAVE, this marking is sometimes absent (e.g., *She like school*) and this is considered one of the core features of AAVE. Further, verbal -s marking also appears in grammatical contexts other than third-person singular (e.g., *The men has wives*) in some varieties of AAVE. There is extensive literature on patterns of -s marking on verbs (Cukor-Avila 1997, Montgomery et al. 1993, Montgomery and Fuller 1996, Poplack and Tagliamonte 1989, 1991, 2005) showing similarities to other nonstandard English dialects.

Another interesting pattern in the verbal system of AAVE is the use of the **zero copula**. As Labov (1969) has explained, the rule for its use is really quite simple. If you can contract *be* in Standard English, you can delete it in AAVE. That is, since 'He is nice' can be contracted to 'He's nice' in Standard English, it can become 'He nice' in AAVE. However, 'I don't know where he is' cannot be contracted to 'I don't know where he's' in Standard English. Consequently, it cannot become 'I don't know where he' in AAVE. We should note that the zero copula is very rarely found in other dialects of English. It is also not categorical in AAVE; that is, there is variation between realization of copula forms and zero copula. Labov (1972) argued for the use of zero copula as a marker of group membership among certain Black youths in Harlem, members of a gang called the Jets. Zero copula use diminished as strength of group membership decreased. There is a wealth of literature on the linguistic factors in copula variation in AAVE; see, for example, Blake 1997, Hazen 2002, Rickford et al. 1991, Weldon 2003.

Still another feature of AAVE has been called **habitual *be*** (also called invariant *be*, or *be₂*). This feature has become a stereotype of Black speech, often imitated in caricatures of AAVE speakers; for example, the US toy store 'Toys "R" Us' has been jokingly called 'We Be Toys' in Harlem, a predominantly African American neighborhood of New York City (see the link to a discussion of this joke in the web links provided in the online materials for this textbook). The feature is called 'invariant' *be* because the copula is not conjugated, but used in the form of *be* for all subjects (i.e., *I be, you be, he/she/it be*, etc.). It is called 'habitual' because it marks an action which is done repeatedly, that is, habitually. Thus the utterance *They be throwing the ball* does not mean that the people in question are (necessarily) currently throwing a ball, but that they often get together and throw a ball back and forth. This differs in meaning from *They (are) throwing the ball*, which indicates something that is happening at the current time. Research on this feature often focuses on its development, which leads us to another important aspect of research on this dialect as a whole: how did it develop, and how does it continue to change?

Development of AAVE

Sociolinguists disagree on how AAVE relates to other varieties of English in the United States, and this is a controversy of long standing. Kurath (1949, 6) and McDavid (1965, 258) argued that AAVE had no characteristics that were not found in other varieties of English, particularly nonstandard varieties spoken by Americans of any color in the south. This is sometimes called the **Anglicist hypothesis** of origin. In this view, AAVE is just another dialect of American English (see Wolfram and Schilling-Estes 2005 for more discussion). That Black speakers may produce greater quantities of certain nonstandard usages is merely a peculiarity of the style of speaking they have adopted.

Wolfram (2003) and Wolfram and Thomas (2002) take a slightly different position, favoring a neo-Anglicist hypothesis that early African Americans maintained certain features of the languages they brought with them while at the same time accommodating to the local dialects of English. Wolfram and Thomas say that such a **substrate** influence (see chapter 5) from the African languages still persists in AAVE, certainly in the variety they examined in Hyde County, North Carolina. Wolfram and Torbert (2006, 228) claim that 'AAE has diverged from European American varieties over the years, so that present-day AAE is now quite different from contemporary benchmark European American dialects. The differences are not due to earlier language history, but to the everyday nature of African American speech during the twentieth century.'

Diametrically opposed to this view is the view of the creolists, for example, Stewart (1967), Dillard (1972), and Rickford (1977, 1997, 1999), who maintain that AAVE is of **creole origin** (see chapter 5), and therefore a variety of English which originated quite independently of Standard English. In this view, AAVE has features that are typical of **creole languages**, particularly the zero copula and habitual *be*, some residual Africanisms, and certain styles of speaking (such as rapping, sounding, signifying, and fancy talk), which look back to an African origin. In this view, AAVE is not a dialect of English but a creolized variety of English (see chapter 5) which continues to have profound differences from the standard variety.

Another issue that intrigues linguists is the **divergence hypothesis**, that is, the claim that AAVE is diverging from other dialects of English, particularly standard varieties (Bailey and Maynor 1989, Butters 1989, Labov and Harris 1986, Fasold et al. 1987; and Wolfram and Thomas 2002). In this view, the English of Blacks and Whites is diverging in certain parts of the United States. Bailey and Maynor (1989) say that they are diverging in the Brazon Valley in Texas, with only Black speakers using constructions like 'He always be tryin' to catch up' and resisting the adoption of post-vocalic *r* in words like *farm*. Butters (1989) argues that there is no solid evidence to support such a claim, pointing out that there are both divergent and convergent features. He says that AAVE is just like any other dialect of English; it has its own innovations but remains strongly influenced by the standard variety. Wolfram (1990, 131) also discusses the idea that these varieties are diverging and concludes that the evidence is 'flimsy.' However, another review of the evidence (Spears 1992) finds some substance. There may actually, as just stated, be both convergence and divergence, for as Wolfram and Thomas say (2002, 24), 'it is quite possible for particular structures, or structures on one level of language organization, to show convergence at the same time that other structures indicate divergence.' Rickford (1999, 274–7) also points to evidence of both convergence and divergence in East Palo Alto, California, with Black adults showing evidence of convergence and Black teenagers of divergence, although whether the latter is mainly an **age-graded** phenomenon is not at all clear. Although most of these studies look at AAVE as the dialect which is changing away from 'White' dialects, another perspective is presented in Van Herk (2008), who suggests that we can also look at this from another perspective, that is, that the Northern Cities Vowel Shift, a vowel shift found across the northern United States, may be a form of linguistic 'white flight' and it is White speakers who are diverging.

Latino Englishes

This section will address the development of ethnic varieties in Latino communities in various parts of the United States. Although the most research has been done on Chicano English, we use the term Latino Englishes to include varieties in Puerto Rican communities and communities which have Latino residents of various backgrounds.

A central issue in the study of ethnic dialects is distinguishing it from learner varieties. For Latino Englishes, it is important to realize that they develop because of the varieties of *English* spoken in a community, not because of Spanish input. That being said, most speakers of Latino English varieties live in communities in which Spanish is spoken, although the speakers of Latino English may themselves be monolingual English speakers or dominant in English (Bayley and Bonnici 2009, 1305). For example, in her work in a Puerto Rican community in New York City, Zentella (1997) distinguishes between Hispanicized English, which is spoken by community members who grew up in Puerto Rico, and Puerto Rican English, which is spoken by second or later generation Latinos in New York City working-class Spanish-speaking communities; although they may share some features, especially phonological features, the former is a form of learner English while the latter is not.

As with AAVE, many morphosyntactic features of other nonstandard American English dialects are found in Latino Englishes, such as **multiple negation** (e.g., 'That ain't gonna never change in L.A. no more,' Fought 2003, 97), **regularization** of irregular past tense verbs (e.g., 'when she striked me with that ...,' Bailey and Santa Ana 2004, 376), and absence of past tense marking (e.g., 'I saw some girl, and she look pretty,' Bailey and Santa Ana 2004, 376). Also, some features of AAVE are used by Latino English speakers, such as habitual *be* (e.g., 'You supposed to be knowing Spanish,' Carter 2013, 79) and zero copula (e.g., 'They feel like they not Latino,' Carter 2013, 83). Morphosyntactic features unique to Latino Englishes are rare; Fought discussed the use of 'could' rather than 'can' when talking about ability, as in 'Nobody believes that you could fix anything' (Fought 2003, 100), and the use of 'tell' to introduce questions was also mentioned (e.g., 'I told Elinore: is that your brother?' Bailey and Santa Ana 2004, 381).

However, it is the phonology of Latino Englishes that is most distinctive from other dialects of English, and one study (Frazer 1996) showed that non-Latino college students, when given recordings of speakers, could readily identify 'Hispanic' (the term used in this study) speakers of English from non-Hispanics. So what are these salient phonological features? Two differences found between Chicano English and the local dialects in their communities that have been found are less frequent **vowel reduction** and **monophthongization** (Fought 2003, Santa Ana and Bayley 2004). Vowel reduction is the use of a /ə/ (i.e., an 'uh' sound), as is common in casual speech, for example, 'because' is not usually pronounced with a long 'e' (/i/) sound in the first syllable. Chicano English speakers would then be more likely to pronounce this word like 'bee-cuz.' Monophthongization is when a **diphthong** is pronounced without the off-glide; so the word 'least,' by many speakers of US English pronounced with an 'y' (/j/) off-glide following the 'e' (/i/) sound, would be pronounced by Chicano English speakers with fewer and shorter glides.

A further issue with the phonology of Latino Englishes is how the speakers sound in comparison to the non-Latino local speakers in their community. Fought (1999, 2003) found that Chicano English speakers who were working class and had gang affiliations did not participate in ongoing sound changes, and similarly Konopka and Pierrehumbert (2008) found that the speakers of what they call 'Mexican Heritage English' were not participating in the **Northern Cities Vowel Shift** (see chapter 8 for a discussion of this change in progress). Wolfram et al. (2004) also found that on the whole Hispanic speakers did not accommodate to the /ai/ monophthongization of local dialect in North Carolina, although some individual speakers did show patterns more similar to the local norms.

However, what is arguably most noticeable about Chicano English is its intonation (Metcalf 1979, Santa Ana and Bayley 2004). Chicano English has more 'glides,' that is, gradual rises or falls in pitch, and the syllable of the pitch rise is also lengthened, producing emphasis. This contrasts with other American English speech patterns which use stress on a syllable for emphasis, as in the following example, adapted from Santa Ana and Bayley (2004, 427):

> He was CHOKing on it (stress on the first syllable of the word 'choking'; typical of most American English dialects)

> He was chooo↑king on it (lengthened 'o' sound and gradual rising pitch; typical of Chicano English)

Even more salient are final pitch contours. In most varieties of American English, there is a step down in pitch at the end of statements, and a step up at the end of questions. In Chicano English, although the overall contour of statements and questions are different, they both tend to end with a glide up and then down at the end of the sentence. Santa Ana and Bayley (2004, 429) note that this intonational feature is often used in stereotypical representations of Mexicans in Hollywood films.

Although exactly how Latino English varieties develop, and why they develop in some communities and not in others, remains a topic for further investigation, one thing is clear: Latino Englishes are identifiable dialects and as such develop in part to construct an ethnic identity. This does not imply that it is the conscious choice of individual speakers, but that the importance of ethnic identity in a community is part of the linguistic forms which are adopted as part of ingroup speech.

This brief overview of research on AAVE and Latino Englishes has raised two broad issues that we will continue to deal with throughout this text. First, language varieties are often associated with particular social groups and as such are used to construct the social identities of speakers (see chapter 11). Second, these associations are often essentialized and used to discriminate (see chapter 13). In the following section, we will look at varieties of another sort, those defined by the context of use rather than by the user alone.

Styles, Registers, and Genres

The study of dialects is further complicated by the fact that speakers can adopt different **styles** and **registers** of speaking, and both spoken and written language can be seen as belonging to different **genres** of language. So while differences in dialect have to do with speakers and their regional or social identities, styles, registers, and genres have to do with different contexts of use. Although the terms style, register, and genre have been used in different ways by different scholars, and there may be overlap between these three terms, we can delineate broad categories which differentiate them (Lee 2001). The term style is most often used to discuss differences in formality; register generally denotes specific ways of speaking associated with particular professions or social groups; and genre is understood as a set of co-occurring language features associated with particular frames (Bauman 2000).

Style

When choosing a style, you can speak very formally or very informally, your choice being governed by circumstances. Ceremonial occasions almost invariably require very formal speech, public lectures somewhat less formal, casual conversation quite informal, and conversations between intimates on matters of little importance may be extremely informal and casual. (See Joos 1962, for an entertaining discussion.) We may try to relate the level of formality chosen to a variety of factors: the kind of occasion; the various social, age, and other differences that exist between the participants; the particular task that is involved, for example, writing or speaking; the emotional involvement of one or more of the participants; and so on. We appreciate that such distinctions exist when we recognize the stylistic appropriateness of *What do you intend to do, your majesty?* and the inappropriateness of *Waddya intend doin', Rex?* While it may be difficult to characterize discrete levels of formality, it is nevertheless possible to show that native speakers of all languages control a range of stylistic varieties. It is also quite possible to predict with considerable confidence the stylistic features that a native speaker will tend to employ on certain occasions. We will return to related issues in chapters 4, 7, and 11.

Exploration 2.4:   Formality in Introductions

Imagine you are introducing a romantic partner to (a) another friend, (b) your parents, (c) your grandparents, (d) a casual acquaintance, or (e) your boss. Do you use different words to describe your relationship, or more or less elaborate ways to perform the act of introducing? (e.g., 'This is Pat,' vs. 'I'd like you to meet my friend Pat' or 'This is my boy/girlfriend Pat.') Compare your own answers with those of other classmates. How might differences in the ideas about the formality of particular relationships (e.g., family members, an employer) account for the different ways people might execute an introduction? Are there different understandings about the level of formality of different linguistic forms used for introductions?

Register

Register is another complicating factor in any study of language varieties. Generally speaking, registers are sets of language items associated with discrete occupational or social groups. Agha (2006, 24) describes a register as 'a linguistic *repertoire* that is associated, culture-internally, with particular social practices and with persons who engage in such practices' (italics in original). Biber and Conrad (2003, 175) distinguish work on registers from other analyses of discourse, saying that they focus on the situational parameters defining the communicative situation. Speakers learn different registers through socialization in different cultural groups within their society. What we refer to as 'legalese' or 'personal ads' are identifiable registers for most people. Use of such registers thus either conforms to the norms for a particular, socially situated way of using language, or is a way of invoking the context usually associated with that register. Of course, one person may control a variety of registers: you can be a stockbroker and an archeologist, or a mountain climber and an economist. A register helps you to construct an identity at a specific time or place.

Genre

A related term is genre, which overlaps in meaning with register but is usually associated with particular linguistic features; thus register focuses more on the social situation, and genre more on the text type (Ferguson 1994; Lee 2001). However, like a register, a genre can also function 'as a routinized vehicle for encoding and expressing a particular order of knowledge and experience' (Bauman 2000, 80). For instance, even if we do not understand all of the words, we all recognize the form of a recipe, a personals ad, a news article, or an infomercial. Thus, while such ways of speaking do require a certain socialization, it is not necessarily socialization into a particular social or occupational group but rather an acquired familiarity with certain norms of language use in particular contexts and for specific functions.

Dialect, style, register, and genre differences are largely independent: you can talk casually about mountain climbing in a local variety of a language, or you can write a formal technical study of wine making. However, speakers have clear ideas about which ways of speaking are considered 'appropriate' for a particular speech event or social context.

Chapter Summary

What is the relationship between a language and a dialect? This chapter seeks to acknowledge many non-linguists' perceptions about this issue while presenting the sociolinguists' stance that particular ways of speaking are considered distinct languages or subordinated dialects because of sociopolitical ideologies and identities, not because of linguistic differences between varieties. While a 'language' is considered an overarching category containing dialects, it is also often seen as synonymous with the standard dialect; yet closer examination of the standard reveals that it is a value-laden abstraction, not an objectively defined linguistic variety. Further, every language has a range of regional dialects, social dialects, styles, registers, and genres. These interrelated concepts are discussed and defined with a focus on how they are part of speakers' identities and social interactions.

Exercises

1. Read the article from *The Independent* titled 'God save the Queen's English: Our language is under threat from ignorance, inverted snobbery, and deliberate "dumbing down".' (You can find this in the links listed for this chapter on the website for this textbook.) Find evidence of the following aspects of the 'standard language myth' referred to in this chapter, notably:
    *   the standard as natural, as evidenced by its widespread use;
    *   the link between the standard and the heritage and identity of its speakers;
    *   the standard as linguistically superior;
    *   the standard as a clearly defined variety with recognizable features.
2. Look at the following examples, and answer the following questions about each: Is this an example of a dialect, style, register, or genre? Does it have a name? How can you describe this variety in terms of its function? What are the linguistic features that make this text identifiable as belonging to a certain category?

- I direct my Executor, hereinafter named, to pay all of my matured debts and my funeral expenses, as well as the costs and expenses of the administration of my estate, as soon after my death as practicable. I further direct that all estate, inheritance, transfer, and succession taxes which are payable by reason under this will, be paid out of my residuary estate; and I hereby waive on behalf of my estate any right to recover from any person any part of such taxes so paid. My Executor, in his sole discretion, may pay from my domiciliary estate all or any portion of the costs of ancillary administration and similar proceedings in other jurisdictions.

- Combine the first four ingredients in a medium bowl. Mix eggs, sugar, and oil in a large bowl; add flour mixture to this bowl and stir until just moistened. Do not over-mix. Pour into a $13'' \times 6''$ baking dish and bake at 350 degrees for 35 minutes, or until a knife inserted comes out clean.

- Tired of having to wipe your tears away when chopping onion? Weary of dicing and slicing for hours? Now you can be tear and fancy free! Introducing the No More Tears Slicer, which lets you slice your prep time in half! With the No More Tears Onion Slicer, you can slice your way through onions, dice vegetables, and slice cheese in minutes! This is one kitchen tool you don't want to do without! Order this time-saving instrument NOW for the TV-price of only $19.99!

- The University of Portlandia is seeking a research fellow to work on the Multilingual Metrolingualism (MM) project, a new five-year NSF-funded project led by Dr Hannelore Holmes. We are seeking a highly motivated and committed researcher to work on all aspects of the MM Project, but in particular on developing a coding system suitable for urban youth language use. Applicants should have a PhD in a relevant area of sociolinguistics or a closely related field. Proficiency in at least one of the following languages is essential: French, Swahili, Mandarin, or Tok Pisin. Candidates must also have good knowledge and understanding of discourse analysis, semiotics, and grammatical analysis. Applicants should demonstrate enthusiasm for independent research and commitment to developing their research career. The post is fixed-term for five years due to funding. The post is available from April 1 or as soon as possible thereafter. Job sharers welcome. The University of Portlandia is an Equal Opportunity Employer.

- Researchers Find Link Between Education, Smartness (*The Onion*, September 3, 2007)

  BOSTON – A study released Tuesday by the Lyman Center for Policy Evaluation and Strategy may have uncovered a link between school-based education and human smartness.

  'Based on these forms we had people fill out, and these charts we came up with, we're pretty sure exposure to education in early life is consistent with higher levels of smartness-having overall,' said Brent Shale, one of the study's coauthors. 'Also, we figured out that the more educated-er people are, the better they are at doing complicated stuff like filling out forms and understanding charts.'

    If the study results are corroborated, the researchers say, it could mean 'a whole new understanding of, you know, what smartness even is.'

3.   Representing dialect. Find a novel that portrays AAVE speakers, such as Nora Zeale Hurston's *Their Eyes Were Watching God* or Mark Twain's *Huckleberry Finn*. What linguistic features are used in the dialogues to represent Black speakers? (Name at least four.) How are they similar to or different from the features discussed in this chapter? (Keep in mind that we have in no way presented a comprehensive list of features of AAVE; you may need to consult other research on AAVE if you want to draw conclusions about whether this fits with linguists' descriptions of the dialect.) Name and describe the features and give examples from the novel you are using.

Do you think this writing represents authentic speech? What do you know about the author that contributes to your position on this?

Further Reading

Biber, Douglas, and Susan Conrad (2009). *Register, Genre, and Style*. New York: Cambridge University Press.

    This volume provides an overview of the definitions and theoretical issues for studying register, genre, and style, as well as methodological issues for the study of these linguistic phenomena.

Crowley, Tony (2003). *Standard English and the Politics of Language*. Basingstoke: Palgrave Macmillan.

    This volume addresses the standard language construct in British history, looking at social issues and educational contexts.

Green, Lisa J. (2002). *African American English: A Linguistic Introduction*. Cambridge: Cambridge University Press.

    This discussion of the features and uses of AAVE is very accessible and a good introduction for anyone interested in this variety, its grammar and its social context.

Hughes, Arthur, Peter Trudgill, and Dominic Watt (2013). *English Accents and Dialects: An Introduction to Social and Regional Varieties of English in the British Isles*. Abingdon: Routledge.

    This fifth edition offers an up-to-date description and discussion of British Isles dialects, including both rural and urban varieties which reflect the contemporary societies of this region.

McDavid, R. I. (1965). American Social Dialects. *College English*, 26: 254–60.

    An early study on social dialects which introduces key issues and addresses the social and educational consequences of societal differentiation through linguistic differences.

Wolfram and Schilling-Estes (2005). *American English: Dialects and Variation*. Oxford: Blackwell.

    A comprehensive discussion both of issues in the study of dialects and of dialects specific to the US context, this text addresses theoretical issues involved in the study of language variation as well as applications of this knowledge to educational contexts.

For further resources for this chapter visit the companion website at
 www.wiley.com/go/wardhaugh/sociolinguistics

References

Agha, A. (2006). Registers of Language. In A. Duranti (ed.), *A Companion to Linguistic Anthropology*. Oxford: Blackwell.

Auer, Peter (2013). Ethnische Marker im Deutschen zwischen Varietät und Stil. *Das Deutsch der Migranten* (*IDS Yearbook 2012*), 9–40.

Auer, Peter, and Inci Dirim (2003). Socio-cultural orientation, urban youth styles and the spontaneous acquisition of Turkish by non-Turkish adolescents in Germany. In J. K. Androutsopoulos and A. Georgakopoulou (eds.), *Discourse Constructions of Youth Identities*. Amsterdam: John Benjamins, 223–46.

Bauer, L. (1994). *Watching English Change: An Introduction to the Study of Linguistic Change in Standard Englishes in the Twentieth Century*. London: Longman.

Bailey, G. and N. Maynor (1989). The Divergence Controversy. *American Speech* 64: 12–39.

Bauman, Richard (2000). Language, Identity and Performance. *Pragmatics* 10(1): 1–5.

Bayley, Robert and Lisa M. Bonnici (2009). Recent Research on Latinos in the USA and Canada, Part 1: Language Maintenance and Shift and English Varieties. *Language and Linguistics Compass* 3(5): 1300–13.

Bayley, Robert and Otto Santa Ana (2004). Chicano English: Morphology and syntax. In Bernd Kortmann, Kate Burridge, Rajend Mesthrie, Edgar W. Schneider, and Clive Upton (eds.), *A Handbook of Varieties of English*. Berlin: Mouton de Gruyter, 374–90.

Biber, D. and S. Conrad (2003). Register Variation: A Corpus Approach. In D. D. Schiffrin, D. Tannen, and H. E. Hamilton (eds.), *The Handbook of Discourse Analysis*. Oxford: Blackwell.

Blake, Rene (1997). Defining the Envelope of Linguistic Variation: The Case of 'Don't Count' Forms in the Copula Analysis of African American Vernacular English. *Language Variation and Change* 9(1), 57–79.

Blommaert, J. (2010). *The Sociolinguistics of Globalization*. Cambridge: Cambridge University Press.

Butters, R. R. (1989). *The Death of Black English: Divergence and Convergence in Black and White Vernaculars*. Frankfurt: Peter Lang.

Carmichael, C. (2002). 'A People Exists and that People Has its Language': Language and Nationalism in the Balkans. In S. Barbour and C. Carmichael (eds.), *Language and Nationalism in Europe*. Oxford: Oxford University Press.

Carter, Phillip (2013). Shared spaces, shared structures: Latino social formation and African American English in the U.S. South. *Journal of Sociolinguistics* 17: 66–92.

Coulmas, F. (1999). The Far East. In J. A. Fishman (ed.), *Handbook of Language and Ethnic Identity*. Oxford: Oxford University Press.

Coupland, N. (2007). *Style: Language Variation and Identity*. Cambridge: Cambridge University Press.

Crowley, Tony (2003). *Standard English and the Politics of Language*. Basingstoke: Palgrave Macmillan.

Cukor-Avila, Patricia (1997). Change and stability in the use of verbal -s over time in AAVE. *Englishes Around the World I*. Amsterdam: John Benjamins, 295–306.

Daily Mail, 'I h8 txt msgs: how texting is wrecking our language.' http://www.dailymail.co .uk/news/article-483511/I-h8-txt-msgs-How-texting-wrecking-language.html# ixzz2uJbwPnOh, (accessed July 10, 2014).

Dillard, J. L. (1972). *Black English: Its History and Usage in the United States*. New York: Random House.

Doetjes, Gerke (2007). Understanding differences in inter-Scandinavian language understanding. In D. Jan and Ludger Yeevaert (eds.), *Receptive Multilingualism. Linguistic Analyses, Language Policies and Didactic Concepts*. Hamburg Studies on Multilingualism, vol. 6. Amsterdam: John Benjamins, 217–30.

Fabricus, A. (2002). Ongoing Change in Modern RP: Evidence for the Disappearing Stigma of t-glottalling. *English World-Wide* 23(1): 115–36.

Fairclough, N. (2001). *Language and Power*. 2nd edn. London: Longman.

Fasold, R. W., W. Labov, F. B. Vaughn-Cooke et al. (1987). Are Black and White Vernaculars Diverging? Papers from the NWAVE XIV panel discussion. *American Speech* 62(1): 3–80.

Ferguson, C. A. (1994). Dialect, Register, and Genre: Working Assumptions about Conventionalization. In D. Biber and E. Finegan (eds.), *Sociolinguistic Perspectives on Register*. Oxford: Oxford University Press.

Fought, Carmen (1999). A majority sound change in a minority community: /u/-fronting in Chicano English. *Journal of Sociolinguistics* 3: 5–23.

Fought, Carmen (2003). *Chicano English in Context*. New York, NY: Palgrave Macmillan.

Foulkes, P. and G. J. Docherty (eds.) (1999). *Urban Voices: Accent Studies in the British Isles*. London: Arnold.

Frazer, T. C. (1996). Chicano English and Spanish Interference in the Midwestern United States. *American Speech* 71(1): 72–85.

Garcia, O. (2009). Education, multilingualism and translanguaging in the 21st century. In T. Skutnabb-Kangas, R. Phillipson, A. K. Mohanty, and M. Panda (eds.), *Social Justice Through Multilingual Education*. Bristol: Multilingual Matters.

Gooskens, Charlotte (2006). Linguistic and extra-linguistic predictors of Inter-Scandinavian intelligibility. *Linguistics in the Netherlands* 23: 101–13.

Greenberg, R. D. (2004). *Language and Identity in the Balkans: Serbo-Croatian and its Disintegration*. Oxford: Oxford University Press.

Harrington, J., S. Palethorpe, and C. I. Watson (2000). Does the Queen Speak the Queen's English? *Nature* 408: 927–8.

Haugen, E. (1966). Dialect, Language, Nation. *American Anthropologist* 68: 922–35. In J. B. Pride and J. Holmes (1972), *Sociolinguistics: Selected Readings*. Harmondsworth, England: Penguin Books.

Hazen, K. (2002). Identity and Language Variation in a Rural Community. *Language* 78(2): 240–57.

Heeringa, W. and J. Nerbonne (2001). Dialect Areas and Dialect Continua. *Language Variation and Change* 13: 375–400.

Heller, M. (2010). The Commodification of Language. *Annual Review Anthropology* 39: 101–14.

Hinton, Linette N. and Karen E. Pollock (2000). Regional variations in the phonological characteristics of African American Vernacular English. *World Englishes* 19(1): 59–71.

Hughes, A., P. Trudgill, and D. Watt (2005). *English Accents and Dialects: An Introduction to Social and Regional Varieties of English in the British Isles*. 4th edn. London: Edward Arnold.

Jannedy, S. (2010). The Usage and Distribution of so in Spontaneous Berlin Kiezdeutsch. *ZAS Papers in Linguistics* 52: 43–62.

Jaspers, J. (2008). Problematizing Ethnolects: Naming Linguistic Practices in an Antwerp Secondary School. *International Journal of Bilingualism* 12(1–2): 85–103.

Joos, M. (1962). *The Five Clocks*. Bloomington, IN: Indiana University Research Center in Anthropology, Folklore, and Linguistics.

Kallmeyer, Werner, and Inken Keim (2003). Linguistic variation and the construction of social identity in a German-Turkish setting. In J. K. Androutsopoulos and A. Georgakopoulou (eds.), *Discourse Constructions of Youth Identities*. Pragmatics & Beyond, vol. 110. Amsterdam: John Benjamins, 29–36.

Kaye, A. S. (2001). Diglossia: The State of the Art. *International Journal of the Sociology of Language* 152: 117–30.

Keim, Inken (1978). *Gastarbeiterdeutsch: Untersuchungen zum sprachlichen Verhalten türkischer Gastarbeiter: Pilotstudie*, vol. 41. TBL Verlag Narr.

King, Robert D. (2001). The poisonous potency of script: Hindi and Urdu. *International Journal of the Sociology of Language* 150: 43–60.

Konopka, K. and J. Pierrehumbert (2008). Vowels in Contact: Mexican Heritage English in Chicago. In *Proceedings of the Sixteenth Annual Symposium about Language and Society – Austin. Texas Linguistic Forum* 52: 94–103.

Kopp, Achim (1999). *The Phonology of Pennsylvania German English as Evidence of Language Maintenance and Shift*. Selinsgrove: Susquehanna University Press.

Kurath, H. (1949). *A Word Geography of the Eastern United States*. Ann Arbor: University of Michigan Press.

Kurpaska, Maria (2010). *Chinese Languages(s): A Look through the Prism of the Great Dictionary of Modern Chinese Dialects*. Berlin: Walter De Gruyter.

Labov, W. (1969). Contraction, Deletion, and Inherent Variability of the English Copula. *Language* 45: 715–62.

Labov, W. (1972). *Language in the Inner City: Studies in the Black English Vernacular*. Philadelphia: University of Pennsylvania Press.

Labov, W. and W. Harris (1986). De Facto Segregation of Black and White Vernaculars. In D. Sankoff (ed.), *Diversity and Diachrony*. Amsterdam: John Benjamins.

Lee, D. Y. (2001). Genres, Registers, Text Types, Domains and Styles: Clarifying the Concepts and Navigating a Path through the BNC Jungle. *Language Learning and Technology* 5(3): 37–72.

Linnes, K. (1998). Middle-Class AAVE versus Middle-Class Bilingualism: Contrasting Speech Communities. *American Speech* 73(4): 339–67.

Lippi-Green, Rosina (2012). *English with an Accent: Language, Ideology and Discrimination in the United States*. 2nd edn. New York: Routledge.

Marshall, J. (2003). The Changing Sociolinguistic Status of the Glottal Stop in Northeast Scottish English. *English World-Wide* 24(1): 89–108.

Mathiot, M. and P. L. Garvin (1975). Functions of Language: A Sociocultural View. *Anthropological Quarterly* 48: 148–56.

Matsuda, M. J. (1991). Voice of America: Accent, Antidiscrimination Law, and a Jurisprudence for the Last Reconstruction. *Yale Law Journal* 100: 1329–407.

McDavid, R. I. (1965). American Social Dialects. *College English* 26: 254–60.

Metcalf, A. A. (1979). *Chicano English*, vol. 21. Arlington, VA: Center for Applied Linguistics.

Milroy, J. (2001). Language Ideologies and the Consequences of Standardization. *Journal of Sociolinguistics* 5(4): 530–55.

Montgomery, Michael, and Janet M. Fuller (1996). What was verbal -s in 19th century African American English? *Focus on the USA* 16: 211.

Montgomery, Michael, Janet M. Fuller, and Sharon DeMarse (1993). 'The black men has wives and sweet harts [and third person plural-s] jest like the white men': Evidence for verbal -s from written documents on 19th-century African American speech. *Language Variation and Change* 5(3): 335–57.

Mugglestone, L. (1995). *'Talking Proper': The Rise of Accent as Social Symbol*. Oxford: Clarendon Press.

Pfaff, Carol W. (1980). Acquisition and development of 'Gastarbeiterdeutsch' by migrant workers and their children in Germany. In E. C. Traugott, R. Labrum, S. C. Shepherd (eds.), *Papers from the Fourth International Conference on Historical Linguistics*. Amsterdam: John Benjamins, 381–39.

Pinker, Steven (2012). False fronts in the language wars. *Slate*. http://www.slate.com/articles/arts/the_good_word/2012/05/steven_pinker_on_the_false_fronts_in_the_language_wars_.html (accessed July 10, 2014).

Poplack, Shana and Sali Tagliamonte (1989). There's no tense like the present: Verbal -s inflection in early Black English. *Language Variation and Change* 1(1): 47–84.

Poplack, Shana and Sali Tagliamonte (1991). African American English in the Diaspora: Evidence from Old-Line Nova Scotians. *Language Variation and Change* 3(3): 301–39.

Poplack, Shana and Sali Tagliamonte (2005). Back to the Present: Verbal –s in the (African American) English Diaspora. In Raymond Hickey (ed.), *Transported Dialects: Legacies of Non-standard Colonial English*. Cambridge: Cambridge University Press, 203–23.

Pranjković, I. (2001). The Croatian Standard Language and the Serbian Standard Language. *International Journal of the Sociology of Language* 147: 31–50.

Rickford, J. R. (1977). The Question of Prior Creolization in Black English. In A. Valdman (ed.), *Pidgin and Creole Linguistics*. Bloomington: Indiana University Press.

Rickford, J. R. (1997). Prior Creolization of African-American Vernacular English? Socio-historical and Textual Evidence from the 17th and 18th Centuries. *Journal of Sociolinguistics* 1(3): 315–36.

Rickford, J. R. (1999). *African American Vernacular English*. Oxford: Blackwell.

Rickford, J. R., A. Ball, R. Blake, R. Jackson, and N. Martin (1991). Rappin on the Copula Coffin: Theoretical and Methodological Issues in the Analysis of Copula Variation in African-American Vernacular English. *Language Variation and Change* 3(1): 103–32.

Rosewarne, D. (1994). Estuary English – Tomorrow's RP? *English Today* 10(1): 3–8.

Salzman , Z., J. Stanlaw, and N. Adachi (2012). *Language, Culture, and Society: An Introduction to Linguistic Anthropology*. 5th edn. Boulder, CO: Westview Press.

Santa Ana, Otto and Robert Bayley (2004). Chicano English Phonology. In B. Kortmann, K. Burridge, R. Mesthrie, E. W. Schneider, and C. Upton (eds.), *A Handbook of Varieties of English*, vol. 1: *Phonology*. Berlin: Mouton de Gruyter, 417–34.

Schüppert, Anja and Charlotte Gooskens (2010). The Influence of Extra-linguistic Factors on Mutual Intelligibility: Some Preliminary Results from Danish and Swedish Pre-schoolers. *Bamberger Beiträge zur Englischen Sprachwissenschaft*. http://www.let.rug.nl/~gooskens/project/pdf/publ_methods_2009b.pdf (accessed July 10, 2014).

Spears, A. K. (1992). Reassessing the Status of Black English (Review Article). *Language in Society* 21: 675–82.

Stewart, W. A. (1967). Sociolinguistic Factors in the History of American Negro Dialects. *Florida FL Reporter* 5(2): 11ff.

Thomas, Eric (2007). Phonological and Phonetic Characteristics of African American Vernacular English. *Language and Linguistics Compass* 1(5): 450–75.

Trudgill, P. (1995). *Sociolinguistics: An Introduction to Language and Society*. 3rd edn. Harmondsworth, England: Penguin Books.

Van Herk, Gerard (2008). Fear of a Black Phonology: The Northern Cities Shift as Linguistic White Flight. *University of Pennsylvania Working Papers in Linguistics* 14(2): 156–61.

Vassberg, Liliane Mangold (1993). *Alsatian Acts of Identity: Language Use and Language Attitudes in Alsace* (No. 90). Clevedon: Multilingual Matters.

Wakelin, M. F. (1977). *English Dialects: An Introduction*. Rev. edn. London: Athlone Press.

Watt, D. J. L. (2000). Phonetic Parallels between the Close-mid Vowels of Tyneside English: Are They Internally or Externally Motivated? *Language Variation and Change* 12: 69–101.

Watt, D. J. L. (2002). 'I Don't Speak Geordie with an Accent, I Speak, like, the Northern Accent': Contact-induced Levelling in the Tyneside Vowel System. *Journal of Sociolinguistics* 6(1): 44–63.

Weldon, T. L. (2003). Revisiting the Creolist Hypothesis: Copula Variability in Gullah and Southern Rural AAVE. *American speech* 78(2): 171–91.

Weldon, T. L. (2004). African American English in the Middle Classes: Exploring the Other End of the Continuum. *NWAV (E): 2004 meeting* Ann Arbor, MI.

Wiese, Heike (2010). Kiezdeutsch: ein neuer Dialekt des Deutschen. In *Aus Politik und Zeitgeschichte* (Issues on Sprache und Gesellschaft, Language, and Society). Edited by the Federal Centre for Political Education.

Wiese, Heike (2012). *Kiezdeutsch: Ein neuer Dialekt entsteht*. München: Verlag C.H. Beck.

Wiese, Heike (2014). Voices of linguistic outrage: Standard language constructs and discourse on new urban dialects. *Working Papers in Urban Language and Literacies* 120: 2–25.

Wolfram, W. (1990). Re-examining Vernacular Black English. *Language* 66: 121–33.

Wolfram, W. (2003). Reexamining the Development of African American English: Evidence from Isolated Communities. *Language* 79(2): 282–316.

Wolfram, W. (2007). Sociolinguistic Folklore in the Study of African American English. *Language and Linguistics Compass* 1(4): 292–313.

Wolfram, W., P. Carter, and B. Moriello (2004). Emerging Hispanic English: New dialect formation in the American South. *Journal of Sociolinguistics* 8: 339–58.

Wolfram, W. and N. Schilling-Estes (2005). *American English: Dialects and Variation*. Oxford: Blackwell.

Wolfram, W. and E. R. Thomas (2002). *The Development of African American English*. Oxford: Blackwell.

Wolfram, W. and E. Thomas (2008). *Development of African American English*. Hoboken: John Wiley & Sons, Inc.

Wolfram, W. and B. Torbert (2006). When Linguistic Worlds Collide (African American English). In W. Wolfram and B. Ward (eds.), *American Voices*. Oxford: Blackwell.

Zentella, Ana Celia (1997). *Growing Up Bilingual*. Oxford: Blackwell.

3

Defining Groups

Key Concepts

How to define a speech community – regions, speakers, and norms

How to define a community of practice – interactions

Social network features and configuration

Social identity and group membership

How beliefs about groups of speakers shape how we use language

Language is both an individual possession and a social possession. We would expect, therefore, that certain individuals would behave linguistically like other individuals: they might be said to speak the same language or the same dialect or the same variety, that is, to employ the same code. In that respect they would be members of the same **speech community**. Sociolinguists have offered different interpretations of this concept. We are faced with the dilemma of wanting to study groups of speakers but lacking a clear definition of what comprises a group. We will discover that just as it is difficult to define such terms as language, dialect, and variety, it is also difficult to define speech community, and for many of the same reasons. Nevertheless, this concept has proved to be invaluable in sociolinguistic work in spite of a certain 'fuzziness' as to its precise characteristics. If we believe that there is an

An Introduction to Sociolinguistics, Seventh Edition. Ronald Wardhaugh and Janet M. Fuller.
© 2015 John Wiley & Sons, Inc. Published 2015 by John Wiley & Sons, Inc.

interaction worth exploring between languages and groups, then we must continue to attempt to define both.

In this chapter, we will present different definitions of speech communities and two other ways in which groups of speakers have been discussed in sociolinguistics, through social networks and communities of practice. Finally, we will link these ideas about how we might define social groups with a framework for studying social identities in order to provide a bridge between individual repertoires and social categories.

Speech Communities

Sociolinguistics is the study of language use within or among groups of speakers. What are groups? The concept of a group is difficult to define but one we must try to grasp. For our purposes, a group must have at least two members but there is really no upper limit to group membership. People can group together for one or more reasons: social, religious, political, cultural, familial, vocational, avocational, and so on. The group may be temporary or quasi-permanent and the purposes of its members may change, that is, its *raison d'être*. A group also may be more than its members, for individuals may come and go; it may be linked to an enduring social category, region, or many other types of associated entities. Group members may also belong to other groups and may or may not even meet face-to-face. The organization of the group may be tight or loose and the importance of group membership is likely to vary among individuals within the group.

We must also be aware that the groups we refer to in various research studies are often groups we have created for the purposes of our research using this or that set of factors. They are useful and necessary constructs but we would be unwise to forget that each such group comprises a set of unique individuals each with complex identities. Consequently, we must be careful in drawing conclusions about individuals on the basis of observations we make about groups that we have defined for our research purposes. Furthermore, to say of any member of such a group that he or she will always exhibit a certain characteristic behavior is to offer a **stereotype**. We talk about such stereotypes as being part of **essentialism**, the idea that people can be placed into fixed social categories and that all members we assign to a category share certain traits which we see as the essence of this category. What sociolinguists (and social scientists) seek to do is not to make such generalizations, but to discover patterns in data which link social factors with language use without ignoring variation within groups and the specific practices and experiences that make up individual identities.

Linguistic boundaries

In sociolinguistics, we need a specific definition of a group in order to do research. The kind of group that sociolinguists have generally attempted to study is called the

speech community (see Patrick 2002 and Morgan 2001, 2006, for a general survey of the research.) For purely theoretical purposes, some linguists have hypothesized the existence of an 'ideal' speech community. This is actually what Chomsky (1965, 3–4) proposes, his 'completely homogeneous speech-community' (see chapter 1 for the discussion of linguistic competence that is related to this). However, such a speech community cannot be our concern: it is a theoretical construct employed for a narrow purpose. Our speech communities, whatever they are, exist in a 'real' world. Consequently, we must try to find some alternative view of speech community, one helpful to investigations of language in society rather than necessitated by abstract linguistic theorizing. However, we must also be aware that the groups we refer to in various research studies are groups we have created for the purposes of our research using this or that set of factors. They are useful and necessary constructs but we would be unwise to forget that each such group comprises a set of unique individuals each with a complex identity (or, better still, identities); the connections to identities will be discussed in more detail below.

Lyons (1970, 326) offers a definition of what he calls a 'real' speech community: 'all the people who use a given language (or dialect).' However, that merely shifts the issue to making the definition of a language (or of a dialect) also the definition of a speech community. If, as we saw in chapter 2, it proves virtually impossible to define language and dialect clearly and unambiguously, then we have achieved nothing. It is really quite easy to demonstrate that a speech community is not coterminous with a language: while the English language is spoken in many places throughout the world, we must certainly recognize that it is also spoken in a wide variety of ways, in speech communities that are almost entirely isolated from one another, for example, in South Africa, in New Zealand, and among expatriates in China. We must ask ourselves in what sense does this modern lingua franca produce a speech community that might be of interest to us, that is, ask what else is shared other than the very language itself. Furthermore, if speech communities are defined solely by their linguistic characteristics, we must acknowledge the inherent circularity of any such definition in that language itself is a communal possession. Speakers do use linguistic characteristics to achieve group identity with, and group differentiation from, other speakers, but they use other characteristics as well: social, cultural, political, and ethnic, to name a few. Our search must be for criteria other than, or at least in addition to, linguistic criteria if we are to gain a useful understanding of 'speech community.'

We should also note that a recognizable single speech community can employ more than one language, whether we use national boundaries to define it (e.g., Switzerland, Canada, Papua New Guinea, all countries with more than one official language), city (or city-state) designations (e.g., Berlin, Singapore, New York City, where multiple languages are used for everyday interactions, education, and commerce), or neighborhood boundaries (e.g., in Little Village in Chicago you can hear both Spanish and English and in San Francisco's Chinatown both Cantonese and English are commonly used). While these speech communities are all defined in terms of geographic areas, as we will see in the discussion below, there are other criteria besides language and region we can use to define speech communities.

Shared norms

One approach to defining a speech community often taken in sociolinguistics is to say that the speakers in such a community share some kind of common feeling about linguistic behavior in that community, that is, they observe certain linguistic **norms**. Such an appeal to norms forms an essential part of Labov's definition of speech community (1972, 120–1):

> The speech community is not defined by any marked agreement in the use of language elements, so much as by participation in a set of shared norms; these norms may be observed in overt types of evaluative behavior, and by the uniformity of abstract patterns of variation which are invariant in respect to particular levels of usage.

This definition shifts the emphasis away from members of a speech community speaking the same to ascribing the same social meanings to particular ways of speaking. Milroy (1987, 13) has indicated some consequences of such a view:

> Thus, all New York speakers from the highest to lowest status are said to constitute a single speech community because, for example, they agree in viewing presence of post vocalic [r] as prestigious. They also agree on the social value of a large number of other linguistic elements. Southern British English speakers cannot be said to belong to the same speech community as New Yorkers, since they do not attach the same social meanings to, for example, (r): on the contrary, the highest prestige accent in Southern England (RP) is non-rhotic. Yet, the Southern British speech community may be said to be united by a common evaluation of the variable (h); *h*-dropping is stigmatized in Southern England … but is irrelevant in New York City or, for that matter, in Glasgow or Belfast.

Thus it is not so much how one speaks as how one evaluates ways of speaking that forms a speech community according to this definition. For the purpose of research, however, this is not a practical definition; values of particular ways of speaking are even less immediately apparent than linguistic patterns. Thus while this idea about shared norms is an important one, it does not easily lead to clearly demarcated speech communities.

Exploration 3.1: Judgments Again

Consider whether you judge each of the following usages acceptable, unacceptable, or maybe acceptable. Then ask yourself why you respond that way, that is, what are you actually responding to? Do you associate these usages with particular groups of speakers? Do you have a perception of regional or social-class difference? Have you been told that particular ways of speaking are 'wrong'? In other words, try to figure out a basis for your judgment (and your willingness to judge). Discuss this with the other members of the class; do you share norms about these utterances, and assign them the same social meanings? Can you explain similarities and differences in judgments in terms of speech community membership?

1. He hurt hisself.
2. She done it.
3. The boy run away last week.
4. To whom did you give it?
5. They ain't got no money left.
6. Can I leave the room now?
7. Just between you and I, I think he's crazy.
8. There's twenty people in the room.
9. Stand over there by them boys.
10. Sally dove in at the deep end.
11. That'll learn you!
12. I'm going to buy me a car.

The concept of the speech community is also somewhat abstract because the particular norms that a community uses may or may not be exclusively linguistic in nature, and along with norms about particular linguistic variables and their social meanings and values, these norms involve evaluations of ways that language is used as well. For any specific speech community, the concept

> reflects what people do and know when they interact with one another. It assumes that when people come together through discursive practices, they behave as though they operate within a shared set of norms, local knowledge, beliefs, and values. It means that they are aware of these things and capable of knowing when they are being adhered to and when the values of the community are being ignored … it is fundamental in understanding identity and representation of ideology. (Morgan 2001, 31)

In other words, we again are using the concept of communicative competence, that is, that speakers within a speech community share a sense of social norms in discourse, along with ideas about the social group identities indexed by various varieties or features of language. One example of how discourse patterns may be significant within a speech community is found in Hymes (2004). He presents analyses of narratives from various Native American groups, showing how, even when they are produced in English, there are distinctive features which can be traced back to narrative structures in the Native American languages. In other words, such speakers use English in special ways to maintain their separate identities within the dominant English-speaking community (see chapter 6 for more on such social dialects).

Gumperz (1971, 114) expresses much the same view of the importance of shared norms, and also notes that the groups may be of various sizes and formed for various purposes:

Most groups of any permanence, be they small bands bounded by face-to-face contact, modern nations divisible into smaller subregions, or even occupational associations or neighborhood gangs, may be treated as speech communities, provided they show linguistic peculiarities that warrant special study.

Thus the relationship between language and social structure is paramount in the development of the concept of the speech community, and this includes the idea that there are different levels of speech communities which correspond to different types of social groups. Gumperz (1971, 115) discusses how linguistic forms can be grouped into dialects, styles, or registers (see discussion in chapter 2 of these various types of varieties). While we may be able to talk about a speech community of speakers of North American English, we can also identify smaller groups with their own norms for interaction related to specific regions, religious organizations, or occupational groups within this larger speech community.

It is also possible for speakers to share certain norms for language when they do not share linguistic systems. For example, in Eastern Europe many speakers of Czech, Austrian German, and Hungarian share rules about the proper forms of greetings, suitable topics for conversation, and how to pursue these, but no common language. They are united in a *Sprachbund* ('speech area'), not quite a speech community, but still a community defined in some way by speech. As we can see, then, trying to define the concept of speech community requires us to come to grips with definitions of other concepts, principally group, language (or variety), and norm.

A single speech community also need not contain only a single language or single variety. Gumperz (1971, 101) points out that 'there are no *a priori* grounds which force us to define speech communities so that all members speak the same language.' As we will see in chapter 4, many societies exist in which bilingualism and multilingualism are the norm, and the use of multilingual discourse may be part of the speech community norms. It is such considerations as these that lead Gumperz to use the term linguistic community rather than speech community. He proceeds to define that term as follows:

> a social group which may be either monolingual or multilingual, held together by frequency of social interaction patterns and set off from the surrounding areas by weaknesses in the lines of communication. Linguistic communities may consist of small groups bound together by face-to-face contact or may cover large regions, depending on the level of abstraction we wish to achieve. (Gumperz 1971, 101)

This brings out another aspect of our definition of speech communities: they are defined partly through their relationships with other communities. Internally, a community must have a certain social cohesiveness; externally, its members must find themselves cut off from other communities in certain ways. The factors that bring about cohesion and differentiation will vary considerably from occasion to occasion. You are a member of one speech community by virtue of the fact that on a particular occasion you identify with North Americans rather than with

Australians; in another context you may distinguish between your Canadian speech community and the norms for speaking in the United States. Thus, it is context and contrast that help us decide what level of speech community is relevant. This approach would suggest that there is an English speech community (because there are French and German ones), a Melbourne speech community (because there are London and Bostonian ones), a Harvard speech community (because there are Oxford and Berkeley ones), a Chicano speech community (because there are others which are Anglo or African American), and so on.

Communities of Practice

As indicated above, one possible definition of a speech community is simply a group of people who interact regularly. Such groups and communities themselves are ever changing, their boundaries are often porous, and internal relationships shift. They must constantly reinvent and recreate themselves. Today's middle class, youth, New Yorkers, women, immigrants, and so on, are not yesterday's nor will they be tomorrow's. The group chosen to identify with will also change according to situation: at one moment religion may be important; at another, regional origin; and at still another, perhaps membership in a particular profession or social class. An individual may also attempt to bond with others because all possess a set of characteristics, or even just a single characteristic (e.g., be of the same gender), or even because all lack a certain characteristic (e.g., not be categorized as 'White'). Language bonding appears to be no different. In one case, command of a particular dialect or language may be a potent marker and, therefore, help create a sense of community and solidarity with others (e.g., a group of Americans abroad); in another case, the lack of such command may exclude you from a community of speakers and mark you in a very different way (e.g., as not being a user of RP or AAVE). However, even sharing the same dialect might be of no significance: if the circumstances require you to discuss astrophysics, your knowledge of the terms and concepts of astrophysics may be more important than the regional or social dialect you speak. Alternatively, speakers of Yoruba may find themselves forming a community with speakers of Japanese and Arabic within an English-speaking foreign-student speech community at a North American or European university.

One way sociolinguists try to get at this dynamic view of social groups is with the idea that speakers participate in various **communities of practice**. Eckert and McConnell-Ginet (1998, 490) define a community of practice as 'an aggregate of people who come together around mutual engagements in some common endeavor. Ways of doing things, ways of talking, beliefs, values, power relations – in short, practices – emerge in the course of their joint activity around that endeavor.' A community of practice is at the same time its members and what its members are doing to make them a community: a group of workers in a factory, an extended family, an adolescent friendship group, a women's fitness class, a Kindergarten classroom, and so on. They add (1998, 490): 'Rather than seeing the individual as some disconnected entity floating around in social space, or as a location in a network, or as a member of a particular group or set of groups, or as a bundle of social characteristics, we need to focus on communities of practice.' (See Meyerhoff and Strycharz 2013 for additional details.) It is such communities of practice that shape individuals, provide them with their identities, and often circumscribe what they can do. Eckert (1998, 2000) used this concept in her research in a Detroit-area high school and Mendoza-Denton (2008) also used it in her work with groups of Latina girls in California. These variationist sociolinguistic studies will be discussed in more detail in chapters 6 and 7.

One study which makes use of the community of practice construct for the study of language and identities is Bucholtz (1999), an investigation of the language of 'nerd girls' in a US high school. Bucholtz (1999, 207) notes the following ways in which the concept of speech community is inadequate for research on language gender:

(a) Its tendency to take language as central.
(b) Its emphasis on consensus as the organizing principle of community.
(c) Its preference for studying central members of the community over those at the margins.
(d) Its focus on the group at the expense of individuals.
(e) Its view of identity as a set of static categories.
(f) Its valorization of researchers' interpretations over participants' own understandings of their practices.

Bucholtz argues that within the community of practice framework, we can define a social group by all social practices, not just language. This concept can also incorporate the idea that there may be conflict within a group about these practices and norms, and thus marginal members of communities, as individuals, can be better included in the analysis. Further, as we will discuss below, this does not put speakers into pre-existing identity categories, but focuses instead on their own construction of identity. Finally, through ethnographic research, it allows for the analysis to focus on how the speakers themselves, not the researcher, enact group memberships.

In this study on nerd girls, Bucholtz notes how the girls both conform to the larger social order (i.e., by focusing on academic achievement) and also resist it (i.e., by rejecting traditional ideas of femininity in dress and appearance). The values of the members of this community of practice are not set norms which define them, but rather are negotiated through ongoing social practices, that is, their interactions serve to define what a nerd is and how the various members of their group fit in this category.

This concept of authenticity in an identity category can also be found in Jones (2011), who writes about the construction of an '(in)authentic lesbian' identity within a lesbian women's community of practice, in which 'girly' practices were deemed less authentic than 'dykey' ones. Another view of authenticity is shown by Meadows (2010), who analyzes the discourse in a community of practice of two

Japanese language learners and how they sought to establish their legitimate connections to an imagined (Japanese) national community.

There are also studies which seek to expand on the community of practice concept of conflict, not consensus, as part of interaction. Davies (2005, 1) argues that the idea of legitimacy is central in community of practice analyses and power structures cannot be ignored: 'While practices may define the community, the community determines who has access to that practice.' Moore (2006) looks at narratives told among high school students in the northwest of England, noting that status inequalities can lead to inequitable allocation of control within a community of practice, and that such hierarchies must be taken into account in the study of community-building and identity construction. (See Gee 2005 for a further discussion of this issue and the usefulness of the community of practice approach for linguistic studies.)

The community of practice framework has also been used to study online communities. Early research explicitly focused on the development of norms; Herring (2001, 622), in an article reviewing research on computer-mediated communication, writes: 'Over time, computer-mediated groups develop *norms* of practice regarding "how things are done" and what constitutes socially desirable behavior; these may then be codified in "Frequently Asked Question" documents (FAQs. ...) and netiquette guidelines.' Other aspects of research which make reference to norm development are within the area of Pragmatics, looking at how (im)politeness expectations are negotiated in online contexts (e.g., Graham 2007, Locher 2010). (See chapter 10 for further discussion of Pragmatics and Politeness Theory.)

Another theme in research employing the community of practice framework and online contexts is the focus on the emergence of communities and the negotiation of individual identities with regard to community membership (Georgakopoulou 2006). For example, Hanh and Kellog (2005) look at how adult English language learners interact online, and emphasize that the community of practice framework allows us to note how negotiation of identities is part of the learning process. Similarly, Peuronen (2011) analyzes data from an online forum for Finnish Christians who participate in extreme sports, showing how they establish their own community as an online group, but also link it to other, wider communities: Christians, Finnish speakers of English, participants in extreme sports, and youth culture. (See also Eckert and McConnell-Ginet 2007 for a further discussion of this aspect of communities of practice, i.e., the positioning of their members with relation to the world beyond the community of practice.)

Social Networks

Another way of viewing how an individual relates to other individuals in society is to ask what **social networks** he or she participates in. That is, how and on what occasions does a specific individual A interact now with B, then with C, and then again with D? How intensive are the various relationships: does A interact more frequently with B than with C or D? How extensive is A's relationship with B in the sense of how many other individuals interact with both A and B in whatever activity brings them together? In a situation in which A, B, C, D, and E are linked in a network, do they all have links to each other or are B, C, D, and E only linked to A but not each other? How people in a social network are linked to each other is one way of viewing social groups as defined by the kinds, frequency, and constellation of social interactions.

Research on social networks in sociolinguistics has proliferated in the last few decades, but is most directly linked to Milroy (1980, 1987; Milroy and Llamas 2013). This work adapted sociological social network theory to sociolinguistic and showed how it could be used in the study of language. You are said to be involved in a **dense social network** if the people you know and interact with also know and interact with one another. If they do not do so, the social network is a **loose** one. You are also said to be involved in a **multiplex social network** if the people within it are tied together in more than one way, that is, not just through work but also through other social activities. (To see diagrams of these different types of networks, see the link in the online companion to this text for *English Language and Linguistics Online*.) People who go to school together, marry each other's siblings, and work and play together participate in dense multiplex networks. In England these are said to be found at the extremes of the social-class structure. Such networks indicate strong social cohesion, produce feelings of solidarity, and encourage individuals to identify with others within the network. On the other hand, middle-class networks are likely to be loose and simplex; therefore, social cohesion is reduced and there are weaker feelings of solidarity and identity.

Milroy (1980) shows that in several working class areas of Belfast, groups with dense, multiplex social networks fostered social solidarity which in turn served to enforce linguistic norms. The differences in social networks could be used to explain differences between different areas that were all categorized as 'working class.' They could also account for gender differences within areas where gender roles and patterns of occupation were quite distinct.

The social networks of particular speakers are not fixed; they can change, just as the ways in which people speak can change over their lifetimes. People also belong to different networks of different strengths. The recent availability of computers, smart phones, and other devices has produced entirely new types of networking which many people now use extensively, and there is now a body of research which looks at how these virtual networks function as speech communities (see Androutsopoulos 2006, Aitchison and Lewis 2003 and Akkaya 2014 for overviews of this research).

Much linguistic behavior seems explicable in terms of network structure and we will see in chapters 7 and 8 how valuable the concept of 'social network' is when we consider matters of language variation and change (see Milroy and Llamas 2013 for additional details). Milroy and Gordon (2008, 119) also point out that the 'concepts of network and community of practice are … closely related, and the differences between them are chiefly method and focus. Network analysis typically deals with structural and content properties of the ties that constitute *egocentric* personal networks ... [but] cannot address the issues of how and where linguistic variants are employed ... to construct local social meanings. Rather, it is concerned with how informal social groups ... support local norms or ... facilitate linguistic change.'

One of the advantages of a social network approach to the study of social groups is that instead of dealing with abstract categories, it looks specifically at who interacts with whom, and how. We will return to this topic and to a discussion of studies employing this framework in chapters 6–8 as we continue to develop our ideas on language variation and sociolinguistic methodologies.

Social Identities

Many of the ideas and issues involved in the study of speech communities, communities of practice, and social networks have been incorporated into the scholarship on language and identity. In chapter 1, we introduced the concept of identity as 'the linguistic construction of membership in one or more social groups or categories' (Kroskrity 2000, 111). Identity may be constructed through a variety of linguistic means. For instance, the use of certain lexical forms or language varieties may contribute to the identification of a speaker, as might particular communicative practices, such as the uses of silence, greeting formulas, or gaze.

A key concept in the study of identities is that identity is not something you *have*, it is something you *do*. Like a community of practice, it is something that finds its basis in interactions. Heller (2007) notes that the concepts of identity, along with those of community and language, are 'heuristic devices which capture some elements of how we organize ourselves, but which have to be understood as social constructs' (2007, 13).

Much of the literature on language and identity is based on the post-structuralist idea that social practices (such as language use) produce and reproduce the social world, including speaker identities. Thus, as Foucault (1980) has argued, the self is not fixed, but is something which is positioned and repositioned through discourse. Consequently, speakers' identities must be continually reconstructed and may be redefined through discourse; they do not exist outside of discourse (see Baxter 2002, drawing on the work of Foucault 1980). For example, an individual's identity as a woman, with a focus on the physical attributes of womanhood, may be brought to the forefront in one interaction (e.g., in a discussion about mammograms), but in another situation this identity may be further defined with regard to professional identity (e.g., while participating in a women's mentoring organization at work). In an online interaction, the gender identity of this same person may be completely irrelevant and unknown to the other participants in the dialogue.

The term 'identity' is used here to describe a primarily social rather than psychological phenomenon: identity is not the source but the outcome of linguistic practice (Bucholtz and Hall 2005). Brubaker and Cooper (2000) note the term identity has been used to mean somewhat contradictory things, either a fundamental 'sameness' of group members or an abiding and foundational aspect of a person's self. In the social constructionist sense, however, the term identity is used to invoke the interactively developed self that is multiple, fragmented, and fluctuating. It is also used to discuss the speakers' identification with social categories of all types, including not only enduring social categories such as 'race' but also situational roles such as 'teacher' and interactional stances of similarity and difference. All of these may be relevant for how speakers define their speech communities, communities of practice, and social networks. So an African American teacher in a majority White school may see herself as a member of a community of practice with the other teachers at the elementary school where she works, but may also construct her identity as different from these colleagues in a discussion of race or White privilege.

Identities are contrastive and fluid; as this last example illustrates, we may identify as similar to a person in one situation, and as different in another. In some cases, identity categorizations may be imposed upon individuals by others (Kroskrity 2000: 113) or they may be severely constrained by others' perceptions (Bucholtz and Hall 2005). The study of language and identity is the study of the linguistic means through which membership assignations are made and how language is used to create, embrace, resist, or alter group boundaries. For instance, Fuller (2012) reports about a girl in a German-English bilingual classroom in Berlin, Germany, who repeatedly attempted to establish her identity as a speaker of German by using this code with her classmates. However, by often replying to her in English, her peers constrained her construction of her bilingual identity.

Issues of identity are particularly salient in work by Rampton (1995, 1999, 2001, 2010) on what he calls **crossing**: 'Language crossing involves code alternation by people who are not accepted members of the group associated with the second language that they are using (code switching into varieties that are not generally thought to belong to them)' (Rampton 2010, 485). The participants in his research are London teenagers, some of whom come from families who came to England from Pakistan or Jamaica, and speak Panjabi or Jamaican Creole in addition to various varieties of English, for example, Asian English, working-class London English dialects, and Standard English varieties. Within multiethnic social networks the teens use all these codes in various ways to index various stances and identities. While these youths have their own speech community, they also participate in other communities which lay claim to them, particularly ethnic communities. They integrate repertoires and adopt (and mock) norms of speaking from these other communities in their youth networks.

Each individual therefore is a member of many different groups. It is in the best interests of most people to be able to identify themselves on one occasion as members of one group and on another as members of another group. Such groups also may or may not overlap. One of the consequences of the intersecting identifications is, of course, linguistic variation: all people do not speak alike, nor does any individual always speak in the same way on every occasion. The variation we see in language must partly reflect a need that people have to be seen as the same as certain other people on some occasions and as different from them on other occasions.

How identities are constructed and manifested is a pervasive issue in sociolinguistics. We will see its relevance to language use in the chapters that follow. In the next chapter, we will address issues of identity with regard to multilingual discourse; chapter 7 will show how the study of identities has been brought into variationist sociolinguistics. Ethnographic approaches to the study of identity will be included in chapter 9, and the role of identities in different approaches to discourse analysis will be addressed in chapter 11. Chapter 12 will include a discussion of research on gender and sexuality identities.

Beliefs about Language and Social Groups

A key aspect of the study of language and social groups is that how languages are evaluated usually has very little to do with their linguistic features, and much more to do with the social status of the groups associated with them. These beliefs about linguistic groups also influence how speakers use particular features and varieties of languages and are thus central to our understandings of social groups and language use.

Many people hold strong beliefs on various issues having to do with language and are quite willing to offer their judgments on these issues (see Bauer and Trudgill 1998, Niedzielski and Preston 1999, and Wardhaugh 1999). They believe such things as certain languages lack grammar, that you can speak English without an accent, that French is more logical than English, that parents teach their children to speak, that primitive languages exist, that English is degenerating and language standards are slipping, that pronunciation should be based on spelling, and so on and so on. Much discussion of language matters in the media concerns such 'issues' and there are periodic attempts to 'clean up' various bits and pieces, attempts that Cameron (1995) calls 'verbal hygiene.' Unfortunately, often people who voice opinion on this do not have any background in linguistics. Wardhaugh has written elsewhere (1999, viii), 'Linguists … know that many popular beliefs about language are false and that much we are taught about language is misdirected. They also know how difficult it is to effect change.' Language beliefs are well entrenched, as are language attitudes and language behaviors.

While sociolinguistic research on language largely focuses on a descriptive, not prescriptive, approach, attitudes, beliefs, and ideologies about language are influences on language use, as well as being areas of study in their own right. Sociolinguists should strive for an understanding of language use and the social context, including ideas about language, because how people behave toward others is influenced not only by actual language use but also by ideals about the standard and ideologies about what kind of person uses language in different ways.

The connections we have discussed in the previous sections indicate that we use language to make ourselves part of particular social groups. We also use language to categorize other people, and judge them, at least partially, according to the social value of the categories to which we assign them. In the next two sections, we will look at two strands of research that address how such lay beliefs about language and social groups are an important part of the study of sociolinguistics.

Ideologies

Errington (2000, 115) describes the study of **language ideologies** as 'a rubric for dealing with ideas about language structure and use relative to social contexts.' Particularly relevant here are ideologies which privilege certain ways of speaking as inherently 'better' than others. While some individuals are sometimes considered to be 'good speakers' of one variety or another, this judgment is usually less about the speaker's proficiency than about the variety itself. That is, there are certain **hegemonic ideologies** about different ways of speaking that dominate in a society and are widely accepted, even by speakers of the varieties which are judged as deficient. These ideologies dictate that certain ways of speaking are indicative of undesirable social traits, for example, poverty or lack of education, or personal characteristics, for example, laziness. Other ways of speaking are associated with more desirable social groups and it is assumed that everyone should want to aspire to speak in these latter ways. Lippi-Green (2012), in a chapter titled *The real trouble with Black English*, discusses this issue, saying that although criticisms of AAVE are often made on the basis of linguistic inferiority, linguistic analyses have shown that AAVE is a rule-governed, systematic language with every bit as much sophistication as any other variety of English. What bothers speakers of Standard English is that they feel that continued use of AAVE is a rejection of mainstream – often perceived as White – middle-class values. We will have more to say about language attitudes toward different languages and their speakers in multilingual contexts in chapter 4, and about how language ideologies play a role in the construction of social identities in chapter 9; chapters 13 and 14 will also address how language ideologies influence the realms of education and policy.

Exploration 3.2:   Slang

Look at the definitions for 'slang' provided on Urban Dictionary, an online dictionary providing definitions posted by users. (Ignore those that have nothing to do with language use; this word can also be used to mean sex, drug dealing, and the past tense of *sling* by some speakers.) What are the ideologies about slang that appear in this forum? To what extent are they about language (and, often, language decay) and to what extent are they about the groups of people associated with the use of slang?

Perceptual dialectology

The study of non-linguists' ideas about the regions, features, and values of dialects has come to be called **perceptual dialectology** (Preston 1989, 1999, 2002a, 2002b, Niedzielski and Preston 1999, Long and Preston 2003). The methodology employed by Preston in his work involved giving people maps of the United States and asking them first to draw dialect regions, and then to label the dialects and describe them in terms of both correctness and pleasantness. What emerges from such work is an understanding of the attitudes people have about the ways of speaking associated with particular regions. It also reveals stereotypes concerning people who live in these regions. Among various interesting findings in these studies we see that speakers may not rate their own dialect highly, and that many dialects (including the speakers' own), are sometimes rated highly for pleasantness but as lacking in correctness, or vice versa. For instance, the findings in Preston (1999) show that respondents from Michigan consistently rated their own dialect as correct, and perpetuated the stereotype of Southerners as speaking incorrect English. However, the Michiganders often rated southern speech as pleasant and friendly (often more friendly than their own region).

One of the interesting findings in some recent research in perceptual dialectology is that regional differences are often intertwined with ideas about other social groups. For instance, Bucholtz et al. (2007) found in a study done among University of California – Santa Barbara students about perceptions of language in the state of California, that although the southern California / northern California divide was prominent for most of the respondents, and stereotypes about the English spoken in these regions abounded, often other factors emerged as significant as well. Speakers of Spanish (mostly referred to as 'Mexicans') were often associated with Los Angeles and San Diego, and speakers of Chinese with the Bay Area. There were also certain areas associated with speakers of AAVE (the Bay Area, and Compton, a largely African American suburb of Los Angeles), but this was less frequent than the references to speakers of Spanish. An interesting finding was that the most common social label was 'hicks,' or other synonymous terms such as 'hillbillies' or 'rednecks;' the authors note that earlier studies have not shown this category to be associated with California by non-Californians.

Research by Alfaraz (2002) also shows the importance of other social factors intertwined with region in the evaluation of speakers of different social groups. This study, carried out in Miami, asked respondents to rate the pleasantness and correctness of various Latin American varieties of Spanish, a variety referred to as Peninsular Spanish, and two varieties of Cuban Spanish, representing the Spanish spoken before and after the Cuban Revolution of 1959. Alfaraz found that association of a particular variety of Spanish with speakers who were of low socio-economic class or were Black correlated with less positive evaluations of the variety. The pre-revolution Cuban Spanish, that is, the variety spoken by these respondents, was evaluated the most positively.

Studies in perceptual dialectology show us that people have far more nuanced beliefs about dialects than simply that they are either 'good' or 'bad.' Further, most people have a more sophisticated understanding of social groups, incorporating information about region, social class, race/ethnicity, and many other levels of identity.

Chapter Summary

In this chapter, we have grappled with how to define the social groups whose language we wish to describe and study in sociolinguistic research, noting that some of the same difficulties in defining what a language is surface in defining what a speech community might be. There is a tendency to look beyond the ways that people speak to define what makes them a community, and to focus on the presence of shared norms. Alternative ways of defining groups, for example, as a community of practice or a social network, are also presented as less abstract means of determining a social group for the purpose of research; both depend on linguistic interaction for their definitions. We also revisit the concept of identities, focusing this time on how identities are linked to social group membership.

Exercises

1. Make a short (15–30 minutes) audio recording of a community of practice you participate in (be sure you have the permission of everyone in the group before you record!). This could be your roommates or family members you live with, some friends you often eat lunch with, a group of co-workers, members of a knitting group, your rugby teammates, and so on; the only criteria is that this must be a group that meets and interacts regularly. Listen to the recording and answer the following questions:
    *   How can you describe the joint endeavor of this group? Do there seem to be common goals of the interaction?
    *   In what ways are the varieties spoken by the individuals in the group different – that is, do they come from different areas or social groups and have linguistic features that are associated with different varieties? Is there ever explicit mention made of speech differences?
    *   In what ways do you see the shared norms of the group – are there particular lexical items or nicknames that are used in this group? Inside jokes? Topics of conversation that recur? In short, try to ascertain what features of the conversation indicate that this is a group that interacts frequently and not a group of strangers.
2. Find a map of the country you live in which has major state or province boundaries but no labels for these regions, and ask ten people to draw dialect

boundaries on the map, name the dialects, and rate them on scales of 1–10 in terms of correctness and pleasantness. Be sure to record relevant information about each of these research participants – for instance, age, sex category identification, nationality, race/ethnicity, socio-economic class identification, occupation, location of residence, region of origin. Answer the following questions about your data:

- Are similar dialect regions identified by all or most of the research participants? Provide an overview of these regions.
- Are there accepted names for different dialects? If so, can you explain how this has come to be the case – are they discussed in popular media, or in school? If not, how can you explain the absence of terms for regional dialects?
- How are different regional dialects evaluated in terms of their correctness and pleasantness?
- How can you account for variation in your data? That is, do particular traits of the research participants (e.g., where they are from) seem to influence how they feel about particular dialects?

Further Reading

Gal, Susan and Judith Irvine (1995). The Boundaries of Languages and Disciplines. How Ideologies Construct Difference. *Social Research* 62: 996–1001.
A foundational article in the study of language ideologies, providing a popular framework for analysis.

Garcia, Ofelia and Joshua A. Fishman (eds.) (2002). *The Multilingual Apple*. 2nd edn. Berlin: Mouton de Gruyter.
This edited volume provides a discussion of many minority language speech communities in New York City, past and present.

Herring, Susan C. (2002). Computer-Mediated Communication on the Internet. *Annual Review of Information Science and Technology*, 36(1): 109–68.
This article provides a descriptive overview of a number of types of computer-mediated communication, and introduces some of the issues involved in sociolinguistic study of these data, including ethical issues for researchers.

Meyerhoff, Miriam and Anna Strycharz (2013). Communities of Practice. In Jack K. Chambers and Natalie Schilling (eds.), *The Handbook of Language Variation and Change*. 2nd edn. Oxford: Wiley-Blackwell, 428–47.
This book chapter defines the concept of community of practice, clearly outlining how it differs from other terms, and discusses its application in research on language variation and change.

Milroy, Lesley and Carmen Llamas (2013). Social Networks. In Jack K. Chambers and Natalie Schilling (eds.), *The Handbook of Language Variation and Change*. 2nd edn. Oxford: Wiley-Blackwell, 409–27.
This book chapter offers an overview of social network theory as it has been applied in the field of sociolinguistics.

Preston, Dennis (1999). *The Handbook of Perceptual Dialectology*, vol. 1. Amsterdam: John Benjamins.

Long, Daniel and Dennis Preston (2002). *The Handbook of Perceptual Dialectology*, vol. 2. Amsterdam: John Benjamins.

These two volumes comprise a wealth of information about studies in perceptual dialectology from a wide variety of languages and cultures, including Japanese, German, French, Dutch, and Turkish as well as both American and British varieties of English.

For further resources for this chapter visit the companion website at

 www.wiley.com/go/wardhaugh/sociolinguistics

References

Alfaraz, G. (2002). Miami Cuban Perceptions of Varieties of Spanish. In Daniel Long and Dennis R. Preston (eds.), *Handbook of Perceptual Dialectology*, vol. 2. Amsterdam: John Benjamins, 1–11.

Aitchison, Jean and Diana Lewis (eds.). (2003). *New Media Language*. London: Routledge.

Akkaya, Aslihan (forthcoming). Language, Discourse and New Media: A Linguistic Anthropological Perspective. *Language and Linguistic Compass* 8.

Androutsopoulos, Jannis (2006). Introduction: Sociolinguistics and computer-mediated communication. *Journal of Sociolinguistics* 10: 419–38.

Bauer, L. and P. Trudgill (eds.) (1998). *Language Myths*. Harmondsworth, England: Penguin Books.

Baxter, Judith (2002). Competing Discourses in the Classroom: A post-structuralist discourse analysis of girls' and boys' speech in public contexts. *Discourse & Society* 13(6): 827–42.

Brubaker, R. and F. Cooper (2000). Beyond 'Identity'. *Theory and Society* 29(1): 1–47.

Bucholtz, M. (1999). 'Why Be Normal?' Language and Identity Practices in a Community of Nerd Girls. *Language in Society* 28: 203–23.

Bucholtz, M. and K. Hall (2005). Identity and Interaction: A Sociocultural Linguistic Approach. *Discourse Studies* 7(4–5): 585–614.

Bucholtz, M., N. Bermudez, V. Fung et al. (2007). Hella Nor Cal or Totally So Cal? The Perceptual Dialectology of California. *Journal of English Linguistics* 35(4): 325–52.

Cameron, D. (1995). *Verbal Hygiene*. London: Routledge.

Chomsky, N. (1965). *Aspects of the Theory of Syntax*. Cambridge, MA: MIT Press.

Davies, Bethan (2005). Communities of Practice: Legitimacy Not Choice. *Journal of Sociolinguistics* 9: 557–81.

Eckert, Penelope (1988). Adolescent Social Structure and the Spread of Linguistic Change. *Language in Society* 17(2): 183–207.

Eckert, Penelope (2000). *Linguistic Variation as Social Practice: The Linguistic Construction of Identity in Belten High*. Oxford: Blackwell.

Eckert, Penelope and Sally McConnell-Ginet (1998). Communities of Practice: Where Language, Gender, and Power All Live. In J. Coates (ed.), *Language and Gender: A Reader*. Oxford: Blackwell.

Eckert, Penelope and Sally McConnell-Ginet (2007). Putting Communities of Practice in Their Place. *Gender & Language* 1: 27–37.

Errington, Joseph (2000). Ideology. *Journal of Linguistics Anthropology* 9(1–2): 115–17.

Foucault, M. (1980). *Power/Knowledge: Selected Interviews and Other Writings.1972–1977*. New York: Pantheon.

Fuller, Janet M. (2012). *Bilingual Pre-teens: Competing Ideologies and Multiple Identities in the U.S. and Germany*. New York: Routledge.

Gee, James Paul (2005). Meaning Making, Communities of Practice, and Analytical Toolkits. *Journal of Sociolinguistics* 9: 590–94.

Georgakopoulou, Alexandra (2006). Postscript: Computer-Mediated Communication in Sociolinguistics. *Journal of Sociolinguistics* 10(4): 548–57.

Graham, Sage Lambert (2007). Disagreeing to Agree: Conflict, (Im)Politeness and Identity in a Computer-Mediated Community. *Journal of Pragmatics* 39: 742–59.

Gumperz, J. J. (1971). *Language in Social Groups*. Stanford, CA: Stanford University Press.

Hanh, T. N. and G. Kellogg (2005). Emergent Identities in On-line Discussions for Second Language Learning. *Canadian Modern Language Review* 62: 111–36.

Heller, M. (2007). *Bilingualism: A Social Approach*. Basingstoke: Palgrave Macmillan.

Herring, Susan (2001). Computer-Mediated Communication. In Deborah Schiffrin, Deborah Tannen, and Heidi E. Hamilton (eds.), *Handbook of Discourse Analysis*. Oxford: Blackwell, 612–34.

Hymes, D. (2004). *'In vain I tried to tell you': Essays in Native American Ethnopoetics*. Lincoln: University of Nebraska Press.

Jones, Lucy (2011). 'The Only Dykey One': Constructions of (In)Authenticity in a Lesbian Community of Practice. *Journal of Homosexuality* 58: 719–41.

Kroskrity, Paul (2000). Identity. *Journal of Linguistic Anthropology* 9(1–2): 111.

Labov, W. (1972). *Sociolinguistic Patterns*. Philadelphia: University of Pennsylvania Press.

Lippi-Green, Rosina (2012). *English with an Accent: Language, Ideology and Discrimination in the United States*. 2nd edn. New York: Routledge.

Locher, Miriam A. (2010). Introduction: Politeness and Impoliteness in Computer-Mediated Communication. *Journal of Politeness Research. Language, Behaviour, Culture* 6: 1–5.

Long, D. and D. R. Preston (eds.) (2003). *Handbook of Perceptual Dialectology*, vol. 2. Amsterdam: John Benjamins.

Lyons, J. (ed.) (1970). *New Horizons in Linguistics*. Harmondsworth, England: Penguin Books.

Meadows, Bryan (2010). 'Like my tutor and stuff, people I would talk to': Laying Claim to Imagined National Communities of Practice in Language Learner Discourse. *Critical Inquiry in Language Studies* 7: 88–111.

Mendoza-Denton, N. (2008). *Homegirls*. Oxford: Blackwell.

Meyerhoff, Miriam and Anna Strycharz (2013). Communities of Practice. In Jack K. Chambers and Natalie Schilling (eds.), *The Handbook of Language Variation and Change*. 2nd edn. Oxford: Wiley-Blackwell, 428–47.

Milroy, L. (1980). Social Network and Language Maintenance. In A. K. Pugh, V. J. Lee, and J. Swann (1980). *Language and Language Use: A Reader*. London: Heinemann Educational Publishers.

Milroy, L. (1987). *Language and Social Networks*. 2nd edn. Oxford: Blackwell.

Milroy, L. and M. Gordon (2008). *Sociolinguistics: Method and Interpretation*. 2nd edn. Oxford: Wiley-Blackwell.

Milroy, Lesley and Carmen Llamas (2013). Social Networks. In Jack K. Chambers and Natalie Schilling (eds.), *The Handbook of Language Variation and Change*. 2nd edn. Oxford: Wiley-Blackwell, 409–27.

Moore, Emma (2006). 'You tell all the stories': Using Narrative to Explore Hierarchy within a Community of Practice. *Journal of Sociolinguistics* 10(5): 611–40.

Morgan, M. M. (2001). Community. In A. Duranti (ed.), *Key Terms in Language and Culture*. Oxford: Blackwell.

Morgan, M. M. (2004). Speech Community. In A. Duranti (ed.), *A Companion to Linguistic Anthropology*. Oxford: Blackwell, 3–33.

Niedzielski, N. and D. R. Preston (1999). *Folk Linguistics*. Berlin: Mouton de Gruyter.

Patrick, P. L. (2002). The Speech Community. In Jack K. Chambers, Peter Trudgill, and Natalie Schilling-Estes (eds.), *The Handbook of Language Variation*. Oxford: Blackwell.

Peuronen, Saija (2011). 'Ride Hard, Live Forever': Translocal Identities in an Online Community of Extreme Sports Christians. In Crispin Thurlow and Kristine Mroczek (eds.), *Digital discourse: Language in the new media*. Oxford: Oxford University Press, 154–76.

Preston, D. R. (1989). *Perceptual Dialectology*. Dordrecht: Foris.

Preston, D. R. (ed.) (1999). *Handbook of Perceptual Dialectology*, vol. 1. Amsterdam: John Benjamins.

Preston, D. R. (2002a). Language with an Attitude. In Jack K. Chambers, Peter Trudgill, and Natalie Schilling-Estes (eds.), *The Handbook of Language Variation*. Oxford: Blackwell.

Preston, D. R. (2002b). Perceptual Dialectology: Aims, Methods, Findings. *Trends in Linguistics Studies and Monographs* 137: 57–104.

Rampton, B. (1995). *Crossing: Language and Ethnicity among Adolescents*. London: Longman.

Rampton, B. (1999). Deutsch in Inner London and the Animation of an Instructed Foreign Language. *Journal of Sociolinguistics* 3(4): 480–504.

Rampton, B. (2001). Crossing. In A. Duranti (ed.), *Key Terms in Language and Culture*. Oxford: Blackwell.

Rampton, B. (2010). Linguistic Ethnography, Interactional Sociolinguistics and the Study of Identities. In C. Coffin et al. (eds.), *Applied Linguistics Methods: A Reader*. London: Routledge, 234–50.

Wardhaugh, R. (1999). *Proper English: Myths and Misunderstandings about Language*. Oxford: Blackwell.

4

Languages in Contact: Multilingual Societies and Multilingual Discourse

Key Concepts

The pervasiveness of multilingualism

Domains of language use

The influence of language ideologies and language attitudes on language use

Multilingual discourse shapes interactions, relationships, and social identities

This chapter will address what happens when languages, or more accurately the speakers of multiple languages, come into contact. Multilingualism is common in societies across the world, despite the perception by many monolinguals that speaking only one language is the norm (see Fuller 2012, 2013 for discussion of what she calls 'the ideology of normative monolingualism'). In many cases, groups of people who speak different languages live near each other; sometimes there are political boundaries that divide them and sometimes they identify as being part of the same nation or state, but in all such cases they have contact and must communicate. (An example of the former situation is the neighboring nations of France and Germany; of the latter, the German and French-speaking regions of Switzerland.) In other cases, there is movement of speakers of one language into an area where another

An Introduction to Sociolinguistics, Seventh Edition. Ronald Wardhaugh and Janet M. Fuller.
© 2015 John Wiley & Sons, Inc. Published 2015 by John Wiley & Sons, Inc.

language is spoken – this is the case for immigration, colonialization, and various scenarios of conquest.

In these latter scenarios, there is likely to be one language which has social dominance, and in this situation **language shift** may occur, that is, speakers shift to speaking the dominant language. In situations of immigration, commonly within three generations, members of the minority group shift to the dominant language. In some scenarios, we have what is called **language maintenance**, that is, both languages continue to be spoken. Giles et al. (1977) proposed a framework within which to assess a language's **ethnolinguistic vitality**, that is, how likely it is to be maintained. They say that we must consider three things about any threatened language: (1) its status: economic, social, and historical; (2) its territorial distribution and concentration together with its population demographics, for example, absolute numbers, birth rates, marriage patterns, and migrations in and out; and (3) its institutional support or lack thereof, both formally, as in the media, education, and government services, and less formally, as in the workplace and in religious, social, and cultural activities.

In the rest of this chapter, we will discuss language use in situations in which there is maintenance, that is, in multilingual communities. We will use the term **multilingual** to refer generally to situations in which there are speakers of more than one language.

Multilingualism as a Societal Phenomenon

In many parts of the world it is just a normal requirement of daily living that people speak several languages: perhaps one or more at home, another in the village, still another for purposes of trade, and yet another for contact with the outside world of wider social or political organization. These various languages are often acquired through simple exposure to the language, although one language or more in a speaker's repertoire may be learned through schooling or in an instructional setting.

One example of a varied multilingual society is present-day India. Mohanty, an Indian sociolinguist, writes of his own linguistic repertoire:

> I use Oriya in my home, English in my work place, Hindi for television viewing, Bengali to communicate with my domestic helper, a variety of Hindi-Punjabi-Urdu in market places in Delhi, Sanskrit for my prayer and religious activities, and some conversational Kui with the Konds for my research in their community. These languages fit in a mutually complementary and non-competing relationship in my life. (Mohanty 2006, 263)

It is unusual in urban Indian society for someone not to use a variety of codes in different contexts and with different interlocutors, and children learn at a young age not only to master several languages but also to master the art of knowing the appropriate language for each social context. Maintaining multiple languages over generations is less common in some other societies and often much less valued. Multilingualism has nonetheless become an expected and increasingly prestigious part of urban cultures across the world. Fuller (2012), in her work in a German-English bilingual classroom in the urban center of Berlin, Germany, notes that many of the children speak two languages at home, sometimes German and English but in some cases English and Spanish, or German and Russian, Hindi, or Setswana. They consider it advantageous to master more languages, often claiming competence in languages to which they have had limited exposure. They also provide positive reinforcement to their classmates as speakers of Serbian, Romanian, or Farsi. This is, of course, not the case everywhere. Fuller notes that the Mexican-American children in her research in rural southern Illinois, USA, who also spoke indigenous languages from Mexico were often hesitant to admit this, and were sometimes teased for their association with these languages. The status of these languages in Mexico was low and there was not a general sense of the value of linguistic diversity in the rural US community in which they lived. Thus while multilingualism can be found almost anywhere, it does not always have positive associations.

Competencies and convergence in multilingual societies

Most people who are multilingual do not necessarily have exactly the same abilities in all the languages (or varieties) they speak; in fact, that kind of parity may be exceptional. As Sridhar (1996, 50) says,

> Multilingualism involving balanced, native-like command of all the languages in the repertoire is rather uncommon. Typically, multilinguals have varying degrees of command of the different repertoires. The differences in competence in the various languages might range from command of a few lexical items, formulaic expressions such as greetings, and rudimentary conversational skills all the way to excellent command of the grammar and vocabulary and specialized register and styles.

Sridhar further specifies that the level of competence in a code is, of course, developed based on the need of the speaker to use a language in a particular domain or for a particular activity. The models for multilingual discourse we will discuss below recognize such factors as topic, speakers, and setting on language choice. They also recognize that context does not *determine* language choice, but merely *influences* it. Speakers draw on the social norms and meanings that are shared in a community, but are not controlled by them.

In such situations, that is, when speakers master multiple languages and use them all in conversation, there may be linguistic consequences. One possibility is the development of what we call **contact languages**, which will be discussed in the next chapter. In other cases, the consequence is diffusion of certain features from one language to the other(s) as a result of the contact situation, particularly certain kinds of syntactic features. This phenomenon has been observed in such areas as the Balkans, the south of India, and Sri Lanka. An early landmark study which reported this is Gumperz and Wilson (1971). They reported that in Kupwar, a small village of about 3,000 inhabitants in Maharashtra, India, there was convergence among the four languages spoken: Marathi and Urdu (both of which are Indo-European), Kannada (a non-Indo-European language), and Telugu (also a non-Indo-European language spoken by only a few people in the village). The languages were distributed mainly by caste. The highest caste, the Jains, spoke Kannada, and the lowest caste, the untouchables, spoke Marathi. People in different castes also needed to speak to one another and to the Telugu-speaking rope-makers. The Urdu-speaking Muslims also needed to be fitted in. Bilingualism or even trilingualism was normal, particularly among the men, but it was Marathi which dominated inter-group communication. One linguistic consequence, however, was that there was some convergence of the languages spoken in the village so far as syntax is concerned, but vocabulary differences were maintained (McMahon 1994, 214–16). It is vocabulary rather than syntax which serves to distinguish the groups, and the variety of multilingualism that has resulted is a special local variety which has developed in response to local needs.

Language ideologies surrounding multilingualism

As we have said, multilingualism is common in many parts of the world and people in those parts would view any other situation as strange and limiting. Nonetheless, there is a long history in certain Western societies of people actually 'looking down' on those who are multilingual. In many of these societies, prestige is attached to only a certain few classical languages (e.g., Classical Greek and Latin) or modern languages of high culture (e.g., English, French, Italian, and German). You generally get little credit for speaking Swahili and, until recently at least, not much more for speaking Russian, Japanese, Arabic, or Chinese. Multilingualism in such societies is often associated with immigrant status, and thus with groups who tend to occupy rather low positions in society. Thus, multilingualism becomes associated with 'inferiority.' One unfortunate consequence of this is that some Western societies go to great lengths to downgrade, even eradicate, the languages that immigrants bring with them while at the same time trying to teach foreign languages in schools. What is more, they have had much more success in doing the former than the latter. We will return to this issue in chapter 14 on language planning and policy, specifically in connection with certain recent developments in the United States.

It is important to note that ideologies about multilingualism are also part of the development of contact linguistics as a field of study, and this influences the terms we use to refer to various contact phenomena. In chapter 2 we used the term variety as a neutral term in referring to ways of speaking, and here we will also use another term, **code**, that, like variety, seeks to avoid the language versus dialect issue. Much of the research on discourse in multilingual contexts uses the term **code-switching** (sometimes written without a hyphen) to avoid the issue of whether people are speaking multiple language or dialects. Many of the theoretical approaches we will discuss can also be applied to data regardless of how we define the status of the relationship, that is, whether it is switching between two distinct languages or between two dialects of one language. However, there is also a growing discussion of the fluidity of codes, and such codes are perhaps better described from an ideological perspective than from a linguistic one (Bailey 2007, Creese and Blackledge 2010). Thus, we will use the term **multilingual discourse** instead of code-switching or code-mixing, as these latter terms imply a normative monolingual ideology which is at odds with current research trends in language contact. Other terms which have been used for this type of discourse are languaging (Jørgensen 2008), translanguaging (Garcia 2009), and metrolingual practices (Otsuji and Pennycook 2011, 2012, Jaworski 2014).

Linguistic landscapes

A recently emerged area of study in the sociolinguistics of multilingual societies is the topic of **linguistic landscapes**, that is, the display of languages in public spaces, including signs, billboards, advertisements, and graffiti. A linguistic landscape is not a straightforward reflection of the official statuses of the languages used, the linguistic diversity present in the city, nor the relationship between languages. Rather, how languages appear in public space provides evidence about underlying ideologies concerning particular codes and their speakers (Hélot et al. 2012). The ways in which languages are used both reflects and impacts their perceived values (Stroud and Mpendukana 2009).

In Berlin, Germany, although German is, of course, the dominant language seen in the linguistic landscape, both English and Turkish (among other languages) are also present, and how they are used provides a perspective on the statuses of these languages. English is frequently used as a lingua franca for speakers of various linguistic backgrounds, for example, in signs in the subways instructing passengers what to do in case of emergency (these are provided in German, English, and French) or in translations of information in tourist attractions (usually only in German and English). However, what is more interesting is the use of English in the names of businesses which are aimed at a primarily native German-speaking audience. A German airline is called *German Wings*, a café has the name *Café Happy Day* (see Figure 4.1), an auto rental agency is named *My Car*, a hairdresser's shop advertises with the slogan *Pimp My Hair* and a club advertises evening entertainment aimed at a female audience with the wording *Zugang zum Mainfloor for ladies only* 'access to the main floor for ladies only.' In most of these cases, the use of English is linked to its status as a prestigious global language which plays an important role in popular culture.

Turkish is used quite differently. In some cases, it appears in contexts in which a Turkish-speaking, as well as a German-speaking, audience is targeted, for example,

Figure 4.1   Linguistic landscapes in Berlin, Germany: Café Happy Day

Figure 4.2   Linguistic landscapes in Berlin, Germany: Your multicultural fresh market

the use of signs with 'welcome' in both German and Turkish (*Willkommen – Hoşgeldinez*) or 'evening dresses 50% off' (*Abendkleider 50% Reduziert – Abiyeler 50% Indirim*). These uses are found exclusively in neighborhoods with high concentrations of Turkish-background residents, unlike the English signs, which can be seen in all districts. Further, Turkish words are often used to sell things that are considered part of Turkish culture, food in particular. In Figure 4.2, we can see how a Turkish grocery store advertises with the words *Helâl et Pazari*; *helâl*, (literally, 'lawful') is readily understood by non-Turkish speakers as meaning food prepared in accordance with Islamic rules. Despite the fact that *pazari* ('market') may not have this same transparency of meaning, this business is clearly using Turkish strategically to attract a varied Berlin clientele. The sign includes a drawing of the Brandenburg Gate – a famous Berlin landmark – and the German description *Ihr multikultereller Frischemarkt* 'Your multicultural fresh market.' Thus the use of Turkish here is not solely, or even primarily, a means of appealing to Turkish-speaking customers, but instead advertising the Turkish nature of the products sold. Thus Turkish is aimed at a particular audience and/or references a specific culture and cuisine. In contrast, English is mostly used without intent to make an association with a specific English-speaking culture; instead, it creates a modern, globalized image for the business.

Such aspects of the linguistic landscape of Berlin bring us to the next topic we wish to explore with regard to multilingualism – the attitudes about particular languages and their speakers. As we will see, the choice of a code is often associated with particular characteristics for the speaker (see also our earlier discussion of this in chapter 3 in our section on ideologies and social groups).

Language attitudes in multilingual settings

Before turning to models which address how speakers use multiple languages in discourse, we must address the issue of attitudes about particular codes. Speakers' choices of code also reflect how they want others to view them. This is apparent from various **matched-guise** experiments that certain social psychologists have conducted. If person A is fluently bilingual in languages X and Y, how is he or she judged as a person when speaking X? How do the same judges evaluate A when A is speaking Y? In matched-guise experiments the judges are unaware that they are judging the same person speaking different language (that is, in different 'guises'). Their judgments are therefore seen as a reflection of their feelings about speakers of X and Y, feelings about such matters as their competence, integrity, and attractiveness.

Lambert, a Canadian social psychologist, developed this technique in order to explore how listeners react to various characteristics in speech. Listeners were asked to judge particular speech samples recorded by bilingual or bidialectal speakers using one language or dialect (one guise) on one occasion and the other language or dialect (the other guise) in identical circumstances. The judgments sought are of such qualities as intelligence, kindness, dependability, ambition, leadership, sincerity, and sense of humor. Since the only factor that is varied is the language or dialect used, the responses provide group evaluations of speakers of these languages and dialects and therefore tap social stereotypes. In one such study, Lambert (1967) reported the reactions of Canadian men and women, referred to as English Canadian and French Canadian according to their dominant language, to subjects who spoke English on one occasion and French on another. Both English Canadian and French Canadian listeners reacted more positively to English guises than French guises. Among eighty English Canadian (EC) and ninety-two French Canadian (FC) first-year college-age students from Montreal, he found (1967, 95–7) that:

- The EC judges rated the female speakers more favorable in their French guises; in particular, they were rated as more intelligent, ambitious, self-confident, dependable, courageous, and sincere than when speaking English.
- Male speakers were rated more favorable in their English guises by EC speakers: they were rated as taller, kinder, more dependable, and more entertaining by the EC male judges, and as taller, more likeable, affectionate, sincere, and conscientious, and as possessing more character and a greater sense of humor by the female EC judges.
- In contrast, FC male speakers were rated lower in integrity and social attractiveness.

The judges were also given the opportunity to compare Continental French (CF) speakers with FC speakers, and Lambert (1967, 7) reports that 'EC judges appear to be less concerned about European French people in general than they are about the local French people; the European French are neither down-graded nor taken as potential social models to any great extent …'

What was most surprising, however, was that the FC judges showed a greater distinction between FC and CF speakers, rating the CF speakers more favorably than the EC speakers, who were rated more favorably than in their FC guises. In other words, they rated members of their own group less favorably on the whole, apparently viewing their own linguistic and cultural group as somewhat inferior to both the English Canadian and the Continental French groups, with this preference apparently stronger in French Canadian males than females. (This study is now nearly fifty years old; it would be surprising if a replication done today would show the same results, in view of the many changes that have occurred in Quebec in recent decades.) This finding can be tied into our discussion in chapter 2 on hegemony; part of this concept is that the dominant group is accepted as rightfully dominant even by members of the groups it dominates.

Other investigators have used the matched-guise technique and report results which clearly indicate that listeners are affected by code choices when they judge what speakers say to them. Certain codes are deemed more appropriate for certain messages than other codes. Code and message are inseparable. The choices we make about the codes we speak influence how we are evaluated. Giles and Coupland (1991, 58) conclude their summary of the work done up to 1990 on the matched-guise technique with the observation that, 'Listeners can very quickly stereotype others' personal and social attributes on the basis of language cues and in ways that appear to have crucial effects on important social decisions made about them.'

Not only are particular languages stereotyped, but the mixture of two or more languages is often, even usually, stigmatized. Many people have a **monoglossic**

ideology, that is, they believe that languages should be kept strictly separate, and this is true of monolingual and multilinguals alike. They may even use derogatory terms to describe what they hear, for example, *Franglais* (French and English in Quebec), *Fragnol* (French and Spanish in Argentina), and *Spanglish* or *Tex-Mex* (Spanish and English in the USA). Such dismissal of the phenomenon demonstrates serious misunderstanding. What we have here is not just a haphazard mixing of two languages brought about by laziness or ignorance or some combination of these. What we have are speakers with a sophisticated knowledge of both languages who are also acutely aware of community norms. These norms require that both languages be used in this way so that speakers can show their familiarity or solidarity. The ability to mix codes in this way is often a source of pride; note, for instance, a number of popular books on *Spanglish* which present it as a desirable way of speaking (Cruz and Teck 1998, Morales 2002, Santiago 2008). These writings show a **pluralist ideology**, in which multiple ways of speaking and being are valued.

Exploration 4.1: Everyday Multilingualism

What varieties of language do you hear in your everyday life? Do all of these varieties have names? What values are assigned to these different ways of speaking, by yourself and others? How do these ideologies and attitudes influence your language use?

Diglossia

Diglossia is the term used to describe a situation in which there are two distinct codes with clear functional separation; that is, one code is employed in one set of circumstances and the other in an entirely different set. Ferguson (1959, 336) has defined diglossia as follows:

> DIGLOSSIA is a relatively stable language situation in which, in addition to the primary dialects of the language (which may include a standard or regional standards), there is a very divergent, highly codified (often grammatically more complex) superposed variety, the vehicle of a large and respected body of written literature, either of an earlier period or in another speech community, which is learned largely by formal education and is used for most written and formal spoken purposes but is not used by any sector of the community for ordinary conversation.

In the same article he identifies four language situations which show the major characteristics of the diglossic phenomenon; in each situation there is a 'high' variety

(H) of language and a 'low' variety (L). Each variety has its own specialized functions, and each is viewed differently by those who are aware of both.

The first situation is in Arabic-speaking countries, in which the two varieties are Classical Arabic (H) and the various regional colloquial varieties (L). The second example is Standard German (H) and Swiss German (L) in Switzerland. Third, Ferguson cites the language situation in Haiti, where the varieties are Standard French (H) and Haitian Creole (L). The fourth is found in Greece with Katharévousa (H) and Dhimotiki or Demotic (L) varieties of Greek. In each case the two varieties coexisted for a long period, sometimes, as with Arabic and Greek, for many centuries. Consequently, the phenomenon of diglossia is not ephemeral in nature; in fact, the opposite is true: it appears to be a persistent social and linguistic phenomenon.

Diglossia has been widely attested across space (e.g., varieties of Tamil in the south of India) and time (e.g., Latin in Europe in the Middle Ages). According to Ferguson (1959, 338), it is likely to come into being when (1) 'there is a sizable body of literature in a language closely related to (or even identical with) the natural language of the community … [and when (2)] literacy in the community is limited to a small elite, [and] … a suitable period of time, of the order of several centuries, passes from the establishment of (1) and (2).'

Domains

A key defining characteristic of diglossia is that the two varieties are kept quite separate in their functions. One is used in one set of circumstances and the other in an entirely different set; these circumstances are called **domains**. For example, the H varieties may be used for delivering sermons and formal lectures, especially in a parliament or legislative body, for giving political speeches, for broadcasting the news on radio and television, and for writing poetry, fine literature, and editorials in newspapers. In contrast, the L varieties may be used in giving instructions to workers in low-prestige occupations or to household servants, in conversation with familiars, in 'soap operas' and popular programs on the radio, in captions on political cartoons in newspapers, and in 'folk literature.' On occasion, a person may lecture in an H variety but answer questions about its contents or explain parts of it in an L variety so as to ensure understanding.

Speakers are unlikely to use an H variety in circumstances calling for an L variety, for example, for addressing a servant; nor do they usually use an L variety when an H is called for, for example, for writing a 'serious' work of literature. If you do the latter, it may be a risky endeavor; it is the kind of thing that Chaucer did for the English of his day, and it requires a certain willingness, on the part of both the writer and the readers, to break away from a diglossic situation by extending the L variety into functions normally associated only with the H. For about three centuries after the Norman Conquest of 1066, English and Norman French coexisted in England in a diglossic situation with Norman French the H variety and English the L. However, gradually the L variety assumed more and more functions associated with the H so that by Chaucer's time it had become possible to use the L variety for a major literary work.

The L variety often shows a tendency to borrow learned words from the H variety, particularly when speakers try to use the L variety in more formal ways. The result is a certain admixture of H vocabulary into the L. On other occasions, however, there may be distinctly different pairs of words, that is, doublets, in the H and L varieties to refer to very common objects and concepts. Since the domains of use of the two varieties do not intersect, there will be an L word for use in L situations and an H word for use in H situations with no possibility of transferring the one to the other. So far as the pronunciation of the two varieties is concerned, the L system will often appear to be the more 'basic.' However, actual circumstances can vary. Whereas the two varieties of Greek have very similar sound systems, there is a considerable difference between Classical Arabic and the colloquial varieties, and a still greater difference between High German and Swiss German.

Language attitudes and ideologies

The H variety is the prestigious, powerful variety; the L variety lacks prestige and power. In fact, there may be so little prestige attached to the L variety that people may even deny that they know it although they may be observed to use it far more frequently than the H variety. Associated with this prestige valuation for the H variety, there is likely to be a strong feeling that the prestige is deserved because the H variety is more 'beautiful,' 'logical,' and 'expressive' than the L variety. That is why it is deemed appropriate for literary use, for religious purposes, and so on. There may also be considerable and widespread resistance to translating certain books into the L variety, for example, the Qur'an into one or other colloquial varieties of Arabic or the Bible into Haitian Creole or Demotic Greek. (We should note that even today many speakers of English resist the Bible in any form other than the King James version.)

This last feeling concerning the natural superiority of the H variety is likely to be reinforced by the fact that a considerable body of literature will be found to exist in that variety and almost none in the other. That literature may also be regarded as reflecting essential values about the culture and, when parts of it are classical literature, deemed worthy of recalling by allusion and quotations on occasions suitable for the employment of H. Speakers of Arabic, for example, gain prestige from being able to allude to classical sources. The folk literature associated with the L variety will have none of the same prestige; it may interest folklorists and it may be transmuted into an H variety by writers skilled in H, but it is unlikely to be the stuff of which literary histories and traditions are made in its 'raw' form.

Language learning

Another important difference between the H and L varieties is that all children learn the L variety; it is also generally the home language. Some may concurrently learn the H variety, but many do not learn the H variety at all; for example, most Haitians have no knowledge at all of Standard French but all can speak some variety of Haitian Creole, although some, as we have said, may deny that they have this ability. The H variety is also likely to be learned in some kind of formal setting, for example, in classrooms or as part of a religious or cultural indoctrination. To that extent, the H variety is 'taught,' whereas the L variety is 'learned.' Teaching requires the availability of grammars, dictionaries, standardized texts, and some widely accepted view about the nature of what is being taught and how it is most effectively to be taught. There are usually no comparable grammars, dictionaries, or standardized texts for the L variety, and any view of that variety is likely to be highly pejorative in nature. When such grammars and other aids do exist, they have in many cases been written by outsiders, for example, 'foreign' linguists. They are also likely to be neither well known to the people whose linguistic usage they describe nor well received by those people, since such works are unlikely to support some of the myths that accompany diglossia, particularly the myth that the L variety lacks any kind of 'grammar.'

The statuses of the H and L varieties

A diglossic situation has by definition prescribed statuses for the H and L varieties. Unlike other types of societal bilingualism, such as situations in which there is a Standard variety and regional dialects, with diglossia no one learns the H variety as their first language in the home. However, in non-diglossic situations, many people learn what is considered the Standard variety as their first language. Further, in diglossia the varieties do not overlap in their functions because of their status differences. In other types of bilingualism, it is possible that either language, or both languages, can be used in a particular domain.

A diglossic pattern of language use can contribute to societal problems if there is a growth of literacy, or when there is a desire to decrease regional and/or social barriers, or when a need is seen for a unified 'national' language. One situation in which we see some of the social issues associated with diglossia is in Haiti. Haitian Creole was eventually recognized as a national language in 1983, with prestigious French, of course, the other. Both languages were made official in 1987. There has been an ongoing debate about the most appropriate orthography (spelling system) for Haitian Creole: about the use of certain letters and accents, and about whether the differences between French and Haitian Creole should be minimized in the orthography for Haitian Creole or whether that orthography should be as transparent as possible in relating letters to sounds, particularly the sounds of the most widespread variety of Haitian Creole. French, though not widely used, has such prestige that, according to Schieffelin and Doucet (1998, 306), virtually any proposal for an orthography for kreyòl has created 'resistance both to the adoption of the orthography and to the use of kreyòl as a medium of instruction in school. The double resistance comes from both the masses and the educated elite minority. The masses see the officialization of written and spoken kreyòl in school as limiting their access to French and, consequently, their social and economic mobility. The elites, who already know kreyòl, do not see the point of teaching it, in any form, in school.'

The linguistic situation in Haiti is intimately tied to power relationships among social groups; this is typical of diglossic situations. Traditionally, the H variety has been associated with an elite and the L variety with everyone else. Diglossia reinforces social distinctions. It is used to assert social position and to keep people in their place, particularly those at the lower end of the social hierarchy. Any move to extend the L variety, even, in the case of Haiti, to make the population literate in any variety, is likely to be perceived to be a direct threat to those who want to maintain traditional relationships and the existing power structure.

The Arabic situation is somewhat different. Many Arabic speakers acknowledge the highly restricted uses of the H variety, but also revere it for certain characteristics that they ascribe to it: its beauty, logic, and richness. Classical Arabic is also the language of the Qur'an. Ferguson has pointed out that choosing one colloquial variety of Arabic to elevate above all others poses a number of problems, so communication between speakers of different varieties of colloquial Arabic requires some mutually intelligible variety. What is commonly referred to as Modern Standard Arabic has emerged, and this variety is described as fairly uniform across countries (Abdelali 2004, Ryding 2005). In some ways, Modern Standard Arabic has taken over the role as the H variety. It is similar to Classical Arabic in structure but differs in style and vocabulary, although both varieties are referred to in Arabic as *al-lugha al-fuSHâ* 'the most eloquent language' (Ryding 2005, 4).

Extended diglossia and language maintenance

What Ferguson describes are 'narrow' or 'classic' diglossic situations. They require the use of very divergent varieties of the same language and there are few good examples. Fishman has broadened or extended the term to include a wider variety of language situations. For Fishman (1980, 3) diglossia is 'an enduring societal arrangement,' extending at least beyond a three-generation period, such that two varieties each have their secure, phenomenologically legitimate, and widely implemented functions. Without diglossia, according to Fishman, language shift within three generations will occur as the languages compete for dominance in various domains. Fishman includes Ferguson's examples, in which the H and L varieties are seen as dialects of the same language, but stipulates that in such cases, the varieties must be 'sufficiently different from one another that, without schooling, the elevated variety cannot be understood by speakers of the vernacular' (1980, 4). Fishman's proposal extends the concept of diglossia to include multilingual situations in which the different languages have quite different functions. For example, one language is used in one set of circumstances and the other in an entirely different set, and such difference is felt to be normal and proper. Fishman gives examples such as Biblical Hebrew and Yiddish for many Jews, Spanish and Guaraní in Paraguay, and even Standard English and Caribbean Creoles.

Rubin (1968) provided a detailed description of the bilingual situation of Paraguay in the middle of the last century. Spanish and Guaraní existed in a relationship that Fishman (1980) calls 'extended diglossic' in which Spanish was the H variety and Guaraní the L variety. Spanish was the language used on formal occasions; it was always used in government business, in conversations with well-dressed strangers, with foreigners, and in most business transactions. People used Guaraní, however, with friends, servants, and poorly-dressed strangers, in the confessional, when they told jokes or made love, and on most casual occasions. Spanish was the preferred language of the cities, but Guaraní was preferred in the countryside, and the lower classes almost always used it for just about every purpose in rural areas. Rubin presents a decision tree to depict the factors involved in language choice in this society, identifying a variety of factors: location (city or country), formality, gender, status, intimacy, seriousness, and type of activity.

Choi (2005) presents data from a questionnaire similar to that used by Rubin and administered to seventy-one residents of the same city in which Rubin did her study, Luque. While Choi's work shows that many of the same factors are at play today in the choices to speak Spanish and Guaraní, some changes can be seen. Overall, more bilingual discourse is reported, and Spanish is used much more in all contexts. The only exception to the latter point is in talking to teachers; more people reported using Guaraní to speak with their teachers in Choi's survey than in Rubin's. This change is undoubtedly due to the increase in the use of Guaraní in education as part of language maintenance efforts. On a national level, it appears that Guaraní is becoming more firmly part of rural life and Spanish more dominant in urban areas. Thus, the language situation in Paraguay appears to become less and less diglossic.

Questioning diglossia

Although the concept of diglossia has been important in the study of multilingualism in a diverse range of societies, the validity of it as a language practice has also been questioned. The relative statuses of the languages may not be exactly as Ferguson depicts; for example, Stępkowska (2012) notes that in Switzerland, Swiss German has long had high prestige and this fact would contradict the usual assumptions about the L code in a diglossic situation. The situation there is further complicated because Swiss German is now the language of instruction in elementary schools.

Another issue is the strict compartmentalization of languages which diglossia requires. Several recent studies have shown the use of colloquial varieties of Arabic mixed with Standard Modern or Classical Arabic (Albirini 2011, Boussofara-Omar

2003, Soliman 2009). Managan (2003) also reports that although the relationship between French and French-based creoles in the Caribbean is often assumed to be diglossic, in Guadeloupe, there is frequent code-switching and nothing resembling diglossia in terms of functional distribution of languages. She also reports that this is a situation of stable bilingualism, which is another challenge to the tenets of the diglossia paradigm, as the claim is that such stable bilingualism can be found only with diglossia.

Even if we embrace the idea of diglossia, it is a concept which fits only a narrow range of social situations. There are many more examples of bilingualism which are clearly not diglossic and we will look at some of these in the pages that follow.

Exploration 4.2:   A Diglossic Situation?

Use the concept of 'diglossia' as a theoretical construct to consider classroom situations in which children who come to school speaking only a regional or social variety of the dominant language, which is well removed from the standard variety, are taught exclusively in that standard variety. Assume that they are taught various uses of the standard, particularly its use in writing, and are constantly informed that the variety they bring with them is 'corrupt,' 'bad,' 'unacceptable,' and so on. (See also chapter 14.) Consider issues of 'power,' 'solidarity,' and 'identity' in doing so. How do factors such as ethnicity, social class, and possibly even gender come into play? What changes might you recommend in language practices in the schools?

Multilingual Discourse

In most multilingual settings, there are no strict or explicit guidelines for what language to speak. People must select a particular code whenever they choose to speak, and they may also decide to switch from that code to another or to mix codes even within sometimes very short utterances. Take, for instance, the following example of English-German multilingual discourse between two pre-teen girls:

1. I: **Iii**, you **knabber** on your finger.
    'Ick, you chew on your finger[nail].'
2. K: No, I don't, this one is broke off.
3. I: **Ekelig**.
    'Gross.'

Until recently, the most common term used in sociolinguistics to refer to this phenomenon was code-switching. However, this term is losing currency, and we choose the term multilingual discourse as a cover term for a number of different linguistic patterns. We will, however, continue to use the term code-switching in the context of the discussion of particular studies that use that term. Our main focus in this section will be models for language choice which focus on the social aspects of multilingual discourse. Researchers on this topic look at a variety of factors, from social and political norms and the linguistic marketplace to social identity and emotions. The subsequent pages will address some major theoretical models which have been suggested that address the underlying principles, often unconscious, that guide speakers in making their linguistic choices.

Although we will not provide an overview of research on **code-switching constraints**, that is, the structural features of multilingual discourse, a brief mention of this topic is warranted here. There has been a great deal of research in this vein and it is not always completely separate from the discussion of social factors. Research on code-switching constraints focuses on switches within a single sentence (called intra-sentential code-switching), such as in the following examples with English and Spanish. These examples show sentences primarily in one language which contain nouns and verbs from another language; these are some of the most common patterns in multilingual discourse.

(While setting up a chess board):
D: Me faltan mi **king** y mi **queen**.
'I am missing my king and my queen.'

(As an explanation for his argument with another student)
S: es que **kickó**, maestra.
'what happened is that he kicked me, teacher.'

Various researchers have proposed models and made predictions about how two languages can be combined. Some of the more popular of these at this time include the Matrix Language Frame (MLF) model (Myers-Scotton 1993, 2002) and work within the Minimalist Program (MacSwan 2014). Most of this research seeks to find universal constraints that apply to all language pairs, but approaches differ. For example, the MLF model is based on the assumption that one of the languages is dominant and provides the grammatical frame, and that only certain types of morphemes can be switched. Work within the Minimalist Program is based on generative syntactic theory and concerns issues such as the union of the two lexicons (MacSwan 2014, 5). Our focus in the rest of this chapter will be the social meanings of such grammatical phenomena.

Metaphorical and situational code-switching

An early seminal work on multilingual discourse is Blom and Gumperz (1972), in which the concepts of situational and metaphorical code-switching are introduced.

Although this distinction is no longer used as a framework for analyses of multi-lingual discourse, the underlying ideas about the meanings of language choices provide the basis for subsequent theories, and are thus introduced here.

Situational code-switching occurs when the languages used change according to the situations in which the speakers find themselves: they speak one language in one situation and another in a different one. What we observe is that one variety is used in a certain set of situations and another in an entirely different set. This kind of code-switching differs from diglossia. In diglossic communities the situation also dictates the choice of variety but the choice is much more rigidly defined by the particular activity and by the relationship between the participants. Diglossia reinforces differences, whereas code-switching tends to reduce them.

As the term itself suggests, **metaphorical code-switching** has an affective dimension to it: the choice of code carries symbolic meaning, that is, the language fits the message. This is illustrated in a quote attributed to Charles V, the Holy Roman Emperor, which indicates attitudes about certain languages being holy, the language of love or male solidarity, or crude or bestial: 'I speak Spanish to God, Italian to women, French to men, and German to my horse.'

Blom and Gumperz' early work set the stage for continued research addressing the question of why speakers switched between languages when and how they did. While many studies have created taxonomies of functions of code-switching (e.g., emphasis, elaboration, and so on), we will focus instead on broader frameworks which seek to provide principles underlying the use of multiple codes in conversation.

Accommodation and audience design

Another framework which has informed current ideas about language choice is Speech Accommodation Theory, later called Communication Accommodation Theory (Giles et al. 1987, 1991, 2007). Speakers sometimes try to accommodate to the expectations that others have of them when they speak, and they may do this consciously and deliberately or be quite unaware of what they are doing. **Accommodation** is one way of explaining how individuals and groups may be seen to relate to each other. One individual can try to induce another to judge him or her more favorably by reducing differences between the two. An individual may even be prepared to sacrifice something to gain social approval of some kind, for example, shift in behavior to become more like the other. This is **convergence** behavior. Alternatively, if you desire to distance yourself from other interlocutors, the shift in behavior will be away from the behavior of another or others. This is **divergence** behavior. Examples would be 'putting on airs and graces' in order to deliberately dissociate yourself from peers, or conversely using slang and nonstandard speech with someone who is speaking a formal, high-status variety.

Giles and Coupland (1991, 60–1) explain speech accommodation as 'a multiply-organized and contextually complex set of alternatives, regularly available to communicators in face-to-face talk. It can function to index and achieve solidarity with or dissociation from a conversational partner, reciprocally and dynamically.' Le Page (1997, 28) extends this definition to put even more emphasis on the speaker's creation of his or her identity: 'we do not necessarily adapt to the style of the interlocutor, but rather to the image we have of ourselves in relation to our interlocutor.' Speaking is not merely a social act that involves others; it is also a personal act in that it helps create the identity one wishes to be seen as having in a particular set of circumstances.

Exploration 4.3:   Accommodation or Mockery?

The concept of accommodation can be used for all levels of language variation, that is, for convergence/divergence in not just distinct languages but also dialects or styles. Think about your own language use; are there instances in which you alter the way you speak to sound more or less like the person to whom you are talking? If you shift your way of speaking to sound more like someone else, where the line between convergence to show solidarity and mocking?

One type of convergent behavior is said to be motivated by how speakers often attempt to deal with listeners through **audience design**, that is, by orienting their speech toward others through code choices. Bell goes so far as to declare that 'Speakers design their style primarily for and in response to their audience' (2001, 143) or occasionally by reference to a third party (referee design) as when the speech of an absent reference group influences language choices. He says that audience design applies to all codes and all speakers, who have what he calls 'a fine-grained ability' to do this (2001, 146). 'Individual speakers use style – and other aspects of their language repertoire – to represent their identity or to lay claim to other identities' (2001, 163). We will take up this perspective below in the section on multilingual identities. We have the ability to present ourselves in different ways. We have control over what is sometimes called speaker design: the use of language 'as a resource in the actual creation, presentation, and re-creation of speaker identity' (Schilling-Estes 2002, 388). Everything we say to others recognizes those others; an individual's speech is not a series of monologs for it is shaped toward and tailored by what others say and do.

Johnson-Weiner (1998) uses accommodation theory to explain differences in language choice between some Old Order Amish and Old Order Mennonite communities in the northeastern United States (mainly New York and Pennsylvania) and Ontario and other New Order communities. The main difference is that the

Old Order communities adhere strictly to use of different varieties of German – Low Pennsylvania German, High Pennsylvania German, and 'Bible German' – and English according to circumstances. They use the varieties of German exclusively within the communities and use English as a contact language with the outside world. Within the New Order communities such as the Beachy Amish and Horning Mennonites there has been a complete shift to English. However, all groups follow strict rules – although not always the same ones – about dress and use (or non-use) of automobiles, electricity, and telephones. Johnson-Weiner says that for the Old Order communities the maintenance of German shows a desire for deliberate divergence from the outside world to the point of rejection. Its use of English accommodates to a necessity to keep that world at bay; it is a way of dealing with that world so as to preserve each community's isolation from it. For communities such as the Beachy Amish and Horning Mennonites, the use of English paradoxically provides both inclusion (convergence) and exclusion (divergence) in that it enables both communication with the outside world and a clear expression to that world of the values of each community, particularly its strong religious beliefs. Burridge (2002) discusses the Ontario group and says that their use of 'Pennsylvania German has always provided an important barrier to the outside world, allowing not only for insider identification, but most importantly for outsider separation. It is one of their main means of remaining detached and isolated from worldly influences. Its loss would also mean the loss of this separate status and, for this group, would be the equivalent of losing their faith' (Burridge 2002, 213).

Accommodation is also a concept used in work done in the Alsace in France. In a study of language use in Strasbourg, Gardner-Chloros (1991) shows among other things how switching between codes, in this case Standard French and Alsatian German, can be an effective neutral compromise for some locals. Speakers can employ code-switching when use of French alone might appear to be too snobbish and Alsatian alone to be too rustic. It is also often necessary when several generations of a family are present and allows for accommodation across the generations. Another investigation (Gardner-Chloros 1997) focused on the use of the two languages in three department stores in Strasbourg: Printemps, a branch of the famous chic Paris store, Magmod, old-fashioned and less luxurious, and Jung, quite provincial in comparison to either of the others. In other words, there is a kind of prestige hierarchy with Printemps at the top, Magmod in the middle, and Jung at the bottom. One would assume that in Printemps French would be the language most likely to be used by shoppers and shop assistants alike, and that Jung would attract most use of Alsatian; Magmod would be somewhere in the middle. Gardner-Chloros found that young French-speaking shoppers in Jung and older Alsatian-speaking shoppers in Printemps code-switched to the other language. There was least code-switching in Magmod. Code-switching goes in both directions: 'up' in Printemps and 'down' in Jung. As she says (1997, 374), it 'is clear ... that the ... assumption that switching reveals a desire to converge to the prestige norm is inadequate. The group which switches more than any other appears to do so in order to fit in with its surroundings, since it is made up of people who are more at ease in the prestige norm, French, than in Alsatian. Accommodation would therefore appear to be as relevant a motive as prestige.'

The Markedness Model

Another theory in the study of language choice is the Markedness Model (Myers-Scotton 1983, 1993, 1998). The main idea of this model is that, for a given interaction, there is an **unmarked choice**, that is, a code which is expected in the specific context. The relative markedness of a code varies by situation. It is an unmarked choice for a citizen to address an inquiry to an official in Bokmål in Hemnesberget, for a teacher to speak Standard German to a visitor in a school in the Gail Valley, Austria, and for a police officer to speak English to someone in a good car in Nigeria. Corresponding marked choices for initial encounters between people who do not know each other in each of the above encounters would be Ranamål, Slovenian, and one of the indigenous Nigerian languages. However, the unmarked choices are these latter languages when locals converse socially in each of these places. Quite often, in fact, local solidarity requires the use of a non-prestige language or variety; or it may require a mixing of two languages. These last observations are important: the unmarked–marked distinction is quite independent of any High–Low, standard–nonstandard, language–dialect, or pure–mixed distinctions. It is entirely dependent on situation.

The Markedness Model does not predict that speakers always use the unmarked code, but rather employs the concept of markedness as a means to analyze code-switching. For example, in a Spanish-English bilingual classroom, the unmarked code for English instruction is clearly and often explicitly English. Using this unmarked code reinforces the status quo relationship between the teacher and the students. If a student switches to Spanish, this marked choice could indicate the student's lack of cooperation in the lesson, or her Spanish utterance could be directed at a peer and thus indicate that this turn is seen as outside of the frame of the lesson, where Spanish is the unmarked choice. The essential point is that all language choices, marked and unmarked, contribute to the relationship between the speakers.

This model is exemplified in a study of a Malawian family living in the United States and the switches between English and Chicheŵa (Myers-Scotton 2002). Everyone in the family (father, mother, and two sons, ages ten and seven – there is also a baby in the family, but he was too young to speak at the time of this recording) speaks both languages fluently. They have lived in the United States for three years. Although English is one of the official languages of their home country, the parents in this family are also invested in having their children learn and maintain Chicheŵa. A quantitative analysis shows that the parents use Chicheŵa as their unmarked code choice, while the children use English. The analysis shows how the children use English to show opposition to their parents (e.g., when one of the sons is objecting to changing the baby) and Chicheŵa to show deference and garner support from their parents. For example, there is a stark contrast between one boy's use of Chicheŵa to address the parents and his switch to English to argue with his younger brother. Similarly, the parents use English to step out of their parental roles, as shown in the following example in which the mother is leaving for work in the English-speaking public sphere, and her language switch parallels her switch in roles.

(Context: Mother is leaving for work; M is Mother, P(eter) is the oldest son; English is in all caps and Chicheŵa is in regular script)
M [to Peter] OK, *ukangoyang'ana ma-*DRINK *amene ali mu-*FRIDGE*-mo.*
'Ok, just go and look at [the] drinks that are in [the] fridge.'
P WHAT COLOR?
M *Upange kaye* CHECK DRINK *usanathile* …
'You should first check [the] drink before you pour [it].'
M … [now on her way out]
Ukachape uyu, AND THEN I'M OUT OF HERE.
'Go and wash this one, and then I'm out of here.'

(Myers-Scotton 2002, 217)

The Markedness Model was originally designed to explain the social motivations of alternation between two distinct languages in spoken conversation, but has also been applied to switching between different varieties of the same language (see the collection of articles in Myers-Scotton 1998) and also literary code-switching (Gross 2000), advertising (Wei-Yu Chen 2006, Micu and Coulter 2010), poetry (Barnes 2011), and film (Barnes 2012).

Exploration 4.4:   The Unmarked Code in the Classroom

When you come into a classroom at your university, what linguistic variety do you expect to hear? (Is this different in foreign language classrooms?) What does it mean if the professor or students speak a different language, a nonstandard dialect, or either more or less formally than you consider 'unmarked'? Compare your expectations with those of your classmates.

Multilingual identities

While the Markedness Model concerns itself with indexing particular role relationships for speakers, there is another approach which regards language choice as a means to construct social identities; we introduced this **social constructionist** (also called social constructivist) approach in the previous chapter. An important aspect of this approach is that identities are not seen as fixed but as fluid, multiple, and culturally constructed. Identities might align with pre-existent categories such as gender, occupation, ethnicity, and so on, but should be thought of as being brought into being through the interaction with others. Furthermore, and of particular importance when looking at multilingual discourse, there is no one-to-one correspondence between language choice and social identity, that is, speaking Spanish in the USA does not necessarily construct the speaker as Latino; in some contexts this may well be the aspect of identity that is constructed, but in others speaking Spanish might serve to construct any number of other things. These other aspects of identity may be related to macrosocial categories, such as age, gender, or social class; or they may be other levels of identity, for example, that of a father, someone with a good sense of humor, or a humble person. Yet another level of identity involves the relationship between speakers, so a language choice may be part of the construction of a close friendship, a boss-employee relationship, or a flirtation.

As within Communication Accommodation Theory, within the social constructionist framework, speakers are said to use language to position themselves vis-à-vis their interlocutors in various ways, including such matters as social values and ideologies about language, speakers, and social norms. Such research on what is called **stancetaking** will be discussed further in chapters 7 and 11.

Bailey (2001, 2005) reports on research done within this framework on Dominican Americans and their use of different varieties of Spanish and English. He describes how Dominican American high-school students in Providence, Rhode Island, negotiate their way among other students of different language backgrounds, mainly other Hispanics and African Americans. They share a language with the former and racial categorization and social-class characteristics with the latter. However, they seek to assert their own separate identity. Consequently, they have developed a code that 'includes distinctive alternation of forms indexing a Dominican American identity. Most salient of these, perhaps, is the alternation between English and Spanish in code-switching' (2005, 259). The Dominican American students do use some speech characteristics of the African American students but such use does not make them 'Black' since their ability to use Spanish, that is, their Spanish ethnolinguistic identity, triumphs over any common identity derived from African descent (2005, 263). While they continue to speak their varieties of Spanish and English, they maintain, at least for now, their separate identity. However, Bailey adds (2005, 270–1) that if succeeding generations of students fail to continue to do so, this could have serious consequences for maintaining a separate Dominican American identity.

Reyes (2005) reports another study in a very different setting, but one also conducted among children of immigrant backgrounds. She provides a somewhat similar example of another code deliberately fashioned to achieve a distinctive identity but which at the same time creates a link with another group of similar status in the community. Reyes worked over a period of four years with small groups of Asian

American teens near Philadelphia's Chinatown. They were mainly American-born children of recent Cambodian, Laotian, and Vietnamese immigrants. These teens identified closely with African American teens from similar low-income backgrounds and participated in many of the styles and activities associated with them, for example, certain types of clothing, accessories, and hair styles, and hip hop culture. They also adopted some of their speech characteristics and created their own hybrid language variety, a mixture of African American English, mainstream English, and contributions from their various Asian languages. They used this variety as 'a resource to fashion their own identities as the Other Asian ... (and) to signal urban youth cultural participation by constructing divisions of identity between youth and adults and between each other' (2005, 527).

Another study of immigrant-background youth, Kallmeyer and Keim (2003), shows how a multiethnic groups of girls in Mannheim use their home languages (mostly contact varieties of Turkish and Italian) along with several varieties of German – local and standard dialects as well as *Gastarbeiterdeutsch* 'guest worker German' – to construct their own identities and also to create caricatures of others. They use these multiple codes to position themselves as different from their parents' generation in order to challenge the ghettoization imposed upon them as youths of migrant background.

Mahootian (2005, 2012), in her work on the use of code-switching in written texts, also addressed how language choice can challenge essentialist ideas about social identity. She analyzes a variety of US sources (e.g., scripted performances, a lifestyles magazine, a short story, and a novel) to address the question of why, given the hegemonic ideology of normative monolingualism, a choice has been made to use multilingual discourse in these contexts. She claims that the use of more than one language in published written language is an intentional strategy to construct not just the identity of the writer as a bilingual but also social categories which challenge those associated with monolingualism.

Another important issue in the study of multilingual discourse and identity has to do with the acceptance by other interlocutors of the identities speakers construct for themselves. Lo (1999) addresses this issue in her analysis of an interaction between a Chinese American (Chazz) and a Korean American man (Ken), in which Chazz uses some utterances in Korean to express both his affiliation with Koreans and his disdain for Vietnamese women. However, perhaps in part because Chazz uses a very derogatory Korean term to refer to Vietnamese women, Ken resists alignment in this exchange, in part by continuing to speak English and not following Chazz's lead and switching to Korean. This pattern of language use constructs a distance between the speaker and the interlocutor while at the same time signaling his lack of participation in using discourses involving ethnic slurs directed at Vietnamese women.

We certainly do use language to construct our social selves, as we can also see in the body of literature on a phenomenon called **crossing** (or sometimes 'styling'; see Rampton 1995, 2001), a concept introduced in chapter 3. In this work, we see how analysis of multilingual discourse is governed by the same principles as work on the use of different dialects of a language. Rampton's work gives examples of London youths who use different varieties of English, including Jamaican Creole English and Asian English, as well as bits of Panjabi, in their interactions within their multiethnic peer groups. Rampton argues that these choices served to denaturalize racial boundaries and the connection of racialized groups with particular ways of speaking, and '... cultivated a spectacular, dynamic, heteroglossic marginality' (Rampton 1995: 507).

Such studies also provide evidence for 'race' as a cultural construct rather than a simple biological reality, as racial group membership is sometimes fluid, contested, or challenged. In another study addressing the social construction of race, Sweetland (2002) describes how a young White woman in the United States uses linguistic features generally associated with African American Vernacular English (AAVE) in order to achieve membership in a group of Blacks, helped in this case by her growing up in an overwhelmingly Black neighborhood. Bucholtz (1999) describes a similar case of a White male student in a California high school where 'an ideologically defined black–white dichotomy ... structures students' social worlds. Yet many European American students symbolically cross this divide through linguistic and other social practices that index their affiliation with African American youth culture, and especially hip hop' (1999, 445). This student drew on features of AAVE – what Bucholtz calls **CRAAVE**, Cross-Race African American Vernacular English – to claim some kind of honorary membership in Black social circles. Bucholtz illustrates how the use of CRAAVE aligns the European American speaker with some African American friends, while at the same time reinforcing stereotypes that associate Black masculinity with physical strength and violence.

Chapter Summary

Chapter 4 explores what happens when languages – or more aptly, speakers of languages – come into contact. There are many different paths to multilingualism, and many different ways of using multiple languages. One pattern of language use we explore is diglossia, in which the two languages differ in terms of their status in society; one is considered more prestigious and is used in more formal contexts, the other is reserved for more casual events and interactions. In many multilingual societies, however, code choice is not so clear, and there is multilingual discourse. Often, the attitudes people have about multilingualism, or about particular languages, influence how the languages are used. We look at three main theoretical approaches to the study of multilingual discourse – Communication Accommodation Theory, the Markedness Model, and the study of language choice as part of the social construction of identity. In this final section, we see how the study of multilingualism and the study of the uses of different dialects of the same language revolve around the same principles.

Exercises

1. The trend in academia has gone from viewing bilingualism as a disadvantage to learning and linguistic ability to viewing it as an advantage in cognitive development (see the websites listed in the links in the online material for this chapter for some background information on this with a focus on bilingualism and cognition.) But what about social advantages and disadvantages? Talk to someone who grew up with two languages and see what they have to say about whether they consider it an advantage or a disadvantage. Here is a preliminary list of questions you might want to ask:
   - Are you glad to be multilingual?
   - Do you continue to use all/both of the languages you know? Describe how and when you use them. Are they used in separate domains or do you use multilingual discourse?
   - Have you ever been ashamed of speaking more than one language, or of being a speaker of a particular language?
   - Do you have different emotional attachments to your different languages?
   - Are there situations when it is very good to be multilingual, and others where it is less good? What are these situations, and what influences how you feel about your language background?
   - If you had children, would you raise them multilingually? Why or why not?

2. Look at the transcript below for a conversation between two young speakers in Berlin, Germany. First read the background information about these speakers, and then, if you would like to hear the conversation, go to the website and click on the link to play the sound file and follow along as you listen. Write a short analysis of the language use by the speakers, using one of the approaches outlined in the chapter.

Sarah and Hans: New Glasses

Sarah and Hans are a heterosexual couple in their early to mid-twenties. They have been together for about two years; they are currently living together temporarily while Sarah looks for a new apartment. Sarah has a German mother but grew up in the United States; she spoke some German growing up but her dominant language is English. She has lived in Germany for about three years. Hans has always lived in Germany and German is his dominant language; he speaks English as a foreign language, having learned it in school. Up until recently, Sarah and Hans almost always spoke German together, but at the time of this recording, Hans was going to be leaving soon for a semester as an exchange student in the United States, and Sarah had been speaking English to him because, as she told the researcher who collected these data, she felt he needed to work on his English.

This segment of the conversation is about halfway through an hour-long recording, during which they have been preparing their evening meal, chatting, and eating.

German words are in **bold**, English in plain font.

1   S: Oh, you know what I had, what I did, I got my eyes checked –
2   H: Oh, where?
3   S: – and my eyes are worse, now, in the last few years, they've gotten worse, especially the right eye. So my right eye has gotten much worse. And um, I need a new, new **Gläser**. Right?
    'lenses'
4   H: M-hmm.
5   S: And it's the same man that I know from 1990, 1989.
6   H: **Wo warst Du, Du warst bei der** –
    'Where were you, you were at the –'
7   S: **Brillenwerkstatt, wo ich meine Brille, wo ich die habe, eigentlich. And um, ja, er sagte, ja, das kostet 300 Mark mit Krankenversicherung. Und ich muss 300 Mark bezahlen.**
    'The Brillenwerkstatt [name of the optician], where I [got] my glasses, where I got these, actually. And um, yeah, he said, yeah, that costs 300 marks with health insurance, And I have to pay 300 marks.'
8   H: **Was kostet mit Krankenversicherung 300 Mark.**
    'What costs 300 marks?'
9   S: **Die neue Gläser für diese Brille.**
    'The new lenses for my glasses.'
10 H: **Echt? Hat er gesagt?**
    'Really? He said that?'
11 S: **Ja ja, wir haben alles aufgerechnet. Alle, ich war da mindesten anderthalb Stunden, er hat alles geprüft, meine Augen, mit die alle verschienden Machinen, die Stigmatismus, die … alle Sachen.**
    'Yeah, yeah, we calculated it all. Everything, I was there at least one and a half hours, he checked everything, my eyes, with all the different machines, my stigmatism, the … everything.'
12 H: **Du musst, du musst trotzdem zum Augenarzt gehen, oder? Weil er dass verschreiben muss, wenn Du was von der Krankenkasse haben willst?**
    'You have to, you have to go to the eye doctor anyway, don't you? So he can prescribe it, if you want to get something from the health insurance?'
13 S: **Um-umm.** {meaning no}
14 H: **Geht nicht Du lasst nur der Optiker machen.**
    'That can't be, that just the optician does it.'
15 S: **Doch. Das is so, auch so wie ich meine Brille gekriegt habe. Ist genau so.**
    'Yes it is. That's how, the way I got my glasses too. Just like that.'

16   H: **Du warst nicht beim Augenarzt.**
      'You didn't go to an eye doctor.'

17   S: **Nee, nie. Nie, Du musst nie da. Er prüft alles da, die haben alles
      da. Es ist ganz super, der Laden, echt. Ich war da schon ein Paar mal.**
      'No, never. You never have to go there. He checks everything, they have
      everything there. It's really great, the shop, really. I've been there a
      couple of times.'

18   H: **Brillenladen in Kreuzberg.**
      'Glasses shop in Kreuzberg [a nearby district of their city].'

19   S: **Ich kenne die auch. Ich kenne den Typ.**
      'I know them too. I knew this guy.'

20   H: **Ich werde irgendwie skeptisch, also.**
      'I'd be skeptical, though.'

21   S: No.

22   H: **Weil der Augenarzt der hat eine Medizinische Ausbildung.**
      'Because a doctor has medical training.'

23   S: **Ich war bei Augenarzt, ich kenne das auch, und die, die machen
      nichts anders. Die machen die selben Tests und so.**
      'I've been to an eye doctor, and I know that too, and they, they don't do
      anything different. They do the same tests and so on.'

24   H: Uh-huh.

25   S: **Aber das Problem ist, ich brauche 300 Mark nächtsten Montag.
      Kannst Du mir das ausleihen?**
      'But the problem is, I need 300 Marks next Monday. Can you lend it to
      me?'

26   H: **Du kriegst eine neue Brille jetzt, oder was?**
      'You're getting a new pair of glasses, or what?'

27   S: **Ja.**

28   H: **Uh-huh.**

29   S: **Ich habe die bestellt.**
      'I ordered them.'

30   H: **Tatsaechlich?**
      'Really?'

31   S: **Ja, Hans, meine Augen sind schlecter, was soll ich tun, ich renne
      blind durch die Gegend!**
      'Yeah, Hans, my eyes have gotten worse, what should I do, I'm running
      around blind!'

32   H: **Aber du siehst, du sagst du siehst immer so viel mit der Brille.**
      'But you see, you saw you see so much with those glasses.'

33   S: No, can you loan me 300 Marks. Do you have it?

34   H: **Natürlich, klar.**
      'Of course, certainly.'

35   S: Do you have that? I thought you had nothing in, on your **Konto.**
                                                                    'account'

36   H: **Ja, ich nehme das von meinem Sparkonto.**
     'Yeah, I'll take it from my savings account.'

37   S: **Geht das? Ist das kein Problem?**
     'Will that work? Is that a problem?'

38   H: **Kein Problem.**
     'No problem.'

39   S: Okay. That's what I wanna know. All your other comments are
     unnecessary.

40   H: Blah-blah-blah.

41   S: So anyway, it's a good thing to go, because I've been having
     headaches a lot lately. And I knew that there was something wrong so I
     went to my xxx

42   H: **Ja, Dein rechtes Auge seiht immer ein bisschen anders aus.**
     'Yeah, your right eye looks a little different.'

43   S: Shut up! It does not.

44   H: **Doch**
     'yes it does.'

45   S: **Nicht wie bei dir.**
     'Not like yours.'

46   H: **Hängt schon fast heraus.**
     'It's almost hanging out.'

47   S: No way. Shut up (laughs)

48   H: (laughs) **Irgendwie dachte ich der fehlt irgendwas an deinem
     Augen.**
     'Somehow I thought there was something wrong with your eye.'

49   S: **Arschloch!**
     'Asshole!'

50   H: **Na na na.**

3. Code-switching and borrowing are said to be different phenomena. Try to
   distinguish between the two, using examples from two languages you know.
   What criteria do the various scholars who have discussed this issue rely on
   most? What disagreements do you find? Is there possibly a continuum here,
   that is, no clear division between the two? You might begin your search for
   answers by consulting Myers-Scotton (2005, 253ff).

Further Reading

Mahootian, Shahrzad (2006). Code Switching and Mixing. *Encyclopedia of Language and
    Linguistics*, 511–27. In Keith Brown (ed.), *Encyclopedia of Language and Linguistics*,
    vol. 2. 2nd edn. Elsevier: Oxford, 511–27.
    An overview of research on code-switching, incorporating different models and
    approaches to the study of social and structural aspects of the use of multiples codes.

Ogay, Tania and Howard Giles (2007). Communication Accommodation Theory: A Look Back and a Look Ahead. In Bryan B. Whaley and Wendy Samter (eds.), *Explaining Communication: Contemporary Theories and Exemplars*. Malwah, NJ: Lawrence Erlbaum Associates, 121–48.

A recent recap of work on Communication Accommodation Theory; does not focus solely on multilingual discourse but looks at accommodation more broadly.

Sebba, Mark, Shahrzad Mahootian, and Carla Jonsson (2011). *Language Mixing and Code-Switching in Writing: Approaches to Mixed-Language Written Discourse. Routledge Critical Studies in Multilingualism*. London: Routledge, Taylor & Francis Group.

This collection of articles presents multilingual data from a wide range of written contexts, including traditional literature and contemporary media relying on computer and cell phone technology. Different methodological approaches to the analysis of these data are addressed.

Snow, D. (2013). Revisiting Ferguson's Defining Cases of Diglossia. *Journal of Multilingual and Multicultural Development* 34(1): 61–76.

A re-examination of the earlier work on diglossia and the proposal of the refinement of the theory to include three different types of diglossia.

Soukup, Barbara (2012). Current Issues in the Social Psychological Study of 'Language Attitudes': Constructionism, Context, and the Attitude–Behavior Link. *Language and Linguistics Compass* 6(4): 212–24.

This review of the literature provides a perspective on how matched-guise research, and attitudinal research more broadly, fits with social constructionist perspectives.

For further resources for this chapter visit the companion website at

 www.wiley.com/go/wardhaugh/sociolinguistics

References

Abdelali, A. (2004). Localization in Modern Standard Arabic. *Journal of the American Society for Information Science and technology* 55(1): 23–8.

Albirini, A. (2011). The Sociolinguistic Functions of Codeswitching between Standard Arabic and Dialectal Arabic. *Language in Society* 40(5): 537–62.

Bailey, B. (2001). Dominican-American Ethnic/Racial Identities and United States Social Categories. *International Migration Review* 35(3): 677–708.

Bailey, B. (2005). The Language of Multiple Identities among Dominican Americans. In S. F. Kiesling and C. B. Paulston (eds.), *Intercultural Discourse and Communication*. Oxford: Blackwell.

Bailey, B. (2007). Heteroglossia and Boundaries. In Monica Heller (ed.), *Bilingualism: Social and Political Approaches*. New York: Palgrave MacMillan, 257–74.

Barnes, L. (2011). The Function and Significance of Bilingual Code-Switching in English Poetry with a Special Focus on the Work of Eliot and Pound. *English Academy Review* 28(1): 23–38.

Barnes, L. (2012). The Role of Code-Switching in the Creation of an Outsider Identity in the Bilingual Film. *Communication* 8(3): 247–60.

Bell, A. (2001). Back in Style: Reworking Audience Design. In P. Eckert and J. R. Rickford (eds.), *Style and Sociolinguistic Variation*. Cambridge: Cambridge University Press

Blom, J. and John J. Gumperz (1972). Social Meaning in Linguistic Structure: Code-Switching in Norway. In John J. Gumperz and Dell Hymes (eds.), *Directions in Sociolinguistics*. New York: Holt, Rinehart and Winston, 407–34.

Boussofara-Omar, N. (2003). Revisiting Arabic Diglossic Switching in Light of the MLF Model and its Sub-models: The 4-M Model and the Abstract Level Model. *Bilingualism: Language and Cognition* 6(1): 33–46.

Burridge, K. (2002). Changes with Pennsylvania German Grammar as Enactments of Anabaptist World View. In N. J. Enfield (ed.), *Ethnosyntax: Explorations in Grammar and Culture*. Oxford: Oxford University Press.

Bucholtz, M. (1999). You Da Man: Narrating the Racial Other in the Production of White Masculinity. *Journal of Sociolinguistics* 3(4): 443–60.

Choi, Jinny K. (2005). Bilingualism in Paraguay: Forty Years after Rubin's Study. *Journal of Multilingual and Multicultural Development* 26(3): 233–48.

Creese, A. and A. Blackledge (2010). Translanguaging in the Bilingual Classroom: A Pedagogy for Learning and Teaching? *The Modern Language Journal* 94(1): 103–15.

Cruz, B. and B. Teck (1998). *The Official Spanglish Dictionary: Un User's Guía to More Than 300 Words and Phrases That Aren't Exactly Español or Inglés*. New York: Fireside.

Ferguson, C. A. (1959). Diglossia. *Word* 15: 325–40. In P. P. Giglioli (ed.), *Language and Social Context: Selected Readings*. Harmondsworth, England: Penguin Books.

Fishman, J. A. (1980). Bilingualism and Biculturism as Individual and as Societal Phenomena. *Journal of Multilingual & Multicultural Development* 1(1): 3–15.

Fuller, Janet M. (2012). *Bilingual Pre-teens: Competing Ideologies and Multiple Identities in the U.S. and Germany*. New York: Routledge.

Fuller, Janet M. (2013). *Spanish Speakers in the USA*. Bristol: Multilingual Matters.

Garcia, O. (2009). Education, Multilingualism and Translanguaging in the 21st Century. In T. Skutnabb-Kangas, R. Phillipson, A. K. Mohanty and M. Panda (eds.), *Social Justice through Multilingual Education*. Bristol: Multilingual Matters.

Gardner-Chloros, P. (1991). *Language Selection and Switching in Strasbourg*. Oxford: Oxford University Press.

Gardner-Chloros, P. (1997). Code-Switching: Language Selection in Three Strasbourg Department Stores. In N. Coupland and A. Jaworski (eds.), *Sociolinguistics: A Reader*. New York: St Martin's Press.

Giles, H., R. Bourhis, and D. M. Taylor (1977). Towards a Theory of Language in Ethnic Group Relations. In H. Giles (ed.), *Language, Ethnicity and Intergroup Relations*. London: Academic Press.

Giles, H. and N. Coupland (1991). *Language: Contexts and Consequences*. Buckingham: Open University Press.

Giles, H., A. Mulac, J. J. Braodac, and P Johnson (1987). Speech Accommodation Theory: The First Decade and Beyond. In Margaret McLaughlin (ed.), *Communication Yearbook 10*. Beverly Hills, CA: Sage, 13–48.

Giles, H., N. Coupland, and J. Coupland (1991). Accommodation Theory: Communication, Context, and Consequences. In H. Giles, N. Coupland, and J. Coupland (eds.), *Contexts of Accommodation: Developments in Applied Sociolinguistics*. Cambridge: Cambridge University Press, 1–68.

Giles, H., and T. Ogay (2007). Communication Accommodation Theory. In B. B. Whaley and W. Samter (eds), *Explaining Communication: Contemporary Theories and Exemplars*. Mahwah, NJ: Lawrence Erlbaum Associates, 325–44).

Gross, S. (2000). Intentionality and the Markedness Model in Literary Codeswitching. *Journal of Pragmatics* 32(9): 1283–303.

Gumperz, J. J. and R. Wilson (1971). Convergence and Creolization: A Case from the Indo-Aryan/Dravidian Border in India. In D. H. Hymes (ed.), *Pidginization and Creolization of Languages*. Cambridge: Cambridge University Press.

Hélot, Christine, Monic Barni, Rudi Jannssens, and Carla Bagna (eds.) (2012). *Linguistic Landscapes, Multilingualism and Social Change*. Frankfurt am Main: Peter Lang.

Jaworski, Adam (2014). Metrolingual Art: Multilingualism and Heteroglossia. *International Journal of Bilingualism* 18: 134–58.

Johnson-Weiner, K. M. (1998). Community Identity and Language Change in North American Anabaptist Communities. *Journal of Sociolinguistics* 2(3): 375–94.

Jørgensen, J. N. (2008). Polylingual Languaging around and among Children and Adolescents. *International Journal of Multilingualism* 5(3): 161–76.

Kallmeyer, W. and I. Keim (2003). Linguistic Variation and the Construction of Social Identity in a German-Turkish Setting. In J. K Androutsopoulos and A. Georgakopoulou (eds.), *Discourse Constructions of Youth Identities*. Amsterdam: John Benjamins, 29–46.

Lambert, W. E. (1967). A Social Psychology of Bilingualism. *Journal of Social Issues* 23: 91–109. In J. B. Pride and J. Holmes (eds.) (1972), *Sociolinguistics: Selected Readings*. Harmondsworth, England: Penguin Books.

Le Page, R. B. (1997). The Evolution of a Sociolinguistic Theory of Language. In F. Coulmas (ed.), *The Handbook of Sociolinguistics*. Oxford: Blackwell.

Lo, A. (1999). Codeswitching, Speech Community Membership, and the Construction of Ethnic Identity. *Journal of Sociolinguistics* 3(4): 461–79.

Mahootian, Shahrzad (2005). Linguistic Change and Social Meaning: Codeswitching in the Media. *International Journal of Bilingualism* 9(3–4): 361–75.

Mahootian, Shahrzad (2012). Resources and Repertoires. In M. Sebba, S. Mahootian, and C. Jonsson (eds.), *Code-Switching in Writing: Approaches to Mixed-Language Written Discourse*. New York: Routledge.

Managan, K. (2003). Diglossia Reconsidered: Language Choice and Code-Switching in Guadeloupean Voluntary Organizations. *Texas Linguistic Forum* 47: 251–61.

MacSwan, J. (2014). *A Minimalist Approach to Intrasentential Code Switching*. New York: Routledge.

McMahon, A. M. S. (1994). *Understanding Language Change*. Cambridge: Cambridge University Press.

Micu, C. C. and R. A. Coulter (2010). Advertising in English in Nonnative English-Speaking Markets: The Effect of Language and Self-Referencing in Advertising in Romania on Ad Attitudes. *Journal of East-West Business* 16(1): 67–84.

Mohanty, A. K. (2006). Multilingualism of the Unequals and Predicaments of Education in India: Mother Tongue or Other Tongue? In O. García, T. Skutnabb-Kangas, and M. E. Torres-Guzmán (eds.), *Imagining Multilingual Schools*. Clevedon: Multilingual Matters.

Morales, E. (2002). *Living in Spanglish: The Search for Latino Identity in America*. New York: St. Martin's Press.

Myers-Scotton, C. (1983). The Negotiation of Identities in Conversation: A Theory of Markedness and Code Choice. *International Journal of the Sociology of Language* 44: 115–36.

Myers-Scotton, C. (1993). *Social Motivation for Code-Switching*. Oxford: Clarendon.

Myers-Scotton, C. (ed.) (1998). *Codes and Consequences: Choosing Linguistic Varieties*. New York: Oxford University Press.

Myers-Scotton, C. (2002). Frequency and Intentionality in (Un)Marked Choices in Codeswitching: 'This Is a 24-hour Country.' *International Journal of Bilingualism* 6(2): 205–19.

Myers-Scotton, C. (2005). *Multiple Voices: An Introduction to Bilingualism*. Oxford: Blackwell.

Otsuji, E. and A. Pennycook (2011). Social Inclusion and Metrolingual Practices. *Journal of Bilingualism and Bilingual Education* 14: 413–26.

Otsuji, E. and A. Pennycook (2012) Unremarkable Hybridities and Metrolingual Practices. In Rani Rubdy and Lubna Alsagoff (eds.), *The Global-Local Interface and Hybridity: Exploring Language and Identity*. Bristol: Multilingual Matters, 83–99.

Rampton, B. (1995). *Crossing: Language and Ethnicity among Adolescents*. London: Longman.

Rampton, B. (2001). Crossing. In A. Duranti (ed.), *Key Terms in Language and Culture*. Oxford: Blackwell.

Reyes, A. (2005). Appropriation of African American Slang by Asian American Youth. *Journal of Sociolinguistics* 9(4): 509–32.

Rubin, J. (1968). *National Bilingualism in Paraguay*. The Hague: Mouton. Excerpted in J. B. Pride and J. Holmes (eds.) (1972), *Sociolinguistics: Selected Readings*. Harmondsworth, England: Penguin Books.

Ryding, K. C. (2005). *A Reference Grammar of Modern Standard Arabic*. Cambridge University Press.

Santiago, B. (2008) *Pardon my Spanglish*. Philadelphia: Quirk Books.

Schieffelin, B. B. and R. C. Doucet (1998). The 'Real' Haitian Creole. In B. B. Schieffelin, K. Woolard, and P. V. Kroskrity (eds.), *Language Ideologies: Practice and Theory*. Oxford: Oxford University Press.

Schilling-Estes, Natalie (2002). Investigating Stylistic Variation. In Jack K. Chambers, Peter Trudgill, and Natalie Schilling-Estes (eds.), *The Handbook of Language Variation*. Oxford: Blackwell.

Soliman, A. (2009). The Changing Role of Arabic in Religious Discourse: A Sociolinguistic Study of Egyptian Arabic. PhD dissertation.

Sridhar, K. K. (1996). Societal Multilingualism. In S. L. McKay and N. H. Hornberger (eds.), *Sociolinguistics and Language Teaching*. Cambridge: Cambridge University Press.

Stępkowska, A. (2012). Diglossia: A Critical Overview of the Swiss Example. *Studia Linguistica Universitatis Iagellonicae Cracoviensis* 129: 199–209.

Stroud, Christopher and Sibonile Mpendukana (2009). Towards a Material Ethnography of Linguistic Landscape: Multilingualism, Mobility and Space in a South African Township. *Journal of Sociolinguistics* 13(3): 363–86.

Sweetland, J. (2002). Unexpected but Authentic Use of an Ethnically-marked Dialect. *Journal of Sociolinguistics* 6(4): 514–36.

Wei-Yu Chen, Cheryl (2006). The Mixing of English in Magazine Advertisements in Taiwan. *World Englishes* 25(3–4): 467–78.

5

Contact Languages: Structural Consequences of Social Factors

Key Concepts

Defining lingua francas

Elaboration and nativization in creole formation

Multiple influences in creole genesis

Features of creole languages

How creole languages differ from mixed languages

Among the many languages of the world are a few that have been assigned a somewhat marginal position in the study of linguistics: the various lingua francas, pidgins, creoles, and so-called mixed languages. Such languages have apparently existed since time immemorial, but we know much less about them than we know about languages that have a long history as standard languages spoken by a dominant group. The history of serious study of such languages goes back only a few decades. Until recently, pidgins and creoles have generally been viewed as uninteresting linguistic phenomena, being notable mainly for linguistic features they have been said to lack (e.g., articles, the copula, and grammatical inflections) rather than those they possess, and those who speak them have often been treated with disdain, even contempt. A major issue in contact linguistics today is the status of such languages, an issue which we will return to below in our discussion of creole languages. At the

An Introduction to Sociolinguistics, Seventh Edition. Ronald Wardhaugh and Janet M. Fuller.
© 2015 John Wiley & Sons, Inc. Published 2015 by John Wiley & Sons, Inc.

center of this controversy is the issue of how different contact languages really are from other languages. For example, English (which is a Germanic language) is notorious for having loanwords from Romance languages which were borrowed during different periods of its development; it clearly changed considerably through language contact. Many, if not most, languages have been influenced at some point in their history by contact with other languages. Although we have certain categories of types of contact languages, as we will discuss in this chapter, it is important to remember than most languages have developed in contexts of language contact. The goal of this chapter is to survey what we find in the literature on language contact, providing an overview of the development of the approach to language contact in sociolinguistics. In the following sections, we will first discuss lingua francas, then turn to a discussion of pidgin and creole languages, and end this chapter with a brief discussion of so-called mixed languages.

Lingua Francas

People who speak different languages and are in contact with each other must find some way of communicating, a **lingua franca**. In a publication concerned with the use of vernacular languages in education published in Paris in 1953, UNESCO defined a lingua franca as 'a language which is used habitually by people whose mother tongues are different in order to facilitate communication between them' (Barotchi 1994: 2211).

At one time or another, Greek koiné and Vulgar Latin were in widespread use as lingua francas in the Mediterranean world and much of Europe. Sabir was a lingua franca of the Mediterranean (and later far beyond); originating in the Middle Ages and dating back at least to the Crusades, it survived into the twentieth century. In other parts of the world, Arabic, Mandarin, Hindi, and Swahili serve as lingua francas. Of these, Arabic is a lingua franca associated with the spread of Islam. Today, English is used in very many places and for very many purposes as a lingua franca, for example, in travel, business, technology, and international relations.

A lingua franca can be spoken in a variety of ways. Not only are they spoken differently in different places, but individual speakers vary widely in their ability to use the languages. English, for example, is for some speakers a native language, for others a second language, and for still others a foreign language (see also the discussion in chapter 13 about English as a lingua franca in Europe). In the last two categories abilities in the language may vary widely from native-like to knowledge of only some bare rudiments. This is certainly the case in India, where even though Hindi is the official language (see chapter 14 for further discussion of this), English, spoken in all kinds of ways, is widely used as a lingua franca.

Kiswahili (the name used by its speakers to refer to what is often called Swahili in Anglophone circles) is a lingua franca of East Africa. On the coast, primarily in Kenya and Tanzania but also as far north as Somalia and as far south as Mozambique, it has long been spoken as a native language (Polomé 1967, 1). However, it also spread as a lingua franca inland and it is used in education in Tanzania, Kenya, Uganda, Rwanda, and Burundi; it is also widely used in politics and other public venues through the Great Lakes region (Kishe 2003).

In North America, Chinook Jargon was used extensively as a lingua franca among native peoples of the coastal northwest, from as far south as northern California and up the coast of British Columbia into Alaska, during the nineteenth century. Its peak was the second half of the 1800s; today it is virtually extinct. Despite the name, Chinook Jargon was an established pidgin, largely based on Chinook (a Native American language of the Northwest) which apparently developed before Europeans arrived but was also used by English and French speakers in the region (Thomason 1983, 820). Even though today hardly anyone can use Chinook Jargon, a few words from it have achieved limited use in English: for example, *potlach* ('lavish gift-giving'), *cheechako* ('greenhorn'), and possibly *high mucky-muck* ('arrogant official') (see Taylor 1981).

Exploration 5.1:   Lingua Francas and Foreign Languages

Have you ever been in a situation where you needed to use a lingua franca? How is this different from a situation in which some people are speaking their native language, and others are speaking that language as a second/ foreign language?

Pidgin and Creole Languages: Definitions

Before delving into the (problematic) definition of pidgins and creoles, we should define other basic terms. Linguists studying pidgins and creoles often use the terms superstrate and substrate to refer the different roles languages play in the development of a contact language. The **superstrate** language (usually only one) is the socially, economically, and politically dominant language in the multilingual context in which the pidgin or creole develops. It is also usually the language which provides the vocabulary for the pidgin or creole, and in that case may also be called the **lexifier language**. Although socially dominant, we must also recognize that the variety of the superstrate language spoken in a particular context was not always what was considered the standard. The European colonists who often provided the superstrate varieties for pidgins and creole languages were very rarely speakers of prestige varieties of their language. Mufwene (2001, 35) describes them as 'defector soldiers and sailors, destitute farmers, indentured laborers, and sometimes convicts ... from the lower strata ... [who] ... spoke nonstandard varieties.'

The **substrate** languages (by definition two or more) are the native languages of the speakers who contribute to the development of these pidgin or creole languages by providing some vocabulary but also phonological systems and grammatical structures. The speakers of these languages are usually socially subordinate to super-strate language speakers. While this social configuration is not necessary for the linguistic development of a pidgin or creole language, exceptions to this pattern are rare (Bakker 2008, Versteegh 2008).

Providing definitions of pidgin and creole languages is no simple matter. Up until fairly late in the twentieth century, what was called the **life cycle model** was widely accepted (see figure 5.1). This model proposes that pidgin languages develop in situations in which speakers have no common language other than the superstrate, but a lack of access to this language. Because of limited input in the superstrate language, they do not simply acquire the superstrate but create a pidgin form of it to use among themselves. While there are many social environments in which a pidgin can arise, the two most common are in situations in which there is either mass migrant labor or increased trade (Winford 2003, 271). In either situation, there are people with a variety of linguistic backgrounds who need to communicate with one another, but one language is very much socially dominant.

Pidgins are thus simplified languages. In some cases, they are used in contexts in which there is continued contact with the lexifier language and a continuum between the pidgin and the lexifier develops, usually ending with the pidgin dis-solving and the lexifier language being spoken. In other contexts, the pidgin expands and becomes stabilized. At this stage, if there is contact with native speakers of the superstrate language, it may again develop a continuum of varieties between the expanded pidgin and the lexifier, with the lexifier language ultimately winning out.

In some cases, the expanded pidgin is used by the children in a community, and it becomes more elaborated and regularized grammatically and acquires registers so that it can be used in all social contexts. It may also become the first language of the next generation. The life cycle model is based on the idea that the distinction between a pidgin and a creole is about nativization, that is, that nativization brought about elaboration. Thus, the generalization was that these two aspects separated pidgins (non-native, simplified languages) from creoles (native, fully elaborated languages). Thus the role of first language acquisition was key to the development of creole languages from pidgin languages.

This model is critical in the **language bioprogram hypothesis** proposed by Bickerton (Bickerton 1981, 1983), which argues that humans are programmed to create languages, and given only input in a simplified pidgin language, they will

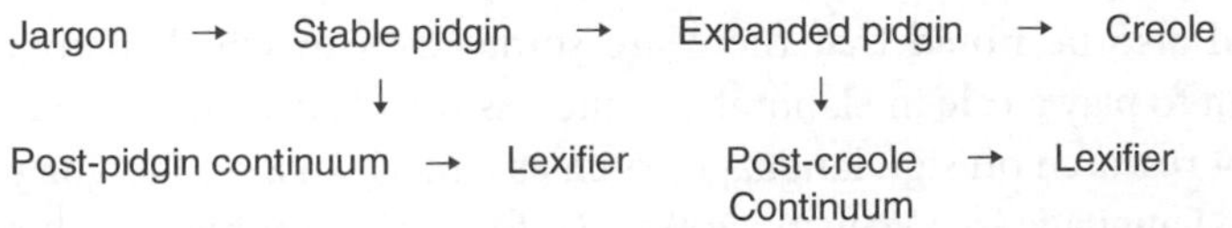

Jargon → Stable pidgin → Expanded pidgin → Creole
            ↓   ↓
Post-pidgin continuum → Lexifier   Post-creole → Lexifier
                                      Continuum

Figure 5.1 The life cycle model of pidgins and creoles

create an elaborated, full-fledged language. Bickerton claims that only this hypothesis adequately explains the similarities among creoles: universal principles of first language acquisition are involved (Bickerton 1983). Typically, creoles are developed by children who find themselves born into a multilingual environment in which the most important language for peer contact is a pidgin. Children are compelled to develop that language because each child has a bioprogram to develop a full language. Children use this bioprogram in the same way wherever they happen to be and the consequence is that 'the grammatical structures of creoles are more similar to one another than they are to the structures of any other language' (1983, 121). Bickerton further develops this thesis, claiming that children have certain innate language abilities that they are actually forced to suppress as they learn languages like English and French. 'It [is] only in pidgin-speaking communities, where there [is] no grammatical model that could compete with the child's innate grammar, that the innate grammatical model [is] not eventually suppressed' (1983, 121). It is in just these circumstances that creoles arise. Bickerton (1977, 49) says that the essential difference between pidgin formation and creole formation is that pidgin formation is second-language learning with restricted input and creole formation is first-language learning, also with restricted input.

Bickerton's hypothesis is not widely accepted, and recent research shows a problem with this proposed chain of events in the life cycle model in general. In a number of creole languages, elaboration appears to develop when expanded pidgins are being spoken by non-native speakers, that is, before nativization occurs. What has been called the **gradualist model** or **gradualism** has been the assumption of much research on creole formation since the late 1980s (e.g., Arends 1993, 1995, Singler 1990, Wekker 1996). Part of the reason for this development is based on methodology; it was not until the 1980s that creolists began to use historical documents as a source of information about earlier forms of creole languages and the social situations in which they arose (Arends and Bruyn 1994, 111)

In general, the finding is that it is not native speakers but the communicative context which gives rise to elaboration. Elaboration occurs when there is a group of speakers who use the code for regular communication; thus, it is discourse which plays the major role in creole development. While no one dismisses the role of first language acquisition in the process, it is no longer generally accepted as the catalyst for grammatical elaboration. One perspective on the roles of adult non-native speakers and child learners is expressed as follows: 'Adults have a creative impact on the language, in expanding the already rich syntactic resources and lexicon; whereas the children have a regularizing impact, particularly as they streamline and condense phonology and generalize grammatical patterns' (Jordan 1991, 195, cited in Bakker 2008, 146).

It should also be noted that there are some cases in which nativization does indeed seem to play a role in elaboration, such as with Hawaiian Creole English and some recent research on sign languages such as American Sign Language and Nicaraguan Sign Language (see Veenstra 2008, 231, for a brief summary of this). However, it does not seem to be a necessary requirement.

If we abandon the idea that elaboration, which is the hallmark of a creole as opposed to a pidgin, necessarily occurs with nativization, then the distinction between a pidgin and a creole becomes less useful. While there are languages which are simplified and non-native which we can call pidgins, and those which are elaborated and native which we can call creoles, there are also other scenarios: elaborated languages which have not undergone nativization, and also processes of nativization and elaboration that occur over many generations. We are left with no simple definitions for, or clear distinction between, pidgin and creole languages, but many interesting questions. We will often use the notation of **P/C languages** to refer to these contact varieties, in keeping with our discussion above about the difficulty in distinguishing between the two.

In the remaining sections of this chapter, we will address how the study of second language acquisition is relevant to our discussion of P/C languages, consider some theories about the process of P/C language development, give an overview of pidgin and creole languages world-wide, and finally present some classic features of these contact varieties. We will also discuss some disputed ideas about a continuum between a Creole and its superstrate language. Finally, we will introduce the basic concepts about mixed languages, and how they are similar to and different from P/C languages.

Connections between P/C languages and second language acquisition

There are two interrelated issues involved in the discussion of the relationship between P/C languages and second language acquisition. First is the issue of the similarities between these two processes; second is the role of second language acquisition in the development of PC languages. We will briefly discuss both of these topics as represented in the study of P/C linguistics.

An early work which discussed second-language learning as 'pidginization' was Schumann (1976), which looked at learners of English and argued that one speaker in particular showed simplification which was evidence of pidginization. While this study was often criticized by both second language acquisition scholars and researchers on P/C languages, it raised the idea of the connection between different types of language contact which has proved to be productive.

Winford (2003) discusses the important ways in which a pidgin can be distinguished from other types of simplified language use such as 'imperfect' second-language learning (**interlanguage**). One important distinction is that pidgins are conventionalized systems of communication, not idiosyncratic production. A pidgin can itself be a target language, that is, something which a speaker is trying to learn. However, both pidgins and interlanguage have a substrate influence (i.e., influence from the speaker's native language). Although it is often recognized that some similar linguistic and cognitive processes are at work in second language acquisition and pidginization, the distinction has been made between the development of an interlanguage spoken by an individual and the sociolinguistic process involving communication between various individuals speaking a second language which forms a pidgin (Siegel 2008, 191).

This leads us to the second issue, the role of second language acquisition in P/C language development. Obviously, some sort of second language acquisition is at work in P/C language development, but the question arises of why the acquisition does not come closer to the target language, that is, why what is called **fossilization** occurs. There is no general answer to this, as pidgin formation scenarios differ, but researchers have raised the issues of social and psychological distance as well a sociohistorical factors which limit the access speakers have to the superstrate/lexifier language (Siegel 2008, 195–6).

The concept of **transfer** in second language acquisition is that learners use features of their first language in the language they are learning. We will discuss below the parallel issue of the influence of the substrate languages in P/C language formation, but again, the issue is the distinction between transfer in an individual interlanguage and the establishment of a transferred feature in a pidgin language spoken by a group of people. (See Siegel 2008 for a more detailed discussion of how the processes of simplification and transfer as discussed in second language acquisition research are relevant for P/C language researchers.)

Pidgin and Creole Formation

If we look at the usual understandings of the processes involved in the genesis of a pidgin (understood as a simplified code) and a creole language (understood as a full-fledged language), we can see that they are almost diametrically opposed to each other in certain important ways. Pidgin formation generally involves some kind of 'simplification' of a language, for example, reduction in morphology (word structure) and syntax (grammatical structure), tolerance of considerable phonological variation (pronunciation), reduction in the number of functions for which the pidgin is used (e.g., you usually do not attempt to write novels in a pidgin), and extensive borrowing of words from local mother tongues. Winford (2003, 302) points out that 'so-called pidginization is really a complex combination of different processes of change, including reduction and simplification of input materials, internal innovation, and regularization of structure, with L1 influence also playing a role.'

On the other hand, creole formation involves expansion of the morphology and syntax, regularization of the phonology, increase in the number of functions in which the language is used, and development of a larger vocabulary. Even though the processes are different, it is still not always clear whether we are talking about a pidgin, an expanded pidgin, or a creole in a certain situation. For example, the terms *Hawaiian Pidgin English* and *Hawaiian Creole English* may be used by even the same creolist (Bickerton 1977, 1983) to describe the same variety. Likewise, Tok Pisin is sometimes called a pidgin, an expanded pidgin, and a creole.

Scholars studying pidgin and creole languages have moved away from using the terms pidginization and creolization. Winford (1997) has pointed out that these terms cover a wide variety of phenomena that are not well understood. He suggests **pidgin formation** and **creole formation** as alternatives so that investigators focus on the specific linguistic input and processes that are involved: 'we should be asking ourselves ... which kinds of linguistic processes and change are common to all ... contact situations and which are not, and how we can formulate frameworks to account for both the similarities and differences in the types of restructuring found in each case' (1997a, 138). A further issue with the term creolization is pointed out by Bakker (2008, 146), who notes that it is used to mean the process of becoming a mother tongue and the process of structural elaboration, which, as discussed above, do not necessarily happen in tandem.

Mufwene (2008, 461) also adds a political dimension to the problems with these terms when applied to varieties developed from European languages in contexts of colonization or slavery, saying 'Usage of the terms *creolization* and *indigenization* to identify their divergence from the European languages from which they developed reflects both a colonial disfranchising attitude toward the populations speaking them and ignorance among linguists of the role that contact has always played in language diversification.'

Theories of creole genesis

In the above sections we have touched upon different perspectives of the central question of P/C languages: how and why do they emerge? This section will provide an overview of ideas about how to answer this question within the framework of the historical development of the field of pidgin and creole studies.

An early perspective on the study of creole languages was that they were structurally similar and that this similarity needed to be explained (although note that this perspective was also challenged, e.g. Muysken 1988, Arends et al. 1995). One theme that emerges in this research is the influence of **linguistic universals** in creole genesis. As mentioned above, one theory by Bickerton is the language bioprogram hypothesis, which focuses on the innate abilities of humans to create language. While this particular theory has not been well accepted, the idea that there are linguistic universals is not a bone of contention among scholars. As noted by Kouwenberg and Singler (2008, 5): 'Virtually no one within creole studies denies a role either to the substrate or to (first) language acquisition. Rather, the questions that engage the field today involve the nature of the interaction of substrate, lexifier, and universal forces.'

In an earlier phase of creole studies, however, there was a sense that Bickerton's position was in opposition to the so-called **substratist** position, which held that the substrate languages held an important role in creole genesis. The idea of a shared substrate seems particularly appropriate to explain many similarities among the

Atlantic Ocean and possibly certain Indian Ocean pidgins and creoles on the one hand and Pacific Ocean pidgins and creoles on the other. The former are said to have an African substrate and the latter an Oceanic one, that is, each contains certain language characteristics of the native ancestral languages of their speakers. In this view Atlantic pidgins and creoles retain certain characteristics of ancestral African languages. African slaves were often multilingual, spoke languages of similar structure but different vocabulary, and tended to treat English and French, and to a lesser extent Portuguese, in the same way. Therefore, the pidgins and creoles are European-language-based and were freshly created in different places. What similarities they have they owe to this fusion of European and African components (see Holm 1988, 2004, and Winford 2003, 16–17).

One theory which focuses on the role of the substrate in creole genesis is the **relexification hypothesis** (Lefebvre 1998, 2004), which is the idea that the phonological form of the superstrate language is used while retaining the semantic and syntactic features from the substrate language; that is, there is substitution of the vocabulary but not the grammatical patterns. This is a strategy for second language acquisition with lack of access to the target language, and leads to variation in the early creole community; in order for a uniform creole to emerge, the process of **leveling** must also occur (see Lefebvre 2001).

Another view of the similarities among Atlantic pidgins and creoles requires us to examine the very beginnings of the pidgin formation process. For example, according to McWhorter (1995, 2000), their similarities can be accounted for if we look back to the beginnings of the slave trade and the existence of English and French slave forts on the West African coast. In these forts contact languages developed, with the most important of these from this point of view being West African Pidgin Portuguese. These contact languages provided the bases for most of the pidgins and creoles that later developed across the Atlantic. This is his **Afrogenesis hypothesis** concerning origin. McWhorter points to the relative paucity of Spanish-based creoles in the New World as evidence which supports this claim as well as to the fact that such creoles are also missing from places we might expect to find them, for example, Puerto Rico and Cuba. (The Spanish creoles that do exist, e.g., Papiamentu, are relexified Portuguese ones.) McWhorter points out that Spain came late to the sugar industry, did not use labor-intensive cultivation systems, sometimes took areas from Portugal, and did not have large slave forts and settlements in Africa. This view of the development of pidgins and creoles is a **monogenetic** view, claiming as it does that a single source accounts for the perceived similarities among the varieties we find.

In contemporary study, most creole scholars would agree that the opposition of universals versus substrate influence is a false dichotomy; most studies today acknowledge multiple influences in P/C language formation. Further, in addition to focus on the contributions of linguistic universals and the substrate languages, there is an increased awareness that we need to also better understand the superstrate-related properties of P/C language structures. While individual studies may focus on one influence or the other, most linguists who study pidgin and creole languages agree that there are multiple factors at play in the development of these contact varieties; the relexification hypothesis does not demand that relexification was the only process that was operative during the creation of pidgins (Winford 2006). Further, processes which influence the development of all other languages also play a role in creole formation. Like all other languages, creoles have complex histories of development which involve multiple factors, language contact being only one of them.

Geographical Distribution

Pidgin and creole languages are distributed mainly, though not exclusively, in the equatorial belt around the world, usually in places with direct or easy access to the oceans. (See the link to *The Atlas of Pidgin and Creole Language Structures* on the website to see a map marking the locations where pidgin and creole languages are spoken.) Consequently, they are found mainly in the Caribbean and around the north and east coasts of South America, around the coasts of Africa, particularly the west coast, and across the Indian and Pacific Oceans. They are fairly uncommon in the more extreme northern and southern areas of the world and in the interiors of continents. Their distribution appears to be fairly closely related to long-standing patterns of trade, including trade in slaves.

A classic source on P/C language distribution is Hancock (1977), a survey that was intended to list each language that had been treated as either a pidgin or a creole whether or not Hancock himself agreed with the classification. The list includes Maltese and Hindi for example, languages which Hancock believes should not be included. Hancock lists 127 pidgins and creoles; those derived from seven common lexifier languages and some examples are given in Table 5.1. (More recently Holm (1989) provides a useful survey of pidgins and creoles, and Smith (1995) lists 351 pidgins and creoles along with 158 assorted mixed languages.)

In addition to these eighty-four languages based on European superstrate languages, Hancock lists another forty-three creoles based on a variety of other languages, for example, Russenorsk (a Russian–Norwegian contact language, now extinct), Chinook Jargon (a virtually extinct contact language of the Pacific Northwest of the United States and Canada, discussed above), Sango (extensively used in the Central African Republic), various pidginized forms of Swahili (a Bantu language) used widely in East Africa, and varieties of Hindi, Bazaar Malay (a variety of Malay in widespread use throughout Malaysia, Singapore, and Indonesia), and Arabic.

For many of these languages, it is not immediately obvious if they are pidgin or creole languages, and some (e.g., Gastarbeiter Deutsch) were never firmly established as pidgins and are no longer in use. However, this list does provide a view of the wide variety of contact languages that have caught the notice of linguists.

Table 5.1　Pidgins and creoles by lexifier language

Lexifier Language	Number Listed	Examples
English	35	Hawaiian Creole, Gullah or Sea Islands Creole (spoken on the islands off the coasts of northern Florida, Georgia, and South Carolina), Jamaican Creole, Guyana Creole, Krio (spoken in Sierra Leone), Sranan and Djuka (spoken in Suriname), Cameroon Pidgin English, Tok Pisin, and Chinese Pidgin English (now virtually extinct)
French	15	Louisiana Creole, Haitian Creole, Seychelles Creole, and Mauritian Creole
Portuguese	14	Papiamentu (used in Aruba, Bonaire, and Curaçao), Guiné Creole, Senegal Creole, and Saramaccan (spoken in Suriname)
Spanish	7	Cocoliche (spoken by Italian immigrants in Buenos Aires)
Dutch	5	US Virgin Islands Dutch Creole (or Negerhollands), now virtually extinct, and Afrikaans (here said to have been creolized in the seventeenth century)
Italian	3	Asmara Pidgin (spoken in parts of Ethiopia)
German	5	Yiddish and whatever still remains of Gastarbeiter Deutsch

Source: based on information from Hancock (1977)

Linguistic Characteristics of P/C Languages

Winford (2003, 307) says that 'creoles constitute a motley assortment of contact vernaculars with different histories and lines of development, though of course they still have much in common … [and] there are no structural characteristics that all creoles share … [and] no structural criteria that can distinguish creoles from other types of language.' This last point has been disputed, most notably by McWhorter, who posits a Creole Prototype (1998, 2005). For a deeper discussion of this debate, see Mufwene (2008) and Ansaldo et al. (2007).

In describing the linguistic characteristics of a pidgin or creole it is difficult to resist the temptation to compare it with the superstrate with which it is associated. In certain circumstances such a comparison may make good sense, as in the linguistic situations in Jamaica and Guyana; in others, however, it seems to make little sense, as in Haiti. In the brief discussion that follows some such comparisons will be made, but they are not meant to be invidious to the P/C language. Each pidgin or creole is a well-organized linguistic system and must be treated as such. You cannot speak Tok Pisin by just 'simplifying' English quite arbitrarily: you will be virtually incomprehensible to those who actually do speak it, nor will you comprehend them. You will instead be using *Tok Masta*, a term used by Papua New

Guineans to describe the attempt which certain Anglophones make to speak Tok Pisin. To use Tok Pisin properly you have to learn it, just as you must learn German or Chinese in order to speak these languages properly. In the next sections, we will discuss some features of P/C languages which illustrate some commonly found characteristics as well as differences across languages.

Phonology

The sounds of a pidgin or creole are likely to be fewer and less complicated in their possible arrangements than those of the corresponding superstrate language. For example, Tok Pisin makes use of only five basic vowels and also has fewer consonants than English. No contrast is possible between words like *it* and *eat*, or *pin* and *fin*, or *sip*, *ship*, and *chip*: the necessary vowel and consonant distinctions (contrasts) are not present. Speakers of Tok Pisin distinguish a ship from a sheep by calling the first a *sip* and the second a *sipsip*. It is also because of the lack of the /p/–/f/ distinction that some written versions of Tok Pisin record certain words with *p* spellings, whereas others record the same words with *f* spellings. So far as speakers of Tok Pisin are concerned, it does not make any difference if you say *wanpela* or *wanfela* ('one'); you will be judged to have said the words in the same way, any difference being no more important to speakers of Tok Pisin than the difference to us between typical North American and British English pronunciations of the middle consonant sound in *butter*. While the numbers of sounds used in pidgins may be smaller than in the corresponding superstrate languages, they also tend to vary more as to their precise quality.

One additional point is worth stressing. A language like English often has complicated phonological relationships between words (or **morphemes**, the small bits of meaning in words) that are closely related, for example, the first vowel in *type* and *typical*, the *c* in *space* and *spacious*, and the different sounds of the 'plural' ending in *cats*, *dogs*, and *boxes*. The technical term for this is **morphophonemic variation**. Such variation is not found in pidgins, but the development of such variation may be one characteristic of subsequent elaboration leading to an expanded pidgin or creole language.

Morphosyntax

In pidgins and creoles there is likely to be a complete lack of inflection in nouns, pronouns, verbs, and adjectives. Nouns are not marked for number and gender, and verbs lack tense markers. Transitive verbs, that is, verbs that take objects, may, however, be distinguished from intransitive verbs, that is, those that do not take objects, by being marked, for example, by a final -*im* in Tok Pisin. Pronouns will not be distinguished for case, so there will be no *I–me*, *he–him* alternations. In Tok Pisin *me* is either 'I' or 'me.' The equivalent of 'we' is either *mipela* ('I and other(s) but not you') or *yumi* ('I and you'). *Yu* is different from *yupela* ('singular' vs. 'plural'), and *em* ('he,' 'she,' or 'it') is distinguished from *ol* ('they' or 'them'). In Tok Pisin there are few required special endings on words, and two of these are actually homophones: *-pela*, a suffix on adjectives, as in *wanpela man* ('one man'), and *-pela*, a plural suffix on pronouns, as in *yupela* ('you plural'). Another is *-im*, the transitive suffix marker on verbs that is mentioned above.

We should not be surprised that there is such a complete reduction of inflection in pidgins. Differences like *one book–two books*, *he bakes–he baked*, and *big–bigger* are quite expendable. In their absence, alternative ways can be found to express the same concepts of number, time, and comparison. Tense marking is often expressed through **periphrastic constructions**, such as the use of *bin* and the unmarked verb for past tense and *bai* and the unmarked verb for the future tense in Tok Pisin (Verhaar 1995).

Syntactically, sentences in pidgins are likely to be uncomplicated in clausal structure. The development of embedded clauses, for example, of relative clauses, is one characteristic of the process of elaboration. Negation may be achieved through use of a simple negative particle *no* in the English-based Krio, for example, *i no tu had* ('It's not too hard') and *pa* in the French-based Seychelles Creole, for example, *i pa tro difisil* ('It's not too difficult'). One particularly interesting feature is the use of pre-verbal particles to show that an action is continuing, that is, to show 'continuous aspect.' We can see this in the use of *de*, *ape*, and *ka* in the following examples taken respectively from English-, French-, and Portuguese-based creoles: *a de go wok* ('I'm going to work' in Krio); *mo ape travaj* ('I'm working' in Louisiana French); and *e ka nda* ('He's going' in St Thomas). What we can see from even these few examples is that creoles associated with quite different superstrate languages apparently use similar syntactic devices. As discussed above, theories of creole genesis have sought to explain such similarities.

Vocabulary

The vocabulary of a pidgin or a creole has a great many similarities to that of the superstrate language with which it is associated. However, the pidgin will be much more limited, and phonological and morphological simplification often leads to words assuming somewhat different shapes. As noted above in the example of *sip* and *sipsip*, it is sometimes necessary to use this **reduplicative** pattern to avoid possible confusion or to express certain concepts, for example, 'repetition' or 'intensification.' When the pidgin is expanded to a creole, it may become more complex in terms of both phonology and morphology, but will of course retain these lexical remnants of its pidgin past. Consequently, in Tok Pisin we find pairs like *tok* ('talk') and *toktok* ('chatter'), *dry* ('dry') and *drydry* ('unpalatable'), *look* ('look') and *looklook* ('stare'), *cry* ('cry') and *crycry* ('cry continually'), *pis* ('peace') and *pispis* ('urinate'), and *san* ('sun') and *sansan* ('sand'). Certain concepts require a somewhat elaborate encoding: for example, 'hair' is *gras bilong het*, 'beard' is *gras bilong fes*, 'feathers' is *gras bilong pisin*, 'moustache' is *gras bilong maus*, 'my car' is *ka bilong me*, and 'bird's wing' is *han bilong pisin*. A pidgin or creole may draw on the vocabulary resources of more than one language. Tok Pisin draws primarily from English but also from Polynesian sources, for example, *kaikai* ('food'), *pukpuk* 'crocodile,' and *guria* 'earthquake,' and even German, because of historical reasons, for example, *rausim* ('throw out'; compare to German *raus* '[get] out'). The source may not always be a 'polite' one, for example, Tok Pisin *bagarap* ('break down') is from the English *bugger up*. So *ka bilong mi i bagarap* is 'My car broke down.' In varieties with African substrate languages, there is also often a noticeable presence of these languages in the vocabulary (e.g., see Turner 1949, on Gullah). Still another source of vocabulary will be innovation. A good example from Winford (2003, 322) is '*as* (<Engl. *arse*) means not just "buttock," but also "cause, foundation." Similarly, *bel* means not just "belly," but also "seat of the emotions".'

From Pidgin to Creole and Beyond

Not every pidgin eventually becomes a creole, that is, undergoes the process of creole formation. In fact, very few do. Most pidgins are lingua francas, existing to meet temporary local needs. They are spoken by people who use another language or other languages to serve most of their needs and the needs of their children. If a pidgin is no longer needed, it dies out. It may also be the case that the pidgin in a particular area must constantly be 'reinvented'; there is no reason to believe, for example, that either Cameroonian Pidgin English or Hawaiian Pidgin English have had uninterrupted histories.

Elaboration occurs only when a pidgin becomes the language of a speech community. We can see how this must have happened in Haiti when French was effectively denied to the masses and the African languages brought by the slaves fell into disuse. We can also see how, while many of the guest workers in Germany may have developed pidginized varieties of German to communicate when necessary with one another, their children did not creolize these varieties but acquired German, since they had to go to school and be educated in German. A full language was available to them so they had no need to creolize Gastarbeiter Deutsch.

The example of Tok Pisin is useful in considering how a pidgin expands and develops into a creole. It was not until the 1960s that the pidgin was nativized, that is, children began to acquire it as a first language; it had been an extended pidgin for previous generations. Mühlhäusler (1982) noted that in Tok Pisin grammatical categories such as time and number had become compulsory, a word-formation component had been developed, devices for structuring discourse were present, and there were opportunities for stylistic differentiation (1982, 449). So far as functions are concerned, Tok Pisin has become symbolic of a new culture; it is now used in many entirely new domains, for example, government, religion, agriculture, and aviation; it is employed in a variety of media; and it is supplanting the vernaculars and even English in many areas (1982, 448–9). Aitchison (1991) has also noted what is happening to Tok Pisin. She points out four kinds of change. One of these is that people speak creoles faster than pidgins and they do not speak them word by word. Consequently, processes of assimilation and reduction can be seen at work in Tok Pisin: *ma bilong mi* ('my husband') becomes *mamblomi*. A second change is the expansion of vocabulary resources: new shorter words are formed, so that *paitman* ('fighter') exists alongside *man bilong pait* ('man of fight'). There is also much borrowing of technical vocabulary from English. A third change is the development of a tense system in verbs. As mentioned above, *bin* is used as a past time marker and *bai*, from *baimbai* ('by and by'), as a future time marker. Finally, greater sentence complexity is now apparent. Some speakers are now able to construct relative clauses because *we* (from 'where') is developing as an introductory marker. In ways such as these, the original pidgin is quickly developing into a fully-fledged language, which we call a creole only because we know its origin. This last point is important: it is only because we know the origins of creoles that we know they are creoles. Mufwene (2008, 460) writes:

> I maintain that there are no particular restructuring processes than can be identified as *creolization* or *indigenization* in the sense of speakers applying a special combination of evolutionary processes that transform a language into a creole or an indigenized variety. Both creole and indigenized varieties have developed by the same restructuring processes that have produced other languages, be they in terms of particular changes in the production of phonological, morphosyntactic, or semantic units, or in terms of selecting particular phonological, morphosyntactic, or semantic-interpretation rules. The varieties are reminders of how languages have changed and speciated several times throughout the history of mankind.

Of course, as mentioned above, while this is a general trend in creole linguistics today, this does not mean that everyone agrees. Some linguists (e.g., McWhorter 2005) still maintain that creole languages have distinct features.

Recent intensive study of pidgins and creoles has revealed how quickly such languages can and do change. Pidgin formation can occur almost 'overnight.' Relexification also seems to be a rapid process. Creole formation can take as little as two generations, although a language can also become elaborated over many generations and still not be spoken as a native language. The particular combination of language and social contact that gives rise to pidgins and creoles, despite a sense that these languages are unusual, seems also to have occurred frequently in the history of the human species.

What this suggests is that many now traditional views about how languages change may need revision (look at chapter 8 for our discussion of this). Such change may not be slow and regular at all, or it may be so only in the absence of certain kinds of language contact. Since contact situations appear to hasten change, the study of pidgins and creoles offers important clues to the kinds of changes that apparently occur. For example, does a contact situation lead to a reduction in inflectional morphology? Does it favor the development of a fixed word order in sentences? Finding answers to questions such as these may provide interesting insights into how languages change.

Creole continuum?

Some scholars of creoles suggest that because a creole can be related to some other dominant (or superordinate) language a **creole** (or post-creole) **continuum** can arise. DeCamp (1971) used this term to discuss Jamaican and Guyanese Creoles because those were situations in which the lexifier language (i.e., English) co-existed with the Creole. This process has become known as **decreolization**, although this term has fallen out of favor with some researchers. For instance, Aceto (1999), Ansaldo et al. (2007) and DeGraff (2001) argue that change in creole languages should be discussed in the same terms as change in other languages. Changes in creole languages are not just a reversion to some past or more standard form.

In discussing the creole continuum in Guyanese English, Bickerton (1975, 24) has proposed a number of terms that may be used to refer to its different parts. He uses the term **acrolect** to refer to educated Guyanese English, a variety which really has very few differences from other varieties of Standard English. He uses the term **basilect** to refer to the variety at the other extreme of the continuum, the variety that would be least comprehensible to a speaker of the standard, perhaps even incomprehensible. **Mesolects** are intermediate varieties. However, these are not discrete entities, and there is variation within them. One important characteristic of these intermediate mesolects is that they blend into one another to fill the 'space' between the acrolect and the basilect. That space is, as we might expect, considerably socially stratified.

Writing of the continuum in Jamaican Creole, DeCamp (1977) has observed that particular speakers often control a span of the spectrum, not just one discrete level within it. He says that the breadth of the span depends on the breadth of the speaker's social activities:

> A labor leader, for example, can command a greater span of varieties than can a sheltered housewife of suburban middle class. A housewife may make a limited adjustment downward on the continuum in order to communicate with a market woman, and the market woman may adjust upward when she talks to the housewife. Each of them may then believe that she is speaking the other's language, for the myth persists in Jamaica that there are only two varieties of language – standard English and 'the dialect' – but the fact is that the housewife's broadest dialect may be closer to the standard end of the spectrum than is the market woman's 'standard.' (DeCamp 1977, 29)

What is particularly important here is the observation that Jamaicans do not perceive the existence of a continuum. Instead, they perceive what they say and hear only in relation to the two ends and make any judgments and adjustments in terms of the two extremes, Standard English or 'the dialect', 'patois', or 'Quashie', as it is

sometimes referred to. Patrick (1999) points out that at least in Kingston the continuum is much more complicated: multi-dimensional rather than uni-dimensional.
The idea of a simple continuum may therefore be little more than a neat theoretical
concept, since the variation found in everyday language use requires taking into
consideration many other explanatory factors.

A continuum can arise only if the two extreme varieties are varieties of the same
language, as with standard X and creolized X (e.g., Standard English and Jamaican
Creole English). When different languages are involved there can be no continuum,
as between Sranan, an English-based creole, and Dutch in Suriname. If the total
society is highly stratified, so that there is little or no contact between the groups
who speak the creolized and superordinate varieties, and/or if these two varieties
have separate and distinct functions in the lives of people, then there will be no
continuum. We will have what has been described as a diglossic situation (see
chapter 4), as in Haiti between Haitian Creole and French. A continuum would
require that there be some kind of continuity in society among the various sub-
groups. It arises from the development of varieties intermediate between the original pidgins and the superordinate variety. The different linguistic situations in
Jamaica and Haiti would therefore suggest that the social situations in these countries are very different, a suggestion which seems to have some validity.

Exploration 5.2:   Another View: 'Broken English'

Saville-Troike (2003, 196) quotes the following from a letter to the editor of
the Trinidad *Guardian*. A report on a Language Arts syllabus had recognized
that most Trinidadians spoke a creole and that English was not their native
language. The letter writer protests as follows:

> If the language of the barrack yard and the market is to be the accepted mode
> of expression in the school-room ... there would be no need for teachers ...
> we could save the high wages of these experts and set them free to go and
> plant peas ... where they can give full vent to this dialect stuff ... What, if
> not broken English, is this dialect? ... I feel that such discussions should be
> banned from our news media as a most damaging ... exercise.

What would you say in a follow-up letter to the editor of the *Guardian*?
Compare your letter with letters that others write. On which points do most
of you agree? How effective are such discussions in newspapers on issues
of this kind in bringing about change?

It is also important to note that not only Patrick (1999) but others such as Le
Page and Tabouret-Keller (1985) reject the idea of the continuum as being altogether

too simplistic. Aceto has also noted the lack of any evidence of a creole continuum or decreolization in some lesser-known English-based creoles in the Caribbean (Aceto 2006, 2010). Patrick (1999), Aceto (1999), and LePage and Tabouret-Keller (1985) claim that in some cases, the concept of the creole continuum results from simplifying and manipulating data rather than trying to confront the evidence in all its complexity. Aceto notes that the creole languages function like other languages in a multilingual society, and that speakers switch in and out of different codes if they have them in their repertoire. All argue that the creole continuum does not explain the linguistic choices that speakers make. It is essentially a uni-dimensional approach to a situation in which all the factors suggest that only a multi-dimensional approach can offer an appropriate account of speakers' linguistic behavior.

Exploration 5.3:   Continua

If the argument is that creole languages are not qualitatively different from other languages without the same type of history of language contact, then we should be able to apply the concepts of the basilect, mesolect, and acrolect to *all* languages. That is, all languages might have a version which is farthest from the standard, a version which is like the standard, and something in-between. How does this work for the variety of English that you speak, or other languages in your speech community? Do you think this concept can be usefully applied to all languages, or should it be abandoned, or reserved only for creole languages?

Other Contact Varieties: Mixed Languages

We can use the term 'contact variety' to refer to a number of different kinds of phenomena, such as dialects of immigrant languages which take on features of the majority languages; for example, what is commonly called Pennsylvania Dutch is a variety of German with lots of lexical borrowing and structural changes which have occurred over the hundreds of years it has been spoken in the United States. While not all of these changes are necessarily due to direct influence from English, because this variety has emerged in a situation of language contact, the label 'contact variety' may be applied. Of course, it is important to remember that no language is completely isolated and it is possible to argue that most languages develop in contexts in which there is some multilingualism. Nonetheless, even if we see this as a matter of degree rather than a clear difference, we can distinguish between languages which show clear features from the languages they are in contact with and those which, for instance, show little beyond **cultural borrowings** in terms of influence from other languages.

There are also cases of the development of languages which seem more clearly to result from a combination of two particular varieties. Thomason (2001) distinguishes these languages from creoles in that there are just two languages involved, and the components of the **mixed language** can be easily traced back to one or the other language. She offers this simple definition: 'A mixed language is a language whose lexical and grammatical structures cannot all be traced back primarily to a single source ("parent") language' (Thomason 2008, 255), noting that this definition draws on the notion of a **language family** used in historical linguistics.

The social circumstances under which mixed languages arise is different from what we know of the social environments in which P/C languages develop. Mixed languages develop when there is widespread bilingualism and thus, unlike pidgins, they do not develop due to a need for a lingua franca.

Bakker (1997) describes one such language, Michif, a mixture of Cree and French spoken mainly in Canada by well under a thousand people of *métis* (First Nation and French) ancestry. Michif is sometimes characterized as a language that mixes Cree verbs and French nouns but probably more accurately is one that uses Cree grammar and French vocabulary. It is a clear marker of group identity for those who use it and emerged to express 'a new ethnic identity, mixed Cree and French. A new language was needed to express that identity. The most obvious way to form a new language was through mixing the two community languages, Cree and French' (Bakker and Papen 1997, 355). Winford (2003, 206) adds that the Michif are an example of 'newly emerged social groups who wanted a language of their own … [and] who saw themselves as distinct from either of the cultural groups from which they descended.'

Another commonly cited example of a mixed language is Ma'a, also called Mbugu, which is spoken in the Usambara Mountains of northeastern Tanzania. In this case, the structure of the language is largely Bantu (the Bantu languages spoken in the region, and by the Ma'a people, are Pare and Shambaa), but the lexicon is at least half from Cushitic languages or Masai, a language related to neither Cushitic nor Bantu. Thomason (2001, 200) reports that earlier descriptions of the language noted more structural features that were not Bantu, so the language cannot be simply described as a Bantu language with borrowings, but is a mixed language.

Media Lengua is another frequently cited case of language mixture, and is described as being of predominantly Quechua grammatical structure and 90 percent Spanish-derived lexicon (Muysken 1981, 52). Like other mixed languages, it is an ingroup language, spoken by people living in villages in the central Ecuador highlands. Muysken describes the motivation for its creation as the desire to express a distinct group identity which was neither acculturated into Spanish-speaking urban society nor completely part of the traditional rural Quechua culture.

These examples, along with those from the chapter 4, show that the different social contexts of multilingualism create different linguistic consequences for the languages in contact. In some cases, language learning occurs, in other cases, new codes such as pidgins, creoles, or mixed languages are formed. The languages which emerge differ from 'regular' languages more in degree than in kind, however, because nearly all languages show signs of language contact through lexical if not structural borrowing. Once again we return to a basic idea presented in chapter 2: languages are both ideologically and linguistically constructed.

Exploration 5.4:   Language Contact Phenomena: Similarities and Differences

From descriptions in this chapter and chapter 4, what do you see as the differences between multilingual discourse, creole languages, and mixed languages? Address this question both in terms of the social situations which give rise to these different language contact phenomena, and in terms of their structural features.

Chapter Summary

While the chapter 4 explored how speakers use their different languages, this chapter investigated how the languages themselves change and develop in different types of multilingual scenarios. The main focus is on pidgin and creole languages, and we explore the different ideas that researchers have about how these languages are formed and why they share certain similarities. A final section introduces another type of contact language, called mixed languages, which both are structurally very different from pidgins and creoles and arise in different types of social scenarios.

Exercises

1. Look at the following questions and answers about pidgin and creole language from Wikianswers.com (see http://wiki.answers.com/Q/What_are_pidgins_ and_creoles). What problems are there with these answers, and how could you improve on them?

    What are pidgins and creoles?
    Answer:
    Pidgins and creoles are two types of artificial language.

    A **pidgin** is formed when two cultures first come into contact with each other; since neither speaks the other's language, an artificial basic language is created as both sides try to communicate. The word itself is a corruption of the English word *business* as pronounced by 19th-century Chinese.

A **creole** is what a pidgin evolves into, if it's maintained for more than one generation. It's named for the Creole people of Louisiana, whose ancestors were African slaves but who weren't permitted to speak their native tongue in the presence of their English- and French-speaking owners. So they invented a form of French-English with a strong African flavor, and passed the new language on to their children.

2. Look at the story at the link below, collected and translated by Peter Patrick, and write a description of how verb marking is done in Jamaican Creole based on these data. How can you tell if verbs are in the present, past, and future tenses? Are there other tenses, moods, or aspects that are marked? http://privatewww.essex.ac.uk/~patrickp/Shots.html

Further Reading

Ansaldo, Umberto, Stephen Matthews, and Lisa Lim (eds.) (2007). *Deconstructing Creole.* Typological Studies in Language series, vol. 3. Amsterdam: John Benjamins.
This volume combines intellectual history with linguistic analysis, presenting both an overview and critical assessment of ideas and theories in creole linguistics as well as theoretically motivated studies of the features of specific creole languages.

Holm, John (2010). Contact and Change: Pidgins and Creoles. In Raymond Hickey (ed.), *The Handbook of Language Contact.* Oxford: Wiley-Blackwell, 252–62.
An excellent brief introduction to the study of pidgin and creole languages, summarizing the themes of research on the development of these varieties.

Lang, George (2009). *Making Wawa: The Genesis of Chinook Jargon.* Vancouver: UBC Press.
A discussion of the origin and social context of the lingua franca spoken widely on the Northwest coast of North America.

Lefebvre, Claire (2006). *Creole Genesis and the Acquisition of Grammar: The Case of Haitian Creole,* vol. 88. Cambridge: Cambridge University Press.
A study of the cognitive processes involved in creole formation as exemplified with data from Haitian Creole.

Matras, Yaron and Peter Bakker (eds.) 2003. *The Mixed Language Debate: Theoretical and Empirical Advances.* Berlin: Walter de Gruyter.
This book examines a range of languages, looking at both social and structural issues, to further refine the definition and description of mixed languages.

For further resources for this chapter visit the companion website at

 www.wiley.com/go/wardhaugh/sociolinguistics

References

Aceto, M. (1999). Looking beyond Decreolization as an Explanatory Model of Language Change in Creole-Speaking Communities. *Journal of Pidgin and Creole Languages* 14(1): 93–119.

Aceto, M. (2006). Statian Creole English: An English-Derived Language Emerges in the Dutch Antilles. *World Englishes* 25(3–4): 411–35.

Aceto, M. (2010). Dominican Kokoy. In D. Schreier, P. Trudgill, E. W. Schneider, and J. P. Williams (eds.) *The Lesser-Known Varieties of English: An Introduction*. Cambridge: Cambridge University Press, 171–94.

Aitchison, J. (1991). *Language Change: Progress or Decay?* 2nd edn. Cambridge: Cambridge University Press.

Ansaldo, Umberto, Stephen Matthews, and Lisa Lim (eds.) (2007). *Deconstructing Creole*. Typological Studies in Language series, vol. 3. Amsterdam: John Benjamins.

Arends, Jacques (1993). Towards a gradualist model of creolization. In Franic Byrne and John Holms (eds.), *Atlantic Meets Pacific: A Global View of Pidginization and Creolization* . Amsterdam: John Benjamins, 371–80.

Arends, Jacques (ed.) (1995). *The Early Stages of Creolization*. Amsterdam: John Benjamins.

Arends, J. and Bruyn, A. (1994). Gradualist and Developmental Hypotheses. In J. Arends, P. Muysken, and N. Smith (eds.) (1995), *Pidgins and Creoles: An Introduction*. Amsterdam: John Benjamins, 111–20.

Arends, J., P. Muysken, and N. Smith (1995). *Pidgins and Creoles: An Introduction*. Amsterdam: John Benjamins.

Bakker, P. (1997). *A Language of Our Own: The Genesis of Michif, the Mixed Cree-French Language of the Canadian Métis*. Oxford: Oxford University Press.

Bakker, Peter (2008). Pidgins versus Creoles and Pidgincreoles. In Silvia Kouwenberg and John Victor Singler (eds.), *The Handbook of Pidgin and Creole Studies*. Oxford: Wiley-Blackwell, 130–57.

Bakker, P. and R. A. Papen (1997). Michif: A Mixed Language Based on Cree and French. In S. G. Thomason (ed.), *Contact Languages: A Wider Perspective*. Amsterdam: John Benjamins.

Barotchi, M. (1994). Lingua Franca. In R. Asher (ed.), *Encyclopedia of Language and Linguistics*, vol. 4. Oxford: Pergamon Press.

Bickerton, D. (1975). *Dynamics of a Creole System*. Cambridge: Cambridge University Press.

Bickerton, D. (1977). Pidginization and Creolization: Language Acquisition and Language Universals. In A. Valdman (ed.), *Pidgin and Creole Linguistics*. Bloomington: Indiana University Press.

Bickerton, D. (1981). *Roots of Language*. Ann Arbor: Karoma Publishers.

Bickerton, D. (1983). Creole Languages. *Scientific American* 249(1): 116–22.

DeCamp, D. (1971). Toward a Generative Analysis of a Post-creole Speech Continuum. In Dell Hymes (ed.), *Pidginization and Creolization of Languages, Proceedings Of A Conference Held at the University of the West Indies, Mona, Jamaica, April, 1968*. Cambridge; Cambridge University Press, 349–70.

DeCamp, D. (1977). The Development of Pidgin and Creole Studies. In A. Valdman (ed.), *Pidgin and Creole Linguistics*. Bloomington: Indiana University Press.

DeGraff, M. (2001). Morphology in Creole Genesis: Linguistics and Ideology. *Current Studies in Linguistics Series* 36: 53–122.

Hancock, I. F. (1977). Appendix: Repertory of Pidgin and Creole Languages. In A. Valdman (ed.), *Pidgin and Creole Linguistics*. Bloomington: Indiana University Press.

Holm, J. (1988, 1989). *Pidgins and Creoles*, 2 vols. Cambridge: Cambridge University Press.

Holm, J. (2004). *Languages in Contact: The Partial Restructuring of Vernaculars*. Cambridge: Cambridge University Press.

Kishe, A. M. (2003). Kiswahili as Vehicle of Unity and Development in the Great Lakes Region. *Language Culture and Curriculum* 16(2): 218–30.

Kouwenberg, Silvia and John Victor Singler (2008). Introduction. In Silvia Kouwenberg and John Victor Singler (eds.), *The Handbook of Pidgin and Creole Studies*. Oxford: Wiley-Blackwell, 1–16.

Lefebvre, C. (1998). *Creole Genesis and the Acquisition of Grammar: The Case of Haitian Creole*. Cambridge: Cambridge University Press.

Lefebvre, C. (2001). The Interplay of Relexification and Levelling in Creole Genesis and Development. *Linguistics* 39(2): 371–408.

Lefebvre, C. (2004). *Issues in the Study of Pidgin and Creole Languages*. Amsterdam: John Benjamins.

Le Page, R. B. and A. Tabouret-Keller (1985). *Acts of Identity*. Cambridge: Cambridge University Press.

McWhorter, J. H. (1995). The Scarcity of Spanish-Based Creoles Explained. *Language in Society* 24: 213–44.

McWhorter, J. H. (1998). *The Word on the Street: Fact and Fable about American English*. New York: Plenum.

McWhorter, J. H. (2000). *The Missing Spanish Creoles: Recovering the Birth of Plantation Contact Languages*. Berkeley: University of California Press.

McWhorter, J. H. (2005). *Defining Creole*. Oxford: Oxford University Press.

Mufwene, S. S. (2001). *The Ecology of Language Evolution*. Cambridge: Cambridge University Press.

Mufwene, S. (2008). Multilingualism in Linguistic History: Creolization and Indigenization. In T. K. Bhatia and W. C. Ritchie (eds.), *The Handbook of Bilingualism*. Oxford: Wiley-Blackwell, 460–88.

Mühlhäusler, P. (1982). Tok Pisin in Papua New Guinea. In R. W. Bailey and M. Görlach (eds.), *English as a World Language*. Ann Arbor: University of Michigan Press.

Muysken, P. C. (1981). Halfway between Quechua and Spanish: The Case for Relexification. In A. R. Highfield and A. Valdman (eds.), *Historicity and Variation in Creole Studies*. Ann Arbor, MI: Karoma Pub.

Muysken, Pieter (1988). Are Creoles a Special Type of Language? In Frederick J. Newmeyer (ed.), *Linguistics: The Cambridge Survey*, vol. II: *Linguistics Theory: Extensions and Implications*. Cambridge: Cambridge University Press, 285–301.

Patrick, P. L. (1999). *Urban Jamaican Creole: Variation in the Mesolect*. Amsterdam: John Benjamins.

Polomé, E. C. (1967). *Swahili Language Handbook*. Washington, DC: Center for Applied Linguistics.

Saville-Troike, M. (2003). *The Ethnography of Communication: An Introduction*. 3rd edn. Oxford: Blackwell.

Schumann, J. H. (1976). Second Language Acquisition: The Pidginization Hypothesis. *Language Learning* 26(2): 391–408.

Siegel, Jeff (2008). Pidgins/Creoles and Second Language Acquisition. In Silvia Kouwenberg and John Victor Singler (eds.), *The Handbook of Pidgin and Creole Studies*. Oxford: Wiley-Blackwell, 189–218.

Singler, John Victor (1990). On the Use of Sociohistorical Criteria in the Comparison of Creoles. *Linguistics* 28: 645–59.

Thomason, S. G. (1983). Chinook Jargon in Areal and Historical Context. *Language* 820–70.

Smith, N. (1995). An Annotated List of Creoles, Pidgins, and Mixed Languages. In J. Arends, P. Muysken, and N. Smith (1995). *Pidgins and Creoles: An Introduction*. Amsterdam: John Benjamins.

Taylor, A. R. (1981). Indian Lingua Francas. In C. A. Ferguson and S. B. Heath (eds.), *Language in the USA*. Cambridge: Cambridge University Press.

Thomason, S. G. (2001). *Language Contact: An Introduction*. Washington, DC: Georgetown University Press.

Thomason, S. G. (2008). Pidgins/Creoles and Historical Linguistics. In Silvia Kouwenberg and John Victor Singler (eds.), *The Handbook of Pidgin and Creole Studies*. Oxford: Wiley-Blackwell, 242–62.

Turner, L. D. (1949). *Africanisms in the Gullah Dialect*. Chicago: University of Chicago Press.

Veenstra, Tonjes (2008). Creole Genesis: The Impact of the Language Bioprogram Hypothesis. In Silvia Kouwenberg and John Victor Singler (eds.), *The Handbook of Pidgin and Creole Studies*. Oxford: Wiley-Blackwell, 219–41.

Wekker, Herman (1996). *Creole Languages and Language Acquisition*. Amsterdam: John Benjamins.

Winford, D. (1997). Creole Formation in the Context of Contact Languages. *Journal of Pidgin and Creole Language* 12(1): 131–51.

Winford, D. (2003). *An Introduction to Contact Linguistics*. Oxford: Blackwell.

Winford, D. (2006). *Revisiting Relexification in Creole Formation*. In L. L. Thornburg and J. M. Fuller (eds.), *Studies in Contact Linguistics: Essays in Honor of Glenn G. Gilbert*. New York: Peter Lang, 231–52.

Verhaar, J. W. (1995). *Toward a Reference Grammar of Tok Pisin: An Experiment in Corpus Linguistics* (No. 26). Honolulu: University of Hawaii Press.

Versteegh, Kees (2008), Non-Indo-European Pidgins and Creoles. In Silvia Kouwenberg and John Victor Singler (eds.), *The Handbook of Pidgin and Creole Studies*. Oxford: Wiley-Blackwell, 158–86.

Part II

Inherent Variety

Variety is the spice of life.

William Cowper

He [John Milton] pronounced the letter R very hard – a certain sign of satirical wit.

John Aubrey

He likes the country, but in truth must own,
Most likes it, when he studies it in town.

William Cowper

Since 'tis Nature's law to change,
Constancy alone is strange.

John Wilmot, Earl of Rochester

Forward, forward let us range,
Let the great world spin for ever down the ringing grooves of change.

Alfred, Lord Tennyson

6

Language Variation

Key Concepts

Dialect regions

Methodology in dialectology: assumptions and challenges

Linguistic variables and social meaning

Defining social class categories and membership

Data collection: how do we know what we have?

What correlations can tell us

This chapter builds on the discussion of varieties in chapter 2 to present a history of variationist sociolinguistic research which focuses on regional and social dialects. Sociolinguists today are generally more concerned with social variation in language than with regional variation. However, if we are to gain a sound understanding of the various procedures used in studies of social variation, we should look at least briefly at previous work in regional dialectology. That work points the way to understanding how recent investigations have proceeded as they have. Studies of social variation in language grew out of studies of regional variation. It was largely in order to widen the limits and repair the flaws that were perceived to exist in the latter that investigators turned their attention to social variation in language. As we will see, there may still be certain limitations in investigating such variation but they are of

An Introduction to Sociolinguistics, Seventh Edition. Ronald Wardhaugh and Janet M. Fuller.
© 2015 John Wiley & Sons, Inc. Published 2015 by John Wiley & Sons, Inc.

a different kind. It is also important to note that even if there are limitations to this kind of work, many sociolinguists regard it as being essentially what sociolinguistics is – or should be – all about. In this view, the study of language variation tells us important things about languages and how they change. This chapter and the two that follow deal with such matters.

Regional Variation

The mapping of regional dialects has had a long history in linguistics (see Petyt 1980, Chambers and Trudgill 1998, and Wakelin 1977). In fact, it is a well-established part of the study of how languages change over time, that is, of **diachronic** or **historical linguistics**. Traditionally, **dialect geography**, as this area of linguistic study is known, has employed assumptions and methods drawn from historical linguistics, and many of its results have been used to confirm findings drawn from other historical sources, for example, archeological findings, population studies, and written records. In this view, languages differentiate internally as speakers distance themselves from one another over time and space; the changes result in the creation of dialects of the languages. Over sufficient time, the resulting dialects might become new languages as speakers of the resulting varieties become unintelligible to one another. So Latin became French in France, Spanish in Spain, Italian in Italy, and so on.

In this model of language change and dialect differentiation, it should always be possible to relate any variation found within a language to the two factors of time and distance alone; for example, the British and American varieties, or dialects, of English are separated by well over two centuries of political independence and by the Atlantic Ocean; Northumbrian and Cockney English are nearly 300 miles and many centuries apart. In each case, linguists working in this tradition try to explain any differences they find with models familiar to the historical linguist, models which incorporate such concepts as the 'family tree' (Latin has 'branched' into French, Spanish, and Italian), phonemic 'split' (English /f/ and /v/ are now distinctive **phonemes** whereas once they were phonetic variants, or allophones, of a single phoneme) or phonemic 'coalescence' (English *ea* and *ee* spellings, as in *beat* and *beet*, were once designated different pronunciations but they have now coalesced into the same sound), the 'comparative method' of reconstruction (English *knave* and German *Knabe* come from the same source), and 'internal reconstruction' (though *mouse* and *mice* now have different vowel sounds, this was not always the case).

Mapping dialects

Dialect geographers have traditionally attempted to reproduce their findings on maps in what they call **dialect atlases**. They try to show the geographical boundaries of the distribution of a particular linguistic feature by drawing a line on a map. Such a line is called an **isogloss:** on one side of the line people say something one way, for example, pronounce *bath* with the first vowel of *father*, and on the other side they use some other pronunciation, for example, the vowel of *cat*. Quite often, when the boundaries for different linguistic features are mapped in this way the isoglosses show a considerable amount of criss-crossing. On occasion, though, a number coincide; that is, there is a bundle of **isoglosses**. Such a bundle is often said to mark a **dialect boundary**. One such bundle crosses the south of France from east to west approximately at the 45th parallel (Grenoble to Bordeaux) with words like *chandelle*, *chanter*, and *chaud* beginning with a *sh* sound to the north and a *k* sound to the south. Quite often, that dialect boundary coincides with some geographical or political factor, for example, a mountain ridge, a river, or the boundary of an old principality or diocese. Isoglosses can also show that a particular set of linguistic features appears to be spreading from one location, a **focal area**, into neighboring locations. In the 1930s and 1940s, Boston and Charleston were the two focal areas for the temporary spread of *r*-lessness in the eastern United States. Alternatively, a particular area, a **relic area**, may show characteristics of being unaffected by changes spreading out from one or more neighboring areas. Places like London and Boston are obviously focal areas; places like Martha's Vineyard in New England – it remained *r*-pronouncing in the 1930s and 1940s even as Boston dropped the pronunciation – and Devon in the extreme southwest of England are relic areas. Wolfram (2004) calls the dialect of such an area a **remnant dialect** and, in doing so, reminds us that not everything in such a dialect is a relic of the past for such areas also have their own innovations. Huntley, a rural enclave in Aberdeenshire, Scotland, where Marshall worked (2003, 2004), is also a relic area.

The Rhenish Fan is one of the best-known sets of isoglosses in Europe, setting off Low German to the north from High German to the south. The set comprises the modern reflexes (i.e., results) of the pre-Germanic stop consonants *p, *t, and *k. These have remained **stops** [p,t,k] in Low German but have become the **fricatives** [f,s,x] in High German (i.e., Modern Standard German), giving variant forms for 'make' [makən], [maxən]; 'that' [dat], [das]; 'village' [dorp], [dorf]; and 'I' [ik], [ix]. Across most of Germany these isoglosses run virtually together from just north of Berlin in an east–west direction until they reach the Rhine. At that point they 'fan,' as in figure 6.1. Each area within the fan has a different incidence of stops and fricatives in these words, for example, speakers in region 2 have 'ich,' 'maken,' 'Dorp,' and 'dat,' and speakers in region 4 have 'ich,' 'machen,' 'Dorf,' and [dat]. The boundaries within the fan coincide with old ecclesiastical and political boundaries. The change of stops to fricatives, called the Second German Consonant Shift, appears to have spread along the Rhine from the south of Germany to the north. Political and ecclesiastical frontiers along the Rhine were important in that spread as were centers like Cologne and Trier. The area covered by the fan itself is sometimes called a transition area (in this case, between Low and High German) through which a change is progressing, in contrast to either a focal or relic area.

Very often the isoglosses for individual phonological features do not coincide with one another to give us clearly demarcated dialect areas. As shown in figure 6.2, while the ideal is that isoglosses coincide as in (a), in reality isoglosses may

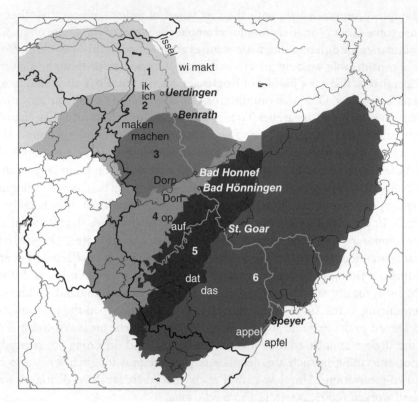

Figure 6.1 The Rhenish Fan

The main kinds of isogloss

Term	Separates	Examples
isolex	lexical items	*nunch* vs *nuncheon*
isomorph	morphological features	*dived* vs *dove*
isophone	phonological features	*put* / pʊt / vs / pʌt /
isoseme	semantic features	*dinner* (mid-day meal) vs (evening meal)

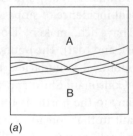

(a)

The expectation
Isoglosses will form neat
bundles, demarcating
dialect A from dialect B.

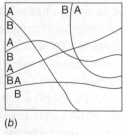

(b)

The reality Isoglosses
criss-cross an area, with
no clear boundary
between A and B.

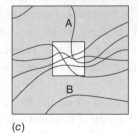

(c)

Focal and transitional On
a larger scale, the isoglosses
are seen to constitute a
transitional area between
the focal areas A and B.

Figure 6.2 Isoglosses

cross-cross as in (b); some examples of how different features of dialects might pattern can be seen in (c). Such patterns are just about impossible to explain using the traditional **family-tree account of language change**. Isoglosses do cross and bundles of them are rare. It is consequently extremely difficult to determine boundaries between dialects in this way and dialectologists acknowledge this fact. The postulated dialect areas show considerable internal variation and the actual areas proposed are often based on only a few key items (or linguistic variables in our terminology). Consequently, as Le Page (1997, 18) says, 'the dialect areas outlined by the isoglosses on the maps were artifacts of the geographer; they had to be matched against such stereotypes as "southern dialect" or "Alemmanic" or "langue d'oc," concepts which often related in the minds of outsiders to just one or two variables characterizing a complete, discrete system.'

Methods in dialectology

There are methodological issues which have caused sociolinguists to question some dialect studies. One of these issues has to do with the **sample** used for the research. First, sampling methods were based on assumptions about who 'representative' speakers of dialects were. For example, the focus was almost exclusively on rural areas, which were regarded as 'conservative' in the sense that they were seen to preserve 'older' forms of the languages under investigation. Urban areas were acknowledged to be innovative, unstable linguistically, and difficult to approach using existing survey techniques. When the occasional approach was made, it was biased toward finding the most conservative variety of urban speech. Ignoring towns and cities may be defensible in an agrarian-based society; however, it is hardly defensible in the heavily urbanizing societies of today's world.

Further, there was a circularity in how social class was addressed; in the data collection for the *Linguistic Atlas of the United States and Canada*, the analysis was partly intended to find out how speech related to social class, but speech was itself used as one of the criteria for assigning membership in a social class. For example, the **informants** chosen for the *Linguistic Atlas of the United States and Canada* were of three types (Kurath 1939, 44), chosen as follows:

Type I: Little formal education, little reading, and restricted social contacts
Type II: Better formal education (usually high school) and/or wider reading and social contacts
Type III: Superior education (usually college), cultured background, wide reading, and/or extensive social contacts

Each of these three types was then sub-categorized as follows:

Type A: Aged, and/or regarded by the field worker as old-fashioned
Type B: Middle-aged or younger, and/or regarded by the field worker as more modern

We should also note that it was the field worker for the *Atlas* who decided exactly where each informant fitted in the above scheme of things. The field worker alone judged whether a particular informant should be used in the study, and Type IA informants were particularly prized as being most representative of local speech.

In England, the Survey of English Dialects carried out between 1950 and 1961 with informants from 313 localities in England and Wales employed similar criteria (Orton et al. 1978, 3):

> The selection of informants was made with especial care. The fieldworkers were instructed to seek out elderly men and women – more often men, since women seemed in general to encourage the social upgrading of the speech of their families – who were themselves of the place and both of whose parents were preferably natives also. They were to be over 60 years of age, with good mouths, teeth and hearing and of the class of agricultural workers who would be familiar with the subject matter of the question-naire and capable of responding perceptively and authoritatively.

Typically, both informants and field workers were male. As Coates (2004, 10–11) says, 'Dialectology … marginalized women speakers. Traditional dialectologists defined the true vernacular in terms of male informants, and organised their ques-tionnaires around what was seen as the man's world.'

Another methodological issue involves basic ideas about language. The data col-lection methodology often used in earlier dialect geography studies assumes that individual speakers do not have variation in their speech; for instance, if they use the word 'pop' to talk about carbonated beverages they never use the term 'soda' to refer to the same thing, or if they merge the vowels in 'pin' and 'pen,' they always do this. This assumption has been called '**the axiom of categoricity**' (Chambers 1995: 25–33) as it treats linguistic variables as if they are categorical in the speech of an individual – and from there it is implied that they are categorical in regional dialects. This is dangerously close to the 'ideal speaker-listener' (referred to in chapter 1) that sociolinguistics eschews. As Gordon (2013, 32–3) observes, not taking variation in the speech of an individual speaker into account leads to an interpretation of the results which is misleading; presenting speakers as using vari-ables categorically is 'taken to represent how languages work rather than how lin-guists work.'

Furthermore, since most of us realize that it is not only where you come from that affects your speech but also your social and cultural background, age, gender, race, occupation, and group loyalty, the traditional bias toward geographic origin alone now appears to be a serious weakness. Then, too, the overriding model of language change and differentiation is an extremely static one, and one that is rein-forced, rather than questioned, by the types of data selected for analysis. Speakers from different regions certainly interact with one another; dialect breaks or bounda-ries are not 'clean'; and change can be said to be 'regular' only if you are prepared to categorize certain kinds of irregularities as exceptions, relics, borrowings, 'minor' variations, and so on. Furthermore, the varieties of a language spoken within large gatherings of people in towns and cities must influence what happens to other varieties of that language: to attempt to discuss the history of English, French, or Italian while ignoring the influences of London, Paris, or Florence would seem to be something like attempting to produce *Hamlet* without the prince!

Dialect mixture and free variation

All of this is not to say that this kind of individual and social variation has gone unnoticed in linguistics. Linguists have long been aware of variation in the use of language: individuals do speak one way on one occasion and other ways on other occasions, and this kind of variation can be seen to occur within even the most localized groups. Such variation is often ascribed to **dialect mixture**, that is, the existence in one locality of two or more dialects which allow a speaker or speakers to draw now on one dialect and then on the other. An alternative explanation is **free variation**, that is, variation of no social significance. However, no one has ever devised a suitable theory to explain either dialect mixture or free variation, and the latter turns out not to be so free after all because close analyses generally reveal that complex linguistic and social factors appear to explain much of the variation.

Exploration 6.1:   Free Variation?

What vowel do you use in the first vowel in the word 'data' (/e/ or /a/), or the initial sound of the words 'economic' (/i/ or /ɛ/) or 'either' (/ai/ or /i/)? Is there any difference in social meaning between the two pronunciations?

Linguistic atlases

There have been some recent developments in linguistic atlas work which hold promise for future discoveries. They result largely from our growing ability to process and analyze large quantities of linguistic data. One, for example, is Kretzschmar's work on the *Linguistic Atlas of the Middle and South Atlantic States* (LAMSAS). He shows (1996) how it is possible to use quantitative methods to demonstrate the probability of occurrence of specific words or sounds in specific areas. Another quantitative survey (Labov et al. 2005) used a very simple sampling technique to survey the whole of North American English in order to produce the *Atlas of North American English* (ANAE), a study of all the cities on the continent with populations of over fifty thousand. This study showed that 'regional dialects are getting stronger and more diverse as language change is continuing and that the structural divisions between them are very sharp, with very tight bundling of the isoglosses' (Labov et al. 2005, 348). (See also links to dialect atlas projects in the US and the UK in the chapter 6 materials on our website companion to this text.)

In still another approach to dialects, this one focusing on how a specific dialect emerged, Lane (2000) used a variety of economic, demographic, and social data from 3,797 residents of Thyborøn, Denmark, covering the years 1890–1996, to reveal how the local dialect 'is the result of a constant situation that led to the formation of a new dialect as a result of massive in-migration … a new system created largely out of materials selected from competing systems in contact and from innovations that indexed the new local linguistic community' (Lane 2000, 287). It was clearly another triumph for an aspiration to achieve a local identity. We can see a similar emphasis on using traditional dialect materials to help us account for current language varieties in recent writings on new Englishes (see Gordon et al. 2004, Hickey 2004, and Trudgill 2004). This discussion of dialect geography raises a number of issues which are important to our concerns. One is the kind of variation that we should try to account for in language. Another has to do with sampling the population among which we believe there is variation. Still another is the collection, analysis, and treatment of the data that we consider relevant. And, finally, there are the overriding issues of what implications there are in our findings for theoretical matters concerning the nature of language, variation in language, the language-learning and language-using abilities of human beings, and the processes involved in language change. It is to these issues that we will now turn, and in doing so, focus on social rather than regional variation in language. The major conceptual tool for investigation of such variation will be the linguistic variable.

The Linguistic Variable

The investigation of social dialects has required the development of an array of techniques quite different from those used in dialect geography. Many of these derive from the pioneering work of Labov, who, along with other sociolinguists, has attempted to describe how language varies in any community and to draw conclusions from that variation not only for linguistic theory but also sometimes for the conduct of everyday life, for example, suggestions as to how educators should view linguistic variation (see chapter 13). As we will see, investigators now pay serious attention to such matters as stating hypotheses, sampling, the statistical treatment of data, drawing conclusions, and relating these conclusions to such matters as the inherent nature of language, the processes of language acquisition and language change, and the social functions of variation.

Possibly the greatest contribution has been in the development of the use of the linguistic variable, the basic conceptual tool necessary to do this kind of work (see Wolfram 1991). As we have just indicated, variation has long been of interest to linguists, but the use of the linguistic variable has added a new dimension to linguistic investigations.

Variants

A **linguistic variable** is a linguistic item which has identifiable **variants,** which are the different forms which can be used in an environment. For example, words like *singing* and *fishing* are sometimes pronounced as *singin'* and *fishin'*. The final sound in these words may be called the linguistic variable (ng) with its two variants [ŋ] in *singing* and [n] in *singin'*. Another example of a linguistic variable can be seen in words like *farm* and *far*. These words are sometimes given *r*-less pronunciations; in this case we have the linguistic variable (r) with two variants [r] and Ø (i.e., 'zero,' or 'null'). There are at least two basically different kinds of variation. One is of the kind (ng) with its variants [ŋ] or [n], or (th) with its variants [θ], [t], or [f], as in *with* pronounced as *with, wit,* or *wif*. In this first case the concern is with which quite clearly distinct variant is used, with, of course, the possibility of Ø, the zero variant. that is, neither. The other kind of variation is a matter of degree, such as the quantity of nasalization of a vowel, rather than its presence or absence. How can you best quantify nasalization when the phenomenon is actually a continuous one? The same issue occurs with quantifying variation in other vowel variables: quantifying their relative frontness or backness, tenseness or laxness, and rounding or unrounding. Moreover, more than one dimension may be involved, for example, amount of nasalization *and* frontness or backness.

An important principle in the analysis of variants is the **principle of accountability**, which holds that if it is possible to define a variable as a closed set of variants, all of the variants (including non-occurrence if relevant) must be counted. So, for instance, in the study of copula usage, the use of a conjugated form of *be* (i.e., *am, is, are*), invariant *be,* and zero copula would all be included in the analysis. While in general this principle applies to grammatical variables, for pragmatically motivated variables such as discourse markers (e.g., *you know, well*) the principle of accountability cannot be applied, as there are no mandatory environments for such particles.

Types of linguistic variables

Linguists who have studied variation in this way have used a number of linguistic variables, many of which have been phonological. The (ng) variable has been widely used; Labov (2006, 259) says it 'has been found to have the greatest generality over the English-speaking world, and has been the subject of the most fruitful study.' The (r) variable mentioned above has also been much used. Other useful variables are the (h) variable in words like *house* and *hospital*, that is, (h): [h] or Ø; the (t) variable in *bet* and *better*, that is, (t): [t] or [ʔ]; the (th) and (dh) variables in *thin* and *they*, that is, (th): [θ] or [t] and (dh): [ð] or [d]; the (l) variable in French in *il*, that is, (l): [l] or Ø; and variables like the final (t) and (d) in words like *test* and *told*, that is, their presence or absence. Vowel variables used have included the vowel (e) in words like *pen* and *men*; the (o) in *dog, caught*, and *coffee*; the (e) in *beg*; the (a) in *back, bag, bad*, and *half*; and the (u) in *pull* (see discussion in chapter 8 on the Northern Cities Vowel Shift, which addresses variation in vowel sounds).

Studies of variation employing the linguistic variable are not confined solely to phonological matters. Investigators have looked at the (s) of the third-person singular, as in *he talks*, that is, its presence or absence; the occurrence or non-occurrence of *be* (and of its various inflected forms) in sentences such as *He's happy, He be happy*, and *He happy*; the occurrence (actually, virtual nonoccurrence) of the negative particle *ne* in French; various aspects of the phenomenon of multiple negation in English, for example, *He don't mean no harm to nobody*; and the beginnings of English relative clauses, as in *She is the girl who(m) I praised, She is the girl that I praised*, and *She is the girl I praised*.

To see how individual researchers choose variables, we can look briefly at three landmark studies carried out in three urban areas by prominent sociolinguists in the 1960s and 1970s: New York City (Labov), Norwich (Trudgill), and Detroit (Shuy et al. and Wolfram).

Variation in New York City

In a major part of his work in New York City, Labov (1966) chose five phonological variables: the (th) variable, the initial consonant in words like *thin* and *three*; the (dh) variable, the initial consonant in words like *there* and *then*; the (r) variable, *r*-pronunciation in words like *farm* and *far*; the (a) variable, the pronunciation of the vowel in words like *bad* and *back*; and the (o) variable, the pronunciation of the vowel in words like *dog* and *caught*. We should note that some of these have discrete variants, for example, (r): [r] or Ø, whereas others require the investigator to quantify the variants because the variation is a continuous phenomenon, for example, the (a) variable, where there can be both raising and retraction of the vowel, that is, a pronunciation made higher and further back in the mouth, and, of course, in some environments nasalization too.

Variation in Norwich

Trudgill (1974) also chose certain phonological variables in his study of the speech of Norwich: three consonant variables and thirteen vowel variables. The consonant variables were the (h) in *happy* and *home*, the (ng) in *walking* and *running*, and the (t) in *bet* and *better*. In the first two cases only the presence or absence of *h*-pronunciation and the [ŋ] versus [n] realizations of (ng) were of concern to Trudgill. In the last there were four variants of (t) to consider: an aspirated variant; an unaspirated one; a glottalized one; and a glottal stop. These variants were ordered, with the first two combined and weighted as being least marked as nonstandard, the third as more marked, and the last, the glottal stop, as definitely marked as nonstandard. The thirteen vowel variables were the vowels used in words such as *bad, name, path, tell, here, hair, ride, bird, top, know, boat, boot,* and *tune.* Most of these had more than two variants, so weighting, that is, some imposed quantification, was again required to differentiate the least preferred varieties, that is, the most nonstandard, from the most preferred variety, that is, the most standard.

Variation in Detroit

One Detroit study (Shuy et al. 1968) focused on the use of three variables: one phonological variable and two grammatical variables. The phonological variable was the realization of a vowel plus a following nasal consonant as a nasalized vowel. The grammatical variables were multiple negation, which we have already mentioned, and pronominal apposition, for example, *That guy, he don't care.* In another study of Detroit speech, Wolfram (1969) considered certain other linguistic variables. These included the pronunciation of final consonant clusters, that is, combinations of final consonants in words like *test, wasp,* and *left, th* in words like *tooth* and *nothing,* final stops in words like *good* and *shed,* and *r*-pronouncing in words like *sister* and *pair.* So far as grammatical variables were concerned, Wolfram looked at matters such as *he talk/talks, two year/years, she nice/she's nice, he's ready/he ready/ he be ready,* and multiple negation as in *He ain't got none neither.*

This brief sample indicates some of the range of variables that have been investigated. The important fact to remember is that a linguistic variable is an item in the structure of a language, an item that has alternate realizations, as one speaker realizes it one way and another speaker in a different way, or the same speaker realizes it differently on different occasions (see the above discussion of the axiom of categoricity) . For example, one speaker may say *singing* most of the time whereas another prefers *singin',* but the first is likely to say *singin'* on occasion just as the second may be found to use the occasional *singing.* What might be interesting is any relationship we find between these habits and either (or both) the social class to which each speaker belongs or the circumstances which bring about one pronunciation rather than the other.

Indicators, markers, and stereotypes

Labov (1972) has also distinguished among what he calls indicators, markers, and stereotypes. An **indicator** is a linguistic variable to which little or no social import is attached. Only a linguistically trained observer is aware of indicators. For example, some speakers in North America distinguish the vowels in *cot* and *caught* and others do not; this is not salient to most non-linguists. On the other hand, a **marker** can be quite noticeable and potent carriers of social information. You do not always have to drop every *g*, that is, always say *singing* as *singin'.* Labov says that 'we observe listeners reacting in a discrete way. Up to a certain point they do not perceive the speaker "dropping his g's" at all; beyond a certain point, they perceive him as always doing so' (Labov 1972, 226). G-dropping is a marker everywhere English is spoken. People are aware of markers, and the distribution of markers is clearly related to social groupings and to styles of speaking. A **stereotype** is a popular and, therefore, conscious characterization of the speech of a particular group: New York *boid* for *bird* or *Toitytoid Street* for *33rd Street*; a Northumbrian *Wot-cher* (What cheer?) greeting; the British use of *chap*; or a Bostonian's *Pahk the cah in Hahvahd Yahd*. Often such stereotypes are stigmatized everywhere, and in at least one reported case (see Judges 12: 4–6 in the Old Testament) a stereotypical pronunciation of *shibboleth* had fatal consequences. A stereotype need not conform to reality; rather, it offers people a rough and ready categorization with all the attendant problems of such categorizations. Studies of variation tend therefore to focus on describing the distributions of linguistic variables which are markers. (Although see Johnstone 2004 for a discussion of stereotypes in Pittsburgh speech.)

Exploration 6.2:   Stereotypes

Are there stereotypes about the variety you speak? Can you give examples of how these stereotypes might be embraced by speakers of that variety, but also stigmatized in a wider context? To what extent do you think these stereotypes are accurate portrayals of local speech?

Social Variation

Once we have identified the linguistic variable as our basic working tool, the next question is how linguistic variation relates to social variation. That is, can we correlate the use of specific linguistics features – r-lessness, for example – with membership in a particular social group?

In order to address this question, the next task becomes one of collecting data concerning the variants of a linguistic variable in such a way that we can draw certain conclusions about the social distribution of these variants. To draw such conclusions, we must be able to relate the variants in some way to quantifiable factors in society, for example, social-class membership, gender, age, ethnicity, and so on. As we will see, there are numerous difficulties in attempting this task, but considerable progress has been made in overcoming them, particularly as studies have built on those that have gone before in such a way as to strengthen the quality of the work done in this area of sociolinguistics.

Social class membership

One factor which has been prominent in sociolinguistic studies of variation is **social class** membership. If we consider 'social class' to be a useful concept to apply in stratifying society – and few indeed would deny its relevance! – we need a way to determine the social class of particular speakers. This raises various difficulties, as in many societies there are not strict guidelines, and terms such as 'middle class' may have many different meanings for the speakers themselves. Further, we must be cautious in any claims we make about social-class structures in a particular society, particularly if we attempt regional or historical comparisons. The social-class system of England in the 1950s was different from what it is today and, presumably, it will be different again in another half century, and all these class systems were and are different from those existing contemporaneously in New York, Brazil, Japan, and so on.

Sociologists use a number of different scales for classifying people when they attempt to place individuals somewhere within a social system. An occupational scale may divide people into a number of categories as follows: major professionals and executives of large businesses; lesser professionals and executives of medium-sized businesses; semi-professionals; technicians and owners of small businesses; skilled workers; semi-skilled workers; and unskilled workers. An educational scale may employ the following categories: graduate or professional education; college or university degree; attendance at college or university but no degree; high school graduation; some high school education; and less than seven years of formal education. Once again, however, some caution is necessary in making comparison across time: graduating from college or university in the 1950s indicated something quite different from what it does today. Income level and source of income are important factors in any classification system that focuses on how much money people have. Likewise, in considering where people live, investigators must concern themselves with both the type and cost of housing and its location.

In assigning individuals to social classes, investigators may use any or all of the above criteria (and others too) and assign different weights to them. Accordingly, the resulting social-class designation given to any individual may differ from study to study. We can also see how social class itself is a sociological construct; people probably do not classify themselves as members of groups defined by such criteria. Wolfram and Fasold (1974, 44) point out that 'there are other objective approaches [to establishing social groupings] not exclusively dependent on socio-economic ranking. ... An investigator may look at such things as church membership, leisure-time activities, or community organizations.' They admit that such alternative approaches are not at all simple to devise but argue that a classification so obtained is probably more directly related to social class than the simple measurement of economic factors. We should note that the concept of **lifestyle** has been introduced into classifying people in sociolinguistics, so obviously patterns of consumption of goods and appearance are important for a number of people in arriving at some kind of social classification. Coupland (2007, 29–30) calls the current era 'late-modernity.' It is a time in which 'Social life seems increasingly to come packaged as a set of lifestyle options able to be picked up and dropped, though always against a social backdrop of economic possibilities and constraints. … Social class … membership in the West is not the straitjacket that it was. Within limits, some people can make choices in their patterns of consumption and take on the social attributes of different social classes. … the meaning of class is shifted.'

In his early work on linguistic variation in New York City, Labov (1966) used the three criteria of education, occupation, and income to set up ten social classes. His class 0, his lowest class, had grade school education or less, were laborers, and found it difficult to make ends meet. His classes 1 to 5, his working class, had had some high school education, were blue-collar workers, but earned enough to own such things as cars. His classes 6 to 8, his lower middle class, were high school graduates and semi-professional and white-collar workers who could send their children to college. His highest class, 9, his upper middle class, were well educated and professional or business-oriented. In this classification system for people in the United States about 10 percent of the population are said to be lower class, about 40 percent working class, another 40 percent lower middle class, and the remaining 10 percent fall into the upper middle class or an upper class, the latter not included in Labov's study. In his later study (2001b) of variation in Philadelphia, Labov used a socio-economic index based on occupation, education, and house value.

In an early study of linguistic variation in Norwich, England, Trudgill (1974) distinguishes five social classes: middle middle class (MMC), lower middle class (LMC), upper working class (UWC), middle working class (MWC), and lower working class (LWC). Trudgill interviewed ten speakers from each of five electoral wards in Norwich plus ten school-age children from two schools. These sixty informants were then classified on six factors, each of which was scored on a six-point scale (0–5): occupation, education, income, type of housing, locality, and father's occupation. Trudgill himself decided the cut-off points among his classes. In doing so, he shows a certain circularity. His lower working class is defined as those who use certain linguistic features (e.g., *he go*) more than 80 percent of the time. Out of the total possible score of 30 on his combined scales, those scoring 6 or less fall into this category. Members of Trudgill's middle middle class always use *he goes*, and that behavior is typical of those scoring 19 or more. His study is an attempt to relate linguistic behavior to social class, but he uses linguistic behavior to assign membership in social class. What we can be sure of is that there is a difference in linguistic behavior between those at the top and bottom of Trudgill's 30-point scale, but this difference is not one that has been established completely independently because of the underlying circularity.

Shuy's Detroit study (Shuy et al. 1968) attempted to sample the speech of that city using a sample of 702 informants. Eleven field workers collected the data by means of a questionnaire over a period of ten weeks. They assigned each of their informants to a social class using three sets of criteria: amount of education, occupation, and place of residence. Each informant was ranked on a six- or seven-point scale for each set, the rankings were weighted (multiplied by 5 for education, 9 for occupation, and 6 for residence), and each informant was given a social-class placement. Four social-class designations were used: upper middle class, those with scores of 20–48; lower middle class, those with scores of 49–77; upper working class, those with scores of 78–106; and lower working class, those with scores of 107–134.

There are some serious drawbacks to using social-class designations of this kind. Bainbridge (1994, 4023) says:

> While sociolinguists without number have documented class-related variation in speech, hardly any of them asked themselves what social class was. They treated class as a key independent variable, with variations in speech dependent upon class variations, yet they never considered the meaning of the independent variable. In consequence, they seldom attempted anything like a theory of why class should have an impact, and even more rarely examined their measures of class to see if they were methodologically defensible.

Woolard (1985, 738) expresses a similar view: 'sociolinguists have often borrowed sociological concepts in an ad hoc and unreflecting fashion, not usually considering critically the implicit theoretical frameworks that are imported.' She adds, 'However, to say that our underlying social theories are in need of examination, elaboration, or reconsideration is not to say that the work sociolinguists have done or the concepts we have employed are without merit.'

Milroy and Gordon (2008) discuss two problematic issues inherent in the study of social class. First, as a concept it combines economic aspects with status ones; this creates particular difficulty when we try to make comparison across communities, as a university professor may have a very different type of status (as well as economic standing) in one community when compared to another. Another issue has to do with mobility between social classes; again we see variation in this across societies, with mobility being greater in, for example, the United States than in the United Kingdom. In short, any categorization of speakers into social class categories must be done with careful attention to the community norms and understandings of economic and status factors. (Go to the online companion for the text for a link to a BBC study about social class in the UK which specifies seven social class categories.)

Exploration 6.3:   Social Class

How would you try to place individuals in the community in which you live into some kind of social-class system? What factors would you consider to be relevant? How would you weigh each of these? What class designations would seem to be appropriate? Where would you place yourself? You might also compare the scale you have devised for your community with similar scales constructed by others to find out how much agreement exists.

Another way of looking at speakers is to try to specify what kinds of groups they belong to and then relate the observed uses of language to membership in these groups. The obvious disadvantage of such an approach is the lack of generalizability of the results: we might be able to say a lot about the linguistic behavior of particular speakers *vis-à-vis* their membership in these groups, but we would not be able to say anything at all about anyone else's linguistic behavior. We can contrast this result with the statements we can make from using the aforementioned social-class designations: they say something about the linguistic usage of the 'middle middle class' without assuring us that there is really such an entity as that class; nor do they guarantee that we can ever find a 'typical' member.

One of the major problems in talking about social class is that social space is multi-dimensional whereas systems of social classification are almost always one-dimensional. As we have seen, at any particular moment, individuals locate themselves in social space according to the factors that are relevant to them at that moment. While they may indeed have certain feelings about being a member of the lower middle class, at any moment it might be more important to be female, or to be a member of a particular church or ethnic group, or to be an in-patient in a hospital, or to be a sister-in-law. That is, creating an identity, role-playing, networking, and so on, may be far more important than a certain social-class membership. This is the reason why some investigators find such concepts as social network and communities of practice attractive. Sometimes, too, experience tells the investigator that social class is not a factor in a particular situation and that something else is more important. For example, Rickford's work (1986) on language variation in a non-American, East Indian sugar-estate community in Cane Walk, Guyana, showed him that using a social-class-based model of the community would be inappropriate. What was needed was a conflict model, one that recognized schisms, struggles, and clashes on certain issues. It was a somewhat similar perspective that Mendoza-Denton (2008) brought to her work among rival Latina groups in a California school where the main issue was Norteña–Sureña rivalry.

One of the problems in sociolinguistics, then, is the tension between the desire to accurately portray particular speakers and to make generalizations about groups of speakers. To the extent that the groups are real, that is, that the members actually feel that they do belong to a group, a description of a social dialect has validity; to the extent that they are not, it is just an artifact. In the extremely complex societies in which most of us live, there must always be some question as to the reality of any kind of social grouping: each of us experiences society differently, multiple-group membership is normal, and both change and stability seem to be natural conditions of our existence. We must therefore exercise a certain caution about interpreting any claims made about 'lower working-class speech,' 'upper middle-class speech,' or the speech of any other social group designated with a class label – or any label for that matter.

Distinguishing among social classes in complex modern urban societies is probably becoming more and more difficult. The very usefulness of social class as a concept that should be employed in trying to explain the distribution of particular kinds of behavior, linguistic or otherwise, may need rethinking.

Social networks

It was for reasons not unlike these that Milroy (1987) preferred to explore social network relationships and the possible connection of these to linguistic variation, rather than to use the concept of social class (see chapter 3 for an introductory discussion of social networks). In her work, Milroy found that it was the network of relationships that an individual belonged to that exerted the most powerful and interesting influences on that individual's linguistic behavior. When the group of speakers being investigated shows little variation in social class, however that is defined, a study of the network of social relationships within the group may allow you to discover how particular linguistic usages can be related to the frequency and density of certain kinds of contacts among speakers. Network relationships, however, tend to be unique in a way that social-class categories are not. That is, no two networks are alike, and network structures vary from place to place and group to group, for example, in Belfast and Boston, or among Jamaican immigrants to London and Old Etonians. But whom a person associates with regularly may be more 'real' than any feeling he or she has of belonging to this or that social class. We will have more to say in chapter 7 about this use of network structure in the study of linguistic variation.

Data Collection and Analysis

Once an investigator has made some decision concerning which social variables must be taken into account and has formed a hypothesis about a possible relationship between social and linguistic variation, the next task becomes one of collecting data that will either confirm or refute that hypothesis. In sociolinguistics, this task has two basic dimensions: devising some kind of plan for collecting relevant data, and then collecting such data from a representative sample of speakers. As we will see, neither task is an easy one.

The observer's paradox

An immediate problem is one that we have previously referred to as the **observer's paradox**. How can you obtain objective data from the real world without injecting your own self into the data and thereby confounding the results before you even begin? How can you be sure that the data you have collected are uncontaminated by the process of investigation itself? This is a basic scientific quandary, particularly observable in the social sciences where, in almost every possible situation, there is one variable that cannot be controlled in every possible way, namely, the observer/ recorder/analyst/investigator/theorist him- or herself. If language varies according to the social context, the presence of an observer will have some effect on that variation. How can we minimize this effect? Even data recorded by remote means, for example, by hidden cameras and sound recorders, may not be entirely 'clean' and will require us to address additional ethical issues which severely limit what we can do and which we would be extremely unwise to disregard. We know, too, that observations vary from observer to observer and that we must confront the issue of the reliability of any observations that we make. Sociolinguists are aware that there are several serious issues here, and, as we will see, they have attempted to deal with them.

The sociolinguistic interview

Unlike the methodology used in dialect geography studies, which often involved explicitly asking speakers to provide linguistic information, the methodology in sociolinguistics is geared toward having the research participants (the term preferred over 'informants' or 'subjects' in sociolinguistics today) provide speech in context. This approach addresses the issues of both non-categorical use and stylistic variation. That is, the interviewer manipulates the context to try to have interviewees focus more or less on how they are speaking. The traditional sociolinguistic interview involves a casual interview, which ideally resembles a conversation more than a formal question and answer session. In addition to trying to make the interviewee feel comfortable enough to talk in a casual speech style, Labov also introduced the 'danger of death' question, in which interviewees were asked to talk about situations in which they had felt themselves to be in serious danger. The idea behind this is that the interviewees would become emotionally involved in the narrative and forget about how they are talking in their involvement with what they are saying.

To get more formal styles of speech, investigators also ask research participants to do various reading tasks: a story passage, lists of words, and **minimal pairs**. Each of these tasks requires an increased level of attention to speech. The texts are designed to contain words which illustrate important distinctions in the regional or social dialect being studied; for instance, if it is known that some speakers in the regional or social group of this speaker pronounce 'cot' and 'caught' with the same vowel, these words, or other words with these vowels, will be present in the reading materials, and be presented as a minimal pair in the final task. Speakers are obviously most likely to pronounce these words differently if they are reading them as a pair. This methodology assumes that if speakers are going to adjust their speaking style, they will use what they consider to be increasingly formal and correct speech in these elicitations.

While many researchers have followed this approach to sociolinguistic fieldwork, sociolinguists continue to rethink and develop data collection methods. For example, the idea that the conversation in a sociolinguistic interview can be described as 'natural' has been challenged, and many linguists recognize 'that there is no one single "genuine" vernacular for any one speaker, since speakers always shape their speech in some way to fit the situation or suit their purposes' (Schilling 2013, 104). Mendoza-Denton (2008, 222–5) also questions the naturalness of such interview-derived data and the usefulness of the danger of death question. She says that in her work using the latter would have been an 'outright *faux pas* … highly suspicious to gang members … very personal, and only to be told to trusted friends.' However, she does admit that 'the sociolinguistic interview paradigm … has yielded replicable results that allow us to contextualize variation in a broader context.' Labov's own recent work (2001a) still distinguishes between casual and careful speech but provides for a more nuanced assessment of how the research participant views the speech situation.

Sampling

Another critical aspect of sociolinguistic research is sampling: finding a representative group of speakers. The conclusions we draw about the behavior of any group are only as good as the sample on which we base our conclusions. If we choose the sample badly, we cannot generalize beyond the actual group that comprised the sample. If we intend to make claims about the characteristics of a population, we must either assess every member of that population for those characteristics or sample the whole population in some way. Sampling a population so as to generalize concerning its characteristics requires considerable skill. A genuine sample drawn from the population must be thoroughly representative and completely unbiased. All parts of the population must be adequately represented, and no part should be overrepresented or underrepresented, thereby creating bias of some kind. The best sample of all is a **random sample**. In a random sample everyone in the population to be sampled has an equal chance of being selected. In contrast, in a **judgment sample** (also known as a **quota sample**) the investigator chooses the subjects according to a set of criteria, for example, age, gender, social class, education, and so on. The goal is to have a certain quota of research participants in each category; for example, if the study aims to look at age and social class, the goal is to include X number of people in each age group from each social class. Sometimes, too, it is the investigator who judges each of these categories, for example, to which social class a subject belongs. A judgment sample, although it does not allow for the same kind of generalization of findings as a random sample, is clearly more practical for a sociolinguist and it is the kind of sample preferred in most sociolinguistic studies (see Chambers 2003, 44–5 and Milroy and Gordon 2008, 30 ff).

In sampling the speech of the Lower East Side in New York City, Labov did not use a completely random sample because such a sample would have produced subjects who were not native to the area, for example, immigrants from abroad and elsewhere in the United States. He used the sampling data from a previous survey that had been made by Mobilization for Youth, a random sample which used a thousand informants. Labov's own sample size was eighty-nine. He used a **stratified sample**, that is, one chosen for specific characteristics, from that survey. He also wanted to be sure that he had representatives of certain groups which he believed to exist on the Lower East Side. When he could not, for various reasons, interview some of the subjects chosen in the sample, he tried to find out by telephoning the missing subjects if his actual sample had been made unrepresentative by their absence. He was able to contact about half of his missing subjects in this way and, on the basis of these brief telephone conversations, he decided that his actual sample was unbiased and was typical of the total population he was interested in surveying.

The Detroit study (Shuy et al. 1968) initially collected data from 702 informants in the city. However, the data used for the actual analysis came from only thirty-six informants chosen from this much larger number. In selecting these thirty-six, the investigators wanted to be sure that each informant used had been a resident of Detroit for at least ten years, was 'representative,' had given a successful interview, and had provided an adequate amount of taped material for analysis. In other words, to any initial biases that might have been created in choosing the first set of 702 informants was added the possibility of still further bias by choosing non-randomly from the data that had become available. This is not to suggest that any such biases vitiate the results: they do not appear to do so. Rather, it is to point out that the kinds of concerns sociolinguists have about data and sources of data have not necessarily been the same as those of statisticians.

Wolfram (1969) chose forty-eight Black informants from those interviewed in the Detroit study. These informants were evenly divided into four social classes used in that study. Each group of twelve was further divided into three age groups: four informants in the 10–12 age group, four in the 14–17 age group, and four in the 30–55 age group. Wolfram also selected twelve White informants from the highest social class in the Detroit project, again by age and sex. Wolfram's study therefore used a total of sixty informants: twenty-four (twelve White and twelve Black) from the upper middle class and thirty-six who were Black and were members of the working classes. Such a sample is very obviously highly stratified in nature.

It is actually possible to use a very small sample from a very large area and get good results. For their *Atlas of North American English* (ANAE) Labov and his co-workers sampled all North American cities with populations over 50,000. Labov (2006, 396) reports that they did this through a telephone survey: 'Names were selected from telephone directories, selecting by preference clusters of family names representing the majority ethnic groups in the area. The first two persons who answered the telephone and said that they had grown up in the city from the age of four or earlier, were accepted as representing that city (four or six persons for the largest cities). A total of 762 subjects were interviewed.' The investigators were very pleased with the results of this sampling procedure for the ANAE.

Apparent time and real time

Investigations may also have a 'time' dimension to them because one purpose of sociolinguistic studies is trying to understand language change. They may be **apparent-time** studies in which the subjects are grouped by age, for example, people in their 20s, 40s, 60s, and so on. Any differences found in their behavior may then be associated with changes that are occurring in the language. **Real-time** studies elicit the same kind of data after an interval of say ten, twenty, or thirty years. If the same informants are involved, this would be in a **panel study**; if different people are used it would be in a **trend study**. Obviously, real-time studies are difficult to do. The study of the Queen's English is one such study (Harrington et al. 2000, mentioned in chapter 2), but she was the sole panel member. The study that replicated Labov's work on Martha's Vineyard (Pope et al. 2007) was a real-time trend study. As we will see in the following pages, most studies of change in progress are apparent-time studies for reasons which should now be obvious.

Exploration 6.4:   Research Design

What are the advantages/disadvantages of: random versus quota sampling; real versus apparent time studies; sociolinguistic interviews versus recordings of naturally occurring data? Think about what kinds of data are collected using these different approaches, and also about what is practical in terms of carrying out research. How are the choices researchers make linked to their research questions?

Correlations: dependent and independent variables

Studies employing the linguistic variable are essentially correlational in nature: that is, they attempt to show how the variants of a linguistic variable are related to social variation in much the same way that we can show how children's ages, heights, and weights are related to one another. However, a word of caution is necessary: correlation is not the same as causation. It is quite possible for two characteristics in a population to covary without one being the cause of the other. If A and B appear to be related, it may be because either A causes B or B causes A. However, it is also possible that some third factor C causes both A and B. The relationship could even be a chance one.

To avoid the problems just mentioned, we must distinguish between **dependent variables** and **independent variables**. The linguistic variable is a dependent variable, the one we are interested in. We want to see what happens to language when we look at it in relation to some factor we can manipulate, the independent variable, for example, social class, age, gender, ethnicity, and so on: as one of these changes, what happens to language? As Chambers (2003, 26) expresses it, 'Socially significant linguistic variation requires correlation: the dependent (linguistic) variable must change when some independent variable changes. It also requires that the change be orderly: the dependent variable must stratify the subjects in ways that are socially or stylistically coherent.'

Quantitative sociolinguistics

This kind of sociolinguistic investigation is often called **quantitative sociolinguistics** (or **variationist** sociolinguistics) and it is, as we have indicated previously, for some sociolinguists the 'heart of sociolinguistics' (Chambers 2003, xix). Quantitative studies must therefore be statistically sound if they are to be useful. Investigators must be prepared to employ proper statistical procedures not only in their sampling but also in the treatment of the data they collect and in testing the various hypotheses they formulate. They must be sure that what they are doing is both valid and reliable. **Validity** implies that, as said by Lepper (2000, 173): 'the researcher must show that what is being described is accurately "named" – that is, that the research process has accurately represented a phenomenon which is recognizable to the scientific community being addressed.' **Reliability** is how objective and consistent the measurements of the actual linguistic data are. Data collection methodology is part of this issue; if only one person collected the data, how consistent was that person in the actual collection? If two or more were involved, how consistently and uniformly did they employ whatever criteria they were using? Bailey and Tillery (2004, 27–8) have identified a cluster of such issues, for example, the effects of different interviewers, elicitation strategies, sampling procedures, and analytical strategies, and pointed out that these can produce significant effects on the data that are collected and, consequently, on any results that are reported. Therefore, there may still be room for improving the reliability of our results.

Serious empirical studies also require experimental hypotheses to be stated *before* the data are collected, and suitable tests to be chosen to decide whether these hypotheses are confirmed or not and with what degree of confidence. (For more discussion of statistical analyses in sociolinguistics, see Bayley 2013 and Tagliamonte 2006.)

Petyt (1980, 188–90) points out how the kinds of figures that sociolinguists use in their tables may be misleading in a very serious way. Sociolinguists stratify society into sub-groups, the members of which are measured in certain ways, and then these measurements are pooled. Individual variation is eliminated. Hudson (1996, 181) offers a similar criticism, declaring that such pooling

loses too much information which may be important. Information about the use of individual variants is lost when they are merged into variable scores, and information about the speech of individuals is also lost if these are included in group averages. At each stage the method imposes a structure on the data which may be more rigid than was inherent in the data, and to that extent distorts the results – discrete boundaries are imposed on non-discrete phonetic parameters, artificial orderings are used for variants which are related in more than one way, and speakers are assigned to discrete groups when they are actually related to each other in more complex ways.

Petyt (1980, 189) provides the data given in figure 6.3. These data come from an investigation of *h*-dropping in West Yorkshire, and the figure shows the means for five sub-groups, that is, social classes. As can be seen, these groups appear to vary quite a bit. However, Petyt points out that, if the range of variation within each sub-group is also acknowledged to be of consequence, there is a considerable overlap among the performances of individuals, so that 'it is not the case that this continuum can be divided in such a way that the members of each social class fall within a certain range, and members of other classes fall outside this.' He indicates the range of individual scores in figure 6.4, and adds that for Classes II and V, there was one individual in each group which provided the lowest and highest figure, respectively. These outliers could be eliminated and the groups would then be more uniform, but their presence shows that the groups are not discrete groups which are unified in their linguistic behavior.

It is quite obvious that if we look only at means in such a case we are tempted to say one thing, whereas if we consider the distribution of responses within each class we may draw some other conclusion. The overriding issue is that there are approved procedures to help investigators to decide how far they can be confident that any differences that they observe to exist among the various classes, that is, among the various means, are due to something other than errors in measurement or peculiarities of distribution. Such procedures require an investigator not only to calculate the means for each class, but also to assess the amount of variation in the responses

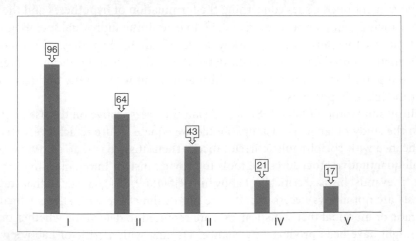

Figure 6.3 H-dropping means for five social groups

Inherent Variety

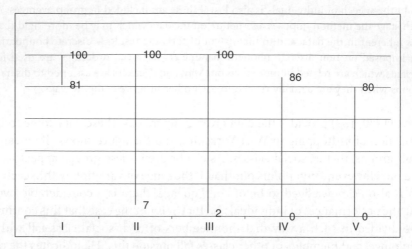

Figure 6.4   H-dropping: within-group ranges for five social groups

within each class, and then to test pairs of differences of means among the classes using a procedure which will indicate what likelihood there is that any difference found occurs by chance, for example, one chance in twenty.

Most social scientists employing statistical procedures regard this last level of significance as a suitable test of a hypothesis. In other words, unless their statistical procedures indicate that the same results would occur by chance in less than one case in twenty, they will *not* say that two groups differ in some respect or on a particular characteristic; that is, they insist that their claims be significant at what they call the 0.05 level of significance. We are also much more likely to find two means to be significantly different if they are obtained from averaging a large number of observations than from a small number.

Whenever you look at results reported by sociolinguists, you should keep in mind the above-mentioned issues concerning the formulation of hypotheses and the collection, analysis, and interpretation of data. In examining individual sociolinguistic investigations, therefore, you must ask what exactly are the hypotheses; how reliable are the methods used for collecting the data; what is the actual significance of results that are reported on a simple graph or histogram; and what do the findings tell us about the initial hypotheses.

Milroy and Gordon (2008, 168) provide another perspective on the use of statistics in the study of language, asking: 'should we equate failure to achieve statistical significance with sociolinguistic irrelevance?' Their answer is that 'statistical tests, like all quantitative procedures are tools to provide insight into patterning in variation. They must be used critically.' Labov himself (1969, 731) has stated that statistical tests are not always necessary: 'We are not dealing here with effects which are so erratic or marginal that statistical tests are required to determine whether or not they might have been produced by chance.' Dealing with a critic of Labov's work, Milroy (1992, 78) says:

It is not surprising that an anti-quantitative linguist should advocate confirmatory statistical testing, but it is very important to understand the proposition put forward here is simply wrong. If Labov's interpretations were suspect (and of course they are not), this would not arise from the fact that he failed to test for significance. There was no reason for him to do so because the claims he wished to make were quite simple … and because in his analysis the same patterns were repeated for every variable studied.

According to Milroy, since this kind of sociolinguistic inquiry is 'exploratory' in nature, it can be likewise 'exploratory' in its quantitative approach. Labov's recent work (2001b) is still exploratory in nature but it is also extremely sophisticated in its sampling, data collection, and hypothesis-testing.

Chapter Summary

In this chapter we present an overview of the development of research on regional dialects, including methodologies used to create dialect maps and study the patterns in local vernaculars. We also introduce the concept of the linguistic variable, which is central to linguistics and variationist sociolinguistics in particular. We review some early important work on regional varieties of English by well-known socio-linguists who were responsible for the growth of the field. Further, we look at social dialects and how they are studied, focusing in particular on social class, and what methodologies have traditionally been used to study this variation.

Exercises

1. As we have said, the (ng) variable, realized as [n] or [ŋ], is generally a noticeable phonological variable throughout the English-speaking world. This task requires you to do some 'field work.' Devise a way of collecting instances of the use of (ng) in naturally occurring discourse. You may want to listen to song lyrics, recorded interviews, talk shows, news reports, and so on. The key is to access both unmonitored speech, that is, talk that is focused on 'content' rather than on 'form,' and more conscious varieties, in which speakers are clearly trying to speak Standard English. After you have collected some data and analyzed what you have, try to figure out how you might improve your results if you were to repeat the task. (You could then repeat it to see what progress you made.) You can be sure that none of the research findings reported in this chapter and in the following two came from first attempts at data collection, but were preceded by such pilot studies!

2. In the following text, identify all of the contexts for the linguistic variable of the copula (that is, the verb *to be*). What are the variants which appear here? (Hint: be sure to include the zero copula variant). Can you describe the contexts in which they occur? (You may wish to consult the description of AAVE from chapter 2, as some usages are from that social dialect.)

Today movie prices are entirely too high. It doesn't make no sense to pay that much, because the picture the people be showing is not worth it. If you going to pay that much for a movie you should at least have a cut on the prices of the food. Not only the food is high, but you cannot sit in a nice clean place. But still you paying that very high price to get inside the place. Another reason you got against paying such a high price is that the people at the movies be throwing popcorn all in your head. You not paying that much money to come to a movie and get food stains all on your clothes and hair.

Further Reading

Chambers, Jack K. and Natalie Schilling (eds.) (2002). *The Handbook of Language Variation and Change*. Oxford: Blackwell.
> This collection of papers on language variation and change presents articles by leading sociolinguistics which address issues of theory and method in sociolinguistic research.

Gordon, Matthew J. (2013). *Labov: A Guide for the Perplexed*. New York: Bloomsbury.
> Written for a general audience, this is an especially good and accessible discussion of Labov's influential work and how it has shaped sociolinguistics.

Milroy, Lesley and Matthew Gordon (2008). *Sociolinguistics: Method and Interpretation*. 2nd edn. Oxford: Blackwell.
> A comprehensive introduction to research in the field of sociolinguistics, with especial foci on phonological variation and style-shifting and code-switching.

Schilling, Natalie (2013). *Sociolinguistic Fieldwork*. Cambridge: Cambridge University Press.
> This is a thorough treatment on research methodology in sociolinguistics, with special attention given to research on speech style, addressing practical, ethical, and theoretical issues.

Tagliamonte, Sali (2012). *Variationist Sociolinguistics: Change, Observation and Interpretation*. Oxford: Wiley-Blackwell.
> A research guide with a primary focus on quantitative research methods with both a treatment of social factors and detailed sections on the analysis of phonological and grammatical variation.

For further resources for this chapter visit the companion website at

 www.wiley.com/go/wardhaugh/sociolinguistics

References

Bailey, G. and J. Tillery (2004). Some Sources of Divergent Data in Sociolinguistics. In C. Fought (ed.) (2004), *Sociolinguistic Variation: Critical Reflections*. New York: Oxford University Press.

Bainbridge, W. S. (1994). Sociology of Language. In R. E. Asher and J. M. Simpson (eds.), *The Encyclopedia of Language and Linguistics*. Oxford: Pergamon.

Bayley, R. (2013) The Quantitative Paradigm. In Jack K. Chambers and Natalie Schilling (eds.), *The Handbook of Language Variation and Change*. 2nd edn. Oxford: Wiley-Blackwell, 85–107.

Chambers, J. K. (1995). *Sociolinguistic Theory: Linguistic Variation and its Social Significance*. Oxford: Blackwell.

Chambers, J. K. (2003). *Sociolinguistic Theory: Linguistic Variation and its Social Significance*. 2nd edn. Oxford: Blackwell.

Chambers, J. K. and P. Trudgill (1998). *Dialectology*. 2nd edn. Cambridge: Cambridge University Press.

Coates, J. (2004). *Women, Men and Language*. 3rd edn. London: Longman.

Coupland, N. (2007). *Style: Language Variation and Identity*. Cambridge: Cambridge University Press.

Gordon, E., L. Campbell, J. Hay et al. (2004). *New Zealand English: Its Origin and Evolution*. Cambridge: Cambridge University Press.

Gordon, M. J. (2013) *Labov: A Guide for the Perplexed*. New York: Bloomsbury.

Harrington, J., S. Palethorpe, and C. I. Watson (2000). Does the Queen Speak the Queen's English? *Nature* 408: 927–8.

Hickey, R. (2004). *Legacies of Colonial English*. Cambridge: Cambridge University Press.

Hudson, R. A. (1996). *Sociolinguistics*. 2nd edn. Cambridge: Cambridge University Press.

Johnstone, B. (2004). Place, Globalization, and Linguistic Variation. In C. Fought (ed.), *Sociolinguistic Variation: Critical Reflections*. New York: Oxford University Press.

Kretzschmar, W. A., Jr (1996). Quantitative Aerial Analysis of Dialect Features. *Language Variation and Change* 8: 13–39.

Kurath, H. (1939). *Handbook of the Linguistic Geography of New England*. Providence, RI: Brown University Press.

Labov, W. (1966). *The Social Stratification of English in New York City*. Washington, DC: Center for Applied Linguistics.

Labov, W. (1969). Contraction, Deletion, and Inherent Variability of the English Copula. *Language* 45: 715–62.

Labov, W. (1972). *Sociolinguistic Patterns*. Philadelphia: University of Pennsylvania Press.

Labov, W. (2001a) The Anatomy of Style Shifting. In P. Eckert and J. R. Rickrods (eds.), *Style and Sociolinguistic Variation*. Cambridge: Cambridge University Press, 85–108.

Labov, W. (2001b). *Principles of Linguistic Change, II: Social Factors*. Oxford: Blackwell.

Labov, W. (2006). *The Social Stratification of English in New York City*. 2nd edn. Cambridge: Cambridge University Press.

Labov, W. (2007). Transmission and Diffusion. *Language* 83(2): 344–87.

Labov, W., C. Boberg, and S. Ash (2005). *The Atlas of North American English*. Berlin: Mouton de Gruyter.

Lane, L. A. (2000). Trajectories of Linguistic Variation: Emergence of a Dialect. *Language Variation and Change* 12: 267–94.

Le Page, R. B. (1997). The Evolution of a Sociolinguistic Theory of Language. In F. Coulmas (ed.), *The Handbook of Sociolinguistics*. Oxford: Blackwell.

Lepper, G. (2000). *Categories in Text and Talk: A Practical Introduction to Categorization Analysis*. London: Sage.

Marshall, J. (2003). The Changing Sociolinguistic Status of the Glottal Stop in Northeast Scottish English. *English World-Wide* 24(1): 89–108.

Marshall, J. (2004). *Language Change and Sociolinguistics: Rethinking Social Networks*. Basingstoke: Palgrave Macmillan.

Mendoza-Denton, N. (2008). *Homegirls*. Oxford: Blackwell.

Milroy, J. (1992). *Language Variation and Change*. Oxford: Blackwell.

Milroy, Lesley (1987). *Language and Social Networks*. 2nd edn. Oxford: Blackwell.

Milroy, Lesley and Matthew Gordon (2008). *Sociolinguistics: Method and Interpretation*, vol. 13. 2nd edn. Chichester: John Wiley & Sons, Ltd.

Orton, H., S. Sanderson, and J. Widdowson (eds.) (1978). *The Linguistic Atlas of England*. London: Croom Helm.

Petyt, K. M. (1980). *The Study of Dialect: An Introduction to Dialectology*. London: André Deutsch.

Pope, Jennifer, Miriam Meyerhoff, and D. Robert Ladd (2007). Forty Years of Language Change on Martha's Vineyard. *Language* 83(3): 615–27.

Rickford, J. R. (1986). The Need for New Approaches to Social Class Analysis in Sociolinguistics. *Language & Communication* 6(3): 215–21.

Schilling, Natalie (2013). *Sociolinguistic Fieldwork*. Cambridge: Cambridge University Press.

Shuy, R. W., W. Wolfram, and W. K. Riley (1968). *Field Techniques in an Urban Language Study*. Washington, DC: Center for Applied Linguistics.

Tagliamonte, Sali (2006). *Analysing Sociolinguistic Variation*. New York: Cambridge University Press.

Trudgill, P. (1974). *The Social Differentiation of English in Norwich*. Cambridge: Cambridge University Press.

Trudgill, P. (2004). *New-Dialect Formation: The Inevitability of Colonial Englishes*. Oxford: Oxford University Press.

Wakelin, M. F. (1977). *English Dialects: An Introduction*. Rev. edn. London: Athlone Press.

Wolfram, W. (1969). *A Sociolinguistic Description of Detroit Negro Speech*. Washington, DC: Center for Applied Linguistics.

Wolfram, W. (1991). The Linguistic Variable: Fact and Fantasy. *American Speech* 66(1): 22–32.

Wolfram, W. (2004). The Sociolinguistic Construction of Remnant Dialects. In C. Fought (ed.), *Sociolinguistic Variation: Critical Reflections*. New York: Oxford University Press.

Wolfram, W. and R. W. Fasold (1974). *The Study of Social Dialects in American English*. Englewood Cliffs, NJ: Prentice-Hall.

Woolard, K. A. (1985). Language Variation and Cultural Hegemony: Toward an Integration of Linguistic and Sociological Theory. *American Ethnologist* 12: 738–48.

7

Three Waves of Variation Studies

Key Concepts

First wave: correlations

Second wave: ethnographic information

Third wave: identity

The role of agency

Social categories versus social networks

Stance: positioning the speaker

Having looked briefly at some of the problems investigators face in using the concept of the 'linguistic variable' to examine linguistic variation in society, we can now turn to some representative quantitative studies. We will look at this work within the perspective of three 'waves' of variation study (Eckert 2012). In these phases of research, there are different perspectives on the relationship between language and society, moving from looking at speech as being driven from the speaker's position in social structure to viewing speakers as agents who construct their social realities. In this chapter, we will look at research findings across all three waves of variationist studies which continue to influence research today.

An Introduction to Sociolinguistics, Seventh Edition. Ronald Wardhaugh and Janet M. Fuller.
© 2015 John Wiley & Sons, Inc. Published 2015 by John Wiley & Sons, Inc.

The First Wave of Variation Studies

Broadly speaking, the **first wave** of studies sought to establish correlations between predetermined macro-level social categories – socioeconomic class, age, race/ ethnicity, and sex – and particular linguistic variables. The Labov (1966) study, discussed in chapter 6, and others carried out in the United States and Great Britain (e.g., Wolfram 1969, Trudgill 1974) showed socioeconomic stratification and 'greater regional and ethnic differentiation at the lower end of the socioeconomic hierarchy as well as greater use of more widespread standard forms' (Eckert 2012, 88). As we mentioned in chapter 6, the focus was on vernacular varieties and how speakers of these varieties moved increasingly toward the standard as they paid more and more attention to their speech. A key concept is that such individual stylistic repertoires mirror the hierarchy of varieties found in the larger society.

Early work on gender variation

One of the earliest studies which included a look at **gender variation** was Fischer's study (1958) of the /n/ variable, that is, pronunciations like *singing* [ŋ] versus *singin'* [n]. We should observe that there is a long history of both the [ŋ] and [n] variants in the language, with the [n] variant stigmatized, or at least associated with less lofty pursuits. The author recalls a student in one of her sociolinguistics courses who claimed that he would use the two pronunciations to mean different things: the less formal *fishin'* meant going out in a boat with a simple fishing pole, whereas the more prestigious-sounding *fishing* meant going fly-fishing. While such a distinction in meaning is by no means widespread (and may have been limited to this one speaker), it is indicative of awareness of this variable being part of communicative competence of many speakers of English.

As part of a study of child-rearing practices in a New England community, Fischer conducted interviews with young children, twelve boys and twelve girls, aged 3–10. He noted their use of *-ing* ([ŋ]) and *-in'* ([n]) in a very formal situation during the administration of the Thematic Apperception Test, in a less formal inter- view, and in an informal situation in which the children discussed recent activities. In the most formal situation, 10/12 (83%) of the girls showed a preference for the *-ing* form, while only 5/12 (42%) of the boys did (Fischer 1958, 48).

Fischer also compared the use of [ŋ] and [n] of a boy described by his teachers as a 'model' boy with that of a boy described as a 'typical' boy. The model boy worked well in school and was described as being popular, thoughtful, and considerate; the typical boy was described as being strong, mischievous, and apparently unafraid of being caught doing something he should not be doing. In the most formal situation these two boys produced the percentages of *-ing* and *-in'* reported in figure 7.1; note that the model boy used far more of the more formal variant. However, Fischer further observed that the model boy also used *-in'* at a higher rate as the formality

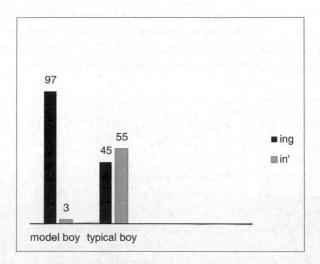

Figure 7.1 'Model' boy versus 'typical' boy: percentages of *-ing* versus *-in'* use

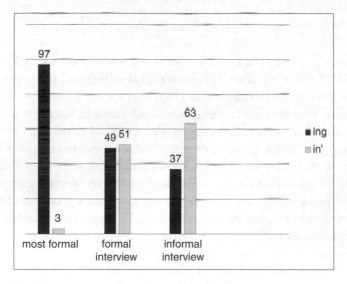

Figure 7.2 'Model' boy's preference for *-ing* versus *-in'* by formality of situation

of the situation decreased, as we can see in figure 7.2. He also observed several other interesting facts. As children relaxed in the most formal situation they produced more instances of *-in'*. Such usage was also associated with specific verbs so that verbs like *hit*, *chew*, *swim*, and *punch*, that is, verbs describing everyday activities, were much more likely to be given *-in'* endings than more 'formal' verbs like *criticize*, *correct*, *read*, and *visit*. Fischer's conclusion (1958, 51) is that 'the choice between the *-ing* and the *-in'* variants appears to be related to sex, class, personality (aggressive/cooperative), and mood (tense/relaxed) of the speaker, to the formality of the conversation and to the specific verb spoken.'

In terms of its findings on gender, this study fit into a pattern of studies which showed that girls/women used more standard variants than boys/men of their same social class in the same social contexts (Macaulay 1977, Trudgill 1972, 1974, Wolfram 1969). We will return to this point below, and again in chapter 8.

Exploration 7.1:   Gender, Standardness, and Formality

What is the relationship between standardness and formality in the use of linguistic features such as the *-in'* suffix, the quotative *like*, or the use of multiple negation? What social factors might contribute to girls or women being more likely to use more standard linguistic features in some contexts? What dangers are there in making generalizations about what motivates girls/women as opposed to boys/men to speak in particular ways?

The fourth floor

Another first wave study, perhaps the most well-known of all, is Labov's small-scale investigation of the (r) variable (Labov 1966). Labov believed that *r*-pronunciation after vowels was being reintroduced into New York speech from above, was a feature of the speech of younger people rather than of older people, was more likely to occur as the formality level in speech increased, and would be more likely at the ends of words (*floor*) than before consonants (*fourth*). He set out to test these hypotheses by walking around three New York City department stores (Saks, Macy's, and S. Klein), which were rather clearly demarcated by the social-class groups to which they catered (high, middle, and low, respectively), and asking the location of departments he knew to be situated on the fourth floor. When the shop assistant answered, Labov would seek a careful repetition of *fourth floor* by pretending not to hear the initial response.

Table 7.1 shows the incidence of *r* use that Labov found among individuals employed in the three stores (Labov 1972, 51). The table shows that 32 and 31 percent of the personnel approached in Saks and Macy's respectively used *r* in all

Table 7.1   Percentage of [r] use in three New York City department stores

	Saks (%)	Macy's (%)	S. Klein (%)
All [r]	32	31	17
Some [r]	30	20	4
No [r]	38	49	79
Number	68	125	71

Source: based on Labov (1972, 51)

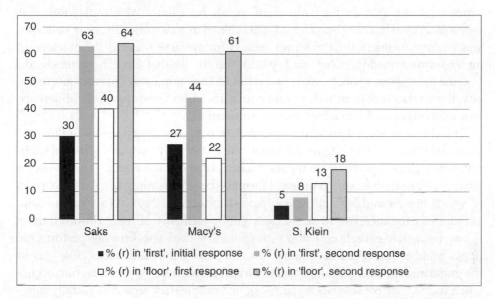

Figure 7.3   Use of (r) pronunciation by department store

possible instances but only 17 percent did so in S. Klein; 79 percent of the seventy-one employees in S. Klein who were approached did not use *r* at all, but only 38 percent of the sixty-eight employees approached in Saks and 49 percent of the 125 employees approached in Macy's were *r*-less.

So far as the position of occurrence of *r*-pronunciation was concerned (i.e., before consonant vs. word final, and first response vs. repeated response), Labov found the distribution reported in figure 7.3. This figure shows that *r*-pronunciation was favored in Saks to a greater extent than in Macy's but much less so in S. Klein. Careful repetition of the utterance nearly always increased *r*-pronunciation, and pronunciation of the *r* was found more often in *floor* than in *fourth* in all circumstances. Labov did not test his findings for statistical significance but the data clearly reveal the patterns just mentioned.

A further analysis of the department store data showed that in Saks it was older people who used *r*-pronunciation less. However, the data from S. Klein on this point were quite inconclusive, and the results from Macy's pointed in a direction completely opposite to that predicted: *r*-pronunciation actually increased with age. This fact led Labov to conclude that members of the highest and lowest social groups tend not to change their pronunciation after it becomes fixed in adolescence but members of middle social groups sometimes do, possibly because of their social aspirations. He tested this last hypothesis later in a more comprehensive study of New York City speech and found good confirmation for it.

Labov has noted that today in New York City pronunciations of words like *car* and *guard* with the *r* pronounced are highly valued. They are associated with the upper middle class even though members of that class do not always use such pronunciations, nor do they use them on all occasions. We should note that r-pronunciation has not always been highly valued in New York City. New York City was r-pronouncing in the eighteenth century but became r-less in the nineteenth, and r-lessness predominated until World War II. At that time r-pronunciation became prestigious again, possibly as a result of large population movements to the city; there was a shift in attitude toward r-pronunciation, from apparent indifference to a widespread desire to adopt such pronunciation.

This desire to adopt a particular pronunciation is, according to Labov, influenced by social class standing. Figure 7.4 shows the use of r by various social classes in different styles of speech, from the most casual type of speech (e.g., telling about a narrow escape from death) to the most formal type (e.g., reading aloud a list of pairs of words like *bit* and *bid* and *pa* and *par*) (Labov 1966, 240). As we can see, the amount of r use increases by social class and by formality of style. However, there is one noticeable exception: Labov's lower middle-class speakers out-perform his upper middle-class speakers on word lists and pairs. Labov calls this a *cross-over* in the graph and explains it as an instance of **hypercorrection**. Hypercorrection occurs when individuals consciously try to speak like people they regard as socially superior but actually go too far and overdo the particular linguistic behavior they are attempting to match. Here, lower middle-class speakers know how prestigious r-pronunciations are and, in reading word lists and lists of pairs, that is, when they are placed in situations which require them to monitor their speech closely, they out-perform their reference group, in this case the next highest social class, the upper middle class.

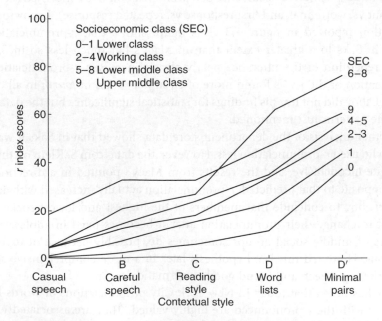

Figure 7.4   Pronunciation of (r) in New York City by social class and style of speech

Labov makes much of this phenomenon of hypercorrection, particularly because it appears to relate to changes that are taking place in the language. However, a word of caution is necessary. Such displays as we find in figure 7.4 are displays of group means. We have no information about the amount of variance about the means so we cannot be sure how comparable they are. We do know they are based on quite small numbers of informants in each case. In addition, we cannot be sure that any two means which differ do so significantly in the statistical sense. The cross-over shown in figure 7.4 could, theoretically at least, be the result of the way the data have been treated. However, the fact that it occurs for both word lists and pairs provides us with some assurance of the correctness of Labov's claims.

Exploration 7.2:   Hypercorrection

There are two different phenomena which can be called 'hypercorrection' – one, as discussed in the context of the Labov study, is hyper-use of a prestigious form; the other is the use of structures which aim to be standard but instead use supposedly standard features in ways that are not prescriptively 'correct.' With this concept in mind, discuss the use of the phrase *between you and I*. Do you use this, hear it frequently, or consider it to be standard? What are the linguistic roots of this construction (contrast with *between you and me*) and why might it be considered a hypercorrection?

Variation In Norwich

The aforementioned work by Trudgill (1974) is also a seminal work of the first wave in **variation studies**. Trudgill investigated sixteen different phonological variables in his work in Norwich, England. He demonstrates, in much the same way as Labov does in New York City, how use of the variants is related to social class and level of formality. Trudgill's analysis of the variables (ng), (t), and (h) shows, for example, that the higher the social class the more frequent is the use of the [ŋ], [t], and [h] variants in words like *singing*, *butter*, and *hammer* rather than the corresponding [n], [ʔ], and Ø variants. However, whereas members of the lower working class almost invariably say *singin'*, they do not almost invariably say *'ammer*. Moreover, although members of the lower working class say *singin'* when they are asked to read a word list containing words ending in -*ing*, they pronounce the (ng) with the [ŋ] variant on the majority of occasions. The data also suggest that, so far as the (ng) variable is concerned, its variant use is related not only to social class but also to gender, with females showing a greater preference for [ŋ] than males, regardless of social-class membership.

(This 1974 study is interesting in still another way. As Trudgill himself later observed (1986, 8), a follow-up analysis of his own pronunciation with each

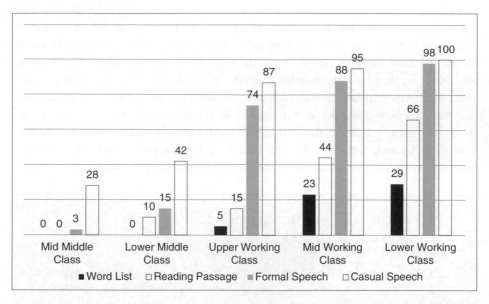

Figure 7.5 Percentage of use of *-in'* in four contextual styles of speech in Norwich

informant showed that his own use of glottal stops shadowed their use by each informant. The more such stops an informant used, the more he himself used such stops. However, his use almost always trailed any other's use. This is a good example of convergent accommodation (see discussion of this in chapter 4). It is also further evidence that the observer-observed relationship is not a neutral one!)

Trudgill (1995, 93–4) uses data such as those presented in a bar graph in figure 7.5 to demonstrate two very important points: First, when style is kept constant, the lower the social class the greater the incidence of the nonstandard variant; thus we see that for each group, the bars increase as the speech style goes from most to least formal. Second, when social class is kept constant, the less formal the style the greater the incidence of the nonstandard variant. Thus we see that the first bar is lower (zero for the first two groups) for the middle-class speakers and gets higher as the social class goes from upper to mid to lower working class. Some increases are negligible and some are considerable. For example, middle middle-class speakers always avoid *-in'* pronunciations in the two most formal styles but 'relax' considerably more in casual style. Upper working-class speakers make a very sharp differentiation between the two reading styles and the two speaking styles. Lower working-class speakers make no real distinction between the two speaking styles and use *-in'* pronunciations almost exclusively in both; however, just like middle working-class speakers, they are conscious that *-ing* pronunciations are used in reading styles and do manage to introduce them on many occasions.

Table 7.2 shows a further breakdown by gender of subjects' performance on the (ng) variable with a score of 000 indicating exclusive use of [ŋ] and a score of 100 indicating exclusive use of [n]. Since the number of informants in each cell is quite

Table 7.2 The (ng) variable in Norwich

Social class[a]	No.	Sex	Style[b]			
			WLS	RPS	FS	CS
MMC	6	M	000	000	004	031
		F	000	000	000	000
LMC	8	M	000	020	027	017
		F	000	000	003	067
UWC	16	M	000	018	081	095
		F	011	013	068	077
MWC	22	M	024	043	091	097
		F	020	046	081	088
LWC	8	M	066	100	100	100
		F	017	054	097	100

[a] Social class: MMC (middle middle class), LMC (lower middle class), UWC (upper working class), MWC (middle working class), LWC (lower working class).
[b] Style: WLS (word list), RPS (reading passage), FS (formal), CS (casual).
Source: based on Trudgill (1974, 94). Copyright © 1974 Cambridge University Press. Reprinted with the permission of Cambridge University Press

small, there is no perfect linear change by gender across the social classes, but we can see that women have lower scores on the whole, indicating use of the more formal [ŋ] variant, and that the scores become higher as social class becomes lower, indicating more use of the informal [n] variant by speakers assigned to lower social-class categories.

Variation in Detroit

A Detroit study (Shuy et al. 1968) and Wolfram's follow-up to that study (1969) are other first wave studies. The Detroit study investigated the use of **multiple negation** as a linguistic variable in that city. It showed that there is a very close relationship between the use of multiple negation and social class. Whereas upper middle-class speakers used such negation on about 2 percent of possible occasions, the corresponding percentages for the other three social classes were as follows: lower middle class, 11 percent; upper working class, 38 percent; and lower working class, 70 percent. From such figures we can make a further observation: it is not that members of the upper middle class *always* avoid multiple negation and members of the lower working class *always* employ it; it may be our impression that such is the case, but the facts do not confirm that impression. No class uses one variant of the variable to the exclusion of the other, regardless of circumstances. Speech within any social class, therefore, is inherently variable, just as it is in society as a whole. However, the analyses of the different variables that were investigated in Detroit clearly show that, although individuals exhibit a certain amount of variation in their linguistic behavior, there is nevertheless a pattern to that behavior. For example, as the situation becomes more formal, an individual's linguistic usage comes closer to standard usage, and the higher the social class of the speaker, the more standard too is the speaker's behavior.

Wolfram's study was an attempt to show how the distribution of linguistic variables correlated with such factors as social class, gender, age, and racial category in Detroit. Wolfram wanted to identify varieties of speech which might be associated with specific social groups in the city, for example, upper middle-class Whites or lower working-class Blacks. His work is based on data collected from forty-eight Black research participants drawn from 702 people who initially took part in the Detroit study. There are two male and two female research participants in each age group (10–12, 14–17, 30–55) in upper middle-, lower middle-, upper working- and lower working-class groups, along with twelve White research participants (two male and two female in each age group, all upper middle class).

Having identified his groups, Wolfram then attempted to show characteristic differences in linguistic behavior. He investigated four phonological variables: word final consonant cluster simplification; medial and final *th*, as in *nothing* and *path*; syllable final *d*; and the occurrence of *r* after vowels. He also investigated four grammatical variables: the zero copula, as in *He tired*; invariant *be*, as in *He be tired*; the -*s* plural, possessive, and third-person singular verbal suffixes, as in *girls*, *boy's*, and *goes*; and multiple negation. Figure 7.6, for example, shows group means for the absence of the third-person singular tense-marking (z). A close inspection of the

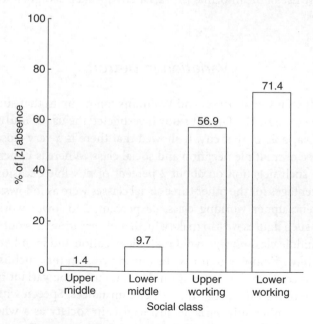

Figure 7.6 Percentage of [z] absence in third-person singular present tense agreement in Detroit Black speech

figure shows that, whereas it is quite possible that the differences between the two groups at each of the ends, that is, between the upper middle and the lower middle classes and between the upper working and the lower working classes, may not be significant, there being only twelve subjects in each group, the difference between the top two groups as a whole and the bottom two groups as a whole, that is, between the middle class and the working class, almost certainly is, and probably at a very high level of significance. There does therefore appear to be a great difference in usage of the (z) between middle-class and working-class people in Detroit.

We can contrast this graph with another from the same study, this one concerned with (r) absence (Wolfram 1969, 110). Figure 7.7 gives us the information we need. Here we find a progressive step-like set of differences. However, without statistical testing we cannot be sure that there is a significant difference between adjacent means, particularly when the groups are small (twelve subjects) and the difference in means is of the order of 61.3 and 71.7 percent. That there is a significant difference between the two groups at each end does seem very likely, but we cannot be sure of the significance of the difference between any adjacent pairs. The data do, however, fall into a very clear pattern and it is such patterns that sociolinguists seek to explain.

Wolfram and Fasold (1974, 80–1) argue that in the case of (r) absence in figure 7.7 we have an example of what they call **gradient stratification**, that is, a regular step-like progression in means which matches social groupings. In the previous case of (z) (figure 7.6), we have **sharp stratification**, that is, a clear break between a particular pair of social groupings. The first kind of stratification is said to be typical

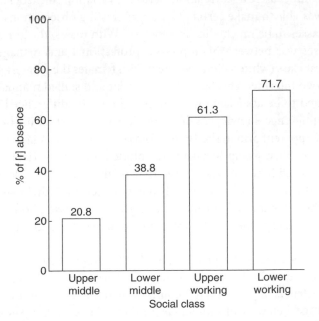

Figure 7.7 Percentage of (r) absence in words like *farm* and *car* in Detroit Black speech

of the distribution of phonological variables; the second kind to be typical of grammatical variables.

Wolfram's general findings in Detroit were that social status was the single most important variable correlating with linguistic differences, with the clearest boundary being between the lower middle and upper working classes, and that in each class females used more standard-language forms than males. Further, older subjects also used fewer stigmatized forms than did younger subjects, and reading style showed the fewest deviations of all from standard-language forms.

Variation in Glasgow

So far we have mentioned several factors that correlate with linguistic variation: social class, age, and gender. Another study which looked at all of these is Macaulay's study (1977) of five variables in Glasgow: the vowels in words such as *hit*, *school*, *hat*, and *now* and the occurrence of glottal stops as replacements for [t] in words like *better* and *get*. Macaulay surveyed sixteen adults, sixteen 15-year-olds, and sixteen 10-year-olds, with equal numbers of males and females represented in each group. His forty-eight subjects were equally divided among four social classes: professional and managerial; white-collar; skilled manual; and semi-skilled and unskilled manual. In the case of children, the occupation of the father was used unless the mother was (or had been) in a 'higher' occupational group. Macaulay counted equal numbers of occurrences of each variable from each speaker as a further control for volubility.

Macaulay found a clear correlation between variation and social class, but in addition he was able to make certain further interesting observations. He found his two lowest classes to be much alike in behavior. With males, the greatest difference between classes was between his top class (professional and managerial) and the second-highest class (white-collar), whereas with females the greatest difference was between the two intermediate classes (white-collar and skilled manual). Increase in age also seemed to be associated with an increase in the difference between social classes, this difference showing itself to be clearly established in the 15-year-olds surveyed (but apparent also in the 10-year-olds). Finally, Macaulay found that when individual rather than group behavior was plotted for each variable, a continuum of behavior was exhibited in each case. That is, there was considerable variation within each of the four classes, with the behavior of certain individuals in each class overlapping the behavior of individuals in neighboring classes; however, the means for most classes, except the two lowest as noted above, were clearly different from each other.

We can conclude from Macaulay's study that the linguistic behavior of individuals forms a continuum in the same way that social organization is continuous. Social classes are constructs imposed on this continuum. If linguistic variation is correlated with the 'average' behavior of individuals in these classes, it will show class differences. This is what we should expect, and it is what happens. However, the linguistic behavior of certain individuals in one class will overlap the linguistic behavior of certain individuals in neighboring classes. What is important in this view is that there is still a certain homogeneity of behavior within the classes. The majority of speakers within the various classes behave like one another even though some individuals do not. This behavior has its own distinctive quality in that its characteristics are not just the result of some individuals behaving like individuals 'above' them and other individuals behaving like individuals 'below' them in the social hierarchy. That is, the members of each social class exhibit certain ranges of behavior on the linguistic variables and, even though the ranges overlap, each social class has a distinctive range for each variable.

Linguistic constraints on variation

We noted above that linguistic variables may correlate not only with social variables but also with other linguistic features, that is, there may be **linguistic constraints** too. In their discussion of linguistic variation, Wolfram and Fasold (1974, 101–5) present data from an earlier study by Fasold (1972) to show that it is possible to state how two or more factors, or constraints, interact to affect the distribution of a variable. In this case they are concerned with deletion of final stops in clusters, for example, the *d* in a word like *cold*, in speech among Blacks in Washington, DC. The data showed that the parenthesized stops were deleted as follows: *san(d) castle*, 83.3 percent deletion; *fas(t) car*, 68.8 percent deletion; *wil(d) elephant*, 34.9 percent deletion; and *lif(t) it*, 25.2 percent deletion. If we look closely at the environments of these stops, we will find that sometimes the stop is preceded by a sonorant (a nasal or *l*) and sometimes by a non-sonorant (a stop or a fricative), and it is followed sometimes by a vowel and sometimes by a consonant (or non-vowel). We can see this distribution more clearly in table 7.3. Wolfram and Fasold point out that the constraint of appearing before a non-vowel has a greater effect than the constraint of appearing after a sonorant, that is, appearance of the stop before a non-vowel leads to a greater amount of deletion than appearance after a sonorant. When both constraints are present we find the highest percentage of deletions: 83.3 percent in *san(d) castle*. When neither constraint is present we have the least: 25.2 percent in *lif(t) it*. In the intermediate cases, appearing before a non-vowel is more important

Table 7.3 Final cluster simplification among Black speakers in Washington, DC

% deleted	Example	Environment
83.3	*san(d) castle*	after sonorant, before non-vowel
68.8	*fas(t) car*	after non-sonorant, before non-vowel
34.9	*wil(d) elephant*	after sonorant, before vowel
25.2	*lif(t) it*	after non-sonorant, before vowel

Source: based on Wolfram and Fasold (1974, 102). Reproduced with the permission of the authors

Table 7.4 Final cluster simplification among Black speakers in Detroit

Social class					
Upper middle	*Lower middle*	*Upper working*	*Lower working*	*Example*	*Environment*
0.07	0.13	0.24	0.34	*burn(ed) up*	*-ed*, before vowel
0.28	0.43	0.65	0.72	*col(d) out*	not *-ed*, before vowel
0.49	0.62	0.73	0.76	*burn(ed) coal*	*-ed*, before consonant
0.79	0.87	0.94	0.97	*col(d) cuts*	not *-ed*, before consonant

Source: based on Wolfram (1969, 59–69)

than appearing after a sonorant. Wolfram and Fasold, therefore, call appearing before a non-vowel a first-order constraint and appearing after a sonorant a second-order constraint. That is, the former exercises a greater influence on a person's linguistic behavior than does the latter.

Constraints may also mix phonological and grammatical features. Wolfram (1969, 59–69) explains a situation in Detroit in which Black speakers also delete final stops in clusters, but in this case make a distinction according to the grammatical function of the stop. In the final cluster in *cold* the *d* has no independent grammatical function – it is part of a single unit of meaning – but in *burned* it marks past tense and is grammatically the *-ed* ending, and therefore has its own meaning. The data are distributed as in table 7.4. In this variety of English the first-order constraint is once again appearance before a vowel or non-vowel (here consonant). Appearance before a vowel inhibits cluster simplification in all cases and appearance before a consonant encourages it. The second-order constraint is appearance as the *-ed* ending. That is, such appearance has a lesser effect than whether or not the following sound is a vowel or consonant. Consequently, the greatest loss of [d] in these examples occurs when the following sound is a consonant and the [d] does not represent the *-ed* grammatical ending. The least loss occurs when the [d] is followed by a vowel and it is the *-ed* ending. This situation is the same for all social classes, but the actual amounts of deletion vary from class to class.

Using information similar to the kind just presented, Wolfram and Fasold (1974, 133–4) go on to show how it is possible to take a phenomenon like cluster simplification and predict certain kinds of linguistic behavior. They distinguish between speakers of Standard English (SE), White nonstandard English (WNS), and what they call Vernacular Black English (VBE). They consider four environments in which cluster simplification can occur: (1) before a word beginning with a consonant (*test program*); (2) before a word beginning with a vowel (*test idea*); (3) before a suffix such as *-ing* (*testing*); and (4) involving a final consonant other than *t* (e.g., *k*) before a suffix such as *-ing* (*risking*). They report their findings (1974, 134) as in table 7.5, with 'always,' 'sometimes,' and 'usually' in that table referring to the pronunciation which they predict will occur. According to such a display, *tes' idea* (for *test idea*) is not a feature of SE; there is a considerable overlap between features

Table 7.5 Final cluster simplification in several varieties of English

Variety of English	Cluster simplification			
SE	sometimes *tes' program*	always *test idea*	always *testing*	always *risking*
Most VBE and some WNS speakers	usually or always *tes' program*	sometimes *tes' idea*	always *testing*	always *risking*
Some WNS Some VBE speakers	always *tes' program*	always *tes' idea*	always *testing*	always *risking*
Some WNS Some VBE speakers	always *tes' program*	always *tes' idea*	usually or always *testing*	usually or always *risking*
Some VBE speakers (especially Deep South children)	always *tes' program*	always *tes' idea*	always *tessing*	always *rissing*

Source: Wolfram and Fasold (1974, 134). Reproduced with permission of the authors

found in WNS and VBE; but it is only in the latter that you find *tessing* (for *testing*) and *rissing* (for *risking*). *Tes' program* (for *test program*), however, is found in all varieties of English but with a different incidence of usage: only 'sometimes' in SE, but 'usually' or 'always' in the other varieties.

Two studies of the French spoken in Montreal are of interest because they suggest some of the complexities we face in trying to describe the distribution of variants of a variable in one case and the persistence of a rare variant in another. The first study is by Sankoff and Cedergren (1971), who report on the (l) variable in Montreal French, that is, the presence or absence of [l] in expressions such as 'he does,' [il fɛ] or [i fɛ], and 'he is,' [il e] or [y e]. They found that in 94 percent of the cases when the (l) was followed by a consonant or a glide it was not produced phonetically, but it went phonetically unrealized in only 57 percent of the cases when it was followed by a vowel. Therefore, before a consonant or glide the (l) is generally not pronounced, but it is pronounced before vowels about two times out of five. However, there is a further constraint. When the (l) is part of an impersonal pronoun, for example, the *l* in *il pleut* ('it's raining') or *il y a* ('there is/are'), that (l) is almost never realized before a consonant or glide; in contrast, a personal *il* ('he') in the same circumstances finds the (l) not realized phonetically about 80 percent of the time. What we find here is that the distribution of the variants of the (l) variable in Montreal French is related to phonological and grammatical factors as well as social ones. The (l) is affected by its relationship to the following phonological segment and whether it occurs in either a personal or impersonal pronoun, when these are even of identical form, that is, *il*.

The second example from Montreal French is Sankoff and Vincent's study (1977) of the use of the negative particle *ne* in verb phrases, or rather its non-use. Martineau and Mougeon (2003, 145–6) say: 'In most varieties of current European French that have been studied, the rate of *ne* deletion still varies as a function of age, social class, sex, and linguistic context. In contemporary Quebec French, however, *ne* deletion is almost categorical in the speech of all age groups, social classes, and both sexes, and in all linguistic contexts.' Consequently, 'Quebec French is ahead of European French in the propagation of sociolinguistic change.' They claim that *ne* deletion began in the nineteenth century. However, Poplack and St-Amand (2007), after an analysis of some 40,000 audio recordings of folk tales, legends, and interviews made in the 1940s and 1950s by 54 Quebeckers born as early as 1846 (and no later than 1893), claim that 'In order for the process of *ne* deletion to have reached near completion by the mid-19th century (barring any as yet undocumented catastrophic event) its rise must have substantially PRE-DATED the 1800s' (2007, 728). Sankoff and Vincent found that *ne* is very rarely used at all in Montreal; in fact, it is not used in about 99.5 percent of the cases in which it would be required in written French. This same deletion is also found in Continental French with estimates from Paris, where the phenomenon is also advanced, running between 25 and 86 percent for deletions. The deletion phenomenon is much more advanced in Montreal, for among the sixty subjects whose speech was analyzed, the woman who deleted least still realized only 8 percent of the *ne*s required by 'standard' treatments of French. However, *ne* has not disappeared entirely from Montreal French. Its use is characteristic of a certain style or effect that speakers wish to achieve. Sankoff and Vincent observe (1977, 303) that '*ne* appears in contexts where speakers are most likely to be aware of speech itself, and to be monitoring their own speech. The topics of language, instruction, discipline, and religion tend to spirit people back to a normative world in which "proper language" becomes very salient.' When speakers do use *ne*, they also tend to use other forms that are rare in Montreal French, for example, *nous* instead of *on* as a subject; *alors* rather than *donc* as a conjunction; and nonreduced forms of *elle* and *elles*. Sankoff and Vincent claim that *ne* persists in Montreal French as a syntactic and stylistic resource which speakers can employ as they see fit. Although many linguists seem to believe that, when a linguistic change has progressed to the point that *ne* deletion has progressed in Montreal, it is best to regard it as lost altogether, Sankoff and Vincent do not agree, claiming that, even at its present extremely low level of use in Montreal, *ne* still has a function to serve. It is still, therefore, a variable feature of Montreal French. Poplack and St-Amand say that the use of *ne* 'has become a sociolinguistic marker of formality. Interestingly, this change seems to have been driven by women, traditionally the exponents of standard speech … *ne* [being considered] a prestige marker of careful speech' (2007, 726). Today, when you learn French as a foreign language, you learn to use *ne*. You must use it in writing French. However, as you become increasingly skilled in listening to spoken French, you will find that you rarely hear *ne*. Your own *je ne sais pas* is likely to give way to *je sais pas* as you become more and more confident about any 'French' identity you take on as you learn the language.

The well-known first wave studies cited above provided a major part of the basis for variationist work in sociolinguistics and the attention it gave to both social and linguistic factors in accounting for language variation. The following sections will show how this type of work evolved as it added other theoretical perspectives and methodologies.

The Second Wave of Variation Studies

While first wave studies focused primarily on attention to speech as a motivation for variation within one speaker' performance, the **second wave** studies began to focus on speaker agency. While maintaining the centrality of vernacular speech, such studies sought to explain the variation using ethnographically determined social categories and cultural norms.

Social networks in Belfast

The work of the Milroys (Milroy and Milroy 1978, and Milroy 1980, 1987) is credited as the beginning of the second wave (Eckert 2012, 91). It looked at certain aspects of speech in three working-class areas in Belfast, Northern Ireland. The Milroys were able to show how a stable set of linguistic norms emerges and maintains itself in a community. Lesley Milroy calls these **vernacular norms**, norms which are 'perceived as symbolizing values of solidarity and reciprocity rather than status, and are not publicly codified or recognized' (1980, 35–6). These norms contrast with middle-class norms, the ones most of us would view as being characteristic of any wide social standard. Consequently, the Milroys looked at working-class speech in three stable inner-city working-class communities in Belfast. The first was Ballymacarrett, in East Belfast, a Protestant area with little male unemployment (because of the stability provided by work in the local shipyard), close male relationships, and a sharp differentiation between men's and women's activities with men working within the area and women working outside. Second was the Hammer, in West Belfast, also a Protestant area. And, finally, the Clonard, also in West Belfast, a Catholic area. In both the Hammer and the Clonard there was considerable male unemployment (about 35 percent), male relationships were less close than in Ballymacarrett, and there was no sharp differentiation between men's and women's activities. Consequently, both the Hammer and the Clonard neighborhoods exhibited less strong social networks within them than did Ballymacarrett, particularly for males.

The Milroys used a modified participant-observer technique, that is, Lesley Milroy became part of the system she studied, being introduced into it as 'a friend of a friend,' and the analysis is based on data collected from forty-six working-class speakers of both sexes with approximately one-third from each community. Being interested in social networks, the Milroys tried to place each informant on a six-point scale which characterized that person's participation in networks. All speakers did so participate, because each of the communities exhibited a pattern of dense and multiplex ties (see chapter 3 if you need to review these concepts). As indicated in chapter 6, a description of a network as dense refers to the fact that many people share the same social contacts, and multiplex to the fact that people are linked to one another in several ways simultaneously, for example, as kin, neighbors, and colleagues. The Milroys' six-point scale for scoring individual network strength used the following factors: membership in a high-density, territorially based cluster; kinship in the immediate neighborhood; working with at least two people of the same sex from the same area; and voluntary leisure-time association with workmates.

The Milroys examined eight linguistic variables and found significant correlations between network strength and linguistic usage on five of these, two at $p < .01$ (that is, there is less than one chance in a hundred that there is no such relationship) and three at $p < .05$ (i.e., there is less than one chance in twenty that there is no such relationship). The two strongest correlations were with the vowel in words like *hat*, *man*, and *grass* (with the vowel being pronounced rather like that of *father*) and the deletion of the fricative *th* [ð] in *mother* and *brother*. The less strong correlations were with the vowel in words like *pull*, *shove*, and *foot* (with the vowel being pronounced rather like that of *but* and *shut*), and the vowel in either monosyllabic words like *peck*, *bet*, and *went* or in the accented syllables of polysyllabic words like *sécond*.

However, a closer inspection of the results by community showed that, with one exception, it was only in Ballymacarrett that there was a significant correlation between the variables and network strength. The greater the network strength, the greater the incidence of the variants identified with the Belfast vernacular. There was also a significant difference in Ballymacarrett between men and women in their use of the vernacular, with men showing a much greater incidence of vernacular usage. The two other communities showed no similar significant differences between men's and women's usage, both ranking below those found in Ballymacarrett, with one exception: young women in the Clonard seemed to prefer certain vernacular variants and seemed to be in the vanguard of extending vernacular norms into that sub-group.

What we see in these working-class communities in Belfast, then, is that the stronger the social network, the greater the use of certain linguistic features of the vernacular. The results support Milroy's (1980, 43) hypothesis that 'a closeknit network has the capacity to function as a norm enforcement mechanism; there is no reason to suppose that linguistic norms are exempted from this process. Moreover, a closeknit network structure appears to be very common ... in low status communities.' She adds that 'the closeknit network may be seen as an important social mechanism of vernacular maintenance, capable of operating effectively in opposition to a publicly endorsed and status-oriented set of legitimized linguistic norms.' Once again, we see how low-status varieties of a language maintain themselves in the face of heavy competition from 'above': they enable those who use them to show their solidarity with one another and achieve some kind of group identity.

Gender variation in the second wave

A second wave study which exemplifies a focus on linguistic variables in gender variation is Cheshire (1978). This study focuses on the (s) variable in the speech of three groups of boys and girls in Reading, England. The (s) variable in this case is the extension of third-person singular verb marking to all other persons, for example, *I knows, you knows, we has,* and *they calls.* The subjects were thirteen boys and twelve girls aged 9–17. They came from three groups of friends: an all-male group (Orts Road boys), a small group of three boys (Shinfield boys), and an all-female group (Shinfield girls). Members of all groups used nonstandard forms with verbs like *know* and *call* on just over half of the possible occasions for use. They used the nonstandard *has,* for example, *we has,* on about a third of the possible occasions and the nonstandard *does* on just under a quarter of the possible occasions for use. The situation with *do* and *does* is complicated by the fact that the nonstandard *he do* is slightly preferred over *he does.* With *have,* Cheshire found that the *has* form occurred only as a full verb ('We has a muck around in there') or before an infinitive ('I has to stop in') but never as an auxiliary (i.e., 'I have got,' not 'I has got').

Further investigation showed that, if a verb took a finite complement, that is, if it was followed by a clause in which the verb is marked for tense, then there was no use of this -s ending with persons other than third-person singular. Consequently, we find 'Oh, I forget what the place is called' and 'I suppose they went to court' in contrast to 'I just lets her beat me' and 'I knows how to stick in the boot.' Moreover, 'vernacular' verbs, that is, commonly used verbs, like *go, kill, boot,* and *learn,* were much more likely to take the -s ending in all forms than other verbs, to the extent that use of *goes, kills, boots,* and *learns* is almost mandatory with such verbs. Cheshire calls these two conditions 'constraints on usage' and points out that they work in opposite directions. Consequently, a verb stem always takes the -s when it is used in the third-person singular, the -s ending is favored in all persons when the verb is a 'vernacular' verb, but the -s is not used at all if the verb has a complement in which the verb in the complement is marked for tense (Cheshire 1978, 62).

Some social factors operate, too, in the pattern of variation. Cheshire devised an index based on ambition, degree of 'toughness' (as indicated by such things as ability to fight and steal), and peer-group status in order to assess the strength of an individual's membership in the boys' vernacular culture. She found that high frequencies of -s usage went with high index scores and low frequencies with low index scores. Girls' vernacular culture had to be defined differently because the girls had different interests from the boys. Girls used the -s ending as much as boys, but did not exhibit the same correlation between frequency of use and index scores. They also shifted their use of the (s) variable toward Standard English norms in formal situations to a greater extent than the boys. Cheshire concluded (1978, 68) that 'variation is controlled by both social and linguistic factors. In boys' speech, variation is governed by norms that are central to the vernacular culture, and are transmitted through the peer group. Variation in the girls' speech appears to be a more personal process, and less rigidly controlled by vernacular norms.' She added that both boys and girls 'are subject to two linguistic constraints on the form of regular present-tense verbs, of which one favours the use of the non-standard verb form, and the other favours the use of the standard form.' Nonstandard forms are not without their attraction; they are said to have **covert prestige** in contrast to the obvious overt prestige of standard forms. They signal that those who use them have no hesitation in identifying with the local community through laying claim to local loyalties. Not for them the attractions of some other identity, which the use of standard forms might indicate.

Cheshire further observes that 'variation in the forms of *have* and *do* appears to be due to linguistic changes in progress.' In the next chapter we will have more to say on this last point and on how studies of variation have been used to indicate not only how much variation exists in a language, but also how such variation can be interpreted to show changes that are occurring.

Kiesling's research (1998) on the use of the (ng) variable among a small group of fraternity men at a university in the United States shows how it might be possible to account for individual differences in usage. He recorded conversations in a variety of settings and found, predictably, that the use of *-in'* was closely related to the type of activity: 75 percent in socializing, 53 percent in interviews, 47 percent in meetings, and 54 percent in reading aloud. The big difference here is between the first activity and the other three. Kiesling focused on the two extremes in his conversational data, socializing and meetings, and was drawn to try to account for the language behavior of three participants who diverged from the usual pattern of decreasing their use of *-in'* as the social situation became more formal, that is, the difference between casual socializing on the one hand and a formal meeting on the other. He concluded that each of the individuals achieved a personal objective in using *-in'* so frequently: for 'Speed' the use of *-in'* symbolized, among other things, values such as hard work, practicality, and freedom as well as a certain rebelliousness and independence; for 'Waterson' its use was likewise emblematic of hard work but was also an appeal to camaraderie and a claim to shared physical power; for 'Mick' the use of *-in'* made the same claim to hard work but also served as an expression of authority and power. Kiesling says that the (ng) variable is here being used to create identity. Although these men are college students they look to working-class modes of behavior in order to express themselves as 'hard working,' 'rebellious,' 'casual,' or 'confrontational,' and they do this through their language choices.

Jocks and burnouts

Any discussion of the second wave of variationist studies would not be complete without the inclusion of Eckert's work on adolescents in a Detroit suburb, work which will also be featured in the discussion of linguistic change in chapter 8 (Eckert 1989, 2000). Her work in a school she calls 'Belton High,' a predominantly White school, but one which was stratified in terms of socio-economic class, showed how students' use of variants associated with suburban versus urban identities correlated with membership in the categories of 'jocks' or 'burnouts', respectively. These named social categories were evoked by the participants in the study; although not all of the students considered themselves as belonging to one group or the other, they still oriented themselves toward these categories, labeling themselves as 'in-betweens.' While these groups correlated to some extent with social class boundaries – with jocks being the college-bound middle class, and burnouts being the more working-class children destined for blue-collar employment after high school, this correlation did not always hold true. Burnout girls used vowel systems which most strongly indicated an urban orientation, while jock girls used vowel systems which were most firmly associated with suburban norms. Eckert (1989, 1998) discusses this finding in terms of the girls' more limited ability to accumulate symbolic capital in other ways; for instance, there was less opportunity for them to show their jock status through participating in sports, or to show their burnout status by working on cars, which were activities boys dominated. This study shows the use of ethnography not only to ascertain the social categories to be used as variables in the study, but also to interpret the findings of the linguistic analysis.

Exploration 7.3:   Social Categories in High School

Were there named social categories such as 'jocks' and 'burnouts' in your high school? If so, what were the terms used, and what were the criteria for being one or the other? Were there any linguistic practices linked to being in one group or the other?

The Third Wave of Variation Studies

What separates **third wave** from second wave studies is the shift in perspective from investigating how language reflects social identity (often articulated in terms of membership in particular social categories) to how linguistic practices are the means through which speakers position themselves as social beings. How do speakers/hearers link linguistic features to particular social meanings? Moreover, these social meanings are not necessarily – in fact, often not at all – related to traditional macrosocial categories such as race, socio-economic class, age, or gender. There is also an increased focus on the mutability of indexical signs because a particular feature may have more than one social meaning, and may be used to index membership in a particular community, mock members of that community, create alignment or distance with an interlocutor, or position the speaker with regard to a larger ideology, attitude, or belief. Consequently, the social meanings of particular ways of speaking are best viewed as interactionally constructed rather than being somewhat statically associated with particular social groups.

Inherent in the third wave approach to variation is a different perspective on the original idea that focus on speech is the key to variation in an individual's performance. In keeping with more social constructionist ideas about language use, sociolinguists studying variation have noted that there are a range of factors which influence speaker choices about what variants to use, and that variation is more than moving up and down the continuum from formal to informal registers (see Schilling 2013 for a more complete discussion of this).

Exploration 7.4:   Variation in Formality/Standardness

In terms of propositional content, the two utterances *She doesn't have any sense* and *She ain't got no sense* are identical, but they are stylistically quite different. Would you use both of these utterances? If so, in what contexts would one be preferable to the other? Is there a difference in meaning? Is the difference between these two utterances simply level of formality, or do they index other social meanings?

Stance

Much recent research uses the concept of **stance** to look at sociolinguistic variation. Although it should be noted that some researchers focus primarily on stance as a means speakers use to position themselves with regard to the ongoing talk, Kiesling (2009) includes in this concept both orientation to talk and relationship to interlocutors. We can therefore conceptualize stancetaking as how interlocutors position themselves with regard to each other, the form and content of an utterance, and ideologies and macrosocial identity categories (see Jaffe 2009). Variation in language use can thus be analyzed as part of stancetaking in addition to being correlated with social variables such as social class, race, and so on, or social networks.

Reports by Podesva (2004, 2007) on the stylistic variation in the speech of a man called Heath in different settings is illustrative of such third wave research. In these studies, features of Heath's speech (aspiration of intervocalic /t/ and falsetto) are analyzed with regard to their use in the construction of a 'diva' personality in one context, and a competent and educated medical student in another. While Podesva notes that the use of falsetto, in particular, may be part of the construction of a gay identity (2007, 494–6), the analysis focuses on how such features are used interactionally to position the speaker. At different points in a conversation with friends, falsetto is part of the style Heath uses to position himself as someone who cares about fashion and grooming, but it is also part of his maneuvers to regain a powerful position in the conversation.

Another study which exemplifies how style and stancetaking work is Goodwin and Alim (2010). This study combines an analysis of stylistic variation with a multi-modal approach to the study of communication, including non-verbal stylizations such as hand gestures and neck-rolling. The analyzed interaction among a group of preadolescent girls shows how members of a clique use all these modes of communication as acts of social aggression toward a girl who 'tags along' with their group but does not really 'belong.' Goodwin and Alim describe one scene as follows:

> Sarah is admonishing her (upper-middle-class) friends to not try to rip her lunch bag open because she must take it home to recycle. Angela, the tagalong girl, responds to this report with a counter move, "Who cares." In response Sarah dismisses what Angela says, with "Whatever! I don't waste my things," and "Don't tell me anything Angela::. Oh my go:d!" Both "Whatever" and "Oh my god" are language forms appropriated from the film *Clueless*. Such expressions are found in what Carmen Fought describes as a "California dialect," which circulates among youth she terms California "Valley Girls" . .... Girls at Hanley School used this term to refer negatively to hyperfeminine white girls. For example, on seeing a teenage white girl strutting around the playground in a short skirt, Angela commented, "Like-totally, Valley Girl."

> Simultaneously with the Valley Girl talk Sarah produces Ghetto Girl gestures, sucking her teeth, rolling her eyes ... and producing a marked neck roll ... a gesture used by some black women across class lines, but generally stigmatized by dominant culture and used as a gesture to index black working-class women. All the other girls laugh at the caricature that is produced, thus displaying their alignment toward the stance taken by Sarah toward Angela. (Goodwin and Alim 2010, 184)

This is not the only instance in which Sarah, herself a marginal member of the clique, uses multi-modal stylizations to ostracize Angela as an outsider based on her racial and social class categorizations. These depictions of Angela serve to push her further away from the group while propelling Sarah to a more central position, despite her own working-class background which contrasts with the higher socio-economic class backgrounds of the other girls. This pattern of interaction, as Goodwin and Alim (2010, 190) note, is not simply a fleeting insult, but part of the cumulative construction of identity: 'not only do these mocking transmodal stylizations and stance displays accomplish a great deal of interactional work that is consequential in the group's immediate, face-to-face interactions (Sarah's indexing of an oppositional stance and negative positioning of Angela in relation to the peer group), but the performance and repetition of these acts, in conjunction with their broader circulation in popular culture and media, may also have longer lasting consequences, helping to create and reify social identities beyond the peer group.'

While third wave studies tend to move away from the sociolinguistic interview as a data source, work by Schilling-Estes (2004) illustrates that interview data also contains stylistic variation which shows speakers' stancetaking. In these data, a young African American man is interviewing a friend who is a Lumbee Indian, and their use of the /r/ variable varies considerably within the interview. Schilling-Estes' analysis shows that different rates of use can be linked to the speakers' orientation to the topic, their ethnic group membership, and their relationship at different points in the interaction.

In sum, third wave studies move away from primarily describing the correlation between linguistic and social variables and instead focus on **speaker agency**, that is, how speakers actively use variation to position themselves in conversation. Further, instead of focusing on such correlations as a consistent social meaning of a particular way of speaking, third wave studies incorporate an awareness of the **mutability of style**; although variationist studies never assumed that using a particular variant always meant the same thing, in the third wave an emphasis on the different interactional meanings of variation has emerged. This must continue to be balanced with the fact that these meanings are rooted in associations with social groups, speaker roles, and societal norms. Eckert (2008, 472) says in this regard, 'While the larger patterns of variation can profitably be seen in terms of a static social landscape, this is only a distant reflection of what is happening moment to moment on the ground.'

Thus while analyzing the interactionally motivated variation of a conversation, we must also continue to be aware of how language varieties and features index ideologies and social categories – not as fixed and static markers, but as social constructions which are just one path within a larger pattern of social norms and indexical relationships.

Chapter Summary

In this chapter we provide an overview of research within the variationist sociolinguistics paradigm, and present this within the framework of what has been described as three waves of variation studies. We describe the developments in both theoretical underpinnings and methodologies across the course of the last six decades of research.

Exercises

1. Choose any two of the studies reported in this chapter and look at them in detail. (You will need to go back to the original articles.) What do they have in common in their underlying assumptions, designs, and methodologies? Are there any key differences? If you were to attempt to replicate one – or both – of the studies, what changes might you make and why? Are there any additional questions you would like to find answers for? Would you expect the overall results to be any different?

2. Select a television program or film that you are already familiar with to do an analysis of final consonant cluster deletion. Choose a short scene (1–2 minutes) that you feel is important in the plot and character development. Write out (transcribe) the dialogue using standard orthography, and then

identify all of the possible contexts for consonant cluster deletion. Listen to the segment you have selected carefully several times, and note when deletion occurs. Make a table showing these data, and write a short discussion (1–2 pages) of your interpretation of the data. Does a high rate of consonant cluster deletion correlate with a particular social variable, for example, race/ethnicity, gender, age, or socio-economic status? Are there ways in which the use of this variable can be associated with the stance of the speakers in this particular interaction? If there is no or very little consonant cluster deletion, what does this indicate to you about how these particular characters are being portrayed? (Make reference to the findings of earlier studies discussed in this chapter as relevant.)

Further Reading

Cameron, Deborah (1996). The Accents of Politics. *Critical Quarterly* 38(4): 93–6.
> An analysis of the speech of some British politicians; defines and discusses the concept of hypercorrection.

Englebreston, Robert (ed.) (2007). *Stancetaking in Discourse*. (Pragmatics & Beyond New Series). Amsterdam: John Benjamins.
> This collection of studies on stance includes a wide variety of data sets and methodologies, including corpus linguistics, conversation analysis, and interactional sociolinguistics.

Johnstone, Barbara and Dan Baumgardt (2004). 'Pittsburghese' Online: Vernacular Norming in Conversation. *American Speech* 79(2): 115–45.
> A recent study addressing the issue of vernacular norms and how they are created through linguistic practices.

Rickford, John R. and Faye McNair-Knox (1994). Addressee-and Topic-Influenced Style Shift: A Quantitative Sociolinguistic Study. In D. Biber and E. Finegan (eds.), *Sociolinguistic Perspectives on Register*. Oxford: Oxford University Press, 235–76.
> An important second wave study which looks at the role of the addressee in stylistic variation in AAVE.

Trudgill, Peter (1972). Sex, Covert Prestige and Linguistic Change in the Urban British English of Norwich. *Language in Society* 1(2): 179–95.
> An early study discussing the concept of covert prestige and its influence in language use and language change.

Zhang, Qing (2008). Rhotacization and the 'Beijing Smooth Operator': The Meaning of a Sociolinguistic Variable. *Journal of Sociolinguistics* 12: 210–22.
> A third wave variationist study which examines variation in rhotacization as part of the construction of social identities related to gender, social class, and urban personas.

For further resources for this chapter visit the companion website at
 www.wiley.com/go/wardhaugh/sociolinguistics

References

Cheshire, J. (1978). Present Tense Verbs in Reading English. In P. Trudgill, (ed.) *Sociolinguistic Patterns in British English*. London: Edward Arnold.

Eckert, P. (1989). *Jocks and Burnouts: Social Categories and Identities in the High School*. New York: Teachers College Press.

Eckert, P. (1998). Gender and Sociolinguistic Variation. In J. Coates (ed.), *Language and Gender: A Reader*. Oxford: Blackwell, 64–75.

Eckert, P. (2000). *Linguistic Variation as Social Practice: The Linguistic Construction of Identity in Belten High*. Oxford: Blackwell.

Eckert, P. (2008). Variation and the Indexical Field. *Journal of Sociolinguistics* 12(4): 453–76.

Eckert, P. (2012). Three Waves of Variation Study: The Emergence of Meaning in the Study of Sociolinguistic Variation. *Annual Review of Anthropology* 41: 87–100.

Fasold, R. W. (1972). *Tense Marking in Black English: A Linguistic and Social Analysis*. Washington, DC: Center for Applied Linguistics.

Fischer, J. L. (1958). Social Influences in the Choice of a Linguistic Variant. *Word* 14: 47–56. In D. H. Hymes, (ed.) (1964), *Language in Culture and Society: A Reader in Linguistics and Anthropology*. New York: Harper & Row.

Goodwin, M. H. and H. S. Alim (2010). 'Whatever (Neck Roll, Eye Roll, Teeth Suck)': The Situated Coproduction of Social Categories and Identities through Stancetaking and Transmodal Stylization. *Journal of Linguistic Anthropology* 20(1): 179–94.

Jaffe, A. (ed.) (2009). *Sociolinguistic Perspectives on Stance*. Oxford: Oxford University Press.

Kiesling, S. F. (1998). Men's Identities and Sociolinguistic Variation: The Case of Fraternity Men. *Journal of Sociolinguistics* 2(1): 69–99.

Kiesling, S. F. (2009) Style as Stance: Can Stance be the Primary Explanation for Patterns of Sociolinguistic Variation? In A. Jaffe (ed.), *Sociolinguistic Perspectives on Stance*. Oxford: Oxford University Press, 171–94.

Labov, W. (1966). *The Social Stratification of English in New York City*. Washington, DC: Center for Applied Linguistics.

Labov, W. (1972). *Sociolinguistic Patterns*. Philadelphia: University of Pennsylvania Press.

Macaulay, R. K. S. (1977). *Language, Social Class, and Education: A Glasgow Study*. Edinburgh: Edinburgh University Press.

Martineau, F. and R. Mougeon (2003). A Sociolinguistic Study of the Origins of *ne* Deletion in European and Quebec French. *Language* 79(1): 118–52.

Milroy, J. and L. Milroy (1978). Belfast: Change and Variation in an Urban Vernacular. In P. Trudgill (ed.), *Sociolinguistic Patterns in British English*. London: Arnold.

Milroy, L. (1980). Social Network and Language Maintenance. In A. K. Pugh, V. J. Lee, and J. Swann, *Language and Language Use: A Reader*. London: Heinemann Educational Publishers.

Milroy, L. (1987). *Language and Social Networks*. 2nd edn. Oxford: Blackwell.

Podesva, R. (2004). On Constructing Social Meaning with Stop Release Bursts. Presented at Sociolinguistic Symposium 15, Newcastle upon Tyne.

Podesva, R. (2007) Phonation Type as a Stylistic Variable: The Use of Falsetto in Constructing a Persona. *Journal of Sociolinguistics* 11(4): 478–504.

Poplack, S. and A. St-Amand (2007). A Real-Time Window on 19th-Century Vernacular French: The *Récits du français québécois d'autrefois*. *Language in Society* 36: 707–34.

Sankoff, G. and H. Cedergren (1971). Some Results of a Sociolinguistic Study of Montreal French. In R. Darnell (ed.), *Linguistic Diversity in Canadian Society*. Edmonton: Linguistic Research Inc.

Sankoff, G. and D. Vincent (1977). l'emploi productif du ne dans le français parlé à Montréal. *Le Français Modern* 45: 243–56.

Schilling, N. (2013). *Sociolinguistic Fieldwork*. Cambridge: Cambridge University Press.

Schilling-Estes, N. (2004). Constructing Ethnicity in Interaction. *Journal of Sociolinguistics* 8(2): 163–95.

Shuy, R. W., W. A. Wolfram, and W. K. Riley (1968). *Field Techniques in an Urban Language Study*. Washington, DC: Center for Applied Linguistics.

Trudgill, P. (1972). Sex, Covert Prestige and Linguistic Change in the Urban British English of Norwich. *Language in Society* 1: 179–95.

Trudgill, P. (1974). *The Social Differentiation of English in Norwich*. Cambridge: Cambridge University Press.

Trudgill, P. (1986). *Dialects in Contact*. Oxford: Blackwell.

Trudgill, P. (1995). *Sociolinguistics: An Introduction to Language and Society*. 3rd edn. Harmondsworth, England: Penguin Books.

Wolfram, W. (1969). *A Sociolinguistic Description of Detroit Negro Speech*. Washington, DC: Center for Applied Linguistics.

Wolfram, W. and R. W. Fasold (1974). *The Study of Social Dialects in American English*. Englewood Cliffs, NJ: Prentice-Hall.

8

Language Variation and Change

Key Concepts

Language variation as change in progress

Stable variation

The role of speakers in language change

Gender and language change; assumptions about gender roles

Changes in an individual's speech over a lifetime – age-grading

Data collection methods for researching language change

Work in sociolinguistics raises a long-standing question: can linguistic change be observed while it is actually occurring? In modern linguistics the answer to that question has usually been a resounding negative. Following the example of two of the founders of the modern discipline, Saussure (1959) and Bloomfield (1933), many linguists have maintained that change itself cannot be observed; all that we can possibly hope to observe are the consequences of change. However, the kinds of studies we looked at in chapters 6 and 7 show that certain kinds of variation in languages can be related to a variety of social factors. Some investigators have been content merely to demonstrate such relationships. Others have developed a strong interest in trying to show how some of that variation underlies changes that are constantly occurring in languages and that some of these changes also have a clear

An Introduction to Sociolinguistics, Seventh Edition. Ronald Wardhaugh and Janet M. Fuller.
© 2015 John Wiley & Sons, Inc. Published 2015 by John Wiley & Sons, Inc.

direction to them. As we will see in this chapter, studies of how certain kinds of variation relate to language change have given a new impetus to work in historical, that is, diachronic, linguistics and therefore to linguistic theory.

The Traditional View

In what we will call the traditional view of language change, the only changes that are important in a language are those that can be demonstrated to have structural consequences. Consequently, over a period of time a distinction between two sounds may be lost in a language, as occurred historically in most varieties of English in the vowels of *meet* and *meat* or *horse* and *hoarse*. In most dialects these once distinct vowels have fallen together (or coalesced). Alternatively, a distinction may be gained where there was none before, as in *a house* with an [s] but *to house* with a [z], or finally in *thin* and *thing*, the [n] and [ŋ]. In each of these cases a single phonological entity became two: there was a structural split. So we can find instances of **phonemic coalescence**, situations in which a contrast existed at one time but was later lost, and instances of **phonemic split**, situations in which there was no contrast at one time but a contrast developed. According to this view of change, that is all we can really say because it is structural considerations alone that are all-important (i.e., do units A and B contrast or do they not?). Variation is either controlled by circumstances, for example, **allophonic** (as when the *p* in *pin* is aspirated but the *p* in *spin* is not), or it is free, that is, random. Internally motivated change in a language is observed through its consequences.

Such change, of course, is not restricted to phonology. The morphology and syntax of a language change in the same way. It is possible, therefore, to write about **internally motivated language change**, that is, histories of languages showing the structural changes that have occurred over periods of time through use of this principle of 'contrast vs. lack of contrast.'

Externally motivated change

A second kind of change in a language is **externally motivated**. This is change brought about through language contact. Changes that occur through borrowing from other dialects or languages are often quite clearly distinguishable, for a while at least, from changes that come about internally. They may be somewhat idiosyncratic in their characteristics or distribution and appear initially to be quite 'marked' in this way, for example, the *schl* and *schm* beginnings of *Schlitz* and *schmuck*, or *Jeanne* with the *J* pronounced like *zh*. There are often good social or cultural reasons for borrowing, and the items that are borrowed are often cultural borrowings for new entities, for example, *pajamas*, *tea*, *perfume*, and *kangaroo*, or learned or scientific words. It should also be kept in mind that internal and external forces for change may work together. Levey et al. (2013) give an example of this from

Canadian French spoken in the bilingual city of Ottawa: the use of *être comme* as a quotative. Because this use is parallel to that of the English *be like* quotative, it could be possibly be an externally motivated change in progress. However, there are enough differences between the patterns in the use of such quotatives in French and English to indicate that the French use is not a simple translation from English, although the occurrence of the English equivalent may have played a role in encouraging bilingual speakers to use the French construction.

Speakers of different languages may have different views about borrowing. English has a long history of borrowing and most present-day English speakers readily accept loanwords. In some societies, however, borrowing is socially, even politically, stigmatized. France is well known for language purity measures, seeking to keep words such as 'email', 'blog', and, more recently, 'hashtag' out of the language. This prohibitive attitudes includes pundits or columnists railing about the demise of French, but also the French cultural ministry has played a role and its website includes a page where people can suggest French-origin words to replace (mostly English) borrowings which are creeping into the language (see link to this page on our companion website). Elsewhere, the speakers of a language may share a preference for borrowings from particular languages which have social or political desirability. Speakers of Hindi may look to Sanskrit for borrowings, and speakers of Urdu look to Arabic. As we will see in the following section, there is also some borrowing – or spread, at least – of phonological and grammatical items through certain areas, but this phenomenon is much more limited – and undoubtedly much harder to explain – than the borrowing of words to describe objects.

Exploration 8.1:   Borrowing

Can you identify lexical items in your language that are recent borrowings? What language(s) have they been borrowed from? Do they refer to things that are new in your culture, or do they replace words that already exist in your language? What are the attitudes about these loanwords – are they considered 'cool' and modern, or as degeneration of the language – or both?

Of these two kinds of change, internally motivated and externally motivated, historical linguists view the former as being far more important, although contact linguistics (see chapters 4 and 5) has become much more widely studied in the past decades. Both of these kinds of change often evoke negative reactions; people tend to react to the consequences of externally motivated change by complaining about the invasion of foreign words, and to internally motivated changes as degradation of the language. The traditional linguistic approach to change has not been very helpful when controversies have arisen. An approach which says that it is languages that change and not speakers that change languages has little to contribute to a better public awareness of what is happening. In sociolinguistics, we focus on how speakers play a role in language change and the social motivations for these developments.

Trees and waves

The traditional view of language change also favors a **family-tree** account of change and of the relationships among languages. Linguists tend to reconstruct the histories of related languages or varieties of a language in such a way that sharp differentiations are made between those languages or varieties, so that at one point in time one thing (that is, a language itself, or a variety, or even a specific linguistic item) splits into two or more, or is lost. More rarely, there is coalescence. The alternative **wave account of language change** and relationships is much less easy to work with. In this approach the various changes that occur must be seen as flowing into and interacting with one another. It is not at all easy to reconcile the need to find contrasts with the desire to maintain a certain fluidity in boundaries. A variant of this latter view of change is that particular changes diffuse throughout a language, sometimes in rather idiosyncratic ways.

It is in the last view of change, through use of the concepts of **wave** and **diffusion**, that we see the possibilities that the study of variation opens up to us for understanding the process of change. The 'family tree' view focuses on the consequences of change and, particularly, on internally motivated language change. But if we believe that languages are changing all the time – and all linguists do hold that belief – we should also be able to see change in progress *if we can recognize it*. If we can interpret the variation we see, or some of it at least, as a wave of change going through a language, and if we can see changes apparently diffusing through sets of similar linguistic items, we may also want to recast or even abandon the traditional Saussurean and Bloomfieldian view of language. To do so, however, we will have to be sure that what we are observing is change and not just random fluctuation. That will be our major concern in the rest of this chapter.

Some Changes in Progress

Before considering language change, we must distinguish between variation and change, for not all variation is a sign of, or leads to, change. There is what Labov (2001, 85) calls 'long-term **stable variation**,' for example, the distribution of the (ng), (th), and (dh) variables previously discussed and such alternatives as the *ask–aks* alternation, the latter as old as the language. Schools sometimes devote considerable time and effort – very often wasted – in attempts to eradicate nonstandard variants of stable variables (see Wolfram and Schilling-Estes 2005 for examples from

American English). Socio-economic class, age, and gender appear to be the factors that affect the distributions of these variables and they continue to operate over long periods of time. Labov adds that his work in Philadelphia showed that the 'primary determinant of the stable sociolinguistic variables is ... social class: the higher the position of a speaker in the social scale, the smaller ... the frequency of nonstandard forms' (2001, 112). However, Dubois and Horvath (1999, 298) warn that their work among Cajuns in Louisiana showed that a 'set of variables cannot be prejudged to be stable sociolinguistic variables because they happen to be stable in the English language as a whole or even in a surrounding dialect.' What appears to be an instance of a stable linguistic variable may actually be a local innovation.

In contrast, change has a direction, being both progressive and linear. Labov points out that language change can be readily observed today: 'In spite of the expansion and homogenization of the mass media, linguistic change is proceeding at a rapid rate ... so that the dialects of Boston, New York, Chicago, Birmingham, and Los Angeles are more different from each other than they were a century ago' (2001, xii). The problem therefore is one of identifying changes that are occurring and then of trying to account for them: what sets them in motion; how they spread; and how they are maintained. These issues have been his concern in some of his most recent publications (1994, 2001, 2007). A similar focus is exemplified in the two brief examples that follow: the spread of a uvular /r/ across languages in Europe and a vowel merger in US English.

Chambers and Trudgill (1998, 170–5) describe the spread of uvular *r* in western and northern Europe. All the languages of this part of the world once had either an apical (i.e., tongue-tip), trilled, or flap *r*, but from the seventeenth century on a uvular *r* spread from Paris to replace these other varieties. This new *r* crossed language boundaries so that it is now standard in French, German, and Danish, and is also found in many varieties of Dutch, Swedish, and Norwegian. It did not cross the Channel into England, nor has it penetrated into Spain or Italy. What you find, however, when you plot the progress of uvular *r*, is the importance of cities in its spread. Uvular *r* seems to be adopted initially by city dwellers, for example, residents of Bergen and Kristiansand in Norway, The Hague in the Netherlands, Cologne and Berlin in Germany, and Copenhagen in Denmark, and then the new use diffuses outwards. Therefore, the strong internal links in the uvular *r* area are those between cities, which form a kind of network. Apparently, uvular *r* spreads from city to city and later into the countryside surrounding each city.

Bailey (1973, 19) has pointed out that the long-standing distinction between the vowels in such pairs of words as *naughty* and *knotty*, *caught* and *cot*, and *Dawn* and *Don* is disappearing in the western United States. For many young speakers the vowel distinction is almost entirely gone, so that even *hawk* and *hock* are homophonous on many occasions. For older speakers, there may be complete loss of the vowel distinction before *t* followed by a vowel, but there is less likely to be such loss before a word final *t* or *n*, and most such speakers still preserve it in the *hawk–hock* pair, that is, before the velar *k*. There is good reason to believe that this merger is now widespread in North America.

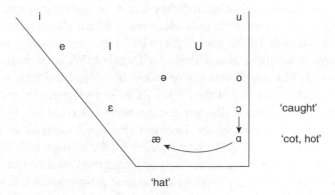

Figure 8.1 The Northern Cities Vowel Shift

The Northern Cities Vowel Shift

Changes in vowel systems are occurring in US English. One ongoing change in the United States is called the Northern Cities Vowel Shift (NCVS), which has lasted several generations and shows no sign of weakening (see Gordon 2002, 254–64). This is a vowel change found in cities settled in a westward movement of people from New York State. It proceeds westward out of the state in a path that includes the cities of Syracuse, Rochester, Buffalo, Cleveland, Toledo, Detroit, Grand Rapids, Chicago, Milwaukee, and Madison. It involves a shift in vowels apparently set in motion by the raising of the vowel in words like *bag* to resemble the vowel in *beg*. The vowel in *hot* fronts to resemble the vowel in *hat* and the vowel in *caught* lowers to resemble the vowel in *cot*, as in figure 8.1, which shows a simplified vowel chart. (For more information on this shift, see the online materials for this chapter for a link to the *Do You Speak* American website, which discusses it.) The NCVS proceeds in a very narrow band as it moves east to west. While its effects are apparent in Detroit, Windsor in Canada across the river is unaffected. Likewise, barely thirty miles to the west of Detroit, Ypsilanti is also largely unaffected because of its large population of migrants from Appalachia. The resultant 'tight Appalachian social network in Ypsilanti serves as an inhibitor to adopting features of the NCS' (Evans 2004, 162).

However, a further study (Evans et al. 2006) did show some acceptance of the NCVS in that area. Appalachian immigrants, particularly young, middle-class women, are taking part in the shift as they become increasingly integrated into the majority speech community. Even some young African American, middle-class women take part in the NCVS: 'they are not linguistically assimilating to the majority surrounding speech norm. Instead, they borrow parts of it as they are seen necessary to social advancement … [they] … are code-switchers' (2006, 195). They continue to identify themselves as African Americans as they 'acquire some aspects of the surrounding majority speech norm, but they do not do it in connection with a loss of home network density … their acquisition … reflects an instrumental rather than integrative motivation and they retain (in the mode popularly known as "code-switching") an ability in the home variety which allows them to maintain local network strength' (2006, 196). Zeller (1997) has described a sound change apparently now in progress in and around Milwaukee, Wisconsin: many speakers pronounce words like *haggle* and *bag* to sound like *Hegel* and *beg*, and *bank* like *benk*. This is another instance of the NCVS. Zeller's investigation showed how it is both age- and gender-related. The younger speakers she recorded, both male and female, have shifted completely and have lost the vowel contrast in such words. Older males and females are also participating in the change with older females leading so that older males are more likely to retain the vowel contrast than older females. The evidence strongly suggests a change in progress: the loss of a contrast in these vowels before a voiced velar stop or nasal.

Change across space: urban centers and physical barriers

All the above are instances of a change diffusing through space (see Britain 2002 for a general discussion). Density of population and the influence of large popula-tion centers appear to be important factors. This gravity model of diffusion holds that large, culturally important cities influence smaller cities they dominate and eventually changes filter down to surrounding rural areas through even smaller towns and communities. A change may even spread directly from one city to another, leapfrogging, as it were, for a while at least, smaller intervening communi-ties. The actual scale may vary, for it is the relative densities of the various places that are important not their absolute size, that is, city > town > village, with later filling of gaps. For example, Britain (2002, 612–16) describes how in the Fens of England such a model explains the diffusion pattern in an area in which there are only two towns, King's Lynn and Wisbech, with populations over 20,000 and only fourteen miles apart. These towns influence the areas that surround them because of the road, rail, and waterway infrastructure and the social services they provide to rural residents. There is actually a dialect divide between the two areas because there are still physical barriers to prevent spatial diffusion.

A physical barrier such as a river or a range of hills can prevent diffusion. (Of course, a river can also become an axis for diffusion.) National boundaries may also act as barriers. The NCVS meets a national boundary in Detroit; it does not cross the river to Windsor in Canada. Boberg has shown that so far as vowel systems are concerned, 'Windsor is just as Canadian as Toronto' (2000, 13). Chambers (2003) points to one very interesting consequence of a national border as a barrier to dif-fusion. He reports that even though children in southern Ontario (and Toronto) may call the final letter of the alphabet 'zee' for a while (influenced no doubt by pre-school television broadcasts originating in the United States), they give up this pronunciation for 'zed' by the time they reach adulthood and this 'declining use of "zee" as people grow older repeats itself in succeeding generations' (2003, 207). A triumph of Canadian identity over gravity!

Change over time or age-grading?

In some of the examples just cited the factor of age seems to be important: younger speakers are observed to use the language differently from older speakers. We might consider such differential use as offering us the key we seek if we want to understand how languages change. Surveys which show age-related differences are usually **apparent time** studies. In such studies, the differences between older speakers and younger speakers is thought to indicate changes in progress. Older speakers' speech reflects the language they used when they were young, so the differences between that and how young people speak today may reflect language changes.

However, not all differences between older and younger speakers are necessarily the result of change. We must be sure that we are not dealing with the phenomenon of **age-grading**, that is, of using speech appropriate to your age group, features which you may no longer use when you are older. How can we be sure that in each of the examples given above the younger people will not change their linguistic ways as they get older, with those changes being in the direction of the use of the groups which are presently described as being older? The just cited use of 'zee–zed' in Canada is clearly an instance of age-grading.

We might consider two other possible cases of age-grading. Miller (2004) reports on a kind of age- and gender-specific speech, *kogyaru*, of certain Japanese adolescent girls called Kogals. Used along with types of dress, hair styling, make-up, and behavior (largely anti-social), this way of speaking establishes group identity. Kogals use certain slang words (e.g., *bakkure* 'play innocent'), some special prefixes (e.g., *mecha kyûto na* 'awesomely cute'), truncated forms (e.g., *mendoi* from *mendokusai* 'pain in the ass' and *maku-ru* 'go to McDonalds') as well as Japanese-English hybrids like *ikemen* from *iketeru* 'cool' and *men* 'men.' They 'party', are assertive, often denigrate boys and men, and are considered to be 'impertinent, vulgar or indecent, egocentric, lacking manners, absurd or devoid of common sense, garish, and without perseverance' (2004, 238). They are, therefore, entirely the opposite of the image of Japanese women as 'repositories of restraint, docility, modesty, and elegance' (2004, 242). The interesting issues here are whether Kogals will persist in such behavior as they get into their 30s and 40s, and whether others adopt their ways, thus spreading *kogyaru* to other social groups.

The second set of examples involves an English usage, the quotative *like*, and there is considerable and growing literature on the topic (see, for example, Dailey-O'Cain 2000, Tagliamonte and D'Arcy 2004, 2007, Barbieri 2005, 2008, and Buchstaller 2006, 2008). Examples of this construction are: 'I'm *like* – give me a break!', 'We're *like* – can't you do it for us?', 'She's *like* – you can't do that!', and 'It's *like* – now I don't know!' This usage is now found throughout North America, in England, and in other English-speaking countries. Tagliamonte and D'Arcy (2007) looked at its use in Toronto. They found the greatest use and range of uses among adolescent girls but both men and women up to the age of 40 also provided instances. They concluded that although *like* usage in Toronto appears to be age-graded, the evidence suggests that *like* was adopted by people while they were adolescents and as the usage caught on these same people increased their own use of it. Those who later adopted *like* increased their range of uses. They suggest that their findings show that this is an instance of a language change in progress rather than just merely one of age-grading.

Exploration 8.2:   Youth Language

Are there certain ways of speaking (pronunciation, vocabulary, or grammatical constructions) that you associate with people older than you, or younger than you? Name some current slang expressions; what would you think if your parents used these expressions? Your professors? What about if your friends *don't* use them? Are these terms that you think you will continue to use as you grow older, so are they part of language change, or things you will abandon, that is, an instance of age-grading? Why?

There are two possible ways of trying to answer the question 'Is this an instance of age-grading or one of a genuine change in progress?' The first way is to survey the same younger people twenty to thirty years later when they become middle-aged to see if they maintain the innovations and really stay quite unlike the present older people; this would be a **real-time panel study**. If there was no change in behavior we could be sure that we had eliminated age-grading as an explanation. The second way is to survey carefully chosen samples drawn from the same population at periods of twenty to thirty years to see if comparable groups have changed their behavior; this would be a **real-time trend study**. As Eckert (1997, 153) says:

> Community studies of variation frequently show that increasing age correlates with increasing conservatism in speech. With just the evidence from apparent time, it is ambiguous whether the language patterns of the community are changing over the years or whether the speakers are becoming more conservative with age – or both. Without evidence in real time, there is no way of establishing whether or not age-stratified patterns of variation actually reflect change in progress.

(See also Bailey et al. 1991, Chambers 2003, 212–25, Chambers and Trudgill 1998, 149–51, and Labov 1994, 76–7, for various points of view on these issues.)

Martha's Vineyard

One study which was able to make use of roughly comparable sets of data from two periods of time is Labov's study (1963) of certain sound changes in progress on

Martha's Vineyard. In this work Labov found that the survey conducted for the *Linguistic Atlas of New England* thirty to forty years before provided him with rich sources of data about the phenomena in which he was interested. The data collection methods of the two surveys, the *Linguistic Atlas* survey and Labov's, differed, but it was possible for Labov to make allowances for these differences in order to achieve the necessary measure of comparability. Although Labov would have preferred to have worked with sound recordings, that possibility did not exist. (However, it does now for future work.)

Martha's Vineyard is a small island lying three miles off the coast of Massachusetts. At the time of Labov's investigation it had a small permanent population of about 6,000 people, but each summer many more thousands came to stay for varying periods of time. Most of the permanent residents lived in the eastern part of the island, the Down-island part, but this area was also the one most favored by the summer visitors. The western part of the island, the Up-island part, was still quite rural with its center Chilmark. The permanent population consisted of Yankees, Portuguese, and Native Americans. The Yankees were descendants of early settlers; the Portuguese were fairly recent newcomers in comparison with the Yankees but had been on the island for several generations; the Native Americans, who lived on a remote headland, Gay Head, were descended from the original occupants of the island.

Labov concentrated his attention on the way those who had grown up on Martha's Vineyard (what we will call 'natives' to this location) pronounced the vowels in the two sets of words: *out, house,* and *trout* and *while, pie,* and *night.* He observed that the first parts of the diphthongs in such words were being centered: [aU] to [əU] and [aI] to [əI], with that centering more noticeable in the first set of words than in the second. He called the variable in the first set the (aw) variable ([aU] or [əU]) and the variable in the second set the (ay) variable ([aI] or [əI]). He set out to collect a large quantity of (aw)s and (ay)s to find out who used the variants of each. He plotted his findings from his sixty-nine natives of Martha's Vineyard on various graphs to examine the relationships between the degree of centralization and such factors as age, ethnicity, occupation, and place of residence. The survey conducted in the 1930s for the *Linguistic Atlas of New England* provided Labov with data for the earlier linguistic situation on the island.

By age level, Labov (1972, 22) found the distribution of the centralized variants shown in figure 8.2. This figure shows that centralization is most obvious in the 31–45 age group. The change was also a little more advanced in those of Yankee descent than among those in the other two groups with which Labov was concerned, but not by much. It was more advanced among those who made a living from fishing than among those who worked in occupations and businesses serving the summer visitors. It was also much more typical of Up-island speech, particularly around Chilmark, the center of the fishing industry, than Down-island speech. The change was therefore most advanced in people in their thirties and early forties who were fishermen living in the Up-island area.

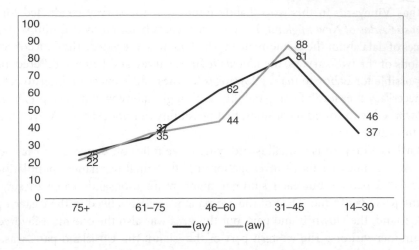

Figure 8.2   Degree of centralization of (ay) and (aw) by age level on Martha's Vineyard

The explanation that Labov offers is that the change was merely an exaggeration of an existing tendency to centralize the first part of the diphthong. This exaggeration is particularly characteristic of those who identified most closely with the island. At the time of the survey for the *Linguistic Atlas*, it appeared that this centralizing tendency was being eliminated. It was virtually extinct in (aw) and in only moderate use in (ay). What had happened apparently was that, instead of eliminating the tendency, residents exaggerated it to show their solidarity and their difference from the summer population. The more you identified with the island, the more you centralized the first part of the diphthong. As Labov says (1972, 36): 'When a man says [rɜit] or [hɜus], he is unconsciously establishing the fact that he belongs to the island: that he is one of the natives to whom the island really belongs.' As further evidence of this fact, Labov divided his informants into three groups according to their feelings about the island: positives, negatives, and neutrals. He found a very striking relationship between such feelings and centralization (1972, 39), as figure 8.3 shows.

If we go back to the original distinction by age, which showed the 31–45 age group in the vanguard of this change, we can see that it is they who had most to gain by identifying with the island. Many of the young were still ambivalent in their feeling: some wanted to leave (and were not inclined to centralize) and some wanted to stay (and did centralize). The very old followed older ways, which did not involve as much centralization. But a person between 31 and 45 was likely to have had to come to terms with life quite recently. That coming to terms quite often meant staying on Martha's Vineyard and showing that commitment by exaggerating centralization, even to the extent of pushing centralizing in (aw) to surpass that in (ay). There was also some evidence that those who had been to the mainland and had returned to the island to live were among the strongest centralizers. Centralization indicated 'Islander' status and local loyalty and solidarity. It had also been fixed on

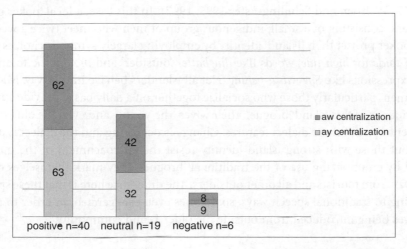

Figure 8.3 Degree of centralization and orientation toward Martha's Vineyard

by the Portuguese and Native Americans, but in their case as marking some kind of equality with the Yankees. Here we can quite clearly see the social motivation of a sound change; in this case, the change is one motivated by a desire to show loyalty to a particular place and solidarity with the people who live there.

Blake and Josey (2003) replicated Labov's study forty years later and, in doing so, took 'into account recent methodological and theoretical developments, both acoustic and social, that have been incorporated into sociophonetic studies' (2003, 452): specifically, they measured formant frequencies and used the **VARBRUL** statistical package. They found that Martha's Vineyard had become an even more popular recreational destination so that the locals had become almost entirely dependent on tourism. Fishing had declined in importance. As they became wealthier, the locals no longer sought to separate themselves from tourists and /ay/ lost its earlier meaning as a local social identifier. Locals are now willing to sound just like tourists.

Pope et al. (2007) also followed up Labov's study of speech on Martha's Vineyard, again some forty years after the original study. Their main purpose was to see the extent to which an apparent-time study which showed a change in progress could be interpreted as also showing a real change in progress. They concluded that 'for variables that lack any strong social index (normally because they are below the level of conscious awareness), inferences for change in progress that have been drawn on the basis of apparent-time data have proved very robust' (2007, 625). However, the actual rate of change may vary, as it did in this case, having speeded up over the forty-year period. (The article also includes a brief discussion of some of the issues involved in attempting to replicate such a study, that is, of trying to 'step into the same river twice.')

A situation similar to the one Labov found in Martha's Vineyard in the 1960s exists still on Ocracoke Island off the coast of North Carolina (Wolfram 1997,

116–17, Wolfram and Schilling-Estes 1995, 1997). In this case, a local 'poker game network' consisting of a small, indigenous group of men who meet twice a week to play poker project their 'island' identity by employing largely symbolic choices such as *hoi toide* for *high tide*, words like *dingbatter* 'outsider' and *mommuck* 'to annoy', and expressions like *She was a-fishing*. Not all islanders behave in this way. Middle-aged men, particularly those who socialize together on a daily basis, provide strongest evidence of this island 'brogue'. Their wives, the young, and even the old are less frequent users of these dialect features. Change is occurring and the dialect is being lost, but those with strong island identity resist the encroachment of the outside world by emphasizing use of the traditional 'brogue'. They mark themselves off in this way from tourists and all other outsiders. The difference here is that these speakers cling to traditional speech ways, sometimes even exaggerated, in order to resist changes being introduced from outside the older island community.

Gender and language change

One generalization that has been made is that changes toward more vernacular forms tend to be led by men, while changes toward the standard tend to be led by women (Romaine 2003) (see below for a discussion of change from above and below, as Labov has called such directions of change). One early study which showed such a pattern is Trudgill's (1972) work in Norwich, England. He offers (1972, 182–3) several possible explanations for women using forms associated with the prestige standard more frequently than men. He suggests that women may be more status-conscious because they are less secure and have less well-developed social networks than men. Their social position is usually inferior to men and they are usually subordinate to them. Men are also judged by what they do, whereas women are rated on how they appear, and an important part of that appearance is their speech. Women have a much greater need to use language to signal their social status than do men. Another important factor in this differential usage is that working-class speech has connotations of 'masculinity' and women often want to dissociate themselves from it for that reason, preferring types of speech which they consider to be markedly more refined. Consequently, Trudgill devoted a considerable part of his research effort to investigating working-class speech and what he calls the 'hidden values associated with non-standard speech [which may be] particularly important in explaining the sex differentiation of linguistic variables' (1972, 183).

Trudgill employed a self-evaluation test to find out what residents of Norwich thought about speech in the city. He asked his informants whether or not they used certain pronunciations and compared the responses they gave him with the actual pronunciations that his informants used. He reports on three variables: (er) as in *ear, here, idea*; (ō) as in *road, nose, moan*; and (ā) as in *gate, face, name*. His findings are shown in table 8.1. In that table 'overreporting' refers to informants claiming to use a prestige variant more often than they are actually observed to use it;

Table 8.1 Percentages of informants overreporting and underreporting variants in Norwich

	(er)			(ō)			(ā)		
	Total	Male	Female	Total	Male	Female	Total	Male	Female
Overreport	43	22	68	18	12	25	32	22	43
Underreport	33	50	14	36	54	18	15	28	0
Accurate	23	28	18	45	34	57	53	50	57

Source: based on Trudgill (1972, 187). Reproduced by permission of Cambridge University Press

'underreporting' is, of course, the opposite. The percentages show that for two of the variables, (er) and (ā), speakers in Norwich overreport their usage; they under-report (ō). However, although the percentages differ for each variable, in all three cases men tend to underreport and women tend to overreport their usages. A further analysis showed that both middle-class and working-class speakers produced very much the same levels of under- and overreporting, so the phenomenon appears to be gender-linked rather than social-class-linked. The same kinds of results appeared when people were asked to make judgments about two pronunciations of *better* ([bɛtə] or [bɛʔə]); in this case, women showed a stronger preference than men for the former, more standard pronunciation.

Trudgill maintains that linguistic changes away from the standard norms are led by men from the upper working class and middle working class, at least in Norwich. In the working class, too, young females aged 10–29 underreported their use in some cases, particularly on the (ō) variable. His general conclusion, therefore, is that nonstandard working-class speech forms are highly valued by males, and by females under 30, but these values are expressed covertly rather than overtly; that is, people may tell you they do one thing but they actually do something else. Trudgill emphasizes that, though it may be correct that in certain communities middle-aged middle-class women and the young are in the forefront of change toward the standard norm, 'in Norwich, at least, there appears to be a considerable number of young WC [working-class] men marching resolutely in the other direction' (1972, 194). They find a certain **covert prestige**, their own form of solidarity, in such behavior. (For somewhat similar behavior among young people in Japan, see Haig 1991.)

Cheshire's (1978) finding in Reading, England, that lower-class boys use more nonstandard syntax than lower-class girls, further supports the thesis that change may be motivated by a desire for identity and solidarity. The 'tougher' the boy, the more nonstandard his use of the -*s* ending on verbs in the present tense. Boys who were not regarded as tough produced a lesser incidence of such nonstandard use. With girls, the more conformist to middle-class values, the lesser the incidence of -*s* endings where they are not found in Standard English. What Reading boys appear to have done is take a particular nonstandard usage in their language, one that actually has a long history in the local dialect but a history which shows that it is being replaced by the usage found in Standard English, and make it into a solidarity marker.

We might actually argue that what we see here is not so much a change in progress but an unconscious resistance to a change being brought in from Standard English. Lacking real-time data, that is, evidence concerning the same phenomenon gathered at two distinct points in time, we cannot be absolutely sure that we are seeing no more than the latter. Cheshire herself acknowledges such a possibility, being prepared to go no further than to say (1978, 58) that: 'Patterns of variation in the forms of the present tense *have* and *do* show that variation in the use of these forms may reflect on-going linguistic changes in the morphology of the verbs.' She adds that whatever change has occurred, it has apparently progressed further with *have* than with *do*.

Another study which grapples with the intertwined issues of gender, language change, and standard language use is Haeri (1994, 1996), which looks at **palatalization** in Cairene Arabic. She distinguishes between weak palatalization in which dental stops are pronounced as **fricatives**, and strong palatalization, in which these sounds are pronounced as **affricates**. She shows evidence that this palatalization is a change in progress, and that women are very clearly leading the change. While upper-class and upper middle-class women use more weak palatalization, which she believes was the first step of the changes in progress, middle middle-class and lower middle-class women have the highest rates of strong palatalization. When looked at in terms of the type of school attended, private versus public, there seems to be a strong tendency for this factor to trump class assignment, as those who attended private schools use more weak palatalization, while those who attended public school use more strong palatalization. Thus there are clear correlations of this linguistic feature with both gender and social class as defined by educational background.

However, another issue here is whether this represents the use of more standard speech. As there is a diglossic situation in Egypt (see chapter 4 to review the discussion of diglossia), Classical Arabic is seen as the high language and Egyptian Arabic as the low language. Palatalization is not a feature of Classical Arabic, so the use of palatalized dental stops is in some sense a change away from the standard language. However, there also exists Standard Egyptian Arabic, and it is this variety that is spoken in Cairo, the nation's capital. Thus, while this innovation is less standard in terms of its relationship to Classical Arabic, it is at the same time part of the regional standard. Haeri does not discuss the specific reasons why women in this society would be the perpetrators of language change, but simply notes that this finding is in keeping with other studies showing women leading linguistic innovation.

There have been many criticisms of some of the interpretations of women's role in language variation and change. Eckert (1989b, 247) notes,

... there is no apparent reason to believe that there is a simple, constant relation between gender and variation. Despite increasingly complex data on sex differences in variation, there remains a tendency to seek a single social construction of sex that will explain all of its correlations with variation . .... This perspective limits the kind of results that can be obtained, since it is restricted to confirming the thesis of a single type of sex effect or, worse, to indicating that there is no effect at all.

As pointed out by Romaine (2003), one basic criticism of general interpretations about sex and language change is of the underlying premises about the nature of sex categories and the nature of language: 'This approach has limited explanatory power since it starts with the categories of male and female and social class as fixed and stable givens rather than as varying constructs themselves in need of explanation' (Romaine 2003, 109). Other problems with assumptions about women's language as reflecting their desire for prestige noted by Romaine include (1) they ignore the role of, and access to, education in the use of standard language features; (2) there is a lack of focus on standard language as something acquired and used in interactions with people outside one's own social (i.e., social class or ethnic) group; (3) they tend not to recognize that women may be norm-makers, that is, linguistic forms become more prestigious when they are used by women; and (4) they do not consider that women may not be seeking out prestigious forms as much as avoiding stigmatized ones. In short, it is overly simplistic to simply attribute to women the motivation of wanting to achieve prestige through standard language. She advocates the use of social networks instead of sex- or class-based categories, and paying attention to ideologies of masculinity and femininity when we attempt to interpret gender variation. We will continue to look at issues of gender in the next section which introduces the concept of the linguistic marketplace.

Language change and the linguistic marketplace

Linguistic marketplace forces may also be at work here: what do individuals want and what will they accept or reject linguistically to satisfy these wants? As the introduction to Bourdieu (1991, 57) says:

> Linguistic utterances or expressions are always produced in particular contexts or markets, and the properties of these markets endow linguistic products with 'value.' On a given linguistic market, some products are valued more highly than others; and part of the practical competence of speakers is to know how, and to be able, to produce expressions which are highly valued on the markets concerned.

The linguistic marketplace refers to how language is used in the give-and-take of social interaction. Language is not just a neutral medium of exchange; its uses take on symbolic value. Some uses are highly valued and others are not. These values are assigned through the various power relationships that exist. RP in England had (and may still have) a high symbolic value. Standard English is more highly valued than nonstandard varieties, at least in many public domains; for ingroup interactions, nonstandard ways of speaking may be more highly valued (see above discussion of covert prestige). High language forms are valued highly in diglossic situations and low language forms are valued not at all. Traditionally, male language uses have been valued more highly than female language uses. (There are many other such market-places that we are involved in as humans, for example, accommodations, dress, food and drink preferences, choices of entertainment, and so on.) As we will see in chapter 14, proponents of critical discourse analysis question the legitimacy of the power relationships that exist in all of the above and argue that sociolinguists should do more than just report on them, as to do so is to offer them tacit support.

Labov (1981, 184), in keeping with research mentioned above, points out that, whenever there is stratification by style and class in linguistic usage, you can also expect differences between men and women, with women showing higher values for preferred variants than men, that is, a preference for forms that have more pres-tige in society. He adds the following corollary: '[it is] important to bear in mind that this shift of women toward higher prestige forms … is limited to those societies where women play a role in public life.' He points out that studies in Tehran and India showed a reverse tendency. Apparently, then, if a woman's status is fixed unal-terably, she has no motivation to change linguistically; only in a society in which status can be changed does the necessary motivation exist. Returning to the just mentioned concept of the 'linguistic marketplace,' we can say that in such cases there are simply no market pressures to change so the status quo is maintained.

Eckert (1989b) suggests that instead of prestige, a better concept for addressing such trends is to look at power relations. She writes,

> So whereas economic explanations focus on the marketplace, they attribute gender differences in language to social forces that could presumably continue to operate on the individual speaker regardless of his or her personal relation to the economy. Since actual power relations between men and women can be expected to lag behind (indeed perhaps be orthogonal to) changes in relative positions in the marketplace, one can expect such a dynamic in language to outlive any number of economic changes. One might argue that the socioeconomic hierarchy, in this case, is the least of women's problems, since their powerless position is brought home to them, in a very real sense, in every interaction. Women's inequality is built into the family, and it continues in the workplace, where women are constantly confronted with a double bind, since neither stereotypic female nor stereotypic male behavior is acceptable. Thus, one might expect that some gender differences in language are more resistant to small-scale economic differences. In particular, the common claim that women are more expres-sive with language (Sattel, 1983) resides in deeper differences than the vagaries of the local economy. (Eckert 1989b, 255)

Another perspective on gender and language, in this case language choice and language shift, is given in a seminal study by Gal (1978, 1979). This body of work focuses on how the inhabitants of Oberwart, a Hungarian enclave in Austria since 1921, shifted from a pattern of stable bilingualism in German and Hungarian to the sole use of German, with young women in the forefront of the change. As Oberwart, about 100 kilometers south of Vienna, grew from a village of 600 to a town of over

5,000 inhabitants, the indigenous bilingual population decreased as a fraction to about a quarter of the total, and many of these, at the time of Gal's research in the community, were peasant farmers. German had become the language of social opportunity and social status, and it was the young women from the bilingual community who showed the most willingness to participate in social change. Hungarian was symbolic of peasant status, and most young people did not want to be peasants. Young bilinguals wanted to pass as monolingual Germans, and children of a bilingual parent and a monolingual German-speaking parent did not learn to speak Hungarian, thus contributing to language shift to German in the region.

An analysis of language use in Oberwart shows that Hungarian was most likely to be used by older people in networks involving many peasant contacts. As the number of peasant contacts and the age of the participants decreased, the amount of German used increased. At the time of Gal's study, and even more so today, German is used in more situations in which Hungarian was once used, and it is used more and more, even by older bilinguals. Young men with strong peasant networks still used Hungarian a great deal, but young women with similar strong peasant networks used German even within these networks. They rejected the use of Hungarian, for it was a clear indicator of peasant status in the community. Young peasant women also preferred not to marry peasant men. They preferred non-peasant, German-speaking workers as spouses. However, the effect of this was that bilingual peasant men married German-speaking peasant women from neighboring villages. The offspring of both kinds of marriage were German-speaking children. It was, therefore, the young women's desire to participate in the social change occurring in Oberwart, and to seek the higher status which the use of German alone seemed to offer, that hastened the change from bilingualism to monolingualism in the community.

What we have seen in all of the above studies are attempts made to isolate the kinds of changes that appear to be occurring in specific places. A close examination of the social context of each change also reveals the particular segment of the community which is most involved in that change and possible motivation for the involvement. These motivations can be various: to try to be like a 'higher' social group or less like a 'lower' one; to mark yourself off from 'outsiders'; to achieve a feeling of 'solidarity' with others; or to react to the pressures of the 'linguistic marketplace.' Women may be more active participants than men in some changes, but the situation may be reversed in others. Although the young are usually in the vanguard of most changes, in some it is the not-so-young who lead. In the next section we will look more closely at the issue of motivation and the actual process of change.

The Process of Change

Labov (1981) has pointed out how difficult it is to get the right kinds of data on which to base claims about linguistic change in progress and how easy it is to make either false claims or incorrect predictions, giving several instances of the latter from

Switzerland, Paris, and Philadelphia (1981, 177–8). He stresses the importance of having good data on which to base claims. Such data can come from studies of a community conducted at different times. However, it is often the case that only a single study is done and the different responses of various age groups are compared and conclusions drawn about changes. As discussed above, such studies are apparent-time studies and ideally require real-time confirmation. Since linguistic usage tends to vary according to the age of the individual, such age-grading must also be taken into account, as we saw, for example, with reference to Canadian uses of 'zee' and 'zed.' Hibya (1996) showed how real-time data can confirm apparent-time data. He was interested in the denasalization of the velar nasal stop in Tokyo Japanese, that is, the use of [g] for [ŋ]. When the data are analyzed by birth year of the research participants, there is an almost completely linear decrease in such use from older speakers to younger ones. But is the loss age-graded? Hibya also had recordings made thirty to forty years earlier of speakers aged between 60 and 80 at that time. Those who would have been over 80 in 1986 showed virtually 100 percent use of [ŋ]. Since in 1986 60- to 80-year-old speakers used [ŋ] between 10 and 40 percent of the time, the change to [g] is confirmed as a real change.

Labov insists that the best studies of change in progress look for different kinds of data sources, are very much concerned with assessing the accuracy of these sources, and are quite cautious in the claims they make. However, he adds that careful surveys of the current state of affairs also enable 'a good deal of the past [to] be reconstructed from the present if we look into the matter deeply enough' (1981, 196). That is, the relationship between **diachronic** (historical) matters and **synchronic** (descriptive) ones is a two-way relationship. There is what Labov calls a 'dynamic dimension' to synchronic structure, so that the past helps to explain the present and the present helps to explain the past.

Change from above and below

After conducting a number of investigations of sound changes in progress, Labov (1972, 178–80) suggests that there are two basic kinds of change: **change from below**, that is, change from below conscious awareness, and **change from above**, that is, change brought about consciously. (Labov says (2006, 203) that in retrospect it might have been clearer for others if he had used the terms *change from within* for *change from below*, and *change from without* for *change from above*.) Change from below is systematic, unconscious change, whereas change from above is sporadic, conscious, and involves issues of prestige. Since change from above is conscious change, we might expect such change to involve a movement toward standard linguistic norms. Change from above may not actually be initiated within the highest social group in society. This group is a kind of reference group to groups lower down in the social scale, and it is among these groups, particularly slightly lower ones, that such change begins. Change from below is unconscious and away from existing norms. As mentioned above, some observers believe that in societies such as ours women may be in the vanguard of the first kind of change and men in the vanguard of the second, because women and men have different motives. In this view, women are motivated to conform to, and cooperate with, those who are socially more powerful, whereas men are more inclined to seek solidarity with peers. Women, therefore, consciously look 'up,' whereas men do not, preferring instead, though they may not be conscious of it, the solidarity they find in the 'masculinity' and 'toughness' of peers and even of those they regard as being 'below' them in society. However, recent work by Labov in Philadelphia (2001) would suggest that such a view is much too simplistic.

It is Labov's view (1994, 23) that 'cities have always been at the center of linguistic innovation.' He decided, therefore, to examine the situation in Philadelphia to see if he could further clarify how and where change begins. He chose Philadelphia because 'it appeared that almost all of the Philadelphia vowels were in motion' (1980, 254–5). He was particularly interested in the fronting and raising of (aw) in words like *out* and *down*, the fronting and raising of (ey) in checked syllables in words like *made* and *pain*, and the centralization of (ay) before voiceless consonants in words like *right* and *fight*. Labov's data came from a telephone survey of the whole city together with intensive network studies of the speech behavior of thirty-six individuals in a few selected neighborhoods. He found that 'the speakers who are most advanced in the sound changes are those with the highest status in their local community … [have] the largest number of local contacts within the neighborhood, yet … [have] the highest proportion of their acquaintances outside the neighborhood' (1994, 261). In Philadelphia the leaders in change were upper working-class women, and men lagged by a generation. He concluded (1994, 262):

> The identification of the innovators of these sound changes allows us to rule out some of the explanations that have been offered in the past for the phenomenon of sound change. Their advanced social position and the high esteem they hold in the local community rule out the traditional charge of careless ignorance of the norms of society. Their reputation as vigorous and effective users of the language, combined with the nature of the vowel shifts themselves, makes any discussion of the principle of least effort beside the point. The central position that they hold in local networks of communication gives new life to the principle of local density, though we cannot project any discontinuity between these speakers and the exponents of the upper middle-class standard that they are leaving behind in their development of local sound changes. Once we are willing to refine our notion of prestige to give full weight to the local prestige associated with the Philadelphia dialect … we must be ready to recognize that such a local prestige, which appears primarily in behavior and rarely in overt reactions, is powerful enough to reverse the normal flow of influence, and allow the local patterns to move upward to the upper middle class and even to the upper class.

Labov's general conclusion (2001) is that the changes that occur essentially arise from the nonconformity of certain upwardly mobile individuals who influence others to adopt their behavior, thus affecting the behavior of the wider community. He also comments on how different segments of society may respond differently in situations of language change. In these data, these conclusions are valid only for Philadelphia and then only for the speech of non-Blacks there. Blacks do not use this vowel system at all, preferring instead that of African American English (AAE). According to Labov, the non-Black vowel system in Philadelphia gains much of its vitality from recent immigration to the city, with an accompanying renewed emphasis on local identification and assertion of local rights and privileges, together with a resistance to allowing the large Black population to have its share of opportunities in the city. He suggests that the future direction of change in the vowel system in Philadelphia will depend very much on social changes that are occurring in the city.

Social network theory and language change

The Milroys (Milroy 1992, and Milroy and Milroy 1992) are two other linguists who are interested in how change begins. For them the key lies in network ties: with strong ties change is slow but weak ties can lead to rapid change. New forms are adopted by innovators with weak ties to more than one group. Some of these innovations are taken up by core members of the groups. Change results. Milroy and Milroy (1992, 9) say that 'groups linked internally mainly by relatively weak ties are susceptible to innovation' and add that 'innovations between groups are generally transmitted by means of weak rather than strong network ties (e.g., through casual acquaintances rather than kin, close friends, or workmates).' They point out (1992, 17) that their conclusion that change begins therefore in the middle of the social-class hierarchy 'is entirely consistent with Labov's finding that innovating groups are located centrally in the class structure, characterized by him as upper-working or lower-middle class. … For in British and American society at least, close-knit, territorially based, kin-oriented networks are located most clearly in the lowest classes, but upper-class networks are in some respects structurally similar, being relatively dense.' Marshall's work (2004) in northeast Scotland also showed that the most revealing factor in determining how individuals changed their speech behavior was the group to which they oriented: 'Those with the most positive orientation to the local rural group resist change.' He adds that those 'who have a higher degree of mental urbanisation, or an attitude of openness to supra-local norms, … are at the forefront of change' (2004, 217).

Many observers have noted the weakening of network ties as social and geographic mobility increased in the late twentieth century. Social contacts increased but became shallower. One consequence for language has been the fairly rapid spread of innovation. Some changes, for example, new slang words, are ephemeral. Others, like accent change, produce more lasting effects. In England the old regional dialects have been much affected. Local varieties adopted linguistic features from influential centers, often with women, particularly younger women, in the vanguard. The results have been the creation of various non-localized norms interposed between the local vernaculars to which many older and less educated speakers still cling and standard RP, itself gradually atrophying.

Exploration 8.3:   Mobility and Language Change

If you have ever moved from one place to another, have you noticed differences in how people talk in one location compared to another? How do you orient yourself to these differences? If you adapt to a new way of speaking associated with a particular location, what are the advantages and disadvantages of changing your way of speaking?

Lifestyle and language change

Eckert's findings (1988, 1989a, 1991, 2000, 2004) from her study of what she calls 'jocks' and 'burnouts' in an almost exclusively White suburban Detroit high school add a further perspective to the study of language change with the concept of **lifestyle**. Jocks are either middle-class students or students with middle-class aspirations, and burnouts are either working-class students or students who wish to identify themselves as such. Jocks tend to be college-bound and white-collar-oriented; burnouts will leave school for the blue-collar workplace. Jocks willingly participate in the activities of the school; burnouts find activities outside school more attractive. We must note that only about one-third of the students readily identified themselves as either jocks or burnouts but the majority leaned one way or the other, although they might describe themselves as 'in-betweens.' In general, on the linguistic variables that were examined (Eckert and McConnell-Ginet 1999), girls ranged far more widely than boys. That is, the difference between jock and burnout girls was greater than that between jock and burnout boys. It would appear that, linguistically, girls were required to do more than boys, that is, to adopt more extreme behaviors in order to establish their places. They developed different practices within the communities within which they functioned. As Eckert says (2000, 35), 'A community of practice is an aggregate of people who come together around some enterprise. United by this common enterprise, people come to develop and share ways of doing things, ways of talking, beliefs, values – in short, practices – as a function of their joint engagement in activity.' The jocks and burnouts had entirely different communities of practice and norms of behavior.

The jock–burnout allegiance was clearly some kind of ideological allegiance which did not align with social class or gender lines. Eckert found that burnouts were much more active than jocks in participating in the NCVS, with the most burned-out burnouts clearly in the lead. They see themselves as part of the developing local urban landscape and are linguistically engaged in it. Jocks, on the other hand, have a wider horizon but also one that leads them to linguistic conservatism. Eckert (2000, 1–2) comments as follows: 'Ultimately, the social life of variation lies in the variety of individuals' ways of participating in their communities – their ways of fitting in, and of making their mark – their ways of constructing meaning in their own lives.' Variation arises from what individuals do with the language as they attempt to come to terms with their surroundings. Mendoza-Denton (2008) found a similar ideological underpinning to the behavior of the Norteñas and the Sureñas in her study of Latina girl groups in a California high school.

Lexical diffusion

Whenever a change begins and whatever its causes, it is not an instantaneous event for the language as a whole. It has to establish itself. A number of linguists (see Wang 1969, 1977) have proposed a theory of change called **lexical diffusion**. According to this theory, a sound change spreads gradually through the words in which the change applies. For example, a change in vowel quality is not instantaneous, affecting at some specific point in time all words in which that vowel occurs, as if you went to bed one night with vowel quality A in those words and got up next morning with vowel quality B. Instead, only some words that have the vowel will be affected initially, then others, then still others, and so on until the change is complete.

According to this view, change does not proceed at a uniform rate throughout the affected vocabulary. Instead, there is an S-curve effect. That is, there is an initial period of slow change in which as few as 20 percent of the relevant words undergo the change, then a shorter period of time of rapid change in which about 60 percent of the affected words show the change, and a final period, again of much the same length as the initial period, in which all or most – there is often a residue – of the remaining 20 percent of relevant words show the change.

This hypothesis allows us to make certain predictions. If a sound change is observed to be occurring in less than a quarter of a set of words which have the necessary conditions for changes, we are probably witnessing the beginning of the process or, of course, the end if the rest of the words already show the change to have occurred. If individual speakers vary in the pronunciation of the words in question with a large proportion pronouncing most of the words one way, an equally large proportion pronouncing most of the words the other way, and a third, but smaller, proportion showing a more even distribution of choices, then we have a change in progress and that change has reached its mid-point. If we plot the distributions of the pronunciations of the individual vocabulary items by individual speakers, we will see much the same phenomenon if there is a change in progress; for example, if it is a sound change, some words will be pronounced by almost everyone with the change, some others without the change, again by almost everyone, and another set will show both variants. This results again in an S-shaped pattern of change.

Labov's view of lexical diffusion is that it has only a very limited role to play in change. He says (1994, 501), 'There is no evidence … that lexical diffusion is the fundamental mechanism of sound change.' It happens but is only a complement – and a small one at that – to regular sound change. The most important factors in linguistic change appear to be long-standing trends in the language, internal variation, and social forces among speakers. These interact and the result is change. According to Labov, the key problem in explaining that change is ascertaining the relevant data in both language and society, and then integrating the resulting observations into a theory of change which will allow us to see how and why change is occurring and plot its course.

Much of Labov's recent work has focused on such issues. In some of that work (2007) he has also tried to sharpen the difference between what he calls the **transmission** of change and the **diffusion** of change. He proposes that 'the contrast between the transmission of change within languages and diffusion of change across languages is the result of two different kinds of language learning … transmission is the product of the acquisition of language by young children … [and] … the limitations of diffusion are the result of the fact that most language contact is largely between and among adults' (2007, 349).

The last three chapters have summarized some major ideas and findings in the study of variationist sociolinguistics, including how the topics of power, solidarity, identity, gender, and social class can be linked to speaker style, dialect, and language development. In the following chapters, we will revisit all of these topics and present other ways of studying them within the field of sociolinguistics.

Chapter Summary

This chapter expands on chapters 6 and 7 and looks at how variation can lead to language change. We review some general ideas about how language change occurs, and then look at research variationist sociolinguists have done on changes in progress, including studies which focus on the role of women in language change. We discuss methodological issues, returning to the concept of apparent time brought up in chapter 7, and also address how social network theory can be used to analyze language variation and change.

Exercises

1. Make a questionnaire which looks at language variation in your region; some sample survey questions for US English are given below. Have a minimum of ten people complete the survey, including at least five in each of two distinct age groups. Are there any patterns that indicate that language change is in progress? If there are differences between the two age groups, what evidence might there be that this is not age-grading? If age is not the variable that explains variation in the answers you got, do you have hypotheses about what other social factors might correlate with different linguistic patterns?

   Questionnaire (thanks to Matthew J. Gordon for these questions)
   - What do you call drinks such as Coca-Cola, Sprite, Dr Pepper?
   - Do you pronounce these two words the same, close, or different? Don, Dawn

- Do you pronounce these two words the same, close, or different? Pen, Pin.
- Is this sentence acceptable in your spoken dialect? 'The car needs washed.'
- Is this sentence acceptable in your spoken dialect? 'He may could arrive today.'
- Is this sentence acceptable in your spoken dialect? 'It sure is hard to tell boys from girls anymore.'
- What do you call rubber sandals that are held on by a strap between your big toe and second toe?
- Is this sentence acceptable in your spoken dialect? 'I did it on accident.'
- What do you call the evening meal?

2. This exercise is most efficiently done in small groups of four to six people. First, your group should discuss what the cultural patterns of surnames are in your culture; for instance, in some cultures traditionally women take the names of their husbands and the children are given this name as well; in other cultures children may be given family names from both parents. Before collecting data, you should discuss some of the local practices in assignment of last names.

Each group member should collect data on the family names of about ten people within three generations of a family; because of the nature of the data we are seeking, they must be people who have children. (You may use your own family if you choose and have information about enough people.) Note the birth names of people, if these names changed if they married, and what the family names given to the children were. Also, compile social information about these people: if they are male or female; their ages; if they married and, if so, at what age; how old they were when they had children; their occupations; how they identify in terms of socio-economic class; their political affiliations; their race/ethnicity; and their nationality.

Do you see changes across time in practices concerning family names? Pool the data with others in your group to see if you can identify social factors which correlate with different naming practices.

Further Reading

Auer, Peter, Frans Hinskens, and Paul Kerswill (eds.) (2005). *Dialect Change: Convergence and Divergence in European Languages*. Cambridge: Cambridge University Press.
This book presents case studies of dialect change across Europe, looking at methodological and social issues in the changes of dialects in contact in England, Germany, Italy, and Scandinavia.

Chambers, Jack K. and Natalie Schilling (eds.) (2013). *The Handbook of Language Variation and Change*. 2nd edn. Oxford: Wiley-Blackwell.
This updated volume addresses issues in data collection and methodology and analysis of change (both internally and externally motivated) in phonology, syntax, and discourse structures and its relationship to social stratification.

Juan Manuel Hernández-Campoy and Juan Camilo Conde-Silvestre (eds). (2012). *The Handbook of Historical Sociolinguistics*. Oxford: Wiley-Blackwell.

Focusing more on the processes of language change, but also incorporating factors such as socio-demographic variables and language attitudes, this book complements the Chambers, Trudgill, and Schilling book to provide a thorough treatment of the social process of language change.

Wagner, Suzanne E. (2012). Age Grading in Sociolinguistic Theory. *Language and Linguistics Compass* 6(6): 371–82.

This review article summarizes the issues and research on the phenomenon of age-grading, looking at definition of the term and the range of linguistic features which have been found to change over time.

For further resources for this chapter visit the companion website at

 www.wiley.com/go/wardhaugh/sociolinguistics

References

Bailey, C.-J. N. (1973). *Variation and Linguistic Theory*. Washington, DC: Center for Applied Linguistics.

Bailey, G., T. Wikle, J. Tillery, and L. Sand (1991). The Apparent Time Construct. *Language Variation and Change* 3: 241–64.

Barbieri, F. (2005). Quotative Use in American English. *Journal of English Linguistics* 33(3): 222–56.

Barbieri, F. (2008). Patterns of Age-Based Linguistic Variation in American English. *Journal of Sociolinguistics* 12(1): 58–88.

Blake, R. and M. Josey, (2003). The /ay/ Diphthong in a Martha's Vineyard Community: What Can We Say 40 Years after Labov? *Language in Society* 32: 451–85.

Bloomfield, L. (1933). *Language*. New York: Henry Holt.

Boberg, C. (2000). Geolinguistic Diffusion and the US–Canada Border. *Language Variation and Change* 12: 1–24.

Bourdieu, P. (1991). *Language and Symbolic Power*. Cambridge, MA: Harvard University Press.

Britain, D. (2002). Space and Spatial Diffusion. In J. K. Chambers, P. Trudgill, N. Schilling-Estes (eds.), *The Handbook of Language Variation*. Oxford: Blackwell.

Buchstaller, I. (2006). Social Stereotypes, Personality Traits, and Regional Perception Displaced: Attitudes Towards the 'New' Quotatives in the UK. *Journal of Sociolinguistics* 10(3): 362–81.

Buchstaller, I. (2008). The Localization of Global Linguistic Variants. *English World-Wide* 29(1): 15–44.

Chambers, J. K. (2003). *Sociolinguistic Theory: Linguistic Variation and its Social Significance*. 2nd edn. Oxford: Blackwell.

Chambers, J. K. and P. Trudgill (1998). *Dialectology*. 2nd edn. Cambridge: Cambridge University Press.

Cheshire, J. (1978). Present Tense Verbs in Reading English. In P. Trudgill, (ed.), *Sociolinguistic Patterns in British English*. London: Edward Arnold.

Dailey-O'Cain, J. (2000). The Sociolinguistic Distribution and Attitudes Toward Focuser *Like* and Quotative *Like*. *Journal of Sociolinguistics* 4(1): 60–80.

Dubois, S. and B. Horvath (1999). When the Music Changes, You Can Change Too: Gender and Language Change in Cajun English. *Language Variation and Change* 11(3): 287–313.

Eckert, P. (1988). Adolescent Social Structure and the Spread of Linguistic Change. *Language in Society* 17: 183–207.

Eckert, P. (1989a). *Jocks and Burnouts: Social Categories and Identities in the High School*. New York: Teachers College Press.

Eckert, P. (1989b). The Whole Woman: Sex and Gender Differences in Variation. *Language Variation and Change* 1: 245–67.

Eckert, P. (1991). Social Polarization and the Choice of Linguistic Variants. In P. Eckert (ed.), *New Ways of Analyzing Sound Change*. New York: Academic Press.

Eckert, P. (1997). Age as a Sociolinguistic Variable. In F. Coulmas (ed.), *The Handbook of Sociolinguistics*. Oxford: Blackwell.

Eckert, P. (2000). *Linguistic Variation as Social Practice: The Linguistic Construction of Identity in Belten High*. Oxford: Blackwell.

Eckert, P. (2004). Variation and a Sense of Place. In C. Fought (ed.), *Sociolinguistic Variation: Critical Reflections*. New York: Oxford University Press.

Eckert, P. and S. McConnell-Ginet (1999). New Generalizations and Explanations in Language and Gender Research. *Language in Society* 28: 185–201.

Evans, B. (2004). The Role of Social Network in the Acquisition of Local Dialect Norms by Appalachian Migrants in Ypsilanti, Michigan. *Language Variation and Change* 16: 153–67.

Evans, B. E., R. Ito, J. Jones, and D. R. Preston (2006). How to Get One Kind of Midwesterner: Accommodation to the Northern Cities Chain Shift. In T. E. Murray and B. L. Simon (eds.), *Language Variation and Change in the American Midland*. Amsterdam: John Benjamins.

Gal, S. (1978). Peasant Men Can't Find Wives: Language Change and Sex Roles in a Bilingual Community. *Language in Society* 7: 1–16.

Gal, S. (1979). *Language Shift: Social Determinants of Linguistic Change in Bilingual Austria*. New York: Academic Press.

Gordon, M. J. (2002). Investigating Chain Shifts and Mergers. In J. K. Chambers, P. Trudgill, N. Schilling-Estes (eds.), *The Handbook of Language Variation*. Oxford: Blackwell.

Haeri, N. (1994). A Linguistic Innovation of Women in Cairo. *Language variation and change* 6(1): 87–112.

Haeri, N. (1996). *The Sociolinguistic Market of Cairo: Gender, Class, and Education*. London: Kegan Paul International.

Haig, J. H. (1991). A Phonological Difference in Male–Female Speech among Teenagers. In S. Ide and N. H. McGloin (eds.), *Aspects of Japanese Women's Language*. Tokyo: Kurosio.

Hibya, J. (1996). Denasalization of the Velar Nasal in Tokyo Japanese. In G. R. Guy, C. Feagin, D. Schiffrin, and J. Baugh (eds.), *Towards a Social Science of Language: Papers in Honour of William Labov*. Amsterdam: John Benjamins.

Labov, W. (1963). The Social Motivation of a Sound Change. *Word* 19: 273–309. In W. Labov (1972), *Sociolinguistic Patterns*. Philadelphia: University of Pennsylvania Press.

Labov, W. (1972). *Sociolinguistic Patterns*. Philadelphia: University of Pennsylvania Press.

Labov, W. (1980). The Social Origins of Sound Change. In W. Labov (ed.), *Locating Language in Time and Space*. New York: Academic Press.

Labov, W. (1981). What Can Be Learned about Change in Progress from Synchronic Description? In D. Sankoff and H. Cedergren (eds.), *Variation Omnibus*. Edmonton: Linguistic Research Inc.

Labov, W. (1994). *Principles of Linguistic Change, I: Internal Factors*. Oxford: Blackwell.

Labov, W. (2001). *Principles of Linguistic Change, II: Social Factors*. Oxford: Blackwell.

Labov, W. (2006). *The Social Stratification of English in New York City*. 2nd edn. Cambridge: Cambridge University Press.

Labov, W. (2007). Transmission and Diffusion. *Language* 83(2): 344–87.

Levey, S., K. Groulx, and J. Roy (2013). A Variationist Perspective on Discourse-Pragmatic Change in a Contact Setting. *Language Variation and Change* 25(2): 225–51.

Marshall, J. (2004). *Language Change and Sociolinguistics: Rethinking Social Networks*. Basingstoke: Palgrave Macmillan.

Mendoza-Denton, N. (2008). *Homegirls*. Oxford: Blackwell.

Miller, L. (2004). Those Naughty Teenage Girls: Japanese Kogals, Slang, and Media Assessments. *Journal of Linguistic Anthropology* 14(2): 225–47.

Milroy, J. (1992). *Language Variation and Change*. Oxford: Blackwell.

Milroy, L. and J. Milroy (1992). Social Networks and Social Class: Toward an Integrated Sociolinguistic Model. *Language in Society* 21: 1–26.

Pope, J., M. Meyerhoff, and D. R. Ladd (2007). Forty Years of Language Change on Martha's Vineyard. *Language* 83(3): 615–27.

Romaine, S. (2003). Variation in Language and Gender. In J. Holmes and M. Meyerhoff (eds.), *The Handbook of Language and Gender*. Oxford: Blackwell.

Sattel, Jack W. (1983). Men, Inexpressiveness, and Power. In Barrie Thorne, Cheris Kramarae, and Nancy Henley (eds.), *Language, Gender, and Society*. Rowley, MA: Newbury House, 119–24.

Saussure, F. de (1959). *Course in General Linguistics*. New York: McGraw-Hill.

Tagliamonte, S. and A. D'Arcy (2004). *He's like, she's like*: The Quotative System in Canadian Youth. *Journal of Sociolinguistics* 8(4): 493–514.

Tagliamonte, S. and A. D'Arcy (2007). Frequency and Variation in the Community Grammar: Tracking a New Change through the Generations. *Language Variation and Change* 19: 199–217.

Trudgill, P. (1972). Sex, Covert Prestige and Linguistic Change in the Urban British English of Norwich. *Language in Society* 1: 179–95.

Wang, W. S.-Y. (1969). Competing Changes as a Cause of Residue. *Language* 45: 9–25.

Wang, W. S.-Y. (ed.) (1977). *The Lexicon in Phonological Change*. The Hague: Mouton.

Wolfram, W. (1997). Dialect in Society. In F. Coulmas (ed.), *The Handbook of Sociolinguistics*. Oxford: Blackwell.

Wolfram, W. and N. Schilling-Estes (1995). Moribund Dialects and the Endangerment Canon: The Case of the Ocracoke Brogue. *Language* 71: 696–721.

Wolfram, W. and N. Schilling-Estes (1997). *Hoi Toide on the Outer Banks: The Story of Ocracoke Brogue*. Chapel Hill: University of North Carolina Press.

Wolfram, W. and N. Schilling-Estes (2005). *American English: Dialects and Variation*. 2nd edn. Oxford: Blackwell.

Zeller, C. (1997). The Investigation of a Sound Change in Progress. *Journal of English Linguistics* 25(2): 142–55.

Part III
Language and Interaction

He [Lord Macaulay] had occasional flashes of silence,
that made his conversation perfectly delightful.

Sydney Smith

My never-failing friends are they,
With whom I converse day by day.

Robert Southey

And, when you stick on conversation's burrs,
Don't strew your pathway with those dreadful urs.

Oliver Wendell Holmes

Part III

Language and Interaction

9
Ethnographic Approaches in Sociolinguistics

Key Concepts

Participant observation

Communicative competence and background knowledge

Rules for everyday interactions

The relationship between macro and micro in ethnographic analyses

---

An underlying assumption in sociolinguistics is that much of communication is directed toward keeping an individual society going; that is, an important function of communication is social maintenance. More recent views hold that language (along with other cultural behavior) does more than just that; it serves to construct and sustain social reality. Thus, the goals of sociolinguistics are not merely to understand the tacit rules and norms of language use that are culturally specific, but should encompass understanding how societies use language to construct those very societies

One broad approach to researching the rules, cultural norms, and values that are intertwined with language use is **ethnography**. Ethnographic research is generally carried out through **participant observation**. Ethnographies are based on first-hand observations of behavior in a group of people in their natural setting. Investigators report on what they see and hear as they observe what is going on around them. As Duranti (1997, 85) says, 'an ethnography is the written description of the

An Introduction to Sociolinguistics, Seventh Edition. Ronald Wardhaugh and Janet M. Fuller.
© 2015 John Wiley & Sons, Inc. Published 2015 by John Wiley & Sons, Inc.

social organization, social activities, symbolic and material resources, and interpretive practices characteristic of a particular group of people.' Ethnographers ask themselves what is happening and they try to provide accounts which show how the behavior that is being observed makes sense within the community that is being observed. As Johnstone (2004, 76) says, ethnography 'presupposes … that the best explanations of human behavior are particular and culturally relative' rather than general and universal. Such studies are also **qualitative** rather than quantitative. In ethnographies of speaking the focus is on the language the participants are using and the cultural practices such language reflects.

Canagarajah (2006, 155) observes that: 'Ethnographers expect to live for an extensive period of time in the community they are studying in order to capture first-hand its language patterns and attitudes. As much as possible, they try not to alter the "natural" flow of life and social relationships of the community, but understand how language works in everyday life.' They are participant-observers and must deal with the basic conundrum of participant observation, which Trusting and Maybin (2007, 578–9) explain as follows: 'Ethnographic work normally requires the researcher to be actively involved in the social action under study, suggesting that this generates insights which cannot be achieved in any other way. But the involvement of the researcher in social action inevitably changes the language practices under study.' This issue may also become more and more important as differences increase between the linguistic and cultural backgrounds of the observer and the observed. It is certainly one that must be confronted by both those who publish ethnographies and those who read them. Mendoza-Denton (2008, 48) addresses this issue directly near the beginning of her ethnographic study of teenage Latina girl groups in a California high school:

> No ethnographer is a blank notepad just as no linguist is a tape recorder. The perceptual filters that we bring to fieldwork situations are powerful indeed, and not always conscious. You will read in the following chapters an account that is my interpretation of years of fieldwork and research with a group of young people who allowed me into their lives, and I will invite you to draw your own conclusions. I have been and will be providing guideposts to show where my ethnographic interpretation might be guided by factors such as my background, social class, and my own subjective and affective reactions to people around me and to events at the time.

She constantly reminds us in her report of the circumstances in which she collected her data and of her involvement in the process.

Three illustrative book-length ethnographic studies are those of Sherzer (1983), Hill and Hill (1986), and Mendoza-Denton (2008). Sherzer describes how the Kuna of Panama use language: their public language of the gathering house, and their use of language in curing and music, in rites and festivities, and in everyday conversation. He points out that the Kuna wait very patiently to take their turns in speaking so that interruptions and overlaps in conversation are rare events.

Hill and Hill describe how the Malinche of Central Mexico use language in their daily lives and in their continuing struggle to preserve their linguistic and cultural identity. Spanish is constantly encroaching on their own language so they have deliberately tried to maintain certain of its features in an almost 'purist' way.

Mendoza-Denton (2008) offers an account of Latina gangs in a California high school. She calls the school, which is located in the San Francisco Bay area, Sor Juana High School. She describes the students as a mixture of well-to-do Euro-Americans, African Americans, Pacific Islanders, Asians, Asian-Americans, and Latinas/Latinos. She was particularly interested in this last group, especially the girls. She focused her research on the Norteñas and the Sureñas, two rival Latina gangs. She studied these groups in depth, having become over a period of time the confidant of members of both groups. She found a strong ideological divide between the groups. The Norteñas were 'northern'-oriented, preferred to speak English, wore red accessories and red lipstick, 'feathered' their hair, favored Motown Oldie music and the numbers XIV, 14, and 4, and, though Hispanic, were mainly US-born. In contrast, the Sureñas were 'southern' (i.e., more Mexican)-oriented, preferred to speak Spanish, wore blue accessories and brown lipstick, ponytailed their hair, favored Mexican bands, pop music, and the numbers XIII, 13, and 3, and were mainly recent immigrants. Mendoza-Denton shows how the members of each group express and reinforce their identities through their various practices and some of the linguistic consequences of such behavior. For example, she found that the preferred use of English or Spanish sometimes concealed a very good knowledge of the dispreferred other language, and that certain linguistic features of Spanish varied according to strength of commitment to the gangs. Mendoza-Denton's study ranges over a wide variety of issues and is a mine of suggestions and insights.

It is important to remember, however, that these studies represent the results of lengthy and time-consuming ethnographic projects. It is also possible to do smaller-scale studies using participant observation, focusing on very specific types of inter-actions in a group and particular linguistic features. For example, a seminal work by Frake (1964) focuses on how to ask for a drink; while this study makes uses of the author's extensive knowledge of the culture, it is illustrative of how a narrowly focused question about linguistic behavior can lead to an insightful analysis of cultural norms. Another important early study by Mitchell-Kernan (1972) discusses particular ways of speaking among some African Americans referred to as 'marking' and 'signifying,' focusing on how cultural knowledge is needed to interpret certain types of implied meanings. A third study which shows this specific focus is Basso (1970), who discusses the meanings of silence in Western Apache. Students wishing to do ethnographic research should note that although a deep understanding of the cultures is necessary for the interpretation of the data in all cases, focusing on very specific elements of communication helps to constrain the scope of these projects.

In the rest of this chapter, we will outline three ethnographic approaches which have been part of the field of sociolinguistics. The first, ethnography of communica-tion, is the main focus of this chapter, as it is by far the most influential and long-standing use of ethnographic concepts and methodologies in the discipline of sociolinguistics. We will also briefly cover ethnomethodology, which we will then take up again in chapter 11 when we delve more deeply into a type of discourse analysis called conversation analysis, which is derived from ethnomethodology. Finally, we will outline the approach called linguistic ethnography, which is a more recently introduced approach in sociolinguistics.

Exploration 9.1:   Cultural Norms in Idioms

In English, we have sayings about how people use language that reveal certain attitudes about language and particular types of speakers. For instance, we say 'Children should be seen and not heard' and 'Loose lips sink ships.' There is a clear trend of sayings which value silence as well as discretion, as in 'Speech is silver, silence is golden' and 'Still waters run deep' (however, linguist Rick Hallett has reported that his grandmother would extend this idiom as follows: ' . . . and are damn dirty, and the devil lies at the bottom.') What idioms do you know about language, in English or any other language? What do they imply about the role of language in society or the desired linguistic behavior of (particular groups of) speakers?

The Ethnography of Communication

As discussed in chapter 1, the study of language involves more than just describing the syntactic composition of sentences or specifying their propositional content. Sociolinguists are interested in the various things that people *do* with that language.

Communicative competence

The term **communicative competence** (introduced in chapter 1) is sometimes used to describe the knowledge of how to use language in culturally appropriate ways. This term was suggested by Hymes (1972) as a counter-concept to Chomsky's linguistic competence, which focused on an ideal hearer-speakers' knowledge of grammaticality of sentences in their native language. Hymes maintained that knowledge of a language involved much more than that. Gumperz (1972, 205) explains the term as follows: 'Whereas linguistic competence covers the speaker's ability to produce grammatically correct sentences, communicative competence describes his ability to select, from the totality of grammatically correct expressions available to him, forms which appropriately reflect the social norms governing behavior in specific encounters.'

Working with an ethnographic or functional approach, we may attempt to specify just what it means to be a competent speaker of a particular language. It is one thing to learn the language of the Subanun, but quite another to learn how to ask for a drink in Subanun (see Frake 1964, mentioned above and discussed in more detail below). To do the first you need a certain linguistic competence; to do the latter you need communicative competence. As Saville-Troike (1996, 363) says:

> Communicative competence extends to both knowledge and expectation of who may or may not speak in certain settings, when to speak and when to remain silent, whom one may speak to, how one may talk to persons of different statuses and roles, what nonverbal behaviors are appropriate in various contexts, what the routines for turn-taking are in conversation, how to ask for and give information, how to request, how to offer or decline assistance or cooperation, how to give commands, how to enforce discipline, and the like – in short, everything involving the use of language and other communicative dimensions in particular social settings.

Hymes (1972, 279) has argued that, in learning a language, children not only must learn how to construct sentences in that language but also must 'acquire knowledge of a set of ways in which sentences are used. From a finite experience of speech acts and their interdependence with sociocultural features, they develop a general theory of the speaking appropriate in their community, which they employ, like other forms of tacit cultural knowledge (competence), in conducting and interpreting social life.' Hymes provides some examples of the kinds of learning that are involved:

> They come to be able to recognize, for example, appropriate and inappropriate interrogative behavior (e.g., among the Araucanians of Chile, that to repeat a question is to insult; among the Tzeltal of Chiapas, Mexico, that a direct question is not properly asked (and to be answered 'nothing'); among the Cahinahua of Brazil, that a direct answer to a first question implies that the answerer has not time to talk, a vague answer, that the question will be answered directly the second time, and that talk can continue).

In learning to speak we are also learning to communicate in ways appropriate to the group in which we are doing that learning; this is sometimes called **language socialization**. These ways differ from group to group; consequently, as we move from one group to another or from one language to another, we must learn the new ways if we are to fit into that new group or to use that new language properly. Communicative competence is therefore a key component of social competence.

A famous study which focuses on communicative competence is found in Frake (1964); it outlines kinds of speech used in drinking encounters among the Subanun of the Philippines. Such encounters are very important for gaining prestige and for resolving disputes. Frake describes how talk, what he calls 'drinking talk,' proceeds in such encounters, from the initial invitation to partake of drink, to the selection of the proper topics for discussion and problems for resolution as drinking proceeds competitively, and finally to the displays of verbal art that accompany heavy, 'successful' drinking. Each of these stages has its own characteristics. Those who are the most accomplished at drinking talk become the *de facto* leaders among the Subanun because successful talk during drinking may be used to claim or assert social leadership. Success gives one a certain right to manipulate others, because it is during such talk that important disputes are settled, for example, disputes which in other societies would have to be settled in the courts. Thus it is clearly not enough to merely be adept at the grammar of the language; you also have to understand the social appropriateness of different constructions. A framework for the systematic study of how talk is used in certain societies is presented in the next section.

SPEAKING

Hymes (1974) has proposed an ethnographic framework which takes into account the various factors that are involved in speaking. An ethnography of a communicative event is a description of all the factors that are relevant in understanding how that particular communicative event achieves its objectives. For convenience, Hymes uses the word SPEAKING as an acronym for the various factors he deems to be relevant. We will now consider these factors one by one (see also the link in our companion website to a short video explaining this acronym).

The **setting and scene** (S) of speech are important. Setting refers to the time and place, that is, the concrete physical circumstances in which speech takes place. Scene refers to the abstract psychological setting, or the cultural definition of the occasion. The Queen of England's Christmas message has its own unique setting and scene, as has the President of the United States' annual State of the Union Address. A particular bit of speech may actually serve to define a scene, whereas another bit of speech may be deemed to be quite inappropriate in certain circumstances. Within a particular setting, of course, participants are free to change scenes, as they change the level of formality (e.g., go from serious to joyful) or as they change the kind of activity in which they are involved (e.g., begin to drink or to recite poetry).

The **participants** (P) include various combinations of speaker–listener, addressor–addressee, or sender–receiver. They generally fill certain socially specified roles. A two-person conversation involves a speaker and hearer whose roles change; a 'dressing down' involves a speaker and hearer with no role change; a political speech involves an addressor and addressees (the audience); and a telephone message involves a sender and a receiver. A prayer obviously makes a deity a participant. In a classroom, a teacher's question and a student's response involve not just those two as speaker and listener but also the rest of the class as audience, since they too are expected to benefit from the exchange.

Ends (E) refers to the conventionally recognized and expected outcomes of an exchange as well as to the personal goals that participants seek to accomplish on particular occasions. A trial in a courtroom has a recognizable social end in view, but the various participants, that is, the judge, jury, prosecution, defense, accused, and witnesses, have different personal goals. Likewise, a marriage ceremony serves a certain social end, but each of the various participants may have his or her own unique goals in getting married or in seeing a particular couple married.

Act sequence (A) refers to the actual form and content of what is said: the precise words used, how they are used, and the relationship of what is said to the actual topic at hand. This is one aspect of speaking in which linguists have long shown an interest, particularly those who study discourse and conversation, and it is one about which we will have more to say in the next two chapters. Public lectures, casual conversations, and cocktail party chatter are all different forms of speaking; with each go different kinds of language and things talked about.

Key (K), the fifth term, refers to the tone, manner, or spirit in which a particular message is conveyed: light-hearted, serious, precise, pedantic, mocking, sarcastic, pompous, and so on. The key may also be marked non-verbally by certain kinds of behavior, gesture, posture, or even deportment. When there is a lack of fit between what a person is actually saying and the key that the person is using, listeners are likely to pay more attention to the key than to the actual content, for example, to the burlesque of a ritual rather than to the ritual itself.

Instrumentalities (I) refers to the choice of channel, for example, oral, written, signed, or telegraphic, and to the actual forms of speech employed, such as the language, dialect, code, or register that is chosen. Formal, written, legal language is one instrumentality; spoken Newfoundland English is another, as is American Sign Language; code-switching between English and Italian in Toronto is a third; and the use of Pig Latin is still another. In Suriname a high government official addresses a Bush Negro chief in Dutch and has his words translated into the local tribal language. The chief does the opposite. Each speaks this way although both could use a common instrumentality, Sranan. You may employ different instrumentalities in the course of a single verbal exchange of some length: first read something, then tell a dialect joke, then quote Shakespeare, then use an expression from another language, and so on. You also need not necessarily change topic to do any of these.

Norms of interaction and interpretation (N) refers to the specific behaviors and properties that attach to speaking and also to how these may be viewed by someone who does not share them (e.g., loudness, silence, gaze return, and so on). For example, there are certain norms of interaction with regard to church services and conversing with strangers. However, these norms vary from social group to social group, so the kind of behavior expected in congregations that practice 'talking in tongues' or the group encouragement of a preacher in others would be deemed abnormal and unacceptable in a 'high' Anglican setting, where the congregation is expected to sit quietly unless it is their time to participate in group prayer or singing. Likewise, a Brazilian and an Anglo-Saxon meeting for the first time are unlikely to find a conversational distance that each finds comfortable, as they may have different ideas about how close one stands when conversing with a stranger.

Genre (G), the final term, refers to clearly demarcated types of utterance; such things as poems, proverbs, riddles, sermons, prayers, lectures, and editorials. These are all marked in specific ways in contrast to casual speech. Of course, in the middle of a prayer, a casual aside would be marked too. While particular genres seem more appropriate on certain occasions than on others, for example, sermons inserted into church services, they can be independent: we can ask someone to stop 'sermonizing'; that is, we can recognize a genre of sermons when an instance of it, or something closely resembling an instance, occurs outside its usual setting.

What Hymes offers us in his SPEAKING formula is a very necessary reminder that talk is a complex activity, and that any particular bit of talk is actually a piece of 'skilled work.' It is skilled in the sense that, if it is to be successful, the speaker must reveal a sensitivity to and awareness of each of the eight factors outlined above. Speakers and listeners must also work to see that nothing goes wrong. When speaking does go wrong, as it sometimes does, that going-wrong is often clearly describable in terms of some neglect of one or more of the factors. Of course, individuals vary in their ability to manage and exploit the total array of factors; everyone in a society will not manage talk in the same way. Nonetheless, conversations can be analyzed in terms of how they fit with social norms for interaction.

Exploration 9.2:   Defining Gossip

How can you define the communicative event of gossiping? Use Hymes' SPEAKING categories to discuss who participates in this type of communication with whom, the characteristic linguistic features, and the social goals.

Ethnography and beyond

In more recent studies, the description of underlying communicative competence and actual language use are combined with critical perspectives and other forms of discourse analysis. For example, Duff (2002) looks at classroom interactions in a multiethnic Canadian high school classroom through ethnography of communication research while also adopting critical and post-structuralist theoretical stances in her analysis. She describes her work as follows:

> This study employed EC [ethnography of communication] to consider how students' identities and interpersonal differences are created and manifested through interaction patterns during classroom discussions. Unlike many past EC studies, I did not provide an indepth structural analysis of the boundaries of the activities (beginning, middle and end) or explicit instruction provided by the teacher about how to participate in different phases of one activity, or explicit sanctions for non-compliance. Nor does the analysis focus on just one type of linguistic structure or framing device. Rather, I combined content and interaction analyses of turn-taking in discussions as parallel manifestations of how knowledge, identities, and differences are established and maintained by members of a classroom 'community.' (Duff 2002, 315)

The analysis, which also includes information about student achievement and attitudes stated in interviews with the researcher, provides a picture of the classroom interaction which is much broader and more nuanced than a description of what occurred in the interactions. For example, some ESL (English as a second language) students, many of whom had Chinese parents or were themselves not born in Canada, participated less in classroom discourse, but were nevertheless high achieving and in many cases performed better academically than their classmates who were born in Canada and had English as their first language. The 'locals' were nonetheless the ones whose voices and perspectives were most often heard in class discussion. Further, a simplistic analysis of turn-taking and the efforts of the teacher to include different students in the discussion fell short of recognizing that despite the good intent of this teacher, she had also contributed to the otherization of some students by calling on them to comment on issues of discrimination and exclusion. As Duff (2002, 315) writes, 'Everyday interactions such as these positioned students within different communities – the very communities students may or may not have wished to venture out of.'

Such an analysis thus draws both on ethnography of communication perspectives and on other types of discourse and content analysis; we will continue to address such issues in the last section of this chapter, on linguistic ethnography, and in the sections on interactional sociolinguistics and critical discourse analysis in chapter 11. In the next section, we will look at what has been called 'ethnomethodology,' and one of its derivatives, conversation analysis.

Ethnomethodology

While it is possible to investigate talk, the various factors that enter into it, and the variety of its functions, and make many sound observations, this does not by any means exhaust all we might want to say on the subject. As indicated at the beginning of the chapter, talk itself is also used to sustain reality and is itself part of that reality. We can therefore look at talk as a phenomenon in its own right. **Ethnomethodology** is that branch of sociology which is concerned, among other things, with talk viewed in this way. (See link in our companion website to an interactive overview of ethnomethodology.)

Ethnomethodologists are interested in the processes and techniques that people use to interpret the world around them and to interact with that world. They are interested in trying to discover the categories and systems that people use in making sense of the world. Therefore, they do not conduct large-scale surveys of populations, devise sophisticated theoretical models of social organization, or hypothesize that some social theory or other will adequately explain social organization. Instead, they focus on the phenomena of everyday existence, actually on various bits and pieces of it, in an attempt to show how those who must deal with such bits and pieces go about doing so. Their methods are entirely inductive. As Leiter (1980, 5) states, 'the aim of ethnomethodology ... is to study the processes of sense making (idealizing and formulizing) that members of society ... use to construct the social world and its factual properties (its sense of being ready-made and independent of perception).' Ethnomethodologists are interested in such matters as how people interact, solve common problems, maintain social contacts, perform routine activities, and show that they know what is going on around them and communicate that knowledge to others.

Ethnomethodologists say that social order does not somehow exist independently of individuals. People must constantly create that order as they use language to give sense to their own behavior and to respond to the behavior of others. The meaning of what one says or does depends entirely on the context of that saying or doing, and the parties understand what has been said or done because they know things about the circumstances of that saying or doing, about each other, about previous similar occurrences and relationships, and about the various possibilities that might follow. There is also the issue of **indexicality**: people are also aware that certain linguistic items (even whole languages) are associated with certain social characteristics so that A – an accent, word, phrase, tone of voice, dialect, and so on – means, or can be taken to mean, B – smartness, foreignness, masculinity, impoliteness, superiority, and so on. In this sense, no utterance is ever 'neutral': it always indexes some characteristic of the speaker. As discussed in chapter 4, there is no one-to-one correlation between a particular code and a social meaning; such meanings are dependent upon context. However, particular ways of speaking may have salient meanings that are likely to emerge, especially among interlocutors from the same speech community.

Background knowledge as part of communication

We can use a simple linguistic example to show that we cannot hope to understand others if we do not share certain background assumptions with those others. Only when there is such sharing is communication possible. In unpublished work, Sacks gives the following example of a two-sentence sequence to illustrate this point: 'The baby cried. The mommy picked it up.' How do we understand these two sentences from a child? How do they communicate? We understand that *mommy* in the second sentence refers to the mother of *baby* in the first, but there is nothing in the structure of the sentences themselves to tell us this. All we have is a connection between *baby* and *mommy* achieved through mention in successive sentences. Sacks claims that in such cases there are what he calls **membership categorization devices** which allow us to assign certain meanings to words like *baby* and *mommy*. In this case, we put the words into a set like *baby, mommy, daddy* rather than one like *baby, child, adult*; consequently, we understand that it is the baby's mother who is involved in the second sentence.

Note that we interpret the following relationship quite differently: 'The baby cried. The adult picked it up.' One assumption we apparently share with others who use such sentences (and with the child who used the original pair) is that the world is ordered in such a way that there are certain categories of relationships that are expressed through language. To interpret particular sentences or sets of sentences, we must have some knowledge of the categories that speakers find relevant (Sacks 1972a, 1972b). This knowledge of membership categorization devices is socially acquired. It is also the kind of knowledge in which ethnomethodologists are interested.

We constantly use such categorizations. They are not unlike labels such as 'jocks' and 'burnouts' discussed in chapters 7 and 8 except that they tend to be covert rather than overt. We constantly label people, places, and events around us and come to rely on such labels to help us deal with what is going on. Such labeling systems must be learned. What exactly is a 'jock,' a 'convenience store,' or a 'tweet'? 'Correct' labeling enables us to negotiate our way in society; 'incorrect' labeling is likely to lead to misunderstanding or possibly even to psychiatric care. If X is indeed a jock and you have correctly identified him as such, you have some idea of what to expect of each other. Misidentification in either direction is likely to produce disorder. If both parties know what a convenience store is and how people usually ask for and give directions, you may be directed to the nearest one. Reference to a tweet is common in many circles, but for speakers who are not in touch with technological advancements, this term may evoke the concept of birdlike noises instead of a type of message.

Commonsense knowledge and practical reasoning

Ethnomethodologists adopt what is called a phenomenological view of the world; that is, the social world is something that is constituted and maintained through people's everyday experiences. In this view, language plays a very significant role in that creating and sustaining. Ethnomethodologists regard 'meaning' and 'meaning-ful activity' as something people accomplish when they interact socially. They focus on what people must do to make sense of, and bring order to, the world around them, and not on what scientists do in trying to explain natural phenomena. Since much of human interaction is actually verbal interaction, they have focused much of their attention on how people use language in their relationships to one another. An important aspect of this is **reflexivity:** the notion that interactions are shaped in relation to the context, while the context is redefined by the ongoing interactions. Further, there is a focus on how people employ what ethnomethodologists call com-monsense knowledge and practical reasoning in the use of language.

Commonsense knowledge refers to a variety of things. It is the understandings, recipes, maxims, and definitions that we employ in daily living as we go about doing things, for example, knowing that thunder usually accompanies lightning; knowing how houses are usually laid out and lived in; knowing how to make a telephone call; knowing that bus drivers do not take checks; knowing that there are 'types' of people, objects, and events, for example, students and professors, classrooms and libraries, and lectures and laboratory sessions. These types help us to classify and categorize what is 'out there' and guide us in interpreting what happens out there. This stock of commonsense knowledge is acquired through experience; but since each person's experience is different from that of everyone else, the knowledge varies from person to person. We also know that it varies, and that some people know more about certain things and others less. The stock itself is not systematic; in fact, it is quite heterogeneous, and often parts of it are inconsistent with other parts – at times even contradictory – but that fact does not usually prove very bothersome to most individuals. In particular circumstances, we draw on the bits and pieces that seem useful; in other circumstances, we look elsewhere in the stock for help and guidance.

Commonsense knowledge also tells us that the world exists as a factual object. There is a world 'out there' independent of our particular existence; moreover, it is a world which others as well as ourselves experience, and we all experience it in much the same way. That world is also a consistent world. Situations and events in it not only occur, they reoccur. Things do not change much from day to day. However, at any one time only bits and pieces of what is out there are relevant to our immediate concerns. We are not required to deal with everything all at once; rather, we must ignore what is irrelevant and focus on what is immediately at issue. So, too, if we ask a question we expect an answer, if we make a request we expect either compliance or a refusal, if we greet someone we expect a reply, and so on. We try to find rational explanations for any deviations from our expectations. This is why certain television programs show people being put into bizarre circumstances in order to amuse an audience, who watch their attempts, and ultimate failures, to provide 'normal' readings for what is happening to them.

Exploration 9.3:   Classroom Language

Teachers and students must cooperate to sustain the 'reality' of the class-room. What are some of the ways in which a teacher and a class cooperate, in your experience? What particular patterns of behavior and types of language recur? What comprises a 'violation'? What changes do you notice between the various levels of schooling, that is, primary, secondary, and college or university? And between types of class, that is, lecture, tutorial, laboratory, seminar, and so on?

Practical reasoning refers to the way in which people make use of their commonsense knowledge and to how they employ that knowledge in their conduct of everyday life: what they assume; what they never question; how they select matters to deal with; and how they make the various bits and pieces of commonsense knowledge fit together in social encounters so as to maintain 'normal' appearances.

It is quite different from logical thinking or the formation and testing of scientific hypotheses, both of which we usually learn in formal settings and have very specialized goals.

Garfinkel and his students: studies in ethnomethodology

In an interesting series of studies, Garfinkel (1972) showed how we conduct our everyday existence in ways that clearly demonstrate how we do not question the kinds of assumptions mentioned above. He did this by creating situations in which his subjects, in this case his students, were not allowed to take certain things for granted; rather, they were required to violate or to question matters which they would normally accept 'routinely.' Needless to say, language was involved in every case.

For example, Garfinkel asked his students to report a conversation and state how the participants understood what they were talking about. To do so, it was necessary not only to interpret what was actually said but also to contrast the said with the unsaid, that is, that which was implied or that which could possibly be inferred, and to make hypotheses about how the various bits and pieces of the conversation fitted together as they did. Each party necessarily had to know a lot about the other party, about the topic, and about the kind of exchange the conversation was; each also had to tolerate considerable inexplicitness in what was actually said. For example, in part of one reported conversation between a husband and wife, the wife's question, 'Did you take him [our son] to the record store?' leads to the following exchange with her husband (1972, 4), with the words actually spoken on the left and the husband's interpretation of these words given on the right:

HUSBAND:	No, to the shoe repair shop.	No, I stopped at the record store on the way to get him and stopped at the shoe repair shop on the way home when he was with me.
WIFE:	What for?	I know of one reason why you might have stopped at the shoe repair shop. Why did you in fact?
HUSBAND:	I got some new shoe laces for my shoes.	As you will remember, I broke a shoe lace on one of my brown oxfords the other day, so I stopped to get some new laces.
WIFE:	Your loafers need new heels badly.	Something else you could have gotten that I was thinking of. You could have taken in your black loafers which need heels badly. You'd better get them taken care of pretty soon.

Garfinkel points out that in such exchanges matters not mentioned or only partially mentioned are still understood, that understanding itself develops as the conversation develops, and that understanding depends on the willingness of each party to work with the other to develop a common scheme of interpretation for what is being talked about. There is common agreement that we have to 'make sense' of what we hear. The shared assumption is that the participants are engaged in a 'normal' social interaction; that assumption will hold until they find very strong contradictory evidence.

When subjects were asked to take part in conversations and to insist that others clarify casual remarks made in those circumstances, the usual reaction of those others was one of either suspicion or hostility. Garfinkel cites two cases that show these consequences quite clearly (1972, 6–7):

Case 1

S: Hi, Ray. How is your girlfriend feeling?
E: What do you mean, how is she feeling? Do you mean physical or mental?
S: I mean how is she feeling? What's the matter with you? (He looked peeved.)
E: Nothing. Just explain a little clearer what do you mean?
S: Skip it. How are your Med School applications coming?
E: What do you mean. How are they?
S: You know what I mean.
E: I really don't.
S: What's the matter with you? Are you sick?

Case 2

On Friday night my husband and I were watching television. My husband remarked that he was tired. I asked, 'How are you tired? Physically, mentally, or just bored?'

S: I don't know, I guess physically, mainly.
E: You mean that your muscles ache, or your bones?
S: I guess so. Don't be so technical.
     (*After more watching.*)
S: All these old movies have the same kind of old iron bedstead in them.
E: What do you mean? Do you mean all old movies, or some of them, or just the ones you have seen?
S: What's the matter with you? You know what I mean.
E: I wish you would be more specific.
S: You know what I mean! Drop dead!

Apparently, conversation proceeds on the assumption that a certain vagueness is normal, that ordinary talk does not require precision, and that many expressions that are used in conversation are not to be taken literally. This vague, imprecise, and non-literal nature of ordinary talk is deemed to be entirely reasonable, and for someone to question it is to act unreasonably.

In another task, students were asked to perform as 'cultural dopes,' that is, to behave as if they were not aware of the social rules that pertained to specific situations; for example, they were asked to try to bargain for standard-priced merchandise. In this case, the greatest problem was that of making the initial move; since you do not bargain for such merchandise, it is difficult to begin the bargaining process because it involves violating a rule of normative behavior. What many students found, though, was that, once this norm was violated, it was possible to bargain in many cases, and that the actual bargaining could be both enjoyable and rewarding.

What is apparent from these various reports is that much of what we take for granted in our dealings with others depends on our accepting the appearances those others try to project. In other words, we accept the world for what it is, and most of what we hear we accept in good faith, and what we doubt we may find hard to confront openly. We accept certain norms; we realize that these vary from occasion to occasion so that different ones may apply in specific instances, but norms do apply. It is our job to find or negotiate the ones appropriate to an occasion – in fact, it is everyone's job!

Ethnomethodology and conversation analysis

Ethnomethodologists have found that naturally occurring conversations provide them with some of their most interesting data. Such conversations show how individuals achieve common purposes by doing and saying certain things and not doing and saying others. They obey certain rules of cooperation, trust, turn-taking, and so on. The type of discourse analysis which focuses on these rules for conversation is called conversation analysis; this will be discussed in more detail, and in relation to other approaches to discourse analysis, in chapter 11. For the moment it suffices to say that people use language not only to communicate in a variety of ways, but also to create a sense of order in everyday life.

Linguistic Ethnography

In recent years **linguistic ethnography** (LE; sometimes also called 'sociolinguistic ethnography') has emerged as a cover term for research which links ethnographic research on ideologies and wider societal norms with the analyses of specific language practices. Creese (2008, 233) explains 'An LE analysis then attempts to combine close detail of local action and interaction as embedded in a wider social world.' Much of this research has been done within the realm of education, and indeed, a major work describing this paradigm (Creese 2008) appears in the *Encyclopedia for Language and Education*. However, it is widely used in other institutional settings (see references cited in Further Reading).

Rampton (2007) describes the methodological tenets of linguistic ethnography as follows:

i)   the contexts for communication should be investigated rather than assumed. Meaning takes shape within specific social relations, interactional histories and institutional regimes, produced and construed by agents with expectations and repertoires that have to be grasped ethnographically; and

ii) analysis of the internal organisation of verbal (and other kinds of semiotic) data is essential to understanding its significance and position in the world. Meaning is far more than just the 'expression of ideas,' and biography, identifications, stance and nuance are extensively signalled in the linguistic and textual fine-grain. (Rampton 2007, 3)

A concept central to this work is that while we can identify **hegemonic ideologies** – for instance, the language ideology of normative monolingualism introduced in chapter 4 – our analysis must necessarily examine how speakers position themselves with regard to such ideologies. That is, we must discover how these ideologies are not only reproduced through language practices but also challenged through the performances of individual speakers or groups of speakers. As noted by Maybin (2009, 76), 'researchers now also frequently draw on social theory which enables them to make important connections between the everyday experiences they are documenting, and societal patterns of power relations, beliefs and values. Students are shown as shaped and constrained by these broader social structures but also as expressing individual agency at a local level and drawing creatively on the cultural resources available.'

In a study of children in a German-English bilingual classroom in Berlin, Germany, Fuller (2012) notes that there is an explicit norm of separation of languages, referenced by everyone: the principal, the teachers, and the students. This norm should dictate that there would be no bilingual discourse in the classrooms, but that is not the reality. However, the children in this study do not simply violate the rule of monolingual discourse and take the consequences; as students in an elite program and speakers of two prestigious languages, they have a great deal to lose if they speak a stigmatized mixed variety. Instead, they often use **flagged code-switching**, that is, switches from one language to the next that are marked by comment, laughter, or repair. These data, collected during English instruction, show that most of the switches occur as singly occurring German lexical items embedded in otherwise English utterances. The students construct themselves as English speakers while simultaneously, by 'slipping' into German, construct themselves as dominant in German. Thereby they access the cultural capital of being an English speaker while simultaneously enjoying the peer solidarity of being a German speaker. Through the flagging of the switches, they can also align themselves with the normative ideology of monolingualism. Such a practice serves to position these bilinguals as part of an educated elite, that is, as English speakers, without sacrificing all of the covert prestige of using the peer language, German.

Other studies conducted within the linguistic ethnography paradigm include research in a variety of educational settings, for example, Copland (2011), a study on teacher training feedback sessions, and Heller (2006), whose research on French schools in Ontario address issues of race/ethnicity, social class, and language ideologies along with language use patterns. Other institutions in which linguistic ethnography has been carried out include residential child care institutions (Palomares and Paveda 2010) and historic societies dealing with the Gullah/Geechee language in the Low Country of South Carolina (Smalls 2012).

Chapter Summary

This chapter returns to the idea of communicative competence which was introduced in chapter 1 and links it to ethnographic approaches to sociolinguistic research, with a particular focus on ethnography of communication. This framework is designed to identify how participants in particular cultural events themselves structure communicative practices, and what underlying assumptions are at work. We also look at ethnomethodology, which is used in conversation analysis, which will be covered in more detail in chapter 11; this methodology focuses on patterns in everyday interactions. Finally, we introduce linguistic ethnography, which is a relatively new approach in sociolinguistics, which integrates the study of linguistic practices in a particular setting with ethnographically gained knowledge about societal norms and ideologies.

Exercises

1. What kind of cultural and linguistic know-how is necessary to perform the following tasks? Imagine you are explaining to someone from a different culture how to carry out these interactions.
    * Asking for a day off work (a) because you are sick; (b) to go to a ball game; (c) to interview for a job with a rival firm.
    * Asking someone you are romantically interested in to go on a date.
    * Asking someone you are not romantically interested in if they want to have dinner (does it matter if this person could interpret this as romantic interest?).
    * Calling a business to find out if they are hiring.
    * Talking to a police officer who has pulled you over on the highway.
2. Building on the discussion in Exploration 9.3, look at the transcript below and discuss the patterns of interaction in this classroom. This is a Spanish-English bilingual classroom in the USA. The teacher is a native speaker of English who speaks Spanish as her second language; the students are all advanced learners of English. This is their ESL lesson. What are some norms for language choice and speaker roles that you can observe in this dialogue?

T = the teacher, S1–S3 are the students

T:	ok. so let's go thru B wh-what's the answer?
S1:	um –
T:	who would you like to play- table tennis
S1:	no, I don't!
T:	you don't what! make a complete sentence.
S1:	/no! I don't like their xxx-/
S2:	/ *¿acaso, vete ¡qué te gusta!?/*
	'/perhaps, get lost, you like it!?/'
S1:	/ *a ya.*/ (.)
	/ oh yes./ (.)
T:	S3, does your best friend like football?
S3:	yeah (.) she does.
T:	she does what?
S1:	*yo le puse ¿no,?* No, he doesn't like football.
	'I put it on, no,? xxx'
S2:	*Yo sé lo hice ésa.*
	'I did that one'
T:	S1, what did you do last night?
S1:	watched (.) I watched a movie that was called (Pirates) (1)
	{lots of background noise during S1's turn}
T:	so S1 what did you do last night tell me again. I couldn't hear you.
S1:	I watched a movie that was called (Pirates) (.)
T:	huuummm what do you want to do next week S2?
S2:	humm eat a lot? I'm going to-
T:	/in a complete sentence/
S2:	*humm yo soy el único que voy ahg {laughs} yo creo que sí maestra!*
	'Hummm I'm the only one that will go ahg {laughs} I think so teacher!'
T:	So, S2, answering the question, what do you want to do next week? How can you say that?. boys (.) girls. *Niños*
	'… Children.'
S2:	umm.
T:	what would you say, if somebody asks you, what do you want to do next week? How can you answer that in a complete-
S2:	/Sentence?/
T:	/sentence/ (.) how can you say that?
S1:	go to a (.) movie?
T:	is that a complete sentence, though?
S1:	go to the movie, watch a movie?
T:	Next (.) week (.) I (.) would like –
S1:	to go to the theaters to watch
T:	/S2 do you/-

S1:   -/ new movie./

T: do you remember when you make a complete sentence (.) from a question if somebody asked you a question and put almost all the words (.) from the 'question into your answer (.) remember how we talked about that? (.5) yeah.-

S1:   */más o menos/ (.) hay tengo hambre!*
/'more or less'/ (.) 'Oh I'm hungry!'

Further Reading

Carbaugh, Donal (2007). Ethnography of Communication. In Wolfgang Donsbach (ed.), *The Blackwell International Encyclopedia of Communication*. Oxford: Blackwell.
A concise overview of the concepts and principles of ethnography of communication research; an excellent basic reference for students interested in pursuing this methodology in their own research projects.

Jacobs, Geert and Stef Slembrouck (2010). Notes on Linguistic Ethnography as a Liminal Activity. *Text & Talk – An Interdisciplinary Journal of Language, Discourse & Communication Studies* 30(2): 235–44.
This article addresses the main methodological and theoretical concerns of linguistic ethnography and the role of researchers in carrying out work within this paradigm.

Saville-Troike, Muriel (2008). *The Ethnography of Communication: An Introduction*. Oxford: Wiley-Blackwell.
A detailed treatment of concepts such as communicative competence, speech communities, language varieties, face, politeness and power, as they are relevant in ethnography of communication research.

Seedhouse, Paul (2004). Conversation Analysis Methodology. *Language Learning* 54(S1): 1–54.
This article outlines the relationship between ethnomethodology and conversation analysis, and the five underlying principles for research in this framework.

Wetherell, Margaret (2007). A Step Too Far: Discursive Psychology, Linguistic Ethnography and Questions of Identity. *Journal of Sociolinguistics* 11(5): 661–81.
This article argues that linguistic ethnography should also address psychological aspects of human interaction, and provides a framework for incorporating discursive psychology into linguistic ethnographic analyses.

For further resources for this chapter visit the companion website at
  🖥 **www.wiley.com/go/wardhaugh/sociolinguistics**

References

Basso, K. H. (1970). 'To Give Up on Words': Silence in Western Apache Culture. *Southwestern Journal of Anthropology* 26(3): 213–30.

Canagarajah, S. (2006). Ethnographic Methods in Language Policy. In T. Ricento (ed.) (2006), *An Introduction to Language Policy*. Oxford: Blackwell.

Copland, F. (2011). Negotiating Face in Feedback Conferences: A Linguistic Ethnographic Analysis. *Journal of Pragmatics* 43(15): 3832–43.

Creese, A. (2008). Linguistic Ethnography. In K. A. King and N. H. Hornberger (eds), *Encyclopedia of Language and Education*, vol. 10. 2nd edn. *Research Methods in Language and Education*. New York: Springer Science+Business Media LLC, 229–41.

Duff, P. A. (2002). The Discursive Co-construction of Knowledge, Identity, and Difference: An Ethnography of Communication in the High School Mainstream. *Applied linguistics* 23(3): 289–322.

Duranti, A. (1997). *Linguistic Anthropology*. Cambridge: Cambridge University Press.

Frake, C. O. (1964). How to Ask for a Drink in Subanun. *American Anthropologist* 66(6:2): 127–32. In P. P. Giglioli (ed.) (1972), *Language and Social Context: Selected Readings*. Harmondsworth, England: Penguin Books.

Fuller, Janet M. (2012). *Bilingual Pre-Teens: Competing Ideologies and Multiple Identities in the U.S. and Germany*. New York: Routledge.

Garfinkel, H. (1972). Studies of the Routine Grounds of Everyday Activities. In D. Sudnow (ed.), *Studies in Social Interaction*. New York: Free Press.

Gumperz, J. J. (1972). Sociolinguistics and Communication in Small Groups. In J. B. Pride and J. Holmes, *Sociolinguistics: Selected Readings*. Harmondsworth, England: Penguin Books.

Heller, M. (2006). *Linguistic Minorities and Modernity: A Sociolinguistic Ethnography*. London: Continuum.

Hill, J. H. and K. C. Hill (1986). *Speaking Mexicano*. Tucson: University of Arizona Press.

Hymes, D. H. (1972). On Communicative Competence. In J. B. Pride and J. Holmes, *Sociolinguistics: Selected Readings*. Harmondsworth, England: Penguin Books.

Hymes, D. H. (1974). *Foundations in Sociolinguistics: An Ethnographic Approach*. Philadelphia: University of Pennsylvania Press.

Johnstone, B. (2004). Place, Globalization, and Linguistic Variation. In C. Fought (ed.), *Sociolinguistic Variation: Critical Reflections*. New York: Oxford University Press.

Leiter, K. (1980). *A Primer on Ethnomethodology*. London: Oxford University Press.

Maybin, Janet (2009). A Broader View of Language in School: Research from Linguistic Ethnography. *Children & Society* 23:70–8.

Mendoza-Denton, N. (2008). *Homegirls*. Oxford: Blackwell.

Mitchell-Kernan, C. (1972). Signifying and Marking: Two Afro-American Speech Acts. In J. J. Gumperz and D. H. Hymes (eds.), *Directions in Sociolinguistics: The Ethnography of Communication*. New York: Holt, Rinehart, and Winston, 161–9.

Palomares, M. and D. Poveda (2010). Linguistic Ethnography and the Study of Welfare Institutions as a Flow of Social Practices: The Case of Residential Child Care Institutions as Paradoxical Institutions. *Text & Talk – An Interdisciplinary Journal of Language, Discourse & Communication Studies* 30(2): 193–212.

Rampton, Ben (2007) Linguistic Ethnography, Interactional Sociolinguistics and the Study of Identities. *Working Papers in Urban Language and Literacies* Paper 43, 1–14.

Sacks, H. (1972a). An Initial Investigation of the Usability of Conversational Data for Doing Sociology. In D. Sudnow (ed.), *Studies in Social Interaction*. New York: Free Press.

Sacks, H. (1972b). On the Analyzability of Stories by Children. In J. J. Gumperz and D. H. Hymes (eds.), *Directions in Sociolinguistics: The Ethnography of Communication*. New York: Holt, Rinehart, and Winston.

Saville-Troike, M. (1996). The Ethnography of Communication. In S. L. McKay and N. H. Hornberger (eds.), *Sociolinguistics and Language Teaching*. Cambridge: Cambridge University Press.

Sherzer, J. (1983). *Kuna Ways of Speaking*. Austin: University of Texas Press.

Smalls, Krystal A. (2012). 'We Had Lighter Tongues': Making and Mediating Gullah/Geechee Personhood in the South Carolina Lowcountry. *Language & Communication* 32(2): 147–59.

Trusting, K. and J. Maybin (2007). Linguistic Ethnography and Interdisciplinarity: Opening the Discussion. *Journal of Sociolinguistics* 11(5): 575–83.

10

Pragmatics

Key Concepts

Form versus function in utterances

How indirect speech functions

The linguistics means of saving or threatening 'face'

Establishing hierarchy with language

The sub-field of linguistics called **pragmatics**, which looks at meanings of utterances in context, is often discussed in contrast with the sub-filed called semantics, which is the study of meaning as part of the language system. Semantics focuses on the meanings of signs, and the relationship between these meanings, and includes the study of meanings of chunks of text. However, when these utterances are interpreted with reference to the context, including the setting, speakers, background knowledge, and so on, this falls into the realm of pragmatics.

Pragmatics is perceived as being distinct from sociolinguistics, but there is some overlap, hence the inclusion of some topics in pragmatics in this textbook. In particular, we incorporate topics which involve how the identities and relationships of speakers influence their linguistic choices and how they are interpreted. This chapter will address four such topics: Speech Act Theory, implicature, Politeness Theory, and pronouns and address terms.

An Introduction to Sociolinguistics, Seventh Edition. Ronald Wardhaugh and Janet M. Fuller.
© 2015 John Wiley & Sons, Inc. Published 2015 by John Wiley & Sons, Inc.

Speech Acts

One thing that many utterances may be said to do is make **propositions**: they do this mainly in the form of either statements or questions, but other grammatical forms are also possible. Each of the following is a proposition: 'I had a busy day today,' 'Have you called your mother?' and 'Your dinner's ready!' Such utterances are connected in some way with events or happenings in a possible world, that is, one that can be experienced or imagined, and in which such propositions can be said to be either true or false. These are **constative utterances**.

A different kind of proposition is the **ethical proposition**, for example, 'Big boys don't cry,' 'God is love,' 'Thou shalt not kill,' 'You must tell the truth,' and even 'Beethoven is better than Brahms.' Just like an ordinary proposition, an ethical proposition may be true or false, although not in the same sense. However, establishing truth and falsity is not the real purpose of an ethical proposition; its real purpose is to serve as a guide to behavior in some world or other. 'Big boys don't cry' is obviously value-laden in a way in which 'Your dinner's ready!' is not.

Another kind of utterance is the **phatic** type, for example, 'Nice day!,' 'How do you do?,' comments about the weather, and so on. According to Malinowski (1923), these are examples of phatic communion, a type of speech in which ties are created by an exchange of words. In such communion the meanings of the words are not the focus of the utterances. Instead, 'they fulfill a social function, and that is their principal aim' (Malinowksi 1923, 315). In phatic communication the actual act of uttering is more important than the content of the particular utterance. Phatic utterances are used to create a sense of solidarity and establish contact between interlocutors, rather than to convey information.

Performatives

Austin (1975), a philosopher, distinguished still another kind of utterance from these, the **performative utterance**. In using a performative utterance, a person is not just saying something but is actually doing something if certain real-world conditions are met. To say 'I name this ship "Liberty Bell"' in certain circumstances is to christen a ship. To say 'I do' in other circumstances is to find oneself a husband or a wife – or a bigamist. To hear someone say to you, 'I sentence you to five years in jail' in still other circumstances is to look forward to a rather bleak future. Such utterances perform acts: the naming of ships, marrying, and sentencing to prison in these cases. A performative speech act changes in some way the conditions that exist in the world.

Austin pointed out that the 'circumstances' mentioned above can be prescribed. He mentions certain **felicity conditions** that performatives must meet to be successful. First, a conventional procedure must exist for doing whatever is to be done, and that procedure must specify who must say and do what and in what circumstances. Second, all participants must properly execute this procedure and carry it through to completion. Finally, the necessary thoughts, feelings, and intentions must be present in all parties. In general, the spoken part of the total act, the actual speech act, will take the grammatical form of having a first-person subject and a verb in the present tense; it may or may not also include the word *hereby*. Examples are 'I (hereby) name,' 'We decree,' and 'I swear.' This kind of utterance is explicitly performative when it is employed in a conventional framework, such as naming ships, making royal proclamations, and taking an oath in court.

There are also less explicit performatives. Declarations like 'I promise,' 'I apologize,' or 'I warn you' have many of the same characteristics as the previously mentioned utterances but lack any associated conventional procedure; for anyone can promise, apologize, and warn, and there is no way of specifying the circumstances quite so narrowly as in naming ships, proclaiming, or swearing an oath. It is also on occasion possible to use other grammatical forms than the combination of first person and present tense. 'Thin ice,' 'Savage dog,' 'Slippery when wet,' and 'Loitering is forbidden' are all very obviously warnings, so to that extent they are performatives. What we can observe, then, is that, in contrast to constative utterances, they are used either appropriately or inappropriately and, if used appropriately, their very utterance is the doing of the whole or part of an action.

Searle's work (1969, 1975, 1999) has addressed what makes an utterance a particular type of speech act. In particular, what makes a promise a promise? For Searle there are five rules that govern promise-making. The first, the propositional content rule, is that the words must predicate a future action of the speaker. The second and third, the preparatory rules, require that both the person promising and the person to whom the promise is made must want the act done and that it would not otherwise be done. Moreover, the person promising believes he or she can do what is promised. The fourth, the sincerity rule, requires the promiser to intend to perform the act, that is, to be placed under some kind of obligation; and the fifth, the essential rule, says that the uttering of the words counts as undertaking an obligation to perform the action. Searle says that neither of the following is a promise: a teacher says to a lazy student, 'If you don't hand in your paper on time, I promise you I will give you a failing grade in the course'; a person accused of stealing money says 'No, I didn't, I promise you I didn't.' The former is a threat, and the latter an assertion. Thus, use of the word 'promise' is neither required nor adequate to make a speech act a promise.

If this view is correct, it should be possible to state the necessary and sufficient conditions for every illocutionary act. Many of these require that the parties to acts be aware of social obligations involved in certain relationships. They may also make reference to certain other kinds of knowledge we must assume the parties have if the act is to be successful. For example, a command such as 'Stand up!' from A to B can be felicitous only if B is not standing up, can stand up, and has an obligation to stand up if A so requests, and if A has a valid reason to make B stand up. Both A and B must recognize the validity of all these conditions if 'Stand up!' is to be used and interpreted as a proper command. We should note that breaking any one of the conditions makes 'Stand up!' invalid: B is already standing up, is crippled (and A is not a faith healer!), B outranks A, or is at least A's equal, or A has no reason that appears valid to B so that standing up appears unjustified, unnecessary, and uncalled for.

These kinds of conditions for illocutionary acts resemble what have been called constitutive rules rather than regulative rules (Rawls 1955). **Regulative rules** are things like laws and regulations passed by governments and legislative bodies: they regulate what is right and wrong and sometimes prescribe sanctions if and when the rules are broken, for example, 'Trespassing is forbidden' or 'No parking.' **Constitutive rules**, on the other hand, are like the rules of baseball, chess, or soccer: they actually define a particular activity in the form of 'doing X counts as Y' so that if, in certain prescribed circumstances, you strike a ball in a particular way or succeed in moving it into a certain place, that counts as a 'hit' or a 'goal.' The rules constitute the game: without them the game does not exist. In the same way, speech acts are what they are because saying something counts as a particular speech act if certain conditions prevail. As Schiffrin (1994, 60) says, 'Language can do things – can perform acts – because people share constitutive rules that create the acts and that allow them to label utterances as particular kinds of acts.'

Locutions, illocutionary acts, and perlocutions

Once we begin to look at utterances from the point of view of what they do, it is possible to see every utterance as a speech act of one kind or other, that is, as having some functional value which might be quite independent of the actual words used and their grammatical arrangement. This means that we can categorize speech acts according to their function, and not their form. For instance, although 'Shut the window' and 'It's cold in here' are quite different in terms of how they express the request to close the window, they are both requests (or can be, given the appropriate context). The utterances we use are **locutions**. The intent of a locution is called an **illocutionary act**. We call the intended purpose of the illocutionary act the **illocutionary force**. A speaker can also use different locutions to achieve the same illocutionary force, as in the example about closing the window mentioned above. Conversely, a speaker can also use one locution for many different purposes – 'It's cold in here' could also be a complaint, an explanation for why the red wine is not at the right temperature, or a request for something other than closing the window (i.e., meaning, 'come here and warm me up!').

Illocutions also often cause listeners to do things. To that extent they are **perlocutions**. If you say 'I bet you a dollar he'll win' and I say 'On,' your illocutionary act of offering a bet has led to my perlocutionary uptake of accepting it. The **perlocutionary force** of your words is to get me to bet, and you have succeeded.

In contrast to Austin, who focuses his attention on how speakers realize their intentions in speaking, Searle focuses on how listeners respond to utterances, that is, how one person tries to figure out how another is using a particular utterance.

Is what is heard a promise, a warning, an assertion, a request, or something else? What is the illocutionary force of a particular utterance?

If we look at how we perform certain kinds of acts rather than at how particular types of utterances perform acts, we can, as Searle (1975) has indicated, categorize at least six ways in which we can make requests or give orders even indirectly. There are utterance types that focus on the hearer's ability to do something ('Can you pass the salt?'; 'Have you got change for a dollar?'); those that focus on the speaker's wish or desire that the hearer will do something ('I would like you to go now'; 'I wish you wouldn't do that'); those that focus on the hearer's actually doing something ('Officers will henceforth wear ties at dinner'; 'Aren't you going to eat your cereal?'); those that focus on the hearer's willingness or desire to do something ('Would you be willing to write a letter of recommendation for me?'; 'Would you mind not making so much noise?'); those that focus on the reasons for doing something ('You're standing on my foot'; 'It might help if you shut up'); and, finally, those that embed one of the above types inside another ('I would appreciate it if you could make less noise'; 'Might I ask you to take off your hat?'). As Searle says (1999, 151), 'one can perform one speech act indirectly by performing another directly.'

What we see in both Austin and Searle is a recognition that people use language to achieve a variety of objectives. If we want to understand what they hope to accomplish, we must be prepared to take into account factors that range far beyond the actual linguistic form of any particular utterance. A speaker's intent, or perceived intent, is also important, as are the social circumstances in which an utterance is made. We can see that this is the case if we consider promises and threats: these share many of the same characteristics, but they must differ in at least one essential characteristic or there would be no distinction.

In the next section, we will address one classic approach to the interpretation of indirect speech, focusing on how understanding context is an integral part of understanding language. Although this material is pragmatic in its content, this focus on context is a core aspect of sociolinguistics.

Exploration 10.1:   Form and Intent

What observations can you make about the relationship between grammatical form and speaker's intent for each of the following utterances?

1.   Have you tidied up your room yet?
2.   When do you plan to tidy up your room?
3.   Don't you think your room's a mess?
4.   Can you go upstairs and tidy up your room?
5.   Would you mind tidying up your room?

6. Go and tidy up your room.
7. If you don't tidy up your room, you don't go out.
8. Tidy up your room and you can have some ice cream.
9. Kids who can't keep their room tidy don't get ice cream.

Each of the above also assumes the existence of an asymmetrical 'power' relationship between speaker and listener. How might you perform this same speech act if speaking to an 'equal,' that is, a roommate or partner you live with?

Implicature

Grice (1975, 45) maintains that the overriding principle in conversation is one he calls the **cooperative principle**: 'Make your conversational contribution such as is required, at the stage at which it occurs, by the accepted purpose or direction of the talk exchange in which you are engaged.' You must therefore act in conversation in accord with a general principle that you are mutually engaged with your listener or listeners in an activity that is of benefit to all, that benefit being mutual understanding.

Maxims

Grice lists four maxims that follow from the cooperative principle: quantity, quality, relation, and manner. The maxim of **quantity** requires you to make your contribution as informative as is required. The maxim of **quality** requires you not to say what you believe to be false or that for which you lack adequate evidence. **Relation** is the simple injunction: be relevant. **Manner** requires you to avoid obscurity of expression and ambiguity, and to be brief and orderly. This principle and these maxims characterize ideal exchanges. Grice points out (1975, 47) that these maxims do not apply to conversation alone. He says:

> it may be worth noting that the specific expectations or presumptions connected with at least some of the foregoing maxims have their analogs in the sphere of transactions that are not talk exchanges. I list briefly one such analog for each conversational category.
>
> 1. *Quantity.* If you are assisting me to mend a car, I expect your contribution to be neither more nor less than is required; if, for example, at a particular stage I need four screws, I expect you to hand me four, rather than two or six.
> 2. *Quality.* I expect your contributions to be genuine and not spurious. If I need sugar as an ingredient in the cake you are assisting me to make, I do not expect

you to hand me salt; if I need a spoon, I do not expect a trick spoon made of
rubber.

3. *Relation.* I expect a partner's contribution to be appropriate to immediate needs
   at each stage of the transaction; if I am mixing ingredients for a cake, I do not
   expect to be handed a good book, or even an oven cloth (though this might be
   an appropriate contribution at a later stage).
4. *Manner.* I expect a partner to make it clear what contribution he is making, and
   to execute his performance with reasonable dispatch.

However, it is also possible to flout these maxims to create what Grice termed
implicature, or implied meaning; this is what occurs in **indirect speech**. That is, a
literal interpretation of the words is not the intended meaning, but rather the hearer
must make an inference based on context. Grice offers the following examples (1975,
51–3). In the first set he says that no maxim is violated, for B's response in each case
is an adequate response to A's remark. The utterances are interpreted as if the
answers are relevant, and thus clear interpretations are available:

A: I am out of petrol.
B: There is a garage round the corner.
A: Smith doesn't seem to have a girlfriend these days.
B: He has been paying a lot of visits to New York lately.

He gives further examples, however, in which there is a deliberate exploitation of a
maxim. For example, a testimonial letter praising a candidate's minor qualities (e.g.,
'his attendance at tutorials has been regular') and entirely ignoring those that might
be relevant to the position for which the candidate is being considered flouts the
maxim of quantity. Other examples are ironic, metaphoric, or hyperbolic in nature:
'You're a fine friend' said to someone who has just let you down; 'You are the cream
in my coffee'; and 'I have a million things to do today.' What we do in understanding
an utterance is to ask ourselves just what is appropriate in terms of these maxims
in a particular set of circumstances. We assess the literal content of the utterance
and try to achieve some kind of fit between it and the maxims. Consequently, the
answer to the question, 'Why is X telling me this in this way?' is part of reaching a
decision about what exactly X is telling me. To use one of Grice's examples (1975,
55), if, instead of Smith saying to you that 'Miss X sang "Home Sweet Home,"' he
says 'Miss X produced a series of sounds that corresponded closely with the score
of "Home Sweet Home,"' you will observe that Smith's failure to be brief helps damn
Miss X's performance.

The theory of implicature explains how, when A says something to B, B will
understand A's remarks in a certain way because B will recognize that A intentionally flouted one of the maxims. B will interpret what A says as a cooperative act of
a particular kind in the ongoing exchange between A and B, but that cooperation
may be shown somewhat indirectly. B will have to figure out the way in which A's
utterance is to be fitted into their ongoing exchange, and B's operating assumption
will be that the utterance is coherent, that sense can be made of it, and that the

principles necessary to do so are available. The task is never an unprincipled one: Grice's maxims provide the necessary interpretive framework within which to establish the relevance of utterances to each other because these 'principles operate even when being flouted' (Levinson 2001, 141). What is left unsaid may be just as important as what is said.

It should be noted that criticisms have been made about the universality of these maxims, and other pragmatic theories have since been proposed to account for indirect speech; see for instance the volumes by Birner and Ward (2006) and Horn and Ward (2008) in Further Reading, below. We present Gricean pragmatics here because it is foundational and also captures some elemental principles of this field; students wishing to focus on such topics should read further!

Exploration 10.2: Implicature

What are the different possible implicatures of the following utterance in the following contexts: what background information do you need to understand them? Are there different possible interpretations of what is meant that can be associated with different cultural backgrounds?

Utterance: 'I'm a vegetarian.'
Context 1: Upon receiving an invitation to dinner.
Context 2: When being offered a sample of beef teriyaki at the supermarket.
Context 3: As offered a portion of an unnamed dish at a potluck.
Context 4: While eating bacon.

The concept of cooperation

When we try to apply any set of principles, no matter what kind they are, to show how utterances work when sequenced into what we call conversations, we run into a variety of difficulties. Ordinary casual conversation is possibly the most common of all language activities. We are constantly talking to one another about this or that. Sometimes the person addressed is an intimate friend, at other times a more casual acquaintance, and at still other times a complete stranger. However, we still manage to converse. Because it is such a commonplace activity, we tend not to think about conversation from the point of view of how it is organized, that is, how particular conversations 'work' is beneath the conscious awareness of most speakers. Scholars who work in pragmatics and discourse analysis seek to make explicit the ways in which we interpret and structure conversation and the everyday knowledge we must possess to do so. All conversation is a cooperative activity in the Gricean sense, one that depends on speakers and listeners sharing a set of assumptions about what is happening. Conversation makes use of the cooperative principle; speakers and listeners are guided by considerations of quantity, quality, and so on, and the process of implicature which allows them to figure out relationships between the said and the unsaid. Grice's principles, therefore, form a fundamental part of any understanding of conversation as a cooperative activity. The maxims are involved in all kinds of rational cooperative behavior: we assume the world works according to a set of maxims or rules which we have internalized, and we generally do our best to make it work in that way. There is nothing special about conversation when we view it in such a way.

However, it should be noted that the concept of 'cooperation' in Gricean pragmatics does not mean that there is no conflict. There is no assumption that people work together to form shared, warm, affectionate exchanges; indeed, some of Grice's examples show quite the opposite. Thus what Grice means by 'cooperation' is 'intent to communicate'. Not answering a question is cooperative in this sense, as is punching someone in the face, or insulting them.

Politeness

Research on politeness in conversation has been dominated by the framework of Politeness Theory (Brown and Levinson 1987). We will introduce the main concepts of this approach, present some research which has been carried out within this framework, and also address some of the challenges the theory faces, particularly from researchers working on non-Western languages such as Japanese and Korean.

Face

The concept of politeness within sociolinguistics owes a great deal to Goffman's original work (1955, 1967) on **face**. In social interaction we present a face to others and to others' faces. We are obliged to protect both our own face and the faces of others to the extent that each time we interact with others we play out a kind of mini-drama, a kind of ritual in which each party is required to recognize the image that the other claims for himself or herself. The consequence is, as Scollon and Scollon (2001, 44) tell us: 'One of the most important ways in which we reduce the ambiguity of communication is by making assumptions about the people we are talking to.' They add: 'Any communication is a risk to face; it is a risk to one's own face, at the same time it is a risk to the other person's. We have to carefully project a face for ourselves and to respect the face rights and claims of other participants. ... "There is no faceless communication"' (2001, 48).

In discussing 'politeness', the concept of interest to them, Brown and Levinson (1987, 61) define face as 'the public self-image that every member wants to claim for himself'. They also distinguish between positive face and negative face. **Positive face** is the desire to gain the approval of others, 'the positive consistent self-image or "personality" ... claimed by interactants' (1987, 61). It is the desire to act out the identity you are claiming for yourself on a particular occasion. **Negative face** is the desire to be unimpeded by others' actions, 'the basic claim to territories, personal preserves, rights to non-distraction ... freedom of action and freedom from imposition' (1987, 61). It might also require others to recognize your positive face, something they may be reluctant to do. Positive face looks to solidarity, but also takes status into account; negative face also acknowledges status as it takes into account the other's right to be left alone to do as they choose. Requests may often show both positive and negative politeness. For instance, when students contact their professors asking for their help with a project, they may acknowledge negative face wants with comments such as 'I know you are very busy' while also acknowledging the professor's positive face by saying 'Since you are an expert in this area, I could benefit from your advice.' Every social encounter requires such **face work**. While the usually assumed goal is to maintain as much of each individual's face as is possible, speakers may also make what are called **face-threatening acts**, that is, speech acts which threaten the positive or negative face of the addressee. Requests are inherently threatening to an addressee's negative face, as are insults to positive face; the study of politeness is how we mitigate such face threats, or not, in different contexts.

Positive and negative politeness

When we interact with others we must be aware of both kinds of face and therefore use different politeness strategies; Brown and Levinson termed this different ways of categorizing politeness strategies as positive and negative politeness. **Positive politeness**, which serves to construct and maintain the positive face of addressees, is most obviously created through the use of compliments, which show appreciation. **Negative politeness**, which caters to the negative face wants of the addressee, is most typically displayed through apologizing for any possible imposition. But these are just the most straightforward connections between particular speech acts and different types of politeness; both positive and negative politeness can be constructed through a variety of linguistic means.

The mitigation of face threats is one aspect which influences the structure of what we say. Saying such things as 'Do you think you might close the window a little?' mitigates a threat to the addressee's negative face more than 'Close the window!' as does 'Excuse me, do you happen to have a minute or two to spare?' rather than 'Come here. We need to talk.' It is also why we sometimes find it difficult to turn down an invitation gracefully as we attempt to preserve the faces of both inviter and invitee. In some languages and cultures, direct refusal is strongly dispreferred. A study by Félix-Brasdefer (2006) on North American speakers of English and Latin American speakers of Spanish shows much more use of direct refusals by the English speakers, although for all speakers directness was conditioned by **social distance**; that is, we are more able to make face-threatening utterances to people with whom we have closer relationships.

Exploration 10.3:   Politely Refusing an Invitation

If you are invited to dinner by a colleague but already have plans for that evening which you cannot change, what is the most polite way to refuse the invitation? Why? What role does saving the face of the person inviting you play in your answer? Here are some options:

1.   Say 'No, I already have plans.' (Do you apologize? Explain why you can't come? Preface this with 'I would love to'?)
2.   Say yes, but don't go.
3.   Say yes, and then call later and say you can't go.
4.   Say thank you but neither accept nor reject the invitation.

We must also acknowledge that in addition to using strategies to minimize face threats to others, we also employ linguistic measures to protect our own positive and negative face. There are, of course, those who say that too much has been made of politeness requirements, for example, Pinker (2007, 392):

> Politeness Theory is a good start, but it's not enough. Like many good-of-the-group theories in social science, it assumes that the speaker and the hearer are working in perfect harmony, each trying to save the other's face. … We need to understand what happens when the interests of a speaker and a hearer are partly in conflict, as they so often are in real life. And we need to distinguish the *kinds* of relationships people have, and how each is negotiated and maintained, rather than stringing all forms of face threat into a single scale, and doing the same with all forms of face saving.

This work by Pinker, and subsequent publications by him and his associates (Pinker et al. 2008, Lee and Pinker 2010) link the study of face and politeness to an issue addressed above, cooperation. We are again reminded that conversation may be less like a carefully choreographed ballet, and more like guerrilla warfare. In the study of politeness in particular, we must remember that the rules are normative rather than categorical; part of our communicative competence is knowing what it means when we do not conform to societal norms for language use.

Politeness world-wide

Brown and Levinson's approach to politeness has been quite revealing when applied to many Western societies. However, (Mills 2003) argues that it encapsulates stereotypical, White, middle-class (and largely female) language behavior. It may also not work so well in other cultures and languages.

A great deal of work has been done on politeness among the Japanese, who are often described by Westerners as being extremely polite people. Martin (1964) has summarized some of the ways in which the Japanese use language to show this politeness:

- honorific forms incorporating negatives (analogous to English 'Wouldn't you like to …?') are more polite than those without negatives;
- the longer the utterance the more polite it is felt to be;
- utterances with local dialect in them are less polite and those with a few Chinese loanwords in them are more polite;
- you are more polite to strangers than to acquaintances;
- your gender determines your use of honorifics, with men differentiating more than women among the available honorifics;
- whereas knowledge of honorifics is associated with education, attitudes toward using them vary with age;
- politeness is most expected when women address men, the young address the old, and members of the lower classes address members of the upper classes, with the last, i.e., class differences, overriding the first two;
- although people may say that it is inappropriate to use honorifics with your relatives, they still use them.

Martin says that there are four basic factors at work here: in choosing the proper, or polite, address term for another, Japanese speakers consider outgroupness, social position, age difference, and gender difference in that order. He observes that anyone who comes to such a complicated system of politeness and address from a simple one may get 'the feeling that Japanese conversation is all formula, with no content' (1964, 407). To the argument that such a complicated system must necessarily give way 'as feudalism is replaced by democracy,' Martin replies that 'we shall probably have speech levels in Japanese … as long as we have plurals in English' (1964, 412).

More recent research has more specifically addressed how the linguistic means of encoding politeness fit into Politeness Theory. Matsumoto (1989) and Ide (1989) both argue that more attention should be given to what they call discernment, which is the speakers' evaluation of and conformity to socially prescribed norms, and less on volition, or speaker intention. Both argue that the concept of face, with its focus on speaker agency and intention, does not offer the best explanation of what is happening. The Japanese are always very much aware of the social context of every utterance they use. They are brought up to use *wakimae* 'discernment,' that is, how to do the right thing socially, so personal face requirements, if any, are pushed into the background. Dunn (2011) supports this observation in research which analyzes business manners training seminars. These seminars are intended to school native speakers of Japanese on appropriate use of honorifics and formal language styles, together with a wide range of other forms of verbal and non-verbal means of encoding politeness. The complexity of the expectations here is extensive, as a simple shift to a particular term of address or formal verb form is in itself not enough; appropriate body language, tone, and pitch of voice must be considered. This training focuses on politeness strategies as 'relatively ritualized acts of social conformity' (Dunn 2011, 3651) rather than as choices speakers must make about how to position themselves vis-à-vis others.

However, Fukada and Asato (2004) disagree on the ritual nature of politeness strategies, arguing that the motivations to maintain the face of oneself and the other are powerful influences in the use of Japanese honorifics. That is, they focus more on speaker agency and personal motivations and less on politeness as part of a formulaic interaction. They write (Fukada and Asato 2004, 1997):

> ... if people do not use honorifics when they are expected to do so, they could sound presumptuous and rude, and in effect, threaten the hearer's face. They could also end up embarrassing themselves; i.e., lose their own face (e.g., when they are speaking in front of an audience and make errors on honorifics). Therefore, proper use of honorifics does appear to have much to do with face preservation contrary to Ide and Matsumoto.

While this debate about the role that desire to maintain face plays in the use of politeness strategies may be inconclusive, it does serve to remind us that although people must be polite everywhere they need not necessarily be polite in the same way or for the same reasons. For example, a recent study (Sreetharan 2004) of the use of a nonstandard variety of Japanese by men in the Kansai (western) region of Japan revealed that, in all-male situations, while young men between the ages of 19 and 23 preferred to use forms of speech that are stereotypically masculine, older men between 24 and 68 tended to avoid such language. Indeed, the older they were, the greater the preference for polite, traditionally feminine forms. They thereby cultivated a polite image, no longer needing to project their masculinity (and the power associated with that) through their language. (Sreetharan discusses this in terms of life stage, and thus age-grading, not change in progress; see chapters 6 and 8 to review research on these ideas within variationist sociolinguistics.)

Another study of eighteen speeches given at five wedding receptions in the Tokyo area (Dunn 2005) showed that the speakers used both the humble forms expected of them at such a function, so as to honor and elevate the bride and groom, along with the ceremonial language appropriate to the occasion. However, such required 'humble' speech was also interspersed with non-humble forms as speakers constantly departed from a 'wedding-speaker' role to a more personal style that reflected the everyday relationships between the speaker and the bride and/or groom. Dunn points out that a complete description of honorific usage in Japanese society must address itself to a wide variety of pragmatic issues, that is, to very specific situations in which language is used to 'accomplish socially meaningful action' (2005, 235).

Research in Africa also shows some orientations toward the concept of face which differ from what are commonly accepted as Western practices. De Kadt (1998) discusses what she calls a 'public' version of face in Zulu interactions with regard to respect strategies. She describes the society as more collectivist than individualistic, and the concept of face that reigns in social interactions as being that of mutual face. This is echoed in research by Grainger et al. (2010) and Kasanga and Lwanga-Lumu (2007) looking at face in South Africa. Grainger et al. argue that interactional deference strategies contribute to group connectedness and thus, again, face must be seen within a collectivist interpretation framework. Kasanga and Lwanga-Lumu look at apologies, noting that they can be used to maintain collective face; they also note that body language and not just verbal utterances are part of the enactment of deference and politeness.

Politeness and indirectness

From our discussion of speech acts, we see that in some cases, indirect speech is perceived as more polite, particularly in speech acts such as requests. This is not always the case, of course, with instances of sarcasm being one example of how indirect speech acts may be less than polite, even insulting. So while not all indirect speech is polite, is polite speech necessarily indirect? While it might be possible to explain that off-record requests (e.g., 'I've got a splitting headache' as a request for an aspirin) are more polite because they allow the addressee the option of interpreting the utterance as merely a request for information and not a request for action, this is not necessarily how speakers view such utterances. Blum-Kulka (1987), based on experimental research in which research participants rated the politeness of requests, argues that on-record, conventionally indirect requests are considered more polite. Conventionally indirect requests include such linguistic forms as 'want' statements, for example, 'I want you to move your car' or 'I would like you to clean the kitchen.' Mild hints such as 'We don't want any crowding' as a request to move your car were not seen as equally polite, nor were bald imperatives such as 'Move your car' (examples from Blum-Kulka 1987, 133). She suggests that conventionally indirect requests are interpreted as polite because they are mitigated, but also because they do not require the work to interpret them that off-record requests require of the addressee.

Félix-Brasdefer (2005) supports this perspective on indirectness and politeness in his research on university students in Mexico. His research, based on the forms of requests used in role-playing tasks, shows that students are more likely to use indirect requests with a professor, that is, in a situation where there is a power difference and social distance between the interlocutors:

. […] quería ver si usted me podría aceptar el trabajo aunque sea dos días tarde.

'[…] I wanted to see if you could accept the paper even if it's two days late'
(Félix-Brasdefer 2005, 69)

However, in scenarios that involved interactions among students (i.e., in situations in which there was not a power difference and less social distance), more direct requests were common, although conventionally indirect 'want' requests were also used:

> Ayúdame a limpiar el baño, POR FAVOR por favor
> 'Help me clean the bathroom, PLEASE please'
>
> Un favor, necesito tus notas para estudiar
> 'A favor, I need your notes to study' (Félix-Brasdefer 2005, 71)

Félix-Brasdefer concludes: 'the present study showed that *on-record* or direct requests are situation-dependent and seem to be the expected behavior among these Mexican subjects in a solidarity politeness system' (Félix-Brasdefer 2005, 76).

Research looking at cross-cultural perspectives on the use of indirect speech involves not just assessing what linguistic constructions are considered more polite, but also what contexts seem to require more politeness, as norms may vary across cultures. Ogiermann (2009) used a discourse completion task to look at request forms in (British) English, German, Polish, and Russian. While there was a clear progression from more direct to less direct in moving eastwards from England to Germany to Poland to Russia, Ogiermann notes that the distinction may lie more in the interpretation of how face-threatening a request is (in this case, a request to get notes from a fellow student after missing class). All languages have linguistic strategies for downgrading the face threat of an utterance, but they are not the same strategies. She summarizes:

> These culture-specific preferences show that cultures differ in the extent to which they assign importance to negative face, thus confirming the validity of the distinction between positive and negative politeness cultures suggested by Brown and Levinson (1987) while, at the same time, showing that emphasis on positive vs. negative face needs is a matter of degree rather than a clear-cut distinction (cf. Ogiermann 2006). The distribution of modifiers further illustrates that although requests were downgraded in all examined languages, the preferences for the various downgrading devices are culture-specific. While the English respondents used consultative devices and the Germans downtoners, Poles and Russians relied more heavily on syntactic downgrading, such as tense and negation. (Ogiermann 2009, 210)

Research looking at requests in English, Hebrew, and Korean (Yu 2002) shows even greater differences, with Korean very different from English and Hebrew. Specifically, while non-conventional indirectness is perceived as polite in English and Hebrew, this is not the case in Korean. This research notes that, as Blum-Kulka (1987) suggested, in some cases indirectness is perceived as less polite because it places the burden of interpretation on the addressee. Byon's research on Korean (2006) also found that direct requests were used with great frequency and that the accompanying honorifics were essential to an interpretation of these utterances as being polite.

We must take into account not just directness in the analysis of politeness, but a wide range of linguistic strategies for negotiating relationships. Recent research on computer-mediated discourse and politeness in a special issue of the *Journal of Politeness Research* seeks to do exactly that, looking at the specific context of online interactions to examine norms and how identity and face are negotiated (Locher 2010). For example, Nishimura (2010) examines the complex interaction between norms for the use of honorifics – which may vary across virtual contexts – and the impact of face-threatening acts, showing that if the norm for honorifics (in this case, non-use) in a familiar, informal, and light-hearted exchange are not violated, the face-threatening act is not disruptive in the online community. If, however, the normative use of honorifics is violated in a face-threatening utterance, this can produce disruption for the interaction for all participants, not just those involved in the particular face-threatening exchange. This research illustrates how online communities are communities of practice which develop their own norms. Darics (2010) looks at ideas about norms in a broader sense in her analysis of interactions of a virtual team in a global management and consultancy company. She finds that the incorporation of practices adapted from spoken interactions (e.g., backchanneling) are used to create community, and that abbreviations common in computer-mediated discourse were avoided to maintain clarity. Both of these practices were seen as politeness strategies, as they are linguistic forms used to minimize face threats.

In the next sections, we will look at how we address each other, using pronouns, titles, names, and other terms, and how these practices are intertwined with the concept of politeness while simultaneously involving issues of power, solidarity, and social identification.

Pronouns

When we speak, we must constantly make choices which determine how we position ourselves in the interaction. One aspect of this positioning involves how we address others. In this section, we will look at the pronominal choice between *tu* **and** *vous* **forms** in languages that require a choice and, more generally, the use of names and address terms. In each case we will see that the linguistic choices a speaker makes indicate the social relationship that the speaker perceives to exist between him or her and the listener or listeners. Moreover, in many cases it is impossible to avoid making such choices in the actual 'packaging' of messages. We will also see that languages vary considerably in this respect, at least in regard to those aspects we will examine.

Tu *and* vous: *power and solidarity*

Many languages have a distinction corresponding to the *tu–vous* (T/V) distinction in French, where grammatically there is a 'singular you' *tu* (T) and a 'formal you' *vous* (V) (the latter often corresponding to, or derived from, a plural form). The T form is sometimes described as the 'familiar' form and the V form as the 'polite' one, although the social meanings of these forms are in reality much more complex than this. Other languages with a similar T/V distinction are Latin (*tu/vos*), Russian (*ty/vy*), Italian (*tu/Lei*), German (*du/Sie*), Swedish (*du/ni*), and Greek (*esi/esis*). English, itself, once had such a distinction, the *thou/you* distinction.

According to Brown and Gilman (1960), the T/V distinction began as a genuine difference between singular and plural. However, a complication arose, which they explain as follows (1960, 25):

> In the Latin of antiquity there was only *tu* in the singular. The plural *vos* as a form of address to one person was first directed to the emperor, and there are several theories ... about how this may have come about. The use of the plural to the emperor began in the fourth century. By that time there were actually two emperors; the ruler of the eastern empire had his seat in Constantinople and the ruler of the west sat in Rome. Because of Diocletian's reforms the imperial office, although vested in two men, was administratively unified. Words addressed to one man were, by implication, addressed to both. The choice of *vos* as a form of address may have been in response to this implicit plurality. An emperor is also plural in another sense; he is the summation of his people and can speak as their representative. Royal persons sometimes say 'we' where an ordinary man would say 'I.' The Roman emperor sometimes spoke of himself as *nos*, and the reverential *vos* is the simple reciprocal of this.

The consequence of this usage was that by medieval times the upper classes apparently began to use V forms with each other to show mutual respect and politeness. However, T forms persisted, so that the upper classes used mutual V, the lower classes used mutual T, and the upper classes addressed the lower classes with T but received V. This latter **asymmetrical T/V** usage therefore came to symbolize a power relationship. It was extended to such situations as people to animals, master or mistress to servants, parents to children, priest to penitent, officer to soldier, and even God to angels, with, in each case, the first mentioned giving T but receiving V.

Symmetrical V usage became 'polite' usage. This polite usage spread downward in society, but not all the way down, so that in certain classes, but never the lowest, it became expected between husband and wife, parents and children, and lovers. Symmetrical T usage was always available to show intimacy, and its use for that purpose also spread to situations in which two people agreed they had strong common interests, that is, a feeling of solidarity. This mutual T for solidarity gradually came to replace the mutual V of politeness, since solidarity is often more important than politeness in personal relationships. Moreover, the use of the asymmetrical T/V to express power decreased and mutual V was often used in its place, as between officer and soldier. Today we can still find asymmetrical T/V uses, but solidarity has tended to replace power, so that now mutual T is found quite often in relationships which previously had asymmetrical usage, for example, father and son, and employer and employee.

This framework of looking at pronouns in terms of power and solidarity can also be used in modern-day languages. Ager (1990, 209) points out that in an advertising agency in Paris everybody uses *tu* except to the owner and the cleaning woman. He adds that in general *tu* is used with intimate acquaintances and people considered to be extremely subordinate, commenting that, 'There is nothing intimate or friendly in the *tu* used by the policeman who is checking the papers of a young person or an immigrant worker.' However, upper-class social leaders still use *vous* widely with intimates: President Giscard d'Estaing in the 1970s used *vous* in talking to everybody in his household – wife, children, and dogs included – and at a later date the well-connected wife of President Chirac addressed her husband with *vous* but he used *tu* to almost everyone.

Bolivia is a Spanish-speaking country with two-thirds of its inhabitants of indigenous descent, mainly Aymara and Quechua. While Spanish is the language of La Paz, many inhabitants prefer to dress in ways that show their indigenous affiliation. Placencia (2001) looked at what happened when such people participated in a variety of service encounters in public institutions, such as hospitals, a government agency, and a city hall, with the service providers being either Whites or indigenous people (White mestizos) who had adopted a Spanish identity in order 'to move up the social ladder' (2001, 199). She was particularly interested in the use of the familiar *tú* and *vos*, and the formal *Usted* and *Ustedes*. Across a variety of different encounters, such as making requests for information and receiving instructions or requests for payment or to move up in a waiting line, she found that, in contrast to White mestizos seeking similar services, 'indigenous persons were generally addressed with the familiar form *tú* or *vos*, were not the recipients of titles or politeness formulas, and, in certain interactions were asked for information or were directed to perform actions with more directness than were their white-mestizo counterparts' (2001, 211–12). Placencia says that social discrimination was quite obviously at work. She adds that 'the use of the familiar form in address to indigenous persons seems to be so ingrained in the linguistic behavior of white-mestizos that they are not even aware of it' (2001, 123). While they thought they were being polite, actual observations showed they were not. Inequality was ingrained beyond the reach of social consciousness.

Another study focusing on how pronouns are used to enact power and solidarity can be found in Ostermann (2003), a study of the use of pronouns in interactions in two institutional settings in Brazil: a police station with an all-female staff, and a feminist crisis intervention center. In this setting, there were fluctuations in the use of the formal and informal pronouns (*você* and *a senhora*) within interactions. The data show that the police officers primarily use the pronouns to enact their institutional power, which often entailed a lack of tolerance for the actions of the crime victims. The workers at the feminist crisis intervention center, in contrast, often employed pronoun switches to align themselves with the female victims without evaluating their behavior. Such positioning will be the focus of the next section.

Pronouns and positioning

Norrby and Warren (2012) present a review of literature on personal pronoun usage in Europe since the 1960s, focusing on French, German, and Swedish. They argue that the concepts of **common ground** and **social distance** are central to the analysis of pronoun usage. Common ground is the focus on sameness; social distance allows us to focus on difference as well. Social distance is a multidimensional concept that relies on affect (i.e., how much you like a person), solidarity (how much you feel you have in common with that person), and familiarity (how well you know the person). Both common ground and social distance are negotiated in interactions; the choice of T or V in a conversation is not dictated through a formula of common ground and social distance; rather, speakers use pronouns to construct their identities and their relationships with their interlocutors.

This ongoing process is illustrated in an article by Keevallik (1999), which provides an interesting account of how school children in Estonia learn to use the T/V system of that language: *sa* (or *sina*) versus *te* (or *teie*). There is considerable variety of usage within the system as factors such as age, town versus country, formality, and changing power relationships are involved. There are also avoidance strategies but these are not always available. The result is that 'singular and plural address in Estonian is actively and creatively used for establishing and maintaining the character of social relations as well as for accomplishing various activities, such as degrading, condemning, or nagging' (1999, 143).

The pronoun system in colloquial Indonesian includes two pronouns which can both signal distance as well as intimacy, *kamu* and *elu* (or its variants, *lu*, *elo*, and *lo*); while both are appropriate for use with intimates and other young people, *kamu* is derived from Standard Indonesian and *elu* and its variants from colloquial varieties. An analysis of contemporary fictional narratives involving two young heterosexual couples shows how these two terms are used in dynamic ways not just to signal but also to construct the shifting levels of intimacy or distance in the relationships (Djenar 2006). Because neither pronoun inherently marks greater social distance than the other, any negotiation involves issues of personal style and orientation toward literary style; the speakers accommodate to each other's style when they wish to narrow the social distance.

This last study moves away from clear categorizations of 'formal' and 'informal' pronouns and leads us to another area of address where there is much ambiguity in terms of social meaning: naming and titles.

Naming and Titles

How do you name or address another? By title (T), by first name (FN), by last name (LN), by a nickname, by some combination of these, or by nothing at all, so deliberately avoiding the problem? What factors govern the choice you make? Is the address process asymmetrical; that is, if I call you *Mr Jones*, do you call me *John*? Or is it symmetrical, so that *Mr Jones* leads to *Mr Smith* and *John* to *Fred*? All kinds of combinations are possible in English: *Dr Smith*, *John Smith*, *Smith*, *John*, *Johnnie*, *Doc*, *Sir*, *Mack*, and so on. Dr Smith himself might also expect *Doctor* from a patient, *Dad* from his son, *John* from his brother, *Dear* from his wife, and *Sir* from a police officer who stops him if he drives too fast, and he might be rather surprised if any one of these is substituted for any other, for example, 'Excuse me, dear, can I see your license?' from the police officer.

In looking at some of the issues involved in naming and addressing, we will first distance ourselves somewhat from English and look elsewhere for what is done. This should allow us to gain a more objective perspective on what we ourselves do in our own language and culture.

A classic study of the Nuer, a Sudanese people, done some ninety years ago, showed some very different naming practices from those with which we are likely to be familiar (Evans-Pritchard 1948). This research showed that every Nuer had a personal or birth name, which was a name given to the child by the parents shortly after birth and retained for life. A personal name could also be handed down, particularly to sons, for a son might be called something equivalent to 'son of [personal name].' Nuer personal names were interesting in what they named, for example, *Reath* 'drought,' *Nhial* 'rain,' *Pun* 'wild rice,' *Cuol* 'to compensate,' *Mun* 'earth,' and *Met* 'to deceive.' Sometimes the maternal grandparents gave a child a second personal name. The consequence was that a child's paternal kin might address the child by one personal name and the child's maternal kin by another. There were also special personal names for twins and children who were born after twins. Males were addressed by their personal names in their paternal villages during boyhood, but this usage shifted in later years when senior males were addressed as *Gwa* 'father' by less senior males, who themselves received *Gwa* from much younger males. Children, however, called everyone in the village by their personal names, older people and parents included.

Every Nuer child also had a clan name, but this name was largely ceremonial so that its use was confined to such events as weddings and initiations. Use of the clan name between females expressed considerable formality, as when a woman used it to address her son's wife. The clan name could also be used by mothers to their small children to express approval and pleasure. Clan names were also used when one was addressed outside one's local tribal area by people from other tribes.

In addition to personal names, which are given, and clan names, which are inherited, the Nuer also had ox names, that is, names derived from a favored ox. A man could choose his own ox name. This was a name which a man used in the triumphs of sport, hunting, and war, and it was the name used among age-mates for purposes of address. Women's ox names came from the bulls calved by the cows they milked. Women's ox names were used mainly among women. Occasionally, young men would address young girls by their ox names as part of flirting behavior or their sisters by these names if they were pleased with them. Married women replaced the ox names with cow names taken from the family herds, and men did not use these names at all.

Evans-Pritchard pointed out a number of further complications in naming and addressing, having to do with the complicated social arrangements found in Nuer life. A person's name varied with circumstances, for each person had a number of names which he or she could use. In addressing another, the choice of name depended both on your knowledge of exactly who that other was (e.g., his or her age and lineage) and on the circumstances of the meeting. Having taken this brief glance at Nuer name and addressing practices, we can now turn our attention to English usage. Brown and Ford's study (1961) of naming practices in English was based on an analysis of modern plays, the naming practices observed in a business in Boston, and the reported usage of business executives and children in the mid-western United States and in 'Yoredale' in England. They report that the asymmetric use of title plus last name and first name (TLN/FN) indicated inequality in power, that mutual TLN indicated inequality and unfamiliarity, and that mutual FN indicated equality and familiarity. The switch from mutual TLN to FN is also usually initiated by the more powerful member of the relationship. Other options exist too in addressing another: title alone (T), for example, *Professor* or *Doctor*; last name alone (LN), for example, *Smith*; or multiple naming, for example, variation between *Mr Smith* and *Fred*. We should note that in such a classification, titles like *Sir* or *Madam* are generalized variants of the T(itle) category, that is, generic titles, and forms like *Mack*, *Buddy*, *Jack*, or *Mate* are generic first names (FN), as in 'What's up, Mate?' or 'Hey, Mack, I wouldn't do that if I were you.'

Address by title alone is the least intimate form of address in that titles usually designate ranks or occupations, as in *Colonel*, *Doctor*, or *Waiter*. They are devoid of 'personal' content. We can argue therefore that *Doctor Smith* is more intimate than *Doctor* alone, acknowledging as it does that the other person's name is known and can be mentioned. Knowing and using another's first name is, of course, a sign of familiarity or at least of a desire for such familiarity. Using a nickname or pet name shows an even greater intimacy. When someone uses your first name alone in addressing you, you may feel on occasion that that person is presuming an intimacy you do not recognize or, alternatively, is trying to assert some power over you. Note that a mother's use of *John Smith* (or, for a greater offense, *John Matthew Smith*) to a misbehaving son reduces the intimacy of first name alone, or first name with diminutive (*Johnny*), or pet name (*Honey*), and consequently serves to signal a rebuke.

Research on news interviews shows how these differences might play out in the public sphere. Both Rendle-Short (2007) and Clayman (2010) show how address terms in news interviews are used to indicate the stances of the speakers. In these politically charged and often combative interactions, the use of a first name by a politician to a journalist may well be a power move as opposed to a friendly overture. In the next section, we will explore other instances of asymmetrical use of terms of address in the enactment of power relationships.

Fluidity and change in address terms

An example from literature which illustrates the constitutive function of both pronoun and address term use for social distance as well as gender can be seen in the work of Mehmet Murat Somer, a Turkish writer. His 'Turkish Delight Mysteries' feature a main character who is a (male) transvestite (henceforth referred to as 'she'). The dialogue in the novels shows the construction of shifting and multiple identities, particularly surrounding social distance, age, and gender. In the English translation of the novels, both English terms and Turkish ones are employed to weave together the tapestry of the many nuanced relationships. The main character is often called *abla* by the transvestites who work in her nightclub, a term which literally means 'older sister' but can be used to show respect and also familiarity when addressing a woman. The male-identifying bouncer who works at the club does not use this term, but instead addresses her with the term *boss*, which reflects more of a power differential and is possibly more masculine. The narrative often includes the protagonist's reaction to being referred to with the informal pronoun *sen*, when she feels that the speaker should be keeping his distance and showing the respect of using the formal *siz*, but also when she or one of the other 'girls' (her way of referring to her transvestite friends) is offended at the age implications of other address terms. In *The Gigolo Murder*, she refers to a close friend as her 'spiritual aunt,' and the friend grimaces: 'She'd have preferred being described as a younger sister' (Somer 2009 25). In another example, the main character is offended by the address term 'uncle': 'The door was opened by a young girl ... "Come in, uncle" she said. I wasn't about to let that one word spoil my mood. "Uncle" indeed!' (Somer 2009, 103). In these cases, it is the implication that the addressee is sufficiently older than the speaker to warrant an address term indicating a generational difference that offends the character.

The fluidity of the gender references made to the main character also shows the constructed nature of gender identity (see chapter 13 for a further discussion of this issue). She is referred to as 'my son' or *abi* ('big brother') by some characters who know her in her professional guise as a computer hacker, but her friends and the girls at her club consistently address her with female terms of address.

This novel also brings up the topics of age and kinship in address terms. As you age and your family relationships change, issues of naming and addressing may arise. For example, knowing how to address your father- or mother-in-law has often been a problem for many people: *Mr Smith* is sometimes felt to be too formal, *Bill* too familiar, and *Dad* pre-empted or even 'unnatural.' There are also issues of address and reference in combined families. Kellas et al. (2008) looks at address terms and terms of reference for family members in English, focusing in particular on stepfamilies. They found four clusters of responses about the terms they used and how these terms positioned themselves within the family structure. They labeled these groups *isolators*, *gatekeepers*, *validators*, and *jugglers*. Isolators used formal terms such as 'stepfather' to maintain social distance to both refer to and address their stepparents and siblings. The gatekeepers referred to their stepfamily with more familiar terms, dropping the 'step,' but addressed them with terms indicating more social distance, for example, calling a stepparent by his or her first name instead of by a kinship term. Although the validators acknowledged in their interviews the difficulty in achieving closeness in combined families, they did use familiar and familial terms with the express intent of constructing closer relationships. The jugglers used similar terms as the validators, but expressed more guilt and confusion about these address terms as they tried to use them to balance the relationships with their stepfamilies without alienating their biological parents. All of these strategies exemplify how address terms can be used to negotiate changing societal norms and personal experiences.

Exploration 10.4: Kinship Terms

What do you call different members of your family – who do you call by their first name, or by a kinship term (e.g, 'Mum') or something else entirely (e.g., a pet name, or a title)? What about in-laws, or more distant relatives? Do you use kinship terms for any people who are not related to you? What do these different forms of address mean about the relationships in terms of power and solidarity?

Chinese comrades

A society undergoing social change is also likely to show certain indications of such change if the language in use in that society has (or had) a complex system of address. One such society is modern China. We will first summarize some research on this carried out in the 1980s (Scotton and Wanjin 1983, and Fang and Heng 1983), and then add a footnote about changes in the use of the same terms since that time. Research from the 1980s showed that the Communist Party of China promoted the use of *tóngzhì* 'comrade' to replace titles for owners and employers, for example, *lǎobǎn* 'proprietor,' and also honorific titles, for example, *xiān·sheng* 'mister.' The party aimed to put everyone on an equal footing through encouraging the use of an address form that implies no social or economic differences and unites all politically. Titles, however, did not entirely disappear from use. Professional titles were still used, for example, *lǎoshī* 'teacher' and *dài-fu* 'doctor,' and skilled workers preferred to be addressed as *shī-fu* 'master.' Table 10.1 shows that *tóngzhì* can be used in a variety of ways (Scotton and Wanjin 1983, 484–5). However, there are clear differences among the choices. *Tóngzhì* is used in situations that are somewhat neutral, that is, when there are no clear indications of power or solidarity and no

Table 10.1 Uses of *tóngzhì* in 1980s China

Combination	Example
Ø + Title	*Tóngzhì* 'Comrade'
Given name + Title	*Wéigúo Tóngzhì* 'Comrade Weiguo'
Modifier + Title	*Lǎo Tóngzhì* 'Old Comrade'
	Xiǎo Tóngzhì 'Young Comrade'
Ø + Title + Title	*Zhǔrèn Tóngzhì* 'Comrade Director'
Family name + Title	*Wáng Tóngzhì* 'Comrade Wang'
Family name + Given name + Title	*Wáng Wéigúo Tóngzhì* 'Comrade Wang Weiguo'
Modifier + Family name + Title	*Lǎo Wáng Tóngzhì* 'Old Comrade Wang'

Source: Scotton and Wanjin (1983, 484–5). Reproduced by permission of Cambridge University Press

familiarity between the parties, for example, to an unknown stranger or to someone whose occupation carries with it no title. *Tóngzhì* can also be used deliberately to keep another at arm's length, as it were. For example, a superior may use *tóngzhì* rather than an inferior's title before offering a rebuke. It can also be used in the opposite direction, from inferior to superior, to remind the superior of shared interests, or between equals who wish to stress their solidarity.

However, many Chinese still preferred the use of a title to the use of *tóngzhì*, for example, *zhǔrèn* 'director' or *zhǎng* 'chief.' There was also widespread use of *lǎo* 'old' and *xiǎo* 'little' in conjunction with last names as polite forms not only between intimates but also to mark social distinctions between non-intimates. An inferior could therefore address a superior by either *Lǎo* + LN or LN + title, with practice varying according to location (Fang and Heng 1983, 499), the first variant being preferred in big cities like Beijing and Shanghai, the second in less egalitarian venues and small towns. Still another form of address used to elderly officials and scholars and showing great deference was LN + *Lǎo*, for example, *Wáng Lǎo*. Some old titles are still used but mainly to accommodate non-Chinese, for example, *tàitai* 'Mrs.' The Chinese address form for a spouse is usually *àiren* 'lover.' The old *xiānsheng* 'Mr' is now applied only to certain older scholars; young teachers are called *lǎoshī* or, if they are professors, *jiàoshòu*. Fang and Heng conclude as follows (1983, 506): 'The address norms in China are indeed extremely complicated. … What we have discussed … [are] … some of the changes in address norms brought about by the Revolution. Taken as a whole, changes in address modes in today's China are unique and drastic. Few countries in the world, we believe, have been undergoing such drastic changes in this respect.' In a later report on the same phenomenon, Ju (1991) points out that *shī-fu* has become somewhat devalued through overextension to those not originally deserving it and that *xiānsheng* has lost its previous derogatory connotations, especially among young people. He concludes (1991, 390): 'China is changing as are its political and cultural systems. Predictably, there will be further changes in its use of its address terms.'

This prediction is indeed borne out; more recent research shows that the use of *tóngzhì* has been rapidly decreasing due to the lack of compatibility between the revolutionary ideology and the contemporary emphasis on a free market economy (Wong 1994). The term has also been appropriated by sexual minority rights activists and has also taken on the meaning of 'gay' among younger speakers (Zhang 2011; Wong 2004, 2005, 2006). It is interesting to note that although the term has fallen into disfavor because of its connection to ideologies which are no longer hegemonic in Chinese society, in Hong Kong it is exactly these indices of respect, equality, and resistance which have prompted its adoption for use by and for sexual minorities; it has then been further re-appropriated by journalists to parody and mock the gay rights movement (Wong 2005).

The history and development of *tóngzhì* highlights the fact that the same term may be used in different ways and different contexts to create different relationships between speakers. Another example can be found in Rendle-Short (2010) in her discussion of the term *mate* in Australian English. She notes that while the usual interpretation of this address term is that it creates an attitude of open friendliness, it can be used in ways that seem to be antagonistic or hostile. Here the focus is on the variation in conversational structure, specifically, whether *mate* is used finally in a sentence, the more typical usage ('how's your day mate') or initially ('Mate, I'm just doing my job'). In the latter, because of its positioning, *mate* serves to mark a transition or problematize speech that has come before the utterance it introduces.

Chapter Summary

In this chapter we introduce three major theoretical frameworks in pragmatics: Speech Act Theory, Grice's maxims, and Politeness Theory. These frameworks are all used to explore how language is used and understood in context. We discuss how each utterance is a speech act, that indirect speech acts can lead to implicature, and that we will use language in different ways to protect our own and others' 'face.' We then turn to pronouns and other terms of address to explore how these aspects of language are used to position the speaker and addressee in the interaction.

Exercises

1. One aspect of naming is how various people are referred to in accounts in newspapers and magazines, and on radio and television, for example, 'John Smith, 53, a retired police officer,' 'Smith's daughter, Sarah, 21, a junior at Vassar,' 'bank Vice-president Smith,' and so on. Examine such naming practices. Look at the various grammatical structures that occur and the kinds of characteristics that are deemed to be relevant concerning the person mentioned. Do any

patterns emerge having to do with gender, age, occupation, social class, and so on? Is it possible that some of this reporting helps give the news item in which it is found a certain slant that it otherwise would not have?

2. Conduct some research on politeness and request forms by collecting examples of requests you hear. Note what is requested, the linguistic form of the request, what the response is, who the speakers are and what their relationship is (or appears to be). Write a short analysis of these data, outlining the linguistic forms you heard and discussing in what cases the most direct and indirect requests are used.

3. Look at the following dialogue in Shakespeare's *Romeo and Juliet* (http://shakespeare.mit.edu/romeo_juliet/full.html), taken from the scene in which Romeo and Juliet meet for the first time and the scene in which Juliet calls for Romeo from her balcony. (If you have never read this play, consult some resources to familiarize yourself with it; some knowledge about the characters will be necessary to complete this exercise.) Look at the use of the formal (you, your) and informal (thou, thy, thee) pronouns in these two scenes and discuss how they are used to construct the identities of and the relationship between these two speakers.

ROMEO
[To JULIET] If I profane with my unworthiest hand
This holy shrine, the gentle fine is this:
My lips, two blushing pilgrims, ready stand
To smooth that rough touch with a tender kiss.

JULIET
Good pilgrim, you do wrong your hand too much,
Which mannerly devotion shows in this;
For saints have hands that pilgrims' hands do touch,
And palm to palm is holy palmers' kiss.

ROMEO
Have not saints lips, and holy palmers too?

JULIET
Ay, pilgrim, lips that they must use in prayer.

ROMEO
O, then, dear saint, let lips do what hands do;
They pray, grant thou, lest faith turn to despair.

JULIET
Saints do not move, though grant for prayers' sake.

ROMEO
Then move not, while my prayer's effect I take.
Thus from my lips, by yours, my sin is purged. {kisses Juliet}

JULIET
Then have my lips the sin that they have took.

ROMEO

Sin from thy lips? O trespass sweetly urged!
Give me my sin again. {kisses Juliet again}

JULIET

You kiss by the book.

JULIET

O Romeo, Romeo! wherefore art thou Romeo?
Deny thy father and refuse thy name;
Or, if thou wilt not, be but sworn my love,
And I'll no longer be a Capulet.

ROMEO

[Aside] Shall I hear more, or shall I speak at this?

JULIET

'Tis but thy name that is my enemy;
Thou art thyself, though not a Montague.
What's Montague? it is nor hand, nor foot,
Nor arm, nor face, nor any other part
Belonging to a man. O, be some other name!
What's in a name? that which we call a rose
By any other name would smell as sweet;
So Romeo would, were he not Romeo call'd,
Retain that dear perfection which he owes
Without that title. Romeo, doff thy name,
And for that name which is no part of thee
Take all myself.

ROMEO

I take thee at thy word:
Call me but love, and I'll be new baptized;
Henceforth I never will be Romeo.

JULIET

What man art thou that thus bescreen'd in night
So stumblest on my counsel?

ROMEO

By a name
I know not how to tell thee who I am:
My name, dear saint, is hateful to myself,
Because it is an enemy to thee;
Had I it written, I would tear the word.

JULIET

My ears have not yet drunk a hundred words
Of that tongue's utterance, yet I know the sound:
Art thou not Romeo and a Montague?

ROMEO
Neither, fair saint, if either thee dislike.

JULIET
How camest thou hither, tell me, and wherefore?
The orchard walls are high and hard to climb,
And the place death, considering who thou art,
If any of my kinsmen find thee here.

ROMEO
With love's light wings did I o'er-perch these walls;
For stony limits cannot hold love out,
And what love can do that dares love attempt;
Therefore thy kinsmen are no let to me.

Further Reading

Bayraktaroğlu, Arin and Maria Sifianou (eds.) (2001). *Linguistic Politeness Across Boundaries: The Case of Greek and Turkish*. Amsterdam: John Benjamins.
This volume contains studies on Greek and Turkish language use which address politeness with regard to various speech acts (compliments, congratulations, giving advice) in particular social contexts (e.g., the classroom, political debates, service encounters).

Birner, Betty J. and Gregory L. Ward (eds.) (2006). *Drawing the Boundaries of Meaning: Neo-Gricean Studies in Pragmatics and Semantics. In Honor of Laurence R. Horn*. Amsterdam: John Benjamins.
This volume deals with issues in pragmatics more broadly, and in particular the boundary between pragmatics and semantics, but provides a detailed look at issues in the study of implicature.

Culpeper, Jonathan (2011). *Impoliteness: Using Language to Cause Offence*. Cambridge: Cambridge University Press.
This text uses some of the theoretical underpinnings of pragmatics (i.e., the concept of 'face' and the use of implicature) to examine impolite speech, arguing that much of communication is not aimed at being polite.

Eelen, Gino, Susan Gal, and Kathryn Ann Woolard (2001). *A Critique of Politeness Theories*. Manchester: St. Jerome.
Looking beyond Brown and Levinson's Politeness Theory, this book offers an overview of different approaches to the study of conversational politeness.

Gass, Susan and Joyce Neu (2006). *Speech Acts Across Cultures: Challenges to Communication in a Second Language*. Berlin: Mouton de Gruyter.
A collection of studies which address methodological and theoretical issues through the examination of data from different linguistic/cultural backgrounds. Includes comparative studies as well as research looking at second language learning of particular speech acts.

Hickey, Leo and Miranda Stewart (2005). *Politeness in Europe*. Clevedon: Multilingual Matters.
This book provides studies on politeness across European countries, including the topics of face, indirectness, and terms of address in particular cultural contexts.

Horn, Laurence and Gregory Ward (eds.) (2008). *Handbook of Pragmatics*. Oxford: Wiley-Blackwell.
This is an excellent collection of papers on topics in pragmatics, including speech acts, implicature, and politeness as covered in this chapter but going far beyond, providing a comprehensive introduction to the major topics in pragmatics.

For further resources for this chapter visit the companion website at

 www.wiley.com/go/wardhaugh/sociolinguistics

References

Ager, D. E. (1990). *Sociolinguistics and Contemporary French*. Cambridge: Cambridge University Press.

Austin, J. L. (1975). *How to Do Things with Words*. 2nd edn. Oxford: Clarendon Press.

Blum-Kulka, S. (1987). Indirectness and Politeness in Requests: Same or Different? *Journal of Pragmatics* 11(2): 131–46.

Brown, R. and M. Ford (1961). Address in American English. *Journal of Abnormal and Social Psychology* 62: 375–85. In J. Laver and S. Hutcheson (eds.) (1972), *Communication in Face to Face Interaction*. Harmondsworth, England: Penguin Books.

Brown, R. and A. Gilman (1960). The Pronouns of Power and Solidarity. In T. A. Sebeok (ed.), *Style in Language*, New York: John Wiley & Sons, Inc. In J. Laver and S. Hutcheson (eds.) (1972), *Communication in Face to Face Interaction*. Harmondsworth, England: Penguin Books.

Brown, P. and S. C. Levinson (1987). *Politeness: Some Universals of Language Use*. Cambridge: Cambridge University Press.

Byon, A. S. (2006). The Role of Linguistic Indirectness and Honorifics in Achieving Linguistic Politeness in Korean Requests. *Journal of Politeness Research* 2: 247–76.

Clayman, Steven E. (2010). Address Terms in the Service of Other Actions: The Case of News Interview Talk. *Discourse & Communication* 4(2): 161.

Darics, E. (2010). Politeness in Computer-Mediated Discourse of a Virtual Team. *Journal of Politeness Research. Language, Behaviour, Culture* 6(1):129–50.

De Kadt, Elizabeth (1998). The Concept of Face and Its Applicability to the Zulu Language. *Journal of Pragmatics* 29: 173–91.

Djenar, D.N. (2006). Patterns and Variation of Address Terms in Colloquial Indonesian. *Australian Review of Applied Linguistics* 29(2):1–22.

Dunn, C. D. (2005). Pragmatic Functions of Humble Forms in Japanese Ceremonial Discourse. *Journal of Linguistic Anthropology* 15(2): 218–38.

Dunn, C. D. (2011). Formal Forms or Verbal Strategies? Politeness Theory and Japanese Business Etiquette Training. *Journal of Pragmatics* 43(15): 3643–54.

Evans-Pritchard, E. E. (1948). Nuer Modes of Address. *The Uganda Journal* 12: 166–71. In D. H. Hymes (ed.) (1964), *Language in Culture and Society: A Reader in Linguistics and Anthropology*. New York: Harper & Row.

Fang, H. and J. H. Heng (1983). Social Changes and Changing Address Norms in China. *Language in Society* 12: 495–507.

Félix-Brasdefer, J. César (2005). Indirectness and Politeness in Mexican Requests. In David Eddington (ed.), *Selected Proceedings of the 7th Hispanic Linguistics Symposium*. Somerville, MA: Cascadilla Proceedings Project, 66–78.

Félix-Brasdefer, J. César (2006). Declining an Invitation: A Cross-Cultural Study of Pragmatic Strategies in American English and Latin American Spanish. *Multilingua – Journal of Cross-Cultural and Interlanguage Communication* 22(3): 225–55.

Fukada, Atsushi and Noriko Asato. (2004). Universal Politeness Theory: Application to the Use of Japanese Honorifics. *Journal of Pragmatics* 36: 1991–2002.

Goffman, E. (1955). On Face-Work: An Analysis of Ritual Elements in Social Interaction. *Psychiatry* 18: 213–31. In J. Laver and S. Hutcheson (eds.) (1972), *Communication in Face to Face Interaction*. Harmondsworth, England: Penguin Books.

Goffman, E. (1967). *Interaction Ritual: Essays in Face-to-Face Behavior*. New York: Anchor Books.

Grainger, K., S. Mills, and M. Sibanda (2010). 'Just Tell Us What To Do': Southern African Face and Its Relevance to Intercultural Communication. *Journal of Pragmatics* 42(8): 2158–71.

Grice, H. P. (1975). *Logic and Conversation*. In P. Cole and J. L. Morgan (eds.), *Syntax and Semantics*, vol. 3: *Speech Acts*. New York: Academic Press.

Horn, Laurence, and Gregory Ward (eds.) (2008). *Handbook of Pragmatics*, vol. 26. Oxford: Wiley-Blackwell.

Ide, S. (1989). Formal Forms and Discernment: Two Neglected Aspects of Linguistic Politeness. *Multilingua* 8: 223–48.

Ju, Z. (1991). The 'Depreciation' and 'Appreciation' of Some Address Terms in China. *Language in Society* 20: 387–90.

Kasanga, L. A. and J. C. Lwanga-Lumu (2007). Cross-Cultural Linguistic Realization of Politeness: A Study of Apologies in English and Setswana. *Journal of Politeness Research. Language, Behaviour, Culture* 3(1): 65–92.

Keevallik, L. (1999). The Use and Abuse of Singular and Plural Address Forms in Estonian. *International Journal of the Sociology of Language* 139: 125–44.

Koenig Kellas, J., C. LeClair-Underberg, and E. L. Normand (2008). Stepfamily Address Terms: 'Sometimes They Mean Something and Sometimes They Don't.' *Journal of Family Communication* 8(4): 238–63.

Lee, J. J. and S. Pinker (2010). Rationales for Indirect Speech: The Theory of the Strategic Speaker. *Psychological Review* 117(3): 785.

Levinson, S. C. (2001). Maxim. In A. Duranti, (ed.), *Key Terms in Language and Culture*. Oxford: Blackwell.

Locher, M. A. (2010). Introduction: Politeness and Impoliteness in Computer-Mediated Communication. *Journal of Politeness Research. Language, Behaviour, Culture* 6(1):1–5.

Malinowski, B. (1923). The Problem of Meaning in Primitive Languages. In C. K. Ogden and I. A. Richards, *The Meaning of Meaning*, London: Routledge & Kegan Paul. Also in J. Laver and S. Hutcheson (eds.) (1972), *Communication in Face to Face Interaction*. Harmondsworth, England: Penguin Books.

Martin, S. (1964). Speech Levels and Social Structure in Japan and Korea. In D. H. Hymes (ed.) (1964), *Language in Culture and Society: A Reader in Linguistics and Anthropology*. New York: Harper & Row.

Matsumoto, Y. (1989). Politeness and Conversational Universals – Observations from Japanese. *Multilingua* 8: 207–22.

Mills, S. (2003). *Gender and Politeness*. Cambridge: Cambridge University Press.

Nishimura, Y. (2010). Impoliteness in Japanese BBS interactions: Observations from Message Exchanges in Two Online Communities. *Journal of Politeness Research. Language, Behaviour, Culture* 6(1):35–55.

Norrby, C. and J. Warren (2012). Address Practices and Social Relationships in European Languages. *Language and Linguistics Compass* 6(4): 225–35.

Ogiermann, Eva (2006). Cultural Variability within Brown and Levinson's Politeness Theory. English, Polish and Russian Apologies. In Cristina Mourón Figueroa and Teresa Iciar Moralejo-Gárate (eds.), *Studies in Contrastive Linguistics*. Santiago de Compostela: Universidade de Santiago de Compostela, Servizo de Publicacións, 707–18.

Ogiermann, E. (2009). Politeness and In-directness Across Cultures: A Comparison of English, German, Polish and Russian Requests. *Journal of Politeness Research* 5(2): 189–216.

Ostermann, A. C. (2003). Localizing Power and Solidarity: Pronoun Alternation at an All-Female Police Station and a Feminist Crisis Intervention Center in Brazil. *Language in Society* 32(3): 351–81.

Pinker, S. (2007). *The Stuff of Thought*. New York: Viking.

Pinker, S., M. A. Nowak, and J. J. Lee (2008). The Logic of Indirect Speech. *Proceedings of the National Academy of Sciences* 105(3): 833–38.

Placencia, M. E. (2001). Inequality in Address Behavior at Public Institutions in La Paz, Bolivia. *Anthropological Linguistics* 43(2): 198–217.

Rawls, J. (1955). Two Concepts of Rules. *Philosophical Review* 64: 3–32.

Rendle-Short, J. (2007). 'Catherine, you're wasting your time': Address Terms Within the Australian Political Interview. *Journal of Pragmatics* 39: 1503–25.

Rendle-Short, J. (2010). 'Mate' as a Term of Address in Ordinary Interaction. *Journal of Pragmatics* 42(5): 1201–18.

Schiffrin, D. (1994). *Approaches to Discourse*. Oxford: Blackwell.

Scollon, R. and S. W. Scollon (2001). *Intercultural Communication: A Discourse Approach*. 2nd edn. Oxford: Blackwell.

Scotton, C. M. and Z. Wanjin (1983). *Tóngzhì* in China: Language Change and its Conversational Consequences. *Language in Society* 12: 477–94.

Searle, J. (1969). *Speech Acts: An Essay in the Philosophy of Language*. London: Cambridge University Press.

Searle, J. (1975). Indirect Speech Acts. In P. Cole and J. L. Morgan (eds.), *Syntax and Semantics*, vol. 3: *Speech Acts*. New York: Academic Press.

Searle, J. (1999). *Mind, Language and Society: Doing Philosophy in the Real World*. London: Weidenfeld and Nicolson.

Somer, Mehmet Murat (2009). *The Gigolo Murder* (translated by Kenneth James Dakan). New York: Penguin Books.

Sreetharan, C. S. (2004). Students, *Sarariiman* (pl.), and Seniors: Japanese Men's Use of 'Manly' Speech Register. *Language in Society* 33: 81–107.

Wong, A. D. (2004). Language, Cultural Authenticity, and the Tongzhi Movement. In *Proceedings of the Twelfth Annual Symposium about Language and Society – Austin*. *Texas Linguistic Forum* 48: 209–15.

Wong, A. D. (2005). The Reappropriation of Tongzhi. *Language in Society* 34(5): 763–93.

Wong, A. D. (2006). Tongzhi, Ideologies, and Semantic Change. In *Proceedings from the Annual Meeting of the Chicago Linguistic Society* 42(1): 303–17.

Wong, Lee (1994). Address Forms in Modern China: Changing Ideologies and Shifting Semantics. *Linguistics* 32(2): 299–324.

Yu, K. A. (2002). Culture-Specific Concepts of Politeness. *Intercultural Pragmatics* 8(3): 385–409.

Zhang, Xiaochi (2011). A Comparative Study of Sino-American Address Terms from an Intercultural Communication Perspective. *International Journal of English Linguistics* 1(1): 54–61.

11

Discourse Analysis

Key Concepts

Local organization of a conversation

Floor management

The role of ethnographic information in analysis of conversational data

What it means to be critical in discourse analysis

In chapter 10 we discussed how the linguistic sub-field of pragmatics is concerned with how utterances are understood in context. The current chapter incorporates some of these same themes, but also draws on ideas from previous chapters about speaker demographics and linguistic varieties, that is, both the societal and the interactional aspects in discourse. Talk is action, and in recent years certain philosophers and social theorists have shown an interest in what utterances do, and claim that part of the total meaning of an utterance is this very doing.

As soon as we look closely at conversation in general, we see that it involves much more than using language to state propositions or convey facts. We also very rarely use language monologically and such uses are clearly marked. The unmarked use is **dialogical**, that is, we speak with another or others in various kinds of verbal give-and-take called conversation. Through conversation we establish and maintain relationships with others while at the same time both reflecting and creating our social reality.

An Introduction to Sociolinguistics, Seventh Edition. Ronald Wardhaugh and Janet M. Fuller.
© 2015 John Wiley & Sons, Inc. Published 2015 by John Wiley & Sons, Inc.

Although there are more approaches to discourse analysis than the three to be discussed here, these three have the closest ties to other themes in sociolinguistics, and the latter two incorporate many types of data and methodologies. In the first section, we will continue in our discussion of ethnomethodology begun in chapter 9 and outline the main tenets of conversation analysis. In the second section, we will look at research within what is called interactional sociolinguistics, and discuss what defines this approach and its major goals. In the third and final section, we will introduce critical discourse analysis, which provides a bridge to the next section of the book on sociolinguistics and social justice.

Conversation Analysis

Some speech is planned, for example, public performances such as commencement addresses, or sometimes we will rehearse a contribution ahead of time for a conversation of great significance, but anyone who has done this knows the conversation then rarely proceeds as planned. Casual conversations are not choreographed to any extent ahead of time and occur in real time. However, such unplanned speech does exhibit certain characteristics: repetitions; simple active sentences; speaker and listener combining to construct propositions; stringing of clauses together with *and* or *but* or the juxtapositioning of clauses with no overt links at all; deletion of subjects and referents; and use of deictics, for example, words such as *this*, *that*, *here*, and *there*. They may also be filled with equivocations (or hedges), that is, words and expressions such as *well, like, maybe, but, sort of, you know, I guess*, and so on. The syntax of unplanned conversation is also not at all that of formal, edited, written prose (see Quaglio and Biber 2006). It is composed of utterances that are often fragmented and overlapping. These are not the complete, non-overlapping sentences which we carefully organize into larger units like the paragraphs, sections, and chapters of a book such as this one. It is the rare person indeed who 'speaks in paragraphs.'

Unplanned speech, however, is not unorganized speech. Unorganized speech would be speech in which anything goes. We obviously cannot say anything to anyone at any time. Nor, as we will now see, can we say what we say in any way that we please. There are specific procedures we must follow as we indulge in the give-and-take of conversation.

In this section we will look at conversation within the ethnomethodological tradition, its gurus being Sacks, Schegloff, and Jefferson (e.g., Jefferson 1988, Sacks 1992, Schegloff 2007, Sacks et al. 1974). Work within this tradition is referred to as **conversation analysis** (henceforth CA). Conversational analysts working within the ethnomethodological tradition point out that, regardless of how many speakers are involved in a conversation, speakers take turns of various lengths with very little overlap, and turn-taking is usually smooth even though it is quite unordered. Further, there appears to be a built-in repair system known to all participants. Consequently, they examine how people manage conversations; how talk proceeds in turns; how one utterance relates to another, often in a paired relationship; how topics are introduced, developed, and changed; and so on. Their concern is the very orderliness of talk; they regard conversation as skilled work in which we all necessarily participate. Their goal is to explain that order and those skills.

This approach is an inductive one and requires a close analysis of large bodies of tape- and video-recorded naturalistic data. In CA, unlike in linguistic ethnography (discussed in chapter 10) or in interactional sociolinguistics (discussed in the next section), the focus is solely on the recorded data and transcripts; any conclusions investigators draw must emerge exclusively from these data. 'As an empirical discipline, conversational analysis allows order to emerge from the data without an intervening layer of theoretical constructs and allows for the determination of the organizing principles that are used and oriented to by the speakers themselves' (Liddicoat 2007, 8).

The primary goal of CA is to unveil conversational structure and its underlying principles. It is also sometimes said that conversations are **locally managed**, that is, they proceed without any conscious plan and the participants simply rely on using the principles that are available to them to achieve any wider objectives they have. Consequently, in Liddicoat's words (2007, 7): 'What participants say is shaped by and for the context in which it occurs and each next bit of talk is understood in the light of what has preceded it. This contextualization is an important procedure for understanding conversational contributions. ... Each turn at talk is the response to some previous talk and, by its utterance, provides a context in which the next turn at talk will be heard. Conversationalists design their talk to demonstrate the sense they have made of the preceding talk and display, through the construction of their talk, their understanding of the talk-so-far.'

Schegloff (2007, 264) summarizes his perspective on the importance of CA as follows:

> All of these organizations of practice (turn-taking, turn organization, action formation, and sequence organization) and others (repair, word selection, and overall structural organization) operate together all the time to inform the participants' co-construction of the observable, actual conduct in interaction that is the prima facie, bottom-line stuff of social life. Only by observing them all together will we understand how the stuff of social life comes to be as it is. Only by understanding them one by one will we get into a position to observe them all together.

This is a very large claim, one we must treat with caution. As Holtgraves (2002, 119) observes, 'the generalizability of their [i.e., conversational analysts'] findings is not known. And it seems likely that there will be cultural variability in many of the regularities that they have uncovered.' In the remaining sections of our discussion of CA, we will address this issue of generalizability of the research on this topic, and look at further challenges to this paradigm in our sections below on interactional sociolinguistics and critical discourse analysis.

Adjacency pairs

One particularly important principle used in CA is the **adjacency pair**. Utterance types of certain kinds are found to co-occur: a greeting leads to a return of greeting; a summons leads to a response; a question leads to an answer; a request or offer leads to an acceptance or refusal; a complaint leads to an apology or some kind of rejection; a statement leads to some kind of confirmation or recognition; a compliment leads to acceptance or rejection; a farewell leads to a farewell; and so on. Some of the pairings provide a choice, for example, you can either accept or reject a compliment. However, not all second parts are equally preferred. Certain types of responses are preferred, for example, acceptances over refusals, answers over non-answers or silence, and so on. A dispreferred choice is a marked choice and may cause disruption to the conversational flow. These **dispreferred responses** tend to require explanations. For example, if a friend asks you, 'Want to go out for a drink tonight?' you might mark your dispreferred rejection of the invitation with a discourse marker, along with an excuse to provide an indirect refusal: 'Oh, I'd love to, but I have to study for a test.' Schegloff (2007, 61) observes that 'It is important throughout this discussion of preference and dispreference to keep clearly in focus that this is a social/interactional feature of sequences and of orientations to them, *not a psychological one* ... "Preferred" and "dispreferred" ... refer to a structural relationship of sequence parts.'

This basic pairing relationship provides the possibilities of both continuity and exchange in that it enables both parties to say something and for these somethings to be related. It also allows for options in the second member of each pair and for a kind of chaining effect. A question can lead to an answer, which can lead to a comment, which can lead to an acknowledgment, and so on. The ring of a telephone (summons) can lead to a response ('Hello') with the rising intonation of a question, which thus requires an answer, and so on. These are purely linear chains. But there can be other types of chains, as when a question–answer or topic–comment routine is included as a sub-routine into some other pair, as shown in the following example. In this four-turn exchange, the first and last turns are a question and answer adjacency pair, with an additional question and answer pair embedded within this sequence:

A: Are you going to Ashok's party Saturday?
B: Are you?
A: Yes.
B: I wasn't sure, but if you're going I'll go.

It has proved possible to plot the structure of many conversations using these ideas of pairing and chaining in order to show how dependent we are on them. We can also show this same dependence by acknowledging what happens when there are violations: not responding to a question; not offering a comment when one is solicited; not acknowledging a request; not exchanging a greeting; and so on. People are considered rude if they do not greet appropriately, for instance. In classroom interaction, teachers expect that students will respond to their questions: lack of response may be penalized in some way.

However, there is some controversy over whether there is such a basic two-part exchange. Another view holds that a basic 'exchange' has three parts: **initiation**, **response**, and **feedback** (IRF). In this view, unless some form of feedback occurs the total exchange is incomplete (see Stubbs 1983; also, see discussion below on CA in classroom settings). Tsui (1989, 561) also argues for such a three-part exchange in which a following move of some kind closes out the sequence: 'a potentially three-part exchange, which may contain nonverbal component parts, is more adequate than an adjacency pair as a basic unit of conversational organization.'

Openings

The beginning of a conversation, or **opening**, will generally involve an exchange of greetings (see Schegloff 1986). Telephone conversations are often opened with each party saying 'hello,' whereas a meeting between strangers might require a more formal sequence, for example, 'I'm X, nice to meet you' – 'A pleasure, my name is Y.' A meeting between close friends may have its own special ritualistic beginning. Much of this preliminary part of a conversation is highly prescribed by cultural setting: how you answer the telephone varies from group to group; greeting exchanges involving the use of names or address terms vary enormously; who speaks first, what a suitable reply is, and what variety of language is employed may also be tightly constrained by circumstances.

To return briefly to the subject of answering the telephone, we can illustrate a little of the variety we find. Schegloff (1968, 1972, 1986) has described a template for telephone openings in American English in terms of four adjacency pairs. First there is the summons and response (the phone ringing and picking up the phone and giving a brief greeting, often just 'hello'). Next comes the identification sequence, which could be something like *Is that Janet?* – *Yeah*. The third part is an exchange of greeting tokens (*hi / hi*) and finally ritualized inquiry after the other's well-being, (e.g., *How are you? Good, you?*). There is, of course, cross-linguistic and cross-cultural variation in the patterns of openings. In Japan, picking up the phone is seen as a 'turn,' and it is the caller who speaks first on the telephone, and, in doing so, identifies him- or herself. In the Netherlands and Sweden (Lindström 1994, Houtkoop-Steenstra 1991) people usually answer the telephone by identifying themselves. In France, a telephone call is an intrusion, so the caller feels some obligation to verify the number, identify himself, and be excused for intruding (Godard 1977).

Taleghani-Nikazm (2002) carried out research on openings of telephone conversations with three different constellations: (1) conversations between native speakers of German in Germany; (2) conversations between native speakers of Farsi in Iran; and (3) conversations between native speakers of German and Iranian non-native speakers of German in Germany. She found that the Iranian 'how are you' sequence tended to be more elaborate and include inquiries after the health of family members, while among native speakers in Germany the ritual inquiry about well-being was sometimes entirely absent; when it was present it was brief and relatively formulaic. When Iranian non-native speakers of German talk on the telephone with native German speakers, they often use the patterns from their native language and therefore inquired extensively after the health of the other's family. Because of this lack of fit between expectations of the two interlocutors, these openings were in some cases less smooth than those between native speakers who spoke exclusively either German or Farsi. In other cases, the native German speakers interpreted the inquiries after family members not as ritualized parts of the opening, but as topic introductions, and provided detailed answers instead of a formulaic response.

Exploration 11.1: New Technology and Openings

How has increased technology, such as caller i.d. and cell phones, changed openings of phone conversations?

Closings

Conversations must also be brought to a satisfactory close (see Aston 1995). An abrupt **closing**, for example, hanging up on someone during a phone call or just simply being somehow accidentally cut off, may lead to dissatisfaction or bewilderment. Quite often the closing itself is ritualistic, for example, both parties simply saying 'goodbye.' But such rituals do not come unannounced: they are often preceded by clear indications that closings are about to occur. All topics have been exhausted and nothing more remains to be said, but it is not quite the time to exchange farewells. It is into such places that you fit **pre-closing signals** which serve to negotiate the actual closing. Such signals can involve an expression like 'Well, I think that's all,' 'I'll let you go now,' or be a brief, deliberate summary of some earlier agreement. They may also include a personal exchange like 'Give my regards to your wife' or 'It was great meeting you'; alternatively, these signals may take the form of a gesture or a physical movement such as rising from a chair or adjusting physical posture in some way. They signal that the conversation is being closed, with final closure waiting only for a ritual exchange. Once conversationalists arrive at the pre-closing stage, specific acknowledgment of that fact must be made if somehow the conversation does not actually close: 'Oh, by the way; I've just remembered,' or 'Something else has just occurred to me.'

An actual closing may involve several steps: the closing down of a topic, for example, 'So that's agreed' or 'One o'clock, then' repeated by the other party or acknowledged in some form; then possibly some kind of pre-closing exchange, for example, 'Okay-Okay'; a possible further acknowledgment of the nature of the exchange, for example, 'Good to see you,' 'Thanks again,' or 'See you soon'; and finally an exchange of farewells, for example, 'Bye-Bye.' The following is an example of such a closing:

A: So, that's agreed?
B: Yep, agreed.
A: Good, I knew you would.
B: Yes, no problem really.
A: Thanks for the help.
B: Don't mention it.
A: Okay, I'll be back soon.
B: Okay, then. Bye. Take care.
A: Bye.

Exploration 11.2:   Pre-Sequences

Closings are not the only speech acts that speakers may feel the need to work up to; we also often see pre-requests or pre-invitations such as *Can I ask you for a favor?* or *Are you doing anything Saturday night?* In what circumstances – that is, with what interlocutors, and with what type of request or invitation – do you use these pre-sequences? How are these sequences related to the concept of 'face' discussed in the last chapter?

Raclaw (2008) examined closings in instant messaging exchange. He discovered two patterns which deviate somewhat from the patterns found in research on face-to-face interactions, both of which may be linked to the medium of communication. The first pattern is the expanded archetype sequence in which a reason for leaving the chat is introduced (and often evaluated by the other interlocutors), as shown in the excerpt below. This expansion of the pre-closing sequences makes sense in the absence of non-verbal cues that one might make use of in face-to-face interaction.

1   fishfood: so like, i love you and all, but i should probably start
2   my homework :/ (9.0)
3   granola: blech, thats stupid (13.0)
4   fishfood: haha homework IS stupid (5.)
4   granola: yet makes you unstupid (3.0)

 5   granola: OR DOES IT (5.0)
 6   fishfood: haha (3.0)
 7   fishfood: okay, I'll see you tomrrow (6.0)
 8   granola: ok see you then (3.0)
 9   fishfood: later! (2.0)
10   granola: byeeeeeeeee
11   fishfood is away (Raclaw 2008, 12)

The second pattern, partially automated closings, goes in the other direction. Instead of providing more elaboration, it makes use of the automated closing to do the work of the final closing statement, as in this example:

1   leetdood: hey, I should probably go to bed. (11.0)
2   paperdoll: Sweet dreams, hun (8.0)
3   leetdood has signed off (Raclaw 2008, 159)

We can see how the medium of communication influences the patterns but the same principles of interaction are being followed: speakers provide notice that they are closing and a ritual reason for signing off just as they do in telephone conversations and in face-to-face exchanges.

Turn-taking

There is another crucial aspect to conversation: the principles of **turn-taking**. Although we engage in turn-taking easily and skillfully in most cases, with not too much interruption and few awkward pauses, this coordination is much more complex than it might appear. Utterances usually do not overlap other utterances, and the gaps between utterances are sometimes measurable in micro-seconds averaging only a few tenths of a second. Turn-taking also applies in a variety of circumstances: between as few as two participants and upward of a dozen; on the telephone as well as in face-to-face interaction; and regardless of the length of particular utterances or how many people want to take a turn. It seems that there must be some system of 'traffic rules' which we are aware of since we manage the taking of turns so well. It is very rare indeed to see turn-taking spelled out in advance, and this is limited to particular speech events, for example, in ceremonies or formal debates in which turns are pre-allocated. Ordinary conversation employs no such pre-allocation: the participants just 'naturally' take turns. We will see, however, that we can offer some account of what actually occurs.

In most conversations – Schegloff (2000, 47–8) admits that there may be exceptions – only one person speaks at a time and that person is recognized to be the one whose turn it is to speak. At the conclusion of that turn another may speak, but there may also be slight overlapping of speaking during the transition between turns. The existence of adjacency pairing assures that there will be turns; however, it does not assure that these turns will be of any particular length. Once a speaker gets a turn to speak, he or she may be reluctant to give up that turn and may employ any one or more of a variety of devices to keep it: avoidance of eye contact with listeners; stringing utterances together in a seamless manner; avoiding the kinds of adjacency pairings that require others to speak; employing gestures and a posture that inhibit others from speaking; and so on. In these ways a speaker can exploit a turn, but such exploitation can be dangerous if carried to the extreme of 'hogging' the conversation, turning it into a speech or a monolog, or just simply boring the listeners by not allowing them the opportunity to participate or possibly even to escape. You must be prepared to give others a turn if you expect to take a turn yourself. Within a conversation, too, 'each turn … can be inspected by co-participants to see what action(s) may be being done through it. And all *series* of turns can be inspected or tracked … to see what course(s) of action may be being progressively enacted through them, what possible responses may be being made relevant, what outcomes are being pursued, what "sequences" are being constructed or enacted or projected' (Schegloff 2007, 3).

There are also certain linguistic and other signals that go with turn-taking. Speakers may signal when they are about to give up a turn in any one of several ways, or by some combination (Duncan 1972, 1974). The final syllable or final stressed syllable of an utterance may be prolonged. The pitch level of the voice may signal closure, for example, by dropping in level on the final syllable. An utterance may be deliberately closed syntactically to achieve a sense of completeness. Words or expressions like 'you know' or 'something' can also be used to indicate the end of a turn. Finally, the body itself, or part of it, may signal closure: a relaxing of posture; a gesture with a hand; or directing one's gaze at the listener. Such cues signal completion and allow the listener to take a turn. They signal what has been called a **transition relevant place**. We must be alert to such places if we want to take a turn. Of course, such places also offer the speaker the opportunity to select the next speaker. When there are several listeners present, a speaker may attempt to address the cues to a specific listener so as to select that listener as next speaker. Speaking is not always a matter of self-selection; sometimes a specific person is clearly being called upon to speak, even on the most informal of occasions. A speaker's use of gaze, that is, looking at a specific individual, or of a name ('honey,' 'John,' or 'coach') or even a plain 'you' may suffice, but such usage varies widely by group and situation (Lerner 2003). Sometimes, when there is no such selection, there is often an embarrassing pause, and, since conversationalists in many cultures abhor silence, someone will usually try to take up the turn as soon as possible.

The control over who speaks in a conversation is called **floor management**. Edelsky (1981) identified different 'floor types,' F1 being linear and hierarchical and F2 being collaborative and egalitarian; he maintained that the former had mostly male participants while the latter had both male and female participants. Itakura and Tsui (2004) present another perspective on this. They used conversations produced by eight mixed-gender pairs of Japanese university students to look at issues of turn-taking and dominance, that is, who gets to control the floor in conversation.

They found that 'male speakers' self-oriented conversational style and female speakers' other-oriented conversational style are complementary and mutually reinforcing rather than competing. In other words, male dominance is not something predetermined and imposed on female speakers. It is instead mutually constructed by the two parties' (2004, 244).

Turn-taking norms may also vary by cultural group. Tannen (1987, 581) identifies a New York conversational style which she labels as **conversational overlap**. She claims that New Yorkers like a lot of talk going on in casual conversation to the extent that they talk while others are talking. In a later book (1994, 62) she adds that it is 'supportive rather than obstructive, evidence not of domination but of participation, not power, but the paradoxically related dimension, solidarity.' It is speech motivated by high involvement rather than disruption. She does admit in the earlier discussion that those unfamiliar with this habit may well consider themselves to be constantly interrupted or even silenced, feeling that their turn-taking principles have been violated. (See also the link in the online materials to interruptions in a presidential candidate debate from 2012 in the United States, showing some very negative attitudes about such overlap and the intentions behind it.)

Repair

As we have noted above, conversation in real life is not like the dialogues we see in books; there are false starts, stammers, errors, and corrections, that is, what we will call **repairs**. Repairs occur when some kind of 'trouble' arises during the course of conversation. An interjection by a listener (e.g., 'Excuse me' or 'what?') may be an attempt to seek some kind of clarification: this is **other-initiated repair**. **Self-repair** occurs when the speaker seeks to clarify in some way what is being said and not being understood, or correct or further elaborate on what has been said. Egbert (1996) reports on an interesting example of other-initiated repair, the use of *bitte* 'pardon' in German. *Bitte* initiates repair but only when there is no mutual gaze between the parties. This use of *bitte* carries over to the telephone where there can be no such mutual gaze. Egbert (2004) looks at how repair can also serve to create membership categorizations among speakers of German. For example, in one conversation she analyzes, a speaker named Tina uses an English phrase, *frat guys*, which is not understood by her interlocutor, although it is unclear if this is because the addressee did not hear what she said or did not understand the term. Tina's response to the request for repair is to translate the phrase into German, thereby positioning herself as possessing language and culture-specific information (about English and college fraternities) that her interlocutor does not have. In another conversation, Tina's pronunciation of the German word *zäh* 'tough' is at first not understood and then repaired, and Tina immediately uses this opportunity to create a different membership categorization for herself: *ja ich komm aus ostfriesland* ('yes i come from east frisia'). This utterance diagnoses the difficulty in comprehension as rooted in Tina's identity as a speaker of a particular German dialect. This research shows that the organization of talk is not just geared solely toward transmitting propositional content, but also integral to our presentations of self and others.

Institutional talk

CA is also concerned with institutional interactions. Research on these settings shows that in certain circumstances some of the principles we customarily use in conversation are not used at all, or are used in special ways, or are used in an 'abnormal' manner. Here we will briefly discuss two such settings, classrooms and doctor's offices.

Teachers and students play different roles in classroom settings and their language choices relate to those roles, as Gardner (2012, 594) explains:

> There appears to be a set of underlying normative practices for turn-taking (teacher dominates next speaker selection, students have limited rights for next speaker selection), sequence organization (teacher produces first-pair parts and has special rights to talk in third position, students predominantly produce second-pair parts), and repair (teachers dominate other initiations of repair, typically following a student answer to their question). However, some research indicates that other conversational resources are exploited in specific ways in classrooms, and teachers appear to have greater access to these than students as a result of their role as teachers.

Overall, the picture that emerges of classroom talk is one in which teachers wield a great deal of power. In traditional, teacher-centered classrooms, the teacher gets to ask most of the questions, and, on the whole, these questions are of a very special kind: they are usually questions to which the teacher already has the answer. The format usually associated with this style of teaching is the above-mentioned IRF sequence (i.e., initiation – response – feedback); the teacher asks a question, a student responds, and the teacher provides feedback on the answer (in some cases, judging the answer to be 'right' or 'wrong'). There are also other characteristics of questioning in the classroom setting which differ from everyday conversation. The questions are quite often addressed to a whole group of listeners and individuals in that group are required to bid for the right to answer. Furthermore, when someone is chosen to answer the question, the whole answering ritual is gone through for the benefit of all participants, not just for the benefit of the one who asked the question. Finally, the questioner actually evaluates the answer as one which is not only right in providing the information that was sought but also right in relation to how the teacher is seeking to develop the topic. However, recent research stresses that as pedagogical changes occur to less teacher-centered, more talk-based and group-work-oriented classroom practices, we have far less information about the structure of conversation in these classroom settings. This is one direction for future research in CA.

Doctor–patient interaction is also full of questioning behavior, but in this case the questions are asked for the purposes of double-checking and eliciting anything that might be relevant to deciding on a particular course of action. Such questioning may also be used for the purpose of classification: the name of a disease given to symptoms that have been elicited, or a course of therapy indicated as a result of psychiatric assessment. In each case the conversation is directed toward establishing relevant 'facts' at a level of certainty that one would never tolerate in ordinary discussion of what happened or is happening.

There is a body of research which looks at how doctors interact with patients and seeks to illustrate how the power differential and conversational structure can influence the effectiveness of medical care. Drew et al. (2001, 67) note that 'the opportunities which patients have to participate and the nature and extent of that participation are closely bound up, in systematic ways, with the design of what doctors say during the interaction. Hence, patient participation should be understood as at least partially the interactional product of doctors' communicative practices and choices – in ways which go beyond what is known already about the differential opportunities which open and closed questions offer patients to contribute and fully to describe their experiences.' This type of research clearly has practical applications, and it is worth noting that Maynard and Heritage (2005) have published an introduction to conversation analysis for medical educators, aimed at helping equip doctors in training to better communicate and understand their interactions with patients, in particular during medical interviews. For example, patients, when describing their symptoms, often provide an explanation of what is called the 'doctorabililty' of their problems, that is, they seek to establish their justification for seeking medical attention. It is important for doctors to understand that patients seek to legitimate their actions as part of their presentation of their symptoms. Maynard and Heritage suggest CA-based reviews of doctor–patient interactions so medical students can learn to identify critical moments in these interviews.

CA does not, however, offer the only way to view conversation. Some researchers even object to the constraints of this approach, arguing that the role of researcher is not simply to describe; see for instance a published discussion of the different viewpoints of scholars of critical discourse analysis and CA (Billig 1999, van Dijk 1999) and post-structural discourse analysis and CA (Baxter 2002a, 2002b, West 2002). We will address these issues later in this chapter, but before doing that, we will introduce two other approaches, interactional sociolinguistics and critical discourse analysis. These approaches incorporate contextual information and information about the speakers into their analyses.

Interactional Sociolinguistics

Gumperz is considered the founder of an approach to analyzing interactions called **interactional sociolinguistics**, which he defines it as '... the search for replicable methods of qualitative analysis that account for our ability to interpret what participants intend to convey in everyday communicative practice' (2003, 4). He maintains that interactive sociolinguistics has its origin in the ethnography of communication, conversation analysis, ethnomethodology, Goffman's work on face and Grice's principles of conversational cooperation. The focus is on diversity and intercultural communication; much of Gumperz' own work focused on how differences in communicative practices can contribute to discrimination (see also Tannen 2005 on the relationship between interactional sociolinguistics and intercultural pragmatics).

Rampton (2007) says that interactional sociolinguistics is one strand of linguistic ethnography (see the discussion in chapter 9) because it looks at a wider context than just the particular interaction being studied. Whereas in CA only the information gleaned from the interaction being analyzed is considered relevant, in interactional sociolinguistics information about the speakers and societal norms or ideologies from ethnographic research or interviews with research participants can also be incorporated.

One example of recent work in this tradition is found in Rampton's work on social class among teenagers at a multiethnic comprehensive school in London. He looked at how the speakers' use of what he describes as 'traditional posh/upper class voices or ... Cockney/vernacular London accents' (2007, 6) indicates how social class is relevant in their worlds. Although the analysis involves a close analysis of the data to identify the features of particular styles, the knowledge of the social meanings of these styles comes from outside of the interactions being studied, that is, from the researcher's own knowledge about ideologies concerning social class and the particular linguistic varieties that exist in London. Further, the researcher's knowledge about the individual speakers and their social and linguistic backgrounds also informs the analysis. In this case, one of the pupils in the classroom, Hanif, frequently performs stylizations of nonstandard English dialects (Cockney and a quasi-Caribbean accent) as well as a 'posh' accent. Teachers do not censor such performances; indeed, they are apparently a receptive audience for many of them. Further, Hanif is not the only student who uses such stylized utterances. Because of his ethnographic research and his understanding of the relationships that exist in the classroom, Rampton (2007, 9) is able to make some generalizations about how these styles are used: 'Cockney seemed to be associated with vigour, passion and bodily laxity, while posh got linked to physical weakness, social distance, constraint and sexual inhibition.' He is also able to make a detailed analysis of particular usages, for example, he is able to show how Hanif, a strong student, uses 'cockneyization' when helping his peers with an assignment. These stylizations do not disrupt work on academic tasks, rather, 'it would be more accurate to describe Hanif as making school knowledge more vernacular and accessible, bringing the science worksheet to life with non-standard accents and a popular TV format' (Rampton 2007, 8). Rampton discusses associations between Cockney and posh speech and different types of power, noting that Cockney speech is linked to a nonconformist power whereas posh speech is more often associated with institutional power (and sometimes mockery of such); however, in all cases the social class associations are key elements in any interpretation of stylistic variation. He summarizes, 'What the analysis shows, in short, is that these kids' everyday practical consciousness was deeply impregnated with the sensibilities that we traditionally associate with social class in Britain' (Rampton 2007, 10). Ethnographically gained knowledge about the school, the repertoires of the pupils, and the values of the various ways of speaking in the wider community is essential to interpreting specific utterances and interactions.

Gafaranga (2010) also links specific interactional practices and macrosocial proc-esses in his research on language shift in a Rwandan community in Belgium. He focuses on a practice of 'medium request,' in which younger speakers will ask someone from an older generation to speak French rather than Kinyarwanda. This request is usually not an explicit request, but rather one made through a code choice, that is, through speaking French. The overall pattern shows that although in many aspects of social life children are expected to conform to adult norms for interaction, in this case adults, who are categorized as bilingual, accommodate to children, who are known to prefer French (see chapter 4 for more discussion of code choice by individuals and in communities). Consequently, the members of this community 'talk language shift into being' (Gafaranga 2010, 249). We have in this research not just an analysis of how speakers use their particular codes, but also information about the sociohistorical context in which their interactions are situated that allows us to understand the social meanings and impact of particular ways of speaking.

Data and methodologies

Work within the interactional sociolinguistics approach is primarily **qualitative**. In most cases, much of the analysis uses data which has been recorded and transcribed, as with CA research. However, interactional sociolinguistic research also draws on data about the wider context in which the conversation takes place and requires the researcher to interpret specific utterance meaning with reference to cultural norms. Thus, in addition to recording and transcribing conversational data, investigators must necessarily include qualitative methods which allow them to gain knowledge of the speech community norms, the repertoires of particular individuals, and the relationships among speakers. Such methods can include ethnographies, interviews, and surveys about language use and attitudes.

Traditionally there has been a focus in sociolinguistics on what has been called 'naturally occurring data,' for example, recordings of people having conversations that they would supposedly have had whether or not they were being recorded. However, many other types of data can be used in discourse studies. Wortham et al. (2011) argue that even interviews which are done in order to gain propositional information from the interviewees contain interactional positionings, and these positionings necessarily involve issues of categorization, power relationships, and identification of selves and others. Their study of interviews about payday muggings in the Latino Diaspora in the United States shows how the people interviewed con-structed social categories of muggers and victims, assigned individuals to these categories, and positioned themselves with respect to them. Although the major focus of these interviews is racial/ethnic categories (i.e., stories about African Americans mugging Mexican immigrants, with stereotypes about the violent tendencies of the former and the latter taking jobs that should go to US citizens), one interview includes a narrative by a young Mexican who characterizes victims as older Mexicans, while youths like himself are capable of defending themselves. The various stances reflect ideas about social structure and stratification and how speakers see themselves with regard to their constructed social realities. The authors conclude: 'Whatever the value of the propositional descriptions they offer, interviewees also position themselves interactionally and evaluate aspects of the social world through the same discourse that they use to refer to and predicate about the topic. By attending to interactional texts, interviewers can sometimes learn about habitual positions that people take in everyday life. ...' (Wortham et al. 2011, 49). Interview data are frequently used in analyses within the interactional sociolinguistics paradigm.

Further, data from computer-mediated discourse and other new media are also increasingly a focus of such research (see Akkaya (in press), Androutsopoulos 2006, and Herring 2008, for overviews of work on these topics). Androutsopoulos (2008) discusses online ethnography as a research method, concluding that the use of an ethnographic perspective in looking at language in digital social life can enhance the analysis of other types of data (interviews and online discourses). Georgakopoulou (2006) also endorses micro-ethnographies in the analysis of computer-mediated communication, specifically to make connections between single communicative events and larger processes, as is the goal of interactional sociolinguistics. She also notes that such data lends itself well to quantitative analysis; such corpus linguistic studies will be discussed in the next section. It should also be noted that some studies employ interviews with users of new media to do meta-analyses about how various types of media are used to do the social work of identity construction and relationship maintenance (Akkaya 2012, Gershon 2010); Thurlow (2006) uses print media discussions of new media to do a similar type of analysis.

Exploration 11.3: What Is Natural?

If we say that we want to get at 'natural' speech, what does that mean? (Look back at the discussion of the observer's paradox in chapter 6 for one perspective on this.) Is the way you speak to your family and close friends the natural way for you to speak in all situations? If you use different languages, dialects, or styles in different contexts, is one or the other more natural than the others? What is the role of context in determining what natural speech is?

Quantitative analyses also have a place within the interactional sociolinguistics paradigm. For example, quantitative work within the framework of audience design (Bell 1984, 2001) clearly represents the spirit of interactional sociolinguistics in the incorporation of social meanings of particular ways of speaking (e.g., their association with particular ethnic groups) and their use in interactions. Schilling-Estes' work on stylistic variation also exemplifies this productive combination of quantitative and qualitative perspectives in bringing macro level factors into discourse analysis (Schilling-Estes 2004).

Contextualization

Gumperz uses the term **contextualization** to discuss how we use our background knowledge to navigate through conversations. 'I use the term "contextualization" to refer to speakers' and listeners' use of verbal and non-verbal signs to relate what is said at any one time and at any one place to knowledge acquired through past experience' (Gumperz 1992, 230). Verbal contextualization cues can include a wide variety of linguistic features; Gumperz mentions prosody, pauses, and tempo in conversation, and also code and lexical choices. (As we discussed in chapter 4, Gumperz has argued that switching from one code to another can be a signal of a switch in the situation, for example, the transition from informal chat between colleagues to addressing a work issue might be marked by a switch in code.) Other research (Schiffrin 1987) has discussed how discourse markers – particles such as *oh*, *well*, or *y'know* – also provide contextualization which helps the listener to understand the utterance it frames. For instance, non-preferred responses (see above) are often prefaced with *oh* or *well*, as in the response to an invitation 'Oh I'd love to, but I have class that night.' A preferred response (acceptance) would more likely occur without such a discourse marker (e.g., 'Sure! What time?').

Androutsopoulos (2000) looks at regiolectal and interlingual spellings in German punk fanzines (i.e., fan magazines). In this context, spellings which index regional dialects are used to indicate a lack of subcultural knowledge (knowledge about punk music) of the person being portrayed. Although a spelling indicating a Germanized pronunciation of English loanwords can have a similar function, that is, it can mark the person attributed with the utterance as being ignorant of punk culture and the (American) English culture it draws on, such a usage can also be a marker of how the concept has been taken into the heart of punk culture: 'the Germanized spelling indicates that a culturally relevant referent has "gone native," is a part of the writer's life-world' (Androutsopoulos 2000, 525). This is the classic understanding of a contextualization cue; it provides the addressees with information that enables them to properly understand how the utterance should be interpreted. As can be seen from these examples, there are various linguistic features, along with extralinguistic cues, which can provide such contextualization.

Stance

Contextualization cues are also seen as the basic tools for **stancetaking**, a concept introduced in chapter 7. Although some of the recent work on stance has come out of variationist work on style, work on stance also fits well within the interactional sociolinguistics paradigm. In any interaction, speakers use language to position themselves in multiple ways. They take a stance toward their own utterances and those of others, toward ideologies referenced in these utterances and toward the speakers themselves. In addition to being linked to work on contextualization cues, work on stance is linked to work on identity construction; as Jaffe (2009, 11) writes: 'Social identity can thus be seen as the culmination of stances taken over time.' There are particular conventional associations of particular ways of speaking in certain contexts, and speakers make use of these to take stances, and through these stances to construct social identities. For instance, using hedges can be linked to a stance of deference, and deference may be linked to femininity (Johnston 2007). However, such interpretations are not fixed, but emerge through dialogical interaction. Consequently, stance is not just subjective but intersubjective; that is, it is not constructed only by the speaker but is a joint construction (Kärkkäinen 2006).

In her work on language choice by teachers in a Corsican school, Jaffe (2007, 2009) shows how the use of French or Corsican positions the teachers with regard to both the content and the form of their utterances, that is, such language choices are stancetaking devices. As Jaffe shows, in order to interpret these stances we must understand the historical and cultural context of the languages and also have information about speaker attitudes, repertoires, and practices. The children in these schools are largely dominant in French, and consequently instruction in and through Corsican has a language revitalization goal. Jaffe claims that teachers strive to construct Corsican as a legitimate language for education and literacy practices, using their positions of authority to lend weight to this stance. A further conversational strategy which creates this stance regarding Corsican is the use of that language for evaluative comments (i.e., within the Initiation – Response – Feedback format for classroom discourse discussed above):

> So, the fact that the teacher uses Corsican for expansions confers on that language the authority embedded in the modeling function of teacher speech, at the same time as it performatively links the child (through his or her expanded utterances) to the code (Corsican) used by the teacher. It too suggests the child should and could have the relationship with Corsican that the teacher does (Jaffe 2007, 75).

However, the relationship between Corsican and French which is constructed within the school – a relationship of equality – is not the relationship that these languages have in the wider society, where French is clearly dominant and Corsican has little practical value. It is also important to note that few of the children come to school proficient in Corsican, so to some extent the teachers' use of Corsican was intertwined with students' positions as non-native speakers and language learners.

In the next section, we will focus more on this aspect of sociolinguistic research, that is, on interactions between speakers with linguistically and culturally different backgrounds.

Intercultural communication

One type of conversational configuration often examined within the interactional sociolinguistics framework is intercultural communication. Verbal exchanges which involve people from different cultural backgrounds can more easily go wrong than those that involve people who share the same cultural background (Gumperz and Cook-Gumperz 1982, 14):

> Many of the meanings and understandings, at the level of ongoing processes of inter-pretation of speaker's intent, depend upon culturally specific conventions, so that much of the meaning in any encounter is indirect and implicit. The ability to expose enough of the implicit meaning to make for a satisfactory encounter between strangers or culturally different speakers requires communicative flexibility.

Not everyone has such communicative flexibility, this ability to cross cultural boundaries. Consequently, when the cross-cultural exchange involves some important matter, for example, a trial, an interview for a position, or a disagreement between employer and employee, there can be a serious breakdown in communication from the lack of such flexibility, as one party finds the other to be 'evasive,' 'confrontational,' 'irrelevant,' 'angry,' 'aloof,' or 'indifferent.' We tend to rely very heavily on our own cultural background in interpreting the talk of others, and it may not be at all easy to understand how this can create difficulties when the others are either complete strangers or come from quite different cultural backgrounds.

Many such situations are also asymmetrical insofar as power is concerned. When the parties to an exchange have both different norms of behavior and claims to power, their intentions toward each other must be our concern. Farfán (2003) recounts a very good example of such inequalities in power between a Mestizo professional middleman buyer and a poor female Hñahñu occasional seller in a marketplace in Mexico. The buyer has better control of Spanish and is socio-economically better off, and can thus potentially not participate in the deal; the seller needs the money she gets for goat skins to survive. The convention is that they should bargain to reach a fair price for the skins because they are 'equal' parties. However, in addition to the inequalities in language, gender, and economic standing, there is consistent violation of the linguistic conventions of buying and selling. The buyer takes control of the opening exchange, manipulates the turn-taking, cuts short the seller's responses, and, in fact, produces what might better be described as a monolog. For the buyer this strategy maximizes his profits; for the seller it provides further confirmation of her oppression. The language use testifies to the fundamental social asymmetry that exists. In the following section, we will look further at certain other possible asymmetries in the distribution of power, and at the views of Fairclough and others like him that sociolinguists should do more than just report on the imbalances they find: they should seek to reduce them.

Exploration 11.4: Cross-Cultural Communication?

Some research on gender differences in language has discussed communication between men and women as cross-cultural communication. One of the foci of this research is misunderstandings, with the claim that men and women have different cultural backgrounds and thus often misinterpret the words of members of the other group. In what ways do you think that this is an accurate way of thinking about male-female interactions, and in what ways does this seem to be in accurate? Give examples, if you can, from your own experience.

Critical Discourse Analysis

Critical discourse analysis (CDA) is an approach which aims to analyze relationships of dominance, discrimination, power, and control in text and talk (Blommaert and Bulcaen 2000, Fairclough 1995, 2013, Wodak and Meyer 2001, van Dijk 1993b, 2003). In cases in which these relationships between different social groups are openly acknowledged (e.g., in discussion of gender differences), it is the role of CDA to point out that they are not natural and inevitable but socially constructed and naturalized. In other instances, asymmetrical social structures may not be explicitly referenced, but are indirectly manifested in language use; for example, articles in parenting magazines may subtly assume an audience of mothers. In these cases, CDA seeks to make these ideologies visible in order to question their validity. Thus CDA, while focused on language, has a social goal. Fairclough (2013, 10) writes:

> Some versions of critiques are only normative or moral, but I take the (Marxist) view that changing the world for the better depends on being able to explain how it has come to be the way it is. It is one thing to critique people's language and practices on the grounds that they are racist, but another to explain why and how racism emerges or becomes virulent amongst certain people in certain circumstances.

The term **Discourse** in this context means more than just text or talk. We use this term (often in the plural) to mean how certain ways of speaking are combined with certain cultural models to produce and reproduce social meanings and structures (see Gee 2014). Gee has called this 'capital "D" Discourse,' to distinguish it from the use of 'discourse' to mean the equivalent of 'conversation.'

The concept of **social power** in CDA is often defined in terms of the ability of a social group or institution to control the actions and the worldview of other groups. Such power can be based on military support, economic resources, or persuasiveness. Integral to this view of power is the concept of **hegemony**. Hegemony refers to power that is achieved through consent; certain groups of people or ways of being are granted social prestige (and thus power) because there is a consensus that they are somehow superior and inherently more valuable. For instance, we can talk about standard languages as being hegemonic, as even speakers of nonstandard varieties have often internalized and naturalized the idea that the standard is superior. The access to and control over public discourse is a main focus of CDA.

Contrasts and critiques

A major difference between CA and CDA is the role that information external to the text plays in the analysis, and also how the analysis is empirically supported. An exchange between researchers in these respective areas (Schegloff and Billig) was featured in *Discourse & Society* in 1999 (Billig 1999), and addressed in particular the issue of the centrality of the textual analysis. As noted in his introduction by the journal editor van Djik, a researcher who is himself associated with CDA, a debate between scholars who employ different approaches does not imply incompatibility of goals between the two approaches; both are concerned with naturally occurring text or talk, both see a detailed analysis of the text itself as part of the process, and both are potentially relevant for looking at the social dimensions of discourse. Of course, one difference is that there are CA researchers who do *not* see such societal critiques as part of their research agenda, and therein lies a key difference: CDA is necessarily aimed at addressing social injustices and discrimination, while CA can, but need not, be.

Methodologies and connections

CDA is not a method of discourse analysis, but a way of viewing the world which influences how text and talk are analyzed. Van Dijk (2001, 352) writes, 'CDA is not so much a direction, school, or specialization next to the many other "approaches" in discourse studies. Rather, it aims to offer a different "mode" or "perspective" of theorizing, analysis, and application throughout the whole field. We may find a more or less critical perspective in such diverse areas as pragmatics, conversation analysis, narrative analysis, rhetoric, stylistics, sociolinguistics, ethnography, or media analysis, among others.'

One way of doing CDA is what is called the discourse historical approach (Wodak and Meyer 2001). This approach looks at discourse with a focus on how it is embedded in the social historical context, and takes into account four levels of context:

1.   the immediate, language or text internal co-text;
2.   the intertextual and interdiscursive relationship between utterances, texts, genres and discourses;
3.   the extralinguistic social/sociological variables and institutional frames of a specific 'context of situation' (middle range theories);
4.   the broader sociopolitical and historical contexts, which the discursive practices are embedded in and related to ('grand' theories). (Wodak and Meyer 2001, 67)

In her study of the construction of an anti-Semitic stereotyped *Feindbild* ('image of the enemy') in Austria, Wodak focuses on particular discourse events in the 1986 presidential campaign of Kurt Waldheim, historical events referenced through intertextuality, and interdiscursive relationships of these discourses with other texts. Wodak (2007) also shows how a pragmatic analysis can be incorporated into CDA in her research on propaganda slogans and rhetoric in the regional election campaign in Vienna in 2001. This study illustrates how pragmatics can help us understand how implicature, allusion, and presupposition work in ideological Discourses. Wodak shows how comments within culturally embedded phrases made by a politician about the president of the Jewish community in Vienna serve to imply criminality and collusion with an international Jewish community and a lack of authentic Austrian identity.

Van Dijk (2003, 2008, 2009) focuses on not just social aspects of discourse but also cognitive ones in his sociocognitive approach to CDA. This includes '... mental representations and the processes of language users when they produce and comprehend discourse and participate in verbal interaction, as well as in the knowledge, ideologies and other beliefs shared by social groups. At the same time, such an approach examines the ways in which such cognitive phenomena are related to the structures of discourse, verbal interaction, communicative events and situations, as well as societal structures, such as those of domination and social inequality. ...' (van Dijk 2009, 64). He notes that his focus is not to imply that analysis should be limited to social and cognitive dimensions to discourse, but proposes these as fruitful for better understanding the relationships between mind, discursive interactions, and society, as well as for understanding particular ideological discourses, such as the discourse of racism (van Dijk 1991, 1992, 1993a). For example, van Dijk (1992) looks at how, in everyday conversations as well as in institutional text and talk, the denial of racism is an essential part of discourses that perpetuate racial prejudices, especially among social elites. As van Dijk notes, '... such discourse signals group membership, white ingroup allegiances and, more generally, the various conditions for the reproduction of the white group and their dominance in virtually all social, political, and cultural domains' (van Dijk 1992, 88).

Lazar (2005, 2007, 2009, 2011) presents a version of CDA she calls feminist critical discourse analysis, which examines in particular how ideologies in discourse perpetuate gender hierarchies. In an examination of a 'Family Life' advertising campaign in Singapore (Lazar 2005), she shows how a discourse of egalitarian gender roles in the family is appropriated within the hegemonic discourse of conservative, asymmetrical gender roles. While being an active, involved father is made acceptable in these advertisements, they do not seriously challenge the underlying ideology in which men are the major breadwinners and women are primarily responsible for child care. Another analysis of advertisements directed at women (Lazar 2009) shows how what at first glance appears to be 'pro-women' sentiments – telling women that they should indulge and pamper themselves, because they are worth it! – presents the concerns of women as trivial and, inevitably, related to improving their appearance (e.g., make-up, bath products, and slimming treatments). Far from challenging any discourses about the low social value of women, this type of advertising reinforces the view of women as being primarily valuable because of their appearances. Lazar discusses how this ideology fits within a putative 'post-feminist discourse,' in which women are presented as having 'arrived' in terms of equality and thus any concerns about their social position are seen as fanatical and old-fashioned; modern women can be concerned with reclaiming femininity through cosmetics, wearing pink, and anointing themselves with floral scents.

Another approach recently combined with CDA is the analysis of large computerized corpora, that is, **corpus linguistics**. In corpus linguistics researchers search such corpora for particular lexical items and collocations; the data may be interpreted critically. Orpin (2005) looked at how words about political corruption were used in a corpus of British newspapers. She noted a drastic growth of such terms since 1985 and was also able to make some generalizations about what words were used to describe activities in particular countries. The more negative terms ('bribery,' 'graft'), which were common in articles about other countries, were increasingly also used to describe the British context. However, certain terms which less clearly indicated criminal behavior, such as 'impropriety' or 'sleaze' were rarely used to describe Italy, and never to talk about events in Pakistan, China, South Korea, India, and Malaysia. These milder terms continued to be used primarily to talk about Britain, while other countries' corruption was described as clearly illegal.

Baker et al. (2008) is another article combining CDA with corpus linguistics for an analysis of British newspapers. The authors examined news articles about refugees, asylum seekers, immigrants, and migrants and how certain collocations are used to create particular representations of people in these categories. By using both of these approaches, they found categories of reference and supported them through a quantitative analysis. Illustrative of the results of such an analysis is the observation, 'A common strategy was to quantify RAS [refugees and asylum seekers] in terms of water metaphors (POUR, FLOOD, STREAM), which tend to dehumanize RAS, constructing them as an out-of-control, agentless, unwanted natural disaster' (Baker et al. 2008, 287).

It should be noted, however, that CDA analyses on newspaper data do not necessarily focus on quantitative analysis of large corpora but may be purely qualitative. Teo (2000) analyzes nine news reports from two Australian newspapers which discuss a Vietnamese gang in Sydney. His analysis includes a general characterization of the newspaper discourse and illustrates how it serves to 'otherize' members of the Vietnamese community. A more detailed analysis of two reports reveals a power discourse in the depiction of the (ethnic) lawbreakers and the (White) police officers. This critique is not merely a critique of journalistic practices, but also of the larger structure of oppression within which such practices occur.

Qualitative analyses in CDA may also look at conversational data. For example, Rogers and Mosley (2008) analyze a discussion among pre-service teachers concerning racial literacy that focuses on children's books and addresses issues of racial representations, definitions of anti-racism, and White privilege. Their conclusions point to the pedagogical benefit of having teachers in training participate in such discussions as part of their preparation for working in a multicultural society.

CDA has also developed a connection to ethnographic research. In a special issue of the journal *Critical Discourse Studies* devoted to the topic, Krzyżanowski (2011) discusses the productive relationship between CDA and ethnography. He notes that bringing ethnographic perspectives to CDA research has emphasized the need to examine the relationship between context and text, and broadened the notion of context to include not just physical or linguistic context but also societal context, including therein social, cognitive, and linguistic aspects and a focus on the producers of the text or speech being studied. This broader perspective has brought about inclusion of concepts such as **interdiscursivity** (see Wodak 2000, Wodak and Meyer 2001). Interdiscursivity involves using discourses from one context in another involving processes of **decontextualization** and **recontextualization**. Such analyses involve recognizing how features of one genre of speech are incorporated into new discursive contexts. Fairclough (2001, 127–36) gives an example of this in an analysis of the Foreword written by the British Prime Minister Tony Blair to the Department of Trade and Industry's White Paper on competitiveness in 1998. Although this is a political text, Blair uses development economic language (such as what might be found in an analysis by the World Bank), combined with political discourse, to represent the 'new global economy' as an inevitable process which is not driven by social agents but is merely part of a world-wide development to which 'we' must respond.

In the next and final part of this book, we will take up some of these issues and look at more research in sociolinguistics which deals with social inequalities. We will examine three topics within the broader topic of social justice: language, gender, and sexuality; language and education; and language planning.

Chapter Summary

This chapter introduces three approaches to the analysis of discourse: conversation analysis (CA), which has grown out of ethnomethodology (discussed in chapter 9); interactional sociolinguistics, an umbrella term for ways of analyzing conversations which incorporate the larger societal norms and values within which they are situated; and critical discourse analysis (CDA), which is a method designed to show how social inequality is reproduced through language use.

Exercises

1. Record some openings and closings of telephone calls on a call-in radio show, and transcribe them. What are the patterns in these exchanges, and how are they different from and similar to openings and closings in conversations between friends, in your experience and in the literature cited in this chapter? That is, how does the relationship between the speakers influence the structure of the conversation?

2. The following transcript is a conversation between two White, US American, female college students; they have just returned to campus after a break for Thanksgiving, a major US holiday. Hooters, Show Me's, and Stix are all bar/restaurants that are known for having female servers who wear revealing clothes. What Discourses about gender are evident in this conversation? What stances do these speakers adopt with regard to the gender norms they discuss? What linguistic features are used to do this stancetaking?

    1. A: oh. Where'd you stay over Thanksgiving?
    2. B: I went to Chicago
    3. A: oh, fun
    4. B: my aunt lives there, and then I, my friend Chelsea, I went and saw her, and then we came back here early, like Saturday night?
    5. A: uh-oh, there's trouble
    6. B: oh, we, it was absolutely out of control
    7. A: ah!
    8. B: we were cra:zy. We went to Hooters and ate
    9. A: mmm. I love their Buffalo wings
    10. B: oh my gosh, we got those? And uhm, but there are these sick girls working there, they were so ugly, I'm like, why are you girls working here? They were just ugly. And they weren't very tan, like they were real pale, and like they were so not cute
    11. A: oh
    12. B: and we were all like, ew
    13. A: pale makes you look bigger, too, if you're gonna run around in little shirts and shorts like that, you'd better be tanned and toned
    14. B: what do they have to wear at Show-Me's?
    15. A: I think the same kind of outfits just different colors
    16. B: really
    17. A: I think their colors are like black and purple or something?
    18. B: really
    19. A: and they have to wear like little tiny shorts and tight little tops
    20. B: I wanna work there {laughs}
    21. A: I could see you workin' there
    22. B: cause I need, it'd be good tips, it'd be good money

23. A: would your house be mad, though, if you like left lookin' like that all the time?
24. B: no, because, there's this one girl that works at Stix, and she wears like, it's like a bra and underwear to work, it's what it looks like
25. A: I hate xxxx
26. B: I hate Stix outfits, I hate 'em, they are so degrading
27. A: they're so trashy looking, like, you walk in and see girls running around like that? And you think, I don't want a hair in my drink, I'm not, it just, it looks trashy
28. B: it's degrading, it's like, ew. I hate it. I absolutely hate going there

Further Reading

Billig, Michael (2008). The Language of Critical Discourse Analysis: The Case of Nominalization. *Discourse & Society* 19(6): 783–800.

Martin, J. R. (2008). Incongruent and Proud: De-vilifying 'Nominalization.' *Discourse & Society* 19(6): 801–10.

Fairclough, Norman (2008). The Language of Critical Discourse Analysis: A Reply to Billig. *Discourse & Society* 19(6): 811–19.

van Dijk, Teun A. (2008). Critical Discourse Analysis and Nominalization: Problem or Pseudo-Problem? *Discourse & Society* 19(6): 821–8.

Billig, Michael (2008). Nominalizing and De-nominalizing: A Reply. *Discourse & Society* 19(6): 829–41.

Fairclough, Norman (2008). A Brief Response to Billig. *Discourse & Society* 19(6): 843–4.
These articles represent an exchange about the perspectives on language central to CDA, and how researchers themselves must be cognizant of how they use language and position themselves in doing their analyses.

Huth, Thorsten (2011). Conversation Analysis and Language Classroom Discourse. *Language and Linguistics Compass* 5(5): 297–309.
An overview of CA research carried out in language classrooms; this body of research addresses issue of language choice as well as conversational structure.

Kotthoff, Helga (2010). Sociolinguistic Potentials of Face-to-Face Interaction. In Ruth Wodak, Barbara Johnstone, and Paul E. Kerswill (eds.), *The SAGE Handbook of Sociolinguistics*. London: Sage Publications, 315–29.
This examines research done within interactional sociolinguistics, ethnography of communication, CDA and CA frameworks and its potential with regard to using analyses of interactions to address issues of social categories and stratification, with a particular focus on gender.

Lazar, Michelle M. (2007). *Feminist Critical Discourse Analysis: Gender, Power and Ideology in Discourse*. Basingstoke: Palgrave Macmillan.
After an introduction from Lazar laying out the main tenets of this approach to discourse analysis, the subsequent chapters present analyses of sexism and gender ideologies in media portrayals from many languages and cultures.

Sidnell, Jack and Tanya Stivers (eds.) (2012). *The Handbook of Conversation Analysis*. Oxford: Wiley-Blackwell.

This book provides an up-to-date presentation of the theory and methods used in conversation analysis, including contributions explaining key terms used in the field. It further addresses research done among particular populations and settings (e.g., *children*, courtrooms) and how CA fits with a variety of academic disciplines.

For further resources for this chapter visit the companion website at

 www.wiley.com/go/wardhaugh/sociolinguistics

References

Akkaya, Aslihan (2012). Devotion and Friendship through Facebook: An Ethnographic Approach to Language, Community, and Identity Performances of Young Turkish-American Women. PhD diss. Carbondale: Southern Illinois University.

Akkaya, Aslihan (in press). Language, Discourse and New Media: A Linguistic Anthropological Perspective. *Language and Linguistic Compass*.

Androutsopoulos, J. K. (2000). Non-standard Spellings in Media Texts: The Case of German Fanzines. *Journal of Sociolinguistics* 4(4): 514–33.

Androutsopoulos, J. K. (2006). Introduction: Sociolinguistics and Computer-Mediated Communication. *Journal of Sociolinguistics* 10(4): 419–38.

Androutsopoulos, J. (2008). Potentials and Limitations of Discourse-Centred Online Ethnography. *Language@ Internet* 5(8).

Aston, G. (1995). Say 'Thank You': Some Pragmatic Constraints on Conversational Closings. *Applied Linguistics* 16(1): 57–86.

Baker, P., C. Gabrielatos, M. Khosravinik et al. (2008). A Useful Methodological Synergy? Combining Critical Discourse Analysis and Corpus Linguistics to Examine Discourses of Refugees and Asylum Seekers in the UK Press. *Discourse & Society* 19(3): 273–306.

Baxter, Judith (2002a). Competing Discourses in the Classroom: A Post-structuralist Discourse Analysis of Girls' and Boys' Speech in Public Contexts. *Discourse & Society* 13(6): 827–42.

Baxter, Judith (2002b). Is PDA Really an Alternative? A Reply to West. *Discourse & Society* 13(6): 853–9.

Bell, A. (1984). Language Style as Audience Design. *Language in Society* 13: 145–204.

Bell, A. (2001). Back in Style: Reworking Audience Design. In P. Eckert and J. R. Rickford (eds.), *Style and Sociolinguistic Variation*. Cambridge: Cambridge University Press

Billig, Michael (1999). Critical Discourse Analysis and Conversation Analysis: An Exchange between Michael Billig and Emanuel A. Schegloff. *Discourse & Society* 10(4): 543.

Blommaert, J. and C. Bulcaen (2000). Critical Discourse Analysis. *Annual Review of Anthropology* 29: 447–66.

Drew, P., J. Chatwin, and S. Collins (2001). Conversation Analysis: A Method for Research into Interactions between Patients and Health-Care Professionals. *Health Expectations* 4(1): 58–70.

Duncan, S. (1972). Some Signals and Rules for Taking Speaking Turns in Conversation. *Journal of Personality and Social Psychology* 23: 283–92.

Duncan, S. (1974). On the Structure of Speaker–Auditor Interaction during Speaking Turns. *Language in Society* 2: 161–80.

Edelsky, C. (1981). Who's Got the Floor? *Language in Society* 10(03): 383–421.

Egbert, M. M. (1996). Context-Sensitivity in Conversation: Eye Gaze and the German Repair Initiator. *Language in Society* 25: 587–612.

Egbert, M. M. (2004). Other-Initiated Repair and Membership Categorization – Some Conversational Events that Trigger Linguistic and Regional Membership Categorization. *Journal of Pragmatics* 36: 1467–498.

Fairclough, Norman (1995). *Critical Discourse Analysis*. London: Longman.

Fairclough, Norman (2001). Critical Discourse Analysis as a Method in Social Scientific Research. In Ruth Wodak and Michael Meyer (eds.), *Methods in Critical Discourse Analysis*. London: Sage Publications, 121–38.

Fairclough, Norman (2013). *Critical Discourse Analysis: The Critical Study of Language*. New York: Routledge.

Farfán, J. A. F. (2003). 'Al fin que ya los cueros no van a correr': The Pragmatics of Power in Hñahñu (Otomi) Markets. *Language in Society* 32: 629–58.

Gafaranga, J. (2010). Medium Request: Talking Language Shift into Being. *Language in Society* 39(02): 241–70.

Gardner, Rod (2012). Conversation Analysis in the Classroom. In Jack Sidnell and Tanya Stivers (eds.), *The Handbook of Conversation Analysis*. Oxford: Wiley-Blackwell, 593–611.

Gee, J. P. (2014). *Social Linguistics and Literacies: Ideology in Discourses*. New York: Routledge.

Georgakopoulou, Alexandra (2006). Postscript: Computer-Mediated Communication in Sociolinguistics. *Journal of Sociolinguistics* 10(4): 548–57.

Gershon, I. (2010). *The Breakup 2.0: Disconnecting over New Media*. Ithaca: Cornell University Press.

Godard, D. (1977). Same Setting, Different Norms: Phone Call Beginnings in France and the United States. *Language in Society* 6: 209–19.

Gumperz, J. J. (1992). Contextualization and Understanding. In A. Duranti and C. Goodwin (eds.), *Rethinking Context: Language as an Interactive Phenomenon*. Cambridge: Cambridge University Press, 229–52.

Gumperz, J. J. (2003). On the Development of Interactional Sociolinguistics. *Language Teaching and Linguistic Studies* 1: 1–10.

Gumperz, J. J. and J. Cook-Gumperz (1982). Introduction: Language and the Communication of Social Identity. In J. J. Gumperz (ed.), *Language and Social Identity*. Cambridge: Cambridge University Press.

Herring, Susan (2008). Computer-Mediated Discourse. In D. Schiffrin, D. Tannen, and H. E. Hamilton (eds.), *The Handbook of Discourse Analysis*. Oxford: Wiley-Blackwell, 612–34.

Holtgraves, T. (2002). *Language as Social Action*. Mahwah, NJ: Lawrence Erlbaum Associates.

Houtkoop-Steenstra, Hanneke (1991). Opening Sequences in Dutch Telephone Conversations. In Deirdre Boden and Don Zimmerman (eds.), *Talk and Social Structure*. Berkeley: University of California Press, 232–50.

Itakura, H. and A. B. M. Tsui (2004). Gender and Conversational Dominance in Japanese Conversation. *Language in Society* 33: 223–48.

Jaffe, A. (2007). Codeswitching and Stance: Issues in Interpretation. *Journal of Language, Identity, and Education* 6(1): 53–77.

Jaffe, A. (ed.) (2009) *Sociolinguistic Perspectives on Stance*. Oxford: Oxford University.

Jefferson, G. (1988). On the Sequential Organization of Troubles-Talk in Ordinary Conversation. *Social Problems* 418–41.

Johnstone, B. (2007). Linking Identity and Dialect through Stancetaking. In Robert Englebretson (ed.) *Stancetaking in Discourse: Subjectivity, Evaluation, Interaction.* Amsterdam: John Benjamins, 49–68.

Kärkkäinen, Elise (2006). Stance Taking in Conversation: From Subjectivity to Intersubjectivity. *Text and Talk* 26(6): 699–731.

Krzyżanowski, M. (2011). Ethnography and Critical Discourse Analysis: Towards a Problem-Oriented Research Dialogue. *Critical Discourse Studies* 8(4): 231–38.

Lazar, Michelle M. (2005). Performing the State Fatherhood: The Remaking of Hegemony. In Michelle Lazar (ed.), *Feminist Critical Discourse Analysis: Gender, Power and Ideology in Discourse.* London: Palgrave Macmillan, 139–63.

Lazar, Michelle M. (2007). Feminist Critical Discourse Analysis: Articulating a Feminist Discourse Praxis. *Critical Discourse Studies* 4(2):141–64.

Lazar, Michelle M. (2009). Entitled to Consume: Postfeminist Femininity and a Culture of Post-critique. *Discourse & Communication* 3(4): 371–400.

Lazar, Michelle M. (2011). The RIGHT to be beautiful: Postfeminist Identity and Consumer Beauty Advertising. In Rosalind Gill and Christina Scharff (eds.), *New Femininities: Postfeminism, Neoliberalism and Subjectivity.* London: Palgrave Macmillan, 31–51.

Lerner, G. H. (2003). Selecting Next Speaker: The Context-Sensitive Operation of a Context-Free Organization. *Language in Society* 32: 177–201.

Liddicoat, A. J. (2007). *An Introduction to Conversation Analysis.* London: Continuum.

Lindström, A. (1994). Identification and Recognition in Swedish Telephone Conversation Openings. *Language in Society* 23: 231–52.

Maynard, D. W. and J. Heritage (2005). Conversation Analysis, Doctor–Patient Interaction and Medical Communication. *Medical Education* 39(4): 428–35.

Orpin, D. (2005). Corpus Linguistics and Critical Discourse Analysis: Examining the Ideology of Sleaze. *International Journal of Corpus Linguistics* 10(1): 37–61.

Quaglio, P. and D. Biber (2006). The Grammar of Conversation. In B. Aartsand and A. McMahon (eds.), *The Handbook of English Linguistics.* Oxford: Blackwell.

Raclaw, Joshua (2008). Two Patterns for Conversational Closings in Instant Message Discourse. *Colorado Research in Linguistics* 21(June): 1–21.

Rampton, Ben (2007). Linguistic Ethnography, Interactional Sociolinguistics and the Study of Identities. *Working Papers in Urban Language and Literacies Paper* 43: 1–14.

Rogers, R. and M. Mosley (2008). A Critical Discourse Analysis of Racial Literacy in Teacher Education. *Linguistics and Education* 19(2): 107–31.

Sacks, H. (1992). *Lectures on Conversation.* Oxford: Blackwell.

Sacks, H., E. A. Schegloff, and G. Jefferson (1974). A Simplest Systematics for the Organization of Turn-Taking for Conversation. *Language* 50: 696–735

Schegloff, E. A. (1968). Sequencing in Conversational Openings. *American Anthropologist* 70(6): 1075–95. In D. H. Hymes and J. J. Gumperz (eds.) (1972), *Directions in Sociolinguistics: The Ethnography of Communication.* New York: Holt, Rinehart and Winston, 346–80.

Schegloff, E. A. (1986). The Routine as Achievement. *Human Studies* 9: 111–52.

Schegloff, E. A. (2000). Overlapping Talk and the Organization of Turn-Taking for Conversation. *Language in Society* 29: 1–63.

Schegloff, E. A. (2007). *Sequence Organization in Interaction.* Cambridge: Cambridge University Press.

Schiffrin, D. (1987). *Discourse Markers*. Cambridge: Cambridge University Press.

Schilling-Estes, N. (2004). Constructing Ethnicity in Interaction. *Journal of Sociolinguistics* 8(2): 163–95.

Stubbs, M. (1983). *Discourse Analysis: The Sociolinguistic Analysis of Natural Language*. Chicago: University of Chicago Press.

Taleghani-Nikazm, C. (2002). A Conversation Analytical Study of Telephone Conversation Openings Between Native and Nonnative Speakers. *Journal of Pragmatics* 34(12): 1807–32.

Tannen, D. (1987). Repetition in Conversation: Toward a Poetics of Talk. *Language* 63: 574–605.

Tannen, D. (1994). *Gender and Discourse*. New York: Oxford University Press.

Teo, P. (2000). Racism in the News: A Critical Discourse Analysis of News Reporting in Two Australian Newspapers. *Discourse & Society* 11(1): 7–49.

Tannen, D. (2005). Interactional Sociolinguistics as a Resource for Intercultural Pragmatics. *Intercultural Pragmatics* 2(2): 205–8.

Thurlow, Crispin (2006). From Statistical Panic to Moral Panic: The Metadiscursive Construction and Popular Exaggeration of New Media Language in the Print Media. *Journal of Computer-Mediated Communication* 11(3): 667–701.

Tsui, A. B. M. (1989). Beyond the Adjacency Pair. *Language in Society* 18: 545–64.

van Dijk, T. A. (1991). *Racism and the Press*. London; New York: Routledge.

van Dijk, T. A. (1992). Discourse and the Denial of Racism. *Discourse & Society* 3(1): 87–118.

van Dijk, T. A. (1993a) *Elite Discourse and Racism*. Newbury Park, CA: Sage Publications.

van Dijk, T. A. (1993b). Principles of Critical Discourse Analysis. *Discourse and Society* 4: 249–83. Also in P. Trudgill and J. Cheshire (eds.) (1998), *The Sociolinguistics Reader*, vol. 1: *Multilingualism and Variation*. London: Arnold.

van Dijk, T. A. (1999). Critical Discourse Analysis and Conversation Analysis. *Discourse & Society* 10(4): 459–60.

van Dijk, T. A. (2001). Multidisciplinary CDA: A Plan for Diversity. In R. Wodak and M. Meyer (eds.), *Methods of Critical Discourse Analysis*. London: Sage Publications.

van Dijk, T. A. (2003). The Discourse-Knowledge Interface. In Gilbert Weiss and Ruth Wodak (eds.), *Critical Discourse Analysis: Theory and Interdisciplinarity*. Houndsmills, UK: Palgrave Macmillan, 85–109.

van Dijk, T. A. (2008). *Discourse and Context: A Sociocognitive Approach*. Cambridge: Cambridge University Press.

van Dijk, T. A. (2009). Critical Discourse Studies: A Sociocognitive Approach. *Methods of Critical Discourse Analysis* 2: 62–86.

West, C. (2002). Peeling an Onion: A Critical Comment on 'Competing Discourses.' *Discourse & Society* 13: 843–51.

Wodak, R. (2000). Recontextualization and Transformation of Meanings: A Critical Discourse Analysis of Decision Making in EU-Meetings about Employment. In S. Sarangi and M. Coulthard (eds.), *Discourse and Social Life*. London: Pearson Education, 185–206.

Wodak, R. (2007). Pragmatics and Critical Discourse Analysis: A Cross-Disciplinary Inquiry. *Pragmatics & Cognition* 15(1): 203–25.

Wodak, R. and M. Meyer (eds.) (2001). *Methods of Critical Discourse Analysis*. London: Sage Publications.

Wortham, S., K. Mortimer, K. Lee, E. Allard, and K. Daniel White (2011). Interviews as Interactional Data. *Language in Society* 40(1): 39–50.

Part IV
Sociolinguistics and Social Justice

It is hard for a woman to define her feelings in language which is chiefly made by men to express theirs.

Thomas Hardy

Men have had every advantage of us in telling their own story. Education has been theirs in so much higher a degree; the pen has been in their hands.

Jane Austen

The awful shadow of some unseen Power
Floats, tho' unseen, amongst us.

Percy Bysshe Shelley

12

Language, Gender, and Sexuality

Key Concepts

Gender and sexuality as socially constructed

How language (use) can be sexist

Gender/sexuality ideologies in Discourses

Generalizations about male and female speech

Power issues in gendered language use

Gender and sexuality identities as socially constructed

A major topic in sociolinguistics is the connection, if any, between linguistic features – the structures, vocabularies, and ways of using particular languages – and the social roles and identities of the men and women who speak these languages. Do the men and women who speak a particular language use it in different ways? (We have already looked at some variationist studies on this topic in chapters 6 through 8.) If they do, do these differences arise from the structure of that language, which would therefore be one kind of confirmation of the Whorfian hypothesis (discussed in chapter 1), or, alternatively, do any differences that exist reflect the ways in which the sexes relate to each other in that society, whatever the reason? Might it be possible to describe a particular language as 'sexist,' or should we reserve such a

An Introduction to Sociolinguistics, Seventh Edition. Ronald Wardhaugh and Janet M. Fuller.
© 2015 John Wiley & Sons, Inc. Published 2015 by John Wiley & Sons, Inc.

description for those who use that language? If the answer to either question is affirmative, what could and should be done?

Such issues generated a considerable amount of thought and discussion in the last decades of the twentieth century and few have been resolved. Further, what began as a focus on the sex of the speaker has shifted to looking at how speakers do gender, and the role of sexuality in language performances has also emerged as an important and interrelated topic. The literature on these issues is now vast; it has been one of the biggest 'growth' areas within sociolinguistics in recent years.

In this chapter we will trace the history of the scholarship on language, gender, and sexuality, encompassing three main topics within this body of research. First, we will look at research that deals with sex and sexism in language systems, and with issues connected to language planning. While it is obviously impossible to separate language systems from language uses, this first section focuses on the former. The latter will be addressed in the second section of this chapter, which looks at how Discourses of gender and sexuality are encoded in language use in both public and private contexts of use. Finally, the third section addresses the topic of most research in this area: how people use language in ways that are linked to their gender and sexuality. Here we will return to some of the ideas about language as a means of constructing identity discussed earlier in chapters 3 and 11.

Defining Terms: Gender, Sex Category, and Sexuality

Before discussing how language, gender, and sexuality are dealt with in sociolinguistics, we need to define the terms gender, sex category, and sexuality to discuss how these concepts are involved in the study of sociolinguistics. **Sex categories** are based on the biological distinction – not always completely clear – between 'male' and 'female.' There may also be additional culturally specific categories that define people who do not fall easily into these first two categories. Native American cultures have a tradition of what has been called 'two spirit' people (Jacobs et al. 1997), and in India there are *hijras* and *kotis*, which are different groups of people who exhibit physical and/or behavioral characteristics of both sex categories; in Indian society, they have a societal role and the linguistic means of constructing such a role in society (Hall 1997, 2005). The term **transgender** is often used in the United States to talk about people who are transitioning or have transitioned from one sex category to another, or have biological attributes of a sex category which does not match their gender (see below) or of both sexes; the term **cisgender** is used to talk about people whose sex category matches their gender. The term transgender may also be used for individuals with biological attributes of both sexes. Thus, while sex categories make references to biological characteristics, and are often perceived as binary and mutually exclusive, they are not entirely in synch with the reality of human diversity and some societies have more than two categories and may accept more fluid membership in sex categories.

On the other hand, **gender**, although based on sex categories, is culturally constructed. What is considered to be masculine or feminine differs from one society to another. It is also usually conceived of as being on a continuum of masculine and feminine, that is, you can be more or less masculine or feminine, while sex categories are generally thought of as being discrete groups so that individuals must firmly and permanently belong to either one or the other category. Within contemporary social theory, gender identities, like other aspects of identity, may change over time, and vary according to the setting, topic, or interlocutors. West and Zimmerman (1987) talk about 'doing gender,' that is, the idea that gender is not something we *have*, but something we *do*. Cameron (2006, 724) says: '*Sex* is a word used in connection with the biological characteristics that mark humans and other animals as either male or female, whereas *gender* refers to the cultural traits and behaviors deemed appropriate for men or women by a particular society.' Elsewhere (1998b, 280–1), she points out that:

> Men and women … are members of cultures in which a large amount of discourse about gender is constantly circulating. They do not only learn, and then mechanically reproduce, ways of speaking 'appropriate' to their own sex; they learn a much broader set of gendered meanings that attach in rather complex ways to different ways of speaking, and they produce their own behavior in the light of these meanings. …

In performances of gender, speakers draw on ideologies about what it means to be a man or a woman; for instance, women may give each other compliments on their appearance, while men exchange ritual insults, speech acts which draw on stereotypes of women seeking solidarity and men constructing hierarchy in conversation. However, performing masculinity or femininity 'appropriately' cannot mean giving exactly the same performance regardless of the circumstances. It may involve different strategies in mixed and single-sexed company, in private and public settings, and in the various social roles (parent, lover, colleague, friend) that someone might regularly occupy in the course of everyday life.

We cannot talk about gender without reference to **sexuality**, or vice versa. Sexuality has to do with an individual's identity in terms of his or her sexual activities. For example, certain types of masculinity rely heavily on heterosexuality while other identities explicitly involve gay masculinity. We also have stereotypes about identity categories such as 'butch' or 'femme' lesbians. Sexual identities are not just about being gay, lesbian, straight, bisexual, transgender, queer, or questioning, of course; they include performances of being available, promiscuous, asexual, or fetishizing certain things, acts, or types of sexual partners. Such aspects of sexual identity are intertwined with gender identity.

The next section will address how languages encode ideas about gender and sexuality, and the broader issue of how ideas about gender and sexuality are produced and reproduced through language. Finally, we will address how speakers' language use can be linked to gender, sex categories, and sexuality.

Exploration 12.1:   Understandings of Sex and Gender

Before reading the definition of the above section, how would you have defined the terms 'sex' and 'gender'? (Why do you think the authors use the term 'sex category' here instead of simply 'sex'?)

How are these terms used in everyday conversations? On forms? In the media? What do these usages reflect about popular understandings of these concepts? How are the ways that these terms are used here different from how they are used in popular culture?

Sexist Language

Can language itself be **sexist**? Work in the 1980s on this topic addressed issues such as the so-called generic 'he' and the use of 'man' or 'mankind' to refer to all people. Penelope (1988) discusses how such usages exclude women and create the mentality that men are the default and the norm, and women are the exception. She gives examples which illustrate how this leads to even gender-neutral words being used to refer to men, for example, a line from Star Trek: 'Our <u>people</u> are the best gamblers in the galaxy. <u>We</u> compete for power, fame, women' (Penelope 1988, 135). Of course, academics were not exempt from such constructions, as she shows with examples from the renowned sociologist Goffman: 'It is here, in this personal capacity, than an <u>individual</u> can be warm, spontaneous and touched by humor. It is here, regardless of <u>his</u> social role, that an <u>individual</u> can show "what kind of guy he is" (Goffman, Encounters, p. 152)' (Penelope 1988, 136). She argues that such linguistic uses perpetuate the invisibility of women (an issue to be discussed further in Exploration 12.2).

Another of the issues involved in answering this question has to do with words that encode sex categories, most commonly sex category–marked names of people in specific occupations, for example, fireman, stewardess, and waitress. While it is not inherently sexist to make reference to the sex category of a person, the problem with such words is that they could influence what professions we see as being appropriate for (only) men or (only) women. If the unmarked form is 'fireman,' it is possible to be a 'firewoman' but this is linguistically marked and suggests that the norm is for a person in this occupation to be a man. This problem has been addressed by the introduction of gender-neutral terms such as *firefighter* and *flight attendant*, common usages in North America. Today, there is a growing awareness, at least in some circles, that subtle, and sometimes not so subtle, distinctions are made in the vocabulary choice used to describe men and women. Consequently, we can understand why there is a frequent insistence that neutral words be used as much as possible, as in describing occupations, for example, *chair(person)*, *letter carrier*, *salesclerk*, and *police officer*. If language tends to reflect social structure and social structure is changing so that judgeships, surgical appointments, nursing positions, and primary school teaching assignments are just as likely to be held by women as by men (or by men as by women), such linguistic changes might be expected to follow inevitably. Focus on such asymmetries in language does two things: it draws our attention to existing inequities and it encourages us to make the necessary changes by establishing new terms and categorizations (e.g., *Ms*), or suggesting modifications for old terms (e.g., changing *policeman* to *police officer*). However, there is still considerable doubt that changing *waitress* to either *server* or *waitperson* or describing Nicole Kidman as an actor rather than as an actress indicates a real shift in sexist attitudes. Reviewing the evidence, Romaine (1999, 312–13) concludes that 'attitudes toward gender equality did not match language usage. Those who had adopted more gender-inclusive language did not necessarily have a more liberal view of gender inequities in language.'

Further, there is not necessarily consensus about what constitutes sexism in language. In a 2001 online discussion about the use of the term *server* (see the link in the online materials), the suggestion that *waiter* is a male term was dismissed by some contributors, who said that this is a neutral term. One writer clearly felt that changing such terms to avoid sexist connotations was silly and unnecessary, writing, 'Similarly, I suppose, the word "President" should have been completely replaced when female corporate executives ascended to that level, right?' The argument made by this poster and others is that what is sexist is not a term such as *waiter* or *actor*, which are gender-neutral terms, but the assumption that we must change the words when women do these jobs. Others pointed out that the issue is that we had gendered pairs of terms such as *waiter–waitress* and there is no such gendered pair for the word *president* in English. The argument here shows that far from there being a wide acceptance of avoiding gender-neutral terms, some people clearly dismiss the idea that language encodes sexism.

In other occupations, words that were often assumed to imply the sex of the person might be prefaced by a gender marker, such as 'male nurse.' We should note that men are increasingly found in the nursing profession, and nurse is less frequently interpreted as implying 'female,' just as the assumption that a doctor is male is no longer the default. However, as we will discuss further below, often the issue is not the labels used but how women or men in particular professions are discussed. For example, although we do not have different words in English for male and female politicians, the appearance of female politicians is often focused on in ways that it usually is not for male politicians (see links in the online materials on this topic).

It should also be noted that language can also encode and perpetuate **heterosexist** attitudes; we will return to this in the section below on language change. This will also be addressed in the section on Discourses of Gender and Sexuality, as much of the research on heteronormativity in language use fits within this approach.

Grammatical gender marking

We must note that grammatical gender marking is more extensive in some languages than it is in English, and presents different problems in attempts to make language more gender neutral. As Mills (2008) notes, the word for 'minister' in French is masculine (*le minister*), so it is difficult to refer to a female minister. Further, the norm in languages such as French and Spanish is to use the masculine plural for groups containing both men and women. While this is traditionally also true in German, some changes have occurred, including more use of the feminine plural ending -*innen* (instead of the masculine plural -*en)* for groups of men and women, and in some cases the introduction of words that do not mark gender for plurals. For example, the plural for 'students,' traditionally *Studenten*, using the masculine -*en* plural ending, was in some cases during the 1980s and 1990s replaced by *StudentInnen*, using the feminine plural suffix -*innen*, but has now been replaced by *Studierende* (literally, 'those who study,' from the verb *studieren* 'to study'). Thus while the form of the language itself may appear to be an impediment to change, in some cases it is possible to work around grammatical gender marking patterns.

One particular bit of sexism in languages that has aroused much comment is the gender systems that so many of them have, the *he–she–it* 'natural' gender system of English or the *le–la* or *der–die–das* 'grammatical' gender systems of French and German. The possible connections between grammatical gender systems (masculine, feminine, neuter) and sex categories (male, female, neither) are various. See Romaine (1999) for some observations and claims concerning these connections, for example, her claim (1999, 66) that 'ideological factors in the form of cultural beliefs about women … enter into gender assignment in [grammatical] systems that are supposedly purely formal and arbitrary.' In English such connections sometimes create problems for us in finding the right pronoun: compare the neutral 'Everybody should hand in their papers in five minutes' to the apparently biased 'No person in his right mind would do that.' Although the singular 'they' in English has come under attack from some prescriptivists, it is now in wide usage, with such sentences as 'I saw someone enter the building, but I didn't know who they were' being common in youth speech in North America.

To return to the cross-linguistic perspective, gender distinctions such as *he–she* can often be avoided so it probably does not follow that languages with gender distinctions must be sexist, which would also be a clear argument in support of the Whorfian hypothesis. It is the people who use languages who are or who are not sexist; Chinese, Japanese, Persian, and Turkish do not make the kinds of gender distinctions English makes through its system of pronouns, but it would be difficult to find evidence to support a generalization that males who speak these languages are less sexist than males who speak English.

Language change

If there is a relationship between language and worldview, regardless of which direction we believe this influence flows, than we would expect that language would reflect (or have formed) changing gender roles. We can see this in some asymmetries of pairs of words. While *actor* and *actress* or *waiter* and *waitress* have few, if any, differences in connotation aside from sex, pairs of terms such as *master–mistress*, *governor–governess,* and *bachelor–spinster* are different in more ways than simply indicating male and female. While a master is the man in charge, the word *mistress* is commonly used to refer to the female lover of a married man. Being a *governor* is an important political position; a *governess* is someone who takes care of children. While *bachelor* has connotations of fun and independence (as in the term *bachelor pad*), *spinster* is an undeniably negative term, calling up the image of an elderly woman living alone with lots of cats. (See Lakoff 1973 for a discussion of these and other such examples.) The interesting thing to note about these asymmetries, however, is that probably most readers of this text do not use the words *mistress, governess, or spinster* at all. If they know these words, they may not be familiar with the connotations cited here, as societal changes have made these terms less prominent and relevant, especially for young people today.

However, gender asymmetries still exist in modern-day English usage. For instance, while it is common to refer to adult females as 'girls,' even in a professional context (for example, a bank employee might tell a customer that 'the girl who handles the housing loans is out today'), such usages occur far less commonly with 'boy' – one rarely hears reference to 'the boy who manages the produce section.' However, the use of 'girl' (sometimes rendered 'grrl') is complicated by feminist reclaiming of the term by some young women, who have embraced the word as a term of empowerment. In another example, we see a clearer asymmetry in the difference between the meaning of 'mothering' a child, which implies nurturing, and 'fathering' a child, which simply implies contributing to the child's conception. However, even here we see some changes, as the term 'parenting' is now used in some contexts in which 'mothering' was used earlier (for example, it is common to refer to 'parenting magazines,' although see below for some comments about the content).

All deliberate attempts to change or modify languages to free them of perceived (hetero)sexism or make them gender-neutral are a form of language planning, which we will discuss further in chapter 14. Sometimes the goal appears to be to force language to catch up to social change; and at other times it seems designed to bring about social change through mandating language change. Whatever it is, it requires us to accept a very Whorfian view of the interrelationship of language and culture. Here is Pauwels' (1998, 228) statement of a similar position:

> The aims of many feminist LP [language planning] efforts are to expose the inequalities in the linguistic portrayal of the sexes which reflect and contribute to the unequal positions of women and men in society and to take action to rectify this linguistic imbalance. Language action … is social action, and to bring about linguistic change is to effect social change.

Some literature on this topic also talks about 'reclaiming' language for women (see especially Lakoff 1990, Penelope 1990, Sellers 1991, and Spender 1985). Spender writes (1985, 3): 'Language helps form the limits of our reality. It is our means of ordering and manipulating the world. It is through language that we become members of a human community, that the world becomes comprehensible and meaningful, that we bring into existence the world in which we live.' She further asserts (1985, 12) that 'the English language has been literally man-made and … is still primarily under male control' and that males, as the dominant group, have produced language, thought, and reality. Penelope (1990) argues that women should be aware of 'the lies of the fathers' tongues' and of the 'Patriarchal Universe of Discourse.' Her view is that women should in a sense reinvent language for their own purposes. In this perspective, ways of speaking that are seen as part of women's repertoires, for example, non-competitive, non-interruptive speech, should be integrated into more contexts of language use. In the final section of this chapter, we will come back to ideas about women's speech and how male-female differences in speech have been studied and perceived.

We should also note that some small changes in heterosexist language practices can also be seen. One example is in reference to partners; some heterosexual married couples will refer to their spouses as 'partners' to avoid indexing the heterosexual privilege of legal marriage. At the same time, as marriage equality is achieved in some regions, the use of the terms 'husband' and 'wife' for same-sex partners is not uncommon, so these terms are no longer reserved for heterosexuals only. Further, in some circles there is objection to the term 'gay marriage,' as can be seen in the words of Liz Feldman (http://www.funnyordie.com/articles/d18ead07bf/one-day-more, accessed July 2, 2014): 'Personally, I am very excited about gay marriage, or, as I like to call it, marriage. Because I had lunch this afternoon, not gay lunch. I parked my car, I didn't gay park it.' However, such changes in both language and worldview are still incipient, and are reflective of policy struggles around marriage equality; language is used to claim or deny legitimacy for same-sex couples.

Exploration 12.2:   Guys and Dolls

A common term used in many varieties of English to address a group of people is 'guys,' as in 'C'mon, you guys, let's go!' For many speakers, this term in the singular is almost exclusively masculine ('I met a guy in the park with a beautiful dog' would imply a male dog owner), but in the plural it can refer to all male referents, a group of both males and females, or an all-female group. Do you use this term? If so, how do you use it, that is, what are the possible referents? If you are female, do you ever object to being referred to with 'guys'? Do you think this usage is inherently sexist, as it uses a male term as the default, like 'mankind'?

Discourses of Gender and Sexuality

Before moving on to the topic of how men and women use language, we would like to address another aspect of how language is used in discussions about men and women, that is, how ideologies about gender, sex categories, sexuality, and so on, are produced and reproduced through language and language use. We use the term **Discourse**, taken from Gee (1999) and his description of Discourse with capital 'D,' as introduced in chapter 11 in our discussion of CDA. Discourse can be described as ways of representing facets of the world, that is, the processes, relations, and structures of the world, as well as feelings, thoughts, and beliefs about the social world (Fairclough 2003). Johnstone (2008) describes Discourse as conventional ways of talking which create and are created by conventional ways of thinking. These connected ways of thinking constitute **ideologies**. Consequently, Discourses have linguistic aspects (conventionalized sets of choices in language) and also ideological aspects (patterns of beliefs and action). Cameron (2008) makes the important point that we do not define ideologies as 'beliefs' or 'attitudes' but as 'representations'; that is, gender 'ideologies' are not distinct from 'truths' about gender. This distinction also focuses on the social aspect of ideologies: whereas 'beliefs' or 'attitudes' are mental constructs, and are individual as opposed to societal, ideologies are cultural manifestations.

Some common Discourses

Discourses about gender and sexuality influence and shape how we think about sex categories and the people who belong in them, as well as other categories having to do with sexuality. Among Discourses of gender and sexuality that we can identify, the discourse of **heteronormativity** is one of the most pervasive (Cameron and Kulick 2003, 2006, Coates 2013, Motschenbacher 2011, Kitzinger 2005). This Discourse requires an assumption of heterosexuality and the stigmatizing of gay and lesbian identities. Milani (2013) illustrates the hegemony of heteronormativity in his study of *meetmarket*, an online dating site for men looking for other men in South Africa. One point he makes is that the term 'straight-acting' is often employed both as a positive presentation of self and a description for what is desired, showing how what is seen as 'heterosexual' behavior is explicitly normative in matters having nothing to do with sex (dress, speech, etc.).

One study showing how heteronormativity begins in primary school is Renold (2000), which addresses how Discourses about girls needing to be attractive to boys, but not 'tarty,' is pervasive, and contrasts with boys' constructions of heterosexuality through fighting, football, homophobia, and misogyny (not aspects of behavior that are aimed at being attractive to girls). Dalley and Campbell (2006) discuss the continuation of this at the high school level, showing strong heteronormative Discourses. Further, this research shows an interesting twist to the perpetuation of privilege of heterosexuality in that the challenge of these hegemonic ideologies only seemed feasible by a group of straight girls. These girls, who identified as 'nerds,' would playact 'lesbianism' in the presence of the normatively heterosexual popular kids, constructing identities for themselves which challenged the gendered expectations for girls in their school. They did not actually identify as lesbians, or have relationships with girls; they were recognized as heterosexual, yet did not conform to normative behavior. The displays of lesbian behavior were clearly performed as challenges to what they saw as homophobic attitudes of the popular crowd. The authors conclude (2006, 25):

> As our article has shown, virtually any move by an individual student or teacher to introduce a queer perspective into classroom discussions was systematically negated, meeting with rejection (exclusion) or negative inclusion by teachers and students alike. Yet at the same time, lesbianism offered a discourse of resistance to five straight girls, the nerds. The nerds also put the straight/gay binary into question: in maintaining both straight *and* queer personas, they posited the possibility of a dynamic and complementary heterosexual/homosexual identity. While adopting this fluid yet counter-hegemonic sexual persona made it possible for these girls to challenge constraining gender roles by being assertive and outspoken about sociosexual matters, such social benefits did not seem to be available to a female friend who self-identified as a lesbian. Gay males also struggled with and against the silencing effects of the heteronormative discourses of the school. Without the protection of a heterosexual persona, however, they could not safely materialise their sexual identities at school. There, they developed strategies to remain hidden, relegating the expression/exploration of their sexual identities to safer zones outside of school.

Heteronormativity has been shown to privilege not only heterosexuals, but also certain gender roles within heterosexuality. Cameron and Kulick (2003) discuss how Discourses of heteronormativity produce what they call the heteronormative hierarchy, which favors monogamous and reproductive heterosexuality in which both partners adhere to normative gender roles. Thus, heteronormativity encompasses many Discourses about gender roles in heterosexual relationships (see Sunderland 2004). For instance, Sunderland (2006) looks at parenting magazines and shows that despite the gender-neutral depiction evoked by the term 'parenting,' the magazines construct a world in which mothers are the main caretakers of children. This Discourse was also apparent in the research on advertising by Lazar (2005) discussed in chapter 11. Another common gendered Discourse has to do with the value of women being linked to their physical appearance, noted in the study of primary school children above. Ohara and Saft (2003) look at data from a Japanese phone-in consultation program and show how this ideology is represented by a female caller who discusses how she dealt with her husband's infidelity by making herself more attractive. This study, which employed in part a membership categorization methodology, which is part of a CA approach, shows how this ideology includes categorizing different types of women. The authors summarize: 'By building on the caller's announcement of self-polishing and explicitly linking it to gender, S is placing the caller in a pre-established type of women, namely, those who react to men's affairs by examining themselves for places that need improvement' (Ohara and Saft 2003, 166). In another study addressing the importance of appearance for teenage girls in Sweden, Ambjörnsson (2005) notes how girls' social relationships are created and maintained through talk about how fat they are; however, the social capital of this type of discourse is available only to girls who are, in fact, slender.

In some cases, the Discourses involve ideologies about other aspects of culture, or language ideologies more broadly. An example of this is given in Cameron (2008), in which she addresses some broader ideas about language, arguing that it is increasingly discussed as a set of skills. She looks at varied texts from the UK about women and men as communicators. She summarizes:

> … what they say about language and gender is essentially similar: each one represents the verbal behavior of men as in some way problematic, and contrasts it unfavorably with the behavior of women in the same situation. In all four texts the "problem" is defined explicitly or implicitly as a lack of skill in using language for the purpose of creating and maintaining rapport with other people. Males in these texts do not spend sufficient time interacting with friends and relatives, do not share their feelings and problems openly, cannot chat to customers in a "natural" manner, and are unable to listen "sympathetically" in group discussions designed to promote learning. These deficiencies are represented as having serious consequences for men, including educational underachievement … unemployment …, personal unhappiness and even premature death. (Cameron 2008, 457)

Her subsequent analyses shows that while explicitly claiming superiority for women, this Discourse implicitly perpetuates traditional stereotypes about women as being more emotional, and so on. Further, it creates a situation in which men who are good communicators by this definition are given extra credit, while women's achievements as communicators are downgraded to being simply part of their 'nature' and thus not an achievement at all.

This chapter has up until now primarily addressed how language, or language use, can be used to represent men and women and how these representations are related to our social world. In the next section, we will move on to the research on how men and women speak, which in the end brings us back to these ideas of Discourses of gender and sexuality.

Deficit, Dominance, Difference, and Identities

Before beginning an historical account of the scholarship on gender and language, we first need to specify what we mean when we talk about differences between men's and women's speech. There are some claims to **gender exclusive language**, that is, situations in which men and women have different ways of speaking that could be deemed different languages, or at least distinct and named dialects of a language. According to Sapir (1929), the Yana language of California contained special forms for use in speech either by or to women. Another claim to sex-exclusive language is found among the Dyirbal people of North Queensland, Australia, who have a special language which is gender-differentiated in a rather novel way (Dixon 1971). The normal everyday language, Guwal, is used by both genders; but, if you are a man and your mother-in-law is present, or if you are a woman and your father-in-law is present, you use Dyalîuy, a 'mother-in-law' variety. This variety has the same phonology and almost the same grammar as Guwal but its vocabulary is entirely different. However, both genders have access to both varieties.

Another Australian aboriginal language, Yanyuwa, a critically endangered language, has gender-differentiated dialects. The dialects use the same word stems but there are different class-marking prefixes on nouns, verbs, and pronouns. According to Bradley (1998), men use one dialect among themselves and women use the other. Men also use men's dialect to speak to women and women use women's dialect to speak to men. Children are brought up in women's dialect with boys required to shift – not always done easily – to men's dialect as they are initiated into manhood. Bradley adds (1998, 16) that: 'If individuals wish to speak Yanyuwa then they are expected to speak the dialect which is associated with their sex – there is no other alternative.' A person can use the other sex's dialect only in very well-defined circumstances such as storytelling, joking, and certain singing rituals.

Another language which is often cited as having different ways of speaking for men and women is Japanese; however, some recent research on this may cause us to question exactly how exclusive the varieties associated with different sexes are. Japanese women show they are women when they speak, for example, by the use of a sentence-final particle *ne* or another particle *wa*. A male speaker refers to himself as *boku* or *ore* whereas a female uses *watasi* or *atasi*. Whereas a man says *boku kaeru* 'I will go back' in plain or informal speech, a woman says *watasi kaeru wa* (Takahara 1991). Children learn to make these distinctions very early in life. However, Reynolds (1998, 306) points out that 'the use of *boku* … by junior high school girls has recently become quite common in Tokyo. Girls who were interviewed in a TV program explain that they cannot compete with boys in classes, in games or in fights with *watasi*. … The use of *boku* and other expressions in the male speech domain by young female speakers has escalated to a larger area and to older groups of speakers.' More recent literature has discussed so-called Japanese women's language as an ideal rather than an existing genderlect (Inoue 2006, Nakamura 2004, 2005).

In the Dyirbal example cited above we may find an important clue as to why there are sometimes different varieties for men and women. One variety may be forbidden to one gender, that is, be taboo, but that gender is apparently nearly always the female gender. This phenomenon has been noted among the Trobriand Islanders, various aboriginal peoples of Australia, Mayans, Zulus, and Mongols, to cite but a few examples. The taboos often have to do with certain kinship relationships or with hunting or with some religious practice, and result in the avoidance of certain words or even sounds in words. They derive from the social organization of the particular group involved and reflect basic concerns of the group. Such concerns quite often lead to women being treated in ways that appear inimical to egalitarian-oriented outsiders.

In addition to ways of speaking which are seen as specific to men or women, there has been some research addressing ways of speaking which are associated with sexual minorities, primarily gay men and lesbians. In a review of the research on gay and lesbian speech, Kulick (2000) notes that up until the 1980s, work focused mostly on lexical items used in particular gay and/or lesbian communities. Subsequent to that, there was a body of research which focused on distinguishing features of gay or lesbian language, with a particular focus on phonology. Some of this research focused on whether research participants could accurately identify gay or lesbian speakers (see Gaudio 1994, Moonwomon-Baird 1997 for examples of two early studies). In a review of this research, Munson and Babel (2007) maintain that while there are certain speech features that are often associated with gay and lesbian speakers, they are not simply imitations of speakers of the opposite sex, but individual features which carry social meanings. Much subsequent research has focused on the communicative practices in **LGBTQ** communities of practice in a social constructionist paradigm, and will be discussed further in our section on identities.

Recognizing the relationship between language and other social practices and structures, we will focus here on what is sometimes called **gender preferential language**. In other words, certain ways of speaking may be preferred by one gender, or are stereotypically associated with being feminine or masculine. We have already mentioned many instances of language behavior varying according to gender (see chapter 7 in particular). Many of these are quantitative studies in which sex is used as one of the variables that are taken into account. As Milroy and Gordon (2003, 100) say, 'Strictly speaking ... it makes sense ... to talk of sampling speakers according to sex, but to think of gender as the relevant social category when interpreting the social meaning of sex-related variation.' We may remember that Fischer's work (discussed in chapter 7) showed how very young boys and girls differ in certain choices they make, as did Cheshire's work in Reading in an older group. Labov's studies in New York and Philadelphia also revealed noticeable gender differences in adult speech. These led him to make some interesting claims about what such differences indicated, for example, about women's role in language change. The Milroys' study (1978) exploring network relationships (see chapter 7) showed certain characteristics of men's and women's speech: how they were alike in some ways but different in others. Gal's (1978) study in the Oberwart of Austria (see chapter 8) showed how it is not only what women say but who they are willing to say it to that is important.

Still other gender-linked differences are said to exist. Women are also said not to employ the profanities and obscenities men use, or, if they do, use them in different circumstances or may be judged differently for using them. (However, the evidence is not conclusive on these issues, and anyone who has ever watched the successful American television series or the later movie *Sex and the City* can see how acceptable certain kinds of language have become even in media still highly controlled in their portrayal of 'normal' behavior.) Women are also sometimes required to be silent in situations in which men may speak. Among the Araucanian Indians of Chile, men are encouraged to talk on all occasions, but the ideal wife is silent in the presence of her husband, and at gatherings where men are present she should talk only in a whisper, if she talks at all.

Some writers are not impressed with such claims. For example, Cameron (1998a, 945–6) says that these findings 'belong to the tradition of empirical sex difference studies that do no more than set out to find statistically significant differences between women's and men's behavior. This research formula has proved as durable as it is dubious (not to say dull).' In this view, merely to observe, count, and graph linguistic phenomena is not enough. An investigator needs some kind of theory about such behavior and some ideas to test before beginning an investigation.

Women's language

Research which seeks to apply social theory and answer questions about the relationship between language and gender/sexuality was launched by a provocative and insightful work by Lakoff in 1973, *Language and Woman's Place*. As this title implies, this work focused on how women's language revealed their place in society – a place that was generally seen as inferior to that occupied by men. This account of what came to be called Women's Language (WL) has in retrospect been called the **deficit model**, as many of the features Lakoff discusses position women as deficient to men: less confident in what they say (e.g., use of tag questions, hedging devices, rising intonation), and less able to participate in serious activities in the social sphere (e.g., empty adjectives, lexicons specific to domestic domains). Empirical studies have shown that some of the features Lakoff suggests are typical of WL are not necessarily present in the speech of women; for instance, empirical work on tag questions has refuted the idea that they are used more by women (Dubois and Crouch 1975, Cameron et al. 1989, and Brower et al. 1979). Holmes (1984) actually found that men were more likely to use tag questions that indicated uncertainty. Furthermore, after analyzing a large corpus of academic data from the University of Michigan, researchers found that 'in the domain of academic speech, there is no specific gender-related effect on speakers' hedging frequencies' (Poos and Simpson 2002, 20).

Still further work by O'Barr and Atkins (1980) showed that in courtroom speech, it was not women who used the features identified by Lakoff as being part of WL, but people who had less institutional power. In a sense this last finding only strengthens the importance of Lakoff's work by confirming that the ways of speaking which are associated with women are associated with a lack of power. This theme of power being encoded and created though language use is one that has wide applications.

Dominance

What has been called the **dominance approach** also addresses power relations between the sexes. Some of this research claims that there is evidence that in cross-gender conversation women ask more questions than men, use more **back-channeling** signals (i.e., verbal and non-verbal feedback to show they are listening) to encourage others to continue speaking, use more instances of *you* and *we*, and do not protest as much as men when they are interrupted. On the other hand, men interrupt more, challenge, dispute, and ignore more, try to control what topics are discussed, and are inclined to make categorical statements. Such behaviors are not characteristic of women in conversations that involve both men and women. In other words, in their interactional patterns in conversation, men and women seem often to exhibit the power relationship that exists in society, with men dominant and women subservient. Work such as that of Fishman (1978) and DeFrancisco 1998 on couples' talk, Zimmerman and West (1975) on gender and interruptions, and West (1984, 1998) on physicians' directives shows how men tend to dominate conversations through interruption and topic control, and to backchannel less than women.

However, more comprehensive research on interruptions shows that this pattern cannot be generalized. James and Clarke (1993) looked at fifty-four studies that addressed the claim that men are much more likely than women 'to use interruption as a means of dominating and controlling interactions' (1993, 268). They report that the majority of studies have found no significant differences between genders in this respect, and that both men and women interrupt other men and women. However, according to James and Clarke (1993, 268), 'A small amount of evidence exists that females may use interruptions of the cooperative and rapport-building type to a greater extent than do males, at least in some circumstances.'

The overarching theme in this research is that men's societal dominance is reproduced in conversations between men and women. Although there are problems with this approach, including that it is somewhat overly simplistic, the idea that larger societal norms influence what happens within a conversation is an enduring concept in the study of language, gender, and sexuality. Context is important in how we use language. Men and women's speech is not the same in private and public spheres, and different roles within an interaction also lead to different ways of speaking. Someone who frequently interrupts in one context may backchannel a lot in another, and this fact must form part of any larger picture we may want to draw of gendered aspects of language use.

Talbot (1998, 133–4) also advocates caution when applying the idea of dominance to gender differences in language: 'A major determinant [of the dominance framework] is that male dominance is often treated as though it is pan-contextual. But … all men are not in a position to dominate all women.' Dominance clearly fails as a universal explanation of gendered language differences.

Difference

Almost concurrently with the focus on dominance in the study of language and gender arose another approach which became known as the **difference, or two**

cultures, approach. Its basic idea was popularized by the psychologist Jonathan Grey in his bestselling book *Men are from Mars, Women are from Venus: The Classic Guide to Understanding the Opposite Sex* (1992) and by the linguist Deborah Tannen in her book *You Just Don't Understand: Women and Men in Conversation* (1990). These works were based on the assumption that men and women speak differently. Their claim is that men learn to talk like men and women learn to talk like women because society subjects them to different life experiences. However, the process of gender differentiation is not the focus of this approach, it is an underlying assumption (and one that has been questioned). The main claim is that men and women have different conversational goals and thus although they may say the same things, they actually mean different things. Maltz and Borker (1982) propose that, in North America at least, men and women come from different sociolinguistic sub-cultures. They have learned to do different things with language, particularly in conversation, and when the two genders try to communicate with each other, the result may be miscommunication. The *mhmm* a woman uses quite frequently means only 'I'm listening,' whereas the *mhmm* a man uses tends to mean 'I'm agreeing.' Consequently, men often believe that 'women are always agreeing with them and then conclude that it's impossible to tell what a woman really thinks,' whereas 'women … get upset with men who never seem to be listening' (1982, 202). They conclude that women and men observe different rules in conversing and that in cross-gender talk the rules often conflict. The genders have different views of what questioning is all about, women treating questions as part of conversational maintenance and men treating them primarily as requests for information; different views of what is or is not 'aggressive' linguistic behavior, with women regarding any sign of aggression as personally directed, negative, and disruptive, and men as just one way of organizing a conversation; different views of topic flow and topic shift; and different attitudes toward problem-sharing and advice-giving, with women tending to discuss, share, and seek reassurance, and men tending to look for solutions, give advice, and even lecture to their audiences.

There is an emphasis on misunderstandings in this approach, caused by differences in conversational goals. For instance, Tannen (1992), who likens speech between men and women to cross-cultural communication, claimed that men seek to establish hierarchy and status through talk, whereas women look to create solidarity and connection.

One consequence of such differences is that men have often devalued women's speech and, as Tannen rightly observes, her difference approach in no way denies the existence of male dominance (1993, 9). Tannen's solution is an interesting one, although one not without its critics. She believes that men and women should try to understand why they speak as they do and try to adapt to each other's styles. However, the self-help nature of her 1990 book *You Just Don't Understand* seems to thrust much of such work onto the shoulders (or tongues?) of women rather than men. Tannen's book was widely acclaimed, so its message obviously resonated with many people, women in particular. As Talbot (1998) observes of the book, with its appearance of objectivity and neutrality and its stress on differences and equality,

Tannen's approach provides a 'comfortable explanation' (1998, 139) for some troublesome issues. Cameron adds (2007, 98) that 'the research evidence does not support the claims made by Tannen and others about the nature, the causes, and the prevalence of male-female miscommunication.' Although such claims may grab our attention, they do not stand up to rigorous scrutiny.

As we can see from the fact that works espousing such a characterization of male-female differences have made the bestseller lists, the claims they make might seem to be valid; however, many sociolinguists remain extremely skeptical. We suggest that their popularity is at least in part because they avoid difficult issues of power relations between the sexes that are brought to the forefront in other approaches (see Cameron 1998c, Talbot 1998). Different ways of speaking are presented as equal but different in this approach, but as we know from discussions of different dialects and attitudes toward them as in chapters 2 and 3, this is a fake neutrality. People evaluate and judge others based on how they speak, and this statement is as true for gendered ways of speaking as it is for social or regional varieties.

Further criticism of the difference approach has been that the analogy to cross-cultural communication and the focus on misunderstanding is misplaced, as it relies on the assumption that most human interactions and socialization are within same-sex groups, something obviously untrue for many people. A related problem which has been pointed out is that this approach reifies the differences between men and women, and men's and women's ways of speaking; but in reality the similarities between male and female speech patterns (to the extent that we can say there are such things) outweigh the differences.

More recently, the concept of 'community of practice' has been used to examine gender issues in language (see chapter 3). According to Eckert and McConnell-Ginet (1998), gender issues are essentially complex and not easy to separate from other issues. They deplore the fact that too often,

> Gender is abstracted whole from other aspects of social identity, the linguistic system is abstracted from linguistic practice, language is abstracted from social action, interactions and events are abstracted from community and personal history, difference and dominance are each abstracted from wider social practice, and both linguistic and social behavior are abstracted from the communities in which they occur. (Eckert and McConnell-Ginet 1998, 485)

In order to understand what is happening when people acquire and use language, we must try to understand the various communities of practice in which people function. Various kinds of differences arise in such circumstances, including gender differences: 'gender is ... produced and reproduced in differential forms of participation in particular communities of practice. ... The relations among communities of practice when they come together in overarching communities of practice also produce gender arrangements' (1998, 491). Individuals participate in various communities of practice and these communities interact in various ways with other communities. Since these processes of participation and interaction are constantly changing, there is also constant reshaping of both individual identity and any kind of group identity, including gender identity. You must learn to be a jock or a burnout, a particular kind of man or a particular kind of woman, and any other kind of socially categorized or gendered person.

Gender and sexuality identities

Work on the social construction of identities has become central to ways of thinking about language, gender, and sexuality in sociolinguistics and linguistic anthropology. As in West and Zimmerman's *Doing Gender* (1987), we focus on gender not as the source of linguistic behavior but as the product of our language performances (see chapters 3 and 4). Identity may be constructed through a variety of linguistic means. For instance, the use of certain lexical forms or language varieties may contribute to the identification of a speaker, just as particular communicative practices, such as silence, greeting formulas, or gaze do. Identity is neither an attribute nor a possession, it is a process of semiosis (Mendoza-Denton 2002). Heller (2007) points out that the concept of identity, along with community and language, are 'heuristic devices which capture some elements of how we organize ourselves, but which have to be understood as social constructs' (Heller 2007, 13).

Work by Bucholtz and Hall (2003, 2004, 2005) outlines an approach to the linguistic construction of social identity that has provided a popular framework for this approach. The term identity is used here to describe what is primarily a social, and not a psychological, phenomenon; we do not speak the way we do because of our identities, but construct our identities using linguistic practices which have social meanings (Bucholtz and Hall 2005). The underlying idea is that identities do not exist outside of the performance of them; thus this work moves away from the common perception that gender and sexuality categories are pre-existing and fixed, and views gender and sexuality identities as fluid and constantly shifting. Individuals are not fixed subjects in a society but position themselves, and are positioned by others, in multiple and sometimes contradictory ways. We speak of identity in terms of intersubjectivity, recognizing the dialogical aspect of the negotiation of identities. Individuals are not solely responsible for their own identity and position vis-à-vis others in an interaction; it is something that is jointly constructed.

Furthermore, a speaker's identification involves social categories of many different types – not just social categories for gender and sexuality such as 'male' or 'gay' but also situational roles such as 'patient' or 'customer' and interactional stances of similarity and difference. What, therefore, are the consequences for gender identity in particular? Gender identity is not separate from other types of identity in two ways. First, it is what has been called **intersectional**; an individual does not construct an identity just as a woman, but as a woman plus other intersecting categories – Latina, middle class, bilingual, straight, mother, urban, and so on. Thus the identity a speaker constructs through language (and other social behaviors) is never just about gender, but about gender and many other types of identity.

Second, if identity is something that must be performed, gender identity might not always be in the forefront of a performance. Everything a man does is not primarily a performance of masculinity; certain ways of speaking may be primarily about constructing an identity as an African American, a professional, or an avid Chicago White Sox baseball fan. While such things may be intertwined with gender identity, gender is not foregrounded in the construction of identity at all times.

There is a large body of literature on the linguistic construction of gender identity, but several themes recur. One is the multiplicity of gender identities. Studies which look specifically at how different linguistic devices are used to construct different masculinities include Bucholtz (1999a), Cameron (1998b), Kiesling (2001) and Sheldon (2008). They use different types of data but share the concept that there are different types of masculinity associated with different ways of speaking to construct particular identities and, as Sheldon and Bucholtz argue, to reify masculine stereotypes. Both Cameron's and Kiesling's articles look at language within male groups and how it is used to construct hegemonic masculinity; Cameron shows how a key component in the conversation she analyzes is used to establish heterosexuality: discussing other men and calling them 'gay.' Kiesling looks at how one member of a fraternity uses different ways of speaking to construct different types of masculinity. Among his frat brothers, he uses confrontational language to put himself at the top of the hierarchy, but with a young woman at a bar he presents himself as an authority figure. Both styles require him to position himself as an expert, albeit in different ways.

Bucholtz' study, which analyzes the narrative of a White teenager who uses CRAAVE (Cross-Race African American Vernacular English), focuses on how a racialized physical masculinity is constructed through language use. This speaker's use of CRAAVE simultaneously constructs him as having an affinity to his African American friends, but also reinforces stereotypes about Black masculinity and its supposed connection to physical strength and toughness.

Sheldon's study looks at an ad for Microsoft which features a 'menacing white biker guy' (Sheldon 2008, 151) who is extolling the virtues of Microsoft's classical music software. He switches between a nonstandard variety of English and a stylized techno-geek register, the former evoking a masculinity based on ideas of physical strength and toughness, the latter based on ideas of technical knowledge as part of masculinity. Sheldon suggests that such use of these contrasting styles and gender ideologies allows the readers of this ad to 'have their cake and eat it too' – that is, they can be knowledgeable about something like classical music, but also be tough and physically strong.

Research on the construction of femininities also focuses on the use of stereotypical ideas about femininity and how speakers position themselves in alignment with, or in opposition to, these dominant ideologies. We mentioned earlier the study which addresses how Swedish girls feel compelled to continually discuss how fat they are as part of their construction of femininity, but that this is a strategy open only to girls who are not actually considered overweight (Ambjörnsson 2005). This study shows how the discourse about weight reproduces stereotypes about body size and femininity. In contrast, Bucholtz (1999b) looks at nerd girls and shows how they use hypercorrect language and displays of knowledge (the latter often associated with masculinity) as part of their construction of nerd girl identity, an identity which challenges hegemonic femininity.

While there is a body of literature which addresses how dominant constructions of masculinity and femininity lead to the silencing of girls in the classrooms (Sadker and Sadker 1994, Swann 2003), there are also studies which show other perspectives on gendered language use in the classroom. Davies (2003) looks at groups of girls and boys in the classroom, and shows that the construction of feminine identities involves cooperation and engagement in academic work. The boys' talk included features of confrontation and the construction of heterosexuality, which, when used in classroom discussion, were a deterrent to academic achievement. Baxter (2002) also shows how girls are not locked into particular ways of speaking, but can resist dominant classroom practices which privilege ways of speaking typically associated with boys. Similar themes are also found in research on gender in the workplace (Holmes 2006), particularly in how gendered language is part of the construction of leadership roles.

The intertwining of gender and sexuality is also apparent in many studies which examine how heteronormativity is reproduced and challenged in conversation. Liddicoat (2011) looks at heteronormative framing in the language classroom, and how several students' valiant attempts to come out (i.e., indicate that they have same-sex partners) are treated as issues of grammatical incorrectness. This theme of normative heterosexuality, discussed above, is also a theme in work by Land and Kitzlinger (2005). They examine data from telephone calls from five lesbian households and show how sexuality is indexed among intimates in similar ways for heterosexual and lesbian women, but in institutional calls, indexing a lesbian identity involves a disruption of the heterosexist assumption. Thus an act of 'coming out' must be continually performed.

Queen (2005) explores how lesbian identity is constructed through joking and on how these interactions revolve around knowledge of both the sexuality of the speakers and stereotypes about lesbians. Far from being accepted as definitive, however, these stereotypes are contested; they can be funny, but they are also a springboard for a negotiation of group and individual identities. In one example, short hair, wearing Birkenstocks, and vegetarianism are presented as identifying characteristics of lesbians, although these are ultimately all challenged in terms of their applicability to themselves and other women they know. Through this conversation their own identities emerge, not simply by positioning themselves with reference to stereotypes but through the interaction itself, thus illustrating how identities are discursively produced. Another article which also examine lesbian identity and authenticity is Jones (2011), in which the category of 'lesbian' is constructed around certain characteristics associated with being 'butch'; being too 'femme' is not seen as authentically lesbian. Again, however, this article shows how these categories and the identities of the speakers are not fixed but emergent from the discourse.

Exploration 12.3:   Labels

Do you have words (slang or standard) for referring to people who are considered to have a particular kind of gender or sexuality identity? For instance, the terms 'butch' and 'femme' are often used to describe lesbians who are considered more masculine or feminine, respectively. Are there other words you use or hear which refer to different ways of being masculine, feminine, gay, straight, and so on? Do these words indicate positive or negative values for the people in the categories they describe?

However, not everyone agrees that the focus on identity is the best way to look at gender and sexuality. In their book-length treatment of sexuality, Cameron and Kulick (2003) adopt a postmodern approach heavily dependent on the ideas of Derrida, Foucault, and Lacan, and argue that a concept they call **desire** should play a central role in trying to understand human behavior since 'desire encompasses more than just the preference for partners of the same or the other sex: it also deals with the non-intentional, non-conscious, and non-rational dimensions of human sexual life. The unconscious and irrational aspects of sexuality may not be manifested on the surface of people's behavior in the same way that their behavior displays the sexual identities they have consciously chosen ("gay," "lesbian," "straight," etc.)' (2003, 140). They argue that the issues of identity and power are less important, an argument that Bucholtz and Hall (2004) reject, claiming that desire is much too vague a concept to be useful and that issues of identity and power are not only relevant but essential in any research on such language varieties.

Research on language, gender, and sexuality has been done in a variety of ways. Although the current focus is on qualitative studies of the linguistic construction of identity, there is also other work on gender and sexuality as variables in variation (as we saw in chapters 6 through 8) and on sexist language and the reproduction of gender/sexuality stereotypes in social Discourses. This range of ways in which we can approach the general topic of language, gender, and sexuality has given rise to controversies and disagreements over the past decades and these continue into the present day. Such discussions should be viewed as a strength in the field, because even without consensus, they guarantee that important issues for language and society continue to be addressed.

Chapter Summary

The research in sociolinguistics on language, gender, and sexuality has been presented here in three main sections. First, we talk about how sexism and hetero-sexism can be encoded in language structure and vocabulary. Second, we look at how language is used to create Discourses of gender and sexuality. The third and most extensive section looks at research on how men and women use language, tracing research trends up to the current focus on language as a means of expressed gender and sexuality identities.

Exercises

1. Look at the following headlines for online articles about stay-at-home parents. Are dads and moms talked about in different ways? What are the differences and similarities? What are some of the underlying assumptions about gender roles that become apparent? What Discourses about gender roles can we see in these headlines, and what inequalities do they represent?

    WALL STREET MOTHER, STAY-HOME FATHERS: As Husbands Do Domestic Duty, These Women Are Free to Achieve. (*New York Times*, http://www.nytimes .com/2013/12/08/us/wall-street-mothers-stay-home-fathers.html, accessed July 2, 2014)

    BREAKING DAD: THE STAY-AT-HOME LIFE: Think tech jobs are booming? Visit a playground on a weekday afternoon and observe the newest wave of the American workforce: the stay-at-home dad. (*Gentlemen's Quarterly*, http://www.gq.com/life/ mens-lives/201311/stay-at-home-dad-fatherhood, accessed July 2, 2014)

    THE OVERHYPED RISE OF STAY-AT-HOME DADS: If anything, men have stopped taking on more responsibility at home in recent years. (*The Atlantic*, http://www .theatlantic.com/business/archive/2013/09/the-overhyped-rise-of-stay-at-home -dads/279279/, accessed July 2, 2014)

    A STAY-AT-HOME DAD NOT WORTH 50K, INTERNET SAYS: (*Good Morning America*,   http://gma.yahoo.com/stay-home-dad-not-worth-50k-internet-says -021629639–abc-news-parenting.html, accessed July 2, 2014)

    WHAT IS A STAY-AT-HOME MOM'S SALARY WORTH? How tasks like driving, cooking and laundry would add up to a $113,568 income. (*Daily Mail*, http://www .dailymail.co.uk/femail/article-2544913/What-stay-home-moms-salary-worth-How -tasks-like-driving-cooking-laundry-add-113-568-income.html,   accessed   July   2, 2014)

    1% WIVES ARE HELPING KILL FEMINISM AND MAKE THE WAR ON WOMEN POSSIBLE: Being a mother isn't a real job – and the men who run the world know it. (*The Atlantic*, http://www.theatlantic.com/politics/archive/2012/06/1-wives-are -helping-kill-feminism-and-make-the-war-on-women-possible/258431/,   accessed July 2, 2014)

GERMAN FAMILY POLICY: PAY TO STAY AT HOME: The government plans a controversial benefit for stay-at-home mothers. (*The Economist*, http://www .economist.com/node/21554245, accessed July 2, 2014)

BEING MR. MOM: Stay-at-Home Dads on Tough, Full-Time Job. (*ABC News Nightline*, http://news.yahoo.com/blogs/nightline-fix-abc-news/being-mr-mom-stay -home-dads-tough-full-154633088.html, accessed July 2, 2014)

STAY-AT-HOME DADS, BREADWINNER MOMS AND MAKING IT ALL WORK: The next time you see a father out shopping with his kids, you might need to check your assumptions. (*NPR*, http://www.npr.org/2013/05/15/180300236/stay-at-home -dads-breadwinner-moms-and-making-it-all-work, July 2, 2014)

2. Write an essay addressing the following question: *What does it mean to say gender and sexuality are 'performed' or 'socially constructed'?* Include references and examples, but explain this in your own words.

Further Reading

Baker, Paul (2008). *Sexed Texts: Language, Gender and Sexuality*. London: Equinox.
   This book offers a review of the literature on language and gender and a main focus on linguistic performance and its role in the construction of gender and sexuality for identities and ideologies. Specific examples from culturally specific representations are included in the discussions of media and interactions.

Cameron, Deborah (2009). Sex/Gender, Language and the New Biologism. *Applied Linguistics* 31(2): 173–92.
   This article examines and refutes arguments that differences between male and female speech are based on biological differences.

Harrington, Kate, Lia Litosseliti, Helen Sauntson, and Jane Sunderland (eds.) (2008). *Gender and Language Research Methodologies*. London: Palgrave Macmillan.
   This edited volume presents introductions to a variety of approaches to studying gender and language, including interactional sociolinguistics, CA, corpus linguistics, CDA, discursive psychology, feminist post-structuralist discourse analysis and queer theory.

Mills, Sara (2008). *Language and Sexism*. Cambridge: Cambridge University Press.
   Following a review of the literature on sexist language, this volume presents a discussion of overt and indirect sexism based on the analysis of texts and conversational data. The author argues that while overtly sexist comments have become easier to identify, and thus are at least in some cases avoided, indirect sexism is extremely common and more difficult to counter, as it relies on contextual and interactional factors to be understood.

Motschenbacher, Heiko (2011). Taking Queer Linguistics Further: Sociolinguistics and Critical Heteronormativity Research. *International Journal of the Sociology of Language* 212: 149–79.
   This article addresses criticism against Queer Linguistics as a post-structuralist approach and makes suggestions for methodologies to empirically study language and sexuality.

Sunderland, Jane (2004). *Gendered Discourses*. London: Palgrave Macmillan.
   A thorough introduction to issues in the study of Discourses of gender and sexuality, and presentation of research and analyses of such Discourses in classrooms, in parenting magazines, in the representation of the British Prime minister, and in children's literature.

For further resources for this chapter visit the companion website at

 www.wiley.com/go/wardhaugh/sociolinguistics

References

Ambjörnsson, Fanny (2005). Talk. In Don Kulick and Anne Meneley (eds.), *Fat: The Anthropology of an Obsession*. New York: Jeremy P. Tarcher/Penguin, 109–20.

Baxter, Judith (2002). Competing Discourses in the Classroom: A Post-structuralist Discourse Analysis of Girls' and Boys' Speech in Public Contexts. *Discourse & Society* 13(6): 827–42.

Bradley, J. (1998). Yanyuwa: 'Men Speak One Way, Women Speak Another.' In J. Coates (ed.), *Language and Gender: A Reader*. Oxford: Blackwell.

Brower, D., M. Gerritsen, and D. de Haan (1979). Speech Differences between Women and Men: On the Wrong Track? *Language in Society* 8: 33–50.

Bucholtz, M. (1999a). You Da Man: Narrating the Racial Other in the Production of White Masculinity. *Journal of Sociolinguistics* 3(4): 443–60.

Bucholtz, M. (1999b). Why be Normal? Language and Identity Practices in a Community of Nerd Girls. *Language in Society* 28: 203–23.

Bucholtz, M. and K. Hall (2003). Language and Identity. In A. Duranti (ed.) (2005), *A Companion to Linguistic Anthropology*. Oxford: Blackwell, 368–94.

Bucholtz, M. and K. Hall (2004). Theorizing Identity in Language and Sexuality Research. *Language in Society* 33: 469–515.

Bucholtz, M. and K. Hall (2005). Identity and Interaction: A Sociocultural Linguistic Approach. *Discourse Studies* 7(4–5): 585–614.

Cameron, D. (1998a). Gender, Language, and Discourse: A Review Essay. *Signs: Journal of Women in Culture and Society* 23(4): 945–73.

Cameron, D. (1998b). Performing Gender Identity: Young Men's Talk and the Construction of Heterosexual Masculinity. In J. Coates (ed.), *Language and Gender: A Reader*. Oxford: Blackwell.

Cameron, D. (1998c). 'Is There Any Ketchup, Vera?': Gender, Power and Pragmatics. *Discourse & Society* 9(4): 437–55.

Cameron, D. (2006). Gender and the English Language. In B. Aarts and A. McMahon (eds.), *The Handbook of English Linguistics*. Oxford: Blackwell.

Cameron, D. (2007). *The Myth of Mars and Venus*. Oxford: Oxford University Press.

Cameron, D. (2008). Gender and Language Ideologies. In J. Holmes and M. Meyerhoff (eds.), *The Handbook of Language and Gender*. Oxford: Wiley-Blackwell, 447–67.

Cameron D. and Kulick D. (2003). *Language and Sexuality*. Cambridge: Cambridge University Press.

Cameron D. and Kulick D. (2006). Heteronorms. In D. Cameron and D. Kulick (eds.), *The Language and Sexuality Reader*. London: Routledge, 165–8.

Cameron, D., F. McAlinden, and K. O'Leary (1989). Lakoff in Context: The Social and Linguistic Functions of Tag Questions. In J. Coates and D. Cameron (eds.), *Women in Their Speech Communities*. London: Longman.

Coates, J. (2013). The Discursive Production of Everyday Heterosexualities. *Discourse & Society* 24(5): 536–52.

Dalley, P. and Campbell, M. D. (2006). Constructing and Contesting Discourses of Heteronormativity: An Ethnographic Study of Youth in a Francophone High School in Canada. *Journal of Language, Identity, and Education* 5(1): 11–29.

Davies, J. (2003). Expressions of Gender: An Analysis of Pupils' Gendered Discourse Styles in Small Group Classroom Discussions. *Discourse & Society* 14(2): 115–32.

DeFrancisco, V. (1998). The Sounds of Silence: How Men Silence Women in Marital Relations. In J. Coates (ed.), *Language and Gender: A Reader*. Oxford: Blackwell.

Dixon, R. M. W. (1971). A Method of Semantic Description. In D. D. Steinberg and L. A. Jakobovits (eds.), *Semantics: An Interdisciplinary Reader in Philosophy, Linguistics and Psychology*. Cambridge: Cambridge University Press.

Dubois, B. L. and I. Crouch (1975). The Question of Tag Questions in Women's Speech: They Don't Really Use More of Them, Do They? *Language in Society* 4: 289–94.

Eckert, P. and S. McConnell-Ginet (1998). Communities of Practice: Where Language, Gender, and Power All Live. In J. Coates (ed.), *Language and Gender: A Reader*. Oxford: Blackwell.

Fairclough, N. (2003). *Analysing Discourse: Textual Analysis for Social Research*. New York: Psychology Press.

Fishman, P. M. (1978). Interaction: The Work Women Do. *Social Problems* 25(4): 397–406.

Gal, S. (1978). Peasant Men Can't Find Wives: Language Change and Sex Roles in a Bilingual Community. *Language in Society* 7: 1–16.

Gaudio R. P. (1994). Sounding Gay: Pitch Proper-Ties in the Speech of Gay and Straight Men. *American Speech* 69: 30–57.

Gee, J. (1999). *An Introduction to Discourse Analysis: Theory and Method*. New York: Routledge.

Hall, Kira (1997). Hijras and the Use of Sexual Insult. In Anna Livia and Kira Hall (eds.), *Queerly Phrased: Language, Gender, and Sexuality*. Oxford: Oxford University Press, 430–57.

Hall, Kira (2005). Intertextual Sexuality: Parodies of Class, Identity, and Desire in Liminal Delhi. *Journal of Linguistic Anthropology* 15 (1): 125–44.

Hall, S. (ed.) (1997). *Representation: Cultural Representation and Signifying Practices*. London: Sage Publications.

Heller, M. (2007). *Bilingualism: A Social Approach*. London: Palgrave Macmillan.

Holmes, Janet (1984). Hedging Your Bets and Sitting on the Fence: Some Evidence for Hedges as Support Structures. *Te Reo* 27: 47–62.

Holmes, Janet (2006). *Gendered Talk at Work*. Oxford: Blackwell.

Inoue, M. (2006). *Vicarious Language: Gender and Linguistic Modernity in Japan*. Berkeley: University of California Press.

Jacobs, S. E., T. Wesley, and S. Lang. (eds.) (1997). *Two-Spirit People: Native American Gender Identity, Sexuality, and Spirituality*. Urbana: University of Illinois Press.

James, D. and S. Clarke (1993). Women, Men, and Interruptions: A Critical Review. In D. Tannen (ed.), *Gender and Conversational Interaction*. New York: Oxford University Press.

Johnstone, B. (2008). *Discourse Analysis*. 2nd edn. Oxford: Blackwell.

Jones, L. (2011). 'The Only Dykey One': Constructions of (In)Authenticity in a Lesbian Community of Practice. *Journal of Homosexuality* 58(6–7): 719–41.

Kiesling, Scott F. (2001). 'Now I Gotta Watch What I Say': Shifting Constructions of Gender and Dominance in Discourse. *Journal of Linguistic Anthropology* 11: 250–73.

Kitzinger, C. (2005). Speaking as a Heterosexual: (How) Is Sexuality Relevant for Talk-in-Interaction. *Research on Language and Social Interaction* 38: 221–65.

Kulick, D. (2000). Gay and Lesbian Language. *Annual Review of Anthropology* 29: 243–85.

Kulick, D. (2003). Language and Desire. In J. Holmes and M. Meyerhoff (eds.), *The Handbook of Language and Gender*. Oxford: Blackwell.

Lakoff, R. T. (1973). Language and Woman's Place. *Language in Society* 2: 45–80.

Lakoff, R. T. (1990). *Talking Power*. New York: Basic Books.

Land, V. and C. Kitzinger (2005). Speaking as a Lesbian: Correcting the Heterosexist Presumption. *Research on Language and Social Interaction* 38(4): 371–416.

Lazar, Michelle M. (2005). Performing the State Fatherhood: The Remaking of Hegemony. In Michelle Lazar (ed.), *Feminist Critical Discourse Analysis: Gender, Power and Ideology in Discourse*. London: Palgrave Macmillan, 139–63.

Liddicoat, A. J. (2011). *An Introduction to Conversation Analysis*. 2nd edn. London: Continuum.

Maltz, D. N. and R. A. Borker (1982). A Cultural Approach to Male–Female Miscommunication. In J. J. Gumperz (ed.), *Language and Social Identity*. Cambridge: Cambridge University Press.

Mendoza-Denton, N. (2002). Language and Identity. In Jack K. Chambers, Peter Trudgill, and Natalie Schilling-Estes (eds.), *The Handbook of Language Variation and Change*. Oxford: Blackwell, 475–99.

Milani, T. M. (2013). Are 'Queers' Really 'Queer'? Language, Identity and Same-Sex Desire in a South African Online Community. *Discourse & Society* 24(5): 615–33.

Mills, S. (2008). *Language and Sexism*. Cambridge: Cambridge University Press.

Milroy, L. and M. Gordon (2003). *Sociolinguistics: Method and Interpretation*. Oxford: Blackwell.

Milroy, J. and L. Milroy (1978). Belfast: Change and Variation in an Urban Vernacular. In P. Trudgill (ed.), *Sociolinguistic Patterns in British English*. London: Arnold.

Moonwomon-Baird, B. (1997). Toward a Study of Lesbian Speech. In Anna Livia and Kira Hall (eds.), *Queerly Phrased: Language, Gender, and Sexuality*. Oxford: Oxford University Press, 202–13.

Motschenbacher, Heiko (2011). Taking Queer Linguistics Further: Sociolinguistics and Critical Heteronormativity Research. *International Journal of the Sociology of Language* 212: 149–79.

Munson, B. and Babel, M. (2007). Loose Lips and Silver Tongues, or, Projecting Sexual Orientation through Speech. *Language and Linguistics Compass* 1(5): 416–49.

Nakamura, M. (2004). Discursive Construction of the Ideology of 'Women's Language': 'Schoolgirl Language' in the Meiji Period (1868–1912). *Nature-People-Society* 36: 43–80.

Nakamura, M. (2005). Construction of 'Japanese Women's Language' as a Symbol of Femininity: After the Second World War (1945–1965). *Nature-People-Society* 39: 1–28.

O'Barr, William M. and Bowman K. Atkins (1980) 'Women's Language' or 'Powerless Language'? In S. McConnell Ginet, R. Borker, and N. Furman (eds.), *Women and Language in Literature and Society*. New York: Praeger, 93–110.

Ohara, Yumiko and Scott Saft (2003). Using Conversation Analysis to Track Gender Ideologies in Social Interaction: Toward a Feminist Analysis of a Japanese Phone-in Consultation TV Program. *Discourse & Society* 14(2): 153–72.

Pauwels, A. (1998). *Women Changing Language*. London: Longman.

Penelope, J. (1988). Prescribed Passivity: The Language of Sexism. In The Nebraska Sociological Feminist Collective (eds.), *A Feminist Ethic for Social Science Research*. Lewiston/Queenston: Edwin Mellen Press, 119–38.

Penelope, J. (1990). *Speaking Freely*. Oxford: Pergamon Press.

Poos, D. and R. Simpson (2002). Cross-Disciplinary Comparisons of Hedging. In R. Reppen, S. M. Fitzmaurice, and D. Biber (eds.), *Using Corpora to Explore Linguistic Variation*. Amsterdam: John Benjamins.

Queen, Robin (2005). 'How Many Lesbians Does It Take …': Jokes, Teasing, and the Negotiation of Stereotypes about Lesbians. *Journal of Linguistic Anthropology* 15(2): 239–57.

Reynolds, K. A. (1998). Female Speakers of Japanese in Transition. In J. Coates (ed.), *Language and Gender: A Reader*. Oxford.

Renold, E. (2000). 'Coming out': Gender, (Hetero)sexuality and the Primary School. *Gender and Education* 12(3): 309–26.

Romaine, S. (1999). *Communicating Gender*. Mahwah, NJ: Lawrence Erlbaum.

Sadker, M. and D. Sadker (1994). Missing in Interaction. In M. Saker and D. Sadker (eds) *Failing at Fairness: How American's Schools Cheat Girls*. Toronto: Maxwell McMillan Canada.

Sapir, E. (1929). Male and Female Forms of Speech in Yana. In S. W. J. Teeuwen (ed.), *Donum Natalicum Schrijnen*. Nijmegen: Dekker & Van de Vegt.

Sellers, S. (1991). *Language and Sexual Difference: Feminist Writing in France*. New York: St Martin's Press.

Sheldon, A. (2008). 'Dis Is Schubert, Tough Guy': Linguistic Construction of Masculinities in a Microsoft Ad. In Jason F. Siegel, Traci C. Nagle, Amandine Lorente-Lapole, and Julie Auger (eds.), *IUWPL7: Gender In Language: Classic Questions, New Contexts*. Bloomington, IN: IULC Publications, 151–160.

Spender, D. (1985). *Man Made Language*. 2nd edn. London: Routledge & Kegan Paul.

Sunderland, Jane (2004). *Gendered Discourses*. London: Palgrave Macmillan.

Sunderland, Jane (2006). *Language and Gender: An Advanced Resource Book*. New York: Routledge.

Swann, J. (2003). Schooled Language: Language and Gender in Educational Settings. In J. Holmes and M. Meyerhoff (eds.), *The Handbook of Language and Gender*. Oxford: Blackwell, 624–44.

Takahara, K. (1991). Female Speech Patterns in Japanese. *International Journal of the Sociology of Language* 92: 61–85.

Talbot, M. M. (1998). *Language and Gender: An Introduction*. Cambridge: Polity Press.

Tannen, D. (1990). *You Just Don't Understand: Women and Men in Conversation*. New York: William Morrow.

Tannen, D. (1992). Rethinking Power and Solidarity in Gender and Dominance. In Claire Kramsch and Sally McConnell-Ginet (eds.), *Text and Context: Cross-Disciplinary Perspectives on Language Study*. Lexington, MA: D.C. Heath, 135–47.

Tannen, D. (1993). *Gender and Conversational Interaction*. New York: Oxford University Press.

Tannen, D. (1998). Talk in the Intimate Relationship: His and Hers. In J. Coates (ed.), *Language and Gender: A Reader*. Oxford: Blackwell.

West, Candace (1984). When the Doctor Is a 'Lady': Power, Status, and Gender in Physician-Patient Encounters. *Symbolic Interaction* 7(1): 87–106. In J. Coates (ed.) (1998), *Language and Gender: A Reader*. Oxford: Blackwell, 396–412.

West, Candace and D. H. Zimmerman (1987) Doing Gender. *Gender and Society* 1(2): 125–51.

Zimmerman, D. H. and C. West (1975). Sex Roles, Interruptions and Silences in Conversation. In B. Thorne and N. Henley (eds.), *Language and Sex: Difference and Dominance*. Rowley, MA: Newbury House.

13

Sociolinguistics and Education

Key Concepts

Language ideologies as an influence on educational programs

Social identities of students as a factor in education

The use of minority languages and dialects in the classroom

Legitimation of minority languages and dialects

Access to English as a global language

Linguists are agreed that no variety of a language is inherently better than any other. They insist that all languages and all varieties of particular languages are equal in that they quite adequately serve the needs of those who use them. (The only exceptions they recognize are pidgin languages, which are by definition restricted varieties; see chapter 5.) A standard variety of a language is 'better' only in a social sense: it has a preferred status; it gives those who use it certain social advantages; and it can increase their opportunities in work and education. Nonstandard varieties tend to produce the opposite effect. These are some of the consequences that follow from elevating one variety and denigrating others, but there is no reason to suppose that any one of the varieties is linguistically more valuable than any other. If the capital cities of England and France had been York and Avignon respectively, Standard English and Standard French today would be quite different from what they actually are, and speakers of Received Pronunciation and Parisian French would in such

An Introduction to Sociolinguistics, Seventh Edition. Ronald Wardhaugh and Janet M. Fuller.
© 2015 John Wiley & Sons, Inc. Published 2015 by John Wiley & Sons, Inc.

circumstances be regarded as speaking somewhat peculiar local dialects that would not be very helpful 'if you want to get on in the world.'

This attitude that linguists have toward different languages and their different varieties is not one that everyone else shares. Many people believe that some languages or varieties *are* better than others, for example, that some languages are particularly 'beautiful,' others 'primitive,' some dialects more 'expressive,' others 'deficient,' and so on. In other words, it is widely believed that you can be advantaged or disadvantaged not just socially or aesthetically, but also intellectually, by the accident of which language or variety of a language you happen to speak. This Discourse is especially prevalent in discussions about education.

Sociolinguists have long been interested in how language plays a role in education, and here the overlap with linguistic anthropology is extensive in terms of the themes addressed and the literature in the field. One prominent scholar is Dell Hymes, whose work on other topics we have already introduced (see the discussion of ethnography of communication in chapter 9). After Hymes' death in 2009, Nancy Hornberger wrote the following tribute to him:

> Early in his career, Hymes called on those of us "for whom 'the way things are' is not reason enough for the way things are" to reinvent anthropology, asking of anthropology what we ask of ourselves – "responsiveness, critical awareness, ethical concern, human relevance, a clear connection between what is to be done and the interests of mankind" (1969:7). Forty years on and more, it is clear that Hymes's scholarship and political advocacy have in no small measure led the way in that task – with a social justice impact reaching beyond anthropology to educational policy and practice and, far more importantly, to the lives and well-being of countless learners and teachers, individuals, and communities around the world. (Hornberger 2011, 316–17)

In this chapter we will take up the relationships among sociolinguistics, education, and social justice. We will address three main topics, all of which involve the hegemony of standard languages and the role education should play with regard to the standard language ideology. First, we will look at issues of social dialects and how ways of speaking associated with lower socio-economic classes and ethnic groups are often viewed as disadvantages in education. Second, we will consider issues of multilingualism in education, again noting that there is a history in many places of viewing minority languages as a disadvantage in terms of education. Finally, we will examine educational issues involved in the growth of English world-wide.

All three of these topics involve the concept of **linguistic inequality**, which is defined by Bonnin (2013, 502) as the unequal social valuation of particular ways of speaking, which, due to the indexical nature of language, reproduces wider social, cultural, and economic inequalities. In the following sections we will revisit ideas we have discussed in previous chapters, for example, standardization (chapter 2), monoglossic ideologies (chapter 4) and critical perspectives on the study of language (chapter 11).

Social Dialects and Education

This section addresses a number of interrelated questions about language and education. What role do children's home dialects and discourse patterns play in their access to educational opportunities? What is the role of schooling vis-à-vis language? Many people would argue that the role of education is to teach children how to use the standard variety. Even if we accept this perspective, how can educational programs make all children's home languages and cultures a resource they can use in learning?

Restricted and elaborated codes

An early perspective on the role of social class in education can be found in the work of Bernstein (1961, 1971, 1972, 1990). Bernstein's views of the relationship between language and culture are influenced by his reading of Whorf (see chapter 1). Bernstein regards language as something which both influences culture and is in turn influenced by culture. A child growing up in a particular linguistic environment and culture learns the language of that environment and that culture, and then proceeds to pass on that learning to the next generation. Bernstein believes that there is a direct and reciprocal relationship between a particular kind of social structure, in both its establishment and its maintenance, and the way people in that social structure use language. Moreover, this relationship is a continuing one; it is socially reproduced and is handed down from generation to generation. For Bernstein, a particular kind of social structure leads to a particular kind of linguistic behavior, and this behavior in turn reproduces the original social structure. Consequently, a cycle exists in which certain social patterns produce certain linguistic patterns, which in turn reproduce the social patterns, and so on.

Individuals also learn their social roles through the process of communication. This process differs from social group to social group, and, because it is different in each social group, existing role differences are perpetuated in society. Of particular concern to Bernstein, therefore, are the quite different types of language that different social groups employ. He claims that there are two quite distinct varieties of language in use in society. He calls one variety **elaborated code** and the other variety **restricted code**. According to Bernstein, these codes have very different characteristics. For example, the elaborated code makes use of 'accurate' – in the sense of standard – grammatical order and syntax to regulate what is said; uses complex sentences that employ a range of devices for conjunction and subordination; employs prepositions to show relationships of both a temporal and a logical nature; shows frequent use of the pronoun *I*; uses with care a wide range of adjectives and adverbs; and allows for remarks to be qualified. According to Bernstein (1961, 169), the elaborated code 'is a language use which points to the possibilities inherent in a complex conceptual hierarchy for the organizing of experience.' In contrast, restricted code employs short, grammatically simple, and often unfinished sentences of 'poor' – meaning nonstandard – syntactic form; uses a few conjunctions simply and repetitively; employs little subordination; tends toward a dislocated presentation of information; is rigid and limited in the use of adjectives and adverbs; makes infrequent use of impersonal pronoun subjects; confounds reasons and conclusions; makes frequent appeals to 'sympathetic circularity,' for example, *You know?*; uses idioms frequently; and is 'a language of **implicit meaning**.'

Bernstein says that every speaker of the language has access to the restricted code because all employ this code on certain occasions; for example, it is the language of intimacy between familiars. However, not all social classes have equal access to the elaborated code, particularly lower working-class people and their children, who are likely to have little experience with it. According to Bernstein (1972, 173), the consequences of this unequal distribution are considerable. In particular, children from the lower working class are likely to find themselves at a disadvantage when they attend school, because the elaborated code is the medium of instruction in schooling. When schools attempt to develop in children the ability to manipulate elaborated code, they are really involved in trying to change cultural patterns, and such involvement may have profound social and psychological consequences for all engaged in the task. Educational failure is likely to result.

Bernstein believes that the British social-class system does not allow the lower working class easy access to the elaborated code. Members of that class most frequently use the restricted code, which limits the intellectual horizons of its speakers. We should note that in Bernstein's view it is the *lower* working class, not the whole of the working class, who are penalized in this way; too often his work is interpreted as a claim about the working class as a whole. Of course, Bernstein and his followers must accept some of the responsibility for this misunderstanding since they generally omit the word *lower* and appear to be discussing the whole of the working class. Rosen (1972) has criticized Bernstein on the ground that he has not looked closely enough at working-class life and language and that many of the key terms in his work are quite inadequately defined, for example, code, class, elaborated, and so on. Many of the arguments also appear to be circular in nature and the hypotheses weak. Labov (1972) has echoed many of these criticisms and added a few of his own. He has argued that one cannot reason from the kinds of data presented by Bernstein that there is a qualitative difference between the two kinds of speech Bernstein describes, let alone a qualitative difference that would result in cognitive and intellectual differences. For example, he says (1970, 84): 'The cognitive style of a speaker has no fixed relation to the number of unusual adjectives or conjunctions that he uses.' A quantitative difference does not establish a qualitative one, particularly if the functions of language are ignored or down-played. In other words, working class speech may be different from middle class speech, but it is not inherently inferior or less well-suited to education. However, this early work raises an issue that is salient in sociolinguistic studies in schools: the relationship between home language and culture and educational practices. (See also the 2009 issue of *Multilingua* for a collection of papers addressing Bernstein's work, and Jones 2013 for a summary and analysis of all of the arguments for and against Bernstein's theory of restricted and elaborated codes.)

Difference not deficit

Many linguists believe that language should not be an issue at all in education. They regard all varieties of a language as equal and say that what we should be doing is teaching everyone to be tolerant and accepting of other varieties (Trudgill 1995, 186–7). This is a perhaps hopelessly utopian view. The inescapable reality is that people do use language to discriminate in every sense of that word. Milroy and Milroy (1999) state that what actually happens is that although public discrimination on the grounds of race, religion, and social class can no longer be done overtly, it appears that discrimination on linguistic grounds is perfectly acceptable, even though linguistic differences may themselves be associated with ethnic, religious, and class differences. Varieties of a language do exist, and people do use these varieties for their own purposes, not all of them to be applauded. As linguists we may deplore this fact, but we would be naive to ignore it.

Fairclough (1995) goes even further in his criticism of any kind of live-and-let-live solution. He criticizes the 'language awareness' approach advocated in various government reports in England in which students are taught Standard English but asked to recognize the legitimacy of other varieties for certain purposes. He says (1995, 225) that this is a doubtful bit of 'social engineering,' that 'passing on prestigious practices and values such as those of standard English without developing a critical awareness of them … implicitly legitim[izes] them,' that it 'dress[es] up inequality as diversity.' Moreover, he claims that it masks that stigmatization of certain varieties is systematic and even institutionalized, not merely the result of individual prejudices. He objects to such an approach because 'it puts linguistics … in the position of helping to normalize and legitimize a politically partisan representation, and turns a social scientific discipline into a resource for hegemonic struggle' (1995, 250). In Fairclough's view, when linguists say that they should not take sides, they are actually taking sides, having been ideologically co-opted – though unwittingly – into the struggle about language and power in society.

The advantages of adopting styles of speech associated with the middle class and giving up those of the working class often seem to teachers to be too obvious to be questioned. They seem directly related to social mobility, which for many seems indisputably positive. Many teachers have actually gone through this process, at least to some extent, themselves. However, for many working-class children, perhaps a large majority, the advantages are not at all obvious. Many see no advantage to buying what the educational system is trying to sell because they find no value in what is being sold: only promises too often broken. As we saw earlier (chapter 7), many members of the working class, including children, find much to be gained from hanging on to their language and resisting attempts that others make to change it. They find solidarity in working-class speech. The prestige it has may be negative and covert, but it is not without its comforts. Moreover, they may be quite aware of what it means to change: almost certain alienation from their peers without necessarily acceptance by social superiors. Attempting to 'speak posh' in Newcastle or Liverpool is almost certain to bring about your social isolation if you attend a local state school. Eckert's work (1989) with jocks and burnouts clearly shows how important identifying with the local area is for the latter group (see discussion of this in chapter 7). In London, Sebba (1993, 33) found that London Jamaican was 'a sign of ethnic identity and solidarity, and [provided] an in-group language for adolescents.' All that may happen from teachers' exhortations to children to adopt a 'better' variety of language is an increase in any linguistic insecurity the children have. The consequences may therefore be quite negative for many children.

A significant study in the role of home dialect and ways of using language is found in the work of Heath (1982, 1983). She looks particularly at practices surrounding literacy in the homes of people in three different communities in the Piedmont area of the Carolinas, USA, which she gives the pseudonyms of Trackton, Roadville, and Maintown. Trackton is a Black working-class farming community, Roadville is a White working-class mill town, and Maintown represents mainstream, middle-class, school-oriented culture. The ways of interacting with books for pre-school children in Maintown are often framed as 'natural' in educational settings, when they are of course cultural. They include behavioral aspects such as being careful with books and sitting quietly while an adult reads aloud, but also ways of using language such as labeling pictures in books, answering questions about what happens in a story, and using allusions to characters and plots from books in conversations outside of story time. Drawing parallels to fiction allows children to also create stories of their own. Thus, children raised in this tradition learn to participate in literacy activities that are parallel to what they will encounter when they begin school: they listen to stories, wait for cues to respond, answer questions about what happened in the book, relate this information to events in their own lives, and perhaps come up with their own stories. All of these activities are useful for participating successfully in school.

Children in Roadville have a different experience with literacy before they begin school. They have a similar orientation to being read to in terms of behavior – they are taught to sit quietly and listen and answer factual questions about the books. However, stories they create themselves are not encouraged and in some cases are treated as lies, that is, they may be reprimanded for this kind of speech. Perhaps most importantly, while they can talk about the plot of a story, they do not have experience decontextualizing it and integrating it into their own lives. Thus while they are equipped to do early tasks surrounding reading in school, they are less prepared to do more advanced work which requires them to answer questions such as 'What would have happened if Character A had done X instead of Y in this story?' or to write creatively.

Trackton children are not systematically exposed to books and printed materials have no special place in their world. They are not socialized to sit and listen quietly while adults tell stories; storytelling is often a collaborative event, and they must compete to make their contributions. They are not asked to label things in books or to answer questions about what happened in stories. They do, however, have more experience with creative storytelling. When they get to school, they are more likely to be seen as having behavioral problems, as they have not been conditioned to sit quietly and listen to stories and answer questions about the stories only when called upon. Although they are probably better equipped to deal with applications of stories to their own lives and analytical treatment of stories, these tasks are usually not asked of children in the early grades, and by the time these children reach the level where these tasks of integration and application are incorporated into instruction, the Trackton children are often already discouraged. If they have often not picked up the comprehension and composition skills required of them up until that point, they will have little opportunity to shine in creative writing.

In short, the only children who have a background that corresponds with what is done in school are the children with a Maintown upbringing. Heath advocates ethnographic research to see how community members orient to literacy in the home, and applying this knowledge to strategies for teaching children.

Exploration 13.1: Who Should Adapt?

Is it the role of children to adapt to the school culture, or for school programs to adapt their teaching methods and curricula to make use of the resources of the children's home languages and cultures? That is, is the role of education to teach children the mainstream language and culture, or to help maintain and value the home languages and cultures? Or neither, or both? What are the practical consequences of any of these answers? Is there room for compromise?

Role of the home dialect in education

One of the issues which is basic to the design of curricula for teaching children who speak a dialect other than the prescribed standard is what role the home dialect will play in the classroom. Siegel (2007) addresses the use of Creoles and nonstandard varieties in education, pointing out multiple problems with forbidding the home language of children. These include the social, cognitive, and psychological disadvantages of being told that one's way of speaking (and being) is wrong and undesired in the school context. Such admonishments lead to children struggling with identity issues surrounding their heritage, insecurity about expressing themselves in front of the teacher and other classmates, and difficulty acquiring literacy skills. He summarizes (Siegel 2007, 67):

It would seem logical that the obstacles mentioned above could be overcome if teachers recognised creoles and minority dialects as legitimate forms of language, if children were allowed to use their own language to express themselves until they learned the standard, and if they learned to read in a more familiar language or dialect. But a different type of logic seems to reign: the vernacular is seen as the greatest barrier to the acquisition of the standard, which is the key to academic and economic success, and therefore the vernacular must be avoided at all costs.

Siegel goes on to outline three different ways in which the home dialects of the children can be incorporated into instruction. In **instrumental programs**, the language is actually used for instruction, for example, the use of Tok Pisin in schools in Papua New Guinea. **Accommodation programs** allow for particular tasks, such as creative writing or oral expression, to be carried out in the home language, as in a reform of secondary education in Jamaica. **Awareness programs** include accommodation activities but also involve explicit learning about different varieties of the language and the social process through which one dialect becomes the standard. Awareness programs also include a contrastive component in which the students learn about the rule-governed natures of all dialects, and contrast the rules and patterns of their own variety with the standard. Wolfram et al.'s work in North Carolina in the United States, discussed below, has a similar orientation.

All such programs require a recognition of the legitimacy of the home dialects of the children. If the teachers and administration do not wish to **legitimate** the dialect, it cannot be used in the classroom. It is possible to both legitimate the dialect and teach the standard, of course, but this requires an ideological stance which allows for **pluralism** and acknowledges linguistic inequality.

Finally, there is a pedagogical issue. Many educators believe that **immersion** in the language or dialect to be used in education, that is, the standard, is the best way for children to learn that variety. However, research does not support this view; while obviously exposure to the standard variety is necessary, complete immersion (or 'submersion') has not been shown to be the most effective way to learn that standard (Craig 2001, Cummins 1988, Rickford and Rickford 2000). Moreover, denying the legitimacy of the children's home language may have a serious negative impact in terms of both social and psychological development.

African American Vernacular English and education

There has been widespread misunderstanding in the United States about AAVE, both of its characteristics and of how it is used (see discussion in chapter 2). This misunderstanding has had a number of unfortunate consequences. Many educators regarded its various distinguishing characteristics as deficiencies: AAVE was not just different from Standard English but restricted cognitive development. For example, Bereiter and Engelmann (1966, 39) stated that such children show 'a total lack of ability to use language as a device for acquiring and processing information. Language for them is unwieldy and not very useful.' In the late 1960s, this view led to certain proposals to teach Black children the standard variety of the language. To remedy the deficiencies they believed to exist, Bereiter and Engelmann proposed a program designed to teach Black children how to speak: for example, how to make statements, to form negatives, to develop polar concepts ('big' and 'little'), to use prepositions, to categorize objects, and to perform logical operations. In this view, children who spoke AAVE suffered from 'verbal deprivation' or 'had no language,' and it was the duty and responsibility of educators to supply them with one. Labov and others have been severely critical of such views, believing that they completely misrepresent the linguistic abilities of Black children. These children speak a variety of English which is different from the standard favored by educators, but it is neither deficient nor unsystematic. Indeed, the variety is both systematic in itself and also related systematically to the standard. Moreover, many Black children live in a rich verbal culture in which linguistic ability is highly prized and in which many opportunities are offered for competition in verbal skill (note the above mention of this in Heath's work on language in Trackton). To assume that such children cannot affirm, negate, categorize, or think logically because they perform poorly in certain extremely inhibiting testing situations is absurd. They must use language all the time in order to get by, and any fair test of linguistic ability shows them to be as skilled as any other children. In addition, there is ample research which shows that verbal proficiency is valued in AAVE linguistic performances (see for example Mitchell-Kernan 1972, discussed in chapter 9); but such verbal skills are different from the ones that many teachers value. That such children need 'compensatory education' for their lack of linguistic ability is a complete misinterpretation of the facts. They may need some help in adjusting to certain middle-class values about how language is used in education, but that is a different matter and is a problem for many non-Black children too. Such views also assume that a major function of schooling is to indoctrinate working-class children in middle-class ways, with language central to this process.

In questioning Bereiter and Engelmann's claim that Black children appear to have no language at all, 'the myth of verbal deprivation,' Labov (1972) points out that, if you put a Black child in front of an adult White interviewer who then proceeds to fire questions at that child, you may expect few responses (1972, 185): 'The child is in an asymmetrical situation where anything he says can literally be held against him. He has learned a number of devices to avoid saying anything in this situation, and he works very hard to achieve this end.' Perhaps nowhere are the inadequacies of Bereiter and Engelmann's program more clearly illustrated than in the following incident recounted by Fasold (1975, 202–3):

> A film showing the corrective program developed by a team of educational psychologists for children alleged to have these language deficiencies was screened for linguists at the 1973 Linguistic Institute in Ann Arbor, Michigan. It contained the following sequence:
>
> Earnest White teacher, leaning forward, holding a coffee cup: 'This-is-not-a-spoon.'
> Little Black girl, softly: 'Dis not no 'poon.'
> White teacher, leaning farther forward, raising her voice: 'No, This-is-not-a-spoon.'

Black child, softly: 'Dis not a 'poon.'
White teacher, frustrated: 'This-is-not-a-spoon.'
Child, exasperated: 'Well, dass a cup!'

The reaction of the linguists, after they had finished applauding and cheering for the child, was a mixture of amusement, incredulity, and anger.

It is quite apparent from the child's final frustrated response that the problem is not language but the meaningless task the child was being asked to do.

A key issue here is the low academic achievement of African American children compared to children of other ethnic groups, often called the **achievement gap**. Rickford (1999a, 305) paints a bleak picture of the school performance of Black third- and fourth-graders in East Palo Alto, California, between 1989 and 1993. Green (2002, 28–9) shows how, in a national study conducted as part of the National Assessment of Educational Progress, about two-thirds of African American fourth-graders in inner city schools were found to be reading below their grade level in the 1990s, and even in the twelfth grade the proportion exceeded two-fifths. (The corresponding rates for White students were 29 percent and 17 percent.) Even for those who regard AAVE as a genuine and inherently non-limiting variety of English, there still remains the problem of how to deal with that variety in the classroom (as discussed in the previous section). The traditional attitude that educators have toward AAVE (and other nonstandard dialects) is that AAVE does not limit its users cognitively but it certainly limits them socially, and one of the purposes of education is the achievement of social equality. (You do not have to be a speaker of AAVE to experience this opinion of your speech, as any Cockney, Scouse, Geordie, New Yorker, or Alabamian knows who has been told his speech sounds poor, slovenly, ugly, bad, or lazy!) But this approach has not been particularly effective. Speakers of nonstandard dialects often value their dialects highly for ingroup interactions and the construction of social identities, and understandably resent attempts to devalue their varieties. Thus, as discussed above, the issue becomes what the role of AAVE should be in the classroom, and this continues to be debated.

Two important events have addressed the issue of race, language, and classroom practices. The by-now famous **Ann Arbor Decision** of 1979 is an example of a successful claim that AAVE is a *bona fide* dialect that schools must recognize. The parents of eleven African American children attending Martin Luther King School in Ann Arbor, Michigan, sued the school board in federal court saying that their children had been denied the 'equal opportunity' to which they were entitled on account of the variety of English they spoke. The judge in the case agreed and ordered the board to take appropriate action to teach the children to read. If that action required the school system to recognize that the children did speak a different variety of the language from that used elsewhere in the school system then the school system had to adjust to the children and not the children to the school system. Although this was not quite a decision in favor of using both AAVE and Standard English, it did give both legal and public recognition to AAVE as an issue that educators could not shy away from.

The second decision involved **Ebonics**, a term particularly popular among those who believe that there are strong connections between AAVE and African languages, specifically Niger-Congo languages (see Williams 1975). On December 18, 1996, the Oakland School Board in California decided to recognize, maintain, and use Ebonics in the classroom so that Black children would eventually acquire fluency in Standard English. In effect, the board declared Ebonics to be a separate language from English, one moreover that was 'genetically based.' (Although this was often interpreted to mean that it was something innate to the race of the speaker, the word 'genetic' was actually intended to refer to language, that is, that Ebonics is descended from African languages.) This decision was supported by a unanimous vote of the Linguistic Society of America at its annual meeting on January 7, 1997, as being 'linguistically and pedagogically sound' (without that organization giving any kind of endorsement to the idea that Ebonics was indeed genetically based; see link in the online materials for this chapter to access the full document). Elsewhere it produced a very strong negative reaction (see Perry and Delpit 1998, Adger et al. 1999, Rickford 1999a, 1999b, 2004, Lakoff 2000, and Baugh 2000). For example, it led to a United States Senate sub-committee hearing in January 1997, and strong opposition from both prominent African Americans (e.g., Jesse Jackson, until he changed his mind after taking time to reconsider the issues) and White conservatives (e.g., Rush Limbaugh). The resulting furor caused the board to drop the word 'Ebonics' from its proposal in April 1997. If nonstandard varieties of English were to have a place in Oakland classrooms, they would have to enter through the back door rather than the front door. (There is now a considerable literature on Ebonics, little of which is very illuminating, for what is said does not explain why this term was selected or what actually happened in Oakland, nor does it recommend what people should do next time something similar happens. The role that linguists played in the dispute has also come in for criticism, as, for example, in Kretzschmar 2008.)

While linguists may try to offer what they regard as correctives to views associated with Bernstein and to false and misleading statements about the language abilities of many African Americans, they may not necessarily be able to provide any solutions to these problems. For example, Alim (2005) describes how difficult it is to deal with the issue of teaching Standard English to Black youths in Haven High, a high school in a small US American city in which opportunities for Blacks are constantly decreasing. Teachers have a poor knowledge of the language of Black youths and do not understand why they resist 'white cultural and linguistic norming' (2005, 195), what Alim calls attempts to 'gentrify' their language. His view is that some kind of balance must be found between the two language varieties; however, he offers no specific suggestions as to how such a balance might possibly be achieved. Perhaps that is not surprising since the problem has proved to be intractable everywhere it has been identified.

Blake and Cutler (2003) look at teacher attitudes about language in general, and AAVE particular, in New York City schools, and their findings show the importance of language ideologies in educational settings. They note (2003, 186), 'The most compelling trend in this study is that teachers' language attitudes appear to be influenced by the philosophies, or lack thereof, of the schools in which they teach.' However, another finding of Blake and Cutler is that while teachers were often open to the idea of using what they recognized as another language in the classroom, they were far less open to the idea that using a nonstandard dialect such as AAVE would be educationally beneficial. 'Forty percent of the teachers in the survey agree that AAVE speakers have to contend with language problems associated with ESL students, with as many agreeing that it is sound to use a students' first language or dialect to teach them the standard language of the community. However, few support programs for dialect speakers or learning strategies employing AAVE as a tool' (Blake and Cutler 2003, 188). In other words, prejudice against dialects seen as deficient conflicted with ascribing a positive value of using the home language as a bridge to learning Standard English.

Applied sociolinguists

While many sociolinguists who work on dialects have been advocates for the speakers of those dialects, and have done work to illustrate the linguistic complexity and social legitimacy of nonstandard varieties, some have gone further and applied their findings to educational issues. Wolfram and his many students and associates have worked on the North Carolina Dialect Awareness Curriculum for decades and have successfully developed a state-approved dialect curriculum now used in public schools in eighth-grade social studies classes. It focuses on language attitudes and how languages are used socially and over time, with a specific focus on North Carolina dialects. (See the link to this project in the online materials for this chapter.) Wolfram advocates a social justice approach to sociolinguistics, arguing that sociolinguists should regard the applications of their work as part of their career obligation (Wolfram 2011).

Siegel (2007, 80) also expresses a similar opinion: 'rather than writing articles calling once again for more teacher training to include sociolinguistics, linguists and applied linguists need to get the message to teachers themselves – by disseminating information in non-technical terms, running workshops, attending educational conferences and meetings, and publishing articles in journals read by teachers. In other words, for linguistic knowledge to have an effect, it will have to go beyond the current boundaries of both linguistics and applied linguistics.'

Exploration 13.2: Sociolinguists at Large

Do you agree that sociolinguists should do applied work, and if so, in what ways should they participate in language planning, policy making, or curricular decisions? What are the pros and cons of this for academics and the communities in which they work?

Multilingual Education

Hornberger and McCay (2010, xv) note that increasingly, multilingual classrooms are the norm, not the exception, the world over, and critical perspectives on language ideologies are integral to the development of both sociolinguistics and language education. This section introduces some of the research and main ideas in this body of research.

Ideologies

A major topic in research on multilingual education is, of course, the language ideologies which inform educational programs, teacher practices, and student participation. We discussed monoglossic and normative monolingual ideologies in chapter 4; research on education in multilingual settings often looks critically at such ideologies. The issues involved here are much the same as those addressed in the last section on nonstandard dialects: the legitimation of the home languages of children, the social identities that are related to these languages, and the issue of exactly how the home language might be used in the classroom.

Wiley and Wright (2004) present a sobering review of minority student education in the United States, noting that the ideologies present are reminiscent of earlier periods in US history with a focus on restriction and social control which is based on racism and linguistic intolerance. Anti-bilingual programs and high-stakes testing (i.e., the use of standardized tests to evaluate student achievement and teacher effectiveness) have negative effects on minority language–speaking children.

Research by Wright and Bougie (2007) addresses the social and psychological advantages of programs which support ideologies of plurality and the value of minority languages spoken by the children in the classroom. They point out that children's self-esteem is higher if their home language is legitimatized in an educational setting. Their research also suggests that **two-way immersion programs**, in which Anglophone children learn a minority language (in their study, Spanish) and minority language–speaking children learn English, are influential in creating more positive evaluations and solidarity across ethnolinguistic group boundaries. Classroom solidarity plays a role in lessening the conceptualization of speakers of other languages, and/or members of other ethnic groups, as 'Other.' They note that the language choices of teachers are an integral part of this process: '… this research supports the specific importance of language and patterns of language use in intergroup contact settings. Consistent use of the minority languages by the teacher can positively contribute to the contact environment in multilingual classroom settings, enhancing the development of friendships and improving dominant-group members' attitudes toward the minority-language group' (Wright and Bougie 2007, 166).

Research carried out in France by Hélot and Young (2006) looks at the ideologies surrounding educating minority language speakers in that country. They describe normative monolingualism as the hegemonic ideology in France (see discussion of French language policy in chapter 14); it has led to a focus on the integration of children with an immigrant background, and not to any appreciation of linguistic diversity. Minority languages such as Breton or Arabic have been introduced into school curricula, but in ways which reflect a strong monolingual bias, for example, Arabic is offered only at the beginning level, rendering this course useless to heritage speakers of Arabic. The ideology here is that education in a minority language is useful only if you are a speaker of French, a position which feeds into the false dichotomy of immigrant versus elite bilingualism, discussed below. These authors advocate the use of language awareness programs so as to address some of the ideological problems they see in French schools.

Use of minority languages in the classroom

As in the case of nonstandard dialects, there has been a long prejudice against the use of minority languages in the classroom. One of the frequently cited reasons against the use of anything but the standard majority language is the idea that the most effective way to learn a second dialect or language is complete immersion. Research on bilingual education has not, however, supported this view. Since the early 1990s, evidence has accumulated that immersing children in the target language is not the most effective means of teaching them that language; instead, bilingual education with some instruction in the home language leads to academic success in the long term. What is often called the **Ramírez Report** (Ramírez et al. 1991), submitted to the US Department of Education, was the result of an eight-year longitudinal study of over 2,300 Spanish-speaking children from 554 classrooms, ranging from kindergarten to sixth-grade, in five different states. It compared different program types and found that the more years of bilingual education children had, the better they performed on English standardized tests in the sixth grade. There are several things to note about this finding. First, the positive effect of bilingual education in test scores was not always found earlier than the sixth grade; acquiring a language for academic success takes time. The long-term effectiveness of first learning to read in one's first language is definitely higher than having children learn to read in a language they are in the process of acquiring. Second, there is a superficially counter-intuitive result that children who have more schooling in Spanish do better on tests in English than children who have more exposure to English. This finding is linked to the first point, that the children who are in bilingual education programs simply have better literacy skills in the long run because they learn to read in a language they speak fluently, as opposed to a language they are learning. Thus, it is not simply exposure to English (sometimes called **time on task**) but the nature of exposure to English that is important.

The next large-scale study, which had similar results, was Thomas and Collier's series of publications based on a five-year study of 210,054 student records for children from kindergarten to twelfth grade across the country (Thomas and

Collier 1995, 1997, Collier and Thomas 2004). Again, they looked at student performance according to the type of program the children were enrolled in and also found that bilingual education programs were more effective in creating successful students in the long run. Further, they found that the more time the students spent learning in the minority language, the better they did. That is, students in programs which were 90 percent in Spanish were the highest achievers, followed by students in programs which were 50 percent in Spanish, with students in programs with fewer years of bilingual education, ESL programs, or English mainstream programs doing less well.

The most successful bilingual programs are two-way immersion programs (also called dual language programs). These programs clearly benefit the children by providing them with instruction in their dominant language and exposing them to English through Anglophone peers; such programs have social and psychological advantages which contribute to academic success. Genesee et al. (2006) also show that English language learners who participate in two-way immersion programs are less likely to drop out of school, have higher long-term academic achievement, and show more positive attitudes on the whole toward school. And for the Anglophone children in these programs, they are not only less likely to discriminate against members of other ethnolinguistic groups, but they also do well academically (Lindholm-Leary 2001). Although the majority language background part of the population in two-way immersion programs has not been studied as extensively, there exists no evidence that there is any negative impact on Anglophone students who are in bilingual programs in the United States, and they have the positive benefit of learning a second language at a young age.

However, even in bilingual education programs, there is a clear ideology about the importance of language purity. Educators frequently debate how languages should be used in multilingual contexts and, in many cases, a strict separation of languages is seen as desirable. Fitts (2006) writes about a Spanish-English dual language program in the USA, and notes some practices which serve to undermine the explicit claim that all of the children at the school are bilingual, for instance, students are categorized according to their 'first language,' which negates the possibility that they might have learned both languages in infancy. Also, it is very common for children to be expected to speak one language or the other, and not both, for instance, only Spanish during instruction in Spanish, and only English during instruction in English. This rarely reflects the reality of language use; for example, Potowski (2004) notes that only 56 percent of the utterances produced by the four students she studied were in Spanish during Spanish instruction. Fuller (2012) notes very different patterns of bilingual discourse in German-English classrooms in Germany and Spanish-English classrooms in the United States, but in neither case did the children categorically (or even mostly) stay in the language of instruction. Many other studies show that regardless of the background of the students or the amount of focus on the minority language, the majority language is used more in peer interactions (Pease-Alvarez and Winsler 1994, Heller 1999, McCarty 2002, Potowski 2004, 2007, Fuller et al. 2007, Palmer 2007).

In cases where teachers or students use bilingual discourse, another issue is *how* the languages are used. Patterns in which the dominant language is used for the content of the instruction and the minority language for comments which support or augment the main focus reproduce language inequalities by relegating the minority language to peripheral functions (see for instance Canagrajah 1995, Martin-Jones and Saxena 1995, 1996, Grima 2000, Martin 2003).

Many sociolinguists advocate a heteroglossic approach to education. García (2009, 2011) uses the term **translanguaging** for discussing an approach to the use of multiple ways of speaking – not just different languages but also different styles and registers – which makes use of all of the students' linguistic resources. However, this is not a widely embraced ideology in education. It requires that educators abandon what are often firmly held and widespread beliefs about the purity of language.

Another ideological issue involved in the use of bilingual discourse in the classroom may have to do with the status of the minority language itself. Even in bilingual programs, the minority language may not command a great deal of respect in comparison with the majority language. Even if the language is valued for ingroup interaction, it may be seen as less relevant for success in the wider society. García (2005) discusses how the term **heritage language** contributes to the ideology which marginalizes minority languages: it makes the language sound like something from the past, and less relevant for contemporary life.

Elite and immigrant bilingualism

Part of the status of bilingualism and the use of two languages has to do with ideas about immigrant bilingualism and elite bilingualism. **Immigrant bilingualism** is usually low status; immigrant languages are associated with poor and disenfranchised segments of society. This association causes many people to associate 'bilingual' with stigmatized identities in society, they then view speaking two languages as something which is not desirable. On the other hand, **elite bilingualism** means speaking two languages which both carry high status. In many countries, speaking an international language such as English (discussed in more detail in the next section) in addition to the national language creates elite bilingualism.

Work by Kanno (2008) on bilingual education in Japan provides an excellent example of how this dichotomy is reproduced in education. In schools which provided bilingual education in Japanese and English (the national language and a prestigious international language, respectively), bilingualism is framed as a resource, and is used to introduce the children to high culture and global imagined communities. In other words, the children are educated with the expectation that they will be successful participants in the global economy. In contrast, the bilingualism of students who are being educated at schools which serve minority language children (i.e., immigrants or returnees, usually of lower socio-economic class) is treated as a deficit. These children are not expected to be competitive players in the global market and 'compared with children of privilege, immigrant and refugee students are socialized into impoverished imagined communities with more limited possibilities' (Kanno 2008, 7). We see echoes of this in Vann et al (2006), where Latina/o students are positioned as future meat factory workers, and Meador (2005), in which immigrant Mexican girls are restricted from the category of 'good students' because of their social class standing and native language.

The distinction between elite and immigrant bilingualism is not a linguistic difference, that is, it is not the case that elite bilinguals are more proficient in their languages than immigrant bilinguals. The perceived difference is cultural: on the one hand, it is low status to speaker a minority language natively, but on the other hand, it is high status to learn a second language (sometimes even that same low-status minority language) if you are a native speaker of the majority language. Thus the bilingualism of some speakers is denigrated, while the bilingualism of other speakers is lauded. In an article discussing the contrast of discourses in the United States about, on the one hand, learning foreign languages to better serve one's country, and on the other hand, voting for English to become the official language of the country so it would be less threatened by other languages, Lo Bianco (2004, 22) writes:

> The bilingualism of immigrants and poor people is often construed as a major social problem threatening national cohesion and endangering security. Cashed-up and professionally organised public campaigns for its restriction result in the intrusion of law and sanction into classrooms, and set teachers and parents at loggerheads, ultimately leading all the way to legal prohibition. For elites, however, the name and the kind of bilingualism they are fostering is an altogether different entity. It is a skill, an esteemed cultural accomplishment, an investment in national capability, and a resource advancing national security and enhancing employment.

Such attitudes about bilingualism create a distinction between so-called elite bilingualism and immigrant bilingualism which is not about language proficiency or the particular languages involved, but about the status of the people who are associated with each category.

Exploration 13.3: 'Research Shows ...'

Why do you think that, despite a consistent line of research which shows the benefits of bilingual education and the use of minority languages and dialects in the classroom, there is still such resistance to this? How do *you* feel about the idea of using a nonstandard dialect or a minority language, either one you speak or one you do not speak, in classrooms in your community? What role do you think ideologies and the emotional attachments we have to different ways of speaking play in attitudes about how children should be taught, and is it possible to change these things with knowledge of research findings?

Education and World-Wide English

In classrooms around the world, some of the same issues arise about whether minority languages should be used, and if so, how they should be incorporated into the instruction. Legitimation of home languages and cultures is balanced against the desire to empower the students by teaching them an instrumentally important majority (or international) language. In this section we will discuss how these issues emerge when learning English as a global language is part of the educational context.

Tan and Tan (2008) look at student attitudes toward Singapore English and Standard English in order to ascertain what is the best pedagogical practice given that the overall goal is for the children to learn Standard English, but they live in an environment where they are exposed to Singapore English, which differs, at times considerably, from the standard. The results from the attitudinal survey showed that the students appreciate the value of Standard English, but that they do not feel that Singapore English is 'bad English.' Use of this variety is an important part of their Singaporean identity. However, such a view of the use of Singapore English is very dependent on context and the interlocutors. Singapore English is considered 'inappropriate' from an English teacher, but less so from a Math teacher. It is the desired code for speaking to friends and family outside an educational context. It is also worth noting that the Standard English guise which was rated most highly was the one spoken with a Singaporean, not American, accent; see the discussion of **glocalization** below. The authors draw parallels to the situation in the United States with Standard English and AAVE, noting that there has been some success in using AAVE in the classroom as a means to help children acquire literacy skills. They interpret the results of their survey as an indication that the use of Singapore English in the classroom might be beneficial.

Circles of English

Despite these parallels, there are some social, linguistic, and political differences between education in contexts with nonstandard dialects and minority languages and those in which English is a global, or **glocal** (global + local), variety with prestige as an international language. To look at these situations, we must first look at some basic concepts in the study of global Englishes.

Kachru (1986) introduced a set of terms for describing the role of English in different countries across the globe. The **inner circle** is described as regions in which English is used for almost all functions by the majority of the population, for example, the United States, the United Kingdom, or Australia. The **outer circle** contains countries in which there are originally non-native but institutionalized uses of English, for example, the Philippines or South Africa. What is called the **expanding circle** comprises countries in which English is learned as a foreign language, and in which it plays an increasingly important role in economic development. The different role of English in these societies contributes to differences in approaches to the use of English in schooling.

In the contexts of both the outer and expanding circles, the concept of glocalization is also relevant. Glocal development means that there is an interaction between global influences and local cultures, that is, there is **hybridization**. The norms of the target standard variety (e.g., British, American, etc.) are not simply adopted because that is what is taught in school; instead, local influences are intertwined with global ones. As Pennycook (2003) argues, globalization is not resulting in either homogenization or heterogenization of English, but is creating new aspects of popular culture, and new social categories and affiliations, which both appropriate global commodities and are locally contextualized. However, these new Englishes create another layer of complexity to multilingual situations. In the next sections we will address some of the resulting problems.

Elite closure

Language often reproduces social inequalities. One way in which this happens is that only certain people have access to languages that allow them to participate in more prestigious segments of society, in which there are often higher economic rewards. The concept of **elite closure** has been used to describe how people with power use language to reproduce their privileged positions; in the words of Myers-Scotton (1993, 149):

> Elite closure is a type of social mobilization strategy by which those persons in power establish or maintain their powers and privileges via linguistic choices. Put more concretely, elite closure is accomplished when the elite successfully employ official language policies and their own non-formalized language usage patterns to limit access of non-elite groups to political position and socioeconomic advancement.

Myers-Scotton used this concept in her work in Africa, where colonial languages (English, French, and Portuguese) are spoken by a minority of the population and limiting participation in higher education and government to those who speak those languages is an effective **gatekeeping** measure. As Myers-Scotton notes, however, elite closure is essentially present everywhere to some extent, but it is more apparent and stronger in cases in which a distinct, colonial language contrasts with local languages, and a relatively small percentage of the population has mastery of the colonial language. The elite language can be any language, but in this section we will focus only on situations in which English is the elite language.

Research by Wright (2002) discusses the historical situation of the status of English in South Africa, as well as the contemporary everyday practices which reproduce the dominance of English. He concludes that there is little challenge to English in its role in economic development, but also that the local languages will continue to be spoken. That is, English will undoubtedly retain its dominance, but not at the expense of local languages. Because of the focus on multilingualism in national language policy, it is possible that high quality English instruction could be made available to the larger population. More people knowing English well would allow continuation in the development in international trade without limiting participation in this economic activity to an elite few. Ridge (2004) notes that the varying levels of exposure to English of the different segments of the population in South Africa make this a challenge, but also advocates providing English education to a larger segment of the population so as to enable more people to participate in the global economy. In an article addressing English language policies in Africa more broadly, Kamwangamalu (2013) endorses dual-medium instruction; he argues for its educational effectiveness but also cautions that the status of the vernacular in society is a crucial key to educational success.

> Most schools in Anglophone Africa use English as the medium of instruction throughout the entire educational system, while others use an indigenous language as instructional medium for the first three years of primary education and then transition to English-medium instruction. Both approaches, however, have failed to spread literacy in English or in the indigenous language, as is evident from the high illiteracy rates in the African continent. There is, therefore, the need to consider an alternative, the proposed dual-medium education consisting of an English-medium stream and a vernacular-medium stream, in each of which the opposite language, English or the vernacular, is taught as a compulsory subject. The advantage of vernacular-medium education is that the vernacular is readily accessible both within and outside of the school compound. However, for vernacular-medium education to succeed locally, particularly in the era of globalization, it must be vested with at least some of the material gains and privileges that are currently associated only with English-medium education. Otherwise, English will continue to serve, as Graddol (2006:38) describes it in his forward-looking book, as 'one of the mechanisms for structuring inequality in developing economies.' (Kamwangamalu 2013, 334–5)

A contrast to the situation in multilingual Africa can be seen in largely monolingual (in terms of local languages) South Korea. English has become a critical part of education and there has been a recent debate about making English an official language of the country (Song 2011). Although no such legislation has yet been proposed, English is an undeniable focus in education. In some cases, businesses insist that applicants for white-collar jobs be able to speak English and they continue to assess the English performance of their employees, even though they may not use English as part of their professional duties. Song describes the situation as elite closure because, although English instruction is offered in all schools, in order to do well on exams and subsequently be admitted to the best universities, students must participate in after-school tutoring programs. Of course, these are accessible only to those who can afford them. As Song notes, this creates a situation in which 'the offspring of the privileged, with "good education," inherit their parents' high socio-economic positions, whereas the offspring of the lower classes, without "good education," inherit their parents' low socio-economic positions' (Song 2011, 44). The established social order in South Korean society is thus perpetuated through English and in the name of globalization.

Exploration 13.4:   Restricted Access

Are there segments of your society which can only be accessed if you master a particular code? Think about such arenas as higher education, white-collar employment, and participation in performing arts and media. Is it possible to compete in these arenas if you do not speak in a mainstream, majority-endorsed way? Also consider the opposite: are there events, activities, and opportunities exclusively for speakers of minority dialects and languages?

English in Europe

We would like to close this chapter with a discussion of the role of English in Europe, particularly within countries in the European Union. English is a lingua franca throughout Europe, just as it is elsewhere in the world. Our focus is on the growing use of English in higher education programs.

English is sometimes described as a threat to the survival of other languages in Europe, and its widespread use challenges the official EU policy on promoting linguistic diversity. It is nonetheless used increasingly in higher education programs (Coleman 2006). There is some speculation about the long-term effects of the increased use of English throughout Europe, including positing the development of a **Euro English** which is distinct from varieties spoken in inner circle countries, (e.g., Jenkins et al. 2001, Mollin 2006) or, at the very least, the emergence of local, communicatively focused uses of English which contrast with a prescriptive focus on norms from the inner circle. House (2003) discusses how English as a lingua franca is spoken by multilinguals and should be embraced as a hybrid variety which may include a variety of underlying worldviews; similar arguments are made by Seidlhofer et al. (2006) and Graddol (2006). In this perspective, native speakers of English from English-speaking countries no longer establish the norms for English in Europe.

In some cases, the spread of English is equated with the spread of capitalism and consumerism. Phillipson (2008) objects to the use of the term 'lingua franca' in this case. He argues that this term evokes a sense of egalitarianism that is not present in a situation in which some are native speakers and others are not, and the language is not neutral but clearly linked to specific cultural traditions and influences. He cautions against the adoption of English as the language of higher education as a response to market forces, and advocates careful policy and planning to prevent it displacing other languages. He notes: 'English as a lingua academica must be in balance with strong local language ecologies, which presupposes strong national language policies. The education system must evolve strategies for students and staff to become effectively trilingual (at least) in a diverse range of languages' (Phillipson 2006, 27).

Bolton and Kuteeva (2012) present a less oppositional view of English in higher education in Sweden in a study in which they surveyed students and academic staff at a Swedish university. The rhetoric of English as a threat is certainly present in the society as a whole and was voiced by the participants in their research, but was not the dominant perspective. One finding was that the use of English parallel to Swedish was a pragmatic reality for those in the natural sciences, and greater use was also reported in the social sciences, with less use found in the study of the humanities and law. There was, on the whole, support among the students for the use of English in instruction, which often occurred in the form of parallel use with Swedish, that is, Swedish was employed to clarify or when students worked together in group work, but English was the medium of lectures. Although 30–40 percent of the students (depending on their area of study) responded that they felt English was a threat to Swedish in terms of the domains of use, very few respondents (ranging from 10 percent in natural sciences to 17 percent in law) felt that the use of English in their education was a disadvantage for them personally, or for the university as a whole.

The example of Europe illustrates that English is not only seen as a threat to other languages in post-colonial contexts or in situations in which it is the dominant language spoken in a community. Its use in education is seen as both necessary for participation in global markets and as a means of creating social inequalities. Once again we see how languages and their uses are inextricably bound.

Chapter Summary

This chapter looks at how linguistic inequality is embedded in education in three different contexts: in cases where students speak nonstandard dialects; in communities where minority languages are spoken; and in countries where English is not a community language but is the medium of education. In all of these contexts, social inequalities are perpetuated by ideologies which privilege certain ways of speaking, and social structures which impede access to high-status codes for some portions of the population.

Exercises

1. Interview a teacher or administrator at a local school and write a short description of the ideologies about and practices in education you discover. Although you may want to add topics to this interview protocol, here is a list of topics to begin with:

- What language varieties are spoken by the children in the school? Is there a clear majority who speak one language, or are there many different codes which are well represented?
- In their free time before and between classes and on the playground, what languages can be heard spoken among the pupils?
- What language(s) are used in instruction? Are they the medium of instruction, the subject of instruction, or both? Are there different programs or classrooms that have different languages (for instance, a few classrooms which offer bilingual instruction, or foreign language classrooms)?
- Is the variety of language used in instruction a contested issue for students, parents, teachers, or administrators? Is this school typical of others in the region? If not, how is it different?
- Do you have suggestions for anything you would change about the language(s) used in instruction at your school?
- Do you feel that most of the children at your school are successful, that is, are prepared to go on to higher levels of education or employment? If so, what do you think is the root of this success? If not, what would need to change to better prepare the students?

2. Write an essay discussing a language awareness curriculum for schools in your region. Include a description of the regional dialects or minority languages which are spoken in the area, and how they are viewed by speakers of the majority language. What exactly would you want to address in a language awareness program? Outline the main points you would like teachers to understand about language variation, language ideologies, and language and social identity. Make some suggestions for what you would like children to do in a unit on language in their region if this was incorporated into the school curriculum. Conclude with a discussion of the potential benefits of such instruction.

Further Reading

Adamson, H. D. (2005). *Language Minority Students in American Schools: An Education in English*. Mahwah, NJ: Erlbaum.

This book introduces the reader to theory in second language acquisition, language policy, and language in society, and then applies this material to the topic of English language learners in the United States. Analysis chapters include a thorough review of bilingual education and nonstandard dialect use in schools.

Cenoz, Jasone and Ulrike Jessner (eds.) (2000). *English in Europe: The Acquisition of a Third Language*, vol. 19. Clevedon: Multilingual Matters.

This volume examines the sociolinguistics, psycholinguistic, and educational aspects of English in Europe. It looks at third language acquisition and how it contrasts with second language acquisition, and presents case studies from regions where most students already speak two varieties when they begin with instruction in English (e.g., Catalonia, Basque Country, Friesland).

Fuller, Janet M. (2009). Multilingualism in Educational Contexts: Ideologies and Identities. *Language and Linguistics Compass* 3(1): 338–58.

> After a brief discussion of the patterns of multilingual language use that have been noted in research in classrooms, this article summarizes research on language ideologies and social identities in a variety of multilingual education contexts, including but not limited to bilingual education programs.

Hélot, Christine and Anne-Marie De Mejía (eds.) (2008). *Forging Multilingual Spaces: Integrated Perspectives on Majority and Minority Bilingual Education.* Clevedon: Multilingual Matters.

> This volume presents case studies from the Americas and Europe looking at the ideologies present in education and the challenges of incorporating multilingualism into the classroom.

Trudell, Barbara (2010). When 'Prof' Speaks, Who Listens? The African Elite and the Use of African Languages for Education and Development in African Communities. *Language and Education* 24(4): 337–52.

> This article examines the role of elite members of African societies in terms of language choices in education, framing these choices in terms of sociopolitical factors which influence curricula.

Wigglesworth, G., R. Billington, and D. Loakes (2013). Creole Speakers and Standard Language Education. *Language and Linguistics Compass* 7: 388–97. doi: 10.1111/lnc3.12035

> This article examines attitudes to creole languages and how these influence their use in educational contexts, and summarizes research on different approaches to the education of speakers of creole languages.

For further resources for this chapter visit the companion website at

 www.wiley.com/go/wardhaugh/sociolinguistics

References

Adger, C. T., D. Christian, and O. Taylor (eds.) (1999). *Making the Connection: Language and Academic Achievement among African American Students.* Washington, DC: Center for Applied Linguistics.

Alim, H. S. (2005). Hearing What's Not Said and Missing What Is: Black Language in White Public Space. In S. F. Kiesling and C. B. Paulston (eds.), *Intercultural Discourse and Communication.* Oxford: Blackwell.

Baugh, J. (2000). *Beyond Ebonics: Linguistic Pride and Racial Prejudice.* New York: Oxford University Press.

Bereiter, C. and S. Engelmann (1966). *Teaching Disadvantaged Children in the Pre-school.* Englewood Cliffs, NJ: Prentice-Hall.

Bernstein, B. (1961). Social Structure, Language and Learning. *Educational Research* 3: 163–76.

Bernstein, B. (1971–5). *Class, Codes and Control,* vols 1–3. London: Routledge & Kegan Paul.

Bernstein, B. (1972). Social Class, Language and Socialization. In P. P. Giglioli (ed.), *Language and Social Context: Selected Readings.* Harmondsworth, England: Penguin Books.

Bernstein, B. (1990). *The Structuring of Pedagogic Discourse*, vol. 4: *Class, Codes and Control*. London: Routledge.

Blake, Rene and Cecilia Cutler (2003). AAE and Variation in Teachers' Attitudes: A Question of School Philosophy? *Linguistics and Education* 14(2): 163–94.

Bolton, Kingsley and Maria Kuteeva (2012). English as an Academic Language at a Swedish University: Parallel Language Use and the "Threat" of English.' *Journal of Multilingual and Multicultural Development* 33(5): 429–47.

Bonnin, Juan Eduardo (2013). New Dimensions of Linguistic Inequality: An Overview. *Language and Linguistics Compass* 7(9): 500–509.

Canagrajah, A. Suresh (1995). Functions of Codeswitching in ESL Classrooms: Socializing Bilingualism in Jaffna. *Journal of Multilingual and Multicultural Development* 16: 173–95.

Coleman, James A. (2006). English-Medium Teaching in European Higher Education. *Language Teaching* 39(1): 1–14.

Collier, Virginia P. and Wayne P. Thomas (2004). The Astounding Effectiveness of Dual Language Education for All. *NABE Journal of Research and Practice* 2(1): 1–20.

Craig, D. R. (2001). Language Education Revisited in the Commonwealth Caribbean. In P. Christie (ed.), *Due Respect. Papers on English and English-Related Creoles in the Caribbean in Honour of Professor Robert Le Page*. Kingston: University of West Indies Press, 61–76.

Cummins, J. (1988). Second Language Acquisition within Bilingual Education Programs. In L. M. Beebe (ed.), *Issues in Second Language Acquisition: Multiple Perspectives*. New York: Newbury House, 145–66.

Eckert, P. (1989). *Jocks and Burnouts: Social Categories and Identities in the High School*. New York: Teachers College Press.

Fairclough, N. (1995). *Critical Discourse Analysis*. London: Longman.

Fasold, R. W. (1975). Review of J. L. Dillard, *Black English*. *Language in Society* 4: 198–221.

Fitts, Shanan (2006). Reconstructing the Status Quo: Linguistic Interaction in a Dual-Language School. *Bilingual Research Journal* 29: 337–65.

Fuller, Janet M. (2012). *Bilingual Pre-Teens: Competing Ideologies and Multiple Identities in the U.S. and Germany*. New York: Routledge.

Fuller, Janet, Minta Elsman, and Kevan Self (2007). Addressing Peers in a Spanish-English Bilingual Classroom. In Kim Potowski and Richard Cameron (eds.), *Spanish in Contact: Educational, Social, and Linguistic Inquiries*. Amsterdam: John Benjamins, 135–51.

García, Ofelia (2005). Positioning Heritage Languages in the United States. *The Modern Language Journal* 89(4): 601–605.

García, Ofelia (2009). Education, Multilingualism and Translanguaging in the 21st Century. In T. Skutnabb-Kangas, R. Phillipson, A. K. Mohanty and M. Panda (eds.), *Social Justice through Multilingual Education*. Clevedon: Multilingual Matters, 140–58.

García, Ofelia (2011). From Language Garden to Sustainable Languaging: Bilingual Education in a Global World. *NABE Perspectives* 34(1): 5–9.

Genesee, F. (ed.) (2006). *Educating English Language Learners: A Synthesis of Research Evidence*. Cambridge: Cambridge University Press.

Graddol, D. (2006). *English Next: Why Global English May Mean the End of 'English as a Foreign Language.'* London: The British Council. http://www.britishcouncil.org/learning-research-english-next.pdf (accessed July 3, 2014).

Green, L. J. (2002). *African American English: A Linguistic Introduction*. Cambridge: Cambridge University Press.

Grima, Antoinette Camilleri (2000). The Maltese Bilingual Classroom: A Microcosm of Local Society. *Mediterranean Journal of Educational Studies* 6: 3–12.

Heath, Shirley Brice (1982). What No Bedtime Story Means: Narrative Skills at Home and School. *Language in Society* 11(1): 49–76.

Heath, Shirley Brice (1983). *Ways with Words: Language, Life and Work in Communities and Classrooms*. Cambridge: Cambridge University Press.

Heller, Monica (1999). *Linguistic Minorities and Modernity: A Sociolinguistic Ethnography*. New York: Longman.

Hélot, Christine and Andrea Young (2006). Imagining Multilingual Education in France: A Language and Cultural Awareness Project at Primary Level. In Ofelia García, Tove Skutnabb-Kangas, and Maria E. Torres-Guzmán (eds.), *Imagining Multilingual Schools: Languages in Education and Glocalization*. Clevedon: Multilingual Matters, 69–90.

Hornberger, Nancy H. (2011). Dell H. Hymes: His Scholarship and Legacy in Anthropology and Education. *Anthropology & Education Quarterly* 42(4): 310–18.

Hornberger, Nancy and Sandra Lee McCay (2010). *Sociolinguistics and Language Education*. Clevedon: Multilingual Matters.

House, Julianne (2003). English as a Lingua Franca: A Threat to Multilingualism? *Journal of Sociolinguistics* 7(4): 556–78.

Hymes, D. (1969). *Reinventing Anthropology*. New York: Random House.

Jenkins, Jennifer, Marko Modiano, and Barbara Seidlhofer (2001). Euro-English. *English Today* 17(4): 13–19.

Jones, Peter E. (2013). Bernstein's 'Codes' and the Linguistics of 'Deficit.' *Language and Education* 27(2): 161–79.

Kachru, Braj B. (1986). The Power and Politics of English. *World Englishes* 5(2–3): 121–40.

Kanno, Yasuko (2008). *Language and Education in Japan: Unequal Access to Bilingualism*. Basingstoke: Palgrave Macmillan.

Kamwangamalu, Nkonko M. (2013). Effects of Policy on English-Medium Instruction in Africa. *World Englishes* 32(3): 325–37.

Kretzschmar, W. A., Jr (2008). Public and Academic Understanding about Language: The Intellectual History of Ebonics. *English World-Wide* 29(1): 70–95.

Labov, W. (1970). The Study of Language in its Social Context. *Studium Generale* 23: 30–87. In P. P. Giglioli (ed.) (1972), *Language and Social Context: Selected Readings*. Harmondsworth, England: Penguin Books.

Labov, W. (1972). *Language in the Inner City: Studies in the Black English Vernacular*. Philadelphia: University of Pennsylvania Press.

Lakoff, R. T. (2000). *The Language War*. Berkeley: University of California Press.

Lindholm-Leary, Kathryn (2001). *Dual Language Education*. Clevedon: Multilingual Matters.

Lo Bianco, J. (2004). Uncle Sam and Mr. Unz. *English Today* 20(3): 16–22.

Martin, Dierdre (2003). Constructing Discursive Practices in School and Community: Bilingualism, Gender and Power. *International Journal of Bilingual Education and Bilingualism* 6: 237–52.

Martin-Jones, Marilyn and Mukul Saxena (1995). Supporting or Containing Bilingualism? Policies, Power Asymmetries, and Pedagogic Practices in Mainstream Primary Classrooms. In James W. Tollefson (ed.), *Power and Inequality in Language Education*. Cambridge, UK: Cambridge University Press, 73–90.

Martin-Jones, Marilyn and Mukul Saxena (1996). Turn-Taking, Power Asymmetries, and the Positioning of Bilingual Participants in Classroom Discourse. *Linguistics and Education* 8: 105–23.

McCarty, Theresa L. (2002). *A Place to Be Navajo: Rough Rock and the Struggle for Self-Determination in Indigenous Schooling*. Nahwah, NJ: Lawrence Erlbaum Associates.

Meador, Elizabeth (2005). The Making of Marginality: Schooling for Mexican Immigrant Girls in the Rural Southwest. *Anthropology and Education Quarterly* 36: 149–64.

Milroy, J. and L. Milroy (1999). *Authority in Language*. 3rd edn. London: Routledge.

Mitchell-Kernan, Claudia (1972). Signifying and Marking: Two Afro-American Speech Acts. In John J. Gumperz and Dell Hymes (eds.), *Directions in Sociolinguistics. The Ethnography of Communication*. New York: Holt, Rinehart, and Winston, 161–69.

Mollin, Sandra (2006). *Euro-English: Assessing Variety Status*, vol. 33. Tübingen: Gunter Narr Verlag.

Myers-Scotton, Carol (1993). Elite Closure as a Powerful Language Strategy: The African Case. *International Journal of the Sociology of Language* 103(1): 149–64.

Palmer, Deborah (2007). A Dual Immersion Strand Program in California: Carrying out the Promise of Dual Language Education in an English-Dominant Context. *The International Journal of Bilingual Education and Bilingualism* 10(6): 752–68.

Pease-Alvarez, Lucinda and Adam Winsler (1994). Cuando el Maestro no Habla Español: Children's Bilingual Language Practices in the Classroom. *TESOL Quarterly* 28: 507–35.

Pennycook, Alastair (2003). Global Englishes, Rip Slyme, and Performativity. *Journal of Sociolinguistics* 7(4): 513–33.

Perry, T. and L. Delpit (eds.) (1998). *The Real Ebonics Debate: Power, Language, and the Education of African-American Children*. Boston: Beacon Press.

Phillipson, Robert (2006). English, a Cuckoo in the European Higher Education Nest of Languages? *European Journal of English Studies* 10(1): 13–32.

Phillipson, Robert (2008). Lingua Franca or Lingua Frankensteinia? English in European Integration and Globalisation. *World Englishes* 27(2): 250–67.

Potowski, Kim (2004). Student Spanish Use and Investment in a Dual Language Classroom: Implications for Second Language Acquisition and Heritage Language Maintenance. *The Modern Language Journal* 88: 75–100.

Potowski, Kim (2007). *Language and Identity in a Dual Immersion School*. Clevedon: Multilingual Matters.

Ramírez, J. D., S. D. Yuen, and D. R. Ramey (1991). *Final Report: Longitudinal Study of Structured English Immersion Strategy, Early-Exit and Late-Exit Programs for Language-Minority Children*. Report submitted to the US Department of Education. San Mateo, CA: Aguirre International.

Rickford, J. R. (1999a). *African American Vernacular English*. Oxford: Blackwell.

Rickford, J. R. (1999b). The Ebonics Controversy in My Backyard: A Sociolinguist's Experience and Reflections. *Journal of Sociolinguistics* 3(2): 267–75.

Rickford, J. R. (2004). Spoken Soul: The Beloved, Belittled Language of Black America. In C. Fought (ed.), *Sociolinguistic Variation: Critical Reflections*. New York: Oxford University Press.

Rickford, J. R. and R. J. Rickford (2000). *Spoken Soul: The Story of Black English*. New York: John Wiley & Sons, Inc.

Ridge, Stanley G. M. (2004). Language Planning in a Rapidly Changing Multilingual Society: The Case of English in South Africa. *Language Problems & Language Planning* 28(2): 199–215.

Rosen, H. (1972). *Language and Class: A Critical Look at the Theories of Basil Bernstein*. Bristol: Falling Wall Press.

Sebba, M. (1993). *London Jamaican: Language Systems in Interaction*. London: Longman.

Seidlhofer, B., A. Breiteneder, and M. L Pitzl (2006). English as a Lingua Franca in Europe: Challenges for Applied Linguistics. *Annual Review of Applied Linguistics* 26: 3–34.

Siegel, Jeff (2007). Creoles and Minority Dialects in Education: An Update. *Language and Education* 21(1): 66–86.

Song, Jae Jung (2011). English as an Official Language in South Korea: Global English or Social Malady? *Language Problems & Language Planning* 35(1): 35–55.

Tan, Peter K.W. and Daniel K. H. Tan (2008). Attitudes Towards Non-Standard English in Singapore. *World Englishes* 27(3/4): 465–79.

Thomas, Wayne P. and Virginia Collier (1995). *Language Minority Student Achievement and Program Effectiveness. Research Summary*. Fairfax, VA: George Mason University.

Thomas, Wayne P. and Virginia Collier (1997). *School Effectiveness for Language Minority Students*. Washington, DC: National Clearinghouse for Bilingual Education.

Trudgill, P. (1995). *Sociolinguistics: An Introduction to Language and Society*. 3rd edn. Harmondsworth, England: Penguin Books.

Vann, R. J., K. R. Bruna, and M. P. Escudero (2006). Negotiating Identities in a Multilingual Science Class. In T. Omoniyi and G. White (eds.), *The Sociolinguistics of Identity*. New York: Continuum, 201–16.

Wiley, Terrence G. and Wayne E. Wright (2004). Against the Undertow: Language-Minority Education Policy and Politics in the 'Age of Accountability.' *Educational Policy* 18(1): 142–68.

Williams, R. (ed.) (1975). *Ebonics: The True Language of Black Folk*. St Louis: Institute of Black Studies.

Wolfram, Walt (2011). In the Profession: Connecting with the Public. *Journal of English Linguistics* 40(1): 111–17.

Wright, Laurence (2002). Why English Dominates the Central Economy: An Economic Perspective on Elite Closure and South African Language Policy. *Language Problems & Language Planning* 26(2): 159–77.

Wright, Stephen C. and Évelyne Bougie (2007). Intergroup Contact and Minority-Language Education Reducing Language-Based Discrimination and Its Negative Impact. *Journal of Language and Social Psychology* 26(2): 157–81.

14

Language Policy and Planning

Key Concepts

The goals of language policies: the government and the people

How planning works (or doesn't)

The roles of ethnic and national identities in language policies

The role of English world-wide

For a final topic we would like to turn our attention to some of the numerous attempts that have been made to influence the form of a language, or to control how a linguistic variety functions in society. We must note that language planning is often done to benefit already powerful sectors of society, as opposed to benefitting all members of society equally. Many planning decisions focus on the issues of hegemony and power which we have discussed in previous chapters, for example, with regard to standardization (chapter 2), critical discourse analysis (chapter 11) and gender and sexuality (chapter 12).

Terminology, Concepts, and Development of the Field

Attempts to change languages, in terms of either their form or their function, are usually described as instances of **language planning**. Because the 'plans' involved

An Introduction to Sociolinguistics, Seventh Edition. Ronald Wardhaugh and Janet M. Fuller.
© 2015 John Wiley & Sons, Inc. Published 2015 by John Wiley & Sons, Inc.

in changing languages often (although by no means always) involve policy decisions, work on language planning is often intertwined with work on **language policy**, and this body of literature is frequently referred to as LPP (Language Policy and Planning; see Hornberger 2006). Hornberger points out that the relationship between policy and planning is complex; planning does not always lead to policy or vice versa, rather they are intertwined processes. She concludes, 'LPP offers a unified conceptual rubric under which to pursue fuller understanding of the complexity of the policy-planning relationship and in turn its insertion in processes of social change' (Hornberger 2006, 25).

Spolsky (2004) offers a definition of language policy which includes three components: the language practices of a community, in particular the patterns of choices of which varieties are used in particular circumstances; language ideologies; and any specific efforts made to influence practices through intervention, planning, and management. As we will see in our further discussion, recognition of language ideologies has become a central aspect of the study of LPP.

Types of language planning

Language planning is an attempt to interfere deliberately with a language or one of its varieties: it is human intervention into natural processes of language change, diffusion, and erosion. That attempt may focus on either its status with regard to some other language or variety or its internal condition with a view to changing that condition, or on both of these since they are not mutually exclusive. The first focus results in status planning; the second results in corpus planning.

Status planning changes the function of a language or a variety of a language and the rights of those who use it. For example, when speakers of a minority language are denied the use of that language in educating their children, their language has no official status. Alternatively, when a government declares that henceforth two languages rather than one of these alone will be officially recognized in all functions, the newly recognized one has gained status. Status itself is a relative concept; it may also be improved or reduced by degrees. So far as languages and their varieties are concerned, status changes are nearly always very slow, are sometimes actively contested, and often leave strong residual feelings. They affect the rights of people to use their language in their daily lives and in their dealings with the state and its various agencies. Even relatively minor changes or proposals for changes can produce such effects, as the residents of many countries, for example, Norway, Belgium, Canada, and India, are well aware.

As a result of planning decisions, a language can achieve one of a variety of statuses (Kloss 1968). A language may be recognized as the sole official language, as French is in France or English in the United Kingdom and the United States. This fact does not necessarily mean that the status must be recognized constitutionally or by statute; it may be a matter of long-standing practice, as it is with English in the two cases cited above. Two or more languages may share official status in some countries, for example, English and French in Canada and in Cameroon; French and Flemish in Belgium; French, German, Italian, and Romansh in Switzerland; and English, Malay, Tamil, and Chinese in Singapore. South Africa has eleven official languages which the state guarantees equal status.

A language may also have official status but only on a regional basis, for example, Igbo, Yoruba, and Hausa in Nigeria; German in Belgium; and Marathi in Maharashtra, India. A language may be a 'promoted' language, lacking official status, but used by various institutions for specific purposes; for instance, English is increasingly used in educational contexts in Germany and Sweden. A tolerated language is one that is neither promoted nor proscribed or restricted, for example, Basque in France, many immigrant languages in Western Europe, and Native American languages in North America. Finally, a discouraged or proscribed language is one against which there are official sanctions or restrictions, for example, Basque in the early years of Franco's regime in Spain; Scots Gaelic after the 1745 rising; Macedonian in Greece. Beginning in the late 1800s, Native American children in the United States were coerced into attending so-called 'Indian Schools,' where they were forbidden to speak their native languages (García 2009, 161).

Planning decisions will obviously play a very large role in determining what happens to any minority language or languages in a country. They can result in deliberate attempts to eradicate such a language, as with Franco's attempt to eliminate Basque from Spain by banning that language from public life. Official neglect may result in letting minority languages die by simply not doing anything to keep them alive. This has been the fate of many Native languages in North America and is likely to be the fate of many more. In France Basque was neglected; in Spain it was virtually proscribed. One interesting consequence is that, while once there were more speakers of Basque in France than in Spain, now the situation is reversed. Instead of neglect there may be a level of tolerance, so that if a community with a minority language wishes to keep that language alive, it is allowed to do so but at its own expense. In 1988 the Council of Europe adopted the European Charter for Regional or Minority Languages that gave some recognition to such languages but really allowed each country to do as it pleased with them.

Corpus planning seeks to develop a variety of a language, usually to standardize it, that is, to provide it with the means for serving every possible language function in society. Consequently, corpus planning may involve such matters as the development of an orthography, new sources of vocabulary, dictionaries, and a literature, together with the deliberate cultivation of new uses so that the language may extend its use into such areas as government, education, and trade. Corpus planning has been particularly important in countries like Indonesia, Israel, Finland, India, Pakistan, and Papua New Guinea.

Governments sometimes very deliberately involve themselves in the standardization process by establishing official bodies of one kind or another to regulate language matters or to encourage changes felt to be desirable. One of the most famous examples of an official body established to promote the language of a country was

Richelieu's establishment of the Académie Française in 1635. Founded at a time when a variety of languages existed in France, when literacy was confined to a very few, and when there was little national consciousness, the Académie Française faced an unenviable task: the codification of French spelling, vocabulary, and grammar. Its goal was to fashion and reinforce French nationality, a most important task considering that, even two centuries later in the early nineteenth century, the French of Paris was virtually unknown in many parts of the country, particularly in the south. Similar attempts to found academies in England and the United States for the same purpose met with no success, individual dictionary-makers and grammar-writers having performed much the same function for English. Since both French and English are today highly standardized, one might question whether such academies serve a useful purpose, yet it is difficult to imagine France without the Académie Française: it undoubtedly has had a considerable influence on the French people and perhaps on their language.

It should also be noted that descriptive grammars and lexicons may be perceived as prescriptive ones. For example, in Germany the *Duden* (a multi-volume reference work on the German language) is considered to dictate what is good German; for instance, the first volume on orthography dictates 'correct' spelling (particularly useful after a spelling reform in 1996). However, like most grammars and dictionaries, the *Duden* also reflects current usage: inclusion in the *Duden* indicates pervasive use of a phrase, rather than 'correctness' in the static sense that is usually associated with the standard. Lippi-Green (2012) also notes the somewhat ambiguous role of dictionaries in this regard, although her concern is the opposite tendency. While pronunciation guides supposedly recognize a variety of possible pronunciations, they clearly do not represent all possible pronunciation variants of a word and thus perpetuate the idea that certain pronunciations are more correct than others. Consequently, the role of reference works in language standardization becomes fuzzy: while they uphold the idea of there being one, or at least very few, correct ways of pronouncing and using words or constructing sentences, they also reflect language change.

Corpus and status planning often co-occur, for many planning decisions involve some combination of a change in status with internal change. For example, as one particular language in Papua New Guinea is developed, all other languages are affected, whether or not the effects are recognized officially.

While much of this discussion of LPP seems based on the idea that planning is done at the level of the government through laws and policies, there is also a body of research that looks at bottom-up approaches to LPP. Educational practices, although often not explicitly identified as language planning, can indeed have an impact on language practices and ideologies. Research by King (1999, 2000), Hornberger and King (1996), and Hornberger and Coronel-Molina (2004) has looked at the effects of heritage language instruction in the Andes for speakers of Quechua. These programs have offered both mother tongue literacy instruction for children who speak Quechua as their first language and programs designed to extend instruction of the language to new speakers. They note that while school-based programs alone cannot reverse language shift, education is a necessary aspect of any local efforts in language maintenance.

In addition to educators, sociolinguists have also been quite involved in many planning activities and surrounding controversies. As we will see in the discussion in the next section on the phases of research, ideas about the role of researchers have changed over time.

Exploration 14.1: Vernacularization

It is rare, but there have been some cases of a language that was 'dead' coming back to life. The most striking and widespread case of this is with Hebrew, which was used only for religious and scholarly purposes but was not spoken natively, but which was revived in Israel as part of the development of national identity. Another example can be found in Manx, spoken on the Isle of Mann. Can you imagine speaking a language other than your native language in casual conversations with family members and friends who share your native tongue? What type of motivation would you need to do this?

The intellectual history of LPP

Haugen (1961) was one of the first people to use the term language planning in his work on language standardization in Norwegian, where he described planning as concerning matters such as orthography, grammar, and lexicon and both prescriptive and descriptive material. Since that time, the scope of the field has broadened to include other aspects of language and society. In an article outlining the historical and theoretical approaches to the field, Ricento (2000) outlines three factors which have shaped research in LPP. The first of these is **macro-sociopolitical** factors, for example, the formation or disintegration of political units (e.g., nations), wars, and population migrations. The second type of factor which influences research is **epistemological**; this refers to developments in theory and paradigms of knowledge which are used in LPP, for example, Marxism, structuralism, or postmodernism. The third type of factor is **strategy**, that is, the social goal of the research. For instance, the aim could be to support current policies being implemented, or to expose inequalities in language planning.

Ricento uses these three factors to look at the history of scholarship on LPP and distinguishes phases in that research since World War II: (1) early work: decolonization, structuralism, and pragmatism; (2) failure of modernization, critical sociolinguistics, and access; and (3) the new world order, postmodernism, and linguistic human rights. We will briefly outline these phases, and present representative material from research around the world.

Ricento (2000, 197) describes the first phase as work conducted with a focus on the macro-sociopolitical state of decolonization within the epistemological framework of **structuralism**, and with a pragmatic aim, that is, with the assumption that language planning and policy could solve language problems which arose during decolonization. Such research involved both status planning, that is, selecting new national languages, and corpus planning to codify those languages. Researchers framed such planning and policy initiatives as being largely non-political and straightforward pragmatic problem-solving; in other words, they were seen as ideologically neutral and serving the desires of the nation as a whole in terms of democratization, modernization, or efficiency. In order to maintain this position, languages were abstracted from their social and historical context (Ricento 2000, 199–200).

The second phase, which began in the 1970s, showed more reflection on decolonization as both the macro-sociopolitical factor and the epistemological factor – one indication of the latter being the introduction of the term **neo-colonial**. There was more discussion of hierarchy and social stratification and how language plays a role in the reproduction of power relationships. This more critical aim led researchers away from the narrow focus on standardization and **graphization** of the first phase of research to an examination of the social, political, and economic consequences of language planning and policies, especially in situations of language contact (Ricento 2000, 202).

Ricento describes the third phase, which began in the mid-1980s under the influence of 'the new world order,' by which he means the breakup of the Soviet Union and the creation of new national identities, the repatriation of colonies such as Hong Kong, the development of new political unions, for example, the European Union, and the globalization of capitalism (2000, 203). **Postmodern theory** also led to an increased focus on ideologies in LPP, and an emerging aim was promoting multilingualism and foreign language learning and defending (minority) language rights.

Data and methods

One issue to be addressed in LPP is identifying the right kinds of data that must go into planning decisions. Planning must be based on good information, but sometimes the kinds of information that go into planning decisions are not very reliable (see Ricento 2006 for a critique of various methods). Census-takers, for example, may have considerable difficulty in determining just who speaks what languages, when, and for what purposes. The census of India has always had this problem. The issues are complex, and gatherers of such information may have great difficulty in getting answers to even simple questions. You also get different answers according to the way you phrase your questions. What is your mother tongue? What was the first language you learned? What languages do you speak? What language do you speak at home? What languages are you fluent in? Do you speak Spanish (French) (German)? And so on. Moreover, the questions and how they are answered may be politically motivated. The different answers are also subject to a variety of interpretations.

Furthermore, it is easier to elicit particular kinds of information at certain times than at other times. During World War II many people in North America apparently suppressed information concerning either a German background or ability to speak German. Recent Canadian censuses show more and more people claiming bilingual ability in English and French, but little assessment is made of such self-reported claims; it is apparently enough that people should wish to make them! Consequently, we must always exercise caution in interpreting untreated data from censuses.

Questions asked at ten-year periods may also produce different answers, partly because there have been objective quantifiable changes but also because less quantifiable and more subjective social or psychological changes have occurred. For instance, members of an immigrant group may have increased in proficiency in the majority language, and this may be reflected in their self-reports of language use; or it could just be that they are increasingly aware of the stigmatization of speaking their minority language, and they may not be willing to admit their continued use of this language in many domains. LPP research must assess the objectivity of the data, and also recognize the diverse goals and consequences of language policies. In the rest of this chapter, we will turn to research on particular languages and national settings to illustrate how these have been addressed in research to date.

LPP and Nationalization

In this section we will look at a variety of linguistic situations in Europe and the former Soviet Union to see some instances of planning. The particular countries we discuss were chosen because they show some of the variety of issues that states engaged in planning face as they continue to make changes. Many other examples could be cited; we have chosen these to illustrate certain points. Other examples would have served just as well, for it is probably true to say that nowhere in the world can you find a country where nothing is being done, either directly or by default, concerning the language or languages of that country.

LPP in Turkey: orthography and purity

Turkey provides a good example of very deliberate language planning designed to achieve certain national objectives and to do this very quickly. When Kemal Atatürk (*ata* 'father'), the 'father of the Turks,' established the modern republic of Turkey, he was confronted with the task of modernizing Turkish. It had no vocabulary for modern science and technology, was written in Arabic orthography, and was strongly influenced by both Arabic and Persian. In 1928 Atatürk deliberately adopted the **Roman script** for his new modern language. This choice symbolically cut the

Turks off from their Islamic past and directed their attention toward both their Turkish roots and their future as Turks in a modern world. Since only 10 percent of the population was literate, there was no mass objection to the changes. It was also possible to use the new script almost immediately as various steps were taken to increase the amount of literacy in the country.

The language reform also aimed to move Turkish away from Arabic and Persian in order to create a 'pure Turkish language.' According to Doğançay-Aktuna (2004, 7), 'the Turkish that was mainly spoken by the masses would be codified and developed to take the place of Ottoman Turkish in administration and education. ... these linguistic modifications would also aid in nation building and modernization by moving from eastern influences to western ones, because the latter were seen as a requirement for national development.'

In addition, the 'Sun Language Theory' was promoted, a theory which claimed that Turkish was the mother tongue of the world and that, when Turkish borrowed from other languages, it was really taking back what had originally been Turkish anyway. This ideology helped to make the language reform swift and successful.

Language planning issues in Turkey reflect the social and political situation. One of the issues, shared with many other languages, involves the ideology of purity of the language, this time with the encroachment of English words (Doğançay-Aktuna 2004, 14ff). Furthermore, English is increasingly used in primary and secondary schools in a variety of programs, and English-medium universities have been established. This development is in keeping with Turkey's claim to be a modern country which can compete in a globalized economy (Doğançay-Aktuna and Kiziltepe 2005, Kirkgöz 2007).

A further issue in LPP in Turkey involves the status of a minority language, Kurdish. There is a history of persecution of Kurds in Turkey and the Kurdish language is discriminated against. Kurdish-speaking children are not allowed to be educated in their home language, nor is Kurdish offered as a subject in schools (Skutnabb-Kangas and Fernandez 2008). The ideologies which support this policy clearly revolve around the idea of an association of a single language, Turkish, with national identity and the lack of value of minority languages.

Exploration 14.2: Language Rights

Are language rights human rights, and does everyone have the right to use their language everywhere? Consider examples such as punishing children for speaking a language other than the dominant language at school, offering court translation services for minority language speakers, and speaking a heritage language (which is not the majority community language) in the home. In what cases are people entitled to use minority languages, and in what cases do you feel they are not?

LPP in the Soviet Union and the post-Soviet era: from Russification to nationalization

In the former Soviet Union there was a great amount of language planning dating from its very founding. One of the most important policies was **Russification**. Needless to say, in a state as vast as the Soviet Union, composed of speakers of approximately 100 different linguistic varieties, there were several different aspects to such a policy. One of these was the elevation of regional and local dialects into 'languages', a policy of 'divide and rule'. Its goal was to prevent the formation of large language blocks and also to allow the central government to insist that Russian be used as a lingua franca. It also led to the large number of languages that flourished in the Soviet Union.

In addition, the **Cyrillic script** was extended to nearly all the languages of the Soviet Union. This orthography further helped to cut off the Muslim peoples of central Asia from contact with Arabic, Turkish, and Persian influences. In the 1930s these peoples were actually provided with Romanized scripts, but Atatürk's Romanization of Turkish (see above) posed a threat in that it made the Turkish world accessible to the Soviet peoples of central Asia. Consequently, Romanization was abandoned in 1940, Cyrillic alphabets were re-imposed, and deliberate attempts were made to stress as many differences as possible among the various languages of the area (e.g., by developing special Cyrillic characters for local pronunciations) as part of the policy of divide and rule. Russification also required the local languages of the Soviet Union to borrow words from Russian when new words were needed. Population migrations, not necessarily voluntary, also spread Russian (and Russians) throughout the country as a whole, for example, into Kazakhstan where Kazakhs became a minority, and into the Baltic republics, particularly Latvia and Estonia. Russian was also promoted as a universal second language and as a language of instruction in the schools. However, there was resistance in such areas as Georgia, Armenia, Azerbaijan, and the Baltic republics.

Pavlenko (2013) discusses some of the misconceptions about Russification that have been perpetuated in scholarly literature. She notes that historiographic research shows that Russian language management was 'laissez-faire' until the late nineteenth century, and that many other languages (e.g., German in the Baltic provinces) were granted autonomy. The goal was not so much to stamp out other languages but to spread Russian throughout the realm. Many of the reforms imposed after the 1863–1864 Polish rebellion had the goal to 'punish rebellious Poles, to counteract Polish influence on Belarussians, Lithuanians, and Ukrainians, and to prevent germanization of Latvians and Estonians and tatarization of Kazakhs' (Pavlenko 2013, 264). Further, the goal was not to turn everyone into Russians, but to exert social control, including marking minorities – assimilation of non-Christians was not desired, and several ethnic groups were allowed to continue with education in their ethnic languages. She summarizes (Pavlenko 2013, 265):

The greatest impact of russification was seen in the territories that became regular Russian provinces, Bessarabia (later Moldova) and Left-bank Ukraine, the territory on the left side of the river Dnieper, incorporated into Russia through the 1654 Treaty of Pereyaslav. The impact was also felt in the Western provinces, Belorussia and Right-bank Ukraine, incorporated into the empire as a result of the 1772–1795 partitions of Poland. In both provinces, the imperial policies delayed standardization of the titular languages and establishment of native-language schooling. Yet the failure to provide Russian-language schooling meant that compactly settled Belorussian and Ukrainian peasants continued to maintain their native languages. Russian was mainly spoken in Belorussian, Bessarabian, and Ukrainian cities, where 19th century industrialization brought in the influx of Russian workers. This urban/rural divide eventually gave rise to language ideologies that linked Russian to modernity and titular languages to back-wardness. The studies to date show that russification in the Russian empire was largely the result of bottom-up processes, such as migration and integration, rather than top-down policies, and usually stopped with ethnic elites, encouraged by social incentives, such as promotion in the imperial service. Nor did it involve a shift to Russian – rather ethnic elites and the educated middleclass in Armenia, Georgia, Estonia, Latvia, Lithuania, and Poland incorporated Russian as an additional language into their mul-tilingual repertoires.

When the Soviet Union eventually fell into disarray at the end of the 1980s the Russification policies had interesting consequences. The Soviet Union had been organized internally by republics constructed primarily on language and ethnicity. It proceeded to divide that way. The Baltic republics of Estonia, Latvia, and Lithuania separated and became distinct states. Moldavia became Moldova and its Moldavian language was finally acknowledged to be what it was, a variety of Romanian, and was renamed Moldavian–Romanian. Georgia, Armenia, and Kazakhstan separated too and proclaimed Georgian, Armenian, and Kazakh as their national languages, even though in the last case only 40 percent of the population were Kazakhs and 37 percent were Russians. The Turkic-speaking republics, deliberate creations within the Soviet Union, also separated and found their main linguistic problem to be how closely they should identify with Turkey itself.

In a study of Latvia, Estonia, Ukraine, and Kazakhstan, Brubaker (2011) notes that ideas about ethnicity and racial categorization have also played a role in how these processes of nationalization have proceeded. In Kazakhstan, **ethnonational** boundaries are perceived as largely racial and nationalization has served to empower the core nation. He describes the situation in Estonia and Latvia, where there has been intergenerational permeability of ethnonational boundaries, as countries where nationalization has served a more assimilative function over time. In the Ukraine, where ethnonational and linguistic boundaries had blurred, nationaliza-tion has involved the process of reshaping cultural practices and identities.

The role of the Russian language continues to be paramount, however, both within and outside areas where Russian is the dominant language. Pavlenko (2013, 268) notes that Russian continues to be an important lingua franca in the geopoliti-cal region. Moreover, in 2002 the Russian parliament passed a law requiring all official languages within the Russian Federation to use the Cyrillic script because various moves toward Romanization, in Tatarstan in particular, were perceived to pose a threat to Russia and Russians (Sebba 2006).

Official monolingualism in France

France serves as a good example of a country which has a single national language and provides limited support to any other languages. Most inhabitants simply assume that French is rightly the language of France. Consequently, they virtually ignore other languages so that there is little national interest in any move to try to ascertain exactly how many people speak Provençal or Breton, or to do anything for, or against, Basque. Likewise, if an immigrant group to France, for example, Algerians or Vietnamese, wants to try to preserve its language, it must try to do so in its own time and with its own resources, since it is widely assumed that French is the proper language of instruction in schools in France. (The only major exception is that German is taught in Alsace; significantly, use of German there is the result of shifting national borders, not immigration.) This situation is little different from the one that existed in the old colonial days, in which it was assumed that the French language and the curriculum of Metropolitan France were entirely appropriate in the *lycées* of colonies such as Algeria and Indo-China (now Vietnam) attended by the more fortunate local children, who might then aspire to higher education in France. France is a highly centralized country with Paris its dominant center even to the extent that when traveling in France you often see signposts indicating exactly how far you are from Paris (actually from the cathedral of Notre-Dame, its symbolic center). Regional languages such as Breton, Basque, Occitan, Flemish, Catalan, Corsican, and Franco-Provençal persist, get varying amounts of state support, and provide local identities to those who maintain them. Such languages may be tolerated but they cannot be allowed to threaten a state unified around French. With the development of the European Union, and its provisions for minority languages, this toleration has become codified but has not greatly improved the status of such languages (see Heidemann 2012 for a discussion of Basque language activism in France).

Multilingual policy in Belgium

Adjacent, and in contrast, to France we have the bilingual country of Belgium. Today, the French-speaking Walloons and the Flemish (whose language is also called Flemish, linguistically a variety of Dutch) coexist in a somewhat uneasy truce in Belgium. The struggle between the Walloons and Flemish in that country has a long history. In 1815 the politically and socially ascendant Walloons in Belgium found themselves returned at the end of the Napoleonic Wars to Flemish rule. William of Holland proceeded to promote Flemish interests and language and limit the power of the French, and the Walloons. He was also a strong Calvinist, and in 1830 both Flemish and Walloon Catholics rebelled and gained independence for Belgium. However, this religious unity between the Flemish Catholics and the Walloon Catholics soon gave way to cleavage along linguistic lines, language proving in this case to be a stronger force for divisiveness than religion for cohesion. The new state became French-oriented and Flemish was banned from the government, law, army, universities, and secondary schools. French-language domination was everywhere, and it was not until the twentieth century that the Flemish, who then comprised a majority of the population, were able to gain a measure of linguistic and social equality. Today's equality, however, is still colored by memories of past discrimination based on language. The Belgians have tried to settle their differences by separating the languages on a territorial basis and regarding Brussels as a bilingual city, even though it is clearly French-dominant. (German is also recognized as an official language but any problems German speakers have are completely overshadowed by Walloon–Flemish issues.) The overall language arrangements have actually increased the differences between the two major groups. Most Belgians have no desire to join either France or the Netherlands but the linguistic situation in Brussels continues to be problematic. It is the capital city, the seat of the European Union, and the home of the North Atlantic Treaty Organization. It is a cosmopolitan city but it is also a French-dominant city in what is traditionally a Flemish-speaking part of the country. The French regard such expansion as perfectly acceptable, but the Flemish regard the encroachment as a threat to both their Flemish identity and the Flemish language. The result is that Belgium is constantly in some kind of political crisis centering on language issues. One perhaps not surprising beneficiary in all of this is the English language, which has become a neutral, 'default' choice in Brussels (O'Donnell and Toebosch 2008). Blommaert (2011) discusses this in terms of language ideology, noting that a monoglossic ideology (see discussion in chapter 4) dominates even in this officially multilingual country. This ideological disdain for linguistic plurality is selective, however, as for Flemish youth English has replaced French as the language used in some domains.

LPP in Post- and Neo-Colonial Contexts

There was a marked difference in the twentieth century in the way in which the old European and central Asian empires broke up and the way in which imperial bonds were loosened elsewhere in South and Southeast Asia and in Africa. When the Austro-Hungarian, Russian, and Ottoman Empires broke up, the result was the emergence of nation-states based primarily on claims about language with a consequent complete redrawing of boundaries. This redrawing did not suit everyone, since many former minorities proved to be no more tolerant of smaller 'captive' language groups than their previous oppressors once they had achieved political recognition as nation-states. When European colonies in Asia and Africa became independent, however, there was no such redrawing of political boundaries. The previous colonies were often peculiar amalgams of language and ethnic groups, since conquest rather than language or ethnicity had accounted for their origins. The colonies became independent states except in a few cases, such as Pakistan, Burma, and Sri Lanka. These countries attempts at becoming autonomous entities were successful, unlike some other such attempts in Africa (i.e., Baifra's attempt to secede from Nigeria and Katanga's from Zaïre). Many of the resultant states have no common language or ethnic identification, and strong internal linguistic and ethnic rivalries, making national planning and consensus difficult to achieve at the best.

One important consequence is that these newer states of Africa and Asia are often multilingual but, as a result of their histories, have elites who speak a European language such as English or French. This language not only serves many as an internal working language but is also still regarded as the language of social mobility. It is both the language that transcends local loyalties and the one that opens up access to the world outside the state. It is unlikely that in these circumstances such outside languages will disappear; rather, it is likely that they will continue to be used and that positions of leadership will continue to go only to those who have access to them, unless present conditions change.

Kenya

In multilingual contexts, an attempt is sometimes made to find a 'neutral' language, that is, a language which gives no group an advantage. In 1974 President Kenyatta of Kenya decreed that Swahili was to become the second official language of the country and the language of national unity, even though most Kenyans did not speak the language; it was not the language of the major city, Nairobi; it was spoken in a variety of dialects and pidgins; the majority of those who did speak it did not speak it well; and English (the other official language) was better known in the higher echelons of government, among white-collar professionals, and so on (Harries 1976). Swahili was chosen over one of the local languages, for example, the president's own Kikuyu, a language spoken by about 20 percent of the population, because the ethnic composition of the country made any other choice too difficult and dangerous. In that respect, Swahili was a neutral language. It was for much the same reason – that it was a neutral unifying language in a state with over 100 indigenous languages – that Swahili was also chosen in Tanzania as the national language, although in this case it was spoken fairly widely as a trade language along the coast and also in the capital, Dar es Salaam. The consequence of the 1974 decree in Kenya is that Swahili is now used much more than it was, but it has not by any means replaced English in those areas of use in which English was previously used.

Although the use of Swahili in Kenya has become a matter of national pride, this does not mean that its extension into certain spheres of life goes unresisted. However, full social mobility in Kenya requires a citizen to be able to use Swahili, English, and one or more local vernaculars since each has appropriate occasions for use.

Although Swahili is used throughout East Africa, it is a native language on only a small part of the coast; elsewhere it is a lingua franca.

Other policy issues relevant in the Kenyan context include the issue of the role and accessibility of English in educational contexts on the one hand, and the use of mother-tongue language learning on the other. There are strong ideologies about English as a language of globalization and upward mobility, but these ideologies are often in conflict with local language loyalties. As noted by Gacheche (2010), although mother-tongue education is the policy in Kenya, it is rarely the practice (see also Jones and Barhuizen 2011). Mother-tongue education is advocated because it has been shown to be beneficial for rural and urban poor children in long-term academic achievement (Lin and Martin 2005). Banda (2009) argues for abandoning monolingual norms and monoglossic ideologies and implementing multilingual education throughout Africa (see also a discussion of this topic in chapter 13).

India

India, with more than a billion people, is another country which has had to face the difficulty of finding a lingua franca. In this case the solution has been to promote Hindi in the **Devanagari script** as the official language that unites the state, but English may also be used for official purposes and in parliament. Twenty-one other languages, including Sanskrit, are recognized as official languages in the nation's constitution (Mohanty 2006). There is a 'three language formula' for schooling (see Hornberger and Vaish 2009, Meganathan 2011), however, the actual choice of languages taught in schools is by no means a simple matter. The policy recommends that the mother tongue be the first language taught, but if children do not speak the regional language as their mother tongue, they may not be educated in their mother tongue. The second language should be either Hindi or English, which is a simple decision if the first language is Hindi, but otherwise not an easy decision at all, since Hindi is a widely used lingua franca which is advantageous to learn and English is a world language with prestige beyond national borders. The third language (introduced later) in some cases therefore must compensate for what has not already been taught; perhaps the regional language, or Hindi, or English; if those are already being learned, then another Indian or European language. Although the policy explicitly promotes multilingualism, it does little to ensure that children will gain literacy in their mother tongue or learn the language(s) necessary for them to be able to pursue certain goals they may have later in life.

Despite its status as an official language and being required in schools, there are serious obstacles to the spread of Hindi in India. There is a considerable difference between literary Hindi and the various regional and local spoken varieties. Gandhi tried to emphasize building Hindi on popular speech so as to bridge the gap between the literary and colloquial varieties and also to unify the regions. In an attempt to overcome some of the difficulties, the Indian government established various groups to develop scientific terminology, glossaries, dictionaries, and an encyclopedia. One noticeable development has been the way in which those entrusted with such tasks, usually the Hindi elite, have looked to Sanskrit in their work: they have followed a policy of **Sanskritization** in their attempts to purify Hindi of English and also increasingly to differentiate Hindi from Urdu, the variety of the language used in Muslim Pakistan. The effects have been particularly noticeable in literary Hindi, which has possibly grown further away from the evolving colloquial varieties as a result of such activities.

The linguistic situation in India is further complicated today in a way in which it was not complicated at the partition of the subcontinent into India and Pakistan (and then later into a third state, Bangladesh). India came into existence as a unitary state. However, local opposition to such centralization was strong and the country was quickly reorganized by states, the first being the Telugu-speaking Andhra state in 1953. Now India has two important levels of government, the central one in New Delhi that looks after common interests, and the other, the state level, with each state government looking after that state's interests and, more importantly, doing so in the language of that state and not in the Hindi or English of the central government.

Hindi is often viewed in India as giving northern Indians unwarranted advantages over Indians elsewhere, as it is related to some of the other northern Indic languages. This feeling is particularly strong in the south of India, where various Dravidian languages are spoken. To that extent, English continues to offer certain advantages. Its use spread throughout the upper social strata everywhere in India in the former imperial regime; now it can be viewed as quite neutral even though, of course, its use may be opposed strongly at an official level, where it is recognized only as an 'auxiliary' language (Inglehart and Woodward 1967). English is used in the higher courts, as a language of parliamentary debate, as a preferred language in the universities, and as a language of publication in learned journals. Although Hindi is promoted as the unifying language of India, many Indians now see such promotion to be at the expense of some other Indian language they speak, or a set of religious beliefs, or the opportunity to acquire a world language like English. Language planning in India, however, is largely confined to elites: the masses, whose needs are more immediate, are largely unaffected. Like any other kind of planning in India, it seems fraught with difficulties, dangers, and unforeseen consequences.

LPP in the United States and Canada

The United States has no official language; Canada has two. Although neighbors, and both once colonized by the British, these countries have gone down very different paths in terms of language policies and planning.

The United States of America

Language planning has become a serious concern in the United States in recent years, particularly as a result of a recognition that there is a large indigenous

Spanish-speaking population and because of continued immigration. A recent source points out that Hispanics comprised 12 percent of the population in 2000, that their proportion in the total population exceeded that of Black Americans in 2002, and that it is estimated that 25 percent of the total population will be of Hispanic origin by 2040 (Huntington 2004, 224). In recent years, too, more and more languages from Asia, Southeast Asia, and the Middle East are represented in the population.

Not only is a language other than English the mother tongue of a great number of residents of the United States, but some of these speakers lack proficiency in English. A 2011 report by the National Center on Immigration Integration Policy, based on the 2010 US Census, categorizes 9 percent of the US population as **Limited English Proficiency** (LEP) (see link to this report on the companion web page for this chapter). Of these speakers, over 60 percent are Spanish speakers, with speakers of Chinese (6.1 percent), Vietnamese (3.3 percent), and Korean (2.5 percent) being the other language groups that comprise more than 2 percent of the LEP population. There are many reasons to account for Spanish speakers being less likely to speak English proficiently, the two most salient being the sheer number and their constant replenishment in the United States (see Fuller 2013, 85ff, for further discussion of Spanish speakers and English learning). One outcome of this situation is an increased demand for services in Spanish, and an increased resentment of such services by monolingual Anglophones.

The United States does not have an official language, although there have been repeated attempts since 1982 to make English the official language. Those in favor of this move believe that the increasing use of languages other than English in the United States and, in particular, the increasing use of Spanish, poses some kind of internal threat. While bills sometimes pass in the House they fail in the Senate, or vice versa, so proponents of Official English laws have turned to state legislation. As of this writing, 31 states have passed some sort of law declaring English the official language (see the web materials for this chapter to find a link to more information on these laws, and a map showing which states have enacted them).

There are three main areas of concern for policies regarding the use of languages other than English in the United States. The first is in education, as discussed in chapter 13 in some detail. The second is in workplace practices and policies. Despite the Equal Employment Opportunity Commission's 1980 guidelines which state that English Only rules are discriminatory if applied without exception, there are frequent court cases in which employees are fired for speaking a language other than English, or claim discrimination because they were told they could not speak another language in the workplace. Del Valle (2009) discusses the issues involved in these policies and suggests that an underlying issue is that individuals described as 'bilingual' in, for example, Spanish and English, are then viewed as having a free choice of which language to speak. In reality there are not only social reasons for choosing one over the other but also issues of proficiency, since few multilinguals have equal proficiencies in all domains. In many cases, the objection to the use of a language other than English is based on the perception that it is 'inappropriate' in some way, or the view that managers must be able to understand what their employees are saying at all times (even, in some cases, during casual conversations while on a break).

The final area in which language policies are disputed has to do with providing services in languages other than English. These services include such things as access to voting materials or driver's license examination forms in other languages. Schmidt (2007, 2009) discusses how the rhetoric against providing these services is that they 'enable' LEP speakers to continue to speak their native languages, when it is in their best interest to not have such services provided so that they will use English. These issues continue to be a battleground in US politics.

Canada

Canada is a country of over 34 million people and, by its new constitution of 1982, a constitutionally bilingual country. However, bilingualism itself continues to be a controversial issue in Canada, as anyone who reads its newspapers or follows political discussions there will know. Canada is a federal country, with its origins in the conquest of the French (of what is now Quebec) by the English in 1759. This conquest was followed by the gradual expansion of the nation to include other British possessions in North America and to fill the prairies to the north of the United States. Although the country dates its 'birth' to 1867 and it was effectively independent from the United Kingdom after that date, its constitution remained an act of the Parliament of the United Kingdom until 1982. Controversies over language rights played a prominent part in discussions leading up to making the constitution entirely Canadian in 1982.

In 1867 the French in Canada seemed assured of opportunities to spread their language and culture throughout the country. Just as English rights in Quebec were protected in the constitution of that year, so French rights outside Quebec seemed to have a strong measure of protection. But that was not to be, as the French soon found in the new province of Manitoba, where French rights were deliberately abrogated. Increasingly, the French in Canada found themselves confined to Quebec, itself dominated by the English of Montreal, and saw the country develop as a country of two nations (or 'two solitudes') with one of them – theirs – in a very inferior position.

The Canadian government appointed a Royal Commission on Bilingualism and Biculturalism in 1963 to look into the resulting situation. The commission's report led to the Official Languages Act of 1969 (reaffirmed in a new form in 1988), which guaranteed the French in Canada certain rights to language everywhere in the country in order to preserve the nation as a bilingual one. The act also appointed an ombudsman, a Commissioner of Official Languages, to report annually to Parliament on progress in implementing new policies. Later, the Constitution Act of 1982 incorporated these language rights guaranteed by statute in 1969 into the constitution. However, if Canada is officially a 'bilingual' country, bilingualism in the two official languages is found mainly in the population of French origin and truly bilingual communities are few, for example, Montreal, Sherbrooke, and the Ottawa-Hull area.

At the same time as the Government of Canada was guaranteeing French rights throughout Canada, the Government of Quebec took measures to minimize the use of English within the province. While the federal government was trying to extend bilingualism in the rest of Canada, the Government of Quebec was trying to restore French **unilingualism** within Quebec. They did this because they found that bilingualism led to unilingualism in English. Outside Quebec, the French in Canada were losing French in favor of English as they went over the generations from being unilingual in French, to being bilingual in French and English, and finally to being unilingual in English. There was mounting evidence that this was also happening within Quebec. However, such moves to restrict the use of English in Quebec, for example, in public education, have come under attack as a violation of rights provided in the new constitution, and in 1984 the Supreme Court of Canada voided those parts of Quebec's Bill 101 of 1977 that restricted certain rights of Anglophones in that province. Quebec does have a variety of language laws to protect French in the province and the authorities are vigilant in enforcing them. Some of those who dislike these laws have moved to other provinces. Others, particularly immigrants, often prefer to learn English rather than French, but between 1971 and 2001 governmental measures have increased the proportion of those who learn French from 29 percent to 46 percent. In spite of such measures, by 2008 less than 54 percent of the population of Montreal, by far the largest city in Quebec, used French as the language of the home, and that fraction was declining. In addition, less than 50 percent had French as their mother tongue.

The basic English–French polarization still exists. The French are still a minority in Canada. Their proportion in the overall population continues to decline, no matter what statistic is used (ethnic origin, mother-tongue use, or language of the home). It is not really surprising, therefore, that in recent years the French within Quebec have toyed with 'separatist' notions, believing that, if they cannot guarantee their future within Canada as a whole, they should at least guarantee it within their home province. The separatist desire increased dramatically in 1990 with the failure that year to reach a countrywide agreement – the so-called Meech Lake Accord – on amending the 1982 constitution. A further attempt at some kind of constitutional settlement failed in 1992 when the Charlottetown Agreement was defeated in a national referendum. However, in 1995 a Quebec referendum on separation from Canada also failed, narrowly though, to gain support for such a move.

The language situation is further complicated by the fact that Canada also has many speakers of First Nation languages (the term used for the languages spoken in these regions before English and French colonization) and it is also a country of immigrants who have flocked mainly to the larger cities, Toronto, Vancouver, and Montreal (see Conrick and Donovan 2010 for a discussion of immigrants and language rights; Ricento and Cervatiuc 2010 and Duff and Li 2009 for discussions of indigenous and immigrant languages rights).

Multilingual Countries and LPP

Some further examples of kinds of planning decisions that have been made in a number of countries in different parts of the world will show how difficult at times planning can be. All of these countries are multilingual and the languages have many different roles in society.

Papua New Guinea

Papua New Guinea has three official languages: Hiri Motu, Tok Pisin, and English. In addition, Ethnologue has this to say about language diversity in this country:

> The number of individual languages listed for Papua New Guinea is 848. Of these, 836 are living and 12 are extinct. Of the living languages, 61 are institutional, 295 are developing, 340 are vigorous, 104 are in trouble, and 36 are dying. (http://www .ethnologue.com/country/PG)

Of the three official languages, Tok Pisin is becoming more and more the first language of many young people, particularly city dwellers. As we saw in chapter 5, Tok Pisin is a creole language which developed out of an English-based pidgin language. Although all children learn English in school and most parents feel that knowledge of English brings great advantages to their children, very little use is made of English outside certain formal contexts, for example, in schools and in certain occupations such as the legal profession. Tok Pisin is now used almost exclusively for purposes of debate in the House Assembly, which is the parliament of Papua New Guinea. It is also frequently used in broadcasting, and increasingly in the press and in education, particularly at the lower levels.

Hiri Motu, another official language of Papua New Guinea, is also pidgin-based. It is identified with Papua and Papuan languages, which are quite different from those in New Guinea. Many people there take great pride in using Hiri Motu, the descendant of Police Mutu, a native-based, pidgin language of the area, rather than Tok Pisin to show local loyalties. The result has been a dramatic increase in the use of Hiri Motu in Papua New Guinea, particularly among separatist-minded Papuans.

In addition to these three official languages, there has also been language planning to use local languages in primary education; according to Klaus (2003), by the end of 2000, 380 indigenous languages were being used in the first years of education across the country. Siegel (1997) notes that the success of this reform is due to community involvement and not to formal governmental policy and implementation.

Singapore

Another example of a multilingual country is Singapore, an independent republic of nearly 5 million people. It is also a small island, situated at the tip of the Malayan peninsula with another large Malay-speaking nation, Indonesia, to its south. The 2010 census showed its population to be approximately 74 percent Chinese, 13 percent Malays, 9 percent Indians, and just over 3 percent others, for example, Eurasians, Europeans, and Arabs. The languages named in the results from the census data include English, Malay, Mandarin, and Tamil; there are also categories for 'Other Chinese dialects' spoken by those categorized as Chinese, and 'Others' for Indians and Malays, showing that the public focus is clearly on these four languages, which all have official status. Malay, Chinese, and Tamil are related to particular segments of the population, while English was clearly chosen because of its international status, particularly important because of Singapore's position as a trading nation. Officially, it is a language of convenience only, a neutral language dissociated from issues of ethnicity (Lee 2002). In terms of policy, English is set apart from the Asian languages with the Mother Tongue Policy, where all children are required to have some proficiency in their 'mother tongue.' Wee (2002) and Wee and Bokhorst-Heng (2005) discuss how the concept of 'mother tongue' is defined in Singapore as the language of the father's ethnic group, and is thus in no way necessarily equivalent to the home language or the first or native language of an individual. Regardless of which language is spoken in the home, children are given an assignment to an ethnic group which is associated with a particular language. In some cases, another Chinese dialect or Indian language, English, or other language is the child's first language.

Despite this Mother Tongue Policy, the most recent census data show an increase in English as 'the language most frequently spoken at home' (see the companion web materials for a link to this document). Among those in the Chinese ethnic group, English designation as the home language rose from 23.9 percent to 32.6 percent from 2000 to 2010; in the Malay group, from 7.9 percent to 17 percent; and among the Indian group, from 35.6 percent to 41.6 percent. Unsurprisingly, across ethnic groups, the younger a person is the more likely they are to speak English. People with post-secondary education are also more likely to speak English than those who have not gained this level of education.

Of the four official languages, Malay is also the national language because of Singapore's position in the Malay world, not because more people in Singapore speak or understand Malay better than any other language. English has become the working language of Singapore: it is the language of the government bureaucracy, the authoritative language of all legislation and court judgments, and the language of occupational mobility and social and economic advancement (see discussion of the 'foreign talent policy' in Wee and Bokhorst-Heng 2005).

The English model chosen is the British one and 'Singlish,' the Singapore variety, finds official disapproval (although, as discussed in chapter 13, it is seen as an important marker of Singaporean identity). A 'Speak Good English' campaign was launched in 2000 (see link to the web page in the online materials for this chapter), after then prime minister Goh Chok Tong said, in his 1999 Rally Day speech, 'We cannot be a first-world economy or go global with Singlish.' Commercials, signs, and other public media were all used to send the message 'Speak Well, Be Understood' (Rubdy 2001, 348). Rubdy describes this campaign as 'creative destruction,' motivated by economic factors. This attempt to root out Singlish by creating a consensus that it is inferior to 'Standard' English ignores the value in terms of identity of Singlish and pits its covert prestige against what the government presents as the best interests of the nation (Rubdy 2001, 353).

This is not the first such public campaign about language planning; beginning in 1979 there was a Speak Mandarin campaign to encourage the Chinese Singaporeans to speak their official mother tongue, and thus unite speakers of different varieties of Chinese (Stroud and Wee 2007, Wee and Bokhorst-Heng 2005). Stroud and Wee (2007) discuss how all such language policies, aimed at reproducing the dichotomy between identity and instrumentalism in language use, need rethinking in the context of multilingual, multiethnic Singapore.

Endangered Languages and the Spread of English

A recurring theme in the discussion of language planning and policies the world over is the role of English in these societies – how it should be taught, who has access to it, whether borrowing from English should be allowed to creep into the language, and how English encroachment on the domains of other languages can be discouraged. In this section, we will focus on this last issue and focus on endangered languages and the spread of English around the world.

Endangered languages

It seems fitting to close a chapter on language planning in various places in the world by mentioning some facts about languages in general. We live in a world of more than 7 billion people and perhaps 6,000 languages (although Gordon (2005) puts the figure at precisely 6,912). Many of these are **endangered** or even dying (see Dorian 1981, 1989, 1998, Fase et al. 1992, Grenoble and Whaley 1998, Mühlhäusler 1996, and Harrison 2007). Harrison's book begins with a challenging opening sentence: 'The last speakers of half of the world's languages are alive today. As they grow old and die, their voices will fall silent. Their children and grandchildren … will either choose not to learn or will be deprived of the opportunity to learn the ancestral language' (2007, 3).

Nettle and Romaine (2000) voice a very similar view, and say that as many as 60 percent of all languages are already endangered, and claim that some of the endangered languages have much to tell us about the natural world, for example, invaluable information about ecological matters, and even perhaps about the nature of reality (see discussion of the Whorfian hypothesis in chapter 1): 'each language … [is] a way of coming to grips with the external world and developing a symbolism to represent it so that it can be talked and thought about' (2000, 69). Harrison (2007, 7) expresses a similar view: 'Language disappearance is an erosion or extinction of ideas, of ways of knowing, and ways of talking about the world and human experience.' Crystal (2000) also deplores the loss of languages but mainly because such loss is loss of knowledge about the possible characteristics of human languages and not because of what such languages might tell us about any other aspect of the world around us.

Estimates of language loss go as high as 95 percent within the new century if nothing is done to stop the decline. It is for just such a reason that the Linguistic Society of America has gone on record as deploring language loss and established a Committee on Endangered Languages and their Preservation to help arrest it. However, we should note that not all linguists agree that they should be out in the field trying to describe – and possibly preserve – threatened languages. Mühlhäusler (1996) goes so far as to argue that linguists are sometimes part of the problem rather than part of the solution. Others agree with him. For example, Newman (2003) argues that since most linguistic investigations focus on 'theoretical' issues, they do little to preserve threatened languages. He says that, above all, such languages need to be thoroughly documented, and this task is even more important than efforts spent in trying to preserve them: 'preservation projects drain resources from the important linguistic task of primary documentation, both in terms of personnel and in terms of research funds' (2003, 6). However, it should be noted that many sociolinguists, and especially linguistic anthropologists, are very much concerned with **language documentation** as well as providing assistance to communities who wish to revitalize their heritage languages (see Gippert et al. 2006 for discussion of such endeavors).

English world-wide

In marked contrast to such language decline, some languages thrive, for example, the Mandarin variety of Chinese, English, Hindi-Urdu, and Spanish (particularly with its spectacular growth in the Americas). One of these, English, has also spread everywhere in the world as a lingua franca (see Crystal 2003, 2004). The United Nations has projected an interesting future for various world languages (see Graddol 2004). Whereas in 1950 about 9 percent of the world's population spoke English natively, with Spanish and then Hindi-Urdu next with about 5 percent each and with Arabic having 2 percent, by 2000 the proportions were just over 6 percent for English, and over 5 percent for Spanish and Hindi-Urdu, with Hindi-Urdu overtaking Spanish. By 2050 the projection is that Hindi-Urdu will overtake English as its proportion reaches 6 percent and that English, Spanish, and Arabic will all hover around 5 percent. However, at all these dates Chinese was, is, and will be used as a native language by an even higher percentage of the world's population. Languages like French (even when promoted by *La Francophonie*), Russian, German, and Japanese, on the other hand, do not thrive in the same way: they win few converts and, as the world's population grows, they decrease proportionally.

As Crystal has pointed out, English spread initially through conquest and then by being in the right place at the right time for use in international relations, the worldwide media, international travel, education, and now communications. He estimates that one-quarter of the world's population have some kind of fluency in the language. Its major appeal is as a lingua franca, a common second language with a certain amount of internal diversity (see Meierkord 2004). In December 2004, a British Council report estimated that 2 billion more people would begin learning English within a decade and by 2050 there would be over 3 billion speakers of English in the world. The main motivation to learn English would continue to be an economic one and an important consequence would be a great increase in bilingualism/multilingualism in English and one or more other languages. (According to this report, Chinese, Arabic, and Spanish would also become increasingly important languages.)

Scientific work is one area in which the English language has become dominant worldwide: 'scientific scholarship is increasingly an English-only domain in international communication (journals, reference works, textbooks, conferences, networking)' (Phillipson 2006, 350). By the end of the twentieth century more than 90 percent of scientific findings were published in English (and even in the humanities the proportion was well over 80 percent). English has also become 'indispensable in prestigious domains such as business, trade, and technology, but in addition has a strong informal base in the global entertainment market and is associated with many lifestyle issues – from "gender mainstreaming," the "sexual revolution," "gay rights," and "political correctness," all the way to "jogging," "[Nordic] walking," "all-inclusive package tours," and "wellness resorts" (these words being used as borrowings from English in many languages)' (Mair 2006, 10).

Not everyone accepts English dominance in even the academic realm of science, where it is well established. In a letter to the prestigious journal *Science* in May 2004, Hayes-Rivas protests as follows: 'Language often leads thought. What will we be losing when all scientists write and think in a language that hems the descriptions of facts and theories into a single subject-verb-object (SVO) order? ... (It has) potential for severely skewing how scientists look at the world, time, space, and causality, perhaps unconsciously closing off areas of investigation. ... At the very least, it is dangerous to assume, without further study, that the effects of such a rigid grammar will be trivial or benign' (2004, 1243). Once again the Whorfian hypothesis is brought to our attention and once again we must ask how it could change anything in what we understand about evolution, relativity, quantum physics, mathematics, genetics, and so on.

A century ago Mencken wrote about the English language in the USA and titled his book *The American Language* (1919); now there are other such languages: Singaporean, Australian, Canadian, Nigerian, South African, and so on. They meet with both approval and disapproval. For example, Lilles (2000, 9) describes Canadian English as a 'fiction (without) any value linguistically, pragmatically, or politically.' The real issue is one of power; should the center (either British or American English) always set the 'standards,' or should these be set locally? As for the situation in India, Gupta (2001, 159) declares: 'We cannot escape the fact that it is impractical, unrealistic, and even futile to talk of British or American norms or models in such a vast and diverse country where millions of people learn, use and interact in English. What we therefore need to do is to accept, recognise and describe adequately all the features of (Standard Indian English) so that a pan-Indian "norm" can be followed and to which no "stigma" is attached.' English can no longer be the possession of small elites; local usages and norms have become important. If a 'good mastery of East African English may be valuable and a source of prestige in Nairobi, but … may be the object of stigmatising reactions in London or New York' (Blommaert 2005, 211), it is those who live in London or New York who should learn to adjust to this new reality.

We must recognize that there are New Englishes, and that English is a rather complex set of varieties of a living language rather than just a 'fixed and dead' entity like Latin. It also lacks a dominant center; it is **pluricentric** and people use it to express both national and local identities (Schneider 2003). There are bodies of literature about many different varieties of English which describe their structures and uses, the ideologies surrounding these structures and uses, and the identities which are constructed through them. For example, Deterding et al. (2008) and Sewell and Chan (2011) discuss the phonology of Hong Kong English, Gisborne (2009) describe its morphosyntax, and Cummings and Wolf (2011) provide a dictionary of Hong Kong English. Evans (2009, 2011) examines the English language speech community in Hong Kong and how this language is used in professional circles. There are similar bodies of research for Indian English, Nigerian English, and Singapore English, to name just a select few.

Exploration 14.3: Englishes

Are some varieties of English better suited than others for international trade, contact across cultures, public media such as signs and newspapers, official documents, or casual conversations? What role do such factors as the ingroup or outgroup status of the intended audience, the repertoires of those involved, and the formality of the interaction or text play in what you deem 'appropriate'? What role do the particular linguistic features of the varieties play?

English has certain resemblances to Latin in its heyday. However, Latin fragmented. Its center did not hold and its various speakers, cut off from one another, went their separate ways. The world in which English functions is very different: it is one in which communications, travel, and interpersonal contacts are relatively easy. Mutual intelligibility of the varieties may be threatened on occasion but it is unlikely to cease.

The spread of English in the world has not gone without critics who regard the language as a clear expression of political, cultural, and economic imperialism and assail all efforts to promote the further use of English in the world, for example, by government-sponsored teaching programs (see Phillipson 1992, 2003, Mühlhäusler 1996, and Pennycook 1998). Writing in the tradition of critical theory (or critical discourse analysis; see chapter 11), such critics cannot conceive of English as a value-free language. As Pennycook says, there is nothing 'neutral' about English use in Hong Kong: 'this image of English use as an open and borrowing language, reflecting an open and borrowing people, is a cultural construct of colonialism that is in direct conflict with the colonial evidence' (1998, 143). Others apply this kind of judgment everywhere English has spread. Mühlhäusler (1996), for example, regards languages like English – others are Bahasa Indonesia and Mandarin Chinese – as 'killer languages' because as national languages of modernization, education, and development they stifle and eventually kill local languages. Dorian (1998, 9) states the case unequivocally: 'Europeans who come from polities with a history of standardizing and promoting just one high-prestige form carried their "ideology of contempt" for subordinate languages with them when they conquered far-flung territories to the serious detriment of indigenous languages.'

House (2003) draws a different conclusion concerning the spread of English in the European Union (see discussion in chapter 13). There, English is spreading because it is an effective lingua franca and she says that this spread may actually strengthen local languages as people seek to maintain local identities. This English is the 'default' language, and it will become increasingly so as the European Union expands. In 2000 the European Commission reported that a survey of European populations showed that close to 80 percent of the populations of the Netherlands, Sweden, and Denmark claimed to be able to speak English. The corresponding percentages for Finland, Luxembourg, and Austria were 50 percent or better, for Belgium, Germany, and Greece about 40 percent, and for France, Italy, Portugal, and Spain they ranged down from 30 to 15 percent. Furthermore, about 87 percent of secondary students were learning English and the proportion for primary students was about 40 percent. Wright (2004, 14) broadens his conclusion beyond the European Union: 'it is not inconceivable that as intergroup communication happens increasingly in English, speakers from the smaller language groups will move from being bilingual in their own language and the national language to being bilingual in their own language and English. This latter bilingualism might be more stable than the former.'

There is a paradox here: linguists are sometimes told that they save languages best by not acting at all; certainly they should do nothing to promote English in the world, or to standardize a language, or possibly to help in any kind of language planning anywhere. Yet, there is no assurance that they will save a single language by not acting. An alternative possibility is that intervention actually slows down decline and loss. However, there is really no hard evidence for either position. Each is essentially ideologically driven: if you believe this you do one thing and if you believe that you do another. We do well to remember that because we are involved in *socio*-linguistic matters, ideology is likely to be at least as potent a factor as scientific findings in determining any approach we may adopt.

Chapter Summary

This final chapter introduces the terms and concepts in language policy and planning and provides an overview of the development of this field of study. We also present discussions of language policies and planning in specific contexts, looking at how language policy can be part of nation-building and the construction of a national identity. A theme through much of this research has to do with policies and planning with regard to multilingualism; it is sometimes fostered, sometimes regulated, and sometimes discouraged, depending on the history and ideological stances in the country.

Exercises

1. Write a report about language policy in the country of your choice, using resources which state statistics and policies, websites or other media which promote particular agendas, and at least two research articles about LPP in this nation. In addition to describing official policies and planning strategies, discuss the underlying ideologies about language implicit in these political actions.

2. Find at least two articles from the popular press about the encroachment of English into the domains or lexicon of another language (for example, how English has edged out German in the European Union, or how German has adopted many English forms in everyday language, business and computer domains, music, etc.). Provide a summary and critique of the arguments presented, including (a) how English is represented (as a necessary evil? A welcome guest? A natural disaster?); (b) how the value of English is discussed; (c) how the value of the non-English language is depicted; (d) what ideas about language purity or heteroglossia are put forth; (e) solutions to the 'problem' of English encroachment.

Further Reading

Brown, N. Anthony (2007). Status Language Planning in Belarus: An Examination of Written Discourse in Public Spaces. *Language Policy* 6: 281–301.

This article looks at signs in Belaruss and how they reflect language ideologies about the roles of Russian and Belaruss. While top-down policy advocates the use of both languages, ideologies can be constructed through both language choice and the positioning of each language in these public displays.

David Cassels Johnson and Thomas Ricento (2013). Conceptual and Theoretical Perspectives in Language Planning and Policy: Situating the Ethnography of Language Policy. *International Journal of the Sociology of Language* 219: 7–21.

This article reviews Ricento's 2000 discussion of the history of language, presenting more recent developments in the field, including information from ethnographies of language policy.

Jenkins, Jennifer (2009). *World Englishes: A Resource Book for Students. 2nd edn*. London: Routledge.

This volume covers the main issues and concepts in the study of varieties of English around the world, with a focus on the development of different varieties. It addresses pidgin and creole languages, nativized English varieties, and English as a lingua franca, both historically and with an eye to the future.

McCarty, Teresa L., Mary Eunice Romero-Little, and Ofelia Zepeda (2006). Native American Youth Discourses on Language Shift and Retention: Ideological Cross-currents and Their Implications for Language Planning. *International Journal of Bilingual Education and Bilingualism* 9(5): 659–77.

This study looks at how the ideologies of community members are integral to language planning and policy, with a focus on youths as integral to the language maintenance efforts.

Ricento, Thomas (ed.) (2006). *An Introduction to Language Policy: Theory and Method*. Chichester: John Wiley & Sons, Ltd.

This book outlines the theories and methodologies, including critiques of different approaches, currently used in LPP research. Included are discussions of ethnographic methods, matched-guise research, social network analyses, language performance testing, and a discourse historical approach.

Shohamy, Elana (2012). *Language Policy: Hidden Agendas and New Approaches*. London: Routledge.

This volume provides an overview of the ideologies and processes in language policies with special foci on education, tests, and the public sphere.

For further resources for this chapter visit the companion website at

 www.wiley.com/go/wardhaugh/sociolinguistics

References

Banda, Felix (2009). Critical Perspectives on Language Planning and Policy in Africa: Accounting for the Notion of Multilingualism. *Stellenbosch Papers in Linguistics* 38: 1–11.

Blommaert, Jan (2005). *Discourse*. Cambridge: Cambridge University Press.

Blommaert, Jan (2011). The Long Language-Ideological Debate in Belgium. *Journal of Multicultural Discourses* 6(3): 241–56.

Brubaker, Rogers (2011). Nationalizing States Revisited: Projects and Processes of Nationalization in Post-Soviet States. *Ethnic and Racial Studies* 34(11): 1785–814.

Conrick, Maeve and Paula Donovan (2010). Immigration and Language Policy and Planning in Québec and Canada: Language Learning and Integration. *Journal of Multilingual and Multicultural Development* 31(4): 331–45.

Crystal, D. (2000). *Language Death*. Cambridge: Cambridge University Press.

Crystal, D. (2003). *English as a Global Language*. 2nd edn. Cambridge: Cambridge University Press.

Crystal, D. (2004). *The Language Revolution*. Cambridge: Polity Press.

Cummings, Patrick Jean and Hans-Georg Wolf (2011). *Hong Kong English*. Hong Kong: Hong Kong University Press.

Del Valle, Sandra (2009). The Bilingual's Hoarse Voice: Losing Rights in Two Languages. In R. Salaberry (ed.), *Language Allegiances and Bilingualism in the US*. Clevedon: Multilingual Matters, 80–109.

Deterding, David, Jennie Wong, and Andy Kirkpatrick (2008). The Pronunciation of Hong Kong English. *English World-Wide* 29(2): 148–75.

Doğançay-Aktuna, S. (2004). Language Planning in Turkey: Yesterday and Today. *International Journal of the Sociology of Language* 165: 5–32.

Doğançay-Aktuna, S. and Z. Kiziltepe (2005). English in Turkey. *World Englishes* 24(2): 253–65.

Dorian, N. C. (1981). *Language Death*. Philadelphia: University of Pennsylvania Press.

Dorian, N. C. (ed.) (1989). *Investigating Obsolescence: Studies in Language Contraction and Death*. Cambridge: Cambridge University Press.

Dorian, N. C. (1998). Western Language Ideologies and Small-language Prospects. In L. A. Grenoble and L. J. Whaley (eds.), *Endangered Languages: Language Loss and Community Response*. Cambridge: Cambridge University Press.

Duff, Patricia A. and Duanduan Li (2009). Indigenous, Minority, and Heritage Language Education in Canada: Policies, Contexts, and Issues. *Canadian Modern Language Review/La Revue canadienne des langues vivantes* 66(1): 1–8.

Evans, Stephen (2009). The Evolution of the English-Language Speech Community in Hong Kong. *English World-Wide* 30(3): 278–301.

Evans, Stephen (2011). Hong Kong English and the Professional World. *World Englishes* 30(3): 293–316.

Fase, W., K. Jaspaert, and S. Kroon (eds.) (1992). *Maintenance and Loss of Minority Languages*. Amsterdam: John Benjamins.

Fuller, Janet M. (2013). *Spanish Speakers in the USA*. Clevedon: Multilingual Matters.

Gacheche, K. (2010). Challenges in Implementing a Mother Tongue-Based Language-in-Education Policy: Policy and Practice in Kenya. *POLIS Journal* 4: 1–45.

García, O. (2009). Education, Multilingualism and Translanguaging in the 21st Century. In T. Skutnabb-Kangas, R. Phillipson, A. K. Mohanty, and M. Panda (eds.), *Social Justice through Multilingual Education*. Bristol, UK: Multilingual Matters, 140–58.

Gippert, Jost, Nikolaus P. Himmelmann, and Ulrike Mosel (eds.) (2006). *Essentials of Language Documentation*, vol. 178. Berlin: Walter de Gruyter.

Gisborne, Nikolas (2009). Aspects of the Morphosyntactic Typology of Hong Kong English. *English World-Wide* 30(2): 149–69.

Gordon, R. G. (ed.) (2005). *Ethnologue: Languages of the World*. Dallas: SIL Publications.

Graddol, D. (2004). The Future of Language. *Science* 303: 1329–31.

Grenoble, L. A. and L. J. Whaley (eds.) (1998). *Endangered Languages: Language Loss and Community Response*. Cambridge: Cambridge University Press.

Gupta, R. S. (2001). English in Post-colonial India: An Appraisal. In B. Moore (ed.), *Who's Centric Now? The Present State of Post-colonial Englishes*. Oxford: Oxford University Press.

Harries, L. (1976). The Nationalization of Swahili in Kenya. *Language in Society* 5(2), 153–64.

Harrison, K. D. (2007). *When Languages Die*. Oxford: Oxford University Press.

Haugen, E. (1961). Language planning in modern Norway. *Scandinavian Studies*, 68–81.

Hayes-Rivas, J. J. (2004). One World Scientific Language? *Science* 304: 1243.

Heidemann, Kai A. (2012). The View from Below: Exploring the Interface of Europeanization and Basque Language Activism in France. *Mobilization: An International Quarterly* 17(2):195–220.

Hornberger, Nancy (2006). Frameworks and Models in Language Policy and Planning. *An Introduction to Language Policy: Theory and Method* 24–41.

Hornberger, N. H. and Coronel-Molina, S. M. (2004). Quechua Language Shift, Maintenance, and Revitalization in the Andes: The Case for Language Planning. *International Journal of the Sociology of Language* 167: 9–68.

Hornberger, N. H. and King, K. A. (1996). Language Revitalisation in the Andes: Can the Schools Reverse Language Shift? *Journal of Multilingual and Multicultural Development* 17(6): 427–41.

Hornberger, N. and Vaish, V. (2009). Multilingual Language Policy and School Linguistic Practice: Globalization and English-Language Teaching in India, Singapore and South Africa. *Compare* 39(3): 305–20.

House, J. (2003). English as a Lingua Franca: A Threat to Multilingualism? *Journal of Sociolinguistics* 7(4): 556–78.

Huntington, S. P. (2004). *Who Are We? The Challenges to America's National Identity*. New York: Simon and Schuster.

Inglehart, R. F. and M. Woodward (1967). Language Conflicts and Political Community. *Comparative Studies in Society and History* 10: 27–45. In P. P. Giglioli (ed.) (1972), *Language and Social Context: Selected Readings*. Harmondsworth, England: Penguin Books.

Jones, Jennifer M. and Gary Barkhuizen (2011). 'It Is Two-Way Traffic': Teachers' Tensions in the Implementation of the Kenyan Language-in-Education Policy. *International Journal of Bilingual Education and Bilingualism* 14(5): 513–30.

King, K. A. (1999). Language Revitalisation Processes and Prospects: Quichua in the Ecuadorian Andes. *Language and Education* 13(1): 17–37.

King, K. A. (2000). Language Ideologies and Heritage Language Education. *International Journal of Bilingual Education and Bilingualism* 3(3): 167–84.

Kirkgöz, Yasemin (2007). Language Planning and Implementation in Turkish Primary Schools. *Current Issues in Language Planning* 8(2): 174–91.

Klaus, David (2003). The Use of Indigenous Languages in Early Basic Education in Papua New Guinea: A Model for Elsewhere? *Language and Education* 17(2): 105–11.

Kloss, H. (1968). Notes Concerning a Language–Nation Typology. In J. A. Fishman, C. A. Ferguson, and J. Das Gupta (eds.), *Language Problems of Developing Nations*. New York: John Wiley & Sons, Inc.

Lee, L. (2002). When English is Not a Mother Tongue: Linguistic Ownership and the Eurasian Community in Singapore. *Journal of Multilingual and Multicultural Development* 23(4): 282–95.

Lilles, J. (2000). The Myth of Canadian English. *English Today* 16(2): 3–9.

Lin, A. M. Y. and Martin, P. W. (2005). From a Critical Deconstruction Paradigm to a Critical Construction Paradigm: An Introduction to Decolonisation, Globalisation and Language in Education Policy and Practice. In A. M. Y. Lin and P. W. Martin (eds.), *Decolonisation, Globalisation: Language-in-Education Policy and Practice.* Clevedon: Multilingual Matters, 1–19.

Lippi-Green, Rosina (2012). *English with an Accent: Language, Ideology, and Discrimination in the United States.* 2nd edn. New York: Routledge.

Mair, C. (2006). *Twentieth-Century English.* Cambridge: Cambridge University Press.

Meganathan, Ramanujam (2011). Language Policy in Education and the Role of English in India: From Library Language to Language of Empowerment. In Hywel Coleman (ed.), *Dreams and Realities: Developing Countries and the English Language.* The British Council, 57–85.

Meierkord, C. (2004). Syntactic Variation in Interactions across International Englishes. *English World-Wide* 25(1): 109–32.

Mohanty, A. K. (2006). Multilingualism of the Unequals and Predicaments of Education in India: Mother Tongue or Other Tongue? In O. García, T. Skutnabb-Kangas, and M. E. Torres-Guzmán (eds.), *Imagining Multilingual Schools.* Clevedon: Multilingual Matters, 262–79.

Mühlhäusler, P. (1996). *Linguistic Ecology: Language Change and Linguistic Imperialism in the Pacific Region.* London: Routledge.

Nettle, D. and S. Romaine (2000). *Vanishing Voices: The Extinction of the World's Languages.* Oxford: Oxford University Press.

Newman, P. (2003). The Endangered Language Issue as a Hopeless Cause. In M. Janse and S. Tol (eds.), *Language Death and Language Maintenance.* Amsterdam: John Benjamins.

O'Donnell, P. and A. Toebosch (2008). Multilingualism in Brussels: 'I'd Rather Speak English!' *Journal of Multilingual and Multicultural Development* 29(2): 154–69.

Pavlenko, A. (2013). Multilingualism in Post-Soviet Successor States. *Language and Linguistics Compass* 7(4): 262–71.

Pennycook, A. (1998). *English and the Discourses of Colonialism.* London: Routledge.

Phillipson, R. (1992). *Linguistic Imperialism.* Oxford: Oxford University Press.

Phillipson, R. (2003). *English-Only Europe? Challenging Language Policy.* London: Routledge.

Phillipson, R. (2006). Language Policy and Linguistic Imperialism. In T. Ricento (ed.), *An Introduction to Language Policy.* Oxford: Blackwell.

Ricento, Thomas (2000). Historical and Theoretical Perspectives in Language Policy and Planning. *Journal of Sociolinguistics* 4(2): 196–213.

Ricento, Thomas (ed.) (2006). *An Introduction to Language Policy: Theory and Method.* Chichester: John Wiley & Sons, Ltd.

Ricento, Thomas and Andreea Cervatiuc (2010). Language Minority Rights and Educational Policy in Canada. In Petrovic, J. E. (ed.), *International Perspectives on Bilingual Education: Policy, Practice, and Controversy.* Charlotte, NC: IAP, 21–42.

Rubdy, Rani (2001). Creative Destruction: Singapore's Speak Good English Movement. *World Englishes* 20(3): 341–55.

Schmidt, R. (2007). Defending English in an English-Dominant World: The Ideology of the 'Official English' Movement in the United States. In A. Duchêne and M. Heller (eds.)

Discourses of Endangerment: Ideology and Interest in the Defence of Languages. New York: Continuum, 197–215.

Schmidt, R. (2009). English Hegemony and the Politics of Ethno-linguistic Justice in the US. In R. Salaberry (ed.), *Language Allegiances and Bilingualism in the US.* Toronto: Multilingual Matters, 132–50.

Schneider, E. W. (2003). The Dynamics of New Englishes: From Identity Construction to Dialect Birth. *Language* 79(2): 233–81.

Sebba, M. (2006). Ideology and Alphabets in the Former USSR. *Language Problems and Language Planning* 30(2): 99–125.

Sewell, Andrew and Jason Chan (2010). Patterns of Variation in the Consonantal Phonology of Hong Kong English. *English World-Wide* 31(2): 138–61.

Siegel, Jeff (1997). Formal vs. Non-formal Vernacular Education: The Education Reform in Papua New Guinea. *Journal of Multilingual and Multicultural Development* 18(3): 206–22.

Spolsky, B. (2004). *Language Policy.* Cambridge: Cambridge University Press.

Stroud, Christopher and Lionel Wee (2007). Consuming Identities: Language Planning and Policy in Singaporean Late Modernity. *Language Policy* 6(2): 253–79.

Tove Skutnabb-Kangas and Desmond Fernandes (2008). Kurds in Turkey and in (Iraqi) Kurdistan: A Comparison of Kurdish Educational Language Policy in Two Situations of Occupation. *Genocide Studies and Prevention* 3(1): 43–73.

Wee, Lionel (2002). When English is Not a Mother Tongue: Linguistic Ownership and the Eurasian Community in Singapore. *Journal of Multilingual and Multicultural Development* 23(4): 282–95.

Wee, Lionel and Wendy D. Bokhorst-Heng (2005). Language Policy and Nationalist Ideology: Statal Narratives in Singapore. *Multilingua* 24(3): 159–83.

Wright, S. (2004). *Language Policy and Language Planning: From Nationalism to Globalisation.* New York: Palgrave Macmillan.

Glossary

accent: a way of speaking, often identified with a region or social group; refers to pronunciation only. Compare with *dialect* and *variety*

accommodation: modifying one's speech to be more similar to or different from the speech of the addressee or hearer; see *convergence* and *divergence*

accommodation program: a type of program in primary and secondary education which uses in the classroom a minority variety spoken by children at home; it is not the language of instruction but pupils are allowed to do certain written or oral tasks in their home variety; compare with *instrumental program*

achievement gap: the disparity in academic performance between different groups of students (often defined by racial or ethnic group membership), usually measured in terms of the dropout rate or standardized test scores

acrolect: a term used in creole linguistics to refer to the form of a creole language which is closest to the superstrate language and a prestige variety; compare with *basilect* and *mesolect*

act sequence: in ethnography of communication research, the term used to refer to the linguistic form and content of the communicative event

adjacency pair: a term used in *discourse analysis* to refer to a single stimulus–response sequence (e.g., a question and an answer, a greeting and another greeting, etc.)

affricate: a sound which combines a stop with a fricative (e.g., the 'ch' sound in English)

An Introduction to Sociolinguistics, Seventh Edition. Ronald Wardhaugh and Janet M. Fuller.
© 2015 John Wiley & Sons, Inc. Published 2015 by John Wiley & Sons, Inc.

African American Vernacular English (AAVE): a variety of US English that is associated with African American speakers and has certain nonstandard features; see *creole origin* and *Anglicist hypothesis*

Afrogenesis hypothesis: a hypothesis about the origins of creole languages which suggests that Portuguese-based pidgins which developed in Africa are the basis of most creole languages

age-grading: the idea that some aspects of language use change over time within the speech of an individual; that is, they may use a particular feature when younger and then not use this feature when they reach adulthood

/ai/ monophthongization: the pronunciation of the diphthong /ai/ (found in words like 'pie' or the pronoun 'I') without the glide (i.e., /a/)

allophone, allophonic variation: an allophone is a phonetic realization of a *phoneme*; allophonic variation is different phonetic realizations which do not change meaning in a particular language (e.g [p] and [pʰ] (i.e., aspirated and unaspirated /p/) in English)

Anglicist hypothesis: the idea that African American Vernacular English grew up in the context of many different English dialects in contact

Ann Arbor decision: a landmark case in which the court ruled that the school district needed to take students' home variety ('Black English') into account when providing education

apparent time: a construct used in sociolinguistic studies which is based on the idea that a speaker's core linguistic features do not change over time, thus comparing the speech of different age groups at a given point in time shows language change

applied: the use of theories, methods, and findings to address issues and solve problems having to do with language in society, the term 'applied linguistics' is used in some cases to refer to language teaching in particular, but may also be used to refer to other domains of application, for instance language policy or translation

asymmetrical T/V: the use of formal (V) and informal (T) pronouns to show a hierarchical relationship, with one speaker using the informal pronoun but receiving the formal and the other using the formal but receiving the informal

audience design: an approach to studying language variation based on the idea that speakers orient their speech based on their audience

awareness program: a type of educational program for children whose home variety is not the variety used in mainstream education; makes use of the home variety of the children for some tasks and also incorporates learning about the social process through which a particular variety becomes the standard and language of education

axiom of categoricity: the idea that a speaker always (i.e., categorically) uses certain linguistic features (compare with *variation*)

backchanneling: the responses interlocutors make to indicate they are listening; includes minimal responses such as *mhm* or *uhuh*, phrases such as *oh, okay*, or *I see*, and non-verbal cues such as nodding or gaze

basilect: a term used in creole linguistics to refer to the variety of a creole language most remote from the prestigious superstrate; compare *acrolect* and *mesolect*

change from above: language change that comes from above the level of consciousness, usually because speakers want to sound like a higher status group; appears in more formal speech first

change from below: language change that occurs without speakers being aware of it; appears in the vernacular first

cisgender: used to refer to people whose sex category is perceived as matching their gender; compare with *transgender*

closing: a term used in *discourse analysis* to describe the turns which end a conversation

code: a word used in sociolinguistics to mean a variety of a language; it is intentionally neutral and does not specify if the variety is a particular dialect (e.g., 'Cockney') or a broader category (e.g., 'English'); compare with *language, dialect, register, genre*, and *style*

code-switching: a term used to describe the use of two or more varieties, or codes, in an interaction; see *code, multilingual discourse*

code-switching constraints: rules which govern the structure of code-switching

common ground: a factor in a relationship which focuses on similarities in background and experience among speakers

commonsense knowledge: understanding of everyday life which allows people to operate in and understand the world around them; relies on a static idea of social reality

communicative competence: the ability to produce and understand utterances which are socially appropriate in particular contexts; contrasts with *competence*

community of practice: a group defined according to interaction around a common endeavor; although speakers may have different linguistic repertoires and backgrounds, common linguistic practices emerge through regular interaction

competence: a person's unconscious knowledge of the grammatical rules of a language; contrasts with *performance* and *communicative competence*

constative utterance: an utterance which is a descriptive statement which can be said to be either true or false

constitutive rules: rules which are necessary to make something what it is, that is, constitute it

construction of social identities: the concept of social identities as not being fixed attributes of the self but as things which emerge out of linguistics (and other social) behavior; see also *social constructionist*

contact languages: a general term used to describe languages which have developed in multilingual contexts; includes *pidgins, creoles,* and *mixed languages*

contextualization: signals (verbal and non-verbal) which help interlocutors to process and interpret the utterances in a conversation

convergence: modifying one's speech so that it resembles that of other interlocutors

conversation analysis (CA): a particular method of *discourse analysis* which studies conversational structure and coherence, based on *ethnomethodology*

conversational overlap: when more than one speaker is talking at the same time in a conversation; may be cooperative or an attempt to interrupt

cooperative principle: from Gricean pragmatics; the principle that participants in a conversation are assumed to be trying to communicate

corpus linguistics: the study of language in real-world texts comprising large, electronically readable corpora, which are analyzed using computerized analytical tools

corpus planning: a type of *language planning* which involves the selection and codification of language norms

correlational studies: research which shows a relationship between a particular *social variable* (e.g., age) and the use of a particular *linguistic variable* (e.g., the lexical item 'ice box'); it does not imply a causal relationship

covert prestige: prestige (of a linguistic variety or form) which is derived from its importance in ingroup interaction; this variety or form does not have prestige in the wider society

CRAAVE: stand for Cross-Race African American Vernacular English; AAVE which is used by non-African Americans who have picked up some features of this dialect, see *crossing*

creole (language): a type of contact language, usually assumed to be elaborated and nativized; compare with *pidgin* and *mixed language*

creole continuum: a construct which is based on the idea that a creole language contains a spectrum of varieties from those most similar to the *superstrate* language to those quite different from it; see *basilect, mesolect,* and *acrolect*

creole formation: the process of the development of a creole language

creole origin: a term used in discussion of the development of African American Vernacular English to refer to the theory that a plantation creole developed on the southern United States during times of slavery, and features of contemporary AAVE can be traced back to this creole language

critical discourse analysis (CDA): an approach to *discourse analysis* which seeks to discover how inequalities are encoded in and reproduced through language use

critical analysis: an analysis that seeks to find underlying ideologies in social practices, particularly those that mask and naturalize the reproduction of inequalities

critical sociolinguistics: the branch of sociolinguistics that examines how language functions in society to reproduce ideologies, particularly those related to social inequalities

crossing: use of a variety associated with a group in which the speaker is not considered a member; see also *CRAAVE*

cultural borrowings: loanwords which are brought into a language because they denote new concepts or items entering the culture

culture: knowledge about how a society works, its values and practices

Cyrillic script: an alphabetic writing system; currently used for Russian among other languages of Europe and Asia

decontextualization: a term used in *discourse analysis* to describe taking language use out of its original context; see also *recontextualization*

decreolization: a concept from creole linguistics which describes a situation in which the standard language which provided the superstrate for the creole language begins to exert influence on the creole, making it become more like the standard; this concept is criticized by some scholars

deficit model: used to refer to work on language and gender which portrays women's language as deficient in comparison with men's language

dense social network: a *social network* in which the people who have ties to ego also have ties to each other; compare with *loose social network*

dependent variable: see under *variable*

descriptive: a systematic analysis of the structure of language as it is spoken in a particular group; compare with *prescriptive*

desire: the concept of sexuality as not just an aspect of identity but also encompassing non-intentional, non-conscious, and non-rational dimensions of human sexual life

Devanagari script: an alphabetic writing system; currently used to write Hindi and Sanskrit, among other languages of India

diachronic (linguistics): the study of languages from a historical perspective *dialect:* the term used to refer to a particular way of speaking a language which is associated with a particular region or social group; compare with *language*

dialect atlas: collections of maps showing regional patterns of language use

dialect boundary: a bundle of *isoglosses*; the border between two varieties of a language

dialect continuum: gradual change of language over space; while the varieties at either end of the continuum may not be mutually intelligible, the adjacent varieties are

dialect geography: the study of regional dialects

dialect mixture: a variety which has features associated with distinct regional dialects

dialogical: involving a dialogue or exchange

difference (or two cultures) approach: in the study of language and gender, an approach which focuses on men and women as members of different sub-cultures, with differences in how they use language

diffusion: the spread of a linguistic feature through a language, region, or period of time

diglossia: the use of two languages (in the original definition, two dialects of the same language) with strict separation by domains

diphthong: a vowel which is comprised by two sounds within one syllable

Discourse(s): language use combined with other social practices which produce and reproduce social categories and their values

discourse analysis: a term used to describe a wide range of approaches to the study of texts and conversation, some of which are sociolinguistic in nature; see *conversation analysis* and *critical discourse analysis*

dispreferred responses: a term used in *discourse analysis* to describe responses to speech acts which are not the unmarked or hoped-for reply; for instance, the refusal of a request

divergence: adjusting one's language use to make it less like that of the interlocutors

divergence hypothesis: the hypothesis that AAVE is becoming less like dialects of American English spoken by White speakers in the same regions

domain: a concept which refers to language use as determined by topic, setting, and speakers; often used to discuss the choice of a particular variety of language *dominance approach:* an approach to the study of language and gender which is based on the idea that men's dominant position in society is reflected and reproduced in conversation

Ebonics: a term for the variety of English which sociolinguistics call *African American Vernacular English*; although the term has not been widely adopted by academics, it is a commonly used term in US society

elaborated code: term used to refer to a variety of language which is used in more formal situations, characterized in part by not being reliant on extralinguistic context to derive meaning; compare with *restricted code*

elite bilingualism: bilingualism which is considered to be socially advantageous, usually involving high-status speakers and prestigious languages

elite closure: a situation in which language policy and the patterns of language use by elite members of society effectively prevents non-elites from access to the linguistic resources they need to gain social, cultural, and economic capital

endangered languages: languages which are in danger of not being spoken any more due to an aging population of speakers and language shift among younger members of the speech community

ends: in ethnography of communication research, the term used to refer to the expected outcome and goals of a particular communicative event

epistemological factors: discussed in language policy and planning research as factors which have to do with the paradigms of knowledge and social theories which are applied in different phases of the development of this field of study

essentialist, essentialism: the view that a single identity category (e.g., 'African American' or 'woman') is synonymous with a pre-existing, homogeneous group, regardless of context

ethical proposition: a term used in pragmatics to describe a proposition which is used to create a value statement

ethnic dialects / ethnolects: dialects associated with particular ethnic groups

ethnography, ethnographic: an approach to research which is an attempt to describe a culture and its practices from an insider's point of view

ethnolinguistic vitality: the potential of a minority language (often one associated with a particular ethnic group) to be maintained

ethnomethodology: an approach to the study of how people organize and understand the social world around them, focusing on the phenomena of everyday activities

ethnonational: the view of national belonging as based on ethnic and racial categorization

Euro English: a term used to describe distinctive varieties of English spoken in Europe, largely by speakers who have English as a second or foreign language

expanding circle: the outermost circle of English, in which speakers learn English as a foreign language and the language plays an increasing role in the economic development of the country; compare with *inner circle* and *outer circle*

externally motivated language change: language change which is motivated by contact with other codes

face: a person's positive self-image

face-threatening act: a speech act which can potentially damage the *face* of the speaker or addressee; see *positive face* and *negative face*

face work: the linguistic efforts made to maintain the face of the speaker or addressee

family-tree account of language change: a conception of language development as being similar to human genealogy, with a mother language and the languages which develop from it being considered sisters

feedback (as part of classroom exchange patterns): the final part of a three-part exchange in which the instructor comments on the *response* given by a student

felicity conditions: a term from Speech Act Theory that describes the situation necessary for a particular speech act to be successfully performed

first wave variation studies: see under *variation studies*

flagged code-switching: the switch from one language to another which is marked through comment, laughter, or repair

floor management: used in *discourse analysis* to refer to how turns are organized in conversation

focal area: in dialect studies, an area which is the source of innovation, usually also economic and cultural centers in a region

fossilization: in second language acquisition, incomplete acquisition of particular aspects of speech which become fixed in a speaker's *interlanguage*

free variation: variation in pronunciation which does not change the meaning of the word; considered rare in sociolinguistics, as *variants* often have different social meanings even if they share denotative meaning

fricatives: sounds made by forcing air through a restricted area of the vocal tract (e.g., /s/ or /f/ in English)

gatekeeping: the practice of preventing certain groups from gaining power by restricting their access to cultural capital; see *elite closure gender:* a socially constructed aspect of identity, linked to ideas about biological *sex categories* but often discussed in terms of 'masculinity' and 'femininity' (as opposed to 'male' and 'female')

gender exclusive language: linguistic features which are used only by members of one gender group or another

gender preferential language: linguistic features which are associated with the way in which members of a particular gender group speak

gender variation: differences in linguistic performance between different gender groups

General American: a term used to refer to a variety of English spoken in North America that is considered 'mainstream,' without strong regional features

genre: a variety of a language which evokes a particular speech event or function; this term/concept is also part of the ethnography of communication research paradigm

glocal, glocalization: developments in language and culture which involve a mixture of global and local influences

glottal stop: a sound produced when air flow is restricted by the glottis closing, as in 'uh-oh!' in English; in some dialects, an *allophone* of /t/

gradient stratification: when the linguistic distinctions between groups is a step-like progression; usually assumed to be typical of phonological variation; compare with *sharp stratification*

gradualist model, gradualism: the idea in the study of pidgin and creole languages that the elaboration of a pidgin happens over several generations, and not necessarily as the result of nativization

grammar: the structure of a language, including its sound system, word order, word formation rules; see also *prescriptive* and *descriptive*

grammatical judgments: the opinions of speakers of a language about whether a particular construction is acceptable in their language

graphization: the development and modification of writing systems

habitual be: the use of the verb form *be* to indicate repeated and habitual action

hegemony, hegemonic ideologies: ideologies which are dominant due to consensus, including the complicity of people for whom the ideologies are not beneficial; although competing ideologies are possible, they must refer to the hegemonic ideology

heritage language: this term is used to refer to a language which is, or has been, spoken by an individual's family; it does not imply any particular level of proficiency in the language, but an association with the language through identification with a cultural group that speaks it

heteronormativity: the underlying assumption that heterosexuality is the norm for all people

heterosexist: ideologies or attitudes which assume and privilege heterosexuality and heterosexuals

historical linguistics: a branch of linguistic which looks at the development of languages over time

hybridization: the process of combining aspects of two different languages, cultures, identities, and so on; involves the inherent assumption of the *essentialist* nature of these original entities

hypercorrection: the use of linguistic forms which overshoot a target which is considered 'correct', producing forms which do not appear in the standard; can also be used to refer to using a particular variant more frequently than speakers of the variety one is trying to emulate

identity: in sociolinguistics, this term is used to mean a socially constructed affiliation with particular social categories which is shifting, multiple, and *dialogical*

ideology: a societal system of ideas and values which underlies cultural behaviors

illocutionary act: a term used in Speech Act Theory to refer to an act performed by making an utterance

illocutionary force: the intended effect of an *illocutionary act*

immersion: a method for teaching a second or foreign language which involves exposure to the target language without use of the learner's first language

immigrant bilingualism: the bilingualism which arises due to migration of individuals and groups from one language area to another; often stigmatized, compare with *elite bilingualism*

implicature: the term from Gricean pragmatics used to refer to the implied meaning of an utterance

implicit meaning: meaning which is not stated explicitly, but which is implied or must be derived from shared knowledge

independent variable: see under *variable*

indexicality: the association of a code or linguistic form with a particular social meaning

indicator: a linguistic feature of a particular variety which is not salient to speakers of that language but can be studied through systematic observation

indirect speech: a speech act that has as its intended meaning an *implicature*, not the literal meaning of the utterance

informant: a term used to refer to speakers of language or dialects who provide linguists with data about their variety; currently preferred term is 'consultant'

initiation (as part of classroom exchange patterns): an utterance by the teacher, often a question, which aims to elicit a *response* from the students

inner circle: in the study of World Englishes, the term used to describe the areas in which English is used in most spheres for the majority of the population; compare with *outer circle* and *expanding circle*

instrumental program: a type of program in primary and secondary education which uses the minority home language of the pupils in instruction; compare with *accommodation program*

instrumentalities: in ethnography of communication research, the term used to refer to the channel of communication and the code used in the communicative event being studies

interactional sociolinguistics: an approach to *discourse analysis* which incorporates the analysis of conversations with attention to broader macro-societal norms, values, and ideologies

interdiscursivity: the incorporation of linguistic material that carries specific meanings or connotations from one *Discourse* or context into another

interlanguage: term used to refer to the developing grammar of a second/foreign language learner

internally motivated language change: a view of language change as being motivated by processes which rely on the structures within the language; compare with *externally motivated language change*

intersectional, intersectionality: the concept that aspects of identity such as gender, ethnicity, or social class (among others) are not independent of each other, or the perspective on identity as including these intertwined aspects

isogloss: a line which marks the distinction between the use of one *variant* and another for a particular linguistic feature

judgment sample: see under *sample*

key: in ethnography of communication research, the term used to refer to the tone, manner, or spirit in which the communicative event takes place

language: a system of signs used for communication; in sociolinguistics, one focus is on how to define the boundaries of such a system. This term is usually taken to mean the superordinate category of a variety which includes dialects, one of which is the standard. See also *code* and *dialect language bioprogram hypothesis:* a hypothesis used in the study of the origins of creole languages which suggests that humans are programmed to create languages, and in the absence of input of a full-fledged language (i.e., with only input from a pidgin) they will elaborate the language according to this bioprogram

language documentation: work done by linguists to make records (e.g., grammar, dictionaries) about languages, especially *endangered languages*

language family: a group of languages considered to have developed from a single source

language ideologies: ideas about language with regard to society; often unconscious ideas about the values of certain ways of speaking

language maintenance: the continued use of a minority language; compare with *language shift*

language planning: efforts to develop a language, or its use, in a particular direction

language policy: legal efforts (making of policies or laws) intended to support language planning

language shift: when speakers cease to use a minority language and instead adopt the majority language for ingroup use; compare with *language maintenance*

language socialization: the process of becoming an active, competent participant in a particular cultural group, viewed as taking place through language practices

legitimate (v.): to assign validity or high status to a particular code

level of significance: a term used in statistical analyses to indicate the probability that the relationship between the variables being analyzed could occur by chance

leveling: the elimination of differences between varieties over time; may lead to the formation of a new, uniform variety

lexical diffusion: a term used to refer to how sound change spreads through the words in a language

lexifier language: the language which contributes most of the lexicon in the development of a pidgin or creole language, usually the socially dominant language and not the native language of any of the speakers; see also *superstrate*

LGBTQ: stands for 'lesbian, gay, bisexual, *transgender* and queer/questioning,' used as an inclusive term which also recognizes diversity

life cycle model: a model of pidgin and creole formation which relies on the idea that a *pidgin* becomes a *creole* when it is spoken to children and becomes their native language; through nativization elaboration ensues

lifestyle: sets of practices which separate individuals into different hierarchically organized groups

Limited English Proficiency (LEP): term used in the US public school system to refer to learners of English

lingua franca: a common language used to communicate in situations in which speakers of different languages interact

linguistic anthropology: the sub-field of anthropology which deals with language as social behavior; overlaps with sociolinguistics

linguistic constraints (on variation): the linguistic context which conditions the use of particular variants

linguistic ethnography: an approach in which ethnography is used to complement an analysis of specific linguistic practices, incorporating microanalyses of conversations with the study of cultural norms and ideologies

linguistic inequality: a situation in which languages have varying levels of social value, and this leads to inequality among different linguistic groups

linguistic landscapes: the visual display of languages through signs, billboards, advertisements, graffiti, and so on

linguistic marketplace: the context in which particular ways of speaking take on different symbolic values

linguistic universals: aspects of language which can be found in all languages

linguistic variable: see *variable*

linguistic variation: a term used to describe the different linguistic forms which can be used to express the same denotational meaning (which generally have different social meanings); see also *variant*

locally managed: used to refer to the emergence and ongoing nature of conversational structure; it is not planned or externally determined but developed by the interlocutors in the ongoing conversation

locution: a meaningful utterance

loose social network: a social network (see definition below) in which the people who have ties to ego do not have ties to each other; compare with *dense social network*

macrolinguistic studies: studies in sociolinguistics which are 'macro' both in the sense that they analyze large amounts of data and that they focus on societal issues

macro-sociolinguistics: the part of sociolinguistics that addresses larger societal patterns of language use (e.g., language attitudes, etc.); compare with *micro-sociolinguistics*

macro-sociopolitical factors: one of three types of factors looked at in language policy and planning research, having to do with social and political developments on a state or national level

manner (maxim): one of the maxims for conversation in Gricean pragmatics; states that utterances should be clear and to the point; violations of this maxim result in *implicature*

marker: a linguistic feature that carries social meaning which is apparent to speakers; compare with *indicators* and *stereotypes*

matched guise: a method to study language attitudes; research participants are asked to judge speakers of different languages, based on a recording of their voices, for a variety of characteristics; unbeknownst to them, the same speaker is given to them in different 'guises' (i.e., speaking two different *codes*)

membership categorization devices: aspects of language which allow us to assign people and things into particular social categories

mesolect: term used to describe the variety of a creole language that is in the mid-range on the continuum between the *superstrate* and the variety furthest from the superstrate; compare *basilect* and *acrolect*

metaphorical code-switching: the use of a code as a means to symbolically redefine the interaction; compare with *situational code-switching*

microlinguistic studies: studies about specific linguistic features used by particular speakers or groups and their social meanings

micro-sociolinguistics: the part of sociolinguistics that addresses the relationship between the use of specific varieties or linguistic features and social structure and categories; compare with *macro-sociolinguistics*

minimal pairs: two words with different meanings but which differ in only one sound, indicating that this particular sound is a phoneme in the language: for instance 'pen' and 'pin' in many dialects of English

mixed language: term used to refer to a type of contact language which is a combination of two languages: the grammar is mostly from one language and the lexicon mostly from the other (although there are variations on and exceptions to this general pattern)

monogenetic, monogenesis: the idea that creole languages all share a single, common origin

monoglossic ideology: the idea that languages are distinct entities and should be kept strictly separate in their use

monophthongization: the pronunciation of a diphthong (a sound including two vowels in one syllable) as a single vowel sound *morpheme:* the smallest grammatical unit which can be assigned semantic meaning

morphophonemic variation: changes in the phonological forms of a morpheme in different linguistic contexts

multilingual, multilingualism: a person able to speak more than one language, or the situation in which speakers can and do speak more than one language

multilingual discourse: the use of linguistic elements from more than one *variety* in a conversation or text

multiple negation: the use of more than one negative particle to indicate negation; in English, this is nonstandard, but it is part of standard grammar in other languages (e.g., French and Spanish)

multiplex social network: a *social network* in which each tie represents several different types of relationship, for example, a relative is also a colleague and a neighbor

mutability of style: the idea that the social meaning of a particular style or variant is not fixed but emerges in the discourse

mutual intelligibility: capability of being understood by both sides; used to discuss different languages or dialects and whether the speakers can understand each other

negative face: a term from Politeness Theory which refers to an individual's desire to not be imposed upon by others; compare with *positive face*

negative politeness: a term from Politeness Theory which refers to the linguistic strategies used by speakers to not threaten the negative face of others; see *face-threatening acts* and *negative face*

neo-colonial: pertaining to the use of a combination of globalization, capitalist enterprise, and cultural imperialism by one country to exert influence over another; draws a parallel to colonialism in which influence is gained through direct military or political dominance

Newscaster English: one term used to refer to what is considered a standard dialect of North American English

norms: although this term may refer to value-laden attitudes about any type of social behavior, here this term is used to refer to ideas about the values of certain ways of speaking

norms of interaction and interpretation: in ethnography of communication research, the term used to refer to the specific behaviors normatively associated with a particular communicative event, and how adherence to or deviation from this set of behaviors might be viewed

Northern Cities Vowel Shift: a chain shift which has been studied in dialects in northern cities of the United States; see link in the online material for chapter 8 for more details of this phonological change in progress

observer's paradox: the aim of sociolinguistic research is to study how people speak when they are not being observed, but the data are only available through systematic observation

opening: term used in *discourse analysis* to refer to the beginning of a conversation

outer circle: in the study of World Englishes, term used to refer to regions in which English is used in many institutions but is, or was originally, a non-native language for most speakers; compare with *inner circle* and *expanding circle*

palatalization: the production of a sound with the tongue in or closer to the palatal position

panel study: a type of real-time study in which the speech of the same research participants from two different points in time is analyzed

participant observation: the process through which a researcher does ethnography, requiring taking part in cultural activities while at the same time noting the activities of others

participants: in ethnography of communication research, the term used to refer to the people who are part of the communicative event being studied

P/C languages: abbreviation for pidgin and creole languages which recognizes the lack of a clear distinction between these two terms

perceptual dialectology: the study of attitudes and view about how people speak in different regions

performance: language in use, that is, actual utterances as they are produced; compare with *competence*

performative utterance: an utterance which performs an action simply by being uttered (e.g., an apology, baptism, or promise); compare with *constative utterance*

periphrastic constructions: a means of expressing grammatical categories which uses a separate word or words instead of an inflection, such as the English future constructions *will* or *going to*

perlocutionary force: the particular effect an utterance has on the addressee or audience

perlocutions: the effect of an *illocution*

phatic, phatic communication: the type of communication which is primarily focused on the interaction as a means to create social connection; the content of the utterance is secondary (e.g., formulaic greetings, discussion of the weather)

phoneme: a perceptually distinctive unit of sound which carries meaning in a particular language (e.g., in English /b/ and /p/ are different phonemes, but /p/ and /pʰ/ (aspirated /p/) are not; see *allophone*

phonemic coalescence: when a contrast between phonemes is lost in a language

phonemic split: when a contrast between two allophones develops into phonemic difference

pidgin (language): a language which develops in a situation of language contact and limited exposure to the target language; compare with *creole language*

pidgin formation: the process through which a *pidgin language* develops

pluralism, pluralist ideology: a way of thinking in which all linguistic varieties, ways of speaking, and ways of being (i.e., cultural behaviors) are valued, not only mainstream or majority cultures and languages

polygenesis: the idea that *creole languages* have multiple origins

positive face: a concept from Politeness Theory that refers to an individual's desire to be appreciated by others

positive politeness: in Politeness Theory, the linguistic strategies used to avoid damaging another's *positive face*; see also *face-threatening act*

postmodern theory: a general term for theoretical developments in the late twentieth century which include an analysis of underlying assumptions and ideological positions in discourse and text

power: the ability to control the actions of one's self and others

practical reasoning: how people apply their *commonsense knowledge* to conduct their lives

pragmatics: a sub-field of linguistics which looks at language meaning as dependent on/derived through context

pre-closing signals: term used in *discourse analysis* to refer to turns which indicate that the speakers are moving toward ending the conversation; see also *closing*

prescriptive: the view that one variety of language is inherently correct and that this way of speaking ought to be imposed on all speakers of that language; compare with *descriptive*

proposition: the sense, or meaning, of a declarative utterance

pluricentric: not having one central focus, but multiple foci

principle of accountability: if it is possible to define a set of *variants*, all members of this set must be taken into account in doing the analysis

qualitative: the term used to refer to studies which do not look at quantitative data; can involve a variety of methodologies, types of data, and epistemological stances

quality (maxim): in Gricean pragmatics, the maxim which indicates that utterances should be truthful; flouting this maxim leads to *implicature*

quantitative: the term used to refer to studies that look at frequency and distribution of particular linguistic features, usually using statistics; the aim is to discover general principles regarding the structure of language in relation to particular *social variables* (see *correlational studies*, above)

quantitative (variationist) sociolinguistics: an approach in sociolinguistics in which the frequency of linguistic features is correlated with social factors

quantity (maxim): in Gricean pragmatics, the maxim which states that utterances should contain all the information required, but not more; violations of this lead to *implicature*

Ramírez Report: a report on the effectiveness of bilingual education submitted to the US Department of Education in 1991, early evidence that longer periods of time in a bilingual educational program were beneficial for English language learners in US schools

random sample: see under *sample*

real time: in sociolinguistics, refers to a study in which data is collected at different points in time to assess language change; compare with *apparent time*

Received Pronunciation: the most common term for the variety of British English which carries the most prestige

recontextualization: the insertion of text or discourse from one context into another; since the meaning is dependent on context, this involves a shift in meaning or communicative purpose

reduplicative, reduplication: the repetition of a linguistic feature to form a new word with a different, often intensified, meaning; for instance, in Jamaican Creole /yɛloyɛlo/ can mean 'very yellow'

reflexivity: the concept that while interactions are shaped by the context in which they occur, they are simultaneously creating the social context

regional dialect: a way of speaking which is associated with residents of a particular geographical region

register: a way of speaking a language which is associated with a particular occupational or activity group

regularization: the development of grammatical paradigms to be uniform, that is, the elimination of forms which do not fit with general rules for grammatical categories; for instance, elimination of irregular past tense verbs in favor of those which apply the regular *-ed* suffix

regulative rules: rules which are stated explicitly and for which there are sanctions if they are broken; not the kind of rules which apply to language

relation (maxim): in Gricean pragmatics, the maxim which states the contributions to conversation should be relevant; flouting this maxim leads to *implicature*

relexification hypothesis: a theory in the study of creole linguistics which suggests that the grammatical structure from a single source language has been essentially translated word for word (i.e., maintaining the structure but changing the lexicon) to create other creole languages: see *monogenesis*

reliability: in research design, the extent to which the means of assessment of the variables produce stable and consistent results

relic area: an area in which older forms of a dialect have been preserved, in contrast with surrounding regions

remnant dialect: a variety spoke in a *relic area*

repair: fixing of a perceived error in an utterance

> *other-initiated repair:* a repair which is suggested by someone other than the speaker of the utterance which is perceived to need fixing
> *self-repair:* a repair which is suggested by the speaker of the utterance which is perceived to need fixing

response (as part of classroom exchange patterns): the second part of an exchange, in which a student answers an *initiation* turn by the teacher

restricted code: term used to refer to a variety of language which is used in informal situations, characterized in part by being reliant on extralinguistic context to derive meaning; compare with *elaborated code*

r-lessness: the lack of pronunciation of an /r/ in post-vocalic position in a word; for instance the word 'car' pronounced as /ka/

Roman script: the alphabetic writing system used for many modern-day languages, including English

Russification: the promotion of Russian language (and culture) through the Soviet Union

sample: the group of research participants in a given study

> *random sample:* a sample in which everyone in the population has an equal chance of being selected; generally impossible to achieve in sociolinguistic studies
> *judgment sample* or *quota sample:* sample in which the researcher begins with certain demographic criteria and selects research participants who fit into these predetermined categories
> *stratified sample:* sampling based on separation of the population into supposedly homogeneous sub-groups; selection of research participants within these groups should be random, and groups at all levels of stratification should be included

sampling: the process of specifying how research participants will be selected

Sanskritization: promotion of words of Sanskrit origin (as opposed to, in particular, English origin) in modern-day Hindi

second wave variation studies: see under *variation studies*

setting and scene: the term used in the ethnographic of communication to refer to the time, place, and cultural description for a particular communicative event

sex categories: social categories which are based on the assumption of biological distinction; typically include 'male' and 'female' but may also include other, culturally specific categories

sexist: distinguishing between the sexes in a way which assumes that all men/women share certain characteristics and implies superiority of one sex over the other

sexuality: identification based on sexual orientation, preferences, and activity; includes but is not limited to identities as heterosexual or *LGBTQ*

sharp stratification: clear-cut differences between two groups in the use of linguistic features, usually associated with grammatical features; compare with *gradient stratification*

situational code-switching: choice of code based on the norms of the situation; compare with *metaphorical code-switching*

social class: hierarchical categories based on social and economic factors

social constructionist: the idea that our social reality (including social identities) are brought into being through social behavior, including language use; see also *construction of social identities*

social dialect, social dialectology: the language spoken within a particular social group, the study of such varieties

social distance: a means of evaluating the relationship between two people based on affect, solidarity, and familiarity

social group: any grouping of people, but most often in sociolinguistics used to refer to socio-economic classes or ethnic groups

social network: described from the perspective of a particular individual (ego), the social connections (called 'network ties') of different types that form their regular interactions and influences: see *dense social network, loose social network,* and *multiplex social network*

social power: the ability of a group or institution to control the acts and worldview of other groups

social variable: see *variable*

society: a general term for a group of people drawn together for particular purpose(s) and who share at least some cultural norms

sociology of language: the study of how social structure can be better understood through the study of language; see *macro-sociolinguistics*

solidarity: a common bond between individuals, usually associated with identification with the same social group

speaker agency: a perspective on language choice and linguistic variation which focuses on the speaker's strategic use (intentional but not necessarily conscious) of particular ways of speaking

speech community: a term used to describe a group of people who share linguistic norms; some definitions also focus on shared speech patterns

stable variation: variation between two or more forms which is not part of ongoing change, but continues to occur as part of formal/informal variation in a language

stance, stancetaking: the use of language to position oneself with regard to other interlocutors as well as attitudes and ideologies being discussed

Standard American English: a term to describe the normatively prescribed dialect of English in the USA

standard language: a dialect of a language which is considered superior to other dialects: *Received Pronunciation* has this status in British English

standard language ideology: the ideology that there is one dialect which is superior to others, and that this is a 'natural' order of things

standardization: the process of recognizing a particular way of speaking as the norm or prestigious, and codifying this dialect

status planning: a type of *language planning* which focuses on changing (usually elevating) the position of a language in a particular society

stereotype: a generalization about members of a group based on the idea that all members of the group will share certain personal characteristics

stereotype (linguistic variable): a linguistic feature which is consciously and commonly associated with a particular social group; may not actually be part of the ways of speaking of members of that group

stops: also called 'plosives,' a term used to refer to sounds which are formed through the stopping of air flowing through the vocal tract; examples from English include /p/ or /t/

strategy factors: factors in language planning and policy research which have to do with the goal of the research

stratified sample: see under *sample*

structuralism: a theoretical framework which analyzes societies in terms of their social systems which exist separate from agents and imagined realities

style: the level of formality in the way of speaking; there are more formal and less formal styles of every variety

substrate: a term used to refer to the native languages of the speakers who participate in the formation of pidgin and creole languages; compare with *superstrate*

substratist: a position in the study of *P/C language* formation that focuses on the role of the substrate languages

superstrate: a term used to refer to the target language in the formation of pidgin and creole languages; see also *lexifier language*, and compare with *substrate*

symmetrical T/V: the reciprocal use of either the informal (T) or formal (V) pronoun form

synchronic (linguistics): the study of a language at a given point of time; compare with *diachronic linguistics*

theoretical: in linguistics, this term is often used to refer to what may also be called 'formal linguistics,' that is, the study of syntax, phonology, and so on, without a focus on social context. In sociolinguistics, this term is also used to make a contrast to *applied* studies; in this case, it means the focus is on theory building rather than how the research can be used to contribute to the community

third wave variation studies: see under *variation studies*

time on task: a term used in the discussion of language learning to discuss the factor of amount of exposure to the target language

transfer: in second language acquisition, the use of features from one's first language in production of the language being acquired

transgender: a term used to refer to people whose gender expression does not match their assigned sex category; independent of sexual orientation

transition relevant place: a moment in a conversation in which a speaker's turn could plausibly end, and the next speaker could begin his or her turn

translanguaging: the incorporation of all aspects of a speaker's repertoire into discourse, including elements from different varieties, registers, and styles

transmission: the acquisition of language by children

trend study: a type of *real-time* study in which different members of the same community are studied at different points of time; compare with *panel study*

tu and vous forms: using the words for the French pronouns, this term is used to refer to all such informal and formal pronoun forms across languages

turn-taking: the switch from one speaker to another within a conversation *two-way (or dual language) immersion:* a type of bilingual education in which half of the pupils in a classroom are speakers of the majority language and half are speakers of the minority language; all students are instructed in both languages

unilingualism: a situation in which only one language is supported in terms of language use in politics, economics, legal contexts, and public social life

unmarked choice: the expected code for a particular situation

validity: in research design, the extent to which the data collected address the research question appropriately

VARBRUL: a set of statistical programs designed to analyze linguistic variation in sociolinguistic research

variable: a unit in language which is subject to *variation*

  dependent variable: a linguistic variable which is assumed to fluctuate with changes in the social factors being studied
  independent variable: a social variable (e.g., age, ethnicity, social class) which is being studied in a sociolinguistic analysis; thought to correlate with particular linguistic variables

variant: a linguistic form which is one of several forms which can be used to express a particular meaning; for example, *wasn't* and *weren't* may both be used in the same linguistic context in some varieties of English (e.g., *I wasn't* or *I weren't*)

variation: the idea that there are a variety of ways of saying things, and which code, lexical item, pronunciation, and so on is used has social meaning

variationist sociolinguistics: see *quantitative sociolinguistics* and *variation studies*

variation studies: one school of research within sociolinguistics

  first wave variation studies: primary focus on the correlation of dependent and independent variables
  second wave variation studies: built on the first wave to include ethnographic information about social factors and speaker agency
  third wave variation studies: shift from looking at how language reflects membership in particular social categories to how language is used to construct social identities

variety: a word used to refer to a particular way of speaking, usually associated with a particular region or group of speakers; see *code, language,* and *dialect*

verbal -s marking: use of the *-s* morpheme on verbs; in Standard English, this is only in third-person singular contexts (e.g., 'she goes'); this may be absent in some dialects of English, or be used in another linguistic context (e.g., 'the preachers likes')

vernacular: a way of speaking that is colloquial and casual; has the connotation of being the native, ingroup way of speaking for a social group

vernacular norms: norms in a vernacular (i.e., nonstandard) variety which are associated with ingroup solidarity as opposed to wider social prestige

vowel reduction: the articulation of an unstressed vowel as a mid-central vowel (i.e., /ə/)

wave account of language change: an approach to the study of language change which uses the metaphor of waves to describe how changes flow and overlap

Whorfian hypothesis: also called the *Sapir Whorf hypothesis*, this hypothesis represents a view of the relationship between language and thought proposed by US linguist Edward Sapir (1884–1939) and his student Benjamin Lee Whorf (1897–1941). It includes the idea that language determines (or at least influences) the way we think, and that distinctions found in one language are not directly translatable into another

worldview: way of seeing the world, or how reality is structured; often used in discussion of the *Whorfian hypothesis*

zero copula: the non-use of a form of the verb 'to be'; a feature of AAVE (e.g., 'they tall' (Standard English, 'they are tall'))

Index

Page numbers referring to figures are in *italics* and those referring to tables are in **bold**.

An Introduction to Sociolinguistics, Seventh Edition. Ronald Wardhaugh and Janet M. Fuller.
© 2015 John Wiley & Sons, Inc. Published 2015 by John Wiley & Sons, Inc.